Lang/Pistone/Schuch/Staringer/Rust/Kc

Introduction to European Tax Law on Direct Taxation

Introduction to European Tax Law on Direct Taxation

edited by
Michael Lang
Pasquale Pistone
Josef Schuch
Claus Staringer

6th edition

Spiramus

Published September 2020 by

Spiramus Press Ltd
102 Blandford Street
London
W1U 8AG

www.spiramus.com

Austria, Germany and Switzerland:
Linde:
978-3-7073-4281-9 (Print)
978-3-7094-1116-2 (E-Book-PDF)
978-3-7094-1117-9 (E-Book-ePub)

All other territories:
Spiramus:
978-1-9135-0721-3 (Print)
978-1-9135-0722-0 (E-Book-PDF)

Preface 6th edition

EU tax law keeps growing mainly through legal interpretation of its principles and rules. A regular update of technical knowledge in this domain is therefore an indispensable tool for mastering its increased complexity. We trust that our readers will welcome our decision to increase the periodicity in the release of the new editions.

Just like the previous editions, also this sixth edition keeps its concise style and selective approach to relevant issues, providing a complete analysis of the key issues of EU direct taxation.

During the past two years the growing role of state aids and EU fundamental rights have confirmed the trend that steers them towards having an equivalent impact on direct taxation as compared to the one traditionally had by fundamental freedoms. The developments of secondary law have been more marginal instead, confirming the difficulties in producing secondary legislation on direct taxes.

This edition contains selected relevant information available as of 30 June 2020 and retains all of the features and tools contained in the previous editions.

From this edition we have invited three more professors from our institute to join us in the role of coordinators of this publication. This reflects our spirit at the Institute for Austrian and International Tax Law of WU Vienna, which brings us altogether in a research group that pursues scientific excellence on European tax law.

The editors and authors are always grateful for comments and suggestions that may further improve the quality and content of forthcoming editions of this textbook. Moreover, we wish to thank *Julie Rogers* for linguistically editing this edition, and *Ivan Lazarov*, who assisted us in reviewing the content throughout the entire production process, allowing this sixth edition to be published according to schedule.

Vienna, 1 July 2020

Michael Lang
Pasquale Pistone
Josef Schuch
Claus Staringer
Alexander Rust
Georg Kofler
Karoline Spies

List of Authors

Mgr. Łukasz Adamczyk

Lawyer and certified Tax Advisor based in Warsaw, with a focus on European and international tax law issues.

Sriram Govind, LL.M. (WU)

Doctoral candidate at the Institute for Austrian and International Tax Law, WU (Vienna University of Economics and Business).

MMag. Matthias Hofstätter

Lecturer and former Research Assistant at the Institute for Austrian and International Tax Law of the WU (Vienna University of Economics and Business); Partner at LeitnerLeitner, Vienna.

Dr. Daniela Hohenwarter-Mayr, LL.M.

Professor at the University of Vienna and St. Gallen; former Research Associate at the Institute for Austrian and International Tax Law of the WU (Vienna University of Economics and Business).

Dr. Dimitar Hristov

Lecturer and former Research Assistant at the Institute for Austrian and International Tax Law of the WU (Vienna University of Economics and Business); Partner at DLA Piper Weiss-Tessbach Rechtsanwälte GmbH.

Ivan Lazarov, LL.M. (KU Leuven)

Research and Teaching Associate at the Institute for Austrian and International Tax Law, WU (Vienna University of Economics and Business).

Dr. Alicja Majdańska

Lawyer and certified Tax Advisor currently working at the tax department of a German DAX 30 MNE; Former Research Associate at the Institute for Austrian and International Tax Law of the WU (Vienna University of Economics and Business).

Alexandra Miladinovic, LL.M. (WU) BSc. (WU)

Research and Teaching Associate at the Institute for Austrian and International Tax Law, WU (Vienna University of Economics and Business).

Prof. Dr. Pasquale Pistone

Academic Chairman of IBFD; Holder of the Jean Monnet *ad personam* Chair in European Tax Law and Policy at WU (Vienna University of Economics and Business); Associate Professor at the University of Salerno; Professor honoris causa at the Ural State Law University and at the University of Cape Town.

Dr. Michael Schilcher

Lecturer and former Research Assistant at the Institute for Austrian and International Tax Law of the WU (Vienna University of Economics and Business); former Tax Consultant; currently Deputy Head of the Department for Income and Corporate Income Tax at the Austrian Federal Ministry of Finance.

Prof. Dr. Karoline Spies

Professor of tax law at the Institute for Austrian and International Tax Law of the WU (Vienna University of Economics and Business).

Dr. Rita Szudoczky

Assistant Professor of tax law at the Institute for Austrian and International Tax Law of the WU (Vienna University of Economics and Business).

Dr. Mario Tenore, LL.M.

Former Lecturer at the Institute for Austrian and International Tax Law of the WU (Vienna University of Economics and Business); currently Senior Associate at Maisto e Associati, Milan (Italy). He holds a PHD (cum laude) in European and International tax law from the Second University of Naples.

Jean-Philippe Van West, LL.M.

Senior Counsel International Tax at PwC Belgium, Guest Professor International and European Tax Law at Free University of Brussels-VUB.

Dr. Sabine Zirngast, LL.M.

Lecturer and former research assistant at the Institute for Austrian and International Tax Law of the WU (Vienna University of Economics and Business); tax consultant; currently assistant professor at the Institute for Financial Management/ Taxation at the University of Klagenfurt.

Stephanie Zolles, LL.M. (WU), BA

Doctoral candidate at the Institute for Austrian and International Tax Law, WU (Vienna University of Economics and Business).

Table of Contents

List of Abbreviations

AEoI	Automatic Exchange of Information
AGI	Allowance for Growth and Investment
AML	Anti-Money Laundering
APA	Advance Pricing Agreement
Art. or Arts.	Article or Articles
ATAD	Anti-Tax Avoidance Directive (Council Directive 2016/1164)
ATAD II	Directive as regards hybrid mismatches with third countries (Council Directive 2017/952 amending Directive (EU) 2016/1164)
BB	Betriebsberater
BEPS	Base Erosion and Profit Shifting
Bulletin	Bulletin for International Taxation
CbC reports	Country-by-Country reports
CbC MCAA	Multilateral Competent Authority Agreement on the Exchange of CbC reports
CCTB	Common Corporate Tax Base
CCCTB	Common Consolidated Corporate Tax Base
CFC	Controlled Foreign Corporation
CFR	European Charter on Fundamental Rights
CFT	Combating the Financing of Terrorism
CJEU	Court of Justice of the European Union
CLO	Central Liaison Office
CMLR	Common Market Law Review
COM	European Commission (formerly Commission of the European Communities)
Council	Council of the European Union
CRS	Common Reporting Standard
DAC	Council Directive 2011/16/EU
DAC 2	Directive 2014/107/EU
DAC 3	Directive 2015/2376/EU
DAC 5	Directive 2016/2258/EU
DB	Der Betrieb

Dispute Resolution Directive	Council Directive (EU) 2017/1852
DStR	Deutsches Steuerrecht
DTC	Double Taxation Convention
EAEC Treaty	European Atomic Energy Community Treaty
EAGF	European Agricultural Guarantee Fund
EAFRD	European Agricultural Fund for Rural Development
EBITDA	Earnings before Interest, Taxes, Depreciation and Amortization
EC	European Community, EC Treaty
ECHR	European Charter of Human Rights
ECOFIN	Economic and Financial Affairs Council
ed.	Edition
ed. or eds.	editor or editors
EEA	European Economic Area
EEC	European Economic Community
EFTA	European Free Trade Area
EGC	European General Court (formerly Court of First Instance)
e.g.	for example
EPA	European Partnership Agreement
EStAL	European State Aid Law Quarterly
ET	European Taxation
etc.	et cetera
et seq.	and the following
EU	European Union
EUR	Euro
EuZW	Europäische Zeitschrift für Wirtschaftsrecht
FATCA	Foreign Account Tax Compliance Act
FJ	Finanz Journal
FR	Finanz-Rundschau
FTT	Financial Transaction Tax
GAAR	General Anti-Abuse Clause/Rule
GBER	General Block Exemption Regulation
GC	General Court
GeS	GeS aktuell (Zeitschrift für Gesellschafts- und Steuerrecht)

HQ	Headquarter
i.e.	that is
Interest and Royalties Directive	Council Directive 2003/49/EC
IP	Intellectual Property
IStR	Internationales Steuerrecht
IWB	Internationales Steuer- und Wirtschaftsrecht
ITPJ	International Transfer Pricing Journal
JFC	Journal of Financial Crime
JIBL	Journal of International Banking Law
JIBLR	Journal of International Banking Law and Regulation
JIFM	Journal of International Financial Markets
JTPF	Joint Transfer Pricing Forum
KYC	Know your Costumer
m.no. or m.nos.	marginal number or marginal numbers
MAATM	Mutual Administrative Assistance in Tax Matters
Merger Directive	Council Directive 90/434/EEC
MLI	Multilateral Convention to Implement Tax Treaty Related Measures to Prevent BEPS
MNE	Multinational Enterprise
MS	Member State of the European Union
OCTs	Overseas Countries or Territories
OECD	Organisation for Economic Co-operation and Development
OECD Model or OECD MC	OECD Model Tax Convention on Income and on Capital
OJ	Official Journal
ÖStZ	Österreichische Steuerzeitung
p. or pp..	page or pages
para. or paras.	paragraph or paragraphs
Parent-Subsidiary Directive	Council Directive 90/435/EEC
PE	Permanent Establishment
R&D	Research and Development
RdW	Recht der Wirtschaft
Recovery Assistance Directive	Council Directive 2001/44/EC

SCE	Societas Cooperativa Europaea
SE	Societas Europaea
SME	Small and Medium-sized Enterprise
StuW	Steuer und Wirtschaft
suppl.	supplement
SWI	Steuer und Wirtschaft International
TEU	Treaty on European Union
TFEU	Treaty on the Functioning of the European Union
TIEA	Tax Information Exchange Agreement
TIN	Taxpayer Identification Number
TNI	Tax Notes International
UCITS	Undertaking for Collective Investment in Transferable Securities
Union	European Union
USD	US-Dollar
VAT	Value Added Tax
v.	versus
WHT	withholding tax
WTO	World Trade Organization
WTJ	World Tax Journal

Chapter 1 – The Sources of EU Law Relevant for Direct Taxation

Łukasz Adamczyk/Alicja Majdańska

I. General Overview
   A. Background
   B. Effects of EU Law
      1. Supremacy
      2. Direct Effect
         a) Direct Effect of the TFEU Treaty Provisions
         b) Direct Effect of the EU Directives' Provisions
      3. Direct Effect of the Provisions of EU International Agreements
      4. EU Institutions

II. Sources of EU Law
   A. Primary Law
      1. Fundamental Freedoms and State Aid
      2. Fundamental Rights
   B. Secondary Law
      1. Level of Harmonization
      2. Directives
      3. Regulations
   C. Soft Law
   D. EU International Agreements
      1. Agreements with third states or international bodies
      2. European Economic Area Agreement
      3. European Partnership Agreements (EPA)
      4. The Arbitration Convention

III. The Enforcement of EU Law
   A. European Union Level
   B. National Level (Preliminary Reference Procedure)
   C. Effectiveness of EU law
      1. Procedural Aspects of Redressing Breaches of EU Law
      2. Remedies against breaches of EU law

I. General Overview

A. Background

1 The roots of the EU can be traced back to the 1950s when three communities were created: the European Coal and Steel Community, the European Economic Community and the European Atomic Energy Community. The European Coal and Steel Community was formed for only a period of 50 years and ceased to exist in 2002. The European Economic Community was set up by the European Economic Community Treaty, signed in Rome on 25 March 1957, also known as the EC Treaty. The European Atomic Energy Community was established by the Treaty establishing the European Atomic Energy Community on 25 March 1957 (hereinafter EAEC Treaty). The European Union was not established until 1992 by the means of the Treaty of Maastricht (hereinafter TEU), which placed all the communities under one umbrella of policies and forms of cooperation. Subsequently, the Treaties of Amsterdam and Nice entered into force in 1999 and 2003, respectively, reforming the EU institutions. The latest package of fundamental changes to EU functioning was adopted by means of the Treaty of Lisbon (which was agreed to in 2007 and entered into force in 2009). Among various changes, the Treaty of Lisbon merged the EU and the European Community (previously the European Economic Community) into the 'Union'. It also subjected the actions of the EU institutions and the Member States, insofar as they apply and implement EU law, to the Charter of Fundamental Rights of the European Union (hereinafter the Charter of Fundamental Rights or the Charter), which enshrines certain fundamental rights that are legally binding at the EU level.

2 As a result, the following four instruments form the foundation of the EU legal system: TEU,[1] TFEU[2] (which is an updated version of the EC Treaty), EAEC Treaty (updated version), and the Charter. Together, the treaties and the Charter form EU primary law. An inherent aspect of EU primary law is the general principles on which the EU legal system is based. They play a key gap-filling role that ensures the coherence of the EU legal system and are taken into account when EU law, as well as national law, measures are interpreted.[3] Notably, in the controversial *Mangold* case, the Court declared the principle of equal treatment to be a general principle of EU law that should guide the interpretation process. Although there has been no specific post-*Mangold* case law developed in the taxation area, this line of reasoning has contributed to the interpretation of the Charter provisions. EU primary law is supplemented by secondary law, which is law made by the EU institutions in the exercise of the powers conferred on them by primary law. It consists of legislative acts (regulations, directives and decisions). Another important element of the EU legal system is soft law, which consists of non-legislative acts (recommendations,

---

1   Consolidated version of the Treaty on European Union, OJ C 326 of 26 October 2012.
2   Consolidated version of the Treaty on the Functioning of the European Union, OJ C 326 of 26 October 2012.
3   Lenaerts/Gutiérrez-Fons, The Constitutional Allocation of Powers and General Principles of EU Law, *Common Market Law Review* 47/6 2010, pp. 1629-1669.

opinions, etc.). In addition, the case law of the CJEU and international treaties signed by the EU are also considered to be a part of the EU legal system.

At the centre of the EU legal system is the concept of an internal market. It is the **3** fundamental EU concept on which the EU legal system rests. It is defined in Art. 26 TFEU as *"an area without frontiers in which the free movement of goods, persons, services and capital is ensured in accordance with the provisions of the Treaties."* Achieving an internal market depends on the four freedoms: the free movement of goods, capital, services, and labour. In addition to the four freedoms, the prohibition on cartel agreements, abuse of dominant market position and State aid prohibition are also aimed at ensuring the protection of the internal market. Finally, 'positive' integration, which implies policy integration (i.e. integration through legislation), plays an important role as well.

Taxation is often seen as a potential obstacle to achieving an internal market and, **4** as a result, is susceptible to infringing the fundamental freedoms. It may distort competition. This is the main reason for a number of directives and regulations in the area of taxation in the EU.

This textbook focuses on an analysis of EU direct taxation. Nevertheless, to ensure **5** a better understanding of its object, especially in respect of structural issues of tax integration in harmonized and non-harmonized fields, and in connection with the implementation of EU law for the purposes of the Charter of Fundamental Rights, when necessary, this chapter also refers to VAT issues.

B. Effects of EU Law

1. Supremacy

As the EC Treaty (the predecessor of the TFEU) was silent on the issue of the **6** relationship between EU law and national legal orders, the CJEU has had to provide clarification. In the Costa v E.N.E.L. case, the Court made it clear that "... *the law stemming from the Treaty ... could not ... be overridden by domestic legal provisions ...*" and in the event of a conflict between an EU law provision and a national provision, the former takes precedence over the latter.[4] Later, the Court further clarified that every national court is obliged to apply EU law "in its entirety and protect rights which the latter confers on individuals and must accordingly set aside any provision of national law which may conflict with it, whether prior or subsequent to" the EU law provision.[5] In addition, the Court held that an EU law provision even takes precedence over a national constitutional provision.[6] According to the subsequent jurisprudence of the CJEU, the national administration is also required to ensure the supremacy of EU law over national law.[7]

---

4   CJEU, 15 July 1964, Case C-6/64, *Costa v E.N.E.L.*, EU:C:1964:66.
5   CJEU, 9 March 1978, Case C-106/77, *Simmenthal*, EU:C:1978:49, para. 21.
6   CJEU, 17 December 1970, Case C-11/70, *Internationale Handelsgesellschaft*, EU:C:1970:114.
7   CJEU, 29 April 1999, Case C-224/97, *Erich Ciola and Land Vorarlberg*, EU:C:1999:212.

2. Direct Effect

7 A **directly effective provision** of EU law confers **legally enforceable rights** on an individual such that that individual may rely on those rights before a national court or a national administrative authority. As a result of the supremacy theory, a national provision that is in conflict with a directly effective EU law provision has to be set aside.

8 A **directly applicable provision** of EU law is **automatically effective** in the national legal order without needing to enact implementation measures. The TFEU expressly recognizes the direct applicability of provisions of EU Regulations. However, the TFEU remains silent on the direct effect of treaty provisions, directives and international agreements concluded by the EU. For this reason, the Court has had to elaborate on these issues.

a) Direct Effect of the TFEU Treaty Provisions

9 The conditions for TFEU provisions having direct effect were spelled out in the landmark case of *Van Gend & Loos*.[8] In the judgment, the Court held that the **EC Treaty (now the TFEU) constitutes more than an international agreement** since the Member States have limited their sovereign rights in certain fields by transferring powers to the EU institutions, creating thereby a new, *sui generis*, system of law. The Court recognized that the provisions of the Treaty are directly effective and that there is no need to implement them into domestic law. As a result, TFEU provisions confer rights and obligations not only on Member States but also on individuals.

10 In order to be directly effective, a TFEU provision has to fulfil the following conditions:

- it must be **clearly** and **precisely** worded; and
- it must be **unconditional** and **independent** from any national implementation measure.

11 Individuals and other persons can therefore directly invoke the TFEU provisions, but only if the provisions meet the above-mentioned conditions.

b) Direct Effect of the EU Directives' Provisions

12 Since Member States are responsible for implementing the directives into domestic law, there is an inherent risk that they will not be implemented or at least not correctly, which might undermine the uniformity of EU law application. Therefore, it is important for individuals to be entitled, in any event, to rely on the 'true meaning' of a directive provision. In the *Van Duyn* case, the Court ruled there that "*it would be incompatible with the binding effect attributed to a directive [...]*"

---

8   CJEU, 5 February 1963, Case C-26/62, *Van Gend en Loos,* EU:C:1985:104.

to exclude in principle, the possibility that the obligation which it imposes may be invoked by those concerned. [...] It is necessary to examine in every case, whether the nature, general scheme and wording of the provision in question are capable of having direct effects on relations between Member States and individuals."[9] In the *Ratti* case, the CJEU established that Member States may not rely on a non-implemented directive against its own citizens (the *estoppel* principle).[10]

Generally, directives should not be applied directly in substantiating obligations to **13** the detriment of an individual (**no reverse vertical direct effect of directive provisions**), however, when there is an abuse of law situation, an individual can be deprived of the EU law rights provided even if there is no specific legal basis under national law for such a denial. This is a new phenomen as regards direct taxation, an area in respect of which, initially, the Court, referring to the anti-abuse provisions of the Merger Directive (art. 15 thereof), ruled that a Member State that has failed to transpose the provisions of a directive into national law cannot rely, as against individuals, upon limitations that might have been laid down on the basis of those provisions.[11] In an apparently striking departure from its previous case law, the Court in the 'Danish' cases[12] acknowledged that *"in the light of the general principle of EU law that abusive practices are prohibited and of the need to ensure observance of that principle when EU law is implemented, the absence of domestic or agreement-based anti-abuse provisions does not affect the national authorities' obligation to refuse to grant entitlement to rights provided for by [the PS Directive and the IR Directive] where they are invoked for fraudulent or abusive ends."*[13] This decision leads to a convergence with VAT case law, in particular the seminal *Halifax* decision, wherein similar Member State rights were recognized.[14] Moreover, in *Italmoda*,[15] the CJEU ruled that Member States may deny rights granted under EU VAT law if the taxable person is participating, or could have known it is participating, in VAT evasion, even if national law contains no basis for such denial.

In addition, the Court clarified that an individual may rely on an unconditional **14** and sufficiently precise provision of a directive if the time limit for implementation has elapsed and the Member State has not implemented the directive[16] or has

---

9   CJEU, 4 December 1974, Case C-41/74, *Van Duyn v Home Office*, EU:C:1974:133.
10   CJEU, 5 April 1979, Case C-148/78, *Publico Ministero v Ratti*, EU:C:1979:110.
11   CJEU, 5 July 2007, Case C-321/05, *Kofoed*, EU:C:2007:408, para. 33.
12   CJEU, 26 February 2019, Joined Cases C-116/16 and C-117/16, *Skatteministeriet v T Danmark* (C-116/16), *Y Denmark Aps* (C-117/16), paras. 70-83.
13   CJEU, 26 February 2019, Joined Cases C-116/16 and C-117/16, *Skatteministeriet v T Danmark* (C-116/16), *Y Denmark Aps* (C-117/16), para. 83.
14   CJEU, 21 February 2006, C-255/02, *Halifax and Others*, EU:C:2006:121.
15   CJEU, 18 December 2014, Joined Cases C-131/13, C-163/13 and C-164/13, *Staatssecretaris van Financiën, v Schoenimport 'Italmoda' Mariano Previti vof* (C-131/13), *Turbu.com BV* (C-163/13) and *Turbu.com Mobile Phone's BV* (C-164/13), EU:C:2014:2455. Similarly, in: CJEU, 22 November 2017, Case C-251/16, *Edward Cussens, John Jennings, Vincent Kingston v T.G. Brosnan*, EU:C:2017:881.
16   CJEU, 19 January 1982, Case C-8/81, *Becker*, EU:C:1982:7.

failed to do so correctly.[17] Consequently, Wattel argues that taxpayers are given a choice: they can either apply a national provision that is contrary to EU law or refer directly to a directive provision. As a result, non-compliance of Member States may result in 'provision shopping'.[18]

15 In principle, an individual may not rely on a non-implemented or incorrectly implemented directive against another individual (**'horizontal direct effect'**). This possibility has been explicitly rejected by the CJEU. Two main arguments support this conclusion. First, the Court emphasized that a directive binds states and not private parties.[19] Second, the requirement for legal certainty prevents the directives from creating obligations for individuals without first being implemented into national law.[20] Nevertheless, a directive might have horizontal and/or inverse vertical effect.[21] This would happen if e.g. an individual brought an appeal on the basis of an EU environmental directive against an environmental permit granted to an undertaking.

16 Moreover, national courts are obliged to ensure that the directive at issue is fully effective. This is achieved through **the principle of interpretation in conformity with EU law**. National courts should follow the method of interpretation that best avoids inconsistency with EU law,[22] both before and after the implementation period has expired.[23] In the doctrine, the principle is also known as the principle of consistent interpretation or of indirect effect. They are required to interpret national law *"as far as possible, in the light of the wording and the purpose of the directive in order to achieve the result pursued by the latter."*[24] As such, it may effect private to private relationships. This principle is subject to restrictions. The principle of interpretation in conformity with EU law applies *"in so far as it is given discretion to do so under national law."*[25] Therefore, an EU-conforming *contra legem* interpretation of national law is not permitted. Moreover, there is no obligation of consistent interpretation if such is contrary to general principles of law, particularly those of legal certainty and non-retroactivity.[26]

---

17 CJEU, 17 October 1996, Joined Cases C-283/94, C-291/94 and C-292/94, *Denkavit International, VITIC Amsterdam and Voormeer*, EU:C:1996:387.
18 Terra/Wattel, *European Tax Law* (2012) p. 82.
19 CJEU, 14 July 1994, Case C-91/92, *Paola Faccini Dori v Recreb Srl.*, EU:C:1994:292, paras. 22-23.
20 CJEU, 7 January 2004, Case C-201/02, The Queen, on the application of Delena Wells v Secretary of State for Transport, Local Government and the Regions, EU:C:2004:12, para. 56.
21 Terra/Wattel, European Tax Law (2012) p. 82.
22 CJEU, 5 October 2004, Joined Cases C-397/01 to C-403/01, Pfeiffer a. o., EU:C:2004:584, paras. 114-119.
23 CJEU, 4 July 2006, Case C-212/04, Konstantinos Adeneler, EU:C:2006:6057, paras. 114-117.
24 CJEU, 13 November 1990, Case C-106/89, Marleasing SA v La Comercial Internacional de Alimentacion SA, EU:C:1990:395, para. 8.
25 CJEU, 10 April 1984, Case C-14/83, Sabine von Colson and Elisabeth Kamann v Land Nordrhein-Westfalen, EU:C:1984:153, para. 28.
26 CJEU, 8 October 1987, Case C-80/86, *Kolpinghuis Nijmegen*, EU:C:1987:431, para. 13; CJEU, 4 July 2006, Case C-212/04, *Konstantinos Adeneler and Others v Ellinikos Organismos Galaktos*, EU:C:2006:443, para. 110.

3. Direct Effect of the Provisions of EU International Agreements

As regards international agreements, the Court has drawn on the doctrine devel- **17** oped in *Van Gend & Loos*. It confirmed the direct effect of specific provisions of EU international agreements as long as they are self-executing, i.e. they meet the two conditions outlined in the case. In addition, the Court added a third require- ment, which addresses the spirit, structure and nature of the agreement, which cannot preclude their direct effect.[27]

In the context of the special role granted to the ECHR in the EU legal system[28] the **18** CJEU has recently reopened the debate on the relationship between international law and EU law. In addressing the effect of international agreements, the Court examines, among other things, whether a sufficient level of protection of the fun- damental rights exists.

In the *Kadi I* case, the CJEU reviewed the lawfulness of a legal act transposing a **19** UN resolution, highlighting the insufficient protection of fundamental rights at the UN level. This seems to represent a departure from the idea of 'distinctive fidelity to international law',[29] which the CJEU adhered to in the past. Neverthe- less, this could also be perceived differently. The CJEU may be opening up the possibility of allowing for the precedence of UN Security Council measures, pro- vided sufficient safeguards for human rights are created.[30]

The balance between the need to combat international terrorism and the protec- **20** tion of the fundamental rights and freedoms of suspected terrorists within the EU legal framework was once again considered in the *Kadi II* case. The CJEU ascer- tained that "*none of the allegations presented (...) are such as to justify the adoption, at European Union level, of restrictive measures (...) either because the statement of reasons is insufficient, or because information or evidence which might substantiate the reason concerned, in the face of detailed rebuttals submitted by the party con- cerned, is lacking.*"[31]

4. EU Institutions

Art. 13 of the TEU establishes, inter alia, the following EU institutions: the Euro- **21** pean Parliament, the Council and the European Commission. These institutions help shape EU direct taxation, although the powers in the field of direct taxation remain mostly in the hands of the Member States.

---

27 CJEU, 9 February 1982, Case C-270/80, *Polydor Limited and RSO Records v Harlequin Records Shops and Simons Records*, EU:C:1982:43, para. 12; CJEU, 11 May 2000, Case C-37/98, Savaş, EU:C:2000:224.
28 CJEU, 18 December 2014, Case Opinion 2/13, EU:C:2014:2454, para. 37 et seq.
29 De Burca, The EU, the European Court of Justice and the International Legal Order after Kadi, *Harv. Int'l L.J.* 2010, p. 47.
30 Kokott/Sobotta, The *Kadi* Case – Constitutional Core Values and International Law – Finding the Balance, *EJIL* 2012, pp. 1015-1016.
31 CJEU, 18 July 2013, Joined Cases C-584/10 P, C-593/10 P and C-595/10 P, *Kadi II*, EU:C:2013:518, para. 163.

22 The **European Parliament** and the **Council** can be seen as two chambers of the legislative branch of the EU with its competences being officially distributed between both institutions. The Treaty of Lisbon has somehow also strengthened the powers of the European Parliament in fields that may be relevant for direct taxation, as the amendment to Arts. 64 and 65 TFEU (ex Arts. 57 and 58 EC) proves. However, some relevant differences can still be noted in comparison to powers given to national legislatures, such as, for instance, the fact that, in principle, the power of legislative initiative is neither for the European Parliament, nor for the Council, but is instead exclusively reserved to the European Commission. Therefore, while the European Parliament can amend and reject legislation, the Commission has to initiate the legislative procedure. A special procedure applies to direct tax matters and requires the unanimity of the Council to issue a directive on direct taxes (Art. 115 TFEU). The European Parliament plays only a consultative role (under the so-called special legislative procedure). According to many, this procedure is seen as hampering progress on important tax initatives. In 2019, the European Commission issued a communication on how to move to Qualified Majority Voting via the use of the general passerelle clause (Art. 192(2) TFEU), or by applying policy-related passerelle clauses. As a result, the Council would share its legislative power with the Parliament, as under the ordinary legislative procedure. Furthermore, a decision at the Council level would be made if consented to by the so-called 'qualified' or 'double majority', i.e. 55% of Member States voting and provided such Member States represent 65% of the European population.[32] As some say, the move to Qualified Majority Voting would make tax policy consistent with the internal market and full accountability of the European Parliament.[33]

23 Besides its competences in the legislative process, the **European Commission** monitors the Member States' compliance with EU law. Whenever it finds that a Member State has not complied with EU law, it may initiate an infringement procedure. This special role has been conferred on the European Commission within the area of State aid. All new aid measures have to be notified to the European Commission. Following the notification, the European Commission initiates a preliminary investigation to decide if a measure may be implemented. The European Commission also has competence to review the authorized aid schemes. In addition, it can examine aid granted without prior authorization (e.g. unlawful aid). If it has serious doubts about the aid's compatibility with EU State aid rules, or where it faces procedural difficulties in obtaining the necessary information, it can initiate a formal investigation procedure (Art. 108(2) TFEU). Moreover, the Commission often issues non-binding soft law measures directed to the Member States.

32　European Commission, Communication from the Commission to the European Parliament, the European Council and the Council. Towards a more efficient and democratic decision making in EU tax policy, Strasbourg, 15 January 2019, COM(2019) 8 final.

33　See Pistone, A Plea for Qualified Majority Voting and the Ordinary Legislative Procedure in European Tax Law, in: van Thiel/ Valente/Raventós-Calvo (eds.), *CFE Tax Advisers Europe – 60th Anniversary Liber Amicorum* (2019) p. 11.

In its capacity as a single judicial body competent to interpret EU law, the role of **24** the **Court of Justice of the European Union** is to ensure that EU law is observed. In doing so, the Court reviews the legality of the acts of the institutions of the European Union (including when it acts as an appellate body in respect of the decisions of the European General Court in domains such as, for instance, State aid), controls the Member States' compliance with obligations under the Treaties and interprets EU law at the request of national courts and tribunals with the aim of ensuring the uniform application and interpretation of EU law. In selected cases it may also decide on the interpretation of a double taxation convention (herein-after: DTC) as an arbitrator. This is only possible, however, when three condi-tions are met, namely: the dispute brought before the CJEU is between Member States, the dispute relates to the subject matter of EU law and the dispute is sub-mitted to the CJEU under a special agreement between the parties.[34] To date, the CJEU has acted as an arbitrator in respect of a DTC only once.[35]

II. Sources of EU Law

A. Primary Law

1. Fundamental Freedoms and State Aid

For about three decades, the most relevant primary law provisions have been the **25** **fundamental freedoms** as interpreted by the CJEU (see Chapter 3, m.no. 190 et seq.), which set limits as to the boundaries for exercising national tax jurisdiction (known as **negative integration**).

More recently, the State aid rules (Arts. 107 and 108 TFEU, ex Arts. 87 and 88 EC) **26** have grown in importance. They have played an increasingly important role in the field of direct taxes, while recent judgments from EU courts have determined the boundaries of the direct effect of such rules on direct taxes and have ensured an effective review of the EU Commission's activity in this domain. (see Chapter 4, m.no. 296 et seq.).

The limited scope of EU law in respect of direct taxation is usually explained in **27** two ways. First, at the time the Treaty of Rome was signed, direct taxes were not apparently seen as necessarily important to the establishment of the internal mar-ket and, consequently, were left outside the scope of the EC Treaty (the predeces-sor to the TFEU).[36] Second, having in mind that direct taxes may serve as useful tools in pursuing various economic or social aims, the Member States' reluctance to give up their competence is understandable. Consequently, direct taxation has

---

34   Art. 273 TFEU.
35   CJEU, 12 September 2017, Case C-648/15, *Austria v Germany*, EU:C:2017:664.
36   It should be noted that the 1953 Tinbergen report, laying down the conceptual grounds for the creation of the EC, did not acknowledge harmonization of direct taxes as necessary in developing the single market.

remained within the competence of Member States. This does not prevent the European Union, however, from taking action in the field of direct taxation.

28 The European Union can only act within the limits of the competences conferred upon it by the Member States in the Treaties to attain the objectives set out therein. This reflects the so-called principle of conferral. The competences of the European Union are divided into three categories: exclusive, shared and supporting competences. Exclusive competence covers areas in which only the European Union can adopt a legal act (e.g. customs). Shared competence covers areas in which either the European Union or Member States can adopt legal acts. If the European Union does not exercise its own competence or has decided not to exercise it, the competence remains with Member States. Among others, the competence over the internal market is shared. Given that direct taxation influences the internal market, it is subsumed under shared competence. Finally, supporting competences only allow the European Union to support, coordinate or complement the actions of Member States. This is true for, inter alia, the areas of culture and education.

29 The exercise of EU competences, also in the field of direct taxation, is limited by two fundamental principles laid down in Art. 5 TEU: proportionality and subsidiarity. The principle of subsidiarity refers only to shared competences and requires that the EU execute its competences *"only if and in so far as the objectives of the proposed action cannot be sufficiently achieved by the Member States."*[37] The principle of proportionality requires that EU action not exceed what is necessary to achieve EU objectives. These two principles are key to tax harmonization.

30 There are a few additional principles that indirectly affect EU competence in the field of (both direct and indirect) taxation and potentially limit the tax sovereignty of Member States. Among these, the prohibition of direct and indirect discriminatory taxation of foreign products and direct and indirect fiscal protection of domestic production play an important role in preventing protectionism (Art. 110 TFEU). The inverse principle is the prohibition of direct or indirect tax subsidies on products exported to another Member State (Art. 111 TFEU). With regard to direct taxation, the prohibition is extended to remissions, repayments, and countervailing charges. However, Member States can obtain authorization from the Commission to introduce such measures.

31 Harmonization of direct and indirect taxation is subject to two separate mechanisms that differ from those of an ordinary EU legislative procedure (so called 'fiscal exclusion' as set forth in **Art. 114 TFEU**). In terms of indirect taxation mechanisms, there is an explicit legal basis for EU competence. Art. 113 TFEU specifically provides for the Council, acting unanimously in accordance with a special legislative procedure and after consulting the European Parliament and

---

37   Art. 5(3) TFEU.

the Economic and Social Committee, to adopt provisions for the harmonization of Member States' rules.[38]

Art. 115 TFEU is seen as the legal basis for harmonization in the field of direct tax-   **32** ation. Although it does not refer to direct taxation *expressis verbis*, it is the only provision that can be applied to harmonization of direct taxes. It authorizes the Council to issue directives to approximate laws, regulations and provisions directly affecting the establishment and functioning of the internal market. Such directives may only be adopted on the basis of **unanimity** in the Council. Therefore, it is rather difficult to push forward European tax harmonization, as every measure has to satisfy all Member States, which, in light of serious differences between national tax policies (for instance, low-tax countries vs. high tax countries), is exceedingly difficult.

Another procedure that can be used for harmonization of (direct and indirect)   **33** taxes is enhanced cooperation. This is seen as a last resort option *"when it has established that the objectives of such cooperation cannot be attained within a reasonable period by the Union as a whole."*[39] The procedure allows at least nine Member States to fully harmonize an area covered by the EU Treaties but not falling within the EU's exclusive competence.[40] The other Member States are not involved in the procedure and do not have to harmonize their laws. The enhanced cooperation procedure has not played a significant role in positive integration in the field of tax law. It has been put forward as an option in respect of implementation of a financial transaction tax and the Common Consolidated Corporate Tax Base, but neither of these proposals has been implemented.

It should be noted that the EC Treaty contained **Art. 293**, which provided that the   **34** Member States had to, to the extent necessary, enter into negotiations to secure the **abolition of double taxation**. Such a provision does not exist in the TFEU. However, as this provision was devoid of direct effect and merely constituted a political declaration,[41] the effect of its deletion should not be overestimated or perceived as an indication that the abolition of double taxation has been removed from the political agenda of the EU.[42]

As a result of the EU's limited competence in the field of direct taxation, positive   **35** integration has not played a dominant role so far. To date, only a limited number of direct tax directives have been adopted on the basis of Art. 115 (see Section II.2.b of this chapter). By contrast, negative integration has had a tremendous impact on the shape of direct taxation amongst Member States.

---

38   Contrary to the other directives in the area of direct taxation, the recent Commission proposal for a directive on the common system of a digital services tax on revenues resulting from the provision of certain digital services relies on Art. 113 as its legal basis.
39   Art. 20(2) TEU.
40   Art. 20 TEU.
41   CJEU, 12 May 1998, Case C-336/96, *Gilly*, EU:C:1998:221, para. 17.
42   See, in this respect, Šemeta, Tax Policy Work Programme, Speech of 16 February 2010, available at http://ec.europa.eu/commission_2010-2014/semeta/headlines/speeches/2010/02/speech_1602b.pdf (accessed 23 October 2015).

2. Fundamental Rights

36 With regard to Member States, fundamental rights are typically protected at three levels: domestic law (usually enshrined in constitutions), EU primary law (mainly the Charter of Fundamental Rights of the European Union)[43] and the ECHR

37 The basis for developing EU fundamental rights in the field of taxation was the *Internationale Handelsgesellschaft*[44] case, which established the standard of legal protection through common principles at the supranational level.[45] Since then, the protection of taxpayer fundamental rights has become even more entrenched.[46]

38 At the EU level, the protection of fundamental rights has developed incrementally. As early as 1969, the Court recognized fundamental rights as part of the general principles of EU law.[47] In its case law, the Court often referred to fundamental rights as stemming from constitutional traditions common to the Member States and to the ECHR.[48]

39 In recognition of the role of fundamental rights within the EU legal system, it was decided to establish a Charter of Fundamental Rights. This was seen as essential *"to make their [fundamental rights] overriding importance and relevance more visible to the Union's citizens."*[49] The text of the Charter of Fundamental Rights was approved in 2000 and, subsequently, in 2009, it entered into force. It is seen as having the same legal status as EU primary law.[50]

40 At the same time, when the Charter of Fundamental Rights entered into force, the EU Commission was given a mandate to negotiate EU accession to the ECHR.[51] The EU's accession to the ECHR has not yet been finalized. Although the draft Accession Agreement of the EU to the ECHR between the 47 Member States of the Council of Europe and the EU was finalized in 2013, the accession was blocked by a negative opinion issued by the CJEU.[52] The Court pointed out, inter alia, that the agreed accession conditions would potentially affect the competences of EU

---

43 The Charter of Fundamental Rights of the European Union, OJ C 83 of 30 March 2010, pp. 389-403.

44 CJEU, 17 December 1970, Case C-11/70, *Internationale Handelsgesellschaft*, EU:C:1970:114.

45 Kofler/Pistone, General Report, in: Kofler/Maduro/Pistone (eds.), *Human Rights and Taxation in Europe and the World* (2011) p. 5.

46 Ibid, p. 7.

47 CJEU, 12 November 1969, Case C-29/69, *Erich Stauder v City of Ulm – Sozialamt*, EU:C:1969:57.

48 See, for example: CJEU, 15 May 1986, Case 222/84, *Johnston*, EU:C:1986:206, paras. 18 and 19; CJEU, 15 October 1987, Case 222/86, *Heylens and Others*, EU:C:1987:442, para. 14; CJEU, 27 Nov. 2001, Case C-424/99, *Commission v Austria*, EU:C:2001:642, para. 45; CJEU, 25 July 2002, Case C-50/00, *P Unión de Pequeños Agricultores v Council*, EU:C:2002:462, para. 39; CJEU, 19 June 2003, Case C-467/01, *Eribrand*, EU:C:2003:364, para. 61; and CJEU, 22 June 2017, Case C-49/16, *Unibet*, EU:C: 2017:491, para. 37.

49 Cologne European Council, 3–4 June 1999, Conclusions of the Presidency, Annex IV–European Council Decision on the drawing up of a Charter of Fundamental Rights of the European Union, para 1.

50 E.g. CJEU, 15 July 2010, Case C-271/08, *Commission v Germany*, EU:C:2010:426, para 37; and CJEU, 4 March 2010, Case C-578/08, *Chakroun*, EU:C:2010:117.

51 Art. 6(2) TEU.

52 Opinion 2/13 of the Court (Full Court), 18 December 2014, EU:C:2014:2454.

institutions and undermine the autonomy of EU law. The Commission is currently exploring how to address the legal issues identified by the CJEU.[53]

The 'regulation' of general principles of EU law has strengthened the role of the **41** principles and rules contained in the national constitutions of the EU Member States. As a result of being shifted from a national to a supranational level, within the framework of the supremacy of EU law over that of EU Member States, they have gained a new dimension. Therefore, this regulated system of protection offers the most modern and comprehensive protection of human rights.

There is a flexible link between the Charter of Fundamental Rights and the Euro **42** pean Convention on Human Rights. To the extent a fundamental right is protected under the European Convention on Human Rights, it enjoys the status of a general principle under EU law. The European Convention on Human Rights constitutes a minimum standard, whereas EU law reaches beyond it and, as such, may ensure stronger protection.[54] This means that case law of the ECtHR remains of great importance to the EU legal framework. As a result, in cases where the CJEU recognizes that a specific provision at stake "*contains rights corresponding to those guaranteed by (...) ECHR. (...) the Charter must therefore be given the same meaning and the same scope as (...) the ECHR, as interpreted by the case-law of the European Court of Human Rights.*"[55] In those cases, the CJEU interprets and applies rights enshrined in the Charter in light of the case law of the ECtHR.

The status of a minimum standard granted to the ECHR also means that the **43** interpretation and application of its provisions may affect the protection granted under the Charter within the EU legal framework. The opposite possibility, i.e. the Charter influencing the ECHR, is not likely. The ECtHR is also not obliged to interpret and apply the Charter.

The national courts have the competence to assess fully the compatibility of any **44** domestic measure that is within the scope of EU law with the Charter of Fundamental Rights.[56] As recent CJEU case law proves, the principles enshrined in the Charter of Fundamental Right may have direct effect in a field covered by EU law. This applies both to vertical and horizontal disputes. In terms of vertical disputes, it is sufficient if it is impossible to interpret the national legislation at issue in a manner consistent with the Charter of Fundamental Rights.[57] Horizontal direct effect of the Charter of Fundamental Rights requires the relevant principle to be mandatory and unconditional.[58]

---

53   Council of the European Union, Council conclusions on the application of the EU Charter of Fundamental Rights in 2016, Brussels, 13 October 2017, 12913/17.
54   Art. 52(3) Charter of Fundamental Rights.
55   CJEU, 5 October 2010, Case C-400/10, PPU, *J. McB. v L. E. Case*, EU:C:2010:582, para. 53; CJEU, 14 Feb. 2008, Case C-450/06, *Varec*, EU:C:2008:91, para. 48.
56   CJEU, 26 February 2013, Case C- 617/10, *Åkerberg Fransson*, EU:C:2013:105, para. 112.
57   CJEU, 13 December 2018, Case C-385/17, *Hein*, EU:C:2018:1018, paras. 48-52.
58   CJEU, 6 November 2018, Case C-684/16, *Max-Planck-Gesellschaft zur Förderung der Wissenschaften e.V. v Tetsuji Shimizu* EU:C:2018:874, paras. 66-74.

45 Nevertheless, the Charter of Fundamental Rights is not an exhaustive list of fundamental rights. It acknowledges the existence of other fundamental rights, beyond its scope. As such, it can be perceived as a basis that aims to enhance legal certainty. It provides a framework that can be expanded within the framework of EU law in the future.[59]

46 The Charter of Fundamental Rights is fully applicable to EU secondary law, such as regulations and directives, as well as decisions of the Commission, EU courts and authorities. In respect of the legal systems of the Member States, it is applied only when the respective bodies 'are implementing Union law'.[60] It should be emphasized that the Charter of Fundamental Rights does not extend the European Union's competences.[61] It entails that EU law cannot restrict the ECHR. The backbone of the Charter of Fundamental Rights is the prohibition of abuse of rights, based on which *"nothing shall be interpreted as implying any right to engage in any activity or to perform any act aimed at the destruction of any of the rights and freedoms recognized in this Charter or at their limitation to a greater extent than is provided for herein."*[62]

47 Although the Charter of Fundamental Rights does not include specific tax provisions, several articles may be relevant to taxpayers. Certain provisions are, in particular, worth mentioning, such as Art. 8 – protection of personal data, Art. 17 – right to property, Art. 20 – equality before the law, Art. 21 – non-discrimination principle, Art. 41 – right to good administration, Art. 42 – right of access to documents, Art. 43 – ombudsman, Art. 45 – freedom of movement and of residence, Art. 47 – right to an effective remedy and to a fair trial, Art. 48 – presumption of innocence and right of defence, Art. 49 – legality and proportionality of criminal offences and penalties, and Art. 50 – right not to be tried or punished twice in criminal proceedings for the same criminal offence (*ne bis in idem*).

48 The scope of application of the Charter of Fundamental Rights has stirred up controversy. Under Art. 51 of the Charter of Fundamental Rights, the Member States are obliged to comply with its whole content only 'when they are implementing Union law'. As a result, the main question has been the meaning of the phrase 'implementing Union law'.

49 In *Iida* the Court pointed out that the Charter of Fundamental Rights is applicable if the national legislation at stake is intended to implement a provision of EU law[63]. It is also important to identify the character of that legislation, and whether it pursues objectives other than those covered by EU law. Finally, it needs to be

---

59   See Pistone, The EU Law Dimension of Human Rights in Tax Matters, in: Brokelind (ed.), *Principles of Law: Function, Status and Impact in EU Tax Law* (2014) p. 102.
60   Art. 51(1) Charter of Fundamental Rights.
61   Ibid, Art. 52(2).
62   Ibid, Art. 54.
63   CJEU, 8 November 2012, Case C-40/11, *Yoshikazu Iida v Stadt Ulm*, EU:C:2012:691.

verified whether there are specific rules of EU law on the matter or capable of affecting it.[64] The wording of the judgment clearly narrows down the potential scope of measures 'implementing Union law' to cases when there is a direct impact of EU law on the national legislation. This has been confirmed in a number of cases related to taxation.

For instance, in the *Chartry* case,[65] the CJEU decided that the Member State does **50** not exercise its rights in implementing EU law by merely requiring a reference to the Constitutional Court for a preliminary ruling if a taxpayer is found to have been deprived of the effective judicial protection guaranteed by Art. 6 of the ECHR.

In the *Belvedere Costruzioni* case,[66] the CJEU decided on the measures the Member **51** States are obliged to introduce to ensure the effectiveness of EU law. In this case, the Court found grounds to apply the Charter of Fundamental Rights, as the Member State was acting in the course of implementing EU law. The CJEU highlighted that *"the obligation to ensure effective collection of European Union resources cannot run counter to compliance with the principle that judgment should be given within a reasonable time, which, under the second paragraph of Article 47 of the Charter of Fundamental Rights of the European Union, must be observed by the Member States when they implement European Union law, and must also be observed under Article 6(1) of the ECHR (...) The facts of the dispute in the main proceedings, which go back about 30 years, show that some of those proceedings have lasted for a much greater number of years. Such a length of proceedings is a priori capable in itself of infringing the reasonable time principle and, moreover, the obligation to ensure the effective collection of the European Union's own resources."*[67]

In the *Åkerberg Fransson*[68] case, the CJEU examined the imposition of penalties **52** in respect of an infringement in the field of value added tax in light of the prohibition of double jeopardy under Art. 50 of the Charter of Fundamental Rights. In that case, the CJEU broadened the scope of the Charter of Fundamental Rights to a field of law that does not fall entirely within the competence of the EU.[69] According to the CJEU, *"The fact that the national legislation upon which those tax penalties and criminal proceedings are founded has not been adopted to transpose Directive 2006/112 cannot call that conclusion into question, since its application is designed to penalise an infringement of that directive and is therefore intended to implement the obligation imposed on the Member States by the Treaty to impose effective penalties for conduct prejudicial to the financial interests of the European*

---

64   Ibid, para. 79.
65   CJEU, 1 March 2011, Case C-467/09, *Chartry*, OJ C 37 of 13 February 2010, pp. 3-3.
66   CJEU, 29 March 2012, Case C-500/10, *Belvedere Costruzioni*, EU:C:2012:186.
67   Ibid, paras. 23 and 25.
68   CJEU, 26 February 2013, Case C- 617/10, *Åkerberg Fransson*, EU:C:2013:105.
69   ECJ Task Force of the CFE, CFE Opinion Statement ECJ-TF 1/2014 of the CFE on the Decision of the European Court of Justice in *Åkerberg Fransson* (Case C-617/10) Concerning Ne Bis in Idem in Tax Law, *ET* 2014.

Union."[70] The CJEU explained indirectly the legally binding force of the Charter and its scope in respect of case law delivered by the European Court of Human Rights. The Court directly referred to the ECtHR's case law for the sake of the case. Last but not least, it emphasized the legal duty of national courts to apply the Charter irrespective of the ECtHR's standing in the domestic legal order.

The scope of jurisdiction of the CJEU was further explained in *IN & JM*, wherein it was pointed out that "*it is for the referring court to indicate to the Court, (…), in what way the dispute pending before it has a connecting factor with the provisions of EU law that makes the preliminary ruling on interpretation necessary for it to give judgment in that dispute.*"[71]

53   The analysis of the CJEU indicates the growing significance of the Charter of Fundamental Rights.[72] As some claim, it is 'the rising star' of EU law.[73] It is likely to play an important role in fields that are highly harmonized, e.g. indirect taxes.[74] In the *Åkerberg Fransson* case, the Court ruled that "*[t]he applicability of EU law entails applicability of the fundamental rights guaranteed by the Charter*" thereby confirming that the Court will not interpret the phrase "*implementing Union Law*" in Art. 51 of the Charter narrowly ("*only when Member States are acting as agents of EU Law*"), but more broadly, as "*in all situations governed by EU law.*"[75] This implies that the Charter of Fundamental Rights might also apply where national law encroaches upon the fundamental freedoms or EU citizenship. This means that, within the scope of tax matters harmonized at the EU level, Member States must adhere to the principles enshrined in the Charter, for instance the principle of equality. This may have important implications on Member States when implementing the EU Directive. For instance, some Member States, when implementing the Parent Subsidiary Directive and the Interest and Royalties Directive, use their discretion to extend the subjective scope of application by including entities that are not listed in the Directive and leave others out. Under the principle of equal treatment, those left out may challenge a Member State to include them as well since otherwise they can be subject to unlawful discrimination.[76]

---

70   CJEU, 26 February 2013, Case C- 617/10, *Åkerberg Fransson*, EU:C:2013:105, paras. 28 and 29.
71   CJEU, 24 October 2019, Joined Cases C-469/18 and C-470/18, *IN & JM*, EU:C:2019:895, para. 24.
72   Poelman, Some fiscal issues of the Charter of Fundamental Rights of the European Union, *Intertax* 2015, p. 178.
73   Professor Ben Terra, of Lund University, Sweden, gave a thorough and stimulating presentation on 'The Rising Star of the Charter' at the one-day seminar 'EU VAT 2015' organized by the School of Economics and Management, Department of Business Law, Lund University.
74   Elgaard, The impact of the Charter of Fundamental Rights of the European Union on VAT law, *World Journal of VAT/GST Law* 2016, pp. 63-91.
75   Van Bockel/Wattel, New Wine into Old Wineskins: The Scope of the Charter of Fundamental Rights of the EU after Åkerberg Fransson, *European Law Review* 2013, p. 866
76   Note, however, that the Court, at least in the employment law area, appears to take a different approach, leaving Member State measures that go beyond a directives' minimum standards outside the scope of the Charter. See CJEU, 19 November 2019, Case 609/17 and 610/17 *TSN*, EU:C:2019:981.

In the *Berlioz* case, the CJEU applied the Charter of Fundamental Rights to the **54** procedure regarding the exchange of information between tax administrations. The CJEU pointed out that *"Directive 2011/16 (...) requires Member States to take necessary measures to obtain the requested information (...) those measures must include arrangements, such as the pecuniary penalty (...). The fact that Directive 2011/16 does not make express provision for penalties to be imposed does not mean that penalties cannot be regarded as involving the implementation of that directive and, consequently, falling within the scope of EU law."*[77] The relevance of the case to the exchange of information between tax administrations is further discussed in Chapter 9 m.no. 698, 768.[78]

The Charter may be also applicable in respect of legal measures to counter VAT **55** fraud and abuse. In the *Taricco* case, the CJEU decided that the extension of the limitation period and its immediate application to VAT fraud suspects do not infringe the fundamental rights of suspects.[79] The issue of the application of fundamental rights in the context of implementing and administering legal measures aimed at countering fraud and abuse was reiterated in the *Surgicare* case.[80] The CJEU confirmed that, in those cases, domestic courts are required to ensure judicial protection of the rights of individuals under EU law, as guaranteed by Art. 47 of the Charter.

Another field that may be affected by the Charter is the collection and use of evi- **56** dence under domestic administrative rules. In the *WebMindLicenses* case,[81] the CJEU pointed out that the use of evidence must comply with the EU's fundamental rights. This means, among other things, that any limitation on the exercise of the rights and freedoms recognized by the Charter must be provided for by law and must respect the essence of those rights and freedoms.

The impact of the Charter, especially Arts. 20 and 21, may be even more far- **57** reaching and fundamental. In *RPO*[82] the Court, for the first time, tested substantive provisions of VAT law against the principle of equality. The Court ruled that the application of a standard VAT rate to digital books available online and a reduced VAT rate to digital books available on CD-ROM, amounts to a different treatment that, however, is justified as all digital services available online are subject to the standard VAT rate.

---

77 CJEU, 16 May 2017, Case C-682-15, *Berlioz Investment Fund*, EU:C:2017:373, paras. 37 – 40.
78 Haslehner, Luxemburg: Exchange of Information and EU Fundamental Rights (C-682/15, *Berlioz Investment Fund S.A.*), in: Lang/Pistone/Rust/Schuch/Staringer/Storck (eds.), *CJEU – Recent Developments in Direct Taxation 2016* (2017).
79 CJEU, 8 September 2015, Case C-105/14, *Ivo Taricco and Others*, EU:C:2015:555.
80 CJEU, 12 February 2015, Case C – 662/13, *Surgicare — Unidades de Saúde SA v Fazenda Pública*, EU:C:2015:89.
81 CJEU, 17 December 2015, Case C-419/14, *WebMindLicenses Kft. v Nemzeti Adó- és Vámhivatal Kiemelt Adó- és Vám Főigazgatóság*, EU:C:2015:832.
82 CJEU, 7 March 2017, Case C-390/15, *Rzecznik Praw Obywatelskich (RPO)*, EU:C:2017:174.

58   Cross-border dispute resolution is another area that may be affected by the Charter of Fundamental Rights, particularly the rights of defence enshrined therein (Arts. 41, 47 and 48). This is likely thanks to the new Arbitration Directive. The national courts may refer a preliminary question to the CJEU with respect to the interpretation and application of the Arbitration Directive.

B. Secondary Law

1. Level of Harmonization

59   As stated in subsection A., when the EC was created, **harmonization** of direct taxes, as such, was not foreseen under the EC Treaty. This likely explains why there is no single EU Regulation entirely devoted to direct taxes.[83] Nevertheless, at a certain stage of development of the Single Market, it became apparent that, at least to some extent, harmonization was required, namely insofar as common rules are indispensable in eliminating obstacles within the internal market. Naturally, there have been different views amongst the Commission and Member States regarding how much harmonization is needed. The introduction of common rules for all EU Member States (known as **harmonization**) in the field of direct taxes has occurred only in a few directives on certain specific issues of company taxation. An alternative means of positive integration is tax coordination, which means making the different tax systems of the Member States consistent with one another without necessarily creating secondary EU law (see Chapter 2 for more on this).

2. Directives

60   Directives can be grouped into three main categories according to their actual function, namely whether they remove a tax obstacle within the internal market, whether they have been designed mainly for the purpose of enhancing tax administration, or whether they are aimed at addressing tax avoidance.

Directives Removing Obstacles

61   Council Directive 90/435/EEC on the common system of taxation applicable in the case of parent companies and subsidiaries of different Member States (**herein-

---

83   However, Art. 7 of Regulation 1612/68 on freedom of movement for workers within the EU requires that all workers who are nationals of a Member State enjoy in the territory of other Member States the same tax benefits as nationals working there (Council Regulation (EC) No 1612/68 of 15 October 1968 on freedom of movement for workers within the Community, OJ, English Special Edition 1968 (II), p. 475). One should also not overlook in this respect the regulations on the Societas Europaea (Council Regulation (EC) No 2157/2001 of 8 October 2001 on the Statute for a European company (SE) accompanied by Council Directive 2001/86/EC of 8 October 2001 supplementing the Statute for a European company with regard to the involvement of employees, OJ L 294 of 10 November 2001, pp. 1-21) and Societas Cooperativa Europaea (Council Regulation (EC) No 1435/2003 of 22 July 2003 on the Statute for a European Cooperative Society (SCE) accompanied by Council Directive 2003/72/EC of 22 July 2003 supplementing the Statute for a European Cooperative Society with regard to the involvement of employees, OJ L 207 of 18 August 2003, pp. 1-24.)

after: The Parent-Subsidiary Directive)[84] was adopted by the Council on 23 July 1990 based on a proposal presented by the Commission in 1969. It allows for, under certain conditions, the elimination of withholding taxes on outbound dividends distributed by a subsidiary to its parent within the EU. Moreover, it prescribes measures so as to avoid economic double taxation of dividends in the hands of a parent company. Since then, the directive has been amended several times (see Chapter 5, m.no. 409 et seq.).[85]

Council Directive 90/434/EEC of 23 July 1990 on the common system of taxation **62** applicable to mergers, divisions, transfers of assets and exchanges of shares concerning companies of different Member States (hereinafter: **The Merger Directive)**[86] was accepted by the Council on 23 July 2003 based on a proposal presented by the Commission in 1969. It provides for deferral (by rollover relief) of tax claims that become due at the level of a company or a shareholder in the case of cross-border mergers, (partial) divisions, transfers of assets and exchanges of shares taking place within the EU. Taxation of capital gains is deferred until a subsequent disposal of the asset (actual realization of profits). On 17 October 2003, the Commission adopted a proposal amending the Merger Directive.[87] A modified version of this proposal was subsequently adopted by the Council (see Chapter 6, m.no. 474 et seq.).[88]

The aim of Council Directive 2003/49/EC of June 2003 on a common system of tax- **63** ation applicable to interest and royalty payments (hereinafter: **The Interest and Royalties Directive)**[89] is to eliminate certain obstacles to the cross-border activity of multinationals. It provides, under certain conditions, for no withholding tax on interest and royalty payments between associated companies (see Chapter 7, m.no. 539 et seq.).

Directives Addressing Tax Avoidance

Council Directive 2016/1164 of 12 July 2016 laying down rules against tax avoid- **64** ance practices that directly affect the functioning of the internal market **(herein-**

---

84 Council Directive 90/435/EEC of 23 July 1990 on the common system of taxation applicable in the case of parent companies and subsidiaries of different Member States, *OJ L 225 of 20 August 1990, pp. 6-9.*
85 Council Directive 2011/96/EU of 30 November 2011 on the common system of taxation applicable in the case of parent companies and subsidiaries of different Member States, OJ L 345 of 29 December 2011, pp. 8-16, as amended.
86 Council Directive 90/434/EEC of 23 July 1990 on the common system of taxation applicable to mergers, divisions, transfers of assets, and exchanges of shares concerning companies of different Member States, *OJ L 225 of 20 August 1990, pp. 1-5.*
87 See COM(2003) 613 final.
88 Council Directive 2009/133/EC of 19 October 2009 on the Common System of Taxation Applicable to Mergers, Divisions, Partial Divisions, Transfers of Assets and Exchanges of Shares Concerning Companies of Different Member States and to the Transfer of the Registered Office of an SE or SCE between Member States (Codified Version), OJ L 310 of 25 November 2009, pp. 34-46; originally Council Directive 2005/19/EC of 17 February 2005 amending Directive 90/434/EEC 1990 on the common system of taxation applicable to mergers, divisions, transfers of assets and exchanges of shares concerning companies of different Member States, OJ L 58 of 4 March 2005, pp. 19-27.
89 Council Directive 2003/49/EC of June 2003 on a common system of taxation applicable to interest and royalty payments, OJ L 157 of 26 June 2003, pp. 49-54.

after: ATAD I)[90] **and** Council Directive amending Directive (EU) 2016/1164 as regards hybrid mismatches with third countries (hereinafter: **ATAD II)**[91] **were implemented with a view to ensuring a coordinated approach of Member States towards the results of the BEPS project. ATAD I forms a part of a wider set of measures developed to prevent aggressive tax planning, enhance tax transparency and create a level playing field for EU taxpayers (Anti-Tax Avoidance Package). Within the Anti-Tax Avoidance Package, in addition to ATAD I, the Commission put forward the** Recommendation on Tax Treaties,[92] the Proposal for a Directive implementing the G20/OECD country-by-country reporting (CbCR),[93] and the Communication on an External Strategy.[94] In terms of ATAD I, it sets forth the following measures: interest limitation rules, an exit tax rule, a GAAR, a CFC rule and a rule on hybrid mismatches. **ATAD II amends ATAD I and supplements it by adopting new rules on hybrid mismatches.** ATAD I needs to be transposed into domestic law by the Member States by 31 December 2018. However, Member States are given the option to comply with the rules on exit taxation (Art. 5) by 31 December 2019. With ATAD II, the implementation period for the rules on hybrid mismatches has also been extended to 31 December 2018, while the implementation period for the rules on reverse hybrid mismatches was extended to 31 December 2021 (Art. 2 ATAD II). Also, Member States may apply national interest limitation rules until 1 January 2024 if they are *"equally effective"* as those of ATAD I (see Chapter 8, m.n. 577 et seq.).

Directives Enhancing Tax Administration

65 Council Directive 77/799/EEC of 19 December 1977 concerning mutual assistance by the competent authorities of the Member States in the field of direct taxation **(hereinafter: The Mutual Assistance Directive)**[95] was issued on 9 December 1977 as the first directive in the field of direct taxes. It dealt with mutual administrative assistance between the competent tax authorities. It authorized them to exchange information (upon request, spontaneously or automatically) relevant in determining a taxpayer's assessment. In 2011, it was replaced by Council Directive

---

90 Council Directive 2016/1164 of 12 July 2016 laying down rules against tax avoidance practices that directly affect the functioning of the internal market, OJ L 193/1 of 19 July 2016.

91 Council Directive (EU) 2017/952 of 29 May 2017 amending Directive (EU) 2016/1164 as regards hybrid mismatches with third countries, OJ L 144 of 7 June 2017.

92 European Commission, Commission Recommendation of 28 January 2016 on the implementation of measures against tax treaty abuse, C(2016) 271 final, Brussels.

93 European Commission, Proposal for a Council Directive amending Directive 2011/16/EU as regards mandatory automatic exchange of information in the field of taxation, COM(2016) 25 final 2016/0010(CNS).

94 European Commission, Communication From The Commission To The European Parliament And The Council on an External Strategy for Effective Taxation, COM(2016) 24 final, Brussels, 28 January 2016.

95 Council Directive 77/799/EEC of 19 December 1977 concerning mutual assistance by the competent authorities of the Member States in the field of direct taxation, *OJ L 336 of 27 December 1977, pp. 15-20.*

2011/16/EU (DAC),[96] which is seen as a key development in the EU framework of cooperation. In keeping with changes in the international tax landscape, it has been subject to subsequent amendments. First, Directive 2014/107/EU (DAC 2)[97] broadened the scope of automatic exchange of information to cover financial account information (interest, dividends, and other income generated, gross proceeds from a sale or redemption and account balances). Next, Directive 2015/2376/EU (DAC 3)[98] introduced automatic exchange of advance cross-border rulings and APAs. Subsequently, Directive 2016/881/EU (DAC 4)[99] imposed an obligation on Member States to exchange CbC reporting on certain financial information. This covers revenues, profits, taxes paid and accrued, accumulated earnings, number of employees and certain assets. Finally, Directive 2016/2258/EU (DAC 5)[100] does not broaden the scope of automatic exchange of information but rather ensures tax authorities have access to beneficial ownership information collected pursuant to the anti-money laundering legislation (see Chapter 9, m.no. 674 et seq.).

Council Directive 2001/44/EC of 15 June 2001 amending Directive 76/308/EEC **66** on mutual assistance for the recovery of claims resulting from operations forming part of the system of financing the European Agricultural Guidance and Guarantee Fund, and of agricultural levies and customs duties and in respect of value added tax and certain excise duties (hereinafter: **The Recovery Assistance Directive**),[101] which established a legal framework for mutual assistance between Member States in recovering claims, initially covered agricultural levies and customs duties as sources of EU revenue (traditional own resources)[102] and was later extended to indirect taxation. As of 1 July 2002, the directive was extended to include the possibility to recover taxes on income and capital, as well as taxes on

---

96 Council Directive 2011/16/EU of 15 February 2011 on administrative cooperation in the field of taxation and repealing Directive 77/799/EEC, OJ L 64 of 11 March 2011, pp. 1–12.

97 Council Directive 2014/107/EU of 9 December 2014 amending Directive 2011/16/EU as regards mandatory automatic exchange of information in the field of taxation, OJ L 359 of 16 December 2014, pp. 1–29.

98 Council Directive (EU) 2015/2376 of 8 December 2015 amending Directive 2011/16/EU as regards mandatory automatic exchange of information in the field of taxation, OJ L 332 of 18 December 2015, pp. 1–10.

99 Council Directive (EU) 2016/881 of 25 May 2016 amending Directive 2011/16/EU as regards mandatory automatic exchange of information in the field of taxation, OJ L 146 of 3 June 2016, pp. 8–21.

100 Council Directive (EU) 2016/2258 of 6 December 2016 amending Directive 2011/16/EU as regards access to anti-money-laundering information by tax authorities, OJ L 342 of 16 December 2016, pp. 1–3.

101 Council Directive 2001/44/EC of 15 June 2001 amending Directive 76/308/EEC on mutual assistance for the recovery of claims resulting from operations forming part of the system of financing the European Agricultural Guidance and Guarantee Fund, and of agricultural levies and customs duties and in respect of value added tax and certain excise duties, OJ L 175 of 28 June 2001, pp. 17-20.

102 Council Directive 76/308/EEC of 15 March 1976 on mutual assistance for the recovery of claims resulting from operations forming part of the system of financing the European Agricultural Guidance and Guarantee Fund, and of the agricultural levies and customs duties, *OJ L 73 of 19 March 1976, pp. 18-23.*

insurance premiums. In 2009, the European Commission put forward a proposal for a completely new directive concerning mutual assistance for the recovery of tax claims.[103] The proposal has already been accepted by the Council and the EU Parliament and was adopted on 16 March 2010 (see Chapter 9, m.no. 782 et seq.).[104]

67 Council Directive (EU) 2017/1852 of 10 October 2017 on tax dispute resolution mechanisms in the European Union (hereinafter: The Dispute Resolution Directive)[105] addresses tax treaty disputes among Member States. It does not replace the Arbitration Convention. Instead, it plays a supplementary role in relation to the Arbitration Convention and provides a dispute resolution mechanism for disputes between Member States over the interpretation and application of treaties. It was implemented in the aftermath of the discussions following the BEPS project, specifically Action 14 of the BEPS Project. It applies to intra-EU disputes relating to income earned in a tax year commencing 1 January 2018 for cases submitted from 1 July 2019. Competent authorities of Member States may agree to apply the Directive to cases submitted earlier or to earlier tax years (see Chapter 10, m.no. 815 et seq.).

Proposals for New Directives

68 A new directive, the text of which has recently been agreed, concerns mandatory disclosure rules, a concept put forward by the OECD under Action 12 of the BEPS Action Plan.[106] A proposal for the so called **directive aimed at boosting transparency in order to tackle aggressive cross-border tax planning** will require intermediaries, such as tax advisors, accountants and lawyers that design and/or promote tax planning schemes to report schemes that are considered potentially aggressive.[107]

69 The European Commission is continuously working on modernizing the EU tax system. In 2016, as a part of the Corporate Tax Reform Package, the common consolidated corporate tax base (CCCTB) project was launched.[108] The project is,

---

103 Proposal of 2 February 2009 for a Council Directive concerning mutual assistance for the recovery of claims relating to taxes, duties and other measures, COM(2009) 28 final. For a detailed analysis on the proposed Directive, see Caram, Enhancing International Cooperation among Tax Authorities in the Assessment and the Recovery of Taxes: The Proposals for New European Directives, *Intertax* 2009, p. 639 et seq.

104 Council Directive 2010/24 of 16 March 2010 concerning mutual assistance for recovery of claims relating to taxes, duties and other measures, OJ L 319/21 of 29 November 2008.

105 Council Directive (EU) 2017/1852 of 10 October 2017 on tax dispute resolution mechanisms in the European Union, OJ L 265 of 14 October 2017, pp. 1–14.

106 OECD, *Mandatory Disclosure Rules, Action 12 – 2015 Final Report*, OECD/G20 Base Erosion and Profit Shifting Project (OECD 2015).

107 The latest draft directive is available online at: http://data.consilium.europa.eu/doc/document/ST-6804-2018-INIT/en/pdf (last accessed 21 April 2018).

108 https://ec.europa.eu/taxation_customs/business/company-tax/common-consolidated-corporate-tax-base-ccctb_en (last accessed 19 April 2018).

in fact, a re-launch of the previously existing CCCTB proposal from 2011 that has been stymied due to the lack of support of all Member States. The new proposal adopts a two-step approach towards CCCTB implementation. It consists of a proposal on a common corporate tax base (CCTB),[109] and on a common consolidated corporate tax base (CCCTB).[110] Its aim is a fairer and better-integrated single market. The proposal relies on the concepts of unitary taxation and formulary apportionment of taxing rights.

Another proposal for a new directive addresses the digital economy. In 2018, the **70** European Commission put forward two proposals for short-term and long-term solutions harmonizing the approach of Member States towards taxation of digital business activities. The short-term solution suggests imposing tax on revenues generated from certain activities where users play a major role in value creation.[111] The long-term solution reflects the need for a common reform of the EU's corporate tax rules for digital activities.[112] The reform would rely on the taxation of profits allocated to a digital platform defined by a taxable 'digital presence' or a virtual permanent establishment in a Member State.

3. Regulations

In contrast to the VAT area,[113] there is no single EU Regulation entirely devoted **71** to direct taxes. However, Art. 7 of **Regulation 1612/68** on freedom of movement for workers within the EU requires that all workers who are nationals of a Member State enjoy in the territory of other Member States the same tax benefits as nationals working there.[114] One should also not overlook in this respect the regulations on the *Societas Europaea*[115] and *Societas Cooperativa Europaea.*[116]

---

109   Proposal for a COUNCIL DIRECTIVE on a Common Corporate Tax Base, COM/2016/0685 final – 2016/0337 (CNS).

110   Proposal for a COUNCIL DIRECTIVE on a Common Consolidated Corporate Tax Base (CCCTB), COM/2016/0683 final – 2016/0336 (CNS).

111   Proposal for a COUNCIL DIRECTIVE on the common system of a digital services tax on revenues resulting from the provision of certain digital services, SWD(2018) 81 – SWD(2018) 82.

112   Proposal for a COUNCIL DIRECTIVE laying down rules relating to the corporate taxation of a significant digital presence, SWD(2018) 81final – SWD(2018)82 final.

113   In order to ensure uniform application of the EU VAT directives, the EU Council enacted Council Implementing Regulation (EU) No 282/2011 of 15 March 2011 laying down implementing measures for Directive 2006/112/EC on the common system of value added tax.

114   Council Regulation (EC) No 1612/68 of 15 October 1968 on freedom of movement for workers within the Community, OJ, English Special Edition 1968 (II), p. 475.

115   Council Regulation (EC) No 2157/2001 of 8 October 2001 on the Statute for a European company (SE) accompanying by Council Directive 2001/86/EC of 8 October 2001 supplementing the Statute for a European company with regard to the involvement of employees, OJ L 294 of 10 November 2001, pp. 1-21.

116   Council Regulation (EC) No 1435/2003 of 22 July 2003 on the Statute for a European Cooperative Society (SCE) accompanying by Council Directive 2003/72/EC of 22 July 2003 supplementing the Statute for a European Cooperative Society with regard to the involvement of employees, OJ L 207 of 18 August 2003, pp. 1-24.

C. Soft Law

72 EU soft law comprises **non-binding recommendations and communications.** These are aimed at promoting Member States' voluntary compliance with EU law (see Chapter 2, m.no. 144 et seq.). As such, these tools play a steering function in tax coordination within the internal market since they promote a consistent interpretation and application of law and contribute to building an internationally accepted tax practice within the internal market.[117] For some time, given their lack of binding character, their relevance has been ignored by some Member States.

73 The EU is increasingly using soft law instruments for the purpose of enhanced coordination of the EU legal framework. In this context, the Recommendations on Tax Treaties and the Communication on External Strategy should be mentioned, which were issued as a part of the EU Anti Avoidance Package. These have supplemented the hard law instruments, i.e. Anti-Tax Avoidance Directive and Revised Administrative Cooperation Directive. The Communication on External Strategy has a particularly wide-ranging impact. Based on this document, the EU Council adopted an EU list of non-cooperative jurisdictions for tax purposes (so called EU tax haven blacklist), supplemented by monitoring and periodic screening of tax policies and also by defensive measures. Another initiative that is worth mentioning is the EU Joint Transfer Pricing Forum (JTPF), which assists and advises the European Commission on transfer pricing tax matters.[118] The JTPF has issued significant guidance and recommendations in this respect.

D. EU International Agreements

1. Agreements with third states or international bodies

74 Art. 217 TFEU (ex Art. 310 EC) clearly entitles the EU to conclude **agreements with third states or international bodies** (hereinafter: 'international agreements'). The EU competence covers both trade and investment agreements. It is, however, not exclusive. Non-direct investments and regimes governing dispute settlement between investors and States are excluded from its scope. As was explained in the CJEU's Opinion 2/15, these two fields falls within the shared competence of the EU and the Member States.[119] The issue of the dispute settlement between investors and States has been the subject of CJEU case law. In the *Achmea* case,[120] the Court made it clear that an arbitration clause in a bilateral investment treaty

---

117 Pistone, Soft Tax Law: Steering Legal Pluralism towards International Tax Coordination, in: Weber (ed.), *Traditional and Alternative Routes to European Tax Integration* (2010) p. 114.

118 For more *see* https://ec.europa.eu/taxation_customs/business/company-tax/transfer-pricing-eu-context/joint-transfer-pricing-forum_en.

119 CJEU, 16 May 2017, Opinion 2/15, *Free Trade Agreement Between the European Union and the Republic of Singapore*, EU:C:2017:376.

120 CJEU, 6 March 2018, Case C-284/16, *Slowakische Republik (Slovak Republic) v Achmea BV*, EU:C:2018:158.

concluded between two EU Member States (intra-EU BIT) is incompatible with EU law and, in particular, the autonomy of the EU legal order. It seems that the Court ruled in this way in order to protect its own jurisdiction. In Opinion 1/17 ('CETA'), however, the Investor-State Dispute Settlement mechanism contained in the Comprehensive Economic and Trade Agreement negotiated between the European Union and Canada was accepted due to the limited scope of application of the ISDS and no risk of undermining the CJEU's position.[121]

The importance of EU international agreements cannot be overstated. Some even **75** open up the application of the fundamental freedoms to non-Member States, e.g. the European Economic Area (EEA). To date, the EU itself has concluded very few international agreements concerning tax law issues directly. Despite this fact, certain provisions in these international agreements may have important consequences for the direct tax systems of Member States.[122] In particular, provisions addressing profit shifting and aggressive tax planning may prevent practices that take advantage of loopholes and mismatches between tax systems in Member States and third states. The issue was recognized and addressed by the European Commission in its Communication on an External Strategy for Effective Taxation.[123] As a result, a framework for a new EU external strategy for effective taxation put forward the inclusion of tax good governance clauses and State aid provisions.[124] These provisions are expected to further promote international standards of transparency, information exchange and fair tax competition.

With respect to the good governance clause, it was agreed that the clause should **76** include the following elements: the standards of transparency, exchange of information and fair tax competition; the OECD/G20 global standard on Automatic Exchange of Information in relation to financial account information; additional standards based on the G20/OECD BEPS project; and Financial Action Task Force international standards on Combating Money Laundering and the Financing of Terrorism and Proliferation. In addition, to ensure its effectiveness, the clause should provisionally apply even before the wider agreement enters into force. Alternatively, the EU should engage in a structured dialogue on tax issues

---

121 CJEU, 30 April 2019, Opinion 1/17, *CETA*, EU:C:2019:341.
122 For more on this issue, see Bezborodov, Freedom of Establishment in the EC Economic Partnership Agreements: in Search of its Direct Effect on Direct Taxation, *Intertax* 2007, pp. 658-712.
123 European Commission, Communication From The Commission To The European Parliament And The Council on an External Strategy for Effective Taxation, COM(2016) 24 final, Brussels, 28 January 2016.
124 To date, several free trade agreements concluded by the EU, e.g. with South Africa (Agreement on Trade, Development and Cooperation between the European Community and its Member States, of the one part, and the Republic of South Africa, of the other part, OJ L 311/3 of 4 December 1999), Mexico (Economic Partnership, Political Coordination and Cooperation Agreement between the European Community and its Member States, of the one part, and the United Mexican States, of the other part, OJ L 276/45 of 28 October 2000) and Korea (Free Trade Agreement between the European Union and its Member States, of the one part, and the Republic of Korea, of the other part, OJ L 127 of 14 May 2011) included rules on the control of public aid.

with the relevant third country, pending entry into force of the agreement. In light of these criteria the Council adopted the EU standard provision on good governance in tax matters for agreements with third countries. It states as follows: *"The Parties recognise and commit themselves to implement the principles of good governance in the tax area, including the global standards on transparency and exchange of information, fair taxation, and the minimum standards against Base Erosion and Profit Shifting (BEPS). The Parties will promote good governance in tax matters, improve international cooperation in the tax area and facilitate the collection of tax revenues."*[125]

2. European Economic Area Agreement

77 The **European Free Trade Area (EFTA)** was created in 1960 as a free trade zone offering an alternative means of economic integration to that of the European Economic Community. **The European Economic Area (EEA)** Agreement was invented as a mechanism allowing Members States of the EFTA to actively participate in the process of European economic integration without losing any political competences. The EEA Agreement entered into force on 1 January 1994. One year later, three Member States of the EFTA (Austria, Finland and Sweden) joined the European Union. Currently, the EFTA consists only of Norway, Lichtenstein, Iceland and Switzerland (the last State is not a member of the EEA since it rejected the EEA Agreement in a referendum in 1992). The EFTA Court is entitled to give opinions on questions referred by the EFTA countries' courts.[126] The **EFTA Court opinions**, unlike the CJEU judgments under Art. 267 TFEU (ex Art. 234 EC), do not bind the national courts. It should be noted that the EFTA countries' courts are not obliged, in any case, to ask the EFTA Court for an opinion and they may freely interpret the EEA Agreement. Nevertheless, generally, the EFTA states' national courts follow the decisions of the EFTA Court.[127] In accordance with Art. 6 EEA, the Agreement has to be interpreted in conformity with the relevant case law of the CJEU and therefore the EFTA Court generally does not diverge from CJEU decisions.[128]

78 The **structure of the EEA Agreement** resembles that of the TFEU. First of all, a prohibition of discrimination on grounds of nationality is provided for.[129] There

---

125 Council of the EU, Tax fraud: Standard provision agreed for agreements with third countries, Press release 290/18, 25.05.2018, available at: http://www.consilium.europa.eu/en/press/press-releases/2018/05/25/tax-fraud-standard-provision-agreed-for-agreements-with-third-countries/pdf (accessed: 15.06.2018).

126 Art. 34 ESA/Court Agreement.

127 One may argue that, as the EFTA Court judgments are frequently cited in the ECJ case law (and vice versa), this makes the officially non-binding opinions of the former more persuasive and gives them more weight.

128 For a notable exception see EFTA Court, 27 June 2014, Case E-26/13, *The Icelandic State v Atli Gunnarsson*.

129 Art. 4 EEA.

are also provisions concerning the fundamental freedoms, as well as on competition and State aid law.[130] In the *Ospelt* case, the CJEU held that *"one of the principal aims of the EEA Agreement is to provide for the fullest possible realization of the free movement of goods, persons, services and capital within the whole European Economic Area, so that the **internal market** established within the European Union is **extended to the EFTA States**"* and, consequently, decided that the provisions of the EEA should be interpreted in a similar fashion as the corresponding provisions of the TFEU.[131] In the *Keller Holding* case,[132] the CJEU applied the EEA to a direct tax case for the first time.

3. European Partnership Agreements (EPA)

Furthermore, the EU and its Member States have concluded several international **79** agreements with third countries for the purpose of making them share to a greater or lesser extent the goals of the internal market. In several (but not all) cases, such agreements contain directly applicable provisions. Examples include the **EPA with Russia** (perhaps the most advanced one so far), EPAs with other economies in transition, the **Euromediterranean Agreement** and agreements with several developing countries.

Although such agreements have not been designed to deal specifically with tax **80** issues, their general wording may, in principle, encompass direct taxes unless they contain a specific carve-out clause.

4. The Arbitration Convention

The Member States concluded the **Arbitration Convention** on 23 July 1990 to **81** provide for binding arbitration when the tax authorities fail to find a solution within two years to double taxation arising within a multinational group due to different views of the tax authorities of the Member States concerned about the prices charged for transactions within this group. It should be noted that, even though the Commission preferred the form of a directive, the Member States selected a form of agreement that does not fall within the jurisdiction of the CJEU. Despite its legal form, it is part of the *acquis communautaire*.[133] This means it is aimed at the removal of possible tax obstacles in cross-border situations within the internal market. This convention is possibly the only example of binding co-ordination in the field of direct taxes (see Chapter 2 m.no. 181 and Chapter 10). The Dispute Resolution Directive (see Chapter 10.) has recently supplemented the Arbitration Convention.

---

130 Art. 8 EEA provides for the free movement of goods, Art. 28 for the free movement of workers, Art. 32 for the freedom of establishment, Art. 36 for the freedom to provide services and Art. 40 for the free movement of capital.
131 CJEU, 23 September 2003, Case C-452/01, *Ospelt*, EU:C:2003:493, paras. 29 and 32.
132 CJEU, 23 February 2006, Case C-471/04, *Keller Holding*, EU:C:2006:143.
133 Hinnekens, The Uneasy Case and Fate of Article 293 Second Indent EC, *Intertax* 2009, p. 604.

III. The Enforcement of EU Law

82   Like every legal system, EU law possesses mechanisms to ensure its proper enforcement. Accordingly, there are **two ways of protecting rights arising from EU law**. Measures incompatible with EU law may be challenged either at the EU level under an infringement procedure or at the national level by nationals invoking directly effective EU law provisions before a national court.[134]

A. European Union Level

83   The Commission serves as the guardian of the Treaties and the watchdog of Member States' compliance with European Union law. Usually, **an infringement procedure** comes into play when a Member State has enacted or kept in force domestic provisions that are incompatible with EU law or if a Member State has failed to implement a directive in a timely or accurate fashion. If an individual whose rights are infringed by a given national provision or by the lack of action taken by a Member State (non-implementation of a directive) makes a complaint to the Commission, it is under no obligation to commence an action, but this complaint may serve as 'inspiration' to initiate an infringement procedure. The Commission has increasingly been employing this procedure in order to tackle potential infringements of the fundamental freedoms by national direct tax provisions. This has resulted in several CJEU cases, some of which are still pending.[135]

84   Once the Commission considers that a Member State has breached EU law, it has the discretion, in accordance with **Art. 258 TFEU** (ex Art. 226 EC), to initiate an **infringement procedure**. As a first step, the Commission needs to notify the Member State involved of its reservations. Once it receives observations from a Member State, it is required to deliver a reasoned opinion. Unless the Member State complies with the position of the reasoned opinion within the period specified, the case may be brought before the CJEU.

85   Under **Art. 260(1) TFEU** (ex Art. 228(1) EC), if the Court finds the Commission action is well founded, the Member State involved is under an obligation to amend its domestic legislation to make it EU-compatible. A failure to do so within a reasonable time triggers another action of the Commission on the basis of **Art. 260(2) TFEU** (ex Art. 228(2) EC). If the Commission considers that the Member State concerned has not taken the necessary steps to comply with the judgment of the Court, it may bring the case before the Court after giving that State the opportunity to submit its observations. If the Court finds that the Member State concerned has not complied with its judgment, it may impose a 'lump-sum or penalty payment'

---

134   It should be noted that, in principle, a Member State national enjoys the right to rely on EU law before a national administrative body, which is, on the other hand, obliged to comply with EU law. However, the administrative body is not entitled to refer a preliminary question to the CJEU.

135   See the list of cases relevant to direct taxation available at: https://ec.europa.eu/taxation_customs/ sites/taxation/files/20171116_court_cases_direct_taxation_en.pdf (accessed 17 April 2018).

on it. The size of the payment is not higher than the amount specified by the Commission to be appropriate in the circumstances.

In accordance with **Art. 259 TFEU (ex Art. 227 EC)**, it is possible for a Member 86 State to bring **a case before the CJEU against another Member State** for its breach of EU law. This procedure has not been frequently employed and, to date, never in direct tax cases.

B. National Level (Preliminary Reference Procedure)

The enforcement of EU law on a national level is governed by the combined prin- 87 ciples of direct effect and supremacy, as well as a preliminary reference procedure. Under **Art. 267 TFEU** (ex Art. 234 EC), the CJEU has jurisdiction to give **preliminary rulings** concerning the interpretation of the TFEU.[136] The aim of this provision is to ensure uniform application of EU law throughout all Member States. When a question concerning the application or interpretation of EU law is raised before a Member State court or a tribunal, it *may* request that the CJEU give a preliminary ruling thereon if it believes that such a ruling is necessary in delivering a decision. However, when such a situation occurs before a court or a tribunal against whose decisions no legal remedies are available under national law (for example, a Supreme Court or a Constitutional Court), it is obliged to pose questions to the CJEU (Art. 267 (3) TFEU). In recent case law, the CJEU confirmed that any reasonable doubt concerning the interpretation of EU law is sufficient to trigger the referral obligation for the last instance court and failure to comply may constitute an infrngment of the EU law attributable to a given Member State.[137]

A national court does not have to make a reference to the CJEU in a case that 88 requires EU law interpretation when the *acte clair* and *acte éclairé* **doctrine** applies. This doctrine was forged in the *CILFIT* case,[138] wherein the Court recognized the national court's discretion to ascertain whether a decision on questions of EU law is necessary to enable it to give judgment.[139] Therefore, once a national court has established that an EU law issue is irrelevant to the outcome of the case, it does not have to refer the case to the CJEU.[140] Moreover, the national court is also under no obligation to do so when *"the EC provision in question has already been interpreted by the Court"* (*acte éclairé*) or *"the correct application of EC law is so obvious as to leave no scope for reasonable doubts"* (*acte clair).*[141]

---

136 By giving a preliminary ruling and interpreting EU law, the CJEU may be going so far as to test the validity of the EU secondary law provisions. See, for example, CJEU, 4 May 2016, Case C-547/14, *Philip Morris*, EU:C:2016:325.
137 CJEU, 8 October 2018, Case C-416/17, *Commission v. France*, EU:C:2018.436.
138 CJEU, 6 October 1982, Case C-283/81, *CILFIT,* EU:C:1984:91.
139 For more on this issue, see Dourado, Is it *Acte Clair?* General Report on the Role played by CILFIT in Direct Taxation, in: Dourado/da Palma Borges (eds.), *The Acte Clair in EC Direct Tax Law* (2008) p. 13 et seq.
140 CJEU, 6 October 1982, Case C-283/81, *CILFIT,* EU:C:1984:91, para. 21.
141 Ibid.

89   The *acte clair* and *acte éclairé* **doctrines** allow a national court a large margin of discretion regarding the necessity of referring a case for a preliminary ruling. On the one hand, it speeds up enforcement of EU law by allowing national courts to decide cases with EU law aspects without time-consuming preliminary references to the CJEU. On the other hand, the national courts in several Member States have reportedly been misusing this doctrine with the result that the CJEU is being excluded from the litigation process even with respect to cases involving unclear EU law issues.[142] Therefore, some commentators suggest that the *acte clair* and *acte éclairé* **doctrines should be reformed by providing new criteria of interpretation that would limit the discretionary power of national courts without shifting an excessive burden onto the CJEU.**[143]

90   As such, the preliminary rulings procedure should operate as a 'dialogue' between the CJEU and national courts. Nevertheless, this past year's experience proves the contrary. In particular, 'open' judgments of the CJEU have been criticized. One of the most striking examples is the *FII* saga. Preliminary questions were referred to the CJEU as many as three times in respect of the same group litigation involving the former UK franked litigation investment income tax system.[144] The reason for this was the difficulty national courts had in deciding their cases on the basis of the answers of the CJEU.[145]

C. Effectiveness of EU law

1. Procedural Aspects of Redressing Breaches of EU Law

91   In the absence of EU measures, a Member State should remedy a breach of EU law on the basis of national provisions, designate the competent courts, as well as set out detailed procedural rules for restitution proceedings (**principle of national procedural autonomy**).[146] This principle, however, is subject to two important limitations. First, *"the substantive and procedural conditions for reparation of loss and damage laid down by the national law of the Member States must not be less favourable than those relating to similar domestic claims"*[147] (**principle of equivalence**). Second, those conditions *"must not be so framed as to make it*

---

142   For more on this issue, see Dourado/da Palma Borges (eds.), *The Acte Clair in EC Direct Tax Law* (2008).

143   For more on this issue, see Vukčević, CILFIT Criteria for the *Acte Clair/Acte Éclairé* Doctrine in Direct Tax Cases of the CJEU, *Intertax* 2012, pp. 654-665.

144   CJEU, 12 December 2006, Case C-446/04, *FII Group Litigation*, EU:C:2006:774; CJEU, 13 November 2012, Case C-35/11, *FII Group Litigation*, EU:C:2012:707; CJEU, 12 December 2013, Case C-362/12, *FII Group Litigation*, EU:C:2006:774.

145   For more on the interaction between national courts and the CJEU, see Sarmiento/Jimenez-Valladolid de L'Hotellerie Fallois (eds.), *Litigating EU Tax Law in International, National and Non-EU National Courts* (2014).

146   CJEU, 16 December 1976, Case C-33/76, *Rewe*, EU:C:1976:167, para. 5; CJEU, 24 September 2002, Case C-255/00, *Grundig Italiana*, EU:C:2002:525, paras. 33 and 42.

147   CJEU, 19 November 1991, Joined Cases C-6/90 and C-9/90, *Francovich*, EU:C:1995:372, para. 43.

virtually impossible or excessively difficult to obtain reparation"[148] (**principle of effectiveness**).

The Court applied the **principle of equivalence** in the *Edis* case, wherein it held   **92**
that if a tax has been imposed in violation of EU law, a taxpayer will be able to
successfully bring an action for recovery of the tax only in accordance with the
national procedural rules that govern the recovery of taxes unduly paid, including
time limits applicable to such actions.[149] The exception to this principle was established in the *Emmot* case, wherein the CJEU ruled that the fact that the provisions
of a directive were not duly (or timely) transposed into national law prevents a
Member State from invoking a time limit provided by its domestic law.[150]

At the core of the dispute in *Weber's Wine World* was an Austrian provision short-   **93**
ening the **time limit for claiming unduly paid taxes** with the exception of taxes
paid in violation of the Constitution. The Court held that the principles set by the
national law regarding time limits applicable to refunds of taxes paid unconstitu-
tionally have to apply also with respect to taxes imposed in violation of EU law.[151]

The **principle of effectiveness** means that domestic procedural law must not   **94**
make it impossible or excessively difficult to enforce rights derived from EU law
at the national level. Therefore, national law is required to ensure the full effectiveness of EU law. This may require that a final administrative decision issued by
a national administrative authority be reversed. In the *Kühne & Heitz* case, the
CJEU ruled that EU law obliges national authorities to "***review a final administrative decision** where an application for such review is made to it, in order to take
account of the interpretation of the relevant provision given in the meantime by the
Court where*

1. *under national law, it has the power to reopen that decision;*
2. *the administrative decision in question has become final as a result of a judgment of a national court ruling at final instance based on a misinterpretation of
   Community law without asking the Court for a preliminary ruling;*
3. *the person concerned complained to the administrative body immediately after
   becoming aware of that decision of the Court."*[152]

The decision in the *Kühne & Heitz* case may prove helpful for a taxpayer in forcing   **95**
the tax authorities to rescind a ruling denying a taxpayer's earlier claim for tax paid
in violation of EU law when it subsequently turns out that the taxpayer's position
was well founded.[153]

---

148   Ibid.
149   CJEU, 15 September 1998, Case C-231/96, *Edis*, EU:C:1998:401, paras. 17-19.
150   CJEU, 25 July 1991, Case C-208/90, *Emmott*, EU:C:1991:333.
151   CJEU, 2 October 2003, Case C-147/01, *Weber's Wine Word*, EU:C:2003:533, para. 117.
152   CJEU, 13 January 2004, Case C-453/00, *Kühne & Heitz*, EU:C:2004:17, para. 28.
153   Dassesse, Dassesse, Taxes paid in violation of EU law: How far back can a taxpayer claim reimburse-
      ment?, *Bulletin* 2004, p. 513.

96 The judgment in the *Kühne & Heitz* case pushed the national courts to ask the CJEU to clarify whether the *res iudicata* principle may override EU law. As a rule, *res iudicata* firmly applies. This was confirmed in the *Kapferer* case, wherein the Court made it clear that a national court is not under an obligation to ignore its procedural provisions in order to void a final court judgment, even where this judgment is contrary to EU law.[154] However, this principle is subject to exceptions that are permanently extended by the CJEU.

97 In the *Lucchini* case, the CJEU decided that EU law precludes the application of a provision of national law that seeks to lay down the principle of *res judicata*, in so far as the application of that provision prevents the recovery of State aid granted in breach of EU law that has been found to be incompatible with the common market in a decision of the Commission that has become final.[155]

98 In the *Fallimento Olimpiclub* case, the CJEU ruled that the interpretation of the *res judicata* principle, pursuant to which final judgments on tax obligations in period X are also binding in period Y, infringes the principle of effectiveness and, therefore, should be ignored.[156]

2. Remedies against breaches of EU law

99 In principle, a taxpayer who has paid taxes in violation of EU law has two kinds of claims at his disposal. Firstly, entitlement to **claim a refund** of charges levied by a Member State in breach of EU law stems from rights conferred on nationals by EU law provisions prohibiting such charges that are directly effective.[157] Secondly, an individual is also entitled to obtain compensation for losses resulting indirectly from the payment of unlawful charges, for example **interest on reimbursed charges** resulting from the lack of availability of sums of money as a result of tax being levied prematurely.[158] This second claim comes into play only as a corollary of a Member State's liability for a breach of EU law.

100 One should not overlook the Court's decision in *Littlewoods Retail and Others* wherein it was held that a taxable person who overpaid tax under national law provisions that are contrary to EU law should be reimbursed together with interest due on the tax payment regardless of whether such interest is granted under national law for overpayment of taxes resulting from a national breach of the constitution.[159] This clear departure from the principle of equivalence in favour of the

---

154 CJEU, 16 March 2006, Case C-234/04, *Kapferer*, EU:C:2006:178.
155 CJEU, 18 July 2007, Case C-119/05, *Lucchini*, EU:C:2007:434.
156 CJEU, 3 September 2009, Case C-2/08, *Fallimento Olimpiclub*, EU:C:2009:506.
157 CJEU, 9 November 1983, Case C-199/82, *San Giorgio*, EU:C:1983:318.
158 CJEU, 13 March 2007, Case C-524/04, *Test Claimants in the Thin Cap Group Litigation*, EU:C:2007:161, para. 112.
159 CJEU, 19 July 2012, Case C-591/10, *Littlewoods Retail and Others*, EU:C:2012:478.

principle of effectiveness has created a genuinely EU law-based right to claim interest on a tax overpayment resulting from national law that is non-compliant with EU law. Consequently, the CJEU ruled that a national provision that limited interest to that which accrued from the day following the date of the claim for repayment of the tax unduly levied breached the principle of effectiveness.[160]

In order to successfully claim remedies for sustained losses, the Member State's liability must first be established. The Court developed the principle of a **Member State's liability for breach of EU law** in *Francovich*, holding that "*it is a principle of Community law that the Member States are obliged to make good loss and damage caused to individuals by breaches of Community law for which they can be held responsible.*"[161] It is settled case law that the following **conditions** have to be met **in order for a Member State to be held liable:**   **101**

1. the rule of law infringed must be intended to confer rights on individuals;
2. the breach of EU law has to be 'sufficiently serious'; and
3. a causal link must exist between the breach of the State's obligation and the loss and damage suffered by the injured parties.

National rules establishing **stringent conditions of liability of a Member State** are unacceptable under EU law, as they could jeopardize the right to compensation for a breach.[162] On the other hand, more lenient state liability conditions are accepted if they ensure a more effective application of EU law.[163]   **102**

In addition, **state liability for breach of EU law** can arise **not only out of activities of legislative organs** of a Member State. In this respect, it should be noted that "*a Member State's failure to fulfil obligations may, in principle, be established under Article 226 EC whatever the agency of that State whose action or inaction is the cause of the failure to fulfil its obligations, even in the case of a constitutionally independent institution.*"[164] Accordingly, the Court has extended the principle of state liability to include the judiciaries of Member States.[165]   **103**

---

160 See also CJEU, Case C-565/11, *Irimie*, EU:C:2013:250.
161 CJEU, 19 November 1991, Joined Cases C-6/90 and C-9/90, *Francovich*, EU:C:1995:372, para. 37.
162 See Jans, in: Obradovic/Lavranos (eds.), *Interface between EU law and national law* (2007) p. 285; see also CJEU, 13 June 2006, Case C-173/03, *Traghetti del Mediterraneo*, EU:C:2006:391.
163 Jans, in: Obradovic/Lavranos (eds.), *Interface between EU law and national law* (2007) p. 286.
164 CJEU, 5 May 1970, Case C-77/69, *Commission v Belgium*, EU:C:1970:34, para. 15. For the sake of clarity, it should be noted that the equivalent to Art. 226 under the TFEU is Art. 258. Pursuant to Art. 258 TFEU: "*If the Commission considers that a Member State has failed to fulfil an obligation under the Treaties, it shall deliver a reasoned opinion on the matter after giving the State concerned the opportunity to submit its observations. If the State concerned does not comply with the opinion within the period laid down by the Commission, the latter may bring the matter before the Court of Justice of the European Union.*"
165 CJEU, 30 September 2003, Case C-224/01, *Köbler*, EU:C:2003:513, CJEU, 9 December 2003, Case C-129/00, *Commission v Italy*, EU:C:2003:656, CJEU, 9 December 2003, Case C-129/00, *Commission v Italy*, EU:C:2003:656; CJEU, 12 November 2009, Case C-154/08, *Commission v Spain*, EU:C:2009:695.

104 **Retroactive effect of the CJEU's decisions** has also contributed to the improved effectiveness of EU law. Decisions of the CJEU also have an influence on assessments of previous years. The CJEU interprets EU law as being effective since it came into force. Nevertheless, restrictions concerning time constraints may exist under national procedural law. In exceptional cases, the CJEU restricts retroactive effect if two essential criteria are fulfilled: (1) those concerned must have acted in good faith; and (2) there must be a risk of serious difficulties e.g. a risk of serious economic repercussions. But it is settled case law that financial consequences that might ensue for a Member State do not, in themselves, justify limiting the temporal effects.[166]

Literature

Baker/Pistone, BEPS Action 16: The Taxpayers' Right to an Effective Legal Remedy Under European Law in Cross-Border Situations, *EC Tax Review* 2016, pp. 335–345; Brokelind (ed.), *Principles of Law: Function, Status and Impact in EU Tax Law* (2014); Brokelind, Case Note on *Åkerberg Fransson* (Case C-617/10), *ET* 2013, p. 281; CFE ECJ Task Force, Opinion Statement ECJ-TF 3/2017 on the Decision of the Court of Justice of the European Union of 16 May 2017 in *Berlioz Investment Fund SA* (Case C-682/15), Concerning the Right to Judicial Review under Article 47 of the EU Charter of Fundamental Rights in Cases of Cross-Border Mutual Assistance in Tax Matters, *ET* (2018); De Burca, The EU, the European Court of Justice and the International Legal Order after *Kadi, Harv. Int'l L.J.* 2010, p. 1; Dourado/da Palma Borges (eds.), *The Acte Clair in EC Direct Tax Law* (2008); Pistone (ed.), *Legal Remedies in European Tax Law* (2009); ECJ Task Force of the CFE, CFE Opinion Statement ECJ-TF 1/2014 of the CFE on the Decision of the European Court of Justice in *Åkerberg Fransson* (Case C-617/10) Concerning Ne Bis in Idem in Tax Law, *ET* 2014; Elgaard, The impact of the Charter of Fundamental Rights of the European Union on VAT law, *World Journal of VAT/GST Law* 2016, pp. 63-91; Gudmundsson, European Tax Law in the relations with the EFTA Countries, *Intertax* 2006, p. 58; Haslehner, Luxemburg: Exchange of Information and EU Fundamental Rights (C-682/15, *Berlioz Investment Fund S.A.*), in: Lang/Pistone/Rust/Schuch/Staringer/Storck (eds.), *CJEU – Recent Developments in Direct Taxation 2016* (2017); Kalloe, EU Tax Haven Blacklist – Is the European Union Policing the Whole World?, *ET* 2018, pp. 47-55; Kofler/Maduro/Pistone (eds.), *Human Rights and Taxation in Europe and the World* (2011); Kokott/Sobotta, The *Kadi* Case – Constitutional Core Values and International Law – Finding the Balance, *EJIL* 2012, p. 1015; Lang/Pistone/Schuch/Staringer (eds.), *Common Consolidated Corporate Tax Base (CCCTB)* (2008); Michel, *Austria v.*

---

166   CJEU, 10 May 2012, Joined Cases C-338/11 and C-347/11, *Santander Asset Management*, EU:C:2012:286, para. 59 et seq.; CJEU, 10 April 2014, Case C-190/12, *Emerging Markets Series of DFA*, EU:C:2014:249, para. 109 et seq.

Germany (Case C-648/15): The ECJ and Its New Tax Treaty Arbitration Hat, *ET* 2018; Mulders, Compensation of losses within the EC, *EC Tax Review* 1996, p. 123; Poelman, Some fiscal issues of the Charter of Fundamental Rights of the European Union, *Intertax* 2015, p. 173;Sarmiento/Jimenez-Valladolid de L'Hotellerie Fallois (eds.), *Litigating EU Tax Law in International, National and Non-EU National Courts* (2014); Spies, The CJEU's approach in direct tax and VAT law: consistencies and divergences, in: Lang/Pistone/Schuch/Staringer/Raponi (eds.), *ECJ – Recent Developments in Value Added Tax 2015* (2016) pp. 135-176; Staringer, Austria: CJEU Pending Case from Austria – *Austria /Germany* (C-648/15), in: Lang/Pistone/Rust/Schuch/Staringer/Storck (eds.), *CJEU – Recent Developments in Direct Taxation 2016* (2017); Terra/Wattel, *European Tax Law* (2005), (2008) and (2012); Vukčević, CILFIT Criteria for the *Acte Clair/Acte Éclairé* Doctrine in Direct Tax Cases of the CJEU, *Intertax* 2012, p. 654; Weber, *Traditional and Alternative Routes to European Tax Integration* (2010).

Chapter 2 – Coordination of Tax Laws and Tax Policies in the EU

Pasquale Pistone/Rita Szudoczky

I. The attribution of competences and the integration of tax systems in the European Union

II. The EU Commission initiatives on tax coordination
   A. General remarks
   B. Coordinating corporate taxation in the EU and beyond
      1. Harmonization of corporate taxation
         a) Past initiatives
         b) Proposals for comprehensive harmonization of corporate income taxation (CC(C)TB)
         c) Proposal for sector-specific tax harmonization: Financial Transaction Tax
      2. Coordination through soft law
         a) Combatting harmful tax competition through the Code of Conduct for Business Taxation
         b) Soft law interpreting the CJEU's case law
         c) Expert forums
         d) Soft law instruments in the area of State aid
      3. Policy towards third countries

III. The BEPS project and the new impetus for the coordination of tax policies in the EU
   A. The role of the EU in global tax coordination and the BEPS project
   B. Impact of BEPS on European Union law: the fight against tax evasion, tax avoidance and aggressive tax planning
      1. General issues
         a) Overview
         b) Conceptual framework
      2. Anti-Tax Avoidance Directive
      3. Administrative cooperation
      4. Dispute resolution
      5. Digital economy
   C. Primary law constraints on the implementation of the BEPS project

I. The attribution of competences and the integration of tax systems in the European Union

105   According to the **principle of conferral**, "the Union shall act only within the limits of the competences conferred upon it by the Member States in the Treaties to attain the objectives set out therein. Competences not conferred upon the Union in the Treaties remain with the Member States" (Art. 5(2) TEU).[1] Since taxation is not mentioned among the competences that the Member States conferred on the Union (see Arts. 3-6 TFEU), it remains within the competence of the Member States. Nonetheless, since the **internal market is part of the shared competence of the Union and the Member States** (Art. 4(2)(a) TFEU),[2] the EU institutions can intervene in the field of taxation as long as national tax measures create obstacles to the internal market. Such intervention may result, for example, in the adoption of Union legislative acts, some of the latest examples of which are Council Directive 2016/1164 of 12 July 2016 laying down rules against tax avoidance practices that directly affect the functioning of the internal market (hereinafter: **ATAD**)[3] (see Chapter 8) and Council Directive 2017/1852 of 10 October 2017 on tax dispute resolution mechanisms in the European Union[4] (see Chapter 10). Furthermore, the sovereignty of the Member States is constrained by the fact that, in tax matters, like in any other policy area, they have to exercise their powers consistent with the supremacy of Union law – in particular, the fundamental freedoms – over national law.

106   When joining the EU,[5] Member States accept the **gradual surrender of their sovereignty** within the framework of a dynamic legal order that is increasingly proceeding towards supranational integration. Legal interpretation of primary EU law, in particular the fundamental freedoms (see Chapter 3) and the State aid rules (see Chapter 4), by the CJEU imposes growing legal constraints on the exercise of national sovereignty by EU Member States. Specifically, EU Member States must set aside national measures that are incompatible with these provisions of primary EU law.

107   In tax matters, the establishment of such limits on the exercise of national sovereignty is also known as **negative tax integration** (see Chapter 1, m.no. 25),[6] as this process gives rise to a convergence of national tax systems, leading to a large extent to effects similar to those of positive tax integration. It is called 'negative'

---

1   Consolidated version of the Treaty on European Union, OJ C 202 of 7 June 2016, p. 13.
2   Consolidated version of the Treaty on the Functioning of the European Union, OJ C 202 of 7 June 2016, p. 47.
3   Council Directive 2016/1164 of 12 July 2016 laying down rules against tax avoidance practices that directly affect the functioning of the internal market, OJ L 193/1 of 19 July 2016.
4   Council Directive (EU) 2017/1852 of 10 October 2017 on tax dispute resolution mechanisms in the European Union, OJ L 265 of 14 October 2017, pp. 1–14.
5   For acceding Member States, the mechanism of adopting the *acquis* of the Union (aka *acquis* communautaire, i.e. the body of EU law that is in force at a certain point in time) implies a unilateral obligation to comply with goals the establishment of which they have not contributed to.
6   Wattel/Marres/Vermeulen (eds.), European Tax Law - *General Topics and Direct Taxation*, Vol. 1, 7th edition (2019) pp. 4-5, 44-45.

integration because it is based on the interpretation of the fundamental prohibitions laid down in the TFEU, i.e. *prohibition* of restrictions on the fundamental freedoms and *prohibition* of State aid.

Positive integration (see Chapter 1, m.nos. 3, 35), on the other hand, involves the   **108**
adoption of common harmonizing rules at the EU level by the Union legislature on the basis of authorizations laid down in the founding Treaties (i.e. legal basis provisions). Such harmonization replaces existing national tax rules with supranational law – in direct taxation in the form of directives – and thus falls within the jurisdiction of the CJEU.

As there is no specific legal basis for the harmonization of direct taxes in the TFEU   **109**
similar to Art. 113 TFEU, which applies in respect of indirect taxes, **Art. 115 TFEU** may be used as a legal basis for harmonizing national direct tax laws with a view to achieving the ultimate aim of the establishment and functioning of the internal market (Art. 3(3) TEU) (see Chapter 1, m.no. 31 et seq.). Under Art. 115 TFEU, **unanimous approval** by EU Member States is necessary for the adoption of harmonizing measures, which can only take the form of directives. Directives adopted on this legal basis must, in addition, comply with the **principle of subsidiarity** (Art. 5(3) TEU), which allows action at the EU level only if no equivalent results for the internal market may be achieved by acting at the national level.

An escape route from the unanimity requirement is offered by **Art. 20 TEU** which   **110**
allows at least nine EU Member States to pursue a stronger integration under **enhanced cooperation** as compared to the levels that otherwise apply within the European Union.[7]

A third set of rules – this time not connected with the functioning of the internal   **111**
market – has gradually been gaining relevance as a benchmark for negative tax integration ever since the EU Charter of Fundamental Rights was given binding force under Art. 6(1) TEU.[8] The EU Charter establishes minimum standards for the **protection of fundamental rights** throughout the Union and shares its core values with the common constitutional tradition of EU Member States and the corresponding principles enshrined in the European Convention on Human Rights (see Chapter 1, m.no. 36 et seq.).

Due to the unanimity requirement for the enactment of harmonizing measures in   **112**
the field of taxation,[9] to date only a few directives could be adopted in the realm of

---

7   See also Arts. 326-334 TFEU.
8   See Charter of Fundamental Rights of the European Union, OJ C 326 of 26 October 2012, pp. 391–407.
9   The EU Commission made an attempt to address this vexed problem of the EU's decision making in the area of taxation, issuing a Communication in January 2019 that started a debate on the gradual transition to qualified majority voting in EU tax policy; see COM(2019) 8 final. For details, see Pistone, A Plea for Qualified Majority Voting and the Ordinary Legislative Procedure in European Tax Law, in: van Thiel/Valente/Raventós-Calvo (eds.), *CFE Tax Advisers Europe – 60th Anniversary Liber Amicorum* (2019) pp. 11-34.

direct taxes on rather specific and fragmented issues (see Chapter 1, m.no. 60 et seq.). In the absence of harmonization, negative integration took the lead in this area. Negative tax integration, however, has some intrinsic flaws. Since it relies on interpretation of primary EU law by the CJEU in individual concrete cases, it yields a **piecemeal approach to the integration of tax systems**.

113   Furthermore, **negative tax integration** is structurally **unable to address disparities** resulting from the differences between the tax systems of the Member States. **Tax disparities** can create unintended **advantages and disadvantages** that are detrimental to the internal market. The most important disadvantage is international (juridical) **double taxation, which is** a consequence of the parallel exercise of tax sovereignty by two or more Member States where **none of them can be held responsible for infringing fundamental freedoms** (see Chapter 3, m.no. 252 et seq.).[10]

114   On the other hand, **tax disparities** can also generate unintended advantages for persons moving across borders or establishing cross-border business structures.[11] Differences or mismatches between the tax systems can open up **arbitrage** opportunities for cross-border businesses that are not available to undertakings operating only domestically. While advantages, including those granted through tax measures, which selectively favour certain undertakings and thereby **distort competition** in the internal market may well constitute prohibited State aid, an advantage that results from disparities between the tax systems has, until present, been held to be **outside the scope of the State aid rules**[12] (see Chapter 4).

115   As disparities cannot be tackled by the fundamental legal norms of the internal market (fundamental freedoms or State aid rules) and harmonization is hampered in the field of direct taxation by the unanimity requirement, such obstacles to the internal market can only be removed through the coordination of the tax systems of the Member States.

116   **Tax coordination in the strict sense** aims at ensuring that national tax systems interact seamlessly and consistently despite the absence of supranational law. Such tax coordination can be achieved by the Member States acting voluntarily at the

---

10   CJEU, 14 November 2006, Case C-513/04, *Kerckhaert and Morres*, EU:C:2006:713; CJEU, 12 February 2009, Case C-67/08, *Block*, EU:C:2009:92; CJEU, 16 July 2009, Case C-128/08, *Damseaux*, EU:C:2009:471.

11   CJEU, 12 July 2005, Case C-403/03, *Schempp*, EU:C:2005:446, para. 45.

12   Commission Decision of 8 July 2009 on the *groepsrentebox* scheme, which the Netherlands is planning to implement (C 4/07 (ex N 465/06)), OJ L 288 of 4 November 2009, pp. 26-39, paras. 115, 117. This has been confirmed by the EU Commission's final decision in the McDonald's case, in which the EU Commission found that the non-taxation of McDonald's profits in Luxembourg did not constitute State aid. Such non-taxation was the result of a mismatch between Luxembourg and US tax law, which caused the profits of McDonald's to be exempt in Luxembourg under the Luxembourg – United States income tax treaty while not being subject to tax in the United States; see Commission Decision (EU) 2019/1252 of 19 September 2018 on tax rulings SA.38945 (2015/C) (ex 2015/NN) (ex 2014/CP) granted by Luxembourg in favour of McDonald's Europe, OJ L 195 of 23 July 2019, pp. 20–39.

national level, through domestic or treaty law. Voluntary action can, on the other hand, be incentivized through soft EU law, or coordination can result from the interpretation of soft Union law by the Member States.[13] The primary objective of this tax coordination is that the EU Member States look across their borders in order to **align their tax rules with those of the other EU Member States.**

Nonetheless, negative and positive integration – even when supplemented by co-ordination as described above – cannot fully compensate for the lack of an autonomous common EU tax policy that could gear the development of Union law on direct taxation in a consistent and coherent manner. Such EU tax policy is absent, as Art. 115 TFEU authorizes the adoption of harmonization measures only for the purpose of achieving the ultimate aim of the proper functioning of the internal market. Thus, the approximation of the tax systems of the Member States cannot follow any autonomous objective (e.g., fiscal, social or regulatory objectives) other than the promotion of the internal market. **117**

Therefore, what remains is a constant struggle to reconcile various national tax policies that pursue different goals but all of which are subject to the legal constraints imposed by supranational EU law. This has put taxation in limbo within the European Union: EU Member States are neither allowed to consistently exercise their national tax policies as they like nor can as much as a hint of a common EU tax policy be found. **118**

The absolute priority of law over policy, which the process of negative integration entails, and the prolonged *impasse* on EU tax policy initiatives fails to achieve systematic solutions to the existing tax problems within the internal market, preserving significant biases in cross-border situations. **119**

Accordingly, the creation of a level playing field in the internal market remains the ultimate goal of all efforts for integrating and coordinating the Member States' tax systems. This involves the removal of all existing tax obstacles, including cross-border discrimination and disparities leading to higher or double taxation, or to double non-taxation, distortions to competition caused by harmful tax regimes of the Member States and excessive compliance costs associated with cross-border business or investment.[14] **120**

Tax coordination in the broadest sense encompasses all the initiatives that pursue this ultimate goal including negative integration, harmonization and coordination. In the following sections, an account of the current coordination efforts in the EU in this broadest sense will be given. **121**

---

13 Pistone, Legal Pluralism and International Taxation in the European Union, in: Weber (ed.), *Traditional and Alternative Routes to European Tax Integration* (2010) p. 98; Pistone, Steering the Development of Direct Taxes towards a Fair Mix of Positive and Negative Integration, in: Lang/Pistone/Schuch/Staringer (eds.), *Horizontal Tax Coordination* (2012) p. 331.
14 See COM(2006) 823 final.

```
                          ┌─────────────────────────┐
                          │    EU  Direct Tax Law    │
                          └─────────────────────────┘
         ┌────────────────────────┼──────────────────┬──────────────┐
         │                        │                  │              │
┌─────────────────────────┐  ┌──────────────┐  ┌──────────────┐
│   Positive Integration   │  │   Negative   │  │ EU International │
│                          │  │ Integration  │  │   Agreements    │
└─────────────────────────┘  └──────────────┘  └──────────────┘
         │                        │                  │
┌──────────────┐         ┌──────────────┐     ┌──────────────┐
│ Harmonization │         │ CJEU Case Law │     │ EEA Agreement │
└──────────────┘         └──────────────┘     └──────────────┘
```

| Directives removing obstacles:
– Parent-Subsidiary
– Merger
– Interest/Royalty | Harmonization of procedural law:
Dispute Resolution Directive

Harmonization of substantive law:
ATAD | Directives enhancing cooperation among tax authorities:
– Mutual Assistance
– Recovery Assistance | Primary Law
– Fundamental Freedoms
– State Aids
– EU Charter
– General principles | EU Association Agreements

EU Free Trade Agreements |

```
                          ┌──────────────┐
                          │ Coordination │
                          └──────────────┘
                 ┌──────────────┴──────────────┐
```

| Binding
(e.g. Arbitration Convention) | Non-Binding
(Soft Law, Communications of the Commission) |

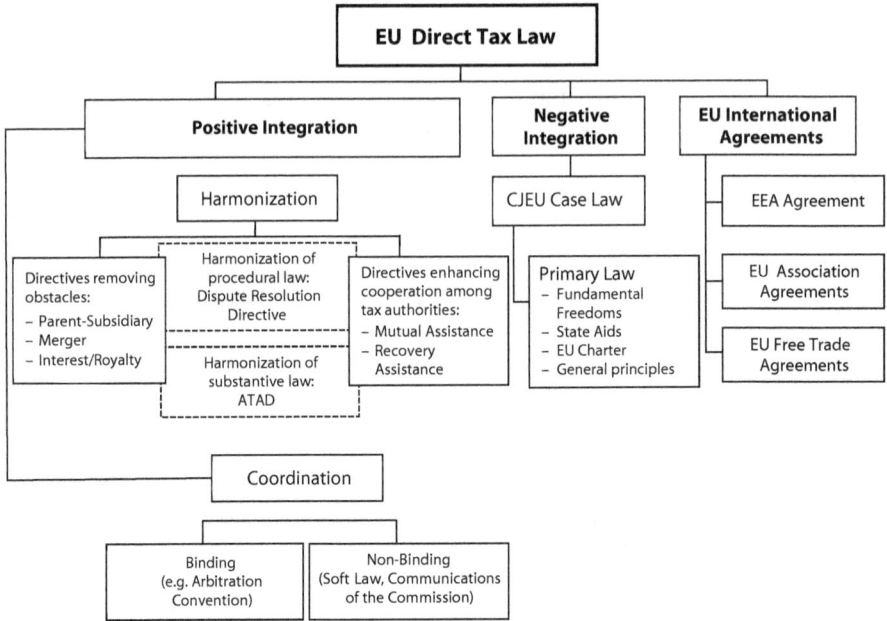

II. The EU Commission initiatives on tax coordination

A. General remarks

123   Historically, the bulk of the coordination efforts in the EU relating to direct taxation concerned corporate taxation. This may be due to the fact that corporate tax obstacles may have been thought to have a greater impact on the internal market and on the exercise of the fundamental freedoms than taxes on individuals.

124   Nevertheless, obstacles to the free movement of workers or the free movement of capital are mostly created by national provisions on individual income taxes or inheritance taxes. Therefore, some efforts have also been made to address cross-border tax obstacles for individuals. These initiatives, however, have scarcely managed to extend beyond non-binding instruments or proposals that quickly get shelved.[15] Good examples of soft law instruments of this kind are the recommendations by the EU Commission on frontier workers[16] and on inheritance

---

15   A rare example of a provision in a binding act of EU law concerning individual income tax is Art. 7(2) of Regulation (EU) No 492/2011 of the European Parliament and of the Council of 5 April 2011 on freedom of movement for workers within the Union (OJ L 141 of 27 May 2011, pp. 1-12), which provides for national treatment for workers of other Member States in terms of tax advantages.

16   Commission Recommendation of 21 December 1993 on the taxation of certain items of income received by non-residents in a Member State other than that in which they are resident, OJ L 039 of 10 February 1994, pp. 22-28.

tax,[17] but also the 2010 Communication by the EU Commission on the removal of cross-border tax obstacles faced by individuals within the internal market.[18]

The following sections take a closer look at the various means of corporate tax coordination. **125**

B. Coordinating corporate taxation in the EU and beyond

1. Harmonization of corporate taxation

a) Past initiatives

The start of the debate about corporate taxation in the EU goes back to the 1960s. **126** It was already recognized at this early stage of the EU's economic integration that differences between the corporate tax systems of the Member States can have an adverse effect on the establishment of the common (internal) market.

After some early studies on the impact of differences in tax systems on the common **127** market, (**Neumark Report** (1962), **Van den Tempel Report** (1970)), the Commission proposed legislation to achieve a certain level of harmonization of the corporate tax systems in the EU. In 1975, the Commission presented a proposal for a directive to harmonize corporate tax rates in a band between 45% and 55%. Two subsequent proposals focussed on loss compensation: one in 1984 on domestic loss carry-forward and the other in 1990 on cross-border loss relief. All these proposals were later withdrawn by the Commission, as they failed to secure support from the Member States.

A rare success in the series of failed attempts to bring about harmonization of **128** corporate taxation in the EU came in 1990. In particular, the Parent-Subsidiary Directive[19] (see Chapter 5), the Merger Directive[20] (see Chapter 6) and the Arbitration Convention[21] (see Chapter 10) were adopted, all on the same day, as the first harmonization and coordination measures in the field of direct taxation.[22]

---

17 Commission Recommendation of 15 December 2011 regarding relief for double taxation of inheritances, OJ L 336 of 20 December 2011, pp. 81-84.

18 COM(2010) 769 final. As a follow-up to this document, an expert group produced two reports; see 'Ways to tackle inheritance cross-border tax obstacles facing individuals within the EU' (KP-04-15-905-EN-N) and 'Ways to tackle cross-border tax obstacles facing individuals within the EU' (KP-01-15-918_EN-N).

19 Council Directive 90/435/EEC of 23 July 1990 on the common system of taxation applicable in the case of parent companies and subsidiaries of different Member States, OJ L 225 of 20 August 1990, pp. 6-9.

20 Council Directive 90/434/EEC of 23 July 1990 on the common system of taxation applicable to mergers, divisions, transfers of assets, and exchanges of shares concerning companies of different Member States, OJ L 225 of 20 August 1990, pp. 1-5.

21 Convention on the elimination of double taxation in connection with the adjustment of profits of associated enterprises (90/436/EEC), OJ T 225 of 20 August 1990, pp. 10-25.

22 The Commission, in 1990, also issued a proposal for a directive on the taxation of interest and royalty payments between associated enterprises. This was eventually adopted as Council Directive 2003/49/EC of June 2003 on a common system of taxation applicable to interest and royalty payments made between associated companies of different Member States, OJ L 157 of 26 June 2003, pp. 49-54 (see Chapter 7).

129   Although the **Ruding Report** (1992) recommended wide-ranging measures – such as the elimination of double taxation on cross-border income flows and approximation of corporate taxes – in the subsequent years the Commission took a cautious approach towards harmonization and chose to tackle only specific problems through specific measures[23] that were more likely to gain political acceptance.

130   A broader strategy on company taxation was presented by the Commission only a decade later, in 2001, in a Communication entitled **"Towards an Internal Market without Tax Obstacles"**.[24] The Commission put forward a **two-track strategy:** besides **targeted measures** aimed at addressing urgent problems in the short- and mid-term (e.g., guidance by the Commission on implementation of the case law of the CJEU on direct taxes, extending the existing direct tax directives, setting up a forum on transfer pricing), a **consolidated corporate tax base** was proposed for the Union-wide activities of EU companies as a **comprehensive** and long-term **solution** that would systematically tackle the majority of the tax obstacles caused by the fact that multiple different tax systems exist in the internal market (i.e. compliance with several different tax regimes, transfer pricing, double taxation and the lack of cross-border loss relief).

131   A new Communication, entitled **"Coordinating Member States' Direct Tax Systems in the Internal Market"**, was released in 2006[25] presenting **coordination** as a **new strategy** aimed at avoiding the inconsistencies that could follow from the unilateral implementation by each Member State of the CJEU's case law on direct taxation. The Communication emphasized that **coordination is also suitable for eliminating** gaps between the tax systems that lead to **unintended non-taxation and** offer room for **abuse.**

b) Proposals for comprehensive harmonization of corporate income taxation (CC(C)TB)

132   In the 2001 Communication "Towards an Internal Market without Tax Obstacles" the EU Commission put the most ambitious project of corporate tax harmonization on the EU's tax agenda, **the common consolidated corporate tax base (CCCTB).** The CCCTB involves drawing up a **single set of rules for calculating the taxable income** of EU companies belonging to a cross-border group and the **consolidation** of the results of the group at the EU level. Consolidation means that **the group is treated as a single entity** for tax purposes; thus, all intra-group transactions are ignored in the calculation of the aggregated profits. The consolidated profits are **apportioned on the basis of a pre-defined formula among the** EU Member States where the companies belonging to the group are active. This profit allocation method is the most revolutionary aspect of the CCCTB, as it means a switch from

---

23   Panayi, *European Union Corporate Tax Law* (2013) p. 20.
24   COM(2001) 582 final.
25   COM(2006) 823 final.

the arm's length method to **formula apportionment** to share the consolidated result of the group. Under the CCCTB, the EU Member States would levy tax on the share of the profits allocated to them at their own national corporate tax rates.

The Commission presented the first proposal for a Directive on a Common Consolidated Corporate Tax Base (CCCTB) in 2011 ('2011 CCCTB Proposal').[26] **133**

With regard to the apportionment of the tax base, the Proposal contained a formula **134** based on labour, capital and sales, each of these factors having equal weight. As the factors included in the formula determine how much profit is to be allocated to the Member States, the selection and weight of the factors is of crucial importance to the Member States.[27] The inability of the Member States to reach a compromise on the definition of the formula doomed the 2011 CCCTB Proposal to fail.

The global efforts to fight tax avoidance and aggressive tax planning of recent years **135** created the right setting for revitalizing the CCCTB. In June 2015, in a Communication on a Fair and Efficient Corporate Tax System in the EU,[28] the EU Commission announced its intention to **relaunch the CCCTB.** The proposals were issued in October 2016.[29] By specifically referring to the effectiveness of the CCCTB in countering tax avoidance schemes, the Commission put the CCCTB in the context of the fight against tax avoidance and base erosion and profit shifting (BEPS). As stated in the Preamble, *"the initiative for a CCCTB should be re-launched in order to address, on an equal footing, both the aspect of business facilitation and the initiative's function in countering tax avoidance."*[30] With such a new image, the Commission tried to make use of the political momentum surrounding BEPS to move the case of the CCCTB forward.

The Commission took a new approach to relaunching the CCCTB in order to avoid **136** the fate of the previous proposal. In particular, the Commission split the original proposal into two parts: a common corporate tax base (CCTB) and a common consolidated corporate tax base (CCCTB) ('2016 CCTB Proposal' and '2016 CCCTB Proposal'), and proposed the introduction of a full-fledged CCCTB in a two steps. In the **first step,** only **a common tax base** would be put in place **without consolidation,** thus achieving a degree of harmonization of direct taxes similar to that achieved in respect of the common value-added tax system through the Sixth Directive in the 1970s. In a **second step,** consolidation of the tax base with formula apportionment would be introduced. Taking into account that under the 2011 Proposal the apportionment formula was the deal breaker, the Commission's

---

26   COM(2011) 121/4.
27   For example, if the formula were to give significant weight to the number of employees and tangible assets, Member States where production facilities are located would be favoured while typical holding jurisdictions – where there are normally only a few employees and mainly intangible assets – would be disadvantaged.
28   COM(2015) 302 final.
29   COM(2016) 685 final and COM(2016) 683 final.
30   Recital 3 of Preamble, COM(2016) 685 final.

strategy is trying to reach a consensus on the less controversial part of the proposal, i.e. the common tax base, while deferring consolidation to a later stage. While a gradual introduction might make the CCCTB more acceptable to the Member States, the risk of this approach is that it will remain half-implemented and result only in a common corporate tax base. That would mean that the greatest benefits of the CCCTB – automatic cross-border loss compensation, the elimination of transfer pricing and the related administrative burden and mitigation of double taxation, which are the consequences of consolidation – would be lost.

137 Further differences between the 2016 and 2011 Proposals are: (i) the scope of the CC(C)TB, (ii) the anti-abuse rules, and (iii) the incentives included in the proposals. As regards the scope, under the 2011 Proposal, the CCCTB regime was optional, meaning that any company could opt into the CCCTB and when it did so, consolidation would have been mandatory for all companies in the EU belonging to the same group ("all-in or all-out" principle). In contrast, under the 2016 CCTB Proposal, the regime is mandatory for certain companies. Such companies are defined through a size-related threshold, i.e. those with total consolidated group revenue exceeding EUR 750 million a year. Thus, large multinational groups that have the greatest capacity for aggressive tax planning are compulsorily included in the scope. Other companies, i.e. small and medium-sized enterprises (SMEs), can opt into the CCTB regime and – as it does not involve consolidation, but only the calculation of the tax base according to the common rules – such an option can be exercised on an individual basis in respect of companies that are part of an SME group (i.e. no "all-in or all-out" principle).

138 As regards anti-abuse rules, the 2016 CCTB Proposal contains an interest limitation rule, a switch-over clause, a controlled foreign companies (CFC) provision, anti-hybrid rules, exit tax and a general anti-abuse clause (GAAR). Some of these rules are new and some have been made stricter in the 2016 CCTB Proposal, aligning the common EU corporate tax regime with domestic corporate tax systems, which have been fortified by compulsory minimum anti-avoidance rules through the ATAD I (see Chapter 8).

139 As regards incentives, one of the key measures that appeared anew in the 2016 CCTB proposal is the Allowance for Growth and Investment (AGI), which is designed to mitigate the notorious debt-bias in the financing of companies (i.e. over-indebtedness of companies due to the fact that interest on debt is tax deductible while dividends on equity are not). The AGI encourages companies under the CCTB to finance their activities through equity rather than debt by granting a defined return for equity, which is deductible from the tax base. The AGI is applied to the increase of equity measured over a rolling 10-year period (incremental-based approach). The other novel provision in the 2016 CCTB Proposal, the Super Deduction for R&D expenses, is different in the sense that it is more than a technical tax provision, insofar as it is aimed at supporting R&D and innovation in the EU. This is in line with the general objective of the CC(C)TB to stimulate growth and investment within the EU. It should be noted that although it is an incentive designed to promote a certain economic function (R&D and innovation) and thus, in principle, could qualify as a selective advantage, it is laid down in EU legislation, which guards it from the reach of the State aid rules.[31]

The 2016 CCTB Proposals also include harmonized transfer pricing rules and provisions on cross-border loss relief in an attempt to remedy the lack of consolidation in the first phase of its introduction. As regards consolidation under the 2016 CCCTB Proposal, an "all-in or all-out" principle applies to a CCCTB group. The Proposal provides for the same formula as under the 2011 proposal, i.e. consisting of labour, assets and sales, whereby equal weight is given to each of these factors. Alternative formulae would apply to certain sectors (e.g. financial services and insurance, oil and gas, shipping and air transport) to better address the specifics of such sectors. Notably, in the Commission's presentation, the consolidation mechanism and formula apportionment are also tools in combatting BEPS. Apportionment of profits based on the formula is more resilient to aggressive tax planning practices, as the Commission claims, than the commonly used transfer pricing methods for allocating profits (i.e. arm's length principle).[32] **140**

Despite the repackaging of the CC(C)TB, there are still serious unresolved controversies about the proposals as the lack of progress since 2016 shows.[33] This comes as no surprise considering what is at stake for the Member States is largely giving up corporate taxation as a means of carrying out their tax policy and most importantly, choosing harmonization instead of tax competition. **141**

c) Proposal for sector-specific tax harmonization: Financial Transaction Tax

The EU Commission sought to bring about harmonization in the financial sector when it proposed a financial transaction tax (FTT), initially in 2011. The Commission reasoned that, as the **financial sector** played a major role in the 2008 financial crisis and received substantial government support to overcome the crisis, the introduction of a separate levy is necessary to ensure that the financial sector **contributes fairly to public finances.** **142**

---

31 The prohibition of State aid under Art. 107(1) TFEU precludes, as its name indicates, the granting of aid by the Member States and not by the Union. Accordingly, when a selective advantage results from a Member State's implementation of secondary Union law, it must be examined whether the advantage is attributable to the Member State or the Union. Only when it is attributable to the Member State can it fall within the scope of Art. 107(1) TFEU. The question of attribution depends on the degree of discretion left by secondary Union law for the Member States. See, to this effect, CJEU, 5 April 2006, Case T-351/02, *Deutsche Bahn*, EU:T:2006:104, paras 101–102; CJEU, 23 April 2009, Case C-460/07, *Puffer*, EU:C:2009:254, para. 70.

32 Explanatory memorandum to the CCTB Proposal, COM(2016) 685 final, p. 2.

33 The new EU Commission's Work Programme 2020 mentions the CCTB and the CCCTB proposals among the pending proposals that will receive priority in 2020; see COM(2020) 37 final, Annex 3.

143 As not all EU Member States supported an EU-wide FTT, the Commission proposed **enhanced cooperation** to adopt the FTT (see above m.no. 110).[34] Achieving unanimity on an FFT, even amongst a smaller circle of 11 Member States that showed a willingness to move ahead under enhanced cooperation, proved, however, to be more difficult than anticipated. The proposal came to a standstill in the Council and, after several years of impasse, the chances for its adoption seem to be slim.[35]

2. Coordination through soft law

a) Combatting harmful tax competition through the Code of Conduct for Business Taxation

144 The coexistence of 28 different tax systems in one integrated market results in significant tax competition between the Member States. Tax competition has a long history in the internal market. On the one hand, it has led to the gradual lowering of corporate tax rates in the EU in combination with the broadening of the tax base. This is a beneficial effect of tax competition, which fosters investor-friendly tax systems. On the other hand, tax competition can also be harmful. When business decisions of market players are influenced by tax, rather than economic, considerations, this can lead to less efficiency (e.g. in the corporate structures of EU businesses) and an increased tax burden on factors of production, which are less mobile than capital (e.g. labour), which in turn, results in unfair tax systems. In addition, harmful tax competition leads to the erosion of national tax bases ("race to the bottom") and thus difficulties in securing sustainable tax revenues for the Member States.

145 Harmful tax competition was intensified in the 1980s when Member States started to offer **targeted tax regimes** that provide considerably lower rates or more favourable tax rules than the general tax system for certain types of income or companies in order to attract foreign capital (e.g. coordination centres, holding company, finance company, and exempt company regimes).

146 In order to tackle harmful tax competition, on 1 December 1997, the Council adopted the **Code of Conduct for Business Taxation**, a **non-binding legal instrument** in the framework of which the Member States made a **political commitment** to repeal harmful tax measures from their tax systems ("roll-back") and not to introduce such new measures ("standstill"). At the same time, the **Code of Conduct**

---

34   COM(2013) 71 final.
35   The last attempt to revive the discussion on the file in the Council was made in May 2019; see http://www.europarl.europa.eu/legislative-train/theme-deeper-and-fairer-internal-market-with-a-strengthened-industrial-base-taxation/file-financial-transaction-tax [accessed 22 July 2020]. The new EU Commission's Work Programme 2020 mentions the FTT proposals among the pending proposals that will receive priority in 2020; see COM(2020) 37 final, Annex 3. The German Presidency of the Council (in the 1 July – 31 December 2020 period) also intends to treat the FTT as a priority on its tax agenda; see CFE's Tax Top 5, 14 April 2020.

Group was established, which reports to the Council and is charged with the task of examining Member States' measures which may fall under the Code (see Chapter 4, m.no. 304 et seq.).

Apart from reviewing potentially harmful tax measures of the Member States (e.g. **147** patent boxes), the Code of Conduct Group also engages in developing overall policies on certain issues, which are to be implemented by the Member States in a coordinated manner (e.g. exchange of tax rulings, treatment of hybrid mismatches). If such coordination through soft law does not lead to the desired outcome, it can be followed by the adoption of hard Union law (as happened in respect of both exchange of tax rulings and hybrid mismatches, see Chapter 9, m.no. 714 et seq. and Chapter 8, m.no. 628 et seq. respectively).[36] Furthermore, the Code of Conduct Group also facilitates the coordination of tax policies beyond the borders of the EU by promoting the adoption of the Code's principles and criteria by third countries. Recently, it has also been charged with developing a coordinated and coherent EU policy towards non-cooperative third-country jurisdictions (see m.no 154 et seq. for more detail on this).

With all these activities, the Code of Conduct Group's work significantly contrib- **148** utes to bringing the tax systems of the Member States closer together by disallowing harmful tax competition measures, designing a coordinated response of the Member States to mismatches and disparities that are exploited by aggressive tax planners and developing coordinated EU tax policy towards third countries. Although the soft law approach to tax coordination that the Code of Conduct represents has proven to be rather effective, it is worth mentioning that the EU State aid rules play an important role in reinforcing the political commitments and gentlemen agreements that characterize the operation of the Code of Conduct. In particular, the Commission has resorted numerous times to the **State aid rules** as a **complementary tool to the Code of Conduct** in limiting the Member States' room to engage in harmful tax competition.[37] This occurred not only in the beginning of 2000s when the Commission started State aid procedures against some measures of the Member States that were listed as harmful tax measures in the Primarolo Report but also more recently in respect of high-profile State aid investigations by the Commission against individual tax rulings that are also being monitored within the Code of Conduct Group.

b) Soft law interpreting the CJEU's case law

As mentioned above, coordination of the Member States' tax systems can be facil- **149** itated by EU soft law, which gives guidance to Member States on how they can

---

36 See on this Nouwe/Wattel, Tax Competition and the Code of Conduct for Business Taxation, in: Wattel/Marres/Vermeulen (eds.), *European Tax Law*, 7th edition (2019) pp. 927-948, at p. 940.
37 Traversa/Flamini, Fighting Harmful Tax Competition through EU State Aid Law: Will the Hardening of Soft Law Suffice?, *EStAL* 2015, pp. 323-331.

eliminate discrimination, disparities and other cross-border tax obstacles to the internal market by acting unilaterally. One of the attempts by the EU Commission in this regard was the issuance of communications (i.e. soft law instruments) interpreting the direct tax case law of the CJEU in order to help the Member States comply with such case law. Within the framework of this coordination process, three Communications have been issued on specific issues: the tax treatment of losses in cross-border situations,[38] exit taxation,[39] and anti-abuse measures.[40] Although the Commission seemed to prefer this route of coordination in 2006–2007, since then it has not issued any new Communications of this kind.

c) Expert forums

150 Expert forums and advisory bodies play an important role in coordinating and approximating the Member States' tax systems. They provide a platform for the exchange of views and sharing of best practices and, in addition, they issue various soft law instruments that contribute to streamlining the tax laws in certain areas and promoting uniform practices.

151 One of these forums was the EU Joint Transfer Pricing Forum ("JTPF"), an **advisory group to the Commission on transfer pricing.**[41] The work of the JTPF contributed to coordination in the area of transfer pricing by promoting **best practices** and recommending solutions aimed at **standardization** and **more uniform application** of the transfer pricing rules within the EU.

152 Another expert forum was set up by the Commission in 2013 in the area of tax good governance. Good governance in the area of taxation is marked by the principles of transparency, exchange of information and fair tax competition. The Platform for Tax Good Governance, Aggressive Tax Planning and Double Taxation is composed of members from the tax authorities of all Member States and organizations representing business, civil society and tax practitioners.[42] The Platform assists the Commission in developing initiatives to promote good governance in tax matters in third countries, to tackle aggressive tax planning and to identify and address double taxation through dialogue and exchange of expertise.

d) Soft law instruments in the area of State aid

153 The use of soft law instruments is most prevalent in the area of State aid. The EU Commission has a longstanding tradition of issuing such instruments – under various names, such as guidelines, frameworks, notices – in the course of its

---

38   COM(2006) 824 final.
39   COM(2006) 825 final.
40   COM(2007) 785 final.
41   The EU Commission established the JTPF in 2002. Its last mandate expired in 2019.
42   The Platform's mandate was last renewed on 16 December 2019.

enforcement of the State aid rules. Most of these instruments are intended to provide guidance on how the Commission is to exercise its discretion under Art. 107(3) TFEU when deciding on the compatibility of State aid measures with the internal market (see Chapter 4, m.no. 370 et seq.). However, from the point of view of tax coordination and negative integration through the State aid rules, the most important soft law instrument in the area of State aid is the Notion of Aid Notice,[43] which has a broader scope and function. It provides **guidance on the interpretation of the concept of State aid**, including fiscal State aid, relying on the Union Courts' case law and the Commission's practice, thereby facilitating a uniform understanding of State aid by the Member States and national authorities. Although soft law instruments do **not have legally binding force**, they can produce indirect legal effects. Specifically, the EU institution issuing such an instrument – which is, in the area of State aid, the EU Commission – may be bound by the terms of the instrument, which follows from the general principle of legitimate expectations.[44]

3. Policy towards third countries

Apart from coordinating the Member State's tax systems, the EU is also committed to contributing to international tax coordination primarily by actively engaging in the BEPS project, taking a lead in implementing the BEPS recommendations (see m.no. 159 et seq.) and promoting standards of tax good governance towards third countries. **154**

Since the Communication on promoting good governance in tax matters was issued in 2009, the EU has sought to convince low-tax third countries to subscribe to the principles of transparency and exchange of information, as well as to abolish tax measures that qualify as harmful according to the Code of Conduct's criteria.[45] At the same time, it was recognized that a coordinated response from the Member States is necessary to have effective counter-measures against base erosion caused by third countries not complying with the minimum standards of tax good governance. Different responses by the Member States are detrimental to the internal market, as businesses may structure arrangements with such third countries through the Member State that has the weakest response (i.e. the lowest level of protection against tax avoidance and profit shifting) and then have access to the rest of the internal market by making use of the free movement provisions.[46] First, the Commission only tried to coordinate the criteria according to which Member States should decide whether a third country complies with minimum **155**

---

43   Commission Notice on the notion of State aid as referred to in Art. 107(1) of the Treaty on the Functioning of the European Union, OJ C 262 of 19 July 2016.
44   See, to that effect, CJEU, 28 June 2005, Joined Cases C-189/02 P, C-202/02 P, C-205/02 P to C-208/02 P and C-213/02 P, *Dansk Rørindustri and Others*, EU:C:2005:408, para. 211.
45   COM(2009) 201 final.
46   COM(2012) 8805 final, Preamble, indent 6.

standards of tax good governance. It also encouraged Member States to draw up **national blacklists** and include third countries on the list on the basis of such criteria.[47] As a second step, the Commission has published an EU-wide list of third country non-cooperative tax jurisdictions compiled from Member States' independent national blacklists ("pan-EU list").[48] However, the **pan-EU list** was still only an interim measure, and the Commission Communication on External Strategy,[49] which was part of the 2016 Anti-Tax Avoidance Package, envisaged a true **common EU list of non-cooperative jurisdictions**. This involved a common EU system for assessing, screening and listing non-cooperative third countries, as well as developing a unified EU response to them in the form of defensive measures. The goal was to replace the medley of national systems with a clear and coherent EU approach in order to enhance legal certainty both for third countries and EU businesses.

156 In November 2016, the Council agreed on the criteria to be used during the screening and listing process: tax transparency, fair taxation, the implementation of OECD BEPS measures and substance requirements for zero-tax countries. The work was carried out during 2017, mainly, in the Code of Conduct Group in regular consultation with the third countries concerned. The Council approved the list, which included 17 jurisdictions, on 5 December 2017. This was in the form of Council Conclusions, i.e. a soft law instrument.[50] The Code of Conduct Group has been charged with continuing the dialogue with the jurisdictions on the list and monitoring the situation in these jurisdictions and in others that have been screened in the process. As a result of the recent February 2020 update, the list contains 12 jursidictions.[51] Jurisdictions that do not yet comply with all international tax standards but committed to reform are considered cooperative and are included in a state of play document (Annex II). Once a jurisdiction meets all of its commitments, it is removed from Annex II. From 2020 onwards, the list is being updated twice a year.

Defensive measures, both in the area of taxation and otherwise, can be applied vis-à-vis the listed jurisdictions. Non-tax defensive measures include restrictions on access for the listed third countries to various EU funds. In the tax area, Member States can apply both administrative measures, such as increasing the risk of audit for taxpayers that have structures involving the listed jurisdictions, and

---

47   COM(2012) 8805 final.
48   COM(2015) 302 final, point 4.1.
49   COM(2016) 24 final.
50   *Council Conclusions 15429/17.*
51   See Taxation: Council revises its EU list of non-cooperative jurisdictions, Council of the European Union, Press Release, 18 Feb. 2020. The EU list of non-cooperative jurisdictions now includes American Samoa, Cayman Islands, Fiji, Guam, Oman, Palau, Panama, Samoa, Seychelles, Trinidad and Tobago, US Virgin Islands, Vanuatu. Furthermore, the Council indicated that Turkey could be included in the list insofar as it does not allow for an effective automatic exchange of information with Cyprus.

legislative measures, such as the non-deductibility of expenses and the application of CFC rules or withholding taxes on transactions with the listed jurisdictions. The defensive measures should be effecive and proportionate. With regard to legislative measures, their effectiveness increases with the level of coordination between the Member States.[52] It should be noted, however, that the application of defensive measures by a Member State vis-à-vis a third country – whether or not the third coutry is listed and whether or not the measure is recommended by EU soft law – may conflict with the requirements of EU primary law, namely the free movement of capital.[53]

Another means of promoting standards of good governance towards third countries is to include good governance clauses in bilateral or regional (free trade, association, etc.) agreements with third countries. The Commission has expressed the need to reinforce such a practice in its Communication on External Strategy.[54] The Commission in the same Communication also envisaged the inclusion of State aid provisions in such agreements. Such provisions would prohibit the most harmful types of subsidies and provide for consultations on harmful subsidies, thereby increasing transparency. The fact that the EU Member States are bound by the rigorous EU State aid rules while their non-EU trading partners are not prevented from subsidizing their local companies through preferential tax regimes or administrative practices – as WTO rules are not very effective in this regard – can create serious distortions in the relationship between the EU and its third country trading partners. Thus, by including State aid provisions into bilateral agreements with third countries the Commission sought to create a level playing field internationally. **157**

The other side of the relationship with third countries includes certain protectionist measures of the EU market. In particular, whilst the ATAD (see further in Chapter 8) establishes stricter limits on CFC legislation within the internal market in order to preserve compatibility with the right of establishment, it leaves the Member States free to apply stricter CFC rules on low-taxed foreign subsidiaries established in third countries. Although the rationale for such rules is to allow for broader compensation of tax advantages arising in legal environments that generally do not include State aid rules, this situation may have a negative impact on free movement of capital. **158**

---

52   For this reason, the Council has specifically invited the Member States to use the EU list of non-cooperative jurisdictions in the application of at least one of the recommended legislative measures as of 2021.

53   In this respect, the Council Conclusions contain the provision that Member States, when taking defensive measures, should ensure they are in line with their obligations under EU law and international law (i.e. any applicable tax treaty); see *Council Conclusions 15429/17*, indent 17. See more in detail, Lazarov, The Compatibility of the EU Tax Haven "Blacklist" with the Fundamental Freedoms and the Charter, in: Martín Jiménez (ed.), *The External Tax Strategy of the EU in a Post-BEPS Environment* (2019) p. 32 et seq.

54   COM(2016) 24 final.

III. The BEPS project and the new impetus for the coordination of tax policies in the EU

A. The role of the EU in global tax coordination and the BEPS project

159 In the aftermath of the 2008 financial crisis, the attention of governments and public opinion focused on the need to counter tax evasion, tax avoidance and aggressive tax planning strategies of large multinational enterprises, the scale of which has exponentially grown in recent decades.

160 The determination to fight this phenomenon culminated first in a global shift towards tax transparency and subsequently in the **OECD/G20 Base Erosion and Profit Shifting (BEPS) Project**, which is an unprecedented plan for achieving **international tax coordination at the global level** in order to constrain tax avoidance, agresssive tax planning and profit shifting techniques. In October 2015, the OECD published the results of its work on a 15-point Action Plan that contains detailed recommendations aimed at changing domestic laws and/or tax treaties in order to keep taxing rights aligned with value creation and effectively countering double non-taxation at the global level.[55]

161 The EU has recognized the dramatic impact of BEPS activities on tax revenues of the Member States and has put forward its own agenda in addition to endorsing general coordination with the OECD.

162 An initial programme to address tax avoidance and profit shifting at the EU level was set out in the Communication issued on 6 December 2012 – thus, even earlier than the first OECD Report on BEPS – which envisaged a whole range of measures, from enacting EU legislation to soft law coordination.[56] The next comprehensive package was issued in March 2015.[57] This package focused on transparency initiatives, translating international initiatives in part to the EU level and addressing EU specific issues. Next, the Commission released a Communication in June 2015 entitled "A Fair and Efficient Corporate Tax System in the European Union: 5 Key Areas for Action".[58] The objectives set out in the Communication, on the one hand, echoed the objectives of the BEPS project (i.e. aligning taxation and economic activity in the EU), emphasizing the need for a strong EU approach to corporate tax avoidance in the EU's external relations. On the other hand, the creation of a growth-friendly and competitive corporate tax environment in the EU was acknowledged as a priority of EU tax policy.

163 As the activity of the EU intensified on this matter, the dilemma became more and more apparent: **what role should the EU play in fighting tax avoidance and**

---

55   OECD, Base Erosion and Profit Shifting http://www.oecd.org/ctp/beps.htm [accessed 22 July 2020].
56   COM (2012) 722 final.
57   COM(2015) 136 final.
58   COM(2015) 302 final.

aggressive tax planning and what should its place be in the global tax coordination effort?

Clearly, the work on curbing tax avoidance, aggressive tax planning and base erosion and profit shifting should be coordinated between the EU and the OECD, instead of having two parallel programmes. Duplicating the work and producing divergent outputs would seriously compromise the efforts towards global coordination of the tax systems while **cooperation and coordination between the two organizations could enhance the chance of success.** **164**

The issue also arises as to **whether the EU should go further than what is recommended under the BEPS Reports** in order to achieve a higher level of coordination or a more effective realization of the goal of fighting BEPS within its Member States. In fact, once the process of tax transparency is complete, arguably there will only be a need for (i) mutual assistance directives within the European Union insofar as they seek stronger administrative cooperation among EU Member States in the assessment and enforcement of taxes and (ii) making dispute settlement more effective by means of general use of international arbitration in tax matters. These steps have, indeed, been taken (see m.no. 179 and 180 et seq, respectively) however, the EU went much further than simply improving administrative cooperation. **165**

First, the **Parent-Subsidiary Directive** was amended by inserting an **anti-hybrid rule**[59] and a **general anti-abuse rule**[60] in order to ensure that the directive does not inadvertently lead to double non-taxation or is not (ab)used for the purpose of shifting profits generated within the EU to low-tax third countries. (see Chapter 5, m.nos. 441, 462). **166**

Second, a whole new directive was adopted,[61] which provides for compulsory domestic anti-avoidance rules to be implemented by the Member States to guarantee a minimum level of protection against tax avoidance throughout the EU (see Chapter 8). **167**

Third, the Commission started to use the State aid rules in the fight against tax avoidance and aggressive tax planning by launching State aid investigations against individual tax rulings, mainly in the area of transfer pricing, that alledgly endorsed tax treatment deviating from the normal application of laws and thus granted selective advantages to certain companies (see Chapter 4, m.no. 309 et seq.). **168**

---

59   Council Directive 2014/86/EU of 8 July 2014 amending Directive 2011/96/ EU on the common system of taxation applicable in the case of parent companies and subsidiaries of different Member States, OJ L 219 of 25 July 2014, pp. 40-41.

60   Council Directive (EU) 2015/121 of 27 January 2015 amending Directive 2011/96/EU on the common system of taxation applicable in the case of parent companies and subsidiaries of different Member States, OJ L 21 of 28 January 2015, pp. 1-3.

61   Council Directive 2016/1164 of 12 July 2016 laying down rules against tax avoidance practices that directly affect the functioning of the internal market, OJ L 193/1 of 19 July 2016.

169 Overall, on the one hand, the EU's actions in the fight against tax avoidance and aggressive tax planning aim to **implement the output of the BEPS project** and tax transparency initiatives on a homogeneous basis throughout the EU. On the other hand, the EU is striving to be a forerunner in this matter and set an example by being first and going beyond the minimum in implementing anti-BEPS measures. In addition, the EU is also seeking to promote wider international coordination in this field by enforcing minimum standards of tax good governance in its external relations. It is also trying to push forward the international agenda on combatting BEPS regarding issues that were not effectively addressed by the BEPS project, e.g. taxation of the digitalized economy (see m.no. 183 et seq).

170 In the following sections, the relationship between the EU and the BEPS project will be analysed in light of a two-way flow of legal issues, namely by looking at (i) how the BEPS project steers tax coordination within the European Union and (ii) the extent to which EU law allows the output of the BEPS project to apply within the European Union.

B. Impact of BEPS on European Union law: the fight against tax evasion, tax avoidance and aggressive tax planning

1. General issues

a) Overview

171 As described above, over the course of the history of coordination of the corporate tax laws and policies of the Member States, a wide range of instruments have been utilized from soft to hard – secondary and primary – law. Notably, the EU's efforts to counter tax avoidance, aggressive tax planning and profit shifting has led to an increased use of secondary law, in particular, harmonizing directives that are either aimed at implementing uniform anti-BEPS measures in the EU or introducing mechanisms that facilitate the resolution of disputes that are likely to rise due to the proliferation of anti-abuse rules in the laws of the Member States.

172 In the following sections, after setting out the conceptual framework, an overview of these renewed harmonization efforts will be provided.

b) Conceptual framework

173 From a theoretical perspective, the developments regarding international tax coordination within the framework of the BEPS project have proved that States are now committed to going beyond simply countering **tax evasion and avoidance,** to actually responding to **aggressive tax planning.**

174 The difference between tax evasion and avoidance is generally clear. While **tax evasion is an open violation of tax law** (which can evolve into its more serious form, generally called tax fraud, in the presence of manoeuvres aimed at hiding

the violation), **tax avoidance** arises in connection with the exploitation of the **friction between form and substance** for the purpose of circumventing the scope of a tax provision. In line with the interpretation provided by the CJEU in the *Emsland-Stärke* case,[62] neither situation enjoys the protection of EU law.

Aggressive tax planning consists of the exploitation of cross-border tax disparities **175** to the advantage of taxpayers, which shift profits out of the country of value creation, often towards low-tax jurisdictions by making use of loopholes and technicalities in the international tax rules and mismatches between the different tax systems. Aggressive tax planning is often aimed at achieving unintended double non-taxation. Anti-avoidance rules are often scarcely effective to counter this phenomenon, especially since aggressive tax planning achieves an undue tax advantage across two different tax jurisdictions.[63]

The dramatic change connected with the BEPS project has strengthened inter- **176** national tax coordination with a view to also countering aggressive tax planning. In the presence of structural similarities to the other phenomena (i.e. fraudulent and abusive practices) that are not eligible for the protection of EU law, coordination in the exercise of tax sovereignty in order to counter aggressive tax planning leads us to conclude that this phenomenon should be treated similarly. This means, in particular, that Member States should be allowed to counter BEPS practices and aggressive tax planning by restricting the exercise of the fundamental freedoms and such restriction, provided that it is proportionate to the objective pursued, should be considered justified, similar to Member State measures aimed at preventing tax avoidance and abuse (see m.no. 187).

2. Anti-Tax Avoidance Directive

The Anti-Tax Avoidance Directive (ATAD) (for a detailed analysis see Chapter 8) **177** was proposed by the Commission in January 2016 and adopted by the Council in June 2016. Taking into account the history of corporate tax harmonization in the EU, i.e. the fact that certain proposals had been pending on the Council's agenda for decades, this proposal has been put in place at lightning speed. This signals the exceptional momentum that surrounds the introduction of anti-avoidance and anti-BEPS measures at this time. As indicated above, the main objective of the ATAD is to bring about a common minimum level of protection for the internal market against tax avoidance practices. It contains five anti-avoidance/anti-BEPS measures that Member States must introduce into their domestic laws, namely an interest limitation rule, exit tax, GAAR, CFC rules and an anti-hybrid rule. The ATAD was amended very soon after its adoption to provide for anti-hybrid rules

---

62   CJEU, 14 December 2000, Case C-110/99, *Emsland-Stärke*, EU:C:2000:695.
63   See further on this Pistone, The Meaning of Tax Avoidance and Aggressive Tax Planning in European Union Tax Law: Some thoughts in connection with the reaction to such practices by the European Union, in: Dourado (ed.), *Tax Avoidance Revisited in the EU BEPS Context* (2017) p. 73 et seq.

in relations with third countries (ATAD II).[64] Member States are required to apply most of these measures as from 1 January 2019 or 1 January 2020.

178 In light of the declared aim of the ATAD, i.e. to coordinate the responses of the Member States in the face of tax avoidance and aggressive tax planning practices in order to avoid unilateral responses by the Member States that would lead to more disparities and further fragmentation of the internal market, the chosen method of minimum harmonization is rather questionable. Minimum harmonization entails that the Member States be allowed to introduce (in domestic law or tax treaties) stricter rules than those laid down in the Directive in order to ensure or safeguard a higher level of protection of their national corporate tax bases. If certain Member States choose to maintain or introduce stricter rules while others stick to the minimum rules of the Directive, it is hard to see how the ATAD will lead to a higher degree of coordination than the status quo.

3. Administrative cooperation

179 While the ATAD lays down substantive tax provisions implementing certain BEPS recommendations in the EU, the Directive on administrative cooperation (DAC)[65] contains procedural provisions that ensure all types of exchange of information (automatic, on request and spontaneous) and other forms of administrative cooperation between the tax administrations of the Member States, thus implementing, within the EU, the results of the global tax transparency efforts. The five successive amendments to the DAC in the last few years indicate the pace of change that we are witnessing today in the area of tax transparency (for details, see Chapter 9). The EU Commission's latest plan in the pipeline is aimed at another amendment of the DAC (DAC 7) in order to improve the rules on joint audits and to provide tax administrations with information on taxpayers who generate income (revenues) through digital platforms.

4. Dispute resolution

180 As mentioned above, the Commission's tax policy program set out in successive Communications was aimed not only at reinforcing the reaction at the EU and Member State level to tax avoidance and aggressive tax planning but also at creating a fairer tax system in the EU for businesses and individuals. Improving the tax climate for EU companies and citizens primarily involves a more comprehensive and effective dispute resolution mechanism designed to resolve double taxation, which is still the greatest burden on cross-border operations and businesses in the EU.

---

64 Council Directive (EU) 2017/952 of 29 May 2017 amending Directive (EU) 2016/1164 as regards hybrid mismatches with third countries, OJ L 144 of 7 June 2017.

65 Council Directive 2011/16/EU of 15 February 2011 on administrative cooperation in the field of taxation and repealing Directive 77/799/EEC, OJ L 64 of 11 March 2011.

A sort of dispute resolution mechanism has already been in place in the EU for **181** quite some time in the form of the **Arbitration Convention,** which the Member States concluded in 1990 with a view to providing for binding arbitration in transfer pricing matters (see Chapter 10). The Arbitration Convention has a limited scope, as it does not address e.g. **double taxation** arising from disputes other than transfer pricing.

Due to its narrow scope and inefficient operation, the Arbitration Convention left **182** a large segment of cross-border tax disputes unsettled and thus double taxation unresolved. The extension of the binding arbitration provided for in the Convention to all disputes concerning the interpretation of tax treaties and leading to double taxation and the improvement of the efficiency of the mechanism fit neatly into the Commission's program of a fairer and more business-friendly tax system in the EU. In October 2017, the Council adopted – this time – a directive to that effect.[66] The Directive does not replace the Arbitration Convention, but provides for an additional and broader framework for settling cross-border tax disputes on income and capital (see Chapter 10). The Directive had to be implemented by 30 June 2019. Several Member States, however, failed to complete the transposition by the deadline.[67]

5. Digital economy

Finding solutions to the problems caused by new business models in the digital **183** economy was the very first action item of the BEPS Action Plan. However, the Final BEPS Report on Action 1 has not proposed any concrete measure that would address the problem of digital enterprises not paying tax on the profits they earn in the market/user jurisdiction in the absence of physical presence (for example, permanent establishment) and thus a tax nexus in that country.

The EU places the problem of the taxation of the digital economy under the umbrella of its fair taxation agenda. The EU Commission issued a Communication on A Fair and Efficient Tax System in the European Union for the Digital Single Market in September 2017.[68] The Commission's goal in this respect is a common **184** EU approach to influence international discussions and develop meaningful solutions to taxing the digital economy as long as global coordination on this matter at the level of the OECD and the Inclusive Framework[69] does not yield results.

---

66 Council Directive (EU) 2017/1852 of 10 October 2017 on tax dispute resolution mechanisms in the European Union, OJ L 265/1 of 14 October 2017.
67 The EU Commission sent reasoned opinions (second step of the infringement procedure under Art. 258 TFEU) to a number of Member States on the matter in November 2019; see https://ec.europa.eu/ commission/presscorner/detail/en/INF_19_6304.
68 COM(2017) 547 final.
69 The Inclusive Framework on BEPS is a forum where interested countries and jurisdictions can work with OECD and G20 members on developing standards on BEPS related issues and review and monitor the implementation of the BEPS Package; see https://www.oecd.org/tax/flyer-inclusive-framework-on-beps.pdf.

185 Accordingly, the Commission, in March 2018, issued two legislative proposals for new rules aimed at ensuring that digital business activities in the EU are taxed in a fair, growth-friendly and sustainable manner.[70] The first proposal aims to reform the corporate tax rules by introducing the notion of taxable "digital presence" or "virtual permanent establishment".[71] These new rules would ensure that profits are taxed where businesses have significant interaction with the users through digital channels even when the businesses are physically not present in that jurisdiction. A "digital presence" or a "virtual permanent establishment" would exist in a Member State if one of the following criteria are met: the digital platform (i) exceeds a threshold of EUR 7 million in annual revenue in a Member State, (ii) has more than 100 000 users in a Member State in a taxable year, or (iii) involves over 3 000 business contracts for digital services between the company and business users in a taxable year. This would be the Commission's preferred long-term solution, which could eventually be included in the rules of the CCCTB. The second proposal puts forward an interim tax on specific revenue from digital activities that escapes the current tax rules entirely.[72] This interim tax was aimed at responding to the demand by some Member States for an immediate solution and preventing unilateral action by the Member States, which could be detrimental to the internal market. The tax would apply to revenue derived from activities where users play a major role in value creation, e.g. revenue from selling online advertising space, from digital intermediary activities that allow users to interact with other users and that can facilitate the sale of goods and services between them, and from the sale of data generated from user-provided information. Tax revenues would be collected by the Member States where the users are located, and the tax would only apply to companies with total annual worldwide revenue of EUR 750 million and EU revenue of EUR 50 million. The Member States could not reach a unanimous agreement on these proposals and agreed to await the result of the OECD's work on the taxation of the digitalized economy, which is expected by the end of 2020. If the OECD/G20 members and the members of the Inclusive Framework cannot reach consensus on a global solution, the EU Commission is likely to revisit the idea of an EU-wide digital tax. In the meantime, the EU Parliament has called for a common EU position in international negotiations and has expressed concern not only that such a position does not seem to exist, but that the positions of the Member States and Commission on the OECD proposals have not been made public.[73]

---

70   Digital Taxation: Commission proposes new measures to ensure that all companies pay fair tax in the EU, European Commission, Press Release IP/18/2041, 21 March 2018.
71   COM(2018) 147 final.
72   COM(2018) 148 final.
73   European Parliament resolution of 18 December 2019 on fair taxation in a digitalised and globalised economy: BEPS 2.0 (2019/2901(RSP)).

Lang et al (Eds), Introduction to European Tax Law on Direct Taxation[6], Linde

C. Primary law constraints on the implementation of the BEPS project

The role of the EU in the fight against tax avoidance and aggressive tax planning **186** is also to ensure that the **responses by the Member States** to such strategies **are in line with EU law, predominantly the fundamental freedoms.**

As **anti-avoidance rules** are normally targeted at cross-border situations, where **187** there is a risk of shifting profits out of the jurisdiction where the profits were generated, there is a risk that such rules will be discriminatory if not on their face, at least, in their concrete application. Nevertheless, discrimination can be **justified by the need to prevent tax avoidance and abuse.** A uniform doctrine regarding abuse has emerged from a long line of CJEU cases covering all areas of tax law (see Chapter 3, m.no. 268 et seq.). Moreover, the abuse doctrine has expanded beyond its original role of justifying prima facie discriminatory measures. The prohibition of abuse is now considered a general principle of EU law that may preclude access to the fundamental freedoms in abusive situations.[74] The EU principle of prohibition of abuse, as interpreted and consolidated by the CJEU, sets a limit on anti-abuse rules that can be introduced in the EU, whether by the Member States or the Union legislature.

In implementing measures recommended under the BEPS project, the Member **188** States and the Union are restrained not only by the EU principle of prohibition of abuse but also the principle of proportionality, which requires that anti-abuse rules that *prima facie* restrict the exercise of the fundamental freedoms be suitable and not exceed what is necessary for the purpose of effectively countering actual cases of abuse. These limits cause significant tension, as abuse seems to have a broader scope in the light of the measures recommended by the BEPS Action Plan than that entailed by the EU principle of prohibition of abuse and abuse in a 'BEPS-sense' can be countered in a less targeted manner than under the EU principle of proportionality.

With regard to other justification grounds, according to settled CJEU case law, in the **presence of an effective system of exchange of information** Member States **cannot** justify restrictions on the fundamental freedoms based on the need to ensure the effectiveness of fiscal supervision (see Chapter 3, m.no. 274).[75] Thus, in an intra-EU context, the **DAC** prevents Member States from relying on this justification when trying to explain a tax provision that discriminates against cross-border situations. Taking into account the **global shift towards tax transparency**

---

74   CJEU, 26 February 2019, Joined Cases C-115/16, C-118/16, C-119/16 and C-299/16, *N Luxembourg,* EU:C:2019:134, paras. 101 and 155.
75   See e.g. CJEU, 6 October 2011, Case C-493/09, *Commission v Portugal,* EU:C:2011:635; CJEU, 11 December 2014, Case C-678/11, *Commission v Spain,* EU:C:2014:2434; CJEU, 9 October 2014, Case C-326/12, *van Caster,* EU:C:2014:2269.

and **the increasing number of international instruments** on the basis of which **exchange of information can be carried out**, we suspect that this justification will not survive in relations between the EU and third countries.

189 In the light of the above, doubts can be raised as regards the conformity of certain elements of the BEPS project with EU law. The fact that some of the BEPS measures have been transformed into secondary EU law with the enactment of the ATAD should not automatically remedy all the potential issues of incompatibility with the fundamental freedoms. The latter constitute primary EU law laid down in the founding treaties that cannot be trumped by the EU legislature adopting conflicting secondary EU law. Having said this, in reality, it is highly unlikely that the CJEU would invalidate any provision of the ATAD on the basis of an infringement of the fundamental freedoms taking into account the Court's self-constrained attitude. In particular, in the Court's view, when *"the EU legislature adopts a tax measure, it is called upon to make political, economic and social choices, and to rank divergent interests or to undertake complex assessments"* and therefore, the EU legislature has to be *"accorded a broad discretion"*.[76] Thus, the Court limits itself to verifying whether any *"manifest error of assessment"* has been made by the EU legislature. With regard to the ATAD, such deference to the EU legislature could risk creating a double standard considering that the measures at issue would be found to be disproportionate restrictions on the fundamental freedoms if enacted by a Member State.

Literature

Weber, *Traditional and Alternative Routes to European Tax Integration* (2010); Lang/Pistone/Schuch/Staringer (eds.), *Horizontal Tax Coordination* (2012); Panayi, *European Union Corporate Tax Law* (2013); Traversa/Flamini, Fighting Harmful Tax Competition through EU State Aid Law: Will the Hardening of Soft Law Suffice? *EStAL* 2015, p. 323; Wattel/Marres/Vermeulen (eds.), *European Tax Law – General Topics and Direct Taxation, Vol. 1, 7th edition* (2019); Dourado (ed.), *Tax Avoidance Revisited in the EU BEPS Context* (2017); Martín Jiménez (ed.), *The External Tax Strategy of the EU in a Post-BEPS Environment* (2019); van Thiel/Valente/Raventós-Calvo (eds.), *CFE Tax Advisers Europe – 60th Anniversary Liber Amicorum* (2019).

---

76   CJEU, 7 March 2017, Case C-390/15, *RPO*, EU:C:2017:174, para. 54.

Chapter 3 – The Relevance of the Fundamental Freedoms for Direct Taxation

Ivan Lazarov

I. Scope

A. General

190 The EU fundamental freedoms form the backbone of the internal market. The main goal of that market is to achieve the most efficient allocation of resources possible within the Union by means of free movement of the factors of production – capital and labour, as well as production outputs – goods and services. To achieve this aim, EU substantive law demands that Member States stay neutral toward private parties that conduct cross-border activities; they shall neither penalize such activities by imposing restrictions, nor create selective incentives by means of illegal State aid. This chapter will focus on the tax related restrictions on cross-border activities; while State aid is discussed later on in the book (see Chapter 4).[1]

191 Even though Member States remain competent in the area of direct taxation, the CJEU has consistently held in its case law that they must nonetheless exercise that competence in line with EU law, *inter alia*, by avoiding restrictions on the fundamental freedoms.[2] Thus, EU law **restrains the tax sovereignty** of the Member States.

192 The central underpinning of EU internal market law is non-discrimination between domestic and cross-border situations. Thus, the **four fundamental freedoms**, namely the free movement of goods, persons, services and capital, are a concrete manifestation of that general principle, enshrined in Art. 18 TFEU.[3] All four freedoms have an impact on direct taxation. However, as the cases on free movement of goods are very few[4] and have not raised any substantive issues in recent years, this chapter will focus only on the free movement of persons, services and capital. Furthermore, it must be pointed out from the onset that the fundamental freedoms come into play only in **cross-border** situations, and only between the Member States (with the exception of the free movement of capital, which also applies with respect to third countries). Hence, **purely internal** direct taxation situations fall outside the scope of Union law, allowing Member States to regulate as they deem fit,[5] subject to a limited number of harmonization measures that apply also in domestic situations (see Chapter 8, m.nos. 603).

---

1   In any event, one and the same measure can often constitute State aid and a restriction of the fundamental freedoms, for example, a residence requirement that favours domestic undertakings – see CJEU, 2 May 2019, Case C-598/17, *A-Fonds*, EU:C:2019:352.

2   See CJEU, 28 January 1986, Case 270/83, *Commission v France ('Avoir Fiscal')*, EU:C:1986:37, para. 13.

3   Consolidated version of the Treaty on the Functioning of the European Union of 13 December 2007, OJ C 326 of 26 October 2012.

4   See, for example, CJEU, 7 May 1985, Case 18/84, *Commission v France*, EU:C:1985:175.

5   CJEU, 13 June 2017, Case C-591/15, *The Gibraltar Betting and Gaming Association Limited and The Queen*, EU:C:2017:449; CJEU, 12 October 2017, Case C-192/16, *Fisher*, EU:C:2017:762.

When the fundamental freedoms are applicable, however, they are **directly effec-** **193** **tive** and have **supremacy** over domestic law (see Chapter 1, m.nos. 6, 7 et seq.). Hence, if national legislation of a Member State goes against EU law, such legislation shall be set aside (principle of supremacy) and the freedoms of movement shall be applied directly instead (principle of direct effect). In practice, the issue of whether there is an inconsistency between domestic and Union law is brought forward to the CJEU either by a national court under the preliminary reference procedure (see Chapter 1, m.no. 87 et seq.) or by the European Commission under an infringement procedure against a Member State (see Chapter 1 m.no. 83 et seq.). The preliminary reference procedure is an especially powerful tool in the hands of taxpayers, as, via the national courts, it is their only effective mechanism to challenge the compatibility of domestic law with EU law.

Once a case on the compatibility of a domestic provision with the fundamental **194** freedoms reaches the Court, it will typically undertake **four steps**. First, the CJEU will examine whether the case falls within the **scope** of the fundamental freedoms, which will require a cross-border element and an entitled person (EU national or company that is governed by the company law of a Member State). Second, the Court will evaluate whether there is a **restriction** of the fundamental freedoms by testing if a cross-border situation is treated worse off than a purely domestic one, provided that both are objectively comparable. Simply put, the Court examines if the entitled person is being 'penalized' either by its home State or by the host State for exercising the fundamental freedoms. Third, the CJEU will check if there is a possible **justification** for setting aside the fundamental freedoms in light of a higher, nobler goal that is worth protecting (e.g. the prevention of tax avoidance). Finally, it will opine on the **proportionality** of the measure by examining if the national provisions are so tailormade that they contribute to the achievement of the higher goal without unduly restricting the fundamental freedoms. Structurally, this chapter will use these steps as guidance. The scheme is as follows:

The steps followed by the CJEU in applying fundamental freedoms

195

1) Scope

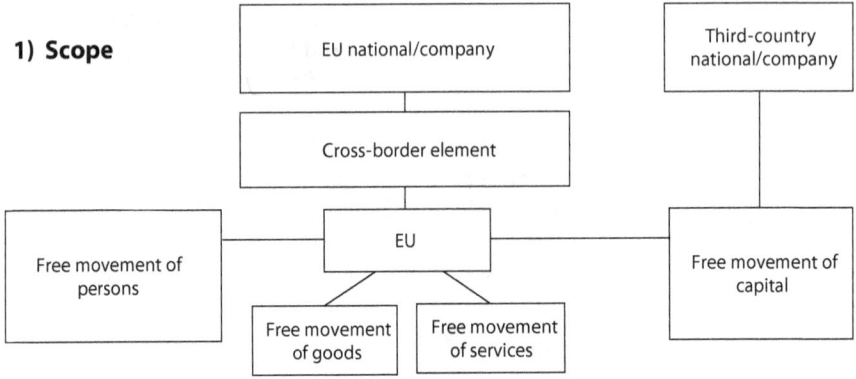

2) Restriction

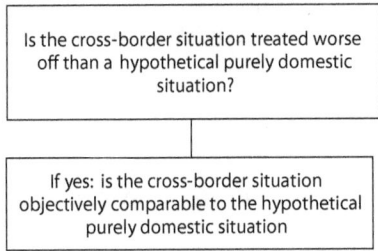

3) Justification

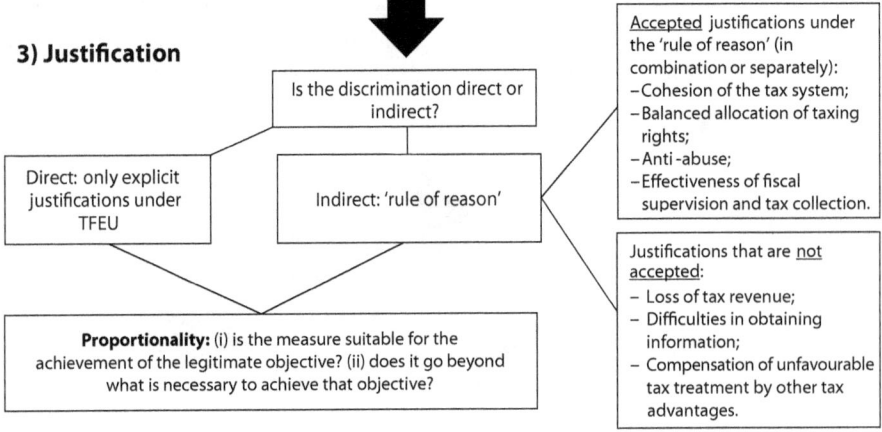

Lang et al (Eds), Introduction to European Tax Law on Direct Taxation⁶, Linde

B. Free Movement of Persons

The free movement of persons can be divided into three main categories; free **196**
movement of **workers,** freedom of **establishment,** and right to **move and reside**
freely in other Member States without pursuing economic activity therein. Each
of these manifestations of the freedom will be examined in turn.

1. Workers

Starting with the **free movement of workers,** Art. 45 et seq. TFEU prohibits dis- **197**
crimination based on the nationality of workers. For the purposes of direct taxation, this entails that the home and the host Member State not treat a worker worse
off because he or she is performing work in a Member State other than the Member State of his or her nationality.

According to the case law, **the term 'worker'** is autonomous and, thus, is not **198**
dependent upon the domestic definition of an employment relationship. Such a
relationship under Union law is defined broadly and entails a situation in which
an individual performs services for and under the direction of another person in
return for which he receives remuneration.[6] The relationship, however, must be
real, genuine and not purely marginal and ancillary.[7]

The CJEU has consistently held that the principle of equal treatment applies to **199**
domestic personal income tax provisions both in inbound and outbound situations. Often **disputes** in respect of direct taxation concern the deductibility of
different kinds of expenses, such as personal allowances and social security
contributions, and the State that has to take into account these expenses in calculating the tax base, or the more favourable treatment of income, originating
domestically.[8]

2. Establishment

Second, concerning **the freedom of establishment,** Art. 49 et seq. TFEU covers, **200**
in essence, two separate situations – the treatment of natural persons, and the
treatment of companies. With respect to natural persons, the freedom entails
the right of an individual to take up and pursue activity in another Member State
as a self-employed person. The key difference between a self-employed person
and a worker is that the former performs services outside a relationship of sub-
ordination.[9] Regarding companies, the freedom of establishment allows foreign
natural and legal persons to set up agencies, branches and subsidiaries in another

---

6   See CJEU, 3 July 1986, Case 66/85, *Lawrie-Blum,* EU:C:1986:284, para. 17.
7   See CJEU, 4 June 2009, Joined Cases C-22/08 and C-23/08, *Vatsouras,* EU:C:2009:344, para. 26.
8   CJEU, 9 February 2017, Case C-283/15, *X,* EU:C:2017:102; CJEU, 24 October 2019, Case C-35/19,
     État belge, EU:C:2019:894.
9   CJEU, 27 June 1996, Case C-107/94, *Asscher v Staatssecretaris van Financiën,* EU:C:1996:251, para. 26.

Member State.[10] It moreover covers instances of merely moving the tax residence of a company without changing its company law status.[11] In essence, the right introduces the possibility to conduct business freely in another Member State on a permanent basis.

201 Although, the distinction between the different freedoms will be discussed in more detail later on in this section, the **acquisition of shares** qualifies under the freedom of establishment only when it leads to the possibility of the shareholder exercising definite influence over the company's decisions.[12] The lack of such definite influence would suggest that the case falls within the scope of free movement of capital, with some peculiarities in third-country situations.[13] This observation is important as, by far, the majority of cases in the area of direct taxation concern the freedom of establishment and the free movement of capital.

202 The tax cases on the freedom of establishment revolve around several issues – the treatment of a permanent establishment (PE) in another Member State,[14] the treatment of groups of companies with foreign subsidiaries and PEs,[15] and cases of exit taxation of individuals[16] and companies.[17]

3. Economically inactive

203 Finally, the free movement of persons also covers individuals moving to another Member State **without the intention of being economically active** therein (e.g. pensioners, students, persons of independent means, etc.). Art. 21 TFEU covers this third category by setting out the right of every national of the EU to move and reside freely within the territory of the Member States, without the need to pursue any professional or other economic activity in the host Member State.[18] The rule of Art. 21 TFEU is of a general character and, therefore, only applies if a more specific provision regulating the case does not apply – e.g. the person is not a worker or self-employed.[19]

---

10   CJEU, 23 February 2006, Case C-471/04, *Keller Holding*, EU:C:2006:143.

11   CJEU, 27 February 2020, Case C-405/18, *AURES Holding*, EU:C:2020:127, para. 25; CJEU, 29 November 2011, Case C-371/10, *National Grid Indus*, EU:C:2011:785, para. 33.

12   CJEU, 20 December 2017, Case C-504/16, *Deister Holding*, EU:C:2017:1009, para. 78.

13   CJEU, 3 October 2013, Case C-282/12, *Itelcar*, EU:C:2013:629, paras. 14-25; CJEU, 24 May 2007, Case C-157/05, *Holböck*, EU:C:2007:297, paras. 9 and 30.

14   CJEU, 28 January 1986, Case 270/83, *Commission v France ('Avoir Fiscal')*, EU:C:1986:37; CJEU, 17 May 2017, Case C-68/15, *X*, EU:C:2017:379, para. 44; for a triangular situation involving a permanent establishment see CJEU, 21 September 1999, Case C-307/97, *Saint-Gobain*, EU:C:1999:438.

15   CJEU, 25 February 2010, Case C-337/08, *X Holding*, EU:C:2010:89; CJEU, 12 June 2018, Case C-650/16, *Bevola*, EU:C:2018:424. Regarding deductibility of costs in connection with holdings in foreign subsidiaries see CJEU, 18 September 2003, Case C-168/01, *Bosal*, EU:C:2003:479.

16   CJEU, 11 March 2004, Case C-9/02, *de Lasteyrie du Saillant*, EU:C:2004:138; CJEU, 21 December 2016, Case C-503/14, *Commission v Portugal*, EU:C:2016:979.

17   CJEU, 29 November 2011, Case C-371/10, *National Grid Indus*, EU:C:2011:785.

18   CJEU, 17 September 2002, Case C-413/99, *Baumbast*, EU:C:2002:493, para. 83.

19   CJEU, 23 April 2009, Case C-544/07, *Rüffler*, EU:C:2009:258, paras. 50-59.

A very typical example of the relevance of Art. 21 to direct taxation is the tax **204** treatment of pensions when the retired person has changed his or her country of residence to another EU Member State.[20] An interesting instance is also highlighted in *Schempp*, wherein the Court found that the rights under Art. 21 and 18 TFEU extend to situations in which the taxpayer himself has not moved across the border but has merely suffered unfavourable tax consequences stemming from the movement of another person (in that case – his former spouse).[21]

C. Free Movement of Services

The free movement of services is dealt with in Art. 56 et seq. TFEU. The definition **205** of **the term 'service'** is rather broad and includes almost any activity provided for remuneration, without the need for the provider to seek profit.[22] The Court, however, has excluded certain public-sector activities. For example, it was decided that education services that are financed, entirely or mainly, by public funds are excluded from the definition of services as, in this instance, the State is fulfilling its duties towards the population and is not seeking to engage in gainful activities.[23] One must note that Art. 56(2) provides for the possibility that the free movement of services might be extended to third country nationals that are established in the Union. However, this provision lacks direct effect and no secondary legislation was adopted to broaden the scope of the freedom.[24]

The free movement of services includes an **active and a passive aspect**, being the **206** freedom to provide and the freedom to receive services, respectively. The freedom entails three **'modes of supply'** within its scope, namely: (i) where the provider moves to another Member State to supply the service, (ii) where the recipient travels to the State of the provider, and (iii) where neither of them moves but the service itself is provided across the border (e.g. digitally).

The **relevance** of the freedom to provide and receive services for direct taxation **207** purposes is often manifested in the issue of the deductibility of expenses incurred in relation to a service received in another Member State.[25] Another example is the application of withholding taxes on a gross basis only with respect to foreign service providers as opposed to an individual tax assessment on a net basis, applied to domestic providers.[26]

20　CJEU, 9 November 2006, Case C-520/04, *Turpeinen*, EU:C:2006:703; CJEU, 19 November 2015, Case C-632/13, *Hirvonen*, EU:C:2015:765.

21　CJEU, 12 July 2005, Case C-403/03, *Schempp*, EU:C:2005:446.

22　CJEU, 18 December 2007, Case C-281/06, *Jundt*, EU:C:2007:816, para. 33.

23　CJEU, 20 May 2010, Case C-56/09, *Zanotti*, EU:C:2010:288, para. 31.

24　A small exception to this rule exists with respect to the freedom to receive services, in respect of which the Services Directive (Directive 2006/123) grants certain rights to third-country individuals who already benefit from rights conferred upon them by Union law – see recital 36 of the Citizenship Directive.

25　CJEU, 28 October 1999, Case C-55/98, *Vestergaard*, EU:C:1999:533; *Zanotti*, supra n. 23.

26　CJEU, 13 July 2016, Case C-18/15, *Brisal and KBC Finance Ireland*, EU:C:2016:549.

D. Free Movement of Capital (and Payments)

208   Art. 63 et seq. TFEU deals with the free movement of capital. According to the Treaty, all restrictions on the movement of capital and payments **between Member States and between Member States and third countries** are prohibited. Thus, this is the only fundamental freedom that applies to not only intra-Community situations but also vis-*à-vis* third States. In that sense, the liberalization of capital is objective and does not depend on the nationality of the capital owner.[27]

209   Special attention in this respect is required regarding **overseas countries or territories (OCTs)**, which are territories that have a special relationship with certain Member States and are listed in Annex II to the TFEU. OCTs must be distingushed from territories the external relations of which a Member State is responsible for, as, in the latter scenario, EU law is applicable in full, unless there is an explicit derogation.[28] Keeping in mind that some OCTs offer a favourable tax regime, it is important to delimit the scope of application of the fundamental freedoms to them. As the Court has pointed out, OCTs have a special status under the Treaties whereby they may only benefit from the freedoms of movement, other than free movement of capital, to the extent that Union law expressly provides for this in Part IV TFEU.[29] Thus, OCTs are, in principle, third countries for the purposes of the fundamental freedoms. The list of OCTs will be substantially reduced after the transitional period concerning the withdrawal of the UK from the Union.

210   There is no definition of **the term "movement of capital"** in the Treaty but the CJEU has confirmed that the nomenclature of capital movements set out in Annex I to Directive 88/361/EEC[30] is relevant to the interpretation of the Treaty provisions.[31] The relevance of movement of capital in the field of direct taxation is often related to the taxation of dividend payments[32] and real property.[33]

E. Order of Priority of the Fundamental Freedoms

211   In general, each of the fundamental freedoms has its own scope of application and a given factual pattern under the preliminary reference procedure would usually

---

27   CJEU, 5 May 2011, Case C-384/09, *Prunus*, EU:C:2011:276, para. 20. However, under the EEA Agreement, the protection of the free movement of capital is subjective, as only capital owners from EEA states are protected – see Art. 40 of the EEA Agreement.

28   CJEU, 2 April 2020, Case C-458/18, *GVC Services (Bulgaria)*, EU:C:2020:266, paras. 30-32.

29   CJEU, 5 June 2014, Joined Cases C-24/12 and C-27/12, *X BV and TBG Limited*, EU:C:2014:1385, paras. 45-46.

30   Council Directive 88/361/EEC of 24 June 1988 for the implementation of Article 67 of the Treaty, OJ L 178 of 8 July 1988, pp. 5-18.

31   See CJEU, 18 December 2007, Case C-101/05, *A.*, EU:C:2007:804.

32   CJEU, 6 June 2000, Case C-35/98, *Verkooijen*, EU:C:2000:294; CJEU, 12 December 2006, Case C-374/04, *Test Claimants in Class IV of the ACT Group Litigation*, EU:C:2006:773; and CJEU, 14 September 2017, Case C-628/15, *The Trustees of the BT Pension Scheme*, EU:C:2017:687.

33   CJEU, 18 December 2014, Case C-133/13, Q, EU:C:2014:2460; CJEU, 30 January 2020, Case C-156/17, *Deka*, EU:C:2020:51.

fall within the scope of a single freedom. There are, however, certain borderline cases where it is difficult to determine what the relevant freedom is, or where it seems that more than one fundamental freedom might be applicable. Besides the obvious relationship between the general equal treatment provision of Art. 18 TFEU and the special rules on the freedoms, which interact under the *lex specialis derogat legi generali* principle,[34] the difficult question is how to resolve an apparent overlap between the four freedoms themselves.

Although, in its earlier case law, the Court took the view that more than one free- **212** dom may apply to a particular situation,[35] more recently, the CJEU has been adopting a 'centre of gravity' approach pursuant to which, although two freedoms may potentially apply, one of the freedoms is of an auxiliary character and, thus, is not examined.[36] These two approaches can be referred to as **the parallel and the predominant application theories.** It has to be noted that, within the internal market, there is generally a **convergence of the fundamental freedoms,** as the CJEU applies the same analytical pattern to all of them. However, delimiting their scope remains important, as Member States are free to treat differently, for tax purposes, activities that fall under different freedoms. For example, the freedom to provide services will often be treated differently from the freedom of establishment.[37] More importantly, the delimitation becomes **crucial in third-country situations** where only the free movement of capital applies. Therefore, based on its practical importance, the subsequent paragraphs will focus on borderline cases related to capital movement.

The most nuanced question is the relationship between the freedom to provide **213** services and the freedom of establishment, on the one hand, and the free movement of capital, on the other. The reason for this is that both the freedom of establishment and of services will often involve, by necessity, an element of capital movement. It would be artificial, however, to *de facto* extend the scope of application of these freedoms to third countries due to the contingent capital movement. Therefore, according to a consistent line of case law, the Court looks at the **object and purpose** of the relevant national legislation to determine the order of priority.[38] In intra-Community cases there is a further step, should the object and purpose be unclear, where the CJEU will look at the concrete facts of the case to decide what the applicable freedom is.[39]

---

34   CJEU, 7 September 2006, Case C-470/04, *N.,* EU:C:2006:525, paras. 27-29.
35   CJEU, 18 November 1999, Case C-200/98, *X and Y,* EU:C:1999:566, para. 30.
36   CJEU, 22 November 2018, Case C-625/17, *Vorarlberger Landes- und Hypothekenbank AG,* EU:C: 2018:939, paras. 24-25.
37   Ibid., paras. 32-37.
38   CJEU, 21 May 2015, Case C-560/13, *Ingeborg Wagner-Raith,* EU:C:2015:347, para. 31; CJEU, 24 November 2016, Case C-464/14, *SECIL,* EU:C:2016:896, para. 31.
39   CJEU, 13 November 2012, Case C-35/11, *Test Claimants in the FII Group Litigation,* EU:C:2012:707, para. 93; CJEU, 28 February 2013, Case C-168/11, *Beker,* EU:C:2013:117, para. 27; and CJEU, 13 March 2014, Case C-375/12, *Bouanich,* EU:C:2014:138, para. 30.

214 With respect to the **freedom of establishment and the free movement of capital**, it is apparent from the case law that one has to first look at the scope of the national legislation and see if it was intended to apply only to shareholders that can exercise definitive influence over a company's decisions.[40] If that is the case, the applicable freedom is establishment, if not – capital. However, often, the national legislation makes no distinction based on whether or not the shareholder is exercising definitive influence. In that scenario, the approach of the CJEU differs depending on whether the situation is intra-Community or concerns a third country. In internal-EU cases, one must look at the concrete percentage of the shareholding and decide, in each individual case, whether that percentage allows for the exercise of definitive influence,[41] unless it is clear from the object of the national legislation that it is, in any event, more intimately connected to the free movement of capital.[42] In a third-country case, when the scope of the national legislation is not restricted to relations of decisive influence, a taxpayer may rely on the free movement of capital even if it holds a substantive participation.[43] This reliance, nonetheless, must not lead to a disguised extension of the freedom of establishment to companies or individuals from third countries. Such a disguised extension will exist if the legislation at hand covers not merely capital movements (e.g. dividend distributions) but also the conditions for access to the market.[44]

215 Regarding the relationship between free movement of **services and capital**, in the *Fidium Finanz* case the Court reached the conclusion that, when a national measure aims to restrict certain financial services provided from a third country, it is unavoidable that such a restriction will also have an impact on the free movement of capital. Therefore, the centre of gravity of the provision, stemming from its purpose, is within the freedom to provide services, which trumps the application of the free movement of capital and, hence, of EU law altogether.[45] The same might hold true if, although the provision does not impede market access *per se*, the level of taxation is set at a prohibitively high level. Moreover, when it comes to financial services, the grandfathering clause of Art. 64(1) TFEU provides for even further possibilities for restrictions even if the situation falls within the scope of the free movement of capital (see m.nos. 279).

216 To summarize, one can claim that the Court is making a logical differentiation between **'pure' capital movements** and substantive **market access** situations

---

40 According to the Court, this requirement will be fulfilled even at a 25% shareholding: CJEU, 31 May 2018, Case C-382/16, *Hornbach-Baumarkt*, EU:C:2018:366, para. 29. At the same time, it will not be fulfilled in respect of a 20% shareholding: CJEU, 7 September 2017, Case C-6/16, *Eqiom*, EU:C: 2017:641, paras. 42-43. This demonstrates the arbitrary character of setting a concrete number in percentage points as a threshold.

41 CJEU, 20 December 2017, C-504/16, *Deister Holding*, EU:C:2017:1009, para. 81.

42 CJEU, 23 January 2014, Case C-164/12, *DMC*, EU:C:2014:20, paras. 28-38.

43 CJEU, 24 November 2016, Case C-464/14, *SECIL*, EU:C:2016:896, para. 41; CJEU, 13 November 2012, Case C-35/11, *Test Claimants in the FII Group Litigation*, EU:C:2012:707, para. 99.

44 CJEU, 24 November 2016, Case C-464/14, *SECIL*, EU:C:2016:896, para. 43.

45 CJEU, 3 October 2006, Case C-452/04, *Fidium Finanz*, EU:C:2006:631, para. 34.

related to establishment and services. Although the former can extend to third countries, the latter does not. Thus, in its rule of priority, the Court emphasizes the purpose of the respective national legislation in deciding if it falls under the free movement of capital or one of the other freedoms.[46]

F. The Fundamental Freedoms under EEA Law

The rules under the EEA Agreement that are identical in substance to those under **217** EU law have to be **interpreted in conformity with the acquis of Union law**.[47] The EFTA Court held in its opinion in the *Fokus Bank ASA*[48] case that the EEA Agreement applies, in principle, in the same way as the EU Treaties in order to expand the internal market to the EEA. The CJEU confirmed these findings, ruling explicitly on the free movement of capital, workers and establishment.[49]

However, sometimes, the different constitutional nature of the EEA may necessi- **218** tate different interpretative results.[50] Such would be the case, for example, concerning the principles of supremacy and direct effect, which are not recognized under EEA law.[51] The same holds true for instances where the wording of the provisions diverge, for example, regarding the free movement of capital, which, in the EEA context, is restricted to EEA situations.

II. Restriction

A. Addressees of the Treaty Provisions

Some of the provisions of the TFEU on the fundamental freedoms are framed such **219** that, on its face, seem to only prohibit discrimination in the **host State**.[52] However, the CJEU has decided that all of the freedoms have a broader scope of application and also apply to the **home State,** which is obliged not to hinder the exercise

---

46   CJEU, 21 January 2010, Case C-311/08, *Société de Gestion Industrielle,* EU:C:2010:26, para. 25; CJEU, 10 February 2011, Case C-436/08 and C-437/08, *Haribo Lakritzen and Österreichische Salinen,* EU:C: 2011:61, para. 35; and CJEU, 11 September 2014, Case C-47/12, *Kronos International,* EU:C:2014:2200, para. 30.

47   CJEU, 6 June 2013, Case C-383/10, *Commission v Belgium,* EU:C:2013:364, para. 71 et seq.; EFTA Court case law; see e.g.: EFTA Court, 23 November 2004, E-1/04, *Fokus Bank ASA,* para. 23; EFTA Court, 12 December 2003, E-1/03, *EFTA Surveillance Authority,* para. 27.

48   EFTA Court, 23 November 2004, E-1/04, *Fokus Bank ASA,* para. 22 et seq.

49   CJEU, 11 June 2009, Case C-521/07, *Commission v Netherlands,* EU:C:2009:360, para. 32 et seq.; CJEU, 5 May 2011, Case C-267/09, *Commission v Portugal,* EU:C:2011:273, para. 50; CJEU, 20 January 2011, Case C-155/09, *Commission v Greece,* EU:C:2011:22, para. 62.

50   EFTA Court, 14 June 2001, E-4/00, *Johann Brändle,* para. 7.

51   EFTA Court, 30 May 2002, E-4/01, *Karlsson,* para. 28; EFTA Court, 3 October 2007, E-1/07, *Criminal proceedings against A,* paras. 40-41. Having in mind that many pieces of secondary EU legislation are EEA relevant and, hence, mandatory in terms of domestic implementation by EEA states, the lack of the abovementioned principles raises important issues when implemented law interacts with purely domestic law.

52   See for example Art. 49(1) TFEU.

of the fundamental freedoms by making cross-board activities less attractive than remaining purely domestic. Hence, the Treaty provisions are 'addressed' to both the home and the host State and have a bilateral scope, unlike Art. 24 of the OECD Model Tax Convention, which only addresses the host state. Under EU law, the home State shall not hinder outbound cross-border activities, while the host State shall not discriminate once these activities are carried out in its territory.

220 Typical examples of national provisions of the **home State** that hinder cross-border activities are exit tax provisions,[53] CFC rules,[54] and domestic group taxation systems that treat an international group less favourably than a purely domestic one.[55] Typical examples of discriminatory national provisions of the **host State** are source taxation on a gross basis for non-residents[56] and less-favourable treatment of a foreign company's PE.[57]

B. The Non-Discrimination Principle

221 The **principle of non-discrimination** is a general principle of EU law and is one of the cornerstones of the internal market. However, unlike other areas where the Court has drifted away from non-discrimination to the broader concept of a 'pure' restriction market access approach,[58] the same development did not occur in the area of direct taxation. The key difference between the two approaches is that, while the non-discrimination principle requires that cross-border situations not be treated worse than entirely domestic ones, the 'pure' restriction principle is not concerned with the existence of actual discrimination but rather with any measure that hinders access to the market or makes this access less attractive. The obvious benefit of the market access approach is that it makes life simpler by removing the need to test if domestic and cross-border situations are comparable, an issue that creates a fair amount of difficulties in tax matters. Nevertheless, applying the idea of 'pure' restrictions to direct taxation seems unreasonable as, essentially, any form of taxation makes access to the market less attractive.[59] Thus,

---

53   CJEU, 7 September 2006, Case C-470/04, *N.*, EU:C:2006:525; CJEU, 29 November 2011, Case C-371/10, *National Grid Indus*, EU:C:2011:785, para. 35; CJEU, 23 January 2014, Case C-164/12, *DMC Beteiligungsgesellschaft*, EU:C:2014:20; CJEU, 21 May 2015, Case C-657/13, *Verder LabTec*, EU:C:2015:331, para. 33.

54   CJEU, 12 September 2006, Case C-196/04, *Cadbury Schweppes*, EU:C:2006:544.

55   CJEU, 13 December 2005, Case C-446/03, *Marks & Spencer*, EU:C:2003:763; CJEU, 25 February 2010, Case C-337/08, *X Holding*, EU:C:2010:89; CJEU, 12 June 2014, Joined Cases C-39/13, C-40/13 and C-41/13, *SCA Group Holding*, EU:C:2014:1758; and CJEU, 22 February 2018, Joined Cases C-398/16 and C-399/16, *X BV and X NV*, EU:C:2018:110.

56   CJEU, 3 October 2006, Case C-290/04, *Scorpio*, EU:C:2006:630, para. 46; and CJEU, 13 July 2016, Case C-18/15, *Brisal and KBC Finance Ireland*, EU:C:2016:549.

57   CJEU, 6 September 2012, Case C-18/11, *Philips Electronics*, EU:C:2012:532, para. 14; and CJEU, 17 May 2017, Case C-68/15, *X*, EU:C:2017:379, para. 40.

58   See the famous examples of CJEU, 20 February 1979, Case 120/78, *Cassis de Dijon*, EU:C:1979:42 and CJEU, 30 November 1995, Case C-55/94, *Gebhard*, EU:C:1995:411.

59   For an extreme example in this respect see Opinion of Advocate General Bobek, 14 December 2017, Case C-382/16, *Hornbach-Baumarkt*, EU:C:2017:974, para. 38. See also Opinion of Advocate General Hogan, 28 November 2019, Case C-565/18, *Société Générale*, EU:C:2019:1029, para. 35.

if the Court adopts this approach, the Member States will have to justify virtually all their tax policies.

It is true that, in some cases, the CJEU has not referred to discrimination but rather to **restrictions**.[60] However, one should not prematurely conclude that the Court has moved from a discrimination to a market access approach. Most recently, in *Deka*, a restriction was subjected to an analysis based on comparability rather than a market access line of reasoning.[61] However, the Court hinted to the fact that the very existence of divergent (non-discriminatory) requirements might result in a restriction of the fundamental freedoms, as *"[residents] would generally be likely to meet all the conditions laid down by the legislation of their State of establishment, whereas [non-residents] would generally be likely to meet only the conditions laid down by their Member State of establishment."*[62] It is striking that a hypothetical comparison is being drawn even in 'exit tax' and CFC cases where, rationally, one would assume that there is nothing to compare with domestically.[63] For direct tax law purposes, therefore, the fundamental freedoms should be regarded as non-discrimination provisions.[64]

222

Hence, it is the principle of non-discrimination that forms the backbone of CJEU case law in tax matters. According to that principle, **comparable situations should not be treated differently**, and different situations should not be treated in the same way,[65] unless doing so is objectively justified. Thus, in order to reach a conclusion that there is a restriction of the fundamental freedoms in direct tax matters, the Court should first determine if the cross-border situation is comparable to a similar domestic situation (or in some rare cases to another cross-border situation). If that is not the case, there can be no restriction, as there can be no discrimination between non-comparable situations. If the situations are indeed comparable, the second issue is whether the cross-border activities are treated less advantageously.[66] Should the answer to both these questions be affirmative, there

223

---

60   See e.g. CJEU, 7 September 2004, Case C-319/02, *Manninen*, EU:C:2004:484, para. 23; CJEU, 9 October 2014, Case C-326/12, *Caster and Caster*, EU:C:2014:2269; CJEU, 8 June 2017, Case C-580/15, *Van der Weegen and Others*, EU:C:2017:429.

61   CJEU, 30 January 2020, Case C-156/17, *Deka*, EU:C:2020:51.

62   Ibid., para. 73 and this is as close to a 'pure restriction' analysis as we have ever seen. In this context, the decision of the Court in *Société Générale* was greatly anticipated, after Advocate General Hogan argued, in his Opinion, that *"the Court's case-law has adopted a narrower definition of the concept of 'restriction' in the field of taxation than in other fields."* See Opinion of Advocate General Hogan, 28 November 2019, Case C-565/18, *Société Générale*, EU:C:2019:1029, para. 48. The Court implicitly confirmed this view, see CJEU, 30 April 2020, Case C-565/18, *Société Générale*, EU:C:2020:318 paras. 34-35.

63   CJEU, 29 November 2011, Case C-371/10, *National Grid Indus*, EU:C:2011:785, para. 37; and CJEU, 12 September 2006, Case C-196/04, *Cadbury Schweppes,* EU:C:2006:544, para. 44.

64   See, in the same sense, Opinion of Advocate General Pitruzzella, Case C-156/17, *Deka*, EU:C:2019:677, paras. 56-57.

65   See e.g. CJEU, 14 November 2006, Case C-513/04, *Kerckhaert-Morres*, EU:C:2006:713, para. 19.

66   It must be noted that, according to the Court, the cross-border situation can be treated differently to the extent that this different treatment is not less advantageous. See CJEU, 3 March 2020, Case C-482/18, *Google Ireland*, EU:C:2020:141, paras. 24-36.

---

is a restriction of the fundamental freedoms. It should be noted that cross-border situations could be treated more favourably than domestic situations, which is called 'reverse discrimination'. Reverse discrimination can have an impact on domestic constitutional law, the State aid rules (see Chapter 4), and in some limited circumstances with respect to Art. 24(1) of the OECD Model Tax Convention,[67] but is perfectly acceptable under the fundamental freedoms.

224 It is settled case law that the Treaty provisions not only cover **direct,** but also **indirect, discrimination**. A measure will be indirectly discriminatory when, on its face, it does not differentiate on grounds of nationality but *de facto* operates at the disadvantage of foreign nationals. A classic example of indirect discrimination is a criterion based on residence, as it is liable to operate mainly to the detriment of nationals of other Member States since, logically, they are more often non-residents. Bearing in mind that the tax systems of the Member States are built on the residence-source principle, it is only natural that, almost universally, cases of direct taxation involve indirect discrimination.[68] Thus, the question arises as to what the **threshold for indirect discrimination is.** Should the domestic measure be intended to put cross-border situations in a less advantageous position, should the discriminatory criterion be intrinsic (e.g. residence) or is it a matter of simple statistics (i.e. the ratio of the affected cross-border versus domestic situations)? It seems, from the Court's most recent decisions in *Vodafone Hungary* and *Tesco*, that the relevant test is not the particular effect of the measure, which might depend on chance, but rather whether it inherently creates discrimination.[69] Accepting this dividing line between indirect discrimination and situations irrelevant to EU law is problematic, as Member States are well positioned to design tax measures that, albeit not discriminatory on their face, have a protectionist effect; e.g. progressive tax on turnover that results in a greater effective tax rate for foreign companies in a given industry thereby favouring domestic production.

225 Concerning **less-favourable treatment,** the Court has recently pointed out that it will depend on the overall (monetary) effect of the measure rather than on a fragmented piece-meal assessment.[70] The CJEU has also examined whether less-favourable treatment in one Member State can be offset by a measure in the other Member

---

67 See para. 15 of the OECD Commentary to Article 24, N. Bammens, *The Principle of Non-Discrimination in International and European Tax Law* (2013), pp. 130-132.

68 There are several cases in the area of gambling where certain Member States have adopted directly discriminatory provisions by explicitly and exhaustively naming domestic casinos, the winnings from which, benefit from a preferential tax regime. CJEU, 6 October 2009, Case C-153/08, *Commission v Spain*, EU:C:2009:618; and CJEU, 22 October 2014, Case C-344/13, *Blanco and Fabretti*, EU:C:2014:2311.

69 CJEU, 3 March 2020, Case C-75/18, *Vodafone Magyarország*, EU:C:2020:139, paras. 52-54; CJEU, 3 March 2020, Case C-323/18, EU:C:2020:140, paras. 72-74.

70 In that respect, for example, the less-advantageous treatment of deductions related to a foreign PE will depend upon the overall company's basis of assessment rather than on a superficial analysis regarding the difference in treatment between a foreign and a hypothetical domestic PE. See CJEU, 17 October 2019, Case C-459/18, *Argenta Spaarbank*, EU:C:2019:871, para. 52.

State, with the effect that the measure of the first State will not constitute a restriction. Taking an example from the case law, in *Denkavit France*,[71] the Court ruled that although withholding tax on passive income did clearly constitute less-favourable treatment, it could be offset by a tax credit in the residence State. Thus, the Court agreed, in principle, that less-favourable treatment in one Member State could be offset in another Member State. In subsequent cases, the CJEU added that for the neutralization argument to succeed, the obligation to credit should stem from a DTC rather than from unilateral domestic legislation,[72] and that the credit should be for the full amount, thus excluding cases where the level of taxation in the source State is higher than that in the State of residence.[73] It is important to note that the neutralization principle is discussed by the Court not at the justification stage, but at the restriction stage of the analysis and, therefore, without recourse to the proportionality test.[74]

C. Comparability

1. General

Knowing that the approach with respect to the restrictions of the fundamental freedoms in the area of direct taxation is based on the non-discrimination principle, one must turn to the **comparability analysis,** as discrimination might occur only between comparable situations. In that respect, the case law of the Court is far from coherent. As some have already noted, the CJEU frequently uses, interchangeably, the comparability and the justification analyses and thus, has not yet developed clear and predictable criteria for the comparability.[75]   **226**

The narrative usually proceeds along these lines: the comparability test will require a comparison between the tax treatment of a person that exercises the fundamental freedoms and a person that operates purely domestically. The **factual cross-border situation** is compared, therefore, with a **hypothetical similar domestic situation**. However, the analysis is not so straightforward in the case law.   **227**

An illuminating example regarding the approach to comparability by the Court is the *Nordea Bank* case, which reaffirmed a steady line of cases that held that treating a cross-border situation worse than a domestic one constitutes a restriction on the fundamental freedoms unless the situations are not objectively comparable or there is a justification.[76] Thus, there is a clear tendency towards a **two-step comparability analysis** – an initial and superficial comparison between domes-   **228**

---

71   CJEU, 14 December 2006, Case C-170/05, *Denkavit Internationaal und Denkavit France,* EU:C:2006:783.
72   See CJEU, 3 June 2010, Case C-487/08, *Commission v Spain,* EU:C:2010:310, para. 66.
73   CJEU, 3 June 2010, Case C-487/08, *Commission v Spain,* EU:C:2010:310, para. 59 et seq.
74   Compare paras. 67 and 68 in *Commission v Spain.* See, in the same sense, Haslehner, 'Avoir Fiscal' and Its Legacy after Thirty Years of Direct Tax Jurisprudence of the Court of Justice', *Intertax* 2016, p. 388.
75   Wattel, Non-Discrimination a la Cour: The ECJ's (Lack of) Comparability Analysis in Direct Tax Cases, *ET* 2015.
76   CJEU, 17 July 2014, Case C-48/13, *Nordea Bank*, EU:C:2014:2087, para. 23 and the case law cited therein.

tic and cross-border situations, and a second 'objective' comparison in light of the aim of the national measure.[77] The first part of the test answers the question of whether there is a restriction, while the second has the role of a quasi-justification (however, without the proportionality test).

229 It is worth noting that the Court did not follow the Opinion of Advocate General Kokott, which was to do away with the objective comparability test and shift the whole analysis to the grounds for justification.[78] Under this two-step approach, the Court sometimes essentially examines the same points twice: once under the comparability analysis and a second time under the justification test.[79] This should come as no surprise, as both the objective comparability and the justification test look at the purpose of the national legislation. As rightfully pointed out by Advocate General Kokott, only the justification test allows for a proportionality analysis and, thus, for striking "*an appropriate balance between the objectives associated with the fundamental freedom and those underlying the ground for differentiation between domestic and cross-border situations.*"[80]

230 Furthermore, the Court's line of reasoning that "*a restriction is permissible only if it relates to situations which are not objectively comparable [...]*"[81] may be questioned as well. A restriction cannot be permissible if it relates to situations that are not objectively comparable. If the situations are not comparable, there is simply no restriction to 'permit' since, under tax law, the restriction analysis is discrimination based and discrimination can occur only between comparable situations.

231 The comparability test often boils down to the question of **whether residents and non-residents are in a comparable situation**. As is generally the case when it comes to the law, the answer is that it depends. Usually the Court will refer to the **aim and purpose of the domestic tax provision** in determining whether it treats residents and non-residents as comparable.[82] Thus, whether a non-resident is comparable to a resident will depend essentially on the aim of the domestic law. Defining the aim of this law, however, is a difficult exercise. This is clearly exemplified

---

77 Wattel, Non-Discrimination a la Cour: The ECJ's (Lack of) Comparability Analysis in Direct Tax Cases, *ET* 2015, p. 543.

78 Opinion of Advocate General Kokott, 13 March 2014, Case C-48/13, *Nordea Bank*, EU:C:2014:153, para. 28. The same was recently reiterated in the Opinion of Advocate General Kokott, 17 October 2019, Case C-405/18, *AURES Holding*, EU:C:2019:879, para. 30

79 *Nordea Bank*, para. 24. Recently, the Court examined the balanced allocation of taxing powers and the prevention of double dips at the comparability rather than the justification stage, thereby confirming Advocate General's Kokott's point that the objective comparability and the justification analysis cannot coexist without creating a fair amount of confusion. CJEU, 27 February 2020, Case C-405/18, *AURES Holding*, EU:C:2020:127, para. 38.

80 *Nordea Bank*, para. 27.

81 CJEU, 17 July 2014, Case C-48/13, *Nordea Bank*, EU:C:2014:2087, para. 23.

82 CJEU, 14 February 1995, Case C-279/93, *Schumacker*, EU:C:1995:31, para. 32; CJEU, 22 March 2018, Case C-327/16, *Jacob*, EU:C:2018:210, para. 78. However, the Court has rejected the possibility for Member States to construct parallel tax systems for domestic and cross-border situations for the purposes of claiming that the situations are not objectively comparable. CJEU, 22 January 2009, Case C-377/07, *STEKO Industriemontage*, EU:C:2009:29, para. 33.

in the *AURES Holding* case wherein the Advocate General and the Court examined the provision of domestic law in question and saw completely different aims, reaching thereby opposite conclusions regarding the objective comparability.[83] Thus, *given that all situations are comparable in some respect, if they are not identical,* the objective comparability test performed by the Court is built around a rather casuistic stream of case law instead of being based upon a coherent principle-based approach. The following pargraphs will examine in greater detail several such streams.

From the perspective of the **home State**, the Court will sometimes look at residence **232** as a factor that might potentially justify a different treatment,[84] while in other instances, it will completely disregard the analysis of comparability and almost presume it.[85] In the latter case, it seems that the Court is drifting towards what AG Kokott suggested in *Nordea Bank* by stating that if a different treatment is applied solely by reason of the fact that a company's registered office is in another Member State, this would deprive Art. 49 TFEU of all meaning.[86] In its more recent case law, however, the Court will first apply a superficial difference in treatment test and then the substantive objective comparability analysis based on the aim of the national legislation.[87]

An example regarding the comparability analysis from the perspective of the **host** **233** **State** was given in the case of *Commission v Greece*.[88] The Court had to decide whether a Greek domestic provision that provided for an exemption from inheritance tax only with respect to residents of Greece was contrary to the free movement of capital. A few points of the comparability analysis are worth noting. First, the Court made no reference to the idea that residents and non-residents are, in principle, not in a comparable situation. Second, it again applied the two-step approach, pursuant to which it first analyses superficial and then objective comparability. Finally, the CJEU analysed objective comparability under the heading 'justifications for a restriction', hence, supporting the view that it looks at objective comparability as a quasi-justification minus proportionality. In other cases, the Court would simply look at the tax advantage and blankly state that residents and non-residents are comparable (e.g. with respect to the deduction of

---

83 Compare Advocate General Kokott's Opinion, 17 October 2019, Case C-405/18, *AURES Holding*, EU:C:2019:879, paras. 26-27 with CJEU, 27 February 2020, Case C-405/18, *AURES Holding*, EU:C:2020:127, para. 38-39.

84 CJEU, 25 February 2010, Case C-337/08, *X Holding*, EU:C:2010:89, para. 23.

85 CJEU, 12 September 2006, Case C-196/04, *Cadbury Schweppes*, EU:C:2006:544; and CJEU, 21 January 2010, Case C-311/08, *Société de Gestion Industrielle*, EU:C:2010:26.

86 CJEU, 12 December 2006, Case C-374/04, *Test Claimants in Class IV of the ACT Group Litigation*, EU:C:2006:773, para. 43; CJEU, 18 June 2009, Case C-303/07, *Aberdeen Property*, EU:C:2009:377, para. 43.

87 CJEU, 27 February 2020, Case C-405/18, *AURES Holding*, EU:C:2020:127; CJEU, 12 June 2018, Case C-650/16, *Bevola*, EU:C:2018:424, para. 21-40; CJEU, 22 March 2018, Case C-327/16, *Jacob*, EU:C:2018:210, para. 78.

88 CJEU, 26 May 2016, Case C-244/15, *Commission v Greece* , EU:C:2016:359 , paras. 28-38.

expenses),[89] even if this is doubtful (in principle, business expenses are to be deducted in the State of residence and not in the source State). The logic of the CJEU seems to be straightforward; as long as the host State is expanding its tax jurisdiction over the income of a non-resident, such a non-resident is in a comparable situation with residents.[90]

234 With respect to **group taxation systems and the treatment of domestic companies with foreign PEs**, the Court has consistently held that a domestic group parent with a domestic group subsidiary is in a situation comparable to a domestic group parent with an EU group subsidiary (or a PE) and that group relief for losses provided only to domestic subsidiaries constitutes discrimination.[91] In the **exit tax cases,** the CJEU held that the situation of a taxpayer who transfers his residence or assets to another Member State is comparable to that of a taxpayer who transfers his residence or assets within the territory of the same Member State as regards the taxation of unrealized capital gains generated within the territory of that State.[92]

235 An instance where the CJEU decided that **a cross-border situation was not comparable to a domestic one** was the *Kronos International* case.[93] There the Court found that a company that was receiving foreign-sourced dividends was not in a situation comparable to a company that was receiving dividends from a domestic source for the purposes of taxation of these dividends at the parent level when the home State was exempting such foreign income. The reasoning of the Court was that the home State could not be required, on top of an exemption, to grant a credit for the corporate income tax paid abroad. Thus, in a situation in which the Member State does not exercise its powers to tax, its obligation does not go so far as to require it to offset the tax burden resulting from the exercise of the tax powers of another Member State or of a third State.[94] Another example where the Court concluded that the comparability is lacking was the recent *X NV* case, wherein it held that currency losses on a shareholding in a subsidiary could be sustained only where the subsidiary was foreign and therefore, for the purposes of such losses, the cross-border situation was not comparable to the domestic one.[95]

236 The existing case law on comparability makes it difficult to formulate a concrete test that the Court follows in practice. As a rule of thumb, one can say that as long as the State is exercising its tax jurisdiction over particular income in both cross-

---

89 CJEU, 13 July 2016, Case C-18/15, *Brisal and KBC Finance Ireland*, EU:C:2016:549, para. 23.

90 See, in the same sense, Haslehner, 'Avoir Fiscal' and Its Legacy after Thirty Years of Direct Tax Jurisprudence of the Court of Justice', *Intertax* 2016, p. 382.

91 CJEU, 13 December 2005, Case C-446/03; *Marks and Spencer*, EU:C:2005:763; CJEU, 25 February 2010, Case C-337/08, *X Holding*, EU:C:2010:89; and CJEU, 2 September 2015, Case C-386/14, *Groupe Steria*, EU:C:2015:524; CJEU, 12 June 2018, Case C-650/16, *Bevola*, EU:C:2018:424.

92 CJEU, 21 May 2015, Case C-657/13, *Verder LabTec*, EU:C:2015:331, para. 38.

93 CJEU, 11 September 2014, Case C-47/12, *Kronos International*, EU:C:2014:2200.

94 Ibid, para. 85.

95 CJEU, 22 February 2018, Joined Cases C-398/16 and C-399/16, *X BV and X NV*, EU:C:2018:110, para. 56.

border and domestic cases, the situations are comparable.[96] There is a notorious example of where this is not the case, i.e. the treatment of final losses incurred by foreign subsidiaries and exempted foreign PEs. Although the home Member State does not have the right to tax the profits of such subsidiaries/PEs, it nevertheless must treat them as objectively comparable for the purposes of taking into account their final losses. Moreover, there is a tendency to differentiate between the issue of comparability for the purposes of finding a 'restriction', where the test is much less rigid, and the question of objective comparability, which is applied as a quasi-justification test. The following sections will deal with specific comparability issues.

2. Permanent Establishment in the Host State

The first such issue is the question of the host State treatment of PEs. In one of the **237** first cases concerning direct taxation (*Avoir Fiscal*)[97] the CJEU had to deal with the question of **whether a domestic PE of a foreign company is in a situation comparable to a domestic company** regarding profits generated domestically. The Court ruled that as long as both PEs and companies were subject to tax on such profits, they were in a comparable situation, and therefore any worse treatment of PEs constituted discrimination.

A later case (*Saint-Gobain*)[98] reaffirmed this with respect to PEs receiving dividends, **238** this time from a **foreign source**. The case concerned a triangular situation whereby a domestic PE of a foreign company was receiving dividend payments from other EU Member States and from third countries. Under domestic tax law, PEs were not granted the same tax credit benefits as those that would have been granted had the foreign shares been held by a domestic company. The CJEU again held that a PE is in a situation comparable to a domestic company, as both are liable to tax on their profits arising from dividend payments. The latter does not change even in situations in which the benefits for the domestic companies stem from the existence of a DTC with a third country rather than from the domestic law itself. According to the Court, in such cases a Member State must unilaterally extend the benefits under a DTC to PEs in order to satisfy the non-discrimination requirement under Union law.

This line of case law has been further confirmed in more recent cases, which spell **239** out explicitly a general principle that companies have the freedom to choose between a subsidiary and a branch in pursuing economic activities in other Member States (**principle of neutrality of legal form**). That choice cannot be impeded by

---

96 A clear example of this line is the Court's view that a CFC rule makes the treatment of a foreign sub-sidiary's income comparable to the treatment of a domestic subsidiary's income – in the latter case the income being taxed directly in the hands of the subsidiary and, in the former, indirectly in the hands of the parent. See CJEU, 26 February 2019, Case C-135/17, *X GmbH*, EU:C:2019:136, para. 67.
97 CJEU, 28 January 1986, Case 270/83, *Commission v France ('Avoir Fiscal')*, EU:C:1986:37.
98 CJEU, 21 September 1999, Case C-307/97, *Saint-Gobain*, EU:C:1999:438.

worse tax treatment of one of the forms.[99] It must be noted, however, that in the *X* case, the Court agreed with AG Kokott that Member States might apply a different tax treatment to PEs as long as that treatment is not less advantageous.[100] Moreover, the principle of neutrality of legal form is a one-way street in the sense that a subsidiary (resident) cannot claim to be treated as a PE (non-resident), as the more-favourable treatment of a PE will amount to reverse discrimination, which is not prohibited by Union law.[101]

240 The principle of neutrality of legal form in the host State (where the PE is established), as discussed in the previous paragraphs, must not be confused with the treatment of the parent company in the home State. In other words, the neutrality of legal form principle is **addressed only to the host State and not the home State**. As is clear from the *X Holding* case, a domestic company with a subsidiary abroad is not in a comparable situation to a domestic company with a PE abroad.[102] The reason is very simple – the home State is exercising taxing rights (potentially) only over the profits generated by a PE in the host State but not over profits generated by a subsidiary. Looking at the situation from the perspective of the host State, the scenario looks different, as the host State exercises taxing rights over both the profits of a PE (limited taxing rights) and a subsidiary (unlimited taxing rights). Thus, the principle of neutrality of legal form binds only the host State since a subsidiary and a PE are comparable only from its point of view. Furthermore, in principle, from the point of view of the home State, a domestic and a foreign PE are not comparable unless the home State has decided to apply the same tax rules with respect to both (e.g. deduction of losses, taxation of profits).[103]

241 There is one **exception** to the rule that domestic PEs (subject to limited tax liability) are in a situation comparable to a domestic company (subject to unlimited tax liability), and that is found in the *Futura Participations* case[104] where the question was whether a domestic PE may take into account losses arising in the HQ State. The Court rejected such a proposition, reasoning that the system is in conformity with the principle of territoriality whereby only profits and losses arising from activities in the PE State are to be taken into account in calculating the tax base of the PE. The CJEU added that such a system cannot entail any discrimination, thus, implicitly accepting that domestic PEs and companies are not in a comparable situation with respect to foreign losses.

---

99   CJEU, 6 September 2012, Case C-18/11, *Philips Electronics*, EU:C:2012:532, para. 14; Opinion of Advocate General Kokott, 17 November 2016, Case C-68/15, *X*, EU:C:2016:886, para. 23; and CJEU, 17 May 2017, Case C-68/15, *X*, EU:C:2017:379, para. 40.

100   Opinion of Advocate General Kokott, 17 November 2016, Case C-68/15, *X*, EU:C:2016:886, paras. 24-25; and CJEU, 17 May 2017, Case C-68/15, *X*, EU:C:2017:379, para. 44.

101   Haslehner, 'Avoir Fiscal' and Its Legacy after Thirty Years of Direct Tax Jurisprudence of the Court of Justice', *Intertax* 2016, p. 385.

102   CJEU, 25 February 2010, Case C-337/08, *X Holding*, EU:C:2010:89, para. 38.

103   CJEU, 17 July 2014, Case C-48/13, *Nordea Bank*, EU:C:2014:2087, para. 24; and CJEU, 17 December 2015, Case C-388/14, *Timac Agro Deutschland*, EU:C:2015:829, paras. 27-28.

104   CJEU, 15 May 1997, Case C-250/95, *Futura Participations*, EU:C:1997:239.

3. Personal Deductions

In *Schumacker*[105], the CJEU developed a specific doctrine applicable in the area of **242** personal deductions for individuals. It decided that granting such deductions is **primarily a matter for the State of residence**. The Court started from the proposition that residents and non-residents are, in principle, not in a comparable situation with respect to personal and family allowances. The reasoning was that, usually, it will be the residence State that is best positioned to determine ability to pay and it will be in the residence State where the predominant part of an individual's income is normally concentrated.[106]

The Court also introduced **exceptions** to this general rule – first, the concept of a **243** so-called **'virtual resident'** – i.e. a situation in which the majority of an individual's income is generated in the host State. In this case, the State of residence is not in a position to grant the personal deductions since the tax base there is too small or non-existent. In that case, the Court concluded that there is no objective difference between the situations of a non-resident and a resident in the host State and, therefore, it will be for the host State to grant the personal deductions.[107] Second, objective comparability will be found when an expense is directly linked to an activity that generates taxable income, e.g. compulsory contributions related to the exercise of a particular profession (e.g. bar association fees).[108]

The line of case law that followed *Schumacker*,[109] has been **delimiting the scope** of **244** such personal deductions to include e.g. costs incurred in obtaining tax advice, mortgage payments, spousal income 'splitting' schemes, contributions to a pension reserve, maintenance payments, allowances corresponding to special costs and extraordinary charges, as well as losses. Notably, what has remained outside the scope of the doctrine is business expenses, professional expenses and social security contributions.[110] The Court has also expanded the *Schumacker* doctrine to third countries with which the EU has special relations, i.e. Switzerland.[111] An interesting perspective on the personal and family allowances line of case law was

---

105   CJEU, 14 February 1995, Case C-279/93, *Schumacker,* EU:C:1995:31.
106   CJEU, 14 February 1995, Case C-279/93, *Schumacker,* EU:C:1995:31, para. 32-35.
107   CJEU, 14 February 1995, Case C-279/93, *Schumacker,* EU:C:1995:31, para. 36-47. When spouses are taxed jointly, their total income should be taken into account in evaluating whether the residence State can grant the personal deductions. CJEU, 22 June 2017, Case C-20/16, *Bechtel,* EU:C:2017:488, paras. 55-59.
108   CJEU, 6 December 2018, Case C-480/17, *Montag,* EU:C:2018:987.
109   CJEU, 14 September 1999, Case C-391/97, *Gschwind,* EU:C:1999:409; CJEU, 16 May 2000, Case C-87/99, *Zurstrassen,* EU:C:2000:251; CJEU, 12 December 2002, Case C-385/00, *De Groot,* EU:C:2002:750; CJEU, 12 June 2003, Case C-234/01, *Gerritse,* EU:C:2003:340; CJEU, 1 July 2004, Case C-169/03, *Wallentin,* EU:C:2004:403; CJEU, 5 July 2005, Case C-376/03, *D.,* EU:C:2005:424; CJEU, 6 July 2006, Case C-346/04, *Conijn,* EU:C:2006:445; CJEU, 18 July 2007, Case C-182/06, *Lakebrink,* EU:C:2007:452; CJEU, 16 October 2008, Case C-527/06, *Renneberg,* EU:C:2008:566; CJEU, 28 February 2013, Case C-168/11, *Beker,* EU:C:2013:117; and CJEU, 9 February 2017, Case C-283/15, *X,* EU:C:2017:102.
110   See CJEU, 31 March 2011, Case C-450/09, *Schröder,* EU:C:2011:198, para. 43 et seq.; CJEU, 23 January 2019, Case C-272/17, *Zyla,* EU:C:2019:49, paras. 30-31.
111   CJEU, 28 February 2013, Case C-425/11, *Ettwein,* EU:C:2013:121.

given in the *X* case,[112] which concerned a situation in which a resident of a Member State (Spain) derived 60% of his income from another Member State (the Netherlands) and 40% from a third country (Switzerland). The question was whether the Netherlands must allow a deduction for negative income related to a dwelling in the State of residence where the person was living but had no income. The Court ruled that the deduction for a dwelling must be provided somewhere or, more precisely, in the Member State where there is sufficient income. If more than one State meets this criterion, the deduction must be given in proportion to the relevant share of income generated.[113]

245　Reading *Turpeinen*[114] and *Hirvonen*[115] together lead to the conclusion that the *Schumacker* logic applies *mutatis mutandis* to non-economic migration of **pensioners** and it is up to the State of former employment (and former State of residence) to provide personal deductions. Typically, a pensioner who changes residence after retirement will have no income in the host State. Hence, he or she will have to be considered a 'virtual resident', *à la Schumacker* in his or her former State of residence, or as the case may be, in multiple former States of residence as in the *X* case.

246　In order to **prevent the double utilization of personal deductions**, the Member State concerned may take into consideration tax advantage that were already granted by another State, provided that, in the end, all personal and family circumstances are duly taken into account.[116]

4. Two Cross-Border Situations

247　The Court's case law lacked consistency as to whether the Treaties prohibit only discrimination between nationals and non-nationals (vertical discrimination) or also between non-nationals and other non-nationals (**horizontal discrimination**). While, for example, in *Cadbury Schweppes*[117] and *Commission v Netherlands*[118] the CJEU clearly compared two cross-border situations, it refused to do so in *D.*[119] and *Haribo*.[120] The statements in both *D.* and *Haribo*, however, were made in a specific factual context; while *D.* concerned extending the benefits of one DTC (between Belgium and Netherlands) to nationals of another Member State (in that case Germany), in *Haribo* the CJEU explicitly envisaged the possibility of treating income from different non-EU countries differently.

112　CJEU, 9 February 2017, Case C-283/15, *X*, EU:C:2017:102.
113　See also Opinion of Advocate General Wathelet, 7 September 2016, Case C-283/15, *X*, EU:C:2016:638, paras. 47-53.
114　CJEU, 9 November 2006, Case C-520/04, *Turpeinen*, EU:C:2006:703.
115　CJEU, 19 November 2015, Case C-632/13, *Hirvonen*, EU:C:2015:765.
116　CJEU, 12 December 2013, Case C-303/12, *Imfeld and Garcet*, EU:C:2013:822, para. 78 et seq.
117　CJEU, 12 September 2006, Case C-196/04, *Cadbury Schweppes*, EU:C:2006:544, paras. 44-45.
118　CJEU, 11 June 2009, Case C-521/07, *Commission v Netherlands*, EU:C:2009:360, para. 43.
119　CJEU, 5 July 2005, Case C-376/03, *D.*, EU:C:2005:424, paras. 49-63.
120　CJEU, 10 February 2011, Joined Cases C-436/08 and C-437/08, *Haribo Lakritzen and Österreichische Salinen*, EU:C:2011:61, para. 48.

A bit more clarity was introduced with the Grand Chamber decision in *Sopora*, **248** wherein the Court concurred with AG Kokott's Opinion that the free movement of workers also precludes discrimination between non-resident workers from different Member States.[121] It is doubtful whether this line of reasoning can be extended to the other freedoms of movement, as there is a textual difference between Art. 45 TFEU and the provisions of the other freedoms.[122] Keeping in mind that the Court never focuses only on the text of the provisions when interpreting EU law, one can expect that a cross-border-to-cross-border comparison can potentially be extended to all four freedoms. This was already suggested with respect to the freedom of establishment by Advocate General Hogan in *GVC Services (Bulgaria)*,[123] a matter that was not addressed in depth by the Court.[124] However, it is also clear from recent case law of the Court that the decision in *D.* stands and there is no horizontal comparison when it comes to the application of DTCs due to their bilateral nature.[125] Hence, as a general principle, Member States **should not discriminate between different EU Member States, unless the difference in treatment arises from a DTC.**

5. Comparability in Third-Country Situations

Keeping in mind that the free movement of capital is applicable not only in intra- **249** Community, but also in third-country situations, the question arises whether there is something peculiar in the comparability analysis with respect to third countries. In the *A.* case,[126] the CJEU came to the conclusion that the **scope** of the free movement of capital is, in principle, **the same** within the EU and with respect to third countries, subject to certain specific provisions of the Treaty (see m.no. 279). If the scope of the freedom is the same, it is likely that the comparability test will also be the same and that the Court will not use different standards for the comparability test in third-country situations.[127]

However, already in *Test Claimants in the FII Group Litigation*, the CJEU held that **250** the **degree of economic integration** that exists between the Member States **may lead to incomparability** between intra-EU and third-country situations.[128] Nevertheless, there has not yet been a case where the CJEU has held that the situations would have been comparable in an intra-Community case but are not when a third country is involved due to the integration between the Member States. For

---

121 CJEU, 24 February 2015, Case C-512/13, *Sopora*, EU:C:2015:108, para. 25.
122 CFE Opinion Statement ECJ-TF 3/2015 on the Decision of the European Court of Justice in *C.G. Sopora* (Case C-512/13), on 'Horizontal Discrimination', *ET* 2016, p. 97.
123 Opinion of Advocate General Hogan, 24 October 2019, Case C-458/18, *GVC Services (Bulgaria)*, EU:C:2019:897, para. 51.
124 CJEU, 2 April 2020, Case C-458/18, *GVC Services (Bulgaria)*, EU:C:2020:266, para. 41.
125 CJEU, 30 June 2016, Case C-176/15, *Riskin and Timmermans*, EU:C:2016:488, para. 31.
126 CJEU, 18 December 2007, Case C-101/05, *A.*, EU:C:2007:804.
127 Recently, Germany tried unsuccessfully to defend the lack of comparability with respect to low tax third countries. See CJEU, 26 February 2019, Case C-135/17, *X GmbH*, EU:C:2019:136, paras. 63-69.
128 CJEU, 12 December 2006, Case C-446/04, *Test Claimants in the FII Group Litigation*, EU:C:2006:774, para. 170.

example, in *SECIL*, the Court applied the well-known *prima facie* and objective comparability two-step approach, without taking into account that the capital movement was from a third country for the purposes of the comparability analysis.[129] Similarly, in *Santander Asset Management SGIIC* (where some of the joint cases were related to non-Member States), the CJEU simultaneously evaluated the comparability of intra-Community and third-country situations and applied the test without any distinction.[130]

251 Therefore, with respect to the comparability analysis, intra-EU and third-country situations are **almost universally comparable**, unless there is a good reason for them not to be. As of yet, no such good reason has emerged. Indeed, the situation is rather different when it comes to the permissible justifications, which, without a doubt, are broader regarding third countries (see m.no. 274 et seq.). However, this is a further step to the analysis that must not be confused with the objective comparability stage.

D. Juridical Double Taxation and the Relevance of DTCs

252 The next issue to be discussed in relation to the restriction analysis is whether juridical double taxation constitutes a restriction of the fundamental freedoms. The short answer is 'no' since the Court has consistently held that, at the current stage of development of EU law, the Member States are under **no obligation to eliminate juridical double taxation** arising from the parallel exercise of their tax sovereignty.[131] It somehow logically stems from this that Member States are free to allocate taxing rights between one another as they deem fit,[132] the Court has no jurisdiction to provide an interpretation of DTCs[133] unless there is a special agreement that provides it with such powers,[134] and the matter of allocation of taxing rights falls outside the scrutiny of the fundamental freedoms.[135] Hence, in principle, juridical double taxation does not constitute a restriction of the fundamental freedoms and DTCs fall outside the scrutiny of the CJEU. This further reinforces the point made above that the restriction analysis in respect of direct taxation is discrimination based, as, although juridical double taxation undoubtedly makes cross-border activities less attractive, it does not involve discriminatory treatment, as it stems from the parallel exercise of taxing powers over one and the same person by more than one Member State.

---

129 CJEU, 24 November 2016, Case C-464/14, *SECIL*, EU:C:2016:896, paras. 48 and 54-55.
130 CJEU, 10 May 2012, Case C-338/11, *Santander Asset Management SGIIC*, EU:C:2012:286, paras. 6 and 23.
131 CJEU, 11 September 2014, Case C-489/13, *Verest and Gerards*, EU:C:2014:2269, para. 18; CJEU, 12 December 2013, Case C-303/12, *Imfeld and Garcet*, EU:C:2013:822, para. 41; and CJEU, 12 February 2009, Case C-67/08, *Block*, EU:C:2009:92, paras. 29-31.
132 CJEU, 12 May 1998, Case C-336/96, *Gilly*, EU:C:1998:221, paras. 30-31.
133 CJEU, 6 December 2007, Case C-298/05, *Columbus Container*, EU:C:2007:754, para. 46.
134 CJEU, 12 September 2017, Case C-648/15, *Austria v Germany*, EU:C:2017:664.
135 CJEU, 21 September 1999, Case C-307/97, *Saint-Gobain*, EU:C:1999:438, para. 56; and CJEU, 30 June 2016, Case C-176/15, *Riskin and Timmermans*, EU:C:2016:488, paras. 20-34.

However, in the Swedish *Bouanich* case,[136] the Court decided that a DTC is not **253** completely irrelevant but forms part of the legal background and **has to be taken into consideration in interpreting the fundamental freedoms**. Furthermore, although the CJEU is not competent to interpret national law (i.e. international treaties and domestic law),[137] it may take into account the application of a DTC in determining the applicable freedom.[138] Finally, it is clear from *Saint-Gobain* that even if Member States are free to allocate taxing rights under a DTC, once these rights are allocated, national law cannot lead to less-favourable treatment.[139] This was reaffirmed in *Verest and Gerards* concerning the application of the exemption with progression method with regard to relief from double taxation.[140] Hence, although the very allocation of taxing rights remains free from the scrutiny of the fundamental freedoms, the exercise of rights so allocated is subject to judicial review by the Court and DTCs have implications both at the justification and the proportionality stages of analysis.[141]

The **take away** from the above analysis is that, first, as long as national law does **254** not discriminate, any juridical double taxation that arises due to the parallel exercise of taxing rights by the Member States is not a restriction of the fundamental freedoms. And second, although, on its face, it seems that the Court is reluctant to test DTCs against the fundamental freedoms, *de facto* it sometimes does so by looking at the national tax treatment once taxing powers are allocated.

E. Economic Double Taxation and the Equivalence of the Exemption and the Credit Method

The stance of the Court concerning economic double taxation is different, since **255** the latter often involves discriminatory treatment; Member States will frequently provide relief only in domestic cases, while treating cross-border activities less advantageously.[142] In that respect, the CJEU was confronted with the question of whether a Member State may apply the exemption method in domestic situations and the credit method in cross-border situations in relieving economic double taxation of a distribution of dividends (once at the level of the company and once at the level of the shareholder).[143] Thus, the question boiled down to whether the

---

136 CJEU, 19 January 2006, Case C-265/04, *Bouanich*, EU:C:2006:51, para. 51.
137 CJEU, 16 July 2009, Case C-128/08, *Damseaux*, EU:C:2009:471, paras. 20 and 22.
138 CJEU, 11 September 2014, Case C-47/12, *Kronos International*, EU:C:2014:2200, para. 33.
139 CJEU, 21 September 1999, Case C-307/97, *Saint-Gobain*, EU:C:1999:438, para. 57.
140 CJEU, 11 September 2014, Case C-489/13, *Verest and Gerards*, EU:C:2014:2210, para. 29 et seq.
141 For a more in-depth analysis of the interplay between the fundamental freedoms and DTCs see Lang, Double Taxation Conventions in the Case Law of the CJEU, *Intertax* 2018, pp. 186-193.
142 CJEU, 24 November 2016, Case C-464/14, *SECIL*, EU:C:2016:896, paras. 48-51; CJEU, 7 September 2004, Case C-319/02, *Manninen*, EU:C:2004:484, para. 20;
143 The Court was also confronted with the opposite scenario where economic double taxation was relieved in domestic situations by using the credit method (including reimbursement of the underlying corporate income tax when the parent was in a loss position), while in cross-border situations the exemption method was applied. CJEU, 11 September 2014, Case C-47/12, *Kronos International*, EU:C:2014:2200.

exemption and the credit method, applied to **avoid economic double taxation, are equivalent measures**. The rationale behind such a differentiation is the desire of a State to protect its own tax revenue from a low corporate tax level abroad via the credit method (the difference will eventually be taxed at the shareholder level). In fact, the previous sentence provides an answer to the question; no, the exemption method and the credit method are not equivalent in terms of the economic result, as only the credit method recaptures the difference in the tax rate.

256   However, in the two *Test Claimants in the FII Group Litigation* cases[144] (and *Haribo* in between)[145] the CJEU concluded that Member States might, in principle, apply the exemption method in respect of the taxation of dividends in domestic situations and the ordinary credit method in cross-border cases. However, in order **not to compromise the equivalence** of the two, the Court imposed certain requirements on the national tax system. First, Member States should not apply lower nominal tax rates for certain companies under its national law, as, in this scenario, under a domestic exemption system, the difference in the rates will not be recaptured at the parent level, while, under a credit system, there will be such a recapture if a similar situation exists involving a foreign subsidiary.[146] Second, the CJEU extended the above line of reasoning to tax systems where, although on its face the nominal rate is fixed, the effective tax rate is typically lower.[147] Moreover, for equivalence to exist, the credit given for the foreign tax must be at least equal to the amount actually paid abroad, capped only by the domestic tax rate, and not for example according to different ratios of income.[148]

257   Finally, the Court also concluded that there must be a **carry-forward of the credit** in fiscal years when the parent has a loss.[149] Without a carry-forward of the tax credit, economic double taxation is suffered in subsequent years when there is a positive tax result. This is due to the fact that, unlike an exemption system, under the credit method, the distributed dividends reduce the losses of the company that receives them. This would have an impact in later years if the parent company becomes profitable again (the carried-forward loss is less than the amount of the dividend). However, if there is no credit carry-forward, the tax that has been paid in the subsidiary State will never be credited, as, in the year when it was suffered, there was no domestic tax to credit against.

---

144   CJEU, 12 December 2006, Case C-446/04, *Test Claimants in the FII Group Litigation*, EU:C:2006:774; and CJEU, 13 November 2012, Case C-35/11, *Test Claimants in the FII Group Litigation*, EU:C:2012:707.

145   CJEU, 10 February 2011, Joined Cases C-436/08 and C-437/08, *Haribo Lakritzen and Österreichische Salinen*, EU:C:2011:61, para. 86 et seq.

146   CJEU, 13 November 2012, Case C-35/11, *Test Claimants in the FII Group Litigation*, EU:C:2012:707, paras. 44-45.

147   Ibid., paras. 46-51.

148   CJEU, 13 March 2014, Case C-375/12, *Bouanich*, EU:C:2014:138.

149   CJEU, 10 February 2011, Joined Cases C-436/08 and C-437/08, *Haribo Lakritzen and Österreichische Salinen*, EU:C:2011:61, para. 158.

III. Justifications

A. General

The fact that a domestic tax measure constitutes a restriction does not per se make **258** it non-permissible under EU law. In contrast, a restriction might be justified under certain conditions. Put in simple terms, there are some **higher, nobler goals** that are worthy of protection and, thus, justify setting aside the economic fundamental freedoms. Some of these higher goals are explicitly provided in the Treaty (public policy, public security and public health), while others have been developed by the Court under the so-called 'rule of reason'. It is worth noting, however, that it is the Member State whose measure is under scrutiny who must put forward a justification, once a restriction is established.[150]

In the area of direct taxation, the **explicit justifications** under the TFEU are of **259** marginal importance for two reasons. First, these justifications are mostly relevant to instances of direct discrimination (which hardly ever occurs in direct taxation), as they are the only grounds for a State to defend a directly discriminatory measure.[151] Second, the Court interprets the explicit grounds extremely narrowly.[152] As such, they are hardly ever successfully invoked under EU law.

Therefore, this section will exclusively deal with the justification grounds that **260** have been recognized (or not) by the Court under the **rule of reason** test. The test was first famously pronounced in *Cassis de Dijon*[153] wherein the CJEU accepted that restrictive measures that are not directly discriminatory might be justified on general grounds of public interest as long as they comply with the principle of proportionality. This creates two obvious questions: (i) which matters of general public interest are worthy of protection, and (ii) when is the proportionality test satisfied. The first question will be dealt with in this section, while the issue of proportionality will be discussed in the last section of this chapter.

B. Justifications Accepted by the CJEU

1. From Cohesion to Balanced Allocation: Consistency Across the Borders

Cohesion of the tax system was accepted for the first time as a justification in **261** *Bachmann*[154] and *Commission v Belgium*,[155] which were decided on the same day and concerned the same provision of Belgian tax law, which allowed for a

---

150 CJEU, 24 October 2019, Case C-35/19, *État belge*, EU:C:2019:894, paras. 37-38.
151 CJEU, 22 October 2014, Case C-344/13, *Blanco and Fabretti*, EU:C:2014:2311, paras. 37-38.
152 See with respect to the definition of 'public order' Opinion of Advocate General Hogan, 24 October 2019, Case C-458/18, *GVC Services (Bulgaria)*, EU:C:2019:897, para. 58.
153 CJEU, 20 February 1979, Case 120/78, *Cassis de Dijon*, EU:C:1979:42.
154 CJEU, 28 January 1992, Case C-204/90, *Bachmann*, EU:C:1992:35.
155 CJEU, 28 January 1992, Case C-300/90, *Commission v Belgium*, EU:C:1992:37.

deduction of insurance contributions only if the insurance company was located domestically. The Court accepted that such a restriction can be justified by the fact that, if the insurance company is located abroad, Belgium will be impeded in exercising taxing rights over the subsequent pension payments. This is the so-called principle of cohesion of the tax system, which requires a nexus between a tax advantage and a future tax levy that offsets it (e.g. what is deducted now must be taxed later for the cohesion justification to work). After this initial broad interpretation, the Court started limiting the scope of the justification and was reluctant to accept it in subsequent years, claiming either an insufficient nexus[156] or that the Member State has given up its taxing rights to offset the advantage under a DTC.[157]

262 16 years after *Bachmann*, the CJEU again accepted the cohesion argument as a **successful** justification in *Krankenheim*.[158] The case concerned a rather standard PE reintegration of losses provision in the HQ country. This was not so much a real cohesion argument but rather reflected the need to justify less favourable treatment the existence of which was questionable.[159] In the *Krankenheim* case, the justification happened to be the cohesion of the tax system. Other examples in which the CJEU again accepted the cohesion argument are *Papillon*,[160] *Test Claimants in the FII Group Litigation*[161] (in both cases the national provisions failed the proportionality test), and the *K.* case,[162] where the cohesion justification was accepted alongside the balanced allocation of taxing rights, and successfully defended by the Member State at the proportionality stage.

263 However, in its most recent case law, the Court either repeatedly rejects the argument based on the cohesion of the tax system[163] or links it to the balanced allocation of taxing rights justification.[164] Thus, there is a **merger between cohesion and the balanced allocation of taxing powers** as grounds for justification, or as the Court notably put it in *Timac Agro Deutschland* (the continuation of the *Krankenheim* saga): "*the requirements of the balanced allocation of powers of taxation and coher-*

---

156 CJEU, 4 July 2013, Case C-350/11, *Argenta Spaarbank NV*, EU:C:2013:447, para. 46 et seq.; and CJEU, 13 March 2014, Case C-375/12, *Bouanich*, EU:C:2014:138, para. 67 et seq.

157 CJEU, 16 April 2015, Case C-591/13, *Commission v Germany*, EU:C:2015:230, para. 74 et seq.

158 CJEU, 23 October 2008, Case C-157/07, *Krankenheim Ruhesitz am Wannsee-Seniorenheimstatt GmbH*, EU:C:2008:588, para. 42 et seq.

159 Wattel, Non-Discrimination a la Cour: The ECJ's (Lack of) Comparability Analysis in Direct Tax Cases, *ET* 2015, p. 552.

160 CJEU, 27 November 2008, Case C-418/07, *Société Papillon*, EU:C:2008:659.

161 CJEU, 13 November 2012, Case C-35/11, *Test Claimants in the FII Group Litigation*, EU:C:2012:707.

162 CJEU, 7 November 2013, Case C-322/11, *K.*, EU:C:2013:716, paras. 64-71.

163 CJEU, 22 February 2018, Joined Cases C-398/16 and C-399/16, *X BV and X NV*, EU:C:2018:110, paras. 43-45; CJEU, 22 June 2017, Case C-20/16, *Bechtel*, EU:C:2017:488, para. 77; CJEU, 26 May 2016, Case C-300/15, *Kohll and Kohll-Schlesser*, EU:C:2016:361, para. 61; CJEU, 21 December 2016, Case C-503/14, *Commission v Portugal*, EU:C:2016:979, para. 64; and CJEU, 2 September 2015, Case C-386/14, *Groupe Steria*, EU:C:2015:524;

164 Opinion of Advocate General Kokott, 13 March 2014, Case C-48/13, *Nordea Bank*, EU:C:2014:153, paras. 42 and 43;

ence of the tax system coincide."[165] Nevertheless, very recently in *Bevola*, the Court again took a step back and accepted the coherence of the tax system as a separate justification.[166]

This leads to the next point regarding the **balanced allocation of taxing powers.** In this respect, the dynamics were completely the opposite; at first, this was accepted as a justification in *Marks & Spencer* but only in combination with other reasons (the need to ensure losses are not taken into account twice and the risk of tax avoidance).[167] Later, in *Oy AA*, the Court admitted that only the balanced allocation argument and the need to combat tax avoidance, in combination, are sufficient as justifications.[168] Finally, in the *X Holding* case,[169] the CJEU went a step further and accepted the need to safeguard the balanced allocation of the power to impose taxes as a justification alone. One can expect that the justification related to ensuring that losses are not taken into account twice will lose its significance in intra-EU situations, as, in the majority of cases, there will be a less-restrictive alternative based on exchange of information between the tax authorities.[170]   **264**

The question in *X Holding* (as a culmination of the *Marks & Spencer* line of case law) was quite straightforward – should a Member State apply a **group tax consolidation** regime only to companies that are tax resident in its territory or should it also extend it to non-resident subsidiaries. Several Member States (including the Netherlands whose national legislation was under scrutiny in the case), claimed that the answer is 'no' because the situations are not comparable. Indeed, it is hard to argue with the point raised by these States that a non-resident subsidiary cannot be integrated into a tax entity in the Netherlands for the simple reason that the country exercises no tax jurisdiction over such a subsidiary. That argument, although not spelled out explicitly in the case, is a manifestation of the territoriality principle. The Court, however, took the view that the situations are comparable but upheld the national legislation under the balanced allocation of taxing powers justification.   **265**

The analysis of the Court in *X Holding* (& co) is at odds with **the idea of territoriality** in *Futura Participations*. Both cases look at essentially the same issue – territorial restrictions of taxing powers: in *X Holding*, regarding foreign subsidiaries (non-residents), and in *Futura Participations*, everything that happens outside the PE State, as it exercises only limited taxing rights. The parent company State is restricted in its taxing powers over a subsidiary abroad in the same way as the PE State with respect to the HQ abroad (or, in fact, other PEs in different countries).   **266**

---

165 CJEU, 17 December 2015, Case C-388/14, *Timac Agro Deutschland*, EU:C:2015:829, para. 47.
166 CJEU, 12 June 2018, Case C-650/16, *Bevola*, EU:C:2018:424, para. 44-51.
167 CJEU, 13 December 2005, Case C-446/03; *Marks and Spencer*, EU:C:2005:763, paras. 43-51.
168 CJEU, 18 July 2007, Case C-231/05, *Oy AA*, EU:C:2007:439, para. 60.
169 CJEU, 25 February 2010, Case C-337/08, *X Holding*, EU:C:2010:89, para. 31 et seq.
170 Opinion of Advocate General Kokott, 27 February 2020, Case C-405/18, *AURES Holding*, EU:C:2020: 127, para. 52.

Nevertheless, while in *Futura Participations* the CJEU found no discrimination due to the principle of territoriality, in *X Holding* it considered the measure restrictive and applied the justifications approach. The shift of the principle of territoriality from the comparability to the justification analysis was explicitly reaffirmed in *Hornbach-Baumarkt*. [171] However, in one of its most recent decisions, the Court took the opposite view, regarding territoriality as a matter of comparability rather than justification.[172]

267 When examining the content of the balanced allocation of taxing powers justification, it is evident where the confusion is coming from. The justification mandates Member States to tax the economic activity that is performed in their territory in harmony (in respect of both profits and losses).[173] Thus, **the concept of balanced allocation of taxing power is a manifestation of the idea of territoriality, only this time at the level of justification rather than comparability**. It stems from this that a country cannot defend its national provisions by balanced allocation of taxing rights if it has decided to exempt particular domestic income but taxes the same income, only this time from a foreign source.[174] Naturally, the territoriality principle and, by extension, the principle of balanced allocation of taxing rights is widely used as a justification also in exit tax cases.[175]

2. Anti-abuse – a justification or a general principle?

268 The question of anti-abuse under the fundamental freedoms has always been a tricky one, as **two opposing forces** are competing. On the one hand, there is the consistent line of case law of the CJEU to the effect that the exercise of the freedoms of movement for the purpose of benefiting from a more favourable legal regime (including tax regime) does not constitute, in itself, abusive behaviour.[176] Hence, the Court leaves scope for tax planning that is not only permissible but also protected under EU law. On the other hand, the Member States try to prevent the erosion of their tax base by means of anti-avoidance rules. Since these rules often only target cross-border situations (as effective tax planning will necessitate a cross-border element), they are seen as restrictions on the fundamental freedoms by the Court. Hence, there is inherent tension between the anti-avoidance rules and the fundamental freedoms.

---

171 CJEU, 31 May 2018, Case C-382/16, *Hornbach-Baumarkt*, EU:C:2018:366, para. 40.

172 CJEU, 27 February 2020, Case C-405/18, *AURES Holding*, EU:C:2020:127, para. 53.

173 Ibid, para. 28; CJEU, 20 October 2011, Case C-284/09, *Commission v Germany*, EU:C:2011:670, para. 77.

174 CJEU, 20 October 2011, Case C-284/09, *Commission v Germany*, EU:C:2011:670, para. 78.

175 For a recent example see CJEU, 21 December 2016, Case C-503/14, *Commission v Portugal*, EU:C: 2016:979, para. 51 et seq. For some peculiarities regarding the application of this justification to the deferral of capital gains taxation under the Merger Directive see CJEU, 22 March 2018, Joined Cases C-327/16 and C-421/16, *Jacob* and *Lassus*, EU:C:2018:210, paras. 81-83.

176 CJEU, 12 September 2006, Case C-196/04, *Cadbury Schweppes*, EU:C:2006:544, para. 38. AG Kokott Opinion, 1 March 2018, Case C-115/16, *N Luxembourg 1*, EU:C:2018:143, paras. 70-73.

Therefore, the Court has developed an **anti-abuse doctrine** that Member States **269** must comply with. Up until relatively recently, the matter was simple: the test of the national anti-tax-avoidance provisions was a matter of fundamental freedoms scrutiny at the justification level. However, on 26 February 2019, the Grand Chamber of the Court came out with two different lines of decisions that are difficult to reconcile. In the first line, the 'Danish' cases, the Court considered anti-abuse, as a general principle of Union law, to be a source of primary law in its own right, thereby making any domestic anti-avoidance provision (or the lack of such) irrelevant.[177] Passing the anti-abuse threshold seemed to be a prerequisite to receiving any benefits stemming from Union law, including the fundamental freedoms.[178] At the same time, in *X GmbH*, the CJEU retained the old formula, pursuant to which anti-abuse is looked at through the prism of a justification, with the resulting focus on the underlying domestic law that follows therefrom.[179] Whether one adopts the former or the latter approach is not merely a theoretical exercise, but has overreaching practical consequences. Under the general principle approach, the domestic legislation remains unimportant, as the factual circumstances of the case are tested against a general principle with its own normative content. Under the justification approach, the attention falls on the compatibility of the domestic legislation with the principle of proportionality. If the domestic legislation fails proportionality, the factual circumstances remain irrelevant. However, both approaches share the same definition of tax avoidance, which answers the question of what Member States are allowed to combat under the justification approach and are obliged to combat under the general principle approach.

Regarding the definition of abuse, it has to be noted that the Court views tax **270** avoidance as an autonomous concept under EU law. This means that, as far as cross-border movement within the scope of EU law is concerned, Member States cannot rely on their domestic definitions of tax avoidance. According to a consistent line of case law, what constitutes an abusive practice is the creation of an artificial arrangement that does not reflect economic reality, the purpose of which is to obtain an unintended tax benefit.[180] Hence, according to the Court, there are **two cumulative elements of tax avoidance** – an objective and a subjective one.

---

177 This had implications also with respect to the need of implementing an explicit anti-avoidance provision under the applicable secondary legislation, since the general principle has direct effect even in the absence of an explicit implementation of an anti-avoidance provision. For the lack of direct effect of anti-avoidance provisions contained in secondary legislation see CJEU, 5 July 2007, Case C-321/05, *Kofoed*, EU:C:2007:408.

178 CJEU, 26 February 2019, Case C-115/16, *N Luxembourg 1*, EU:C:2019:134, para. 155; CJEU, 26 February 2019, Case C-116/16, *T Danmark*, EU:C:2019:35, para. 122. The creeping influence of the general principle in the area of taxation could have been foreseen by the decision in *Cussens*. See CJEU, 22 November 2017, Case C-251/16, *Cussens and Others*, EU:C:2017:641, para. 30.

179 CJEU, 26 February 2019, Case C-135/17, *X GmbH*, EU:C:2019:136, para. 73.

180 CJEU, 12 September 2006, Case C-196/04, *Cadbury Schweppes and Cadbury Schweppes Overseas*, EU:C:2006:544, para. 55; CJEU, 20 December 2017, Joined Cases C-504/16 and C-613/16, *Deister Holding and Juhler Holding*, EU:C:2017:1009, para. 60; CJEU, 26 February 2019, Case C-116/16, *T Danmark*, EU:C:2019:35, para. 81; CJEU, 26 February 2019, Case C-135/17, *X GmbH*, EU:C:2019:136, para. 73.

271 For the **objective element** to be satisfied, the arrangement at hand must be characterized by artificiality; while existing in the legal world, it should not reflect economic reality. The concrete test will depend on whether the arrangement under scrutiny is related to an entity or a transaction. When it comes to an entity, the Court has ruled that in order to reflect economic reality, an entity should be engaged in economic activity (be it even marginal, such as the holding of shares or providing financing) and should physically exist in terms of staff, premises and equipment.[181] If a Member State claims that a transaction, rather than an entity, is fictitious, the CJEU takes a different approach by benchmarking the transaction under suspicion against the arm's length principle as a standard for genuine activity,[182] unless the transaction in question was fully fictitious and occurred only on paper; for example, no services were actually provided.[183] In the latter case, the objective element will be, by definition, satisfied.

272 The **subjective test** will require that the taxpayer engage in the artificial arrangement for the essential purpose of obtaining an unintended tax benefit.[184] Hence, it presupposes a mental element of the taxpayer whereby its actions (the creation of the artificial arrangement) are directed towards a particular result – an unintended tax benefit – and this result is the foreseen and desired consequence of the action.

273 It is interesting to note that, in some judgments, the Court sees anti-avoidance as **connected with the balanced allocation of taxing rights** between the Member States.[185] In this respect, one might wonder whether the Court considers that it is an implicit requirement that the economic activity concerned be performed specifically in the State that is invoking its anti-abuse provisions. Furthermore, recent developments in international tax law, related to the adoption of the BEPS action plans and their subsequent implementation in the EU via ATAD, are challenging the view of the CJEU on anti-abuse by introducing a broader concept of tax avoidance in secondary legislation (See Chapter 8, m.no. 646 et seq.).[186]

---

181 CJEU, 20 December 2017, Joined Cases C-504/16 and C-613/16, *Deister Holding and Juhler Holding,* EU:C:2017:1009; and CJEU, 12 September 2006, Case C-196/04, *Cadbury Schweppes,* EU:C:2006:544, para. 67.

182 CJEU, 13 March 2007, Case C-524/04, *Test Claimants in the Thin Cap Group Litigation,* EU:C:2007: 161, paras. 71-83. CJEU, 21 January 2010, Case C-311/08, *SGI,* EU:C:2010:26, para. 71; CJEU, 31 May 2018, Case C-382/16, Hornbach-Baumarkt, EU:C:2018:366. Note that in the *SGI* and *Hornbach-Baumarkt* cases the anti-avoidance justification was bundled together with balanced allocation of taxing powers.

183 CJEU, 5 July 2012, Case C-318/10, *SIAT,* EU:C:2012:415, paras. 41-42.

184 CJEU, 22 November 2017, Case C-251/16, *Cussens and Others,* EU:C:2017:641, para. 53; CJEU, 21 February 2006, Case C-255/02, *Halifax,* EU:C:2006:121, para. 75.

185 CJEU, 20 December 2017, Joined Cases C-504/16 and C-613/16, *Deister Holding and Juhler Holding,* EU:C:2017:1009, para. 96. CJEU, 21 January 2010, Case C-311/08, *SGI,* EU:C:2010:26, para. 69.

186 Opinion of Advocate General Kokott Opinion, 1 March 2018, Case C-115/16, *N Luxembourg 1,* EU:C:2018:143, para. 64.

3. Effectiveness of Fiscal Supervision and Tax Collection

The **effectiveness of fiscal supervision** and tax collection is a justification that rarely withstands the scrutiny of the Court in intra-Community situations, which enjoy, to some degree, a presumption of effectiveness.[187] This is predominantly due to the numerous possibilities for administrative assistance between the tax authorities of the different Member States (see Chapter 9). There are, however, several examples of when the Court has accepted the justification also within the European Union. **274**

In *Futura Participations*, the Court agreed that the host State might require a PE to draw up its tax accounts according to its own domestic rules in order to ensure effective fiscal supervision.[188] The CJEU also accepted this argument in the more recent case of *Sparkasse Allgäu*. This case concerned a German bank with a branch in Austria, which had to notify the German tax authorities in the event of the death of a German tax resident holding assets in the Austrian branch of the bank. The strict Austrian bank secrecy legislation, at the time, provided for criminal penalties in the event of a breach. Nevertheless, the Court held that Germany is free to impose such a notification requirement due to the need for effective fiscal supervision related to the imposition of inheritance tax.[189] **275**

This justification is, however, more relevant in relations between Member States and **third countries,** concerning the free movement of capital. The landmark case in this respect is the *A.* case,[190] which concerned Swedish national legislation that provided for an exemption of dividends stemming from domestic subsidiaries, EEA subsidiaries and subsidiaries in countries with which Sweden had an exchange of information agreement. The exemption, thus, did not apply with respect to Switzerland, as there was no exchange of information agreement in place. It is peculiar to note that seven other Member States intervened in the case, all supporting the position of Sweden, which was symptomatic of the rising fight against further liberalization of the movement of capital to and from third-countries. The Court eventually accepted that third-country situations are materially different when there is no exchange of information agreement. Thus, the possibility to justify a restrictive measure *vis-à-vis* third-countries based on the effectiveness of fiscal supervision is broader in comparison to a similar capital movement within the Union. **276**

Nevertheless, in order to rely successfully on the lack of exchange of information with third countries, the relevant Member State must demonstrate that there is a **277**

---

187 CJEU, 6 October 2011, Case C-493/09, *Commission v Portugal,* EU:C:2011:635, para. 46; and CJEU, 27 January 2009, Case C-318/07, *Pershe,* EU:C:2009:33.
188 CJEU, 15 May 1997, Case C-250/95, *Futura Participations,* EU:C:1997:239, paras. 23-35.
189 CJEU, 14 April 2016, Case C-522/14, *Sparkasse Allgäu,* EU:C:2016:253, para. 29.
190 CJEU, 18 December 2007, Case C-101/05, *A.,* EU:C:2007:804.

real need to obtain information in order to grant a tax advantage.[191] Simply put, a Member State cannot 'hide' behind the lack of exchange of information to justify any restriction to the movement of capital; instead, it has to prove that there is a material fact that has to be verified. The same logic was extended to assistance with respect to enforcement of taxes, in respect of which the CJEU has held that in order to rely on the lack of a mutual assistance agreement, the Member State has to show that such assistance is indeed needed in the first place.[192]

278   The Court has also found that the need to ensure **effective collection of taxes** is an acceptable justification with respect to the means of taxation. Namely the CJEU has agreed that, as far as the temporary provision of services is concerned (e.g. free movement of services), withholding tax is an appropriate means of taxation for non-residents even if it is not applied to residents.[193] Recent case law, however, has upheld that such withholding taxes cannot be imposed on a gross basis but must allow for deduction of related business expenses.[194] Nevertheless, once the activity reaches a degree of permanence (as a rule of thumb when it triggers a PE) the difference in treatment can no longer be justified based on the need for effective collection of taxes.[195]

4. 'Standstill (Grandfather) Clause' in Third-Country Situations

279   Art. 64 TFEU contains a special provision applicable in third-country situations allowing Member States to **continue to apply discriminatory national provisions** in the area of the free movement of capital, provided that the restriction existed on 31 December 1993. This provision concerns specific types of capital movement, namely those that involve direct investments, the provision of financial services, or the admission of securities to the capital market. Art. 64 TFEU does not contain a justification in the strict sense but rather a specific limitation on the scope of capital liberalization to and from third-countries.

280   The standstill clause represents a **derogation** from the fundamental principle of the free movement of capital and, thus, must be interpreted strictly.[196] However, a

---

191   See e.g. CJEU, 11 June 2009, Case C-521/07, *Commission v Netherlands*, EU:C:2009:360, para. 43 et seq.; and CJEU, 28 February 2013, Case C-544/11, *Petersen*, EU:C:2013:124, para. 57 et seq.

192   CJEU, 10 February 2011, Joined Cases C-436/08 and C-437/08, *Haribo Lakritzen and Österreichische Salinen*, EU:C:2011:61, para. 73.

193   CJEU, 3 October 2006, Case C-290/04, *FKP Scorpio*, EU:C:2006:630; and CJEU, 18 October 2012, Case C-498/10, *X NV*, EU:C:2012:635; para. 42.

194   CJEU, 13 July 2016, Case C-18/15, *Brisal and KBC Finance Ireland*, EU:C:2016:549, para. 55; CJEU, 2 June 2016, Case C-252/14, *Pensioenfonds Metaal en Techniek*, EU:C:2016:402. For criticism of this approach by the Court see Ribeiro, Did the ECJ Go Too Far in *Brisal* (Case C-18/15)?, *ET* 2017, pp. 496-502; Smit, International Income Allocation under EU Tax Law: Tinker, Tailor, Soldier, Sailor, *EC Tax Review* 2017, p. 71.

195   CJEU, 19 June 2014, Joined Cases C-53/13 and C-80/13, *Strojírny Prostějov*, EU:C:2014:2011, paras. 48-49.

196   CJEU, 21 May 2015, Case C-560/13, *Ingeborg Wagner-Raith*, EU:C:2015:347, paras. 21 and 42.

national measure adopted after 31 December 1993 does not automatically fall outside the scope of Art. 64 TFEU. Subsequent provisions that are, in substance, identical to the previous legislation or limit an existing restriction of capital movement, still fall within the scope of the standstill provision. By contrast, legislation based on an approach that is different from that of the previous law is no longer covered by the grandfather clause.[197] Moreover, the national measure must remain substantially unchanged in terms of its personal and material scope in the context of the overall legislation.[198] It is also the understanding of the Court that the national provision should be maintained without interruption between the reference date in 1993 and the present in order to be covered by Art. 64.[199] The CJEU has observed that the applicability of the grandfather clause depends on the effect of the national legislation, rather than its aim.[200] Thus, even if the domestic provision has a broader scope of application than that envisaged under Art. 64 TFEU, this does not preclude the application of the standstill clause; e.g. if the national legislation restricts not only movement in relation to direct investment but also portfolio investments, the Member States can rely on Art. 64 TFEU to restrict direct investment.[201]

The standstill clause has gained importance in the area of direct taxation in terms **281** of its applicability to **direct investment** and the **provision of financial services**. The CJEU has had to define, therefore, both terms. The Court understands the term 'direct investment' as an investment of any kind undertaken by natural or legal persons, serving to establish or maintain lasting and direct links between the investor and the undertaking that allow the investor to participate in the management of the company or in its control.[202] Regarding financial services, the CJEU has decided that the term covers both the acquisition of units in investment funds and the receipt of funds deriving from such funds,[203] as well as opening securities accounts.[204] However, a causal link must exist between the capital movement and the provision of financial services; thus, even if a pension fund receives dividends from its acquisition of shareholdings, this cannot be regarded as a financial service that such pension fund provides to the insured persons.[205]

197　See CJEU, 12 December 2006, Case C-446/04, *Test Claimants in the FII Group Litigation*, EU:C:2006:774, para. 192; CJEU, 10 April 2014, Case C-190/12, *Emerging Markets Series of DFA*, EU:C:2014:249, para. 48.

198　CJEU, 20 September 2018, Case C-685/16, *EV*, EU:C:2018:743, para. 82.

199　CJEU, 18 December 2007, Case C-101/05, *A*, EU:C:2007:804, paras. 48-49.

200　CJEU, 15 February 2017, Case C-317/15, *X*, EU:C:2017:119, para. 21.

201　CJEU, 26 February 2019, Case C-135/17, *X GmbH*, EU:C:2019:136, paras. 32-34.

202　CJEU, 24 May 2007, Case C-157/05, *Holböck*, EU:C:2007:297; para. 32 et seq.; CJEU, 10 May 2012, Case C-338/11, *Santander Asset Management SGIIC*, EU:C:2012:286, paras. 75-76; Opinion of Advocate General Wathelet, 7 February 2018, Case C-685/16, *EV*, EU:C:2018:70, paras. 77-83.

203　CJEU, 21 May 2015, Case C-560/13, *Ingeborg Wagner-Raith*, EU:C:2015:347, paras. 34, 43, 46 et seq.

204　CJEU, 15 February 2017, Case C-317/15, *X*, EU:C:2017:119, para. 27.

205　CJEU, 13 November 2019, Case C-641/17, *College Pension Plan of British Columbia*, EU:C:2019:960, paras. 108-109.

C. Justifications Not Accepted by the CJEU

1. Loss of Tax Revenue

282 The Court has **never accepted** the potential loss of tax revenue in cross-border situations as an overriding reason of public interest that can justify restrictive measures, in itself. The CJEU considers that when one Member State loses revenue, another State gains revenue (in an ideal world).[206] The answer is not that straightforward, however, once one takes a closer look at the principle of a balanced allocation of taxing rights. This principle provides that Member States are at liberty to apply restrictive national measures as long as these measures are aimed at ensuring that the economic activities performed in a State's territory are to be taxed in that State (see m.no. 264 et seq.). Thus, in fact, a State might defend itself against base erosion but only within the scope of that justification and subject to the conditions applicable to it (e.g. it must not have given up taxing powers over the same type of income domestically).

2. Difficulties in Obtaining Information

283 The 'difficulties in obtaining information' argument is the unfortunate twin brother of the 'effectiveness of fiscal supervision' justification. It delimits the boundaries beyond which the justification no longer works. As was already mentioned, the Court has been reluctant to accept that difficulties in obtaining information can act as a justification within the European Union for a simple reason – according to the Court there are no such difficulties due to the existence of the Mutual Assistance Directive (see Chapter 9). In principle, the Member States may obtain any information necessary regarding the collection of taxes by requesting that the taxpayer provide sufficient data that can be varified through the Directive – thus there is a presumption of effectiveness in exchanging information within the European Union.[207] Consequently, whenever a Member State has tried to justify a discriminatory provision on the basis that difficulties in obtaining information exist, the CJEU always denies the justification.[208] Furthermore, the Court has **never accepted practical difficulties** in obtaining information from certain Member States as a justification ground, pointing out that it is up to the Member States to make the instrument more effective.[209]

---

206 CJEU, 7 September 2004, Case C-319/02, *Manninen,* EU:C:2004:484; and CJEU, 10 April 2014, Case C-190/12, *Emerging Markets Series of DFA,* EU:C:2014:249, para. 103.

207 CJEU, 27 January 2009, Case C-318/07, *Persche,* EU:C:2009:33, paras. 51-72.

208 There is one theoretical possibility of relying on the need for effectiveness of fiscal supervision in the context of difficulties in obtaining information in intra-Community situations, which is, namely, Art. 17 of the Mutual Assistance Directive on the limits to the exchange of information obligation between the Member States. However, this has never been successfully invoked.

209 See CJEU, 9 October 2014, Case C-326/12, *Caster and Caster,* EU:C:2014:2269, para. 56; CJEU, 11 December 2014, Case C-678/11, *Commission v Spain,* EU:C:2014:2434, para. 61. This 'fundamentalist' approach to administrative cooperation was heavily criticized recently – see Ribeiro, Did the ECJ Go Too Far in *Brisal* (Case C-18/15)?, *ET* 2017, p. 500.

Concerning third countries, it seems that Member States will have increasing **284** difficulty in relying on the effectiveness of fiscal supervision due to the proliferation of international exchange of information agreements. The push for a global automatic exchange of information (AEoI) standard at the OECD level can be expected to further this trend and one can anticipate that the effectiveness of fiscal supervision justification will gradually fade also *vis-à-vis* cooperative third countries.[210]

3. Compensation of Unfavourable Tax Treatment by Other Tax Advantages

In some cases, governments have argued that discrimination may be compen- **285** sated for through other tax advantages. This argument has never been accepted by the CJEU as a justification. The Court has held that a less-favourable treatment cannot be justified on the basis of other advantages, even if such advantages actually exist.[211] In other words, **no balancing exercise between advantages and disadvantages** in a Member State is permissible, beyond instances of cohesion (see m.no. 261) and neutralization (see m.no. 225).

D. Combination of Justifications by the CJEU

If one looks at the case law of the Court, it seems that sometimes one reason, in **286** isolation, is deemed insufficient to justify discriminatory domestic measures. In several cases the Court has considered that some grounds, on their own, were not convincing enough. However, the CJEU has ruled that several justifications might **cumulatively serve as an overriding reason** of public interest. As will be shown, however, subsequent cases have often not supported this view. The Court has come to the rightful conclusion that increasing the quantity of justifications does not necessarily lead to a better legal argument.

Notorious examples, in this respect, are *Marks & Spencer*,[212] *Oy AA* [213] and *X* **287** *Holding*.[214] The Court started with three cumulative justifications in *Marks & Spencer*, reduced them to two in *Oy AA* and, eventually, had to admit that only one can suffice in *X Holding*. What we can observe in these cases, however, is the gradual refinement of the Court of the actual scope of the balanced allocation of taxing powers justification concerning cases of group taxation.

210　A residual area where the justification can still apply in full is the jurisdictions that have been blacklisted by the Union as non-cooperative (see Chapter 2 m.nos. 155).

211　CJEU, 28 January 1986, Case 270/83, *Commission v France ('Avoir Fiscal')*, EU:C:1986:37, para. 21; CJEU, 1 July 2010, Case C-233/09, *Dijkman*, EU:C:2010:397, para 43; CJEU, 10 April 2014, Case C-190/12, *Emerging Markets Series of DFA*, EU:C:2014:249, para. 62 et seq.; and CJEU, 9 October 2014, Case C-326/12, *Caster and Caster*, EU:C:2014:2269, para. 31.

212　CJEU, 13 December 2005, Case C-446/03; *Marks and Spencer*, EU:C:2005:763.

213　CJEU, 18 July 2007, Case C-231/05, *Oy AA*, EU:C:2007:439, para. 60

214　CJEU, 25 February 2010, Case C-337/08, *X Holding*, EU:C:2010:89.

288   It seems that there is also a **tendency** toward cumulative justifications in the case law between balanced allocation of taxing rights and territoriality,[215] and between balanced allocation and anti-abuse.[216] It is doubtful whether stacking these justifications adds any value to the analysis. Concerning the first pair, both balanced allocation of taxing rights and territoriality 'look' at the same phenomenon – jurisdiction to tax. The only difference is that territoriality looks at it at the comparability stage (*Futura Participations* and *AURES Holding*) while balanced allocation looks at it at the justification stage (*X Holding*). Merging balanced allocation and anti-abuse is, however, certainly problematic, as the scope of these justifications is rather different; while the latter targets intentional behaviour aimed at circumventing tax that is normally due (tax avoidance), the former aims to protect the taxing powers of a Member State over the economic activity that took place in its territory even in circumstances that fall short of abuse (a typical example would be a disparity between the tax systems or an exit tax case).

IV. Proportionality

289   Finding a justification that is acceptable to the Court is only the first step in defending discriminatory domestic legislation against the fundamental freedoms. The final stage of the test addresses the proportionality of the measure. A restrictive domestic provision is proportionate if it satisfies **two conditions**: (i) it is suitable to achieving the higher goal protected (the overriding reason of public interest) and (ii) does not go beyond what is necessary to achieve that goal. These conditions are referred to herein as the suitability and necessity tests.

290   The **suitability test** is generally easier to satisfy, as it merely requires that there be a clear and coherent nexus between the measure and the higher goal protected, in the sense that the measure is apt to contribute to the achievement of the goal. For example, in the *Blanco and Fabretti* case the Court found that, although combating compulsive gambling is an acceptable justification related to public health, only taxing winnings from foreign casinos is not apt to contributing to the achievement of that objective, and thus fails the suitability test.[217] More recently, the CJEU ruled that confining measures targeted at environmental protection to the national territory makes such measures inappropriate in terms of achieving their objective, as the matter of environmental protection has a cross-border element.[218]

---

215   CJEU, 29 November 2011, Case C-371/10, *National Grid Indus*, EU:C:2011:785, para. 46; CJEU, 16 April 2015, Case C-591/13, *Commission vs Germany*, EU:C:2015:230, paras. 65 and 69 et seq; CJEU, 21 May 2015, Case C-657/13, *Verder LabTec*, EU:C:2015:331, para. 42 et seq.

216   CJEU, 20 December 2017, Joined Cases C-504/16 and C-613/16, *Deister Holding and Juhler Holding*, EU:C:2017:1009, para. 96; and CJEU, 21 January 2010, Case C-311/08, *Société de Gestion Industrielle*, EU:C:2010:26, para. 69;

217   CJEU, 22 October 2014, Case C-344/13, *Blanco and Fabretti*, EU:C:2014:2311, paras. 44 and 46.

218   CJEU, 22 November 2018, Case C-679/17, *Huijbrechts*, EU:C:2018:940, para. 34.

Compliance with the **necessity test** is much trickier, as it requires Member States **291** to apply the least discriminatory measure that is necessary to achieving the goal. This is the orthodox way of explaining necessity but does not say much. In fact, it is easier to understand and more accurate to say that to comply with the necessity test, a domestic measure must be **tailor-made** such that it catches only those practices that fall within the scope of the justification. This will depend on the justification in each case: (i) if an anti-abuse measure, it must catch only abusive practices but not the genuine exercise of the freedoms of movement; (ii) if the balanced allocation of taxing rights is invoked, the measure cannot completely avoid taking into account foreign losses or the deduction of expenses, merely because they were incurred abroad; (iii) if the effectiveness of fiscal supervision is relied on, the measure must target only cases where fiscal supervision is impeded but not instances where information can be obtained from the foreign tax authorities, the taxpayer, or where obtaining information is irrelevant. In other words, the national legislation must not be too general in nature; rather it has to be carefully drafted and precisely aimed at the objective of the justification. The following paragraphs will provide some concrete examples in this respect.

Starting with the **effectiveness of fiscal supervision and tax collection**, the Court **292** has held that the taxpayer must be given the possibility to produce relevant documentary evidence under a procedure that is not too formal.[219] With respect to third countries, the CJEU maintains that there is no need for the exchange of information agreement to be equivalent in its effect to the Mutual Assistance Directive but rather it has to allow for a sufficient level of cooperation, depending on the case at hand.[220] Furthermore, an obligation on non-resident taxpayers to appoint a domestic tax representative for the purposes of collecting information and withholding taxes is not proportionate, as the foreign company might carry out the related tasks itself.[221] Concerning the effective collection of taxes, the Court held that retention at source is proportionate when the non-resident derives income from the State only on a temporary basis.[222]

Regarding the **balanced allocation of taxing rights** justification, the Court has **293** not been particularly consistent. First, with respect to exit taxation, both *National Grid Indus*[223] and *N.*[224] concerned exit taxation of uncrystallised capital gains with

---

219   CJEU, 11 October 2007, Case C-451/05, *Elisa*, EU:C:2007:594; see as well CJEU, 27 November 2008, Case C-418/07, *Société Papillon*, EU:C:2008:659, para. 54 et seq.; and CJEU, 9 October 2014, Case C-326/12, *Caster and Caster*, EU:C:2014:2269, para. 49;

220   CJEU, 10 February 2011, Joined Cases C-436/08 and C-437/08, *Haribo Lakritzen and Österreichische Salinen*, EU:C:2011:61, paras. 73-74; and CJEU, 10 April 2014, Case C-190/12, *Emerging Markets Series of DFA*, EU:C:2014:249, para. 88.

221   See CJEU, 29 September 2011, Case C-387/10, *Commission v Austria*, EU:C:2011:625, para. 27 et seq.

222   CJEU, 19 June 2014, Joined Cases C-53/13 and C-80/13, *Strojírny Prostějov*, EU:C:2014:2011, para. 48 et seq.

223   CJEU, 29 November 2011, Case C-371/10, *National Grid Indus*, EU:C:2011:785, para. 58;

224   CJEU, 7 September 2006, Case C-470/04, *N.*, EU:C:2006:525. Recently, the Court also upheld its case law regarding exit taxation of natural persons with respect to the EU-Switzerland agreement. See CJEU, 26 February 2019, Case C-581/17, *Wächtler*, EU:C:2019:138.

the only difference being that the taxpayer in *National Grid Indus* was a legal entity and, in the *N.* case, was a natural person. However, in the former case, the Court concluded that the home State should not take into account a decrease in an asset's value after a change of residence, while in the latter, it must take into account such a decrease and not doing so would be disproportionate. It seems that, following *Commission v Portugal*, the Court has aligned the treatment of natural and legal persons by ruling that the State of former residence is also not obliged to take into account any subsequent capital losses with regard to individuals.[225] However, at the same time, the Court held that the home Member State must indeed provide a credit for subsequent losses when taxation is deferred in the context of the Merger Directive, coming to the opposite conclusion to the one under *National Grid Indus* and *Commission v Portugal*.[226]

294 Second, concerning group taxation, the proportionality analysis in *Marks & Spencer*[227] regarding the **'finality of losses'** argument is one that is challenging to understand not only from a technical point of view (when losses are 'final') but also conceptually. The idea of the Court is that when a foreign subsidiary[228] or a PE exhausts all options for its losses to be taken into account in the host State and has no income in that State (i.e. the losses are 'final'), the State of the parent must consider the remaining final losses.[229] It seems that the Court is of the understanding that a measure based on the balanced allocation of taxing rights will be disproportionate if it results in a situation in which losses are not offset anywhere. However, it is hard to comprehend why the Member State of the parent has to provide relief for losses that have nothing to do with it or with any economic activity performed in its territory.[230] It is precisely the essence of the principle of the balanced allocation of taxing rights that a Member State must exercise tax jurisdiction over profits and losses in harmony. Thus, a national measure that excludes losses of foreign subsidiaries and exempted PEs is precisely tailormade to the principle of a balanced allocation of taxing rights. It seems that the underlying idea behind this line of case law is the understanding of the Court that losses have to be deducted

---

225   CJEU, 21 December 2016, Case C-503/14, *Commission v Portugal*, EU:C:2016:979, paras. 55-56.

226   CJEU, 22 March 2018, Joined Cases C-327/16 and C-421/16, *Jacob* and *Lassus*, EU:C:2018:210, paras. 82-83. For a more detailed explanation as to the difference between *Lassus*, on the one hand, and *National Grid Indus* and *Commission v Portugal*, on the other, see Opinion of Advocate General Wathelet, 15 November 2017, Joined Cases C-327/16 and C-421/16, *Jacob* and *Lassus*, EU:C:2017:865, paras. 84-94.

227   CJEU, 13 December 2005, Case C-446/03; *Marks and Spencer*, EU:C:2005:763, para. 54 et seq.

228   For the final losses doctrine to apply, the foreign subsidiary might be indirectly owned to the extent that the subsidiary and the sub-subsidiary are established in the same Member State. See CJEU, 19 June 2019, Case C-608/17, *Holmen AB*, EU:C:2019:511, paras. 20-33.

229   CJEU, 12 June 2018, Case C-650/16, *Bevola*, EU:C:2018:424, paras. 63-64. However, when all options for taking into account foreign losses will be exhausted is a recurring question under the case law. It remains unclear whether the matter concerns legal or factual impossibility. See, for example, CJEU, 19 June 2019, Case C-607/17, *Memira Holding*, EU:C:2019:510.

230   Wattel, Non-Discrimination a la Cour: The ECJ's (Lack of) Comparability Analysis in Direct Tax Cases, *ET* 2015, p. 549.

somewhere.[231] Strikingly, at the same time, the Court accepts that there is no obligation on Member States to remedy international double taxation,[232] which is essentially the same phenomenon. In one case, it arises due to the parallel exercise of taxing powers (double taxation) and, in the other, because of the parallel non-exercise of taxing powers (double non-deduction).[233]

Fortunately, the proportionality test in **anti-abuse** cases is easier to follow, to the **295** extent that anti-avoidance is seen as a justification (as mentioned in m.no. 269 when abuse is treated as a general principle, there is no proportionality test). It is the Court's view that the national anti-avoidance measure has to be drafted such that it allows for an individual assessment of the existence of tax avoidance, as defined by the CJEU. Thus, neither a general presumption of abuse is allowed, nor national legislation that is so broad that it encompasses, alongside abusive practices, the genuine exercise of the fundamental freedoms.[234] In other words, the anti-abuse provision must allow all 'good' cases to fall outside its scope in order to be proportionate. There are a few other elements to the proportionality test when relying on the anti-abuse justification. First, the State must provide an opportunity to the taxpayer to provide a commercial justification for the transaction and, second, any tax adjustment by the authorities must not go beyond the arm's-length standard when the case concerns related enterprises.[235] Moreover, the Court recently went as far as ruling that a private party must be given the opportunity to put forward commercial reasons for deviating from the arm's-length principle, based on its economic interest to have a financially successful subsidiary.[236] There are enough reasons to consider that such broad interpretation of the 'commercial justifications' requirement might erode the arm's length principle.

Literature

Schön, The Concept of Abuse of Law in European Taxation: A Methodological and Constitutional Perspective, *Working Paper of the Max Planck Institute for Tax Law and Public Finance* No. 2019-18; Ismer/Kandel, A Finale Incomparabile to the Saga of Definitive Losses? Deduction of Foreign Losses and Fundamental Freedoms After Bevola and Sofina, *Intertax* 2019; Bundgaard/Schmidt/Laursen/Aarup, European Union – When Are Domestic Anti-Avoidance Rules in Breach of Primary and Secondary EU Law? – Comments Based on Recent ECJ Decisions, *ET* 2018; Cordewener, Anti-Abuse Measures in the Area of Direct Taxation: Towards

---

231 Ibid, p. 549.
232 CJEU, 12 February 2009, Case C-67/08, *Block,* EU:C:2009:92.
233 Wattel, Non-Discrimination a la Cour: The ECJ's (Lack of) Comparability Analysis in Direct Tax Cases, *ET* 2015, pp. 549-550.
234 CJEU, 20 December 2017, Joined Cases C-504/16 and C-613/16, *Deister Holding and Juhler Holding,* EU:C:2017:1009, paras. 61-62.
235 CJEU, 3 October 2013, Case C-282/12, *Itelcar,* EU:C:2013:629, paras. 37-38.
236 CJEU, 31 May 2018, Case C-382/16, *Hornbach-Baumarkt,* EU:C:2018:366, para. 56.

Converging Standards under Treaty Freedoms and EU Directives?, *EC Tax Review* 2017; de Groot, Case *X* (C-283/15) and the Myth of '*Schumacker*'s 90% Rule, *Intertax* 2017; Dourado, The EU Free Movement of Capital and Third Countries: Recent Developments, *Intertax* 2017; Freyer, The Proportionality Principle under EU Tax Law: General and Practical Problems Caused by Its Extensive Application, Parts 1 and 2, *ET* 2017; Lang, Double Taxation Conventions in the Case Law of the CJEU, *Intertax* 2018; Peeters, *Kieback*: When *Schumacker* Emigrates, *EC Tax Review* 2016; Schön, Neutrality and Territoriality – Competing or Converging Concepts in European Tax Law? *BIT* 2015, p. 271; Smit, International Income Allocation under EU Tax Law: Tinker, Tailor, Soldier, Sailor, *EC Tax Review* 2017; Wattel, Non-Discrimination à la Cour: The ECJ's (Lack of) Comparability Analysis in Direct Tax Cases, *ET* 2015; Weber/da Silva, *From Marks & Spencer to X Holding. The Future of Cross-border Group Taxation* (2011); Werner Haslehner, 'Avoir Fiscal' and Its Legacy after Thirty Years of Direct Tax Jurisprudence of the Court of Justice, *Intertax* 2016; Zalasiński, Tax Rules Applicable without Distinction and the EU Internal Market Freedoms – An Analysis of Recent Case Law Regarding Taxation of Investment Income, *ET* 2017.

Chapter 4 – The State Aid Provisions of the TFEU in Tax Matters

Alexandra Miladinovic[1]

---

1   This chapter was co-authored by Marie-Ann Kronthaler and Yinon Tzubery in the 4th edition of this book but has been substantially reworked from the fifth edition onwards.

I. Background to the EU Prohibition of State Aid

296 The competition policy of the EU was developed to ensure **fair competition, proper functioning of markets and a competitive economy** within the internal market. Similar to competition rules applicable to cartels, abuse of dominance, forms of commercial cooperation and merger control, State aid control is part of the EU **rules on competition**. The State aid prohibition is laid down in **Art. 107(1) of the Treaty on the Functioning of the European Union (hereinafter TFEU)**,[2] which provides: "*Save as otherwise provided in the Treaties, any aid granted by a Member State or through State resources in any form whatsoever which distorts or threatens to distort competition by favouring certain undertakings or the production of certain goods shall, in so far as it affects trade between Member States, be incompatible with the internal market.*" In short, it prohibits the provision of **advantages**, in any form, by national **public authorities** to **undertakings** on a **selective basis**. In particular, Art. 107(1) TFEU only applies to aid granted by Member States, which means that Union aid is not covered by the prohibition.[3] Nevertheless, the latter might have repercussions on the international arena, such as WTO law, where other prohibitions on subsidies exist.[4]

297 In general, prohibited State aid exists if **four cumulative conditions** are fulfilled:[5] First, the measure confers an advantage on its recipients that puts them in a more favourable position than other undertakings or relieves them of charges that are normally borne by undertakings. Second, the advantage is granted by the state or through State resources. Third, the advantage conferred is selective in that it favours "*certain undertakings or the production of certain goods*". Fourth, the measure affects competition and trade between Member States.

298 For more than two decades now, the Commission has been applying the prohibition against State aid under Art. 107(1) TFEU to tax matters. In addition to the State aid rules laid down under primary EU law, it has been using an array of "soft law" instruments, such as communications, notices and other non-binding instruments, to tackle harmful tax competition, promote good governance and combat corporate tax avoidance. In contrast to hard law, soft law is typically characterized by having no binding force.[6] One of the most relevant soft law instruments in the area of State aid provided by the Commission is the Notice on the notion of State aid as referred to in Art. 107(1) TFEU (hereinafter: Notion of aid notice).

---

2   Consolidated version of the Treaty on the Functioning of the European Union of 13 December 2007, OJ C 326 of 26 October 2012.

3   Englisch, Equality under State aid rules and VAT, *World Journal of VAT/GST Law* 8/2019, p. 22.

4   Hofmann, in: Hofmann/Micheau (eds.), *State aid law of the European Union* (2016) p. 36 et seq.

5   Commission Notice on the notion of State aid as referred to in Article 107 (1) of the Treaty on the Functioning of the European Union (hereinafter: Notion of aid notice), OJ C 262 of 19 July 2016, para. 5.

6   See Art. 288 TFEU.

The Commission published the Notion of aid notice to ensure that its decisions **299** were predictable and that equal treatment was guaranteed. The Notice repealed and replaced the former Commission Notice on the application of the State aid rules to measures relating to direct business taxation (hereinafter: Notice on business taxation) of 1998.[7] The Notion of aid notice, having a broader scope than the previous notice, provides further clarification on State aid concepts in general, includes recent jurisprudence and gives substantial guidance on fiscal State aid in particular. With the guidelines provided therein, the Commission aims to clarify its understanding of the State aid rules and sets out how they should be construed with regard to issues that have not yet been decided by the General Court (GC) or the Court of Justice (CJEU).[8]

Soft law instruments, such as the Notion of aid notice, establish rules of practice **300** designed to produce external effects.[9] Despite the fact that they have not been attributed legally binding force, the CJEU has held that the Commission is bound by the acts it adopts on its own.[10] In adopting rules of conduct and announcing that they will apply to the cases to which they relate, the Commission imposes a limit on the exercise of its discretion.[11] After issuing such rules, the Commission can no longer depart from them without having regard to the general principles of law, such as the principle of equal treatment or the protection of legitimate expectations.[12] To the extent that the Commission does not observe the self-binding effect of its own rules or give valid reasons for the departure in an individual case, it is infringing on the right to good administration, which is laid down in Art. 41 of the EU Charter.

In principle, the prohibition against State aid serves a **dual purpose**: First, it **prevents** **301** **waste** of public resources via inefficient subsidies and therefore helps Member States manage their budgets more wisely and employ the correct priorities.[13] Second, it **prevents the crowding out of efficient private investments** by preserving a competitive and open internal market. Competition, in turn, contributes to spurring more growth in the internal market and the achievement of overall welfare gains.[14]

Nevertheless, State subsidies are **not always** a negative phenomenon. Public **302** intervention is **fully justified** – and in fact needed – where it is put in place to target **market failures** and thereby complement, not replace, private spending.[15] Therefore, State aid may be required **to provide goods and services that the market would not deliver** on fair and equal terms. "**Good aid**" should be granted if there

---

7   Commission Notice on the application of the State aid rules to measures relating to direct business taxation (hereinafter: Notice on business taxation), OJ C 384 of 10 December 1998.
8   Notion of aid notice, para. 3 et seq.
9   Stefan, *Soft Law in Court* (2013) p. 15 et seq.
10   CJEU, 28 June 2005, Joined Cases C-189/02 P, *Dansk Rørindustri v Commission*, EU:C:2005:408, para. 210.
11   Ibid., para. 211; see also Stefan, *Soft Law in Court* (2013) p. 167 et seq.
12   Ibid., para. 209.
13   Hofmann, in: Hofmann/Micheau (eds.), *State aid law of the European Union* (2016) p. 10 et seq.
14   Ibid., p. 6-9.
15   Communication on EU State aid Modernisation, COM (2012) 209 final of 8 May 2012, para. 12.

is no better market alternative and it aims to **induce its beneficiaries** to undertake necessary economic activities that they would not undertake without the aid.[16] For this reason, the prohibition of State aid is not absolute and provides for **exceptions under Art. 107(2) and (3) TFEU**.

303 The TFEU gives the **Commission** the responsibility, under a system of **prior authorization**, to make sure that Member States only conceive and design aid measures that help companies produce goods and services that would **otherwise not be provided in the internal market**, and not measures that **distort competition** by strengthening particular regions or sectors to the detriment of the economy as a whole.[17] Member States **must not put** their proposed aid **into effect** until the Commission has **approved** it.[18] The Commission's decision is subject to a two-tier judicial review by the GC and the CJEU.[19]

II. The Code of Conduct

304 The **Code of Conduct for Business Taxation**, adopted by the Council of Economics and Finance Ministers (ECOFIN), constitutes an important soft law instrument concluded with the intention of preventing harmful tax competition.[20] The Code of Conduct is **not legally binding**, but rather a **political commitment** made by the Member States.[21] In establishing the Code, the Council emphasized that *"some of the tax measures covered by this code may fall within the scope of the provisions on State aid."*[22] Regarding the relationship between the Code of Conduct and the State aid rules, it is important to emphasize that both may apply in parallel and that the *"qualification of a tax measure as harmful under the code of conduct does not affect its possible qualification as a State aid."*[23]

305 With the Code of Conduct, the Member States have undertaken not to introduce new tax measures that are harmful (standstill obligation) and to re-examine their existing laws and established practices in order to eliminate harmful measures quickly (rollback obligation).[24] Even though the obligations and the scope of application of the State aid rules and Code of Conduct seem to be quite similar, there are major differences in terms of the legal consequences. In particular, the obligation to recover the amount of illegal aid granted by a Member State exists only under State aid law.

---

16   Quigley, *European State aid law and policy* (2015) p. 255.
17   Council Regulation (EU) 2015/1589 laying down detailed rules for the application of Article 108 of the Treaty on the Functioning of the European Union (hereinafter: Procedural Regulation), OJ L 248 of 24 September 2015, para. 2.
18   Art. 108(3) TFEU; Art. 3 Procedural Regulation.
19   Art. 256(1) TFEU; Hancher, in: Hancher et al. (eds.), *EU State aids* (2016) para. 1-053.
20   Council Resolution on the code of conduct for business taxation (hereinafter: Code of Conduct), OJ C 2/2 of 6 January 1998.
21   Moutarlier, in: Richelle et al. (eds.), *State aid and business taxation* (2016) p. 77.
22   Code of Conduct, para. J.
23   Notice on business taxation, para. 30.
24   Code of Conduct, paras. C and D.

As mentioned, the Commission is not bound by any solutions of the Code of **306** Conduct Group particularly due to the soft-law character of the Code. Since the Code was not issued by the Commission, there is no self-binding effect.[25] It does, however, have major influence on the Commission's practice. When the Code of Conduct Group declared that the IP box regimes established in some Member States were harmful because they did not comply with the modified nexus approach endorsed, the States concerned agreed to amend their existing regimes.[26] Although the Commission clearly expressed doubts as to the compatibility of IP box regimes with State aid rules,[27] it stopped pursuing further investigations as soon as political agreement was reached among the Member States.[28] Nevertheless, it must be kept in mind that neither the declaration of the circumstances in which IP box regimes are not considered harmful for the purposes of the Code of Conduct, nor the fact that the amendments were endorsed by the Council have any binding effect on the Commission's capacity to initiate State aid proceedings.[29]

III. The Application of the Prohibition of State Aid in Tax Matters

For decades, the Commission has been applying the State aid prohibition, which **307** is part of competition law, to tax matters. While the Commission did not initially pay particular attention to tax law, in recent years it has been increasingly challenging Member States' tax measures under the State aid rules.

As will be further discussed in Section V.B., State aid can be granted through var- **308** ious means. In tax matters, the typical form of aid is granted via legislation, i.e. a legal provision that applies to a group of taxpayers that display specific characteristics. As with any other legal norm, it is generally applicable and addresses the group of taxpayers in an abstract way ("general" State aid). State aid can also be granted through targeted measures that individually address particular taxpayers ("targeted" State aid), such as advance pricing agreements (APA), tax rulings, and tax assessment notices issued by tax administrations. In recent years, there has been a shift from scrutinizing "general" State aid towards examining "targeted" State aid. The following section focuses, in particular, on the Commission's recent approach to scrutinizing targeted State aid.

In 2014, hundreds of tax rulings issued by Luxembourg tax authorities were **309** leaked and made available to the public following a journalistic investigation. The normal function of tax rulings is to establish, in advance, the application of national

---

25 See para. 307 of this Chapter.
26 Council, 16846/14 FISC 233 ECOFIN 1196 of 11 December 2014.
27 Press Release, IP/14/309 (24 March 2014).
28 Commission Communication, COM(2015) 302, p. 10; Panayi, *Advanced issues in International and European tax law* (2015) Chapter 5.6.
29 Wittmann, Patent boxes and their compatibility with European Union State aid rules, in: Kerschner/ Somare (eds.), *Taxation in a global digital economy* (2017) p. 423 et seq.

tax law to a particular case and to lay down the methods through which transfer pricing for intra-group transactions within a corporate group is to be determined to be considered at arm's length in order to provide legal certainty to taxpayers.[30] The revelation accused Luxembourg authorities of granting favourable tax treatment to multinational enterprises via this tool.[31]

310 The incident, commonly known as the "Luxembourg Leaks" or "LuxLeaks", motivated the Commission to open a number of investigations against Luxembourg and other Member States in respect of their tax ruling practices.[32] The Commission's inquiry led to the initiation of formal investigation procedures with regard to tax rulings granted by Belgium (Belgian Excess Profit Tax Scheme),[33] Ireland (Apple),[34] Luxembourg (Fiat, Amazon, McDonalds, Engie)[35] and the Netherlands (Starbucks, IKEA, Nike).[36] In all of the cases yet to be decided,[37] the Commission has concluded that the rulings issued in favour of multinational enterprises by the respective tax administrations constituted illegal State aid, with the result that it has ordered the recovery of up to EUR 13 billion. Except for the decision in the McDonalds case, which was decided in favour of Luxembourg,[38] the Commission's decisions were appealed and brought before the GC. The GC issued decisions in the Fiat, Starbucks and Apple cases,[39] albeit with different results: While the GC upheld the decision in the Fiat case, it annulled the Commission's decision in the Starbucks and Apple cases. Although the GC agreed with the Commission's arguments in substance, it found that the Commission had not succeeded in providing sufficent proof of the existence of a selective advantage.[40] The decision concerning the Fiat case was appealed and is now pending before the CJEU.[41]

---

30   Notion of aid notice, para. 169; Lyal, Transfer pricing rules and State aid, 38 *Fordham Int'l L.J.* 2015, p. 1017.
31   Jaeger, From Santander to Luxleaks – and back, EStAL 3/2015, p. 355.
32   Giraud/Petit, Tax rulings and State aid qualification: should reality matter?, EStAL 2/2017, p. 233.
33   Press Release, IP/15/4080 (3 February 2015); GC, 14 February 2019, Joined Cases T-131/16 and T-263/16, *Belgium v Commission (Magnetrol)*, EU:T:2019:91.
34   Press Release, IP/14/663 (11 June 2014).
35   Press Release, IP/14/663 (11 June 2014); Press Release, IP 15-5166 (11 June 2015); Press Release, IP 15-6221 (3 December 2015); Press Release, IP 16-3085 (19 September 2016).
36   Press Release, IP/14/663 (11 June 2014); Press Release, IP 17-5343 (18 December 2017), Press Release, IP 19-322 (10 January 2019).
37   So far, negative decisions have been issued in the Amazon (Press Release IP 17-3701, 4 October 2017), Apple (Press Release IP 16-2923, 30 August 2016), Belgian Excess Profit Scheme (Press Release IP 16-42, 11 January 2016), Starbucks and Fiat cases (Press Release IP 15-5881, 21 October 2015).
38   Press Release, IP/18/5831 (19 September 2018).
39   GC, 24 September 2019, Joined Cases T-755/15 and T-759/15, *Fiat Chrysler Finance Europe*, EU:T:2019:670; GC, 24 September 2019, T-760/15 and T-636/16, *Starbucks Manufacturing Emea BV*, EU:T:2019:669; GC, 15 July 2020, T-778/16 and T-892/16, *Ireland and Apple Sales International v Commission*, ECLI:EU:T:2020:338.
40   GC, 24 September 2019, Joined Cases T-760/15 and T-636/16, *Starbucks Manufacturing Emea BV*, EU:T:2019:669, para. 559; GC, 15 July 2020, T-778/16 and T-892/16, *Ireland and Apple Sales International v Commission*, ECLI:EU:T:2020:338, para. 312.
41   Appeal Case before the Court of Justice C-885/19 P and C-898/19 P.

To clarify its current approach, the Commission published a Working Paper on State aid and tax rulings, which explains its own understanding of arm's length pricing and provides guidance on how a market-based outcome is to be determined correctly in order to be in line with Art. 107 TFEU.[42] Moreover, the Commission states that the OECD Transfer Pricing Guidelines, which have been established on the basis of international consensus, provide useful guidance on how to achieve such an outcome. According to the Commission, a tax ruling endorsing an arrangement based on the OECD Transfer Pricing Guidelines "*is unlikely to give rise to State aid.*"[43] In this respect, it must be noted that, as with all soft law instruments it issues, the Commission is bound by its own guidance provided in the Working Paper and may not depart from it without having regard to the general principles of EU law.[44]   **311**

The Commission's decisions in the transfer pricing cases have been heavily criticized both from a legal and political perspective.[45] Shortly after the final decisions in the rulings cases were issued, the U.S. Treasury published a White Paper addressing the Commission and challenging its recent decision-making practice.[46] Moreover, while the Commission is arguing that the arm's length principle is inherent in Art. 107(1) TFEU, it has proposed formulary apportionment in the re-launch of the Common Consolidated Corporate Tax Base (CCCTB) proposal.[47] Global formulary apportionment is considered an alternative to a system based on the arm's length principle and might therefore even conflict with primary EU law.[48]   **312**

In the wake of the "LuxLeaks" and following recent OECD developments in the course of the base erosion and profiting shifting (BEPS) project,[49] the Commission proposed a tax transparency package to fight tax evasion and avoidance, which was adopted by the Council. It consists, among other things, in mandatory automatic exchange of tax rulings and country-by-country (CbC) reporting to enhance transparency in the field of transfer pricing.[50]   **313**

---

42 DG Competition Working Paper on State aid and tax rulings, 3 June 2016 (hereinafter: Working Paper).

43 Notion of aid notice, para. 173; Working Paper, para. 18; Nicolaides, State aid rules and tax rulings, EStAL 3/2016, p. 420.

44 For the self-binding effect of soft law see also Stefan, *Soft Law in Court* (2013) p. 167 et seq.

45 Gonzalez, State aid and tax competition: comments on the EC's decisions on transfer pricing rulings, EStAL 4/2016, p. 556 et seq.

46 US Treasury, White Paper. The European Commission's recent State aid investigations of transfer pricing rulings, 24 August 2016.

47 Proposal for a Council Directive on a Common Corporate Tax Base, COM(2016) 683 final 2016/0336 of 25 October 2016.

48 OECD, *Transfer pricing guidelines for multinational enterprises and tax administrations* (2017) p. 39 et seq.; see also Llinares/Madelpuech, Apple and the CCCTB: can the European Commission have both? *Tax Notes Int'l* 2017, p. 557.

49 BEPS OECD Action Plan and BEPS Final Reports.

50 See Chapter 9 for further on this point.

IV. General Issues Raised by the Application of State Aid in Tax Matters

A. The Prohibition of State Aid and Direct Taxation. Harmonization of Direct Taxes through the Backdoor?

314 Since the Member States did not want to give up their sovereignty in direct tax matters when establishing and acceding to the EU, competence in respect of direct tax law, as opposed to indirect tax law, has remained, to a great extent, with the Member States. According to Art. 115 TFEU, a unanimous vote by the Member States is required to reach agreement to harmonize legislation concerning direct taxation. The persistent fruitless attempts to conclude the CCCTB, for example, show that it is very difficult to achieve consensus among the EU Member States. Nevertheless, the Member States need to respect EU principles and cannot use their tax sovereignty as an excuse to disregard the main rules, particularly the State aid prohibition.

315 The Commission has been increasingly focussing on identifying aid within individual corporate taxation. However, looking into each ruling and dictating how the Member States' tax authorities should apply national tax laws arguably constrains the tax sovereignty that Member States continue to want to retain. For this reason, the Commission has been heavily criticized for extending its competences conferred by the TFEU. With merit, it has been argued that direct tax law is secretly being harmonized through the application of competition law to individual direct taxation despite the reluctance of the Member States in this regard.

316 For the sake of completeness, it must be mentioned that, in fact, there is a legal competence under Art. 116 TFEU allowing the Council to adopt directives by way of a majority vote (instead of unanimity) in matters falling under the exclusive competence of the Member States to eliminate distortions of competition created by "*a difference between the provisions [...] in Member States.*" If the distortive effect of disparities were to be considered serious enough, the Council could rely on this authorization. However, this legal basis has not been utilized in the tax law area to date.[51]

B. The Prohibition of State Aid and Indirect Taxation

317 For many years, the focus on fiscal State aid was mainly in the field of **direct business taxation**. However, the Commission has started to apply the principles laid down in the former Notice on business taxation in analyzing certain cases in the area of **indirect taxation** as well.[52]

---

51 Wattel, in: Richelle et al. (eds.), *State aid and business taxation* (2016) p. 70.
52 Report on the implementation of the Commission notice on the application of the State aid rules to measures relating to direct business taxation, COM(2004)434 of 9 February 2004, para. 71.

As indirect taxes are mostly harmonized within the EU, the crucial question **318** may be the extent to which a measure can be attributable to the State.[53] **VAT, in particular,** has been extensively harmonized through EU legislation that must be implemented by all Member States.[54] The same is true for **excise taxes**, which have also been harmonized at the EU level.[55] As a rule, a measure granted by a State on the basis of a provision transposed into national law in accordance with its obligation to implement EU legislation may not be qualified as State aid.[56] This applies for both mandatory provisions in a directive, as well as options included therein that the Member States can choose to apply.[57] Only where EU legislation leaves room for discretion to unilaterally grant specific advantages, can the measure be imputable to the Member State and, therefore, State aid could arise.[58]

C. The Prohibition of State Aid and the Fundamental Freedoms

The prohibition of State aid, like the prohibition of discrimination (Art. 18 TFEU), **319** the freedom of establishment (Art. 49 TFEU), and the free movement of services (Art. 56 TFEU), capital (Art. 63 TFEU) and workers (Art. 45 TFEU), has been designed to ensure that free competition in the internal market is not distorted. While the State aid rules are aimed at ensuring that Member States do not provide selective advantages to certain undertakings to the detriment of others, the fundamental freedoms are designed to remove barriers to the free movement of services, goods, capital and persons.[59]

It is important to stress that the scope of the prohibition on State aid is much **320** broader than that of the fundamental freedoms. The latter prohibit discrimination of cross-border activities carried out by individuals, as well as undertakings, in inbound and outbound situations. By contrast, the State aid prohibition is also applied in purely domestic situations and disallows any form of discrimination that involves the granting of an advantage to particular undertakings.[60] However, the prohibition of State aid and the fundamental freedoms can be seen as two sides of the same coin: Measures that put, for instance, resident undertakings in a better position than non-resident ones typically do not fall within the ambit of the fundamental freedoms, but may be covered by the scope of the State aid rules.

---

53   Englisch, EU State aid rules applied to indirect tax measures, *EC Tax Review* 2013/1, p. 15.
54   CJEU, 23 April 2009, Case C-460/07, *Puffer*, EU:C:2009:254, para. 70.
55   E.g. Energy taxation Directive 2003/96/EC, OJ L 283/51 of 27 October 2003.
56   CJEU, 5 April 2006, Case T-351/02, *Deutsche Bahn AG v Commission*, EU:T:2006:104, paras. 101-103; Terra, Value Added Tax and State aid law in the EU, in: van Arendonk (eds.), *VAT in an EU and International perspective* (2011) p. 316.
57   Quigley, *European State aid law and policy* (2015) p. 33.
58   Notion of aid notice, para. 44.
59   Micheau, Fundamental freedoms and State aid rules under EU law: the example of taxation, *ET* 2012, p. 213.
60   Szudoczky, Convergence of the analysis of national tax measures under the EU State aid rules and the fundamental freedoms, *EStAL* 3/2016, p. 363 et seq.

321 As mentioned, the Commission is the competent authority to assess the compatibility of State aid. To ensure a consistent application of the State aid rules, the CJEU has held that where an aid measure violates another provision of the Treaty, e.g. the fundamental freedoms, the Commission cannot find it to be compatible with the internal market.[61] Nevertheless, the fact that the Commission has authorized a measure does not automatically render the measure immune from a potential conflict with the fundamental freedoms. In the *A-Fonds* case, the CJEU decided that, due to the division of powers, the national courts cannot rule, in particular, on the compatibility of a criterion with the fundamental freedoms, if this criterion is part of a State aid scheme.[62] Otherwise, the national courts would indirectly have to assess the compatibility of the scheme with the fundamental freedoms, a decision which lies solely within the competence of the Commission. Considering the discrimination-based approach under the State aid rules, overlaps with the restrictions under the fundamental freedoms cannot be excluded. In case of doubt, the national courts might decide to refrain from assessing measures with respect to their compatibility with the fundamental freedoms, which seems counterproductive to the principle of effectiveness of EU law.

322 Yet, it is possible that a national measure will fall under the scope of both the fundamental freedoms and the State aid prohibition, for instance, in respect of a tax imposed only on non-resident undertakings.[63] The consequences of this overlap are yet to be decided.[64] In particular, the result of a dual infringement of both the fundamental freedoms and the State aid rules could be problematic when it comes to legal consequences because of their opposite effects: An infringement of the State aid prohibition requires the Member State concerned to recover the aid, including interest, at a rate fixed by the Commission, from all undertakings that have received the benefit. Recovery is ordered upon a negative decision of the Commission and is to be implemented retroactively for a period of up to 10 years despite any statute of limitations (see section VIII. D. of this Chapter).[65] As regards aid that has not yet been awarded, the standstill obligation applies, which obliges the Member State to stop granting the aid concerned. In contrast to the State aid consequence, where the beneficiaries' advantage is removed and neutralized, the primacy of the fundamental freedoms may force the Member States to extend the application of the more advantageous rule to all taxpayers.[66] For example, a breach of the fundamental freedoms allows undertakings that have paid the tax at issue and hence were placed at a disadvantage to be reimbursed by the Member State

---

61 CJEU, 19 September 2000, Case C-156/98, *Commission v Germany*, EU:C:2000:467, para. 78.

62 CJEU, 2 May 2019, Case C-598/17, *A-Fonds*, EU:C:2019:352, para. 52 et seq.

63 CJEU, 22 March 1977, Case 74/76, *Iannelli & Volpi*, EU:C:1977:51, para. 9.

64 CJEU, 17 November 2009, Case C-169/08, *Presidente del Consiglio dei Ministri v Regione Sardegna*, EU:C:2009:709.

65 Art. 16 Procedural Regulation; see also Notice from the Commission – Towards an effective implementation of Commission decisions ordering Member States to recover unlawful and incompatible State aid (hereinafter: Recovery notice), OJ C 272 of 15 November 2007, para. 39.

66 Lang, Seminar J: Steuerrecht, Grundfreiheiten und Beihilfeverbot, *IStR* 2010, p. 578 et seq.

in ongoing proceedings.[67] The issue of the application of legal consequences in a situation of overlapping applicability of both the State aid rules and the fundamental freedom provisions is yet to be resolved by the CJEU.[68]

In order to provide clarity and avoid overlap, the CJEU developed the "severability **323** test" according to which elements of State aid that lead to preferential treatment of e.g. particular domestic products should be addressed under the State aid rules and not under the fundamental freedoms.[69] As the Court stated in *Iannelli & Volpi*, "*those aspects of aid which contravene specific provisions of the Treaty other than Articles 107 and 108 [...] may be so indissolubly linked to the object of the aid that it is impossible to evaluate them separately so that their effect on the compatibility or incompatibility of aid viewed as a whole must therefore of necessity be determined in the light of the procedure described in Article 108.*"[70]

Even though the application of the severability test has been repeatedly confirmed **324** in later jurisprudence, the interplay between the fundamental freedoms and the State aid prohibition is still not perfectly clear.[71] For example, it could be questioned whether approval of an aid measure may constitute a proper justification ground based on the rule of reason.[72]

V. The Prohibition of State Aid under Art. 107(1) TFEU

As explained in section I., four conditions need to be fulfilled for a measure to be **325** considered State aid. Thus, to fall under Art. 107(1) TFEU, a Member State must (1) grant an advantage (2) out of State resources to (3) particular undertakings on a selective basis and (4) this advantage might distort competition and affect trade. Before taking a deeper look at these four criteria, the notion of "undertaking" needs to be explained, since only undertakings are covered by the scope of the State aid prohibition.

A. Undertaking

The prohibition of State aid applies only when the beneficiary, regardless of its **326** legal form of organization or means of being financed, is engaged in economic

---

67 There are only limited exceptions where breach of legal force could be required; see CJEU, 18 July 2007, Case C-119/05, *Lucchini*, EU:C:2007:434, para. 63.

68 Micheau, Fundamental freedoms and State aid rules under EU law: the example of taxation, *ET* 2012, p. 213; Opinion of Advocate General Kokott 16 April 2015, Case C-66/14, *Finanzamt Linz* [2015], para. 4.

69 CJEU, 22 March 1977, Case 74/76, *Iannelli & Volpi*, EU:C:1977:51, para. 14.

70 Ibid.

71 E.g. CJEU, 23 April 2002, Case C-234/99, *Nygard*, EU:C:2002:244, para. 56; GC, 31 January 2001, Case T-197/97, *Weyl Beef Products BV*, EU:T:2001:28, para. 77; GC, 13 May 2015, Case T-511/09, *Niki Luftfahrt GmbH*, EU:T:2015:284, para. 216; see also Szudoczky, *The sources of EU law and their relationships: lessons for the field of taxation* (2013) p. 659 et seq.

72 Staes, The combined application of the fundamental freedoms and the EU State aid rules: in search of a way out of a maze, *Intertax* 2014, p. 118.

activities. Moreover, the concept of "undertaking" is not necessarily limited to separate legal entities. An economic unit, consisting of several separate legal entities, may be considered to be the relevant "undertaking" as well.[73] An economic activity, in this regard, is any activity consisting in offering goods and services on a given market.[74] Therefore, the notion of "undertaking" in Art. 107(1) TFEU must be interpreted accordingly.

327 Hence, the performance of economic activities and the existence of an "undertaking" presupposes the existence of a market.[75] It can be debated though whether this criterion is the most suitable for the application of the State aid rules since the decision about the creation of markets might depend on the Member States' own (legislative) choices.[76] Therefore, e.g. establishing a monopoly, cannot act as a shield from State aid scrutiny.[77] Usually, the economic activity is carried out **directly** in a given market. However, economic activities could also be carried out **indirectly** by an entity exercising control over an operator who is directly engaged in the market. Thus, the mere holding of shares, even controlling shareholdings, is insufficient to automatically characterize the entity holding those shares as being an undertaking in the sense of Art. 107(1) TFEU.[78] However, if the controlling entity actually **exercises its control** by being directly or indirectly involved in the management of the controlled undertaking, it must be regarded as taking part in the economic activity carried on by the latter. In such cases, the controlling entity must be considered, in itself, as an undertaking within the meaning of Art. 107(1) TFEU.[79]

328 **Non-profit organizations** or **public enterprises** may also fall within the scope of Art. 107(1) TFEU to the extent that they take part in economic life.[80] This consequence is required because economic activities performed by such companies may be in competition with private profit-making operators.[81] In recent jurisprudence, the CJEU has held that even churches benefitting from tax exemptions on the basis of international agreements may fall within the ambit of the rule to the extent they engage in economic activities.[82]

---

73 Notion of aid notice, para. 11; CJEU, 16 December 2010, Case C-480/09 P, *AceaElectrabel Produzione SpA v Commission*, EU:C:2010:787, paras. 47 to 55; CJEU, 10 January 2006, Case C-222/04, *Cassa di Risparmio di Firenze SpA and Others*, C EU:C:2006:8, para. 112.

74 CJEU, 12 September 2000, Joined Cases C-180/98 to C-184/98, *Pavlov and others*, EU:C:2000:428, para. 74 et seq.; CJEU, 1 July 2008, Case C-49/07, *MOTOE*, EU:C:2008:376, para. 22.

75 Notion of aid notice, para. 12 et seq.

76 Ibid., para. 13 et seq.

77 Ibid,. para. 188.

78 Ibid., para. 16.

79 CJEU, 10 January 2006, Case C-222/04, *Cassa di Risparmio di Firenze SpA*, EU:C:2006:8, para. 109 et seq.

80 Notion of aid notice, para. 8 et seq.

81 CJEU, 10 January 2006, Case C-222/04, *Cassa di Risparmio di Firenze SpA*, EU:C:2006:8, para. 123.

82 CJEU, 27 June 2017, Case C-74/16, *Congregación de Escuelas*, EU:C:2017:496; see Nicolaides, Not even the church is absolved from State aid rules: the essence of economic activity, *EStAL* 4/2017, p. 527 et seq.

With regard to the application of the State aid prohibition to public enterprises, **329** Art. 106(2) TFEU establishes specific conditions. Thus, undertakings entrusted by a Member State with the operation of **services of general economic interest** or **having the character of a revenue-producing monopoly** are subject to Art. 107 TFEU. However, to secure their proper functioning, Art. 106(2) TFEU provides for a limitation on the applicability of the State aid prohibition in so far as it hinders the performance of the particular tasks assigned to them. Nevertheless, this limitation must not affect the development of trade to an extent that would be contrary to the interests of the Union.

Consequently, tax privileges or other benefits granted to **private persons, non-** **330** **profit organizations and public enterprises that do not engage in economic activity** are not covered by Art. 107(1) TFEU. It should be noted that, for the purpose of applying Art. 107(1) TFEU to an aid scheme, it is sufficient that the scheme benefits certain undertakings, even if it may also benefit persons or entities that are not undertakings.[83]

B. Advantage

In general terms, aid is an **advantage** or **benefit** that improves the economic or **331** financial situation of an undertaking. Moreover, an economic advantage is characterized by the fact that a private undertaking could not have received the aid under normal conditions in the market without intervention by the State.[84]

Art. 107(1) TFEU provides for "form neutrality", meaning that the Commission **332** and the GC/CJEU examine the compatibility of aid with the internal market not in terms of the form that it may take, but in terms of its effect.[85] The State aid prohibition therefore applies not only to subsidies but also to measures by which the public authorities mitigate the charges normally included in the budget of the undertaking since, in both instances, the recipient's financial position improves in comparison to others.[86] Hence, State measures that, in various forms, confer on recipients an advantage by means of e.g. direct payments, state guarantees or benefits in kind (positive aid) or relieve them of charges that are normally inherent in the cost of their economic activities e.g. through tax exemptions (negative aid), may be covered by Art. 107(1) TFEU.[87]

---

83   CJEU, 15 December 2005, Case C-66/02, *Italy v Commission*, EU:C:2005:768, paras. 91-92.
84   Notion of aid notice, para. 66.
85   Ibid., para. 67.
86   Quigley, *European State aid law and policy* (2015) p. 15.
87   CJEU, 15 March 1994, Case C-387/92, *Banco Exterior de España*, EU:C:1994:100, para. 14; CJEU, 8 September 2011, Joined Cases C-78/08 to C-80/08, *Paint Graphos*, EU:C:2011:550, para. 46; CJEU, 15 November 2011, Joined Cases C-106/09 P and C-107/09 P, *Commission v Gibraltar*, EU:C:2011:732, para. 72.

333 Fiscal State aid typically is granted in the form of negative aid, i.e. by means of an indirect grant of aid through the tax system. Therefore, in order to determine whether a **tax measure** may constitute an economic advantage, it must be established whether the resulting tax burden is **lower** than that which similar undertakings normally would be liable to pay.[88]

334 **Tax advantages** resulting in State aid may lead to a reduction of an undertakings' overall tax liability in various ways, including:[89]

- A reduction in the **tax base** (such as special deductions, special or accelerated depreciation);
- A total or partial reduction in the **amount of tax** (such as tax exemption or a tax credit); or
- **Deferment of tax collection, cancellation** or special **rescheduling** of tax debt.

335 However, a **refund of taxes** unduly collected does not constitute State aid, because it does not involve a transfer of public funds or forgoing revenue.[90] The same is true for **obligations on national authorities to compensate for damage they have caused to certain undertakings** since this is not considered to be an advantage.[91]

336 Recent developments in the jurisprudence indicate a tendency for the criterion of "advantage" not to be clearly distinguishable from the "selectivity" criterion,[92] especially as it is not strictly examined separately in each case.[93] Rather, both the examination of the existence of an advantage and the selectivity test are merged into one step of the State aid assessment, converging in the examination of a "selective advantage".[94] Hence, with regard to tax measures, the distinction between the two elements of advantage and selectivity is not clear cut.[95] The conflation of the two criteria raises particular issues in terms of presumed selectivity in cases of individual aid. Due to the similarity of the two conditions, it not entirely clear how to provide proof of the existence of an advantage that presumes selectivity.[96]

---

88 Quigley, *European State aid law and policy* (2015) pp. 8 and 50; CJEU, 8 September 2011, Joined Cases C-78/08 to C-80/08, *Paint Graphos*, EU:C:2011:550, para. 45; CJEU, 8 September 2011, Case C-279/08, *Commission v Netherlands* EU:C:2011:551, paras. 67, 86; CJEU, 24 January 2013, Case C-73/11, *Frucona Kosice*, EU:C:2013:32, para. 69.

89 Notice on business taxation, para. 9.

90 Quigley, *European State aid law and policy* (2015) p. 108.

91 CJEU, Joined Cases C-106-120/87, *Asteris*, EU:C:1988:457, para. 23 et seq.; Notion of aid notice, para. 71.

92 See, e.g., GC, 24 September 2019, Joined Cases T-755/15 and T-759/15, *Fiat Chrysler Finance Europe*, EU:T:2019:670, para. 122.

93 See also CJEU, 15 November 2011, Joined Cases C-106/09 P and C-107/09 P, *Commission v Gibraltar*, EU:C:2011:732; CJEU, 17 November 2009, Case C-169/08, *Presidente del Consiglio dei Ministri v Regione Sardegna*, EU:C:2009:709.

94 Lang, in: Richelle et al. (eds.), *State aid and business taxation* (2016) p. 28 et seq.

95 Lang, State aid and taxation: recent trends in the case law of the ECJ, *EStAL* 2/2012, p. 418.

96 M.no. 353.

C. State Origin

Furthermore, Art. 107(1) TFEU requires that the advantage granted be **directly** **337** **or indirectly financed by State resources and imputable to the Member State**.[97] Thus, the criterion of State origin involves two separate conditions that must be cumulatively fulfilled.[98] First, the benefit must be a burden on the public budget and either directly granted by a public authority (e.g. **central government institutions, regional or local bodies** in the Member States) or indirectly provided by **private companies that are controlled by the State**.[99] Second, the condition of imputability must be fulfilled. Thus, a measure needs to be attributable to a Member State. With regard to companies on which the State exerts influence, it is necessary that the State be involved in the adoption of the measure.[100] Where a measure is required to be taken due to an obligation under EU law, the measure is not imputable to the Member State.[101]

A **loss of tax revenue is equivalent to consumption of State resources** in the **338** form of fiscal expenditure.[102] Granting tax relief entails a loss of resources for the State in that it forgoes revenue and therefore there is a **burden on the public budget**.[103] For this reason, it is evident that **tax benefits are always granted from State resources**. From an economic point of view, it does not make a difference whether the State levies taxes and then grants the resources to certain undertakings or whether the State abstains from levying taxes with regard to certain undertakings in the first place.[104] Moreover, as tax measures are usually the responsibility of national authorities, the advantage stems from State intervention and the condition of imputability is satisfied.

In addition, it must be noted that a tax measure cannot escape categorization as **339** aid where the beneficiary is subject to a specific additional or different charge that is **unconnected** with the aid in question.[105] The State resources criterion must be assessed at the level of each **individual recipient**, without taking into account the induced effect of the measure in economic or budgetary terms.[106] Therefore, the fact that an aid scheme has a **positive overall effect on budget revenue** is not sufficient to rule out the condition of financing through State resources.[107]

---

97 CJEU, 13 March 2001, Case C-379/98, *Preussen Elektra*, EU:C:2001:160, paras. 58-62.
98 Szyszczak, in: Hofmann/Micheau (eds.), *State aid law of the European Union* (2016), p. 65.
99 Fort, EU State aid and tax: an evolutionary approach, *ET* 2017, p. 375.
100 Notion of aid notice, para. 40.
101 Quigley, *European State aid law and policy* (2015) p. 32.
102 Nicolaides, Grants versus fiscal aid: in search of economic reality, *EStAL* 3/2015, p. 415.
103 GC, 27 January 1998, Case T-67/94, *Ladbroke v Commission*, EU:T:1998:7; CJEU, 15 December 2005, Case C-66/02, *Italy v. Commission*, EU:C:2005:768.
104 Quigley, *European State aid law and policy* (2015) p. 24 et seq.
105 CJEU, 8 December 2011, Case C-81/10 P, *France Télécom SA*, EU:C:2011:811, para. 43.
106 Fort, EU State aid and tax: an evolutionary approach, *ET* 2017, p. 375.
107 Commission Decision 2003/757/EC, *Belgian Coordination Centers*, OJ L 282 of 30 October 2003, p. 25.

D. Selectivity

340 The **main criterion**, and the **constituent factor**[108] in applying Art. 107(1) TFEU to tax measures, is selectivity. The measure must be **selective** in that it favours *"certain undertakings or the production of certain goods."* In other words, it has to be determined whether there is a specific **"target group"** that benefits from the measure whilst other economic agents do not. Otherwise, if a measure does not favour particular undertakings only, but applies to all undertakings with the same legal and factual characteristics, it is general in nature.[109] General measures fall outside the scope of Art. 107(1) TFEU.

341 The phrase "**production of certain goods**" may be misleading, since it seems to restrict the application of Art. 107(1) TFEU only to production branches in the manufacturing industry. The notion **"certain undertakings"** indicates, however, that a measure is also selective when its eligibility criteria **set a group of beneficiaries apart** from other economic agents based on **common features, with the result that they are excluded** from receiving the same benefit.[110] A tax incentive is therefore considered to be selective if it is **limited to certain taxpayers or categories of taxpayers based on common features and at the same time excludes other taxpayers that are legally and factually comparable in respect of the object of the tax concerned.**[111]

342 Such categories could be, for example, certain sectors of the economy (**sectorial aid**),[112] certain business functions within a branch (**horizontal aid**), **public undertakings** carrying out an economic activity,[113] **large** or **multinational companies**,[114] **exporters**,[115] sectors that are subject to **international competition**,[116] **offshore companies**,[117] and **non-resident companies** providing certain services (e.g. financial services) within a group.[118] The same is true for measures that apply only to companies that were **set up after a certain date**, in that existing companies are excluded from receiving the aid.[119]

---

108 CJEU, 6 September 2006, Case C-88/03, *Portugal v Commission*, EU:C:2006:511, para. 54.

109 Bacon, *European Union law of State aid* (2017) para. 2.129.

110 Report on implementation, C(2004) 434 of 9 February 2004, Box No. 5; CJEU, 6 September 2006, Case C-88/03, *Portugal v Commission*, EU:C:2006:511, para. 56; Lang, State aid and taxation: recent trends in the case law of the ECJ, *EStAL 2012*, p. 420.

111 CJEU, 8 September 2011, Joined Cases C-78/08 to C-80/08, *Paint Graphos*, EU:C:2011:550, para. 49.

112 CJEU, 15 December 2005, Case C-148/04, *Unicredito Italiano*, EU:C:2005:774; paras. 44-48; CJEU, 15 December 2015, Case C-66/02, *Italy v Commission*, EU:2005:768, paras. 94-98.

113 CJEU, 27 June 2017, Case C-74/16, *Congregación de Escuelas*, EU:C:2017:496.

114 Report on implementation, C(2004) 434 of 9 February 2004, Box No. 5.

115 CJEU, 21 December 2016, Case C-20/15, *World Duty Free Group SA*, EU:C:2016:981.

116 Commission Decision 97/239/EC, *Maribel bis/ter case*, OJ L 95 of 4 December 1996, p. 25.

117 CJEU, 15 November 2011, Joined Cases C-106/09 P and C-107/09 P, *Commission v Gibraltar*, EU:C:2011:732, para. 107.

118 Notice on business taxation, para. 26.

119 Report on implementation, C(2004) 434 of 9 February 2004, Box No. 5.

A selective advantage may be provided through tax provisions of a **legislative,** 343
regulatory or **administrative** nature, or as a result of a **discretionary practice** on
the part of the tax authorities.[120] Thus, the misapplication of a tax provision by the
tax authorities to the advantage of a taxpayer also constitutes a selective measure.[121] Although, there is no requirement that the tax authority act arbitrarily in
order for a measure to be selective, having a margin of discretion in applying a legal
provision would suffice.[122] If, however, the degree of latitude of the competent
authorities does not go beyond implementation of objective criteria related to the
nature or general scheme of the tax system, the discretion may be justified.[123]

Further, it needs to be stressed that advance pricing agreements or tax rulings are 344
not considered to be selective, as such, only because they are obtained on an individual basis. A ruling can just be a selective measure in the event that it results in
unequal treatment where certain undertakings are favoured over others.[124] In
principle, one can say that if rulings are used to clarify the applicable national tax
law and the tax authority is only anticipating the decision it would, in any event,
reach at a later stage and the possibility to obtain a ruling is generally available to
all taxpayers, then they do not conflict with State aid law.[125]

In general, one can distinguish between different types of selectivity. First, a dis- 345
tinction can be drawn between material and regional selectivity.[126] While material
selectivity distinguishes between certain undertakings within a Member State as
a whole, regional selectivity makes a distinction between different regions of a
Member State. Apart from that, a further differentiation must be made between
de jure and de facto selective measures.[127] Measures are de jure selective if the
different treatment is based on formal criteria laid down in national legislation.
De facto selectivity exists where a measure is selective in its effect even though it
applies on the basis of apparently objective and general legal terms.[128]

In order to differentiate between general and selective measures a "selectivity test" 346
is performed. The Commission and the EU Courts apply the "derogation test" in
determining material selectivity, which is comprised of three steps. In a first step,
the Member State's "common" or "normal" tax system is identified, which is the
relevant point of reference that serves as the basis for comparison.[129] Secondly, it

---

120 Notice on business taxation, para. 12.
121 Schön, in: Richelle (eds.), *State aid and business taxation* (2016) p. 5.
122 CJEU, 26 September 1996, Case C-241/94, *Commission v France*, EU:C:1996:353, paras. 23-24; Bacon,
      European Union law of State aid (2017) para. 2.126.
123 CJEU, 18 July 2013, Case C-6/12, *P Oy*, EU:C:2013:525, paras. 22-26, 32.
124 Bacon, *European Union law of State aid* (2017) para. 2.127.
125 Lang, Tax rulings and State aid law, *British Tax Review* 2015, p. 394 et seq.
126 Notion of aid notice, para. 119.
127 Ibid., para. 121.
128 CJEU, 15 November 2011, Joined Cases C-106/09 P and C-107/09 P, *Commission v Gibraltar*, EU:C:
      2011:732, para. 75; Bacon, *European Union law of State aid* (2017) para. 2.119.
129 Notion of aid notice, para. 128.

must be determined whether the tax measure at issue deviates from the "normal" tax system, such that it differentiates between economic operators in a comparable factual and legal situation in light of the objectives of the tax system in the Member State concerned.[130] This comparability examination depends on the nature or general scheme of the relevant Member State's tax system.[131] If the taxpayers are comparable and a derogation exists, the measure is considered prima facie selective. In a final step, it must be examined whether the derogation or differentiation within that system may be justified by the *"nature or general scheme of the tax system,"* that is to say, whether it *"results directly from the basic or guiding principles of the tax system in the Member States concerned."*[132] If the different treatment is justified, the measure is not considered to be selective and does not fulfil Art. 107(1) TFEU.[133]

347 The application of the three-step test requires determining a certain point of reference. In other words, a benchmark needs to be identified based on which the different treatment or derogation can be established. Obviously, however, problems in applying the derogation test arise if a specific benchmark does not exist. In the *Gibraltar* case, the government of Gibraltar amended its corporate income tax regime to avoid an allegation that it was providing selective advantages to particular offshore undertakings. The system was replaced by a combination of different tax rules introduced in such a way that their combined application actually affected only domestic companies and effectively resulted in a lower tax burden for comparable offshore undertakings. In this case, the CJEU held that although the measure seems to be general in nature and appears to apply for all undertakings, this compilation of tax rules confers a de facto selective advantage. Moreover, it clarified that selectivity cannot depend on the regulatory technique of a Member State.[134] As a result, the Court confirmed that unlawful aid had been awarded, but the provision had failed the benchmark test. It is for this reason that some, in the literature, view this landmark decision as a sign of a change in the

---

130 CJEU, 22 December 2008, Case C-487/06 P, *British Aggregates v Commission*, EU:C:2008:757, para. 82; CJEU, 8 September 2011, Joined Cases C-78/08 to C-80/08, *Paint Graphos*, EU:C:2011:550, para. 49; CJEU, 15 November 2011, Joined Cases C-106/09 P and C-107/09 P, *Commission v Gibraltar*, EU:C: 2011:732, para. 75; CJEU, 7 March 2012, Case T-210/02 RENV, *British Aggregates Association v Commission*, EU:T:2012:110, para. 49. By contrast, in CJEU, 8 November 2001, Case C-143/99, *Adria-Wien Pipeline*, EU:C:2001:598, para. 41 the Court held that comparability should be assessed in light of the objective pursued by the measure in question.

131 Lang, State aid and taxation: recent trends in the case law of the ECJ, *EStAL* 2012, p. 418.

132 CJEU, 6 September 2006, Case C-88/03, *Portugal v Commission*, EU:C:2006:511, para. 81.

133 Notion of aid notice, para. 128; CJEU, 8 November 2001, Case C-143/99, *Adria-Wien Pipeline*, EU:C:2001:598, para. 42; CJEU, 22 December 2008, Case C-487/06 P, *British Aggregates v Commission*, EU:C:2008:757, para. 83; CJEU, 15 November 2011, Joined Cases C-106/09 P and C-107/09 P, *Commission v Gibraltar*, EU:C:2011:732, para. 145.

134 CJEU, 15 November 2011, Joined Cases C-106/09 P and C-107/09 P, *Commission v Gibraltar*, EU:C: 2011:732, paras. 91-93, 100-104; later repeated in CJEU, 21 December 2016, Case C-20/15, *World Duty Free Group SA*, EU:C:2016:981, para. 79 and most recently in CJEU, 28 June 2018, Case C-203/16 P, *Dirk Andres*, EU:C:2018:506, para. 88 et seq.

paradigm from a derogation approach towards a discrimination test similar to the test applied with regard to the fundamental freedoms.[135]

In applying the selectivity test to measures providing regional preferential treatment, a tax benefit to undertakings in a specific region of a Member State would always be considered selective, as it deviates from the generally applicable national tax system. Therefore, the three-step test needs to be applied merely in the context of the particular regional system, i.e. what needs to be examined is whether taxpayers are treated equally solely within that region and not within the whole State. Consequently, to determine regional selectivity, the reference point needs to be adjusted.[136]   **348**

In order for a regional tax system to be considered the benchmark under the selectivity test, the regional authority, such as a federal State or municipality, must enjoy sufficient institutional, procedural and economic autonomy to establish its own tax system in defining the economic environment in which undertakings operate.[137] To have regional autonomy, three conditions must be fulfilled.[138] First, the regional authority needs to have, by constitution, a political and administrative status separate from the national government (institutional autonomy). Second, the measure must be adopted such that no central government is authorized to directly intervene in this decision (procedural autonomy).[139] Finally, the financial consequences of the benefits given to undertakings in the region must not be offset by aid or subsidies from other regions or the central government (economic and financial autonomy).[140]   **349**

As mentioned, a prima facie selective measure may be justified by the **nature or general scheme of the tax system** if it reflects the basic logic or guiding principles of that system.[141] This is true with regard to measures the economic rationale of which makes them **necessary to the system's functioning and effectiveness.**[142] In general, Member States impose taxes either to generate revenue or to pursue other goals, like penalizing or incentivizing certain behaviour.[143] In this context, a distinc-   **350**

---

135   Lang, State aid and taxation: recent trends in the case law of the EC, *EStAL* 2/2012, p. 414 et seq.; Lang, in: Richelle (eds.), *State aid and business taxation* (2016) p. 27 et seq.; Lyal, Transfer pricing rules and State aid, 38 *Fordham Int'l L.J.* 2015, p. 1039; Szudoczky, Convergence of the analysis of national tax measures under the EU State aid rules and the fundamental freedoms, *EStAL* 3/2016, p. 363 et seq.; see however, Schön, in: Richelle (eds.), *State aid and business taxation* (2016), p. 9 et seq.

136   Bacon, *European Union law of State aid* (2017) para. 2.137.

137   CJEU, 6 September 2006, Case C-88/03, *Portugal v Commission*, EU:C:2006:511, para. 67; CJEU, 11 September 2008, Joined Cases C-428/06 to C-434/06, *UGT-Rioja*, EU:C:2008:488, paras. 54-55.

138   Report on implementation, C(2004) 434 of 9 February 2004, Box No. 6; CJEU, 6 September 2006, Case C-88/03, *Portugal v Commission*, EU:C:2006:511, para. 67.

139   CJEU, 11 September 2008, Joined Cases C-428/06 to C-434/06, *UGT-Rioja*, EU:C:2008:488, para. 96.

140   Ibid., para. 67.

141   Notice on business taxation, paras. 16, 26; CJEU, 6 September 2006, Case C-88/03, *Portugal v Commission*, EU:C:2006:511, para. 83.

142   Notice on business taxation, para. 23.

143   Schön, in: Richelle (eds.), *State aid and business taxation* (2016), p. 5 et seq.

tion must be made between, on the one hand, internal objectives that are inherent to the tax system (with regard to income tax this would, for example, be its progressive nature on the basis of the ability to pay principle, or preventing tax avoidance or double taxation) and, on the other hand, **external objectives** that are assigned to a particular tax scheme (e.g. environmental objectives within the income tax regime).[144] At the level of the comparability examination, the tax system's **internal objectives** may dictate whether different taxpayers are comparable or rather in different factual and legal situations, and therefore treated differently without this being considered prohibited State aid. However, the objectives upon which the national tax system is built play a decisive role at the justification level as well: Internal objectives can be invoked to justify a different treatment of comparable taxpayers. In contrast to internal objectives, **external objectives cannot justify a selective measure**. The fact that a selective measure is based on objective criteria does not suffice to prove that it is consistent with the logic of the system concerned.[145]

351 The Commission lists the following **examples** of measures that may be justified by the nature of a tax system:[146] the **progression of income tax rates** and **specific provisions on the taxation of small and medium-sized enterprises (SMEs)** because they may fulfil the redistributive purpose of a tax system in accordance with the ability to pay principle; **tax exemption for non-profit-making undertakings** because profit tax cannot be levied if no profit is earned; and **tax exemption for cooperatives** that distribute all their profits to their members, provided that tax is levied at the level of the latter. By contrast, with regard to a Finnish income tax provision, the CJEU held that the objective of maintaining employment would be "unrelated" and therefore extrinsic to the income tax system.[147]

352 The nature or general scheme of the tax system plays a major role both in determining whether undertakings are in a comparable legal and factual situation, as part of the second step of the selectivity test, and whether a prima facie selective tax measure may be justified, as part of the third step of the selectivity test. However, there is a procedural distinction between the stages of the three-step selectivity test concerning **the burden of proof**. While the Commission must prove that the first and second steps of the selectivity test have been fulfilled, it is up to the Member State concerned to show that a *prima facie* selective measure is actually justified by the nature of its tax system as part of the third step.[148] Moreover, for tax measures to be justified, it is also necessary to ensure that those measures

---

144 Notice on business taxation, para. 26; CJEU, 6 September 2006, Case C-88/03, *Portugal v Commission*, EU:C:2006:511, paras. 52, 81; CJEU, 18 July 2013, Case C-6/12, *P Oy*, EU:C:2013:525.

145 Report on implementation, C(2004) 434 of 9 February 2004, Box. No. 8.

146 Notice on business taxation, paras. 24-27.

147 CJEU, 18 July 2013, Case C-6/12, *P Oy*, EU:C:2013:525, para. 27 et seq.

148 Notice on business taxation, para. 23; Report on implementation, C(2004) 434 of 9 February 2004, para. 35, Box No. 7; CJEU, 29 April 2004, Case C-159/01, *Netherlands v Commission*, EU:C:2004:246, paras. 43, 77; CJEU, 15 November 2011, Joined Cases C-106/09 P and C-107/09 P, *Commission v Gibraltar*, EU:C:2011:732, paras. 146, 151.

are consistent with the **principle of proportionality** and do not go beyond what is necessary, in that the legitimate objective being pursued could not be attained through less far-reaching measures.[149]

The burden of proof concerning the selectivity criterion that lies with the Commission differs depending on the type of aid.[150] In contrast to aid schemes or "general" aid measures, such as legal provisions or regulations, there is presumed selectivity in terms of advantages conferred by individual aid or "targeted" aid measures, such as tax rulings or tax assessments.[151] In the *MOL* case, the CJEU held that, in cases of individual aid, *"the identification of the economic advantage is, in principle, sufficient to support the presumption that it is selective."*[152] However, it is unclear whether the Commission's burden of proof is actually alleviated in matters concerning individual aid, particularly since the advantage and selectivity criteria are very difficult to distinguish. Apart from individual aid, the existence of a broad margin of discretion may also lead to a presumption of selectivity.[153] Thus, if a provision provides too much leeway for the tax authorities, the provision may be prima facie selective.[154] The fact that discretion is not sufficiently limited might cause different treatment through a discretionary practice in the application of the rule.[155] Therefore, the CJEU has decided that justification depends on the discretion being limited by objective criteria related to the tax system.[156]   **353**

Due to their sovereignty in the area of direct taxation, it falls within the competence of the Member States, or infra-State bodies having fiscal autonomy, to decide on appropriate economic policies, designate bases of assessment and, in particular, spread the tax burden as they see fit across the different economic sectors.[157] In other words, **Member States have the sovereignty to establish their tax systems' internal objectives.**[158] Nevertheless, the internal objectives must be **consistently applied in implementing the tax system.**[159] It is therefore for up to the Member State concerned to introduce and apply **appropriate control and monitoring procedures** in order to ensure that specific tax measures are consistent with the logic and general scheme of the tax system and to prevent undertakings from taking actions for the sole purpose of taking advantage of the benefits provided by the tax system.   **354**

---

149 CJEU, 8 September 2011, Joined Cases C-78/08 to C-80/08, *Paint Graphos*, EU:C:2011:550, paras. 73-75.
150 CJEU, 4 June 2015, Case C-15/14 P, *Commission v MOL*, EU:C:2015:362, para. 60.
151 See also Gormsen, *European State Aid and Tax Rulings* (2019) p. 52 et seq.
152 CJEU, 4 June 2015, Case C-15/14 P, *Commission v MOL*, EU:C:2015:362, para. 60.
153 Notion of aid notice, para. 123.
154 Ibid., para. 123 et seq.
155 Ibid., para. 124.
156 CJEU, 18 July 2013, Case C-6/12, *P Oy*, EU:C:2013:525, para. 27.
157 Notice on business taxation, para. 13; CJEU, 15 November 2011, Joined Cases C-106/09 P and C-107/09 P, *Commission v Gibraltar*, EU:C:2011:732, para. 97.
158 Notice on business taxation, paras. 24-27.
159 Rossi-Maccanico, The Gibraltar judgement and the point on selectivity in fiscal aids, *EC Tax Review* 2009, p. 74.

355 The fact that a measure is alien to the inherent logic of a tax system does not mean that it is selective, since such a measure could be general in nature.[160] A **general measure** is the opposite of a selective measure. A tax benefit will not be considered selective if it is *"applicable without distinction to all economic operators"* that fall under its scope and are factually and legally comparable.[161] However, it is not necessary that all economic agents enjoy the tax reduction equally, i.e. to the same extent, for it to be considered general.[162] An example of a general measure would be a uniform reduction in income tax rates.[163] Obviously, in this instance, it is an inevitable consequence that companies earning more profits will benefit more in relative terms than companies with lower profits.[164]

356 The Commission and the CJEU follow an **effects-based approach** in determining whether a tax measure is selective or general, taking into account only the effects of the measure.[165] Hence, the reason why a Member State implements an aid measure, the goals it wishes to achieve and how it plans to achieve its goals do not matter.

357 The notion of selectivity is constantly evolving. Recent jurisprudence reveals that the concept of selectivity has been widened extensively, making the distinction between general measures and selective measures more difficult in practice.[166] In the *World Duty Free* case, a provision under Spanish corporate tax law was at stake, which provided that undertakings resident in Spain could deduct goodwill from their tax base in the event of the acquisition of at least 5 % of the shares of a foreign company. However, a deduction for goodwill was not available in respect of acquisitions of shareholdings in domestic companies. The GC considered that the measure was not selective since the tax advantage was accessible to all undertakings. Moreover, in its view, an advantage is not selective if it is not directed at a particular category of undertakings but rather at a particular type of transaction. Since the Commission had not identified such a category of undertakings exclusively benefitting from the measure, the GC annulled the Commission decision. However, the CJEU disagreed and held that, in performing the selectivity assessment, it is necessary to establish *"whether the situation of operators benefiting from the measure is comparable with that of operators excluded from it"* and if so, whether a different treatment is suffered.[167] According to the CJEU, it is not necessary, though, to define a particular category of undertakings that are favoured

---

160 CJEU, 15 November 2011, Joined Cases C-106/09 P and C-107/09 P, *Commission v Gibraltar*, EU:C: 2011:732, para. 81.

161 CJEU, 18 July 2013, Case C-6/12, *P Oy*, EU:C:2013:525, para. 18.

162 Bacon, *European Union law of State aid* (2017) para. 2.129.

163 CJEU, 15 November 2011, Joined Cases C-106/09 P and C-107/09 P, *Commission v Gibraltar*, EU:C: 2011:732, para. 83.

164 Bacon, *European Union law of State aid* (2017) para. 2.129.

165 Notice on business taxation, para. 15; CJEU, 8 December 2011, Case C-81/10 P, *France Télécom SA*, EU:C:2011:811, para. 17; CJEU, 15 November 2011, Joined Cases C-106/09 P and C-107/09 P, *Commission v Gibraltar*, EU:C:2011:732, paras. 87-88.

166 Nicolaides, Excessive widening of the concept of selectivity, *EStAL* 1/2017, p. 62 et seq.

167 CJEU, 21 December 2016, Case C-20/15, *World Duty Free Group SA*, EU:C:2016:981.

by a tax measure.[168] From this judgement, it can be derived that the selectivity criterion can be satisfied even where the measure is available to all undertakings and its application merely depends on the choice of undertakings to perform the transaction concerned.[169]

E. Distortion of Competition and Effect on Trade

As mentioned, State aid control is part of EU competition law. Therefore, a tax **358** measure is considered State aid only if it is a **cause of distortion of competition** that **affects trade between Member States**. These two distinct criteria are inextricably linked to each other.[170]

Not only actual, but also **potential, distortions of competition** that are **liable to** **359** **affect trade** are caught by Art. 107(1) TFEU.[171] This is due to the fact that, according to the procedure laid down in Art. 108(3) TFEU, Member States have to inform the Commission **in advance** of any plans to grant or alter State aid, which requires the Commission to make a decision **before** the real effects of an aid measure on the market can be determined. It is therefore sufficient that aid be **capable of distorting competition** or **affecting trade**.

Competition is considered distorted and intra-EU trade affected if the aid in ques- **360** tion **strengthens the competitiveness of the recipient**, for instance, by reducing its operating costs in comparison to its competitors.[172] Hence, it is not necessary that public support helps the recipient expand its market share; it suffices if the aid allows the recipient to maintain a stronger position than it would have had without it.[173] Neither the fact that the recipient's share in the market is very small, nor that the recipient does not export at all or exports all its products outside the EU can alter this conclusion.[174]

The reason why measures that strengthen the position of undertakings that are **361** involved in domestic trade only also fall within the scope of Art. 107(1) TFEU is that such aid may still influence trade between Member States by **reducing the opportunities** for undertakings from other Member States to **penetrate the domestic market**. Furthermore, fortifying the domestic market position of an

168 Ibid., para. 94.
169 The CJEU referred the case back to the GC, as it should not have required the Commission to define a particular category of undertakings that are favoured by the measure, but instead should have determined whether the Commission had analysed the measure's discriminatory effect. For the practical significance of the decision see Derenne, Commission v World Duty Free Group a.o.: selectivity in (fiscal) State aid, quo vadis curia?, *Journal of European Competition Law & Practice* 2017, p. 311 et seq.
170 CJEU, 15 June 2000, Joined Cases T-298/97, T-312/97 etc., *Alzetta Mauro*, EU:T:2000:151.
171 CJEU, 10 January 2006, Case C-222/04, *Cassa di Risparmio di Firenze SpA*, EU:C:2006:8, para. 140.
172 Notion of aid notice, paras. 187, 190.
173 Ibid., para. 189.
174 Ibid., paras. 189, 192; CJEU, 17 September 1980, Case 730/79, *Commission v Philip Morris*, EU:C:1980:209, para. 11.

undertaking that is not involved in intra-EU trade may enable that undertaking to **penetrate the markets of other Member States in the future.**[175]

362 The wide scope of potential causes of distortion of competition that affect trade between Member States leads to the result that **whenever aid is granted by a Member State to certain undertakings, these two criteria are fulfilled.** Thus, these conditions are usually not examined thoroughly by the Commission and the CJEU in the State aid assessment and are simply **assumed to be fulfilled.**[176] Nevertheless, there are limited cases in which the conditions are not satisfed. If State support is granted in respect of activities that have purely a local impact and it is unlikely to attract customers from other Member States, such as public funding for the main purpose of addressing a medial emergency, there may not be an effect on intra-EU trade or a distortion of competition.[177]

363 It needs to be pointed out that the existence of comparable or rival tax rules in other Member States possibly distorting competition or affecting trade is not relevant in the assessment of State aid. Therefore, it cannot be argued that the tax measure concerned could be perceived as bringing charges in the relevant sector that are more in line with those of its competitors in other Member States. Each measure must be assessed individually in the context of the tax system of the State concerned.[178]

VI. Exemptions from the Prohibition of State Aid under Art. 107(2) and (3) TFEU

364 The State aid prohibition applies if all conditions of Art. 107 (1) TFEU are satisfied. Most issues, in practice, concern the fulfillment of the four conditions and, in particular, the actual conferral of a selective advantage. Pursuant to Art. 107(1) TFEU, State aid is **generally incompatible** with the internal market and thus prohibited. However, this prohibition is neither absolute nor unconditional. Art. 107(2) and (3) TFEU provide for exemptions according to which – despite fulfillment of the four conditions – State aid *must* or *may be* **considered compatible** with the internal market.[179] If compatible aid remains unnotified and is put into effect

---

175 CJEU, 10 January 2006, Case C-222/04, *Cassa di Risparmio di Firenze SpA*, EU:C:2006:8, para. 143; CJEU, 8 September 2011, Joined Cases C-78/08 to C-80/08, *Paint Graphos*, EU:C:2011:550, para. 80.

176 Report on implementation, C(2004) 434 of 9 February 2004, para. 22; Quigley, *European State aid law and policy* (2015) p. 79 et seq.

177 For further examples, see Press Release, IP/15/4889 (29 April 2015).

178 Notice on business taxation, para. 15; Report on implementation, C(2004) 434 of 9 February 2004, para. 24, Box No. 4.

179 The COVID-19 outbreak caused some serious disturbances in the EU economy. To mitigate the economic consequences of the pandemic, the Commission adopted a temporary framework based on Art 107 (3) lit b TFEU that enables the Member States to use the full flexibility foreseen by the State aid rules. For the time being, main parts of the framework are in place until the end of 2020, yet extensions might be possible. In addition to Art 107 (3) TFEU and the temporary framework, the Member States may rely on the legal exemption of Art 107 (2) lit b of the TFEU to grant aid that compensates companies for the damages caused by this exceptional occurrence. Since the beginning

without prior approval of the Commission, it is technically unlawful and subject to recovery.[180] Yet, there is a difference in the amount that has to be recovered: While in cases of aid that is compatible with the internal market only the interest must be paid, recovery of incompatible aid encompasses the entire amount of aid including interest (see section VIII.D. of this Chapter).

Consequently, the granting of aid is not automatically contrary to the TFEU. Hence, after assessing the conditions of Art. 107(1) TFEU and concluding that all four conditions have been fulfilled, it needs to be examined whether the measure in question is compatible with the internal market. The State aid prohibition applies only if it does not fall under Art. 107(2) or (3) TFEU. However, it must be emphasized that the CJEU has been consistently reaffirming that both exceptions to the general rule in Art. 107(1) TFEU must be construed narrowly.[181] **365**

A. Legal Exemptions under Art. 107(2) TFEU

Art. 107(2) TFEU specifies three instances in which aid is **automatically compatible** with the internal market (**legal exemption**). Hence, the following types of aid are *ex lege* seen as compatible: **366**

- aid having a **social character**, granted to individual customers, provided that such aid is granted without discrimination in terms of the origin of the products concerned;
- aid to make good damage caused by **natural disasters or exceptional occurrences**; and
- aid granted to the economy of certain areas of the **Federal Republic of Germany** affected by the division of Germany, insofar as such aid is required to compensate for the economic disadvantages caused by that division.[182]

With regard to **social aid**, the beneficiaries are usually lower income groups that need financial support, such as aged people, children and disabled persons. Aid given to individuals is not subject to State aid rules. Nevertheless, Art. 107(2) TFEU ensures that the beneficial effect indirectly granted to undertakings when favouring certain customer groups does not undermine the exemption. **367**

Concerning **natural disasters or exceptional occurrences**, it is necessary that the aid be granted to beneficiaries suffering from substantial and unpredictable circum- **368**

---

of the outbreak, the Member States have adopted, on the basis of these provisions, different kinds of State aid, comprising, in particular, various measures in the area of taxation. For example, the Commission approved, on the basis of the temporary framework, certain aid schemes notified by Italy to support companies affected by the COVID-19 outbreak through tax waivers and tax credits. See Press Release IP/20/1210 (26 June 2020).

180 See section VIII.D. of this Chapter.
181 CJEU, 30 September 2003, Case C-301/96, *Germany v Commission*, EU:C:2003:509, para. 71; CJEU, 29 April 2004, Case C-278/00, *Greece v Commission*, EU:C:2004:239, para. 81.
182 Aid in relation to the division of Germany has not been authorized in the past decade and is thus of little practical relevance.

stances that are out of the ordinary,[183] e.g. tornadoes, wars or serious pandemics, such as the COVID-19 outbreak.[184] Regarding the damage covered by the aid, the CJEU has held that only economic disadvantages directly caused by the catastrophe qualify for compensation.[185]

369   If a measure is covered by one of these enumerated types of aid, it is definitely compatible with the internal market and automatically exempted from the State aid prohibition. This does **not absolve the Member States of their obligation to notify** their plans to the Commission before they are put into effect. The Commission only has to examine whether the aid measure in question falls within the ambit of Art. 107(2) TFEU. If the conditions are properly met, the Commission has no margin of discretion and has to authorize the aid.[186]

B. Discretionary Exemptions under Art. 107(3) TFEU

370   Art. 107(3) TFEU defines five instances in which State aid *may be* compatible with the internal market. In this scenario, State aid is not automatically exempted but **may be authorized by the Commission.** Thus, whenever the Commission examines aid schemes notified by Member States, it is bound by Art. 107(3) TFEU and may only authorize those measures listed. Any other kind of aid must be rejected if all of the conditions of Art. 107(1) TFEU are fulfilled. Therefore, the following measures *may* be considered compatible with the internal market:

- aid to promote the **economic development of areas** where the standard of living is abnormally low or where there is serious underemployment;
- aid to promote the execution of an **important project** of common European interest or to **remedy a serious disturbance** in the economy of a Member State;
- aid to facilitate the **development of certain economic activities or of certain economic areas,** where such aid does not adversely affect trading conditions to an extent contrary to the common interest;
- aid to promote **culture and heritage conservation** where such aid does not affect trading conditions and competition in the EU to an extent that is contrary to the common interest; and
- other categories of aid as may be specified by **decision of the Council** acting by a qualified majority on a proposal from the Commission.

371   Compared to the types of aid enumerated in Art. 107(2) TFEU, the Commission enjoys a wider margin of discretion in relation to aid measures covered by Art. 107(3) TFEU.[187] In general, the **Commission,** as the competent authority in EU State aid

---

183   The notion was first expressly defined by GBER, Reg. 651/2014 of 17 June 2014.

184   Fn 179.

185   E.g., CJEU, 29 April 2004, Case C-278/00, *Greece v Commission*, EU:C:2004:239, para. 49.

186   Orzan, in: Hofmann/Micheau (eds.), *State aid law of the European Union* (2016) p. 234 et seq.

187   CJEU, 8 March 1988, Joined Cases 62 and 72/87, *Exécutif régional wallon and SA Glaverbel v Commission*, EU:C:1988:132, para. 34.

matters, is exclusively responsible to decide on the compatibility of State aid. The exercise of its discretion involves an economic and social assessment in an EU context.[188] Further, the Commission has to examine whether the measure in question infringes other provisions of the TFEU, including the fundamental freedoms, and provisions of secondary law. Additionally, the Commission should respect its own authorization practice in order to ensure equal treatment of the Member States. Its decisions are **subject to review by the GC and the CJEU, respectively.** However, the Court must restrict itself to examining whether the assessment of the Commission was based on a *"manifest error or misuse of powers"* (see section VIII.C. of this Chapter).[189]

To make the exercise of the discretionary power more transparent and predicta- **372** ble and to ensure **legal certainty** for undertakings and authorities, the Commission has issued a number of guidelines, communications and notices.[190] These publications include the criteria it uses when deciding on the compatibility of aid under Art. 107(3) TFEU. Although most acts are not legally binding and are only intended to indicate the Commission's view on the application of its discretion, they nevertheless form rules of practice from which the Commission may not depart in an individual case without giving reasons that are compatible, in particular, with the principle of equal treatment.[191] In addition, the Commission has adopted the General Block Exemption Regulation (GBER), a legally binding act declaring certain categories of aid compatible with the internal market (see section VII. of this Chapter).

VII. De minimis Limitation and General Block Exemption Regulation

According to Art. 109 TFEU, the Council may make appropriate regulations for **373** the application of Arts. 107 and 108 TFEU. In particular, it may determine the conditions for the application of the notification requirement of Art. 108(3) TFEU and the categories of aid exempted from this procedure. The Commission may adopt regulations relating to the categories of State aid that the Council has exempted from the notification requirement.[192]

---

188 CJEU, 17 September 1980, Case C-730/79, *Commission v Philip Morris*, EU:C:1980:209, para. 24.

189 CJEU, 14 March 1973, Case 57/72, *Westzucker*, EU:C:1973:30, para. 14; CJEU, 14 January 1997, Case C-169/95, *Spain v Commission*, EU:C:1997:10, para. 34; CJEU, 12 December 2002, Case C-456/00, *Commission v France*, EU:C:2002:753, para. 41; CJEU, 23 February 2006, Joined Cases C-346/03 and C-529/03, *Atzeni and others*, EU:C:2006:130, para. 84.

190 For example, Guidelines on Regional Aid for 2014-2020 (RAG), OJ C 209/1 2013 of 23 July 2013; Guidelines on State Aid for Environmental Protection and Energy 2014-2020, OJ C 200/1 2014 of 28 June 2014; Framework for State aid for research and development and innovation, OJ C 198/1 2014 of 27 June 2014.

191 CJEU, 28 June 2005, Joined Cases C-189/02 P, *Dansk Rørindustri v Commission*, EU:C:2005:408, para. 209.

192 Art. 108(4) TFEU.

374 On that basis, Council Regulation No. 994/98 was adopted, which authorizes the Commission to adopt so-called Block Exemption Regulations.[193] Among others, it authorizes the Commission to decide that certain measures are exempt from notification even if they would otherwise meet the criteria of Art. 107(1) TFEU, provided that the aid granted to the same undertaking over a given period of time does not exceed a certain fixed amount.[194] Based on this empowerment, the Commission adopted the **regulation on the application of Arts. 107 and 108 TFEU to *de minimis* aid.**[195]

375 Generally speaking, *de minimis* aid is not State aid within the meaning of Art. 107 TFEU since the aid amount is considered to be too low to have an effect on trade or competition in the internal market.[196] According to the *de minimis* regulation, **measures will be exempt from the notification requirement if the total amount of aid granted by a Member State to a single undertaking does not exceed EUR 200 000 over any period of three fiscal years.**[197]

376 This general rule is subject to several exceptions. For example, the ceiling of the *de minimis* exemption is higher with regard to undertakings providing services of general economic interest[198] and lower for undertakings performing road freight transport for hire or reward.[199] Some sectors, such as agricultural and fishery production, are excluded from the *de minimis* exemption.[200] The regulation also exempts from its scope aid to export-related activities,[201] as well as aid contingent upon the use of domestic over imported goods.[202] Specific conditions apply for aid in the form of a loan, capital injection, risk finance or guarantee.[203]

377 Although the measure does not need to be notified, Art. 6 of the *de minimis* regulation imposes particular monitoring obligations on the Member States. Accordingly, the Member States shall grant *de minimis* aid only after having checked that

---

193   Art. 1 Council Regulation (EC) No. 994/98 of 7 May 1998 on the application of Articles 92 and 93 of the Treaty establishing the European Community to certain categories of horizontal State aid (hereinafter: Council Reg. No. 994/98).

194   Art. 2 Council Reg. No. 994/98.

195   Commission Regulation (EU) No. 360/2012 of 25 April 2012 on the application of Articles 107 and 108 of the Treaty on the Functioning of the European Union to *de minimis* aid granted to undertakings providing services of general economic interest (hereinafter: SGEI Regulation); Commission Regulation (EU) No. 1407/2013 of 18 December 2013 on the application of Articles 107 and 108 of the Treaty on the Functioning of the European Union to *de minimis* aid (hereinafter: De minimis Regulation).

196   Staviczky, Cumulation of State aid, *EStAL* 1/2015, p. 121 et seq.; CJEU, 8 May 2013, Case C-197/11, *Libert*, EU:C:2013:288, para. 81.

197   Art. 3(2) para. 1 *De minimis* Regulation.

198   Art. 2(2) SGEI Regulation; for the provision of services covered the ceiling is EUR 500 000 per undertaking for 3 years.

199   Art. 3(2) *De minimis* Regulation; for road freight transport, the ceiling is EUR 100 000 per undertaking for 3 years.

200   Art. 1(1)(a)-(c) *De minimis* Regulation.

201   Ibid., Art. 1(1)(d).

202   Ibid., Art. 1(1)(e).

203   Ibid., Art. 4(3)-(6).

the total amount of aid the beneficiary has received does not exceed the relevant ceiling. Alternatively, the Member State may choose to set up a central register containing complete information on *de minimis* aid.

For the purposes of transparency, equal treatment and effective monitoring, **378** the *de minimis* limitation applies only to aid in respect of which it is possible to calculate precisely the gross grant equivalent *ex ante* using market interest rates without the need to undertake a risk assessment ("transparent aid").[204] Aid in the form of tax expenditure is considered transparent if the underlying instrument provides for a cap ensuring that the relevant ceiling is not exceeded.[205] In practice, however, the calculation of the exact amount of aid might prove to be difficult.[206]

In addition, Council Regulation No. 994/98 also authorizes the Commission to **379** adopt regulations declaring certain categories of aid compatible with the internal market and exempting them from the notification requirement under particular conditions.[207] The categories specified include aid in favour of SMEs, R&D, environmental protection, employment, training and regional aid. Under this authorization, the Commission adopted the General Block Exemption Regulation (GBER), declaring certain categories of aid compatible with the internal market, provided that all requirements are properly met.[208]

With the GBER, the Commission has exempted particular categories of aid sub- **380** ject to certain conditions from the notification requirement, allowing for implementation without prior authorization. In terms of measures falling under the GBER (but also under the *de minimis* regulation), the Commission only exercises its general ex post monitoring function. The GBER conditions are derived from market experience and the Commission's decision-making practice and define eligible beneficiaries, as well as the maximum intensity of the aid. Currently, approximately 95% of all Member States' aid measures, with a combined annual expenditure of over EUR 28 billion, are implemented under the GBER.[209] The GBER rules for environmental tax reductions are of major relevance in the field of tax law.[210]

Measures that fall under the GBER can be implemented directly, without prior **381** approval, when the following conditions are satisfied: the measure must fulfil all

---

204 Ibid., para. 14.
205 Ibid., para. 15.
206 For example, CJEU, 27 June 2017, Case C-74/16, *Congregación de Escuelas*, EU:C:2017:496, para. 83 et seq.
207 Art. 1 Council Reg. No. 994/98 last amended by 2015/1588 of 13 July 2015.
208 Commission Regulation (EU) No. 651/2014 of 17 June 2014 declaring certain categories of aid compatible with the internal market in application of Articles 107 and 108 of the Treaty, OJ L 187 of 26 June 2014, pp. 1-78 (hereinafter: GBER). Last amended by No. 2017/1084 of 14 June 2017.
209 Available at http://europa.eu/rapid/press-release_MEMO-17-1342_en.htm.
210 Art. 44 GBER.

common provisions, reporting and monitoring requirements and must satisfy specific provisions, which are different for each aid category. Although there is no notification obligation for measures covered by the GBER, Member States must report every aid granted under the GBER within 20 days following its entry into force. The case law indicates that the GBER conditions are interpreted very strictly.[211] However, if the GBER conditions are not met, this does not mean that the measure is incompatible State aid; it only means that the notification obligation applies.

VIII. The State Aid Control System under Art. 108 TFEU

A. Overview of the Procedural Aspects of State Aid

382 Art. 108 TFEU provides for the procedural rules of the EU State aid control system. In 2015, Council Regulation No. 2015/1589 (hereinafter: Procedural Regulation) was adopted, laying down detailed rules for the application of Art. 108 TFEU.[212] Under this system, a clear distinction has to be made between **existing aid and new aid**. This differentiation is of great relevance as Art. 108 TFEU provides for different procedures for these two categories.

383 **Existing aid** is aid that was in operation before the establishment of the EU or before the date the Member State concerned acceded to the EU (**accession date**).[213] With regard to existing State aid, only a *pro futuro* monitoring procedure of the Commission under Art. 108(3) TFEU takes place. Existing State aid is considered to be lawful and may be granted as long as the Commission does not find it incompatible with the internal market, after having performed the formal investigation procedure under Art. 108(2) TFEU. Hence, a negative decision concerning existing aid, is directed at the future and obliges the Member State to stop granting the aid that was previously accepted.

384 **Individuals** who have concerns about an existing aid may give notice to the Commission and propose that an investigation procedure be initiated.[214] However, they have no right to claim the initiation of a formal investigation procedure under Art. 108(2) TFEU. Furthermore, if the Commission initiates an investigation procedure and finds that an existing aid measure is not, or is no longer, in line with the internal market, this negative decision only has **effect for the future (*ex nunc*)**. If the Member State continues to apply the incompatible State aid measure, a request for recovery is possible.[215]

---

211 CJEU, 21 July 2016, Case C-493/14, *Dilly's Wellnesshotel*, EU:C:2016:577; CJEU, Pending Case C-585/17, *Dilly's Wellnesshotel*.
212 This Regulation replaced Council Regulation (EC) No. 659/1999 of 22 March 1999 laying down detailed rules for the application of Article 93 of the EC Treaty.
213 Art. 1(b) Procedural Regulation comprises an exhaustive list of all the forms of existing aid.
214 Ibid., Art. 24(2).
215 CJEU, 15 March 1994, Case C-387/92, *Banco Exterior de España*, EU:C:1994:100, para. 20.

New aid means all aid that is not existing aid.[216] Therefore, aid that is introduced **385** *after* a Member State's accession to the EU is new aid. The same holds true for any substantial alterations of existing aid.[217] With regard to new aid, a stricter State aid procedure applies (see section VIII.B. of this Chapter): the Member States must first notify their proposed plans to the Commission and obtain its authorization before implementation. Thus, Art. 108(3) TFEU provides for **the prohibition of implementation or a standstill obligation**, meaning that the Member State's authorities and courts may not implement the intended measures prior to the Commission's approval.[218]

The **purpose of this preventive review procedure** for new aid is to enable the Com- **386** mission to evaluate measures before they are implemented to prevent undesirable burdens on the internal market. Even if the unlawfully granted measure is discovered at an early stage and can be tackled, it can be very difficult to restore the *ex-ante* competitive situation and undo the negative effects caused by the measure. Therefore, Art. 108(2) TFEU and the Procedural Regulation provide for a formal investigation procedure that is to be started by the Commission if the suspicion of State aid still exists after a preliminary investigation.

B. Notification and the Standstill Obligation

As to new aid, the procedural demands are higher. Art. 108(3) first sentence TFEU **387** provides that the Member States must inform the Commission of any plans to grant or alter new aid (**notification obligation**). The notification obligation is quite far-reaching: the Member States have to notify any measure that attracts the suspicion of State aid.[219] The notification has to take place in a timely manner so that the Commission can decide on the measure before it is put into effect. Hence, there is a **prohibition of implementation** of the notified measure as long as it is not declared compatible with the internal market by the Commission or is deemed to have been declared compatible.[220] This so-called **standstill obligation** is provided for in **Art. 108(3) TFEU** and is effective during the whole investigation procedure until the final decision is made.

If that aid is implemented without prior notification, it is at least formally il- **388** legal. For aid to be implemented or put into effect, it is not necessary that the aid actually be paid to the beneficiary. Thus, the conferment of powers enabling the aid to be granted without further formality is enough to fulfil this requirement. Therefore, measures (potentially) constituting State aid should be notified to the

---

216 Ibid., Art. 1(c).
217 Kekelekis, Stretching the concept of existing aid alterations and the new role of national courts in State aid proceedings, *EStAL* 2/2017, p. 291 et seq.
218 Art. 3 Procedural Regulation.
219 Art. 2 Procedural Regulation.
220 Ibid., Art. 3.

Commission before their **legal adoption** in the respective Member State.[221] In this respect, the Commission has recommended that Member State authorities include a reserve clause into the new legislation whereby implementation of the measure takes place only after the Commission has finally decided on its character.[222]

389 However, there are a number of **exceptions** to the notification requirement.[223] Notification is not necessary in respect of *de minimis* aid and aid covered by the GBER. Moreover, there is no (additional) notification requirement if the aid is granted on the basis of an authorized aid scheme.[224] These exceptions reduce the administrative burden of the Member States and save the Commission from dealing with a high number of routine State aid cases.

390 According to the case law of the CJEU, the standstill obligation in Art. 108(3) TFEU is **directly applicable in the Member States** and confers rights on **individuals** that the national courts are bound to safeguard.[225] All **national authorities**, i.e. the legislator, tax authorities and the national courts are addressed by the standstill obligation.[226] Thus, none of them should apply a national provision suspected to be unlawful aid.[227] Therefore, aid must not be granted even if other beneficiaries have already received it. By contrast, Art. 107(1) TFEU does not provide for such a direct effect. Hence, a business liable to pay a tax cannot rely on the argument that the exemption enjoyed by another business constitutes State aid within the meaning of Art. 107(1) TFEU in order to avoid paying the tax.[228]

391 If the national court has doubts whether a measure fulfils all the criteria of Art. 107(1) TFEU, it may request that the **CJEU give a preliminary ruling** on the subject under Art. 267 TFEU.[229] A national court of last instance, however, has to refer the question to the CJEU for a preliminary ruling. The Commission has pointed out that Member States may also request assistance by asking for legal or economic information, especially where the application of Art. 107(1) TFEU raises particular difficulties.[230]

---

221 Nicolaides/Kekeleus/Buyshes, *State aid policy in the European Community: a guide for practitioners* (2005) p. 58.

222 Commission, 23rd Report on competition policy 1993, p. 250.

223 Commission notice on the enforcement of State aid law by national courts (hereinafter: Enforcement notice), 2009/C 85/01 of 9 April 2009, para 15.

224 According to Art. 1(b)(iii) Procedural Regulation, individual aid granted on the basis of an authorized scheme is considered existing aid.

225 CJEU, 15 July 1964, Case 6/64, *Costa v E.N.E.L.*, EU:C:1964:66, p. 1273; CJEU, 11 December 1973, Case 120/73, *Lorenz*, EU:C:1973:152, para. 8; CJEU, 21 November 1991, Case C-354/90, *Fédération Nationale du Commerce Extérieur des Produits Alimentaires and Others v France*, EU:C:1991:440, paras. 11-12; CJEU, 11 July 1996, Case C-39/94, *SFEI and Others*, EU:C:1996:285; Enforcement notice, para. 24.

226 CJEU, 15 April 2010, Case C-511/08, *Heinrich Heine*, EU:C:2010:189.

227 Ibid.

228 CJEU, 15 June 2006, Case C-393/04, *Air Liquide*, EU:C:2006:403.

229 Enforcement notice, para. 67.

230 Ibid., para. 77 et seq.

Under the control system of State aid, there is a **"triangle of power"** consisting of **392** the European Commission, the CJEU, and the national courts:[231] While the supervision of new and existing aid lies in the hands of the Commission, which therefore plays an integral part in any State aid procedure, its decisions are subject to review by the GC.[232] Decisions of the GC can, in turn, be appealed before the Court of Justice. National courts, however, have to ensure the effectiveness of the notification obligation and safeguard the rights that individuals enjoy resulting from the direct effect of the standstill obligation.

C. Commission Decisions and Judicial Review

After receiving notification of a new measure, the Commission initiates a **pre-** **393** **liminary examination procedure** that has to result in a decision within a period of two months.[233] If, after the preliminary examination, the Commission comes to the conclusion that the notified measure does not constitute aid (no aid decision) or that the measure is aid but falls under an exception provided for by the TFEU, it gives a decision thereon (decision not to raise objections).[234] If the Commission, after a preliminary examination, still has doubts about the compatibility of the aid and cannot definitely conclude that the aid is not contrary to the State aid prohibition, it will decide to initiate the formal investigation procedure pursuant to Art. 108(2) TFEU.[235] The rules providing for the formal investigation procedure apply for both existing aid and the new aid regime.[236]

The formal investigation procedure ends with a **final decision** by the Commis- **394** sion.[237] It may either decide that the proposed measure is not considered aid at all (**no aid decision**), is aid that is compatible with the internal market (**positive decision**), needs to be modified in order to be regarded as compatible (**conditional decision**), or is incompatible with the internal market (**negative decision**). Like any other legal act, the final decision is subject to review by the EU Courts under Art. 263 TFEU and therefore must be sufficiently reasoned.[238] If the requirement of proper reasoning according to Art. 296 TFEU is not fulfilled, the decision runs the risk of being annulled for lack of motivation.[239]

---

231 Sutter, The *Adria Wien Pipeline* case and the State aid provisions of the EC treaty in tax matters, *ET* 2001, p. 249.
232 Enforcement notice, para. 92.
233 CJEU, 11 December 1973, Case 120/73, *Lorenz*, EU:C:1973:152, para. 4; Art. 4(5) Procedural Regulation.
234 Art. 4(2) and (3) Procedural Regulation.
235 Ibid., Art. 4(4).
236 The formal investigation procedure is provided for in Arts. 6-9 Procedural Regulation.
237 Ibid., Art. 9.
238 For the requirements of the decision initiating the formal investigation procedure see Art. 6 Procedural Regulation.
239 GC, 21 March 1996, Case T-230/94, *Farrugia v Commission*, EU:T:1996:40; CJEU, 21 January 2003, Case C-378/00, *Commission v Parliament/Council*, EU:C:2003:42.

395 To challenge the final decision of the Commission before the GC by means of an action for annulment as regulated by Art. 263 TFEU, the respective parties must make it clear that they are **directly and individually concerned** in terms of Art. 263(4) TFEU by the Commission's decision. However, not only the actual recipient itself, but also potential aid recipients may challenge a negative or conditional decision if they were identified or at least readily identifiable at the time of the adoption of the decision.[240] Moreover, as concerns competitors of the beneficiary, they must demonstrate that they have a significant role in the State aid procedure and that their position in the market is significantly affected by the aid to have legal standing.[241] By contrast, Member States are privileged under Art. 263(2) TFEU and do not need to meet particular requirements.[242]

396 The assessment of whether a new measure (but also existing aid) fulfilling Art. 107(1) TFEU is compatible with the internal market according to Art. 107(2) and (3) TFEU lies within the exclusive power of the Commission, but is subject to review by the EU Courts.[243] As to the scope of **judicial review**, it needs to be distinguished: the CJEU exercises a comprehensive review of whether a measure falls within the scope of Art. 107(1) TFEU.[244] As a matter of principle, the notion of aid is a legal concept that needs to be interpreted based on objective factors. Contrary to Art. 107(2) and (3) TFEU, there is no margin of discretion and thus it is subject to full judicial review. A limited judicial review applies only if an assessment that is technical or complex in nature is necessary in assessing the requirements of Art. 107(1) TFEU. In such a scenario, the Court does not substitute its own assessment for that of the Commission. The scope of judicial review is also limited within the framework of Art. 107(2) and (3) TFEU, where complex economic and social assessments are involved. In this context, limited review means that judicial review is confined to examining whether the Commission complied with the rules of procedure and the duty to give reasons, verify the accuracy of the facts relied on and establish whether there has been an error in law, manifest error in the assessment of facts or misuse of powers.[245]

D. The Consequences of Unlawful Aid

397 If the Commission detects, *ex officio*, or following a complaint from a third party (e.g. competitors), that aid is in place that is not duly notified and therefore constitutes formally unlawful aid, the **Commission** starts the procedure against the

---

240 CJEU, 28 June 2018, Case C-203/16 P, *Dirk Andres*, EU:C:2018:506, paras. 40-58.
241 CJEU, 28 January 1986, Case C-169/84, *Cofaz*, EU:C:1986:42, para. 25; CJEU, 23 May 2000, Case C-106/98 P, *Comité d'entreprise de la Société française de production and others*, EU:C:2000:277, para. 40. However, the requirement of active participation and the effect on the market position is not yet fully clear; see Pastor-Merchante, The protection of competitors under State aid law, *EStAL* 4/2016, p. 535.
242 CJEU, 14 November 1984, Case C-323/82, *Intermills*, EU:C:1984:345, para. 16.
243 Enforcement notice, para. 92.
244 Nehl, in: Hofmann/Micheau (eds.), *State aid law of the European Union* (2016) p. 435 et seq.
245 GC, 16 July 2014, Case T-309/12, *Zweckverband Tierkörperbeseitigung v Commission*, EU:T:2014:676, para. 96.

Member State.[246] The mere fact that the measure was not notified does not auto-matically mean that it is also incompatible with the internal market.[247] If it is not notified on time, the aid is at least formally unlawful because of the breach of the notification and standstill obligation. However, the Commission is obliged to examine the compatibility of the aid with the internal market to determine whether the aid measure is materially unlawful, as well.[248] Therefore, the Com-mission may issue the following decisions regarding unlawful aid: On the one hand, it may find that the measure not duly notified is aid that is compatible with the internal market (**unnotified *but* compatible aid**). In such a case, the aid is only formally, but not materially, unlawful. On the other hand, it may come to the conclusion that the aid not notified is not compatible with the internal market (**unnotified incompatible aid**). In this event, the aid is both formally and materi-ally unlawful. The differentiation between these two types of illegal aid is of major importance, since the ultimate consequences – the recovery of aid – are dependent on the type of unlawful aid.[249] Whereas aid that is both formally and materially unlawful is subject to recovery with regard to the amount of aid received includ-ing interest, formally unlawful aid is subject to interest recovery only.

Art. 16 of the Procedural Regulation stipulates that where negative decisions are taken in cases of unlawful aid, effective competition needs to be restored and aid has to be recovered. The purpose of recovery is to re-establish the situation in the market that would have existed had the unlawful aid not been granted. Recov-ery is not meant to be a penalty, but a consequence of the finding that the aid is unlawful.[250] **398**

If, following a formal investigation procedure, the Commission finds that the un-notified aid measure is incompatible with the internal market, i.e. formally and materially unlawful, it issues a **recovery decision** and requires the Member State concerned to recover the aid including interest from the beneficiary. By means of a recovery decision, the **Commission may only provide for recovery of aid that is both formally and materially unlawful** but not for aid which is just formally unlawful.[251] Formerly authorized aid that has later been declared incompatible as a result of a negative Commission decision, after having performed an investiga-tion, is not subject to recovery in respect of the amounts granted prior to the negative decision, as it was not materially unlawful at that time. However, all amounts of aid that were granted by the Member State after its status changed through the decision are subject to recovery since the measure is then both for-mally and materially unlawful. **399**

246 Art. 24(2) Procedural Regulation; Pastor-Merchante, The protection of competitors under State aid law, *EStAL* 4/2016, p. 536.
247 CJEU, 5 October 1994, Case C-47/91, *Italy v Commission*, EU:C:1994:358.
248 CJEU, 14 February 1990, Case C-301/87, *France v Commission*, EU:C:1990:67, para. 11.
249 Ghazarian, Recovery of State aid, *EStAL* 2/2016, p. 228 et seq.
250 Recovery notice, para. 13 et seq.
251 CJEU, 14 February 1990, Case C-301/87, *France v Commission*, EU:C:1990:67, para. 11.

400 The recovery decision is directly applicable for the Member State addressed, which has to ensure full recovery under its domestic procedural laws.[252] Due to its direct applicability, the specifications of the recovery order supersede conflicting national law, especially with regard to provisions on legal force or interest rates. When ordering recovery, the Commission is not required to provide the exact amount that is to be recovered. It is sufficient for the decision to include enough information to enable the Member State addressed to calculate the amount without too much difficulty.[253] It needs to be added that if the Member State concerned fails to implement a recovery decision, the Commission may initiate infringement proceedings pursuant to Art. 258 TFEU.

401 In general, the recovery of aid also includes interest to compensate for the advantage in time, i.e. the interest advantage. According to Art. 14(2) Procedural Regulation, the Member State must order the aid recipient to pay interest at a level fixed by the Commission for the period of unlawfulness.[254] The aid to be recovered thus includes interest payable from the date on which the unlawful aid was at the disposal of the beneficiary until the date of its recovery.[255] This way, the advantage in time gained by the premature receipt of the aid is neutralized.[256]

402 In its *CELF* judgement, the CJEU clarified that in respect of formally unlawful aid, national courts must order recovery of interest even where the aid is compatible with EU law and the Commission has issued a positive decision.[257] Thus, interest needs to be recovered because the aid should have been granted at a later point in time – after notification and the Commission's subsequent decision – and causes competitors to suffer from the measures' effects earlier than they would have had to.[258] However, since Art. 16 Procedural Regulation only applies to negative decisions and the Commission cannot issue such decisions if aid is only formally unlawful but compatible with the internal market, the consequences of formally unlawful aid depend solely on national law. This fact might reduce the effectiveness of both the notification and standstill obligation.

403 When implementing the recovery decision, the Member States must, in the absence of relevant EU law provisions, follow the **procedural and substantive provisions of their national law**.[259] Hence, the application of national procedural law must comply with the requirements of the principles of effectiveness and equivalence. The principle of **effectiveness** provides that national proceedings

---

252 Recovery notice, para. 46.
253 CJEU, 8 December 2011, Case C-81/10 P, *France Télécom SA*, EU:C:2011:811, para. 102.
254 Recovery notice, para. 39; CJEU, 12 February 2008, Case C-199/06, *CELF*, EU:C:2008:79, para. 55.
255 Art. 16(2) Procedural Regulation.
256 Commission Regulation No. 271/2008 fixing recovery interest rates.
257 CJEU, 12 February 2008, Case C-199/06, *CELF*, EU:C:2008:79, paras. 50-55.
258 Enforcement notice, para. 39.
259 Art. 14(3) Procedural Regulation.

may not render practically impossible, or disproportionately aggravate, the exercise of rights conferred on the basis of EU legislation.[260] The principle of **equivalence** requires that national proceedings for the enforcement of claims under EU law may not be less favourable than proceedings in purely national matters. In this way, **minimum standards** are set for the effective enforcement of claims based on Art. 108(3) TFEU.

The enforcement of the recovery order depends on the procedural rules and remedies available in the respective Member State's legal system and is thus different in each State.[261] What is also worth mentioning is that actions of annulment pursuant to Art. 263 TFEU against the recovery decision do not have the effect of suspending the decision according to Art. 278 TFEU, which means that the national courts must order recovery even though the decision has been appealed. That is why, in the Apple case, for example, Ireland was obliged to recover the aid although the appeal had been filed. Only the CJEU may, upon application of the party, decide to suspend implementation while the Court proceedings are pending. **404**

Nonetheless, there are **limitations to the recovery** of State aid.[262] First, Art. 17 Procedural Regulation provides that the Commission can only order recovery of unlawful and incompatible aid granted within a period of **ten years**. According to Art. 17(2) Procedural Regulation, the limitation period begins to run from the day on which the unlawful aid was awarded to the beneficiary.[263] However, any action taken by the Commission interrupts the limitation period, which then starts running afresh. Secondly, recovery does not have to take place if it would contradict general principles of EU law,[264] such as the principle of legitimate expectations or the principle of legal certainty, or if it is **absolutely impossible** for the Member States to recover the aid.[265] **405**

It should be noted that the **principle of legitimate expectations** is one of the most commonly invoked pleas against recovery orders, but rarely succeeds before EU Courts.[266] According to the CJEU, beneficiaries cannot enjoy protection and rely on this principle unless the measure has been granted in compliance with the procedure laid down in Art. 108 TFEU. The CJEU held that a diligent business operator should normally be able to determine whether that procedure has been **406**

---

260 Birnstiel, Recovery of unlawful State aid, *EStAL* 3/2012, p. 645 et seq.
261 CJEU, 11 December 1973, Case 120/73, *Lorenz*, EU:C:1973:152, para. 8 et seq.
262 Recovery notice, para. 17.
263 CJEU, 8 December 2011, Case C-81/10 P, *France Télécom SA*, EU:C:2011:811, paras. 80-81.
264 Recovery notice, para. 17; see also Rzotkiewicz, The general principle of EU law and their role in the review of State aid put into effect by Member States, *EStAL* 3/13, p. 464 et seq.
265 CJEU, 23 February 1995, Case C-349/93, *Italy v Commission*, EU:C:1995:53, para. 12; CJEU, 4 April 1995, Case C-348/93, *Commission v Italy*, EU:C:1995:95, para. 16.
266 Saavedra Pinto, The 'narrow' meaning of the legitimate expectations principle in State aid law versus the foreign investor's legitimate expectations, *EStAL* 2/2016, p. 273 et seq.

followed.[267] This shows that the actual scope of protection of undertakings' expectations is quite restricted.[268] Accordingly, legitimate expectations are acknowledged only in limited circumstances, e.g. in the event of assurance of a measure's compatibility resulting either from a positive action or inaction involving the Commission or the EU Courts (e.g. a positive decision on the same measure in the past, an extraordinary delay of a Commission decision concerning recovery and the Commission's interpretation of a CJEU decision that offers grounds to believe that the measure is in accordance with State aid law).[269]

407 Generally speaking, the necessity to recover unlawful State aid has been criticized as curtailing economic prosperity in the internal market. In the long run, exposure to retroactive payment demands could discourage economic players from pursuing business within the EU, in particular in cases where undertakings have relied in good faith on tax rulings that were structurally designed to achieve legal certainty as to the application of the rules. Besides, recovery could be particularly problematic in the area of tax law.[270] With regard to tax measures, recovery takes the form of retroactive taxation. However, retroactive taxation based on primary law without any legal basis in national tax law might conflict with the rule of law, which is also a general EU principle.[271]

---

267 CJEU, 11 November 2004, Joined Cases C-183/02 P and C-187/02 P, *Demesa and Territorio Histórico de Álava*, EU:C:2004:701, paras. 44-45; CJEU, 8 December 2011, Case C-81/10 P, *France Télécom SA*, EU:C:2011:811, para. 59.

268 Pistone, *Legal remedies in European tax law* (2009) p. 255 et seq.

269 Hancher/Ottervanger/Slot, EU State aids, 5th edition (2016) para. 26-017; CJEU, 22 June 2006, Joined Cases C-182/03 and C-217/03, *Belgium and Forum 187 v Commission*, EU:C:2006:416, paras. 153-155; CJEU, 24 November 1987, Case 223/85, *Rijn-Schelde-Verolme v Commission* (1987), 901; Commission Decision of 9 March 2004 on an aid scheme implemented by Austria for a refund from the energy taxes on natural gas and electricity in 2002 and 2003, C(2004)325, OJ L 190 of 22 July 2005, para. 66.

270 Kokott, Steuerrecht und unionsrechtlicher Beihilfebegriff, in: Lang (ed.) *Europäisches Steuerrecht* (2018) p. 555 et seq.

271 Bal, Tax Rulings, State Aid and the Rule of Law, in: Van Brederode (ed.), *Ethics and Taxation* (2020) p. 374 et seq.

IX. Overview of the Procedural Treatment of State Aid

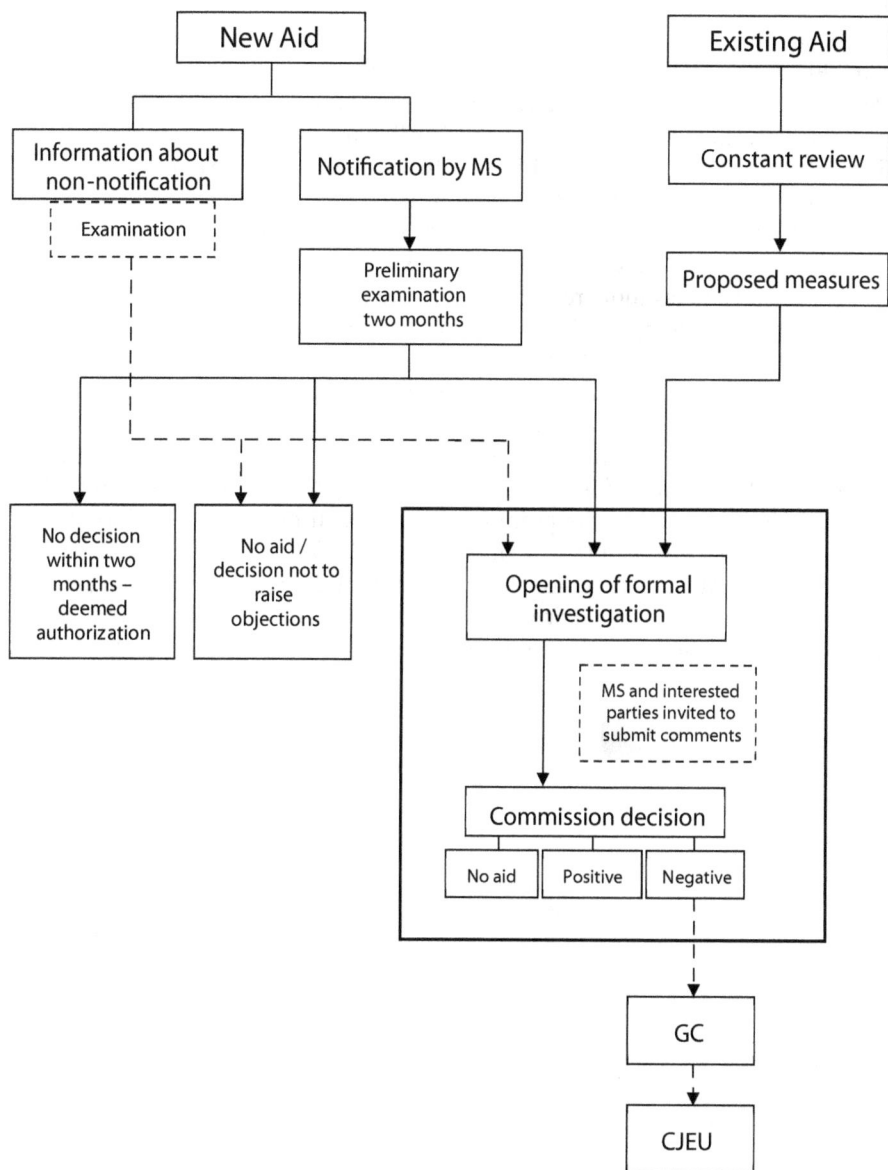

```
┌─────────────────┐                        ┌─────────────────┐
│     New Aid     │                        │  Existing Aid   │
└─────────────────┘                        └─────────────────┘
         │                                          │
  ┌──────┴──────┐                                   │
┌───────────────┐   ┌───────────────┐      ┌─────────────────┐
│ Information    │   │ Notification  │      │ Constant review │
│ about          │   │ by MS         │      └─────────────────┘
│ non-notification│  └───────────────┘               │
└───────────────┘           │                        │
  ┌ ─ ─ ─ ─ ─ ┐             │              ┌─────────────────┐
  │Examination│    ┌───────────────┐       │Proposed measures│
  └ ─ ─ ─ ─ ─ ┘    │  Preliminary  │       └─────────────────┘
                   │  examination  │
                   │  two months   │
                   └───────────────┘
```

- **New Aid**
  - **Information about non-notification**
    - Examination
  - **Notification by MS**
    - Preliminary examination two months
- **Existing Aid**
  - **Constant review**
    - **Proposed measures**

- **No decision within two months – deemed authorization**
- **No aid / decision not to raise objections**
- **Opening of formal investigation**
  - MS and interested parties invited to submit comments
  - **Commission decision**
    - No aid
    - Positive
    - Negative

- **GC**
- **CJEU**

408 **Literature**

Bacon, *European Union law of State aid*, 3rd edition (2017); Englisch, Equality under State aid rules and VAT, *World Journal of VAT/GST Law* 8/2019, p. 22; Fort, EU State aid and tax: an evolutionary approach, *ET* 2017, p. 375; Giraud/ Petit, Tax rulings and State aid qualification: should reality matter?, *EStAL* 2/2017, p. 233; Gormsen, *European State Aid and Tax Rulings* (2019); Hancher/Ottervanger/ Slot (eds.), *EU State aids*, 5th edition (2016); Hofmann/Micheau (eds.), *State aid law of the European Union* (2016); Jaeger, From *Santander* to Luxleaks – and back, *EStAL* 3/2015, p. 355; Kokott, *Das Steuerrecht der Europäischen Union* (2018); Lang, Seminar J: Steuerrecht, Grundfreiheiten und Beihilfeverbot, *IStR* 2010, p. 579; Lang, State aid and taxation: recent trends in the case law of the ECJ, *EStAL* 2/2012, p. 418; Lang, Tax rulings and State aid law, *British Tax Review* 2015, p. 394; Lyal, Transfer pricing rules and State aid, *Fordham Int'l L.J.* 2015, para. 1017; Micheau, Fundamental freedoms and State aid rules under EU law: the example of taxation, *ET* 2012, p. 213; Nicolaides, State aid rules and tax rulings, *EStAL* 3/2016, p. 420; Quigley, *European State aid law and policy*, 3rd edition (2015); Richelle/Schön/ Traversa (eds.), *State aid and business taxation* (2016); Rossi-Maccanico, The *Gibraltar* judgement and the point on selectivity in fiscal aids, *EC Tax Review* 2009, p. 74; Rust/Micheau (eds.), *State aid and tax law* (2013); Szudoczky, Convergence of the analysis of national tax measures under the EU State aid rules and the fundamental freedoms, *EStAL* 3/2016, p. 363; Szudoczky, *The sources of EU law and their relationships: lessons for the field of taxation* (2014) p. 659.

Chapter 5 – The Parent-Subsidiary Directive

Mario Tenore

I.   Aims of the Directive

409   Council Directive 2011/96/EU of 30 November 2011 (recast)[1] on the common system of taxation applicable in the case of parent companies and subsidiaries of Member States (hereinafter "the Directive") deals with the elimination of economic double taxation arising within a group of companies from **cross-border distributions of profits,** as well as the avoidance of double non-taxation resulting from the combined effect of the exemption of dividends in the Member State of the parent and the deductibility of the same dividends at the level of subsidiary in its Member State of residence.

410   The fourth preamble to the Directive affirms the need to create within the EU *"conditions analogous to those of an internal market"* and to *"ensure the effective functioning of the common market …."* The **elimination of economic double taxation** is a necessary precondition to achieving the aforementioned objectives. Accordingly, the Directive provides – under certain conditions – an exemption from withholding tax in the State of the subsidiary, as well as an obligation for the State of the parent company to either exempt or grant an underlying tax credit (offsetting the taxes paid at the level of the subsidiary). The Directive relieves the two layers of tax levied in the hands of the parent company upon the distribution of profits, i.e. the withholding tax in the State of the subsidiary and the corporate tax levied in the hands of the parent company on the profits so received in its State of residence.[2] Due to the elimination of the withholding tax in the State of the subsidiary, it can be concluded that the elimination of **juridical double taxation** is also an indirect effect of applying the Directive.

411   After an initial draft proposal delivered in 1969, the Directive was finally **adopted in 1990,**[3] together with Council Directive 90/434/EEC of 23 July 1990 on the common system of taxation applicable to mergers, divisions, transfers of assets and exchanges of shares concerning companies of different Member States (hereinafter

---

1   The Directive recasts Council Directive 90/435/EEC on the common system of taxation applicable in the case of parent companies and subsidiaries of different Member States, OJ L 225, 22 September 1990 without entailing a material amendment of the rules contained in this Directive. The recast was necessary since Directive 90/435/EEC has been amended several times and further amendments may possibly be made in the future. The recast was also necessary (i) to update the Annexes to Directive 90/435/EEC and (ii) to redraft the wording of the second subparagraph of Art. 4(3) of Directive 90/435/EEC for the purpose of clarifying that the rules referred to therein are adopted by the Council acting in accordance with the procedure provided for in the TFEU.

2   It follows that the income remains taxed only once in the hands of the subsidiary in its State of residence.

3   The final version of the Directive departed from the 1969 draft proposal in at least two respects. First, whilst the 1969 Draft proposal envisaged the exemption method exclusively, the final version of the Directive left the Member States free to decide between the exemption and the indirect credit method in order to relieve economic double taxation. Second, the final version of the Directive contained no option for the parent company to consolidate the profits of the foreign subsidiary, with a view to making such a company comparable to a foreign permanent establishment.

the "Merger Directive")[4] and Convention 90/436/EEC of 23 July 1990 on the Elimination of Double Taxation in Connection with the adjustment of Profits of Associated Enterprises (hereinafter the "Arbitration Convention").[5] Since then, the original text has been modified a number of times.

The first revision triggered by **amending Directive 2003/123/EC** (hereinafter **412** "the 2003 amending Directive")[6] dealt with the practical problems that had arisen since the early 1990s.[7] The 2003 amending Directive broadened, inter alia, the scope of the Directive by extending it to permanent establishments, as well as to the SE.[8]

Further amendments to the Directive were made following the adoption of **413** (i) **Council Directive 2014/86/EU of 8 July 2014** (hereinafter the "2014 amending Directive"), to be implemented by 31 December 2015, which has modified, inter alia, Art. 4(1)(a) of the Directive with a view to countering double non-taxation resulting from the combined effect of the exemption of dividends in the Member State of the parent and the deductibility of the same dividends at the level of the subsidiary in its Member State of residence and (ii) **Council Directive 2015/121 of 27 January 2015** (hereinafter the "2015 amending Directive"), which, inter alia, introduced a general anti-abuse clause in Art. 1(1) and 1(2) of the Directive.

II. Subjective Scope

A. Definition of "Company of a Member State"

Art. 2(1)(a) of the Directive defines the subjective scope of the Directive and **414** includes a definition of the term "**company of a Member State**", which must be met both at the level of the parent company and at the level of the distributing entity. The term "company of a Member State" includes any company that meets the following cumulative requirements:

---

4   Council Directive 90/434/EEC of 23 July 1990 on the Common system of taxation applicable of mergers, divisions, partial divisions, transfers of assets and exchange of shares concerning companies of different Member States and to the transfer of the registered office, of an SE or SCE, between Member States, OJ L 225 of 20 August 1990.

5   Convention 90/436 of 23 July 1990 on the elimination of double taxation in connection with the adjustment of profits of associated enterprises, OJ L 225 (1990).

6   Council Directive 2003/123/EC of 22 December 2003 amending Directive 90/435/EEC on the common system of taxation applicable in the case of parent companies and subsidiaries of different Member States, OJ L 007 of 13 January 2004.

7   The amendment of the Directive was also envisaged by the Commission in its Communication "Company Taxation in the Internal Market", COM(2001) 582 final, SEC (2001) 1681.

8   The amending Directive also introduced other substantive changes to the 1990 version of the Directive, namely the gradual reduction to 10 % of the minimum holding threshold, the treatment of profits derived by subsidiary companies that are regarded as transparent for tax purposes in the State of the parent, and finally the abolition of transitional and special regimes.

a. it takes one of the forms listed in the annex (hereinafter the "Annex") to the Directive [Art. 2(a)(i) of the Directive];

b. it resides for domestic tax purposes in a Member State; furthermore, under any double taxation convention (DTC) concluded with non-EU Member States, such a company may not be regarded as resident in any of those states [Art. 2(a)(ii) of the Directive]; and

c. it is subject to one of the corporate taxes listed in Art. 2, without the possibility of an option or of being exempt [Art. 2)(a)(iii) of the Directive].

It is doubtful whether, although not expressly mentioned, the application of the Directive is subject to the condition that the parent company also qualify as the beneficial owner of the dividends. In particular, in the recent Danish cases, the Court incidentally mentioned that, where the beneficial owner of dividends paid is resident for tax purposes in a third State, the source State may refuse to apply the exemption at source even in the absence of abuse.[9] Based on the above, it can be inferred that, in pan-European situations, the beneficial ownership requirement is *per se* a condition for the application of the Directive.[10]

415 Under (a) and (b), the Directive adopts a **list-based approach**. With regard to (a), the Annex to the Directive lists the legal forms. In respect of certain states, the list includes, however, a residual entity clause that allows for the application of the Directive to any company constituted under the law of such countries and subject to corporate tax therein.[11] Investment funds and pension funds are not listed, save for a few exceptions.[12] In respect of certain states, the list also includes public and private entities that are subject to corporate tax and carry on business activities. In the *Gaz de France* case the Court pointed out the exhaustive nature of the list; accordingly, the application of the Directive may not be extended by analogy to other forms of companies, even if these companies were later included by virtue of the 2003 amending Directive.[13]

416 With regard to (b), Art. 2 of the Directive lists the **types of corporate tax**. This article also includes a residual clause, which refers "to any other tax which may be

---

9   CJEU, 26 February 2019, Joined Cases C-116/16 to C-117/16, *Skatteministeriet v. T Danmark and Y Denmark Aps*, EU:C:2019:135, para. 111.

10 On this point, Advocate General Kokott rejected this conclusion. In her Opinion, delivered on 1 March 2018, she relied on a strictly literal interpretation of the Directive (see para. 86 of the Opinion, "*[...] the approach of the Parent-Subsidiary Directive differs from that of the Interest and Royalties Directive and therefore deliberately avoids using the term 'beneficial owner'*)."

11 See the annex to the Directive, for example, letters (b), (c), (e), (f), (i), (j) and (k).

12 See letters (p) and (s) listing the Luxembourg "Association d'épargne pension" and the Netherlands "Fonds voor gemene rekening", respectively. See Maisto, The 2003 amendments to the EC Parent-Subsidiary Directive: What's next?, *EC Tax Review* 2004, p. 172.

13 CJEU, 1 October 2009, Case C-247/08, *Gaz de France*, EU:C:2009:600. See also CJEU, 2 April 2020, Case C-458/18, *GVC Services (Bulgaria)» EOOD*, EU:C:2020:266, para. 35, wherein the CJEU took the position that a company incorporated and subject to corporation tax in Gibraltar is not eligible for the withholding tax exemption envisaged in the Directive.

substituted for any of the above taxes." The list under (b) is intended to define the subjective scope of the Directive and is only relevant for the purpose of interpreting the term "**company of a Member State**". Accordingly, the list does not affect the objective scope of the Directive, i.e. the taxes covered by the Directive (e.g. exemption in the State of residence should also be extended to taxes other than those listed even if not classified as corporate tax). In addition to listing the types of corporate taxes, Art. 2(a)(iii) also dictates a subject-to-tax requirement. The latter requirement was recently clarified in the *Wereldhave* [14] case in which the Court clarified that the subject-to-tax requirement laid down in Art. 2(a)(iii) of the Directive contemplates two conditions: (i) a positive condition, i.e. the relevant company must be liable to tax, and (ii) a negative condition, i.e. the relevant company must not be exempt from tax and not have the possibility of an option for an exemption (para. 31). This double requirement excludes from the scope of application of the Directive companies that are not actually liable to pay one of the listed taxes (para. 32), such as investment funds that are subject to a zero corporate tax rate, which is equivalent, in practical terms, to a full exemption from tax (paras. 33-34). [15]

Lastly the condition under (b) above requires the company to be resident in a Member State both under domestic and tax treaty law. Such a requirement prevents the application of the Directive even if a company is resident, for domestic law purposes, in a Member State but is considered to be a resident of a non-EU Member State under the tie-breaker rule contained in the DTC concluded with that non-EU Member State. [16] It is not compulsory for a company to meet the three requirements in the same Member State, [17] unless this is expressly set forth in the Annex (e.g. let b) contains a residual clause which refers to „other companies constituted under Belgian law subject to Belgian corporate tax"). The Directive also applies to companies that are constituted under the law of a certain Member State and are subject to corporate tax in a different Member State. The wording of certain residual entity clauses provided in the Annex to the Directive, however, seems to

417

---

14   CJEU, 8 March 2017, Case C-448/15, *Belgische Staat v Wereldhave Belgium Comm. VA and Others*, EU:C:2017:180.

15   For a comprehensive analysis of the decision, see Arginelli, *The Subject-to-Tax Requirement in the EU Parent-Subsidiary Directive* (2011/96) *ET* 2017.

16   Art. 4(3) OECD MC (2017 Version) provides for a tie-breaker rule that applies when a company is considered resident under the domestic law of both contracting States. In such a case, the provision states that the competent authorities of the Contracting States shall endeavour to determine by mutual agreement the Contracting State of which such person shall be deemed to be a resident for the purposes of the Convention, having regard to its place of effective management, the place where it is incorporated or otherwise constituted and any other relevant factors. In the absence of such agreement, such person shall not be entitled to any relief or exemption from tax provided by this Convention except to the extent and in such manner as may be agreed upon by the competent authorities of the Contracting. The vast majority of double tax conventions contemplate the old version of Art. 4(3) OECD MC (2014 Version) under which the company must be regarded as resident only in the State in which its place of effective management is located.

17   Terra/Wattel, *European Tax Law* (2019) p. 225.

be more restrictive, requiring that the company be constituted under the law of a Member State and be subject to corporate tax in that same State.[18]

B. Definition of "Parent Company"

418   Art. 3(1)(a) defines "**parent company**" as a company that holds at least a 10 % stake in the capital of a company of another Member State; both companies must fulfil the requirement provided for in Art. 2. The participation in the latter company may also be held wholly or partially through a permanent establishment.[19]

419   The CJEU held in the *Les Vergers du Vieux Tauves SA* case that the concept of a holding in the capital of a company of another Member State does not include the **holding of shares in usufruct**. The usufruct arrangement is not such as to endow the company receiving the dividends with the "status of shareholder", even if the usufruct holder were to be attributed the voting powers and would *de facto* not differ from a shareholder in this respect.[20]

420   The wording of Art. 3(1)(a) does not clarify whether the holding stake may be held indirectly, i.e. through an intermediate company, although the prevailing opinion in the literature is against this interpretation.[21]

421   Art. 3(2) gives the Member States the opportunity to derogate twice from Art. 3(1)(a). First, Member States may replace – by means of a bilateral agreement – the criterion of a holding in the capital of the subsidiary with that of voting rights. Second, Member States may also make the application of the Directive subject to an **uninterrupted holding period** requirement of at least two years.

422   The first derogation takes into account the fact that many Member States do make reference in their domestic law to the **voting rights requirement** whereas the second derogation is meant to prevent abusive constructions, such as securities lending schemes, aimed at obtaining the more favourable tax regime provided for in the Directive.

423   The **holding period requirement** may be relevant for both outgoing and ingoing flows of dividends, i.e. for profits distributed to foreign parent companies and for

---

18   See Annex, let. i "*companies under Greek law known as 'ανώνυμη εταιρεία', 'εταιρεία περιορισμένης ευθύνης (E.Π.E.)' and other companies constituted under Greek law subject to Greek corporate tax*" (emphasis added).

19   The scenario in which the participation is held through a permanent establishment will be dealt with in m.no. 456 et seq.

20   CJEU, 22 December 2008, Case C-48/07, *Les Vergers du Vieux Tauves SA*, EU:C:2008:758, para. 41.

21   See Maisto, The 2003 amendments to the EC Parent-Subsidiary Directive: What's next?, *EC Tax Review*, 2004, p. 176, according to whom indirect holdings should not be covered "*due to the fact that the lowering of the minimum holding satisfied by itself the desire to broaden the scope of the Directive.*" A statement that seems to accept the relevance of indirect holdings can be found in the Commission Communication COM 2011(714) Final, Proposal for a Council Directive on a common system of taxation applicable to interest and royalty payments made between associated companies of different Member States, p. 8.

profits received by domestic parent companies, respectively. Vice versa, it is possible for a Member State to set a holding period requirement exclusively for outgoing flows of profits or – alternatively – exclusively for incoming flows of profits. Finally, it is even possible for a Member State to provide for different holding periods for outbound and inbound distributions.[22]

The CJEU clarified the application of the holding period requirement in joined **424** cases **Denkavit-Vitic-Voormeer.**[23] The CJEU pointed out that Member States cannot make the grant of the exemption under Art. 5(1) of the Directive subject to the condition that the holding period be met at the moment the profits are distributed. The CJEU acknowledged that However, since the Directive is silent on procedures, it is not for the Court to impose a particular arrangement on the Member States. Having said that it can be inferred that from a procedural standpoint, Member States are free to choose whether to apply the exemption (i) immediately at the time of the payment and revoke the benefits if the holding period is not met or (ii) upon a subsequent refund of the withholding tax once the holding period requirement is met.

C. Definition of "Subsidiary Company"

Art. 3(1)(b) defines the term "**subsidiary company**" as a company the capital of **425** which the holding of the "parent", as defined in Art. 3(1)(a), is included. The 2003 amending Directive introduced Art. 4(1)(a) in order to clarify that when the State of the parent company considers the subsidiary transparent for tax purposes "on the basis of that State's assessment of the legal characteristics of that subsidiary arising from the law under which it is constituted ...," this State is nevertheless obliged to eliminate economic double taxation when taxing the profits when they arise and to regard as irrelevant for tax purposes the subsequent distribution of profits.

Art. 4(1)(a) eliminates therefore any possibility of economic double taxation, which **426** could **temporarily** persist due to the fact that taxation of profits when they arise occurs prior to the time of the actual distribution of dividends.[24] By contrast, the Directive does address the situation in which the parent company is regarded as transparent under the domestic tax law of the subsidiary State (as may be the case due to application of CFC legislation, if any).

---

22 It is, however, possible that, due to the existence of different holding requirements, as well as different holding periods in the Member States, the Directive regime may be applicable solely in one State, e.g. the State of the subsidiary, and not in another State, i.e. the State of the parent. See Terra/Wattel, *European Tax Law* (2019) p. 231.

23 CJEU, 17 October 1996, Joined Cases C-283/94, C-291/94 and C-292/94, *Denkavit, VITIC and Voormeer*, EU:C:1996:387.

24 This result was achieved by the domestic law of most States even prior to the addition of Art. 4(1)(a) in the Directive. See Maisto, The 2003 amendments to the EC Parent-Subsidiary Directive: What's next?, *EC Tax Review* 2004, p. 175.

D. Definition of "Permanent Establishment"

427　The 2003 amending Directive included a definition of the term "**permanent establishment**", which was needed in the light of the broader scope of the Directive. The term "permanent establishment" is defined in Art. 2(b) as "*a fixed place of business situated in a Member State through which the business of a company of another Member State is wholly or partly carried on ....*"

428　The definition of Art. 2(b) refers to what is known as a **material permanent establishment**, defined in Art. 5(1) OECD MC. Moreover, such a definition requires the profits of a permanent establishment to be subject to tax in the Member State where the permanent establishment is located both under domestic and treaty law. The Directive does not envisage other types of permanent establishment provided for in Art. 5 OECD MC, such as the agency permanent establishment or construction permanent establishment dealt with in the OECD MC in Art. 5(3) and Art. 5(5), respectively. The definition contained in Art. 2(b) of the Directive should consider the treaty developments of EU Member States. For example, assume that EU Country A and EU Country B have both signed the OECD Multilateral Convention[25] and both have chosen Option A in Art. 13 of such Convention.[26] In such a case, if all the requirements are met for the application of the Directive, the broader treaty definition of permanent establishment resulting therefrom should also affect the definition of permanent establishment contained in Art. 2(b) of the Directive (with regard to intercompany dividend distributions involving the aforementioned countries). This conclusion relies on the fact that Art. 13 tackles the use of specific activity exemptions in order to artificially avoid the existence of a permanent establishmentand is thus aimed at countering a particular instance of abuse (i.e. fragmentation of the activities). Given that the Directive does not preclude the application of "agreement-based provisions required for the prevention of fraud or abuse" (see Art. 1(2) of the Directive), the broader definition of permanent establishment contained in the treaty between EU Country A and EU Country B should prevail over the definition of permanent establishment contained in Art. 2(b) of the Directive.

III. Objective and Territorial Scope

429　The analysis of the **objective scope** of the Directive will be divided into three main parts. The first part deals with the interpretation of the terms "distribution of profits" and "distributed profits". The second and third parts contribute to defining the objective and **territorial scope** of the Directive. In particular, the second part

---

25　*Multilateral Convention to Implement Tax Treaty Related Measures to Prevent Base Erosion and Profit Shifting* (24 Nov. 2016).

26　Under Option A, the specific activity exemption is limited to circumstances in which the activity is of a "preparatory or auxiliary" nature, which requires a subjective analysis based on the concrete facts and circumstances of the case.

deals with a plain-vanilla bilateral situation involving a qualifying parent company and its subsidiary. This situation will be analysed taking into account separately the perspective of the two States involved, i.e. the parent company State and the subsidiary State. The third part deals with situations involving the presence of a permanent establishment – located in a State other than that of the subsidiary – to which the distributed profits are attributable.

A. The Terms "Distribution of Profits" and "Distributed Profits"

The Directive uses the terms "**distribution of profits**" and "**profits distributed**" **430** in Art. 1(1) and Art. 4(1), respectively, instead of making reference to the term "dividends". The terms "distribution of profits" and "profits distributed", however, are not defined in those provisions or elsewhere in the Directive. One must therefore wonder whether the terms have to be interpreted according to the domestic law of the Member States, or vice versa, and whether they should be given an autonomous interpretation regardless of any domestic law meaning.[27] The latter interpretation should be preferred, although it would not be possible to depart entirely from the characterization of the income under domestic law, insofar as the latter is relevant in establishing whether or not certain items of income are taxable.[28]

The terms "distribution of profits" and "profits distributed" have a **broader scope** **431** than the term "dividends". It has been argued that the term includes any kind of transfer of benefits – without consideration – from a qualifying subsidiary, resident in a Member State, to its qualifying parent company, resident in another Member State.[29] It has also been argued that the Directive covers deemed distributions of profits such as those resulting from the application of thin capitalization rules, as well as those resulting from the application of transfer pricing rules. Such an expansive interpretation of the Directive seems therefore in line with one of its main goals, i.e. the elimination of economic double taxation.[30] On the other hand, one may argue that this interpretation contrasts with the *Les Vergers du*

---

27   According to Maisto, in: Maisto/Weber (eds.), *EU Income Tax Law: Issues for the Years Ahead* (2013), "*In favour of the commercial law qualification, one can observe that the Directive makes express reference to Member States' tax laws in order to define the Directive's subjective scope. Qualification of profits under commercial law is also favoured by the existence of common accounting principles in the Member States and by the existence of common rules on the annual accounts of companies in the Member States. On the contrary, reference to tax laws (either of the state of residence or of the subsidiary or of the parent company) would imply a hidden transfer to the Member State to define the scope of application of the Directive by determining the magnitude of the concept of "profits distributed", thereby jeopardizing a uniform application of the Directive throughout the European Union. This would of course be in contrast with the aim of the Directive.*"

28   Helminen, *The Dividend Concept in International Tax Law* (1999) p. 74.

29   *Ibid.*

30   *Ibid.*

Vieux Tauves SA decision where the CJEU required that the dividends must be received in the capacity of shareholder under commercial law.[31]

432 The Directive is silent in respect of **disagreements** between the Member States concerning the characterization of certain types of income as profits distributed within the meaning of either Art. 4 or Art. 5 of the Directive.[32] These cases are not dealt with by the EU Arbitration Convention and it is unclear whether they can be addressed by the recently approved Council Directive (EU) 2017/1852 of 10 October 2017 on tax dispute resolution mechanisms in the European Union, since Art. 1 of such directive refers to disputes arising from "*the interpretation and application of agreements and conventions that provide for the elimination of double taxation of income and, where applicable, capital.*"

433 In cases concerning **deemed distributions of profits,** it is necessary to distinguish situations in which the parent company has a qualifying holding in the capital of the subsidiary from situations in which no such holding exists.[33] Such a distinction appears relevant for the purpose of applying Art. 4 and Art. 5 of the Directive, which deal with the elimination of economic double taxation in the State of the parent company and with the exemption from withholding tax in the State of the subsidiary, respectively.

434 Unlike Art. 5, Art. 4 of the Directive makes reference to the term "**by virtue of association**", making it explicit that benefits provided by reason thereof are granted to the extent the qualifying parent company has a holding in the capital of the qualifying subsidiary. It has been argued that the absence of such a holding would render the Directive exclusively binding for the State of the subsidiary.[34]

435 However, since the *Les Vergers du Vieux Tauves SA* case, this position should no longer have merit: the CJEU has indeed held that the application of the Directive requires **a holding relationship** between the companies involved. As a result, the benefits of the Directive should not apply insofar as this condition is not met

---

31 According to Maisto, in: Maisto/Weber (eds.), *EU Income Tax Law: Issues for the Years Ahead* (2013), "*Les Vergers du Vieux Tauves has set the scene for an autonomous definition of the expression "holding in the capital". Such definition rests entirely on the civil law qualification of the relationship between the recipient of the income and the paying entity. Accordingly, its meaning is not influenced by tax considerations. It is expected that this conclusion of the Court – which conflicts with Advocate-General Mischo's Opinion in Lankhorst Hohorst (Case C-324/00) [29] – shall also influence the meaning of the term "distributed profits [...] The meaning of this latter term should also be found on the basis of the civil law qualification: the close relationship between the notion of holding in the capital and that of distributed profits would indeed make it difficult to accept a different* solution."

32 Thömmes/Nakhai, in: Thömmes/Fuks (eds.), *EC Corporate Tax Law* (loose leaf) p. 26.

33 *Ibid.*

34 It has been argued that such an interpretation would allow for the application of Art. 5 of the Directive to deemed distributions of profits resulting from transfer pricing adjustments made between sister companies. See Maisto, The 2003 amendments to the EC Parent-Subsidiary Directive: What's next?, *EC Tax Review* 2004, p. 177.

(e.g. with regard to deemed distributions of dividends that result from secondary transfer pricing adjustments between sister companies).[35]

B. Application of the Directive in the State of the Parent Company

In defining the objective scope of the Directive, Art. 1, let. a) includes "*distribution*   **436** *of profits received by companies which come from their subsidiaries of other Member States.*" Art. 1(a) must be read together with Art. 4 and Art. 6, which impose two distinct obligations on the Member State of the parent company.

Art. 4 affirms the obligation on the State of the parent company to eliminate eco-   **437** nomic double taxation arising in respect of such an inbound distribution of profits. In particular, the State of the parent company is given the option to either **exempt** the profits received by the parent or tax such profits while granting a **tax credit for the corporate tax** (so called "indirect tax credit") paid by the subsidiary and any lower-tier subsidiary, insofar as, in respect of each tier, the requirements set out in Art. 2 and Art. 3 are fulfilled.[36]

The choice of either option reflects the **fiscal policy** pursued by the Member State   **438** concerned.[37] In any event, Member States must **exercise the choice** between the exemption method and the credit method in a way that complies with **primary law**. In this respect, they may not disregard the case law of the CJEU, such as the *FII Group Litigation* cases,[38] when the State of the parent applies the exemption method to a domestic distribution and the imputation credit for inbound distributions, and the *Kronos* case for the opposite situation.[39]

Lastly, Art. 4(1) of the Directive also provides for an exception whereby the State   **439** of the parent is not obliged to relieve economic double taxation if the profits result

---

35   See Tenore, Taxation of dividends: a comparison of selected issues under Article 10 OECD MC and the Parent-Subsidiary Directive, *Intertax* 2010, p. 222.

36   On 22 September 2011 the Economic and Monetary Affairs (ECON) Committee in the European Parliament issued a report on the recast of the Parent-Subsidiary Directive proposing a minimum taxation requirement. According to this proposed amendment, the State of the parent company (or where the PE that receives the "distributed profits" is located) should refrain from taxing such profits only if they have been taxed in the country of the subsidiary at a corporate tax rate not lower than 70% of the average corporate tax rate in the EU, or should tax these profits at a corporate tax rate of not lower than 70% of the EU average corporate tax rate (i.e. 16%, which amounts to 70% of the profits being taxed at the average EU corporate tax rate of 23.2%), while allowing a deduction of the tax paid in the State of the distributing subsidiary. This measure was meant to avoid the shifting of income to low-tax jurisdictions, but it was ultimately rejected by the Council.

37   In particular, the exemption method will achieve capital import neutrality (CIN), whereas the credit method will achieve capital export neutrality (CEN).

38   CJEU, 12 December 2006, Case C-446/04, *Test Claimants in the FII Group Litigation*, EU:C:2006:774; CJEU, 13 November 2012, Case C-35/11, *Test Claimants in the FII Group Litigation*, EU:C:2012:707.

39   CJEU, 11 September 2014, Case C-47/12, *Kronos International Inc. v Finanzamt Leverkusen*, EU:C: 2014:2200.

---

from the **liquidation of the subsidiary.** The CJEU clarified in the *Punch Graphix* case that the notion of "liquidation" as used in Art. 4(1) of the Directive must be interpreted in line with the definition of "merger" dictated by the Merger Directive. The CJEU reached this conclusion relying on the fact that (i) the proposal for the Directive was submitted by the European Commission on the same day as that of the Merger Directive and that (ii) both directives have the same objective to abolish restrictions, disadvantages or distortions arising in particular from the tax provisions of the Member States for the operations covered by those directives, governing different types of transnational cooperation between companies, and constituting *"according to the legislature's plan, a whole, in that they complement each other."*[40]

1. The Exemption Method

440 With regard to the **exemption method** under Art. 4(1)(a) of the Directive, the CJEU held in the *Cobelfret* case[41] that the rule is sufficiently clear and unconditional; therefore, it does not need to be implemented in domestic law and taxpayers may rely on this provision directly before national courts.[42]

441 The 2014 amending Directive amended Art. 4(1)(a) in order **to counteract double non-taxation** arising notably from the exemption of the income in the parent's State of residence and the deduction of the same income in the subsidiary's State of residence. Art. 4(1)(a) provides therefore that the State of residence of the parent company is to exempt the profits paid by the subsidiary resident in the other Member State if such profits are not deductible in the hands of the latter company. In the opposite case (the profits are deductible), Art. 4(1)(a) requires the parent's State of residence to refrain from applying the exemption and imposes on that State an **obligation to tax the dividends** received by the parent company. Art. 4(1)(a) of the Directive raises some interpretative issues, such as how to define the term "distributed profits" or what if the payment is not effectively deducted or has been partially deducted in the other State. The obligation to tax raises some issues of coordination with the recently approved Council Directive amending Directive (EU) 2016/1164 as regards hybrid mismatches with third countries (hereafter "ATAD 2") as regards hybrid mismatches with third countries[43] (See Chapter 8 for further on this). In this respect, it must be observed that ATAD 2 expressly provides that, insofar as the Directive is applicable *"there should be no scope for the application of the hybrid mismatch rules provided for in*

---

40   CJEU, 18 October 2012, Case C-371/11, *Punch Graphix*, EU:C:2012:647, p. 35.

41   CJEU, 12 February 2009, Case C-138/07, *Cobelfret*, EU:C:2009:82.

42   In the *Cobelfret* decision, the Court clarified that the Belgian dividends deduction system led to *de facto* taxation of the foreign dividends not compatible with the aforesaid provision since it reduced the losses of the parent company. On the same issue, see also CJEU, 4 June 2009, Joined Cases C-439/07 and C-499/07, *KBC Bank NV*, EU:C:2009:339.

43   See m.nos. 628.

this Directive."[44] The obligation to tax also raises issues of coordination with tax treaties between EU Member States, in which case the Directive should prevail.

Art. 6 of the Directive prevents the Member State of the parent company from charging an inbound withholding tax on the profits received by such a company. **442**

2. The Indirect Credit Method

Should the State of residence of the parent company opt for the **indirect credit method**, it will be obliged to allow a deduction – from the taxes due by that company – of the lesser of the corporate tax paid by the subsidiary in its State of residence and the corporate tax that would be levied in the case of purely internal distributions of profits. **443**

The Member State of the parent company has the obligation to extend such a credit to corporate tax paid by **any lower subsidiary**, provided that the company can be regarded as a "company of a Member State" and as a "subsidiary" under Art. 2 and Art. 3 of the Directive, respectively. In particular, the minimum holding threshold will have to be satisfied by each subsidiary having regard exclusively to its holding stake in the capital of the lower-tier subsidiary. **444**

The **extension of the indirect tax credit** to corporate tax paid by the lower-tier subsidiaries prevents economic double taxation, which would otherwise arise due to the fact that both the exemption method and the credit method may apply. For example, where a Member State (MS A) exempted the inbound distribution of profits received by a company resident therein from its subsidiary resident in another Member State (MS B), economic double taxation would not be eliminated should the former company pay the dividends on to its parent company resident in a third Member State (MS C), which relieves economic double taxation by means of the indirect credit method. Due to the exemption applicable in the former Member State (MS A), there would be no foreign corporate tax to offset the tax liability of the parent company resident in MS C.[45] **445**

With respect to the indirect foreign tax credit, the Directive is silent on the **procedural and administrative issues** that could arise, such as the tracing of the profits distributed along the chain of companies. Neither does the Directive contain any guidance concerning the use of the excess foreign tax credit, which might arise, for example, when the foreign corporate tax rate is higher than the domestic rate. All these issues are to be dealt with under the domestic law of the Member States. **446**

---

44   See Recital 30 to Council Directive (EU) 2017/952 of 29 May 2017 amending Directive (EU) 2016/1164 as regards hybrid mismatches with third countries, OJ L 144 of 7 June 2017; Chapter 8, m.no. 666.
45   Terra/Wattel, *European Tax Law* (2019) pp. 245-246.

3. Tax Treatment of Charges Connected to the Holding in the Subsidiary

447 Art. 4 (3) is **not clearly worded**.[46] The provision entails two different periods with different scopes. Art. 4(3), first paragraph, provides for the option for the Member States to deny the deduction of any **charges relating to the holding or losses** connected to the distribution of profits. In addition, Art. 4(3), second paragraph, provides that whenever **management charges** are determined by virtue of a flat rate, the amount so determined may not exceed 5 % of the profits distributed by the subsidiary. Accordingly, depending on whether the State of the parent company exempts the inbound distribution of profits or grants an underlying foreign tax credit, this State will accordingly reduce either the amount of the profits exempted therein or the foreign dividends for the purpose of calculating the amount of the underlying foreign tax credit, by the same percentage, i.e. 5 %.

448 It is doubtful, however, whether the scope of Art. 4(3), second part is strictly limited to "**management costs**" or, vice versa, whether it also applies to other costs, such as interest expenses deriving from the loan taken out to finance the purchase of the holding. A broad interpretation of Art. 4(3), second paragraph, can be derived from the *Bosal Holding* case,[47] where the CJEU implicitly admitted that it is possible for Member States to limit the deduction of interest expenses as a result of the exercise of the option granted to such states in Art. 4(3). In the recent *Argenta Spaarbank* case,[48] the CJEU held that Art. 4(2) of the Directive should be given a narrow interpretation, as it only grants Member States the right to deny the deduction of costs "relating to the holding" but does not allow Member States to preclude parent companies from deducting interest paid in respect of all the loans of a parent company (whether or not relating to the loan) up to an amount equal to the profit generated by its holdings in its subsidiaries.

449 With regard to the 5 % ceiling, the CJEU held in the *Association française des entreprises privées* case that the levying of additional taxes, such as a 3% contribution applied in addition to French corporate tax, would be in breach of the Directive. According to the Court, the levying of such a contribution would trigger double taxation at the level of the parent company due to the fact that 5 % of the dividends is already subject to corporate tax.

---

46   Brokelind, The Proposed Amendments to the Parent-Subsidiary Directive: Some progress, *ET* 2003, p. 455.

47   CJEU, 18 September 2003, Case C-168/01, *Bosal Holding*, EU:C:2003:479.

48   CJEU, 26 October 2017, Case C-39/16, *Argenta Spaarbank NV*, EU:C:2017:813, para. 45.

C. Application of the Directive in the State of the Subsidiary

1. Exemption of Outbound Dividends

Art. 1(b) includes in the objective scope of the Directive – inter alia – the **distributions of profits by subsidiary companies** in favour of their parent companies resident in other Member States. This provision must be read together with Art. 5 of the Directive, which contains the obligation for the Member State of the subsidiary to exempt such a distribution of profits from withholding tax.[49]   **450**

Such rules align the taxation of dividends in the State of the subsidiary with that of capital gains derived from the alienation of participations, normally also exempt from tax under the provisions of Art. 13(5) OECD MC. By **exempting distributions of profits from withholding tax,** the Directive prohibits the State of the subsidiary from collecting a second layer of tax, in addition to corporate taxes levied in the hands of the subsidiary itself, thus preventing economic double taxation.[50]   **451**

The Directive is silent in respect of the **procedural issues** concerning the application of the exemption from withholding tax in the State of the subsidiary. In particular, Art. 5 of the Directive does not affirm explicitly whether such a State is obliged to exempt the distribution of profits at the time of the payment, or vice versa, whether it is allowed to levy a withholding tax at the time of the actual distribution – according to domestic and tax treaty law – although it is under an obligation to refund the taxes so levied upon an application of the parent company. Just like the procedural issues arising in respect of the holding period, such issues are also to be dealt with in the domestic law of the Member States concerned. However, while enjoying national procedural autonomy, Member States must still comply with the principles of equivalence and effectiveness (see Chapter 1), not imposing requirements that, although not discriminatory, make it more burdensome or stricter for the parent company to obtain a withholding tax exemption.   **452**

2. Definition of "Withholding Tax"

There is no definition of "**withholding tax**" in Art. 5 nor elsewhere in the Directive.[51] The term "withholding tax" in Art. 5(1) of the Directive is not limited to specific types of national taxes. Moreover, the nature of a tax, duty or charge must   **453**

---

49 Art. 5 of the Directive was substantially revised by the 2003 amending Directive, which eliminated the reference to a minimum holding threshold of 25 %, which had to be met by the parent in order to claim the exemption from withholding tax in the State of the subsidiary. It must be remarked that in the absence of the qualifying requirements for the withholding tax exemption the State of the subsidiary is nonetheless still obliged to apply its domestic law in a non-discriminatory manner. See CJEU, 18 June 2009, Case C-303/07, *Aberdeen Property*, EU:C:2009:377, para. 76.

50 As we have seen in m.no.436 et seq., the State of the parent will be obliged either to exempt or to grant an indirect foreign tax credit.

51 The term "withholding tax" is also found in Art. 6 of the Directive.

be determined by the Court, under Community law, according to the objective characteristics by which it is levied, irrespective of its classification under national law.[52] The uncertainty resulting from the absence of such a definition has resulted in robust case law of the CJEU, including, amongst others, the *Epson* case,[53] the *Athinaiki Zithopiia* case,[54] the *Océ Van Der Grinten* case[55] and, lastly, the *X* [fairness tax] case.[56]

454   In the light of previous case law, the CJEU held that, in order to regard a tax on income levied in the State of the subsidiary as a "withholding tax" prohibited under Art. 5 of the Directive, **three conditions must be cumulatively met.**[57] In particular, the Court held that any tax on income received in the State in which dividends are distributed is a withholding tax on distributed profits where (i) the chargeable event for the tax is the payment of dividends or of any other income from shares, (ii) the taxable amount is the income from those shares and (iii) the taxable person is the holder of the shares.[58]

455   The case law above shows the tendency of the CJEU to prefer a **substance-over-form approach** in defining the term "withholding tax".[59] The term is in fact interpreted "autonomously", i.e. regardless of any definition contained in the domestic law of the Member States. In this respect, the CJEU has echoed settled case law according to which *"the nature of a tax, duty or charge must be determined by the Court, under Community law, according to the objective characteristics by which it is levied, irrespective of its classification under national law."*[60]

---

52   CJEU, 25 September 2003, Case C-58/01, *Océ Van Der Grinten*, EU:C:2003:495, para. 46.

53   CJEU, 8 June 2000, Case C-375/98, *Epson*, EU:C:2000:302. The **Epson** case dealt with the compatibility of Portuguese succession and donation tax with Art. 5 of the Directive, which was levied upon the payment of dividends by companies having their seat in Portugal. In the literature, see Da Camara, *ET* 2001, p. 309.

54   CJEU, 4 October 2001, Case C-294/99, *Athinaiki Zithopiia*, EU:C:2001:505. The *Athinaiki Zithopiia* case concerned compensatory tax charges applicable in Greece upon the distribution of dividends in the hands of Greek subsidiaries, insofar as such dividends were distributed out of exempt income or income taxed under a more favourable regime. In the literature, see Stavropoulos, *ET* 2002, p. 97.

55   CJEU, 25 September 2003, Case C-58/01, *Océ Van Der Grinten*, EU:C:2003:495. In the **Océ Van Der Grinten** case the CJEU endorsed the application of a withholding tax on the repayment of the underlying tax credit, to which Dutch shareholders of UK companies were entitled under Art. 10(3) of the UK–Netherlands double tax convention. According to the CJEU, the application of a withholding tax on the repayment of the tax credit did not mirror the application of withholding tax on distributed profits. In the literature, see European Team of the IBFD, *ET* 2003, p. 396.

56   CJEU, 17 May 2017, Case C-68/15, *X v Ministerraad*, EU:C:2017:379 in which the Court held that the Belgian levy known as "fairness tax" was not contrary to Art. 5 of the Directive *"given that the taxable person for the purposes of a tax such as the 'fairness tax' is not the holder of the shares but the distributing company [...]".*

57   CJEU, 26 June 2008, Case C-284/06, *Burda*, EU:C:2008:365.

58   See also CJEU, 24 June 2010, Joined Cases C-338/08 and C-339/08, *P. Ferrero e C. SpA v Agenzia delle Entrate – Ufficio di Alba* and *General Beverage Europe BV v Agenzia delle Entrate – Ufficio di Torino 1*, EU:C:2010:364, para. 26.

59   Terra/Wattel, *European Tax Law* (2019) p. 255.

60   CJEU, 13 February 1996, Joined Cases C-197/94 and C-252/94, *Bautiaa and Société française maritime*, EU:C:1996:47, para. 39.

D. Application of the Directive to Permanent Establishments

Art. 1 (c) and (d) deal with: **456**

- distributions of profits **received by permanent establishments** located in a State other than that of the subsidiary (Art. 1(c)); and
- distribution of profits by subsidiary companies to permanent establishments located in another Member State and belonging to parent companies resident in a Member State, **whether or not resident** in the same Member State of the distributing subsidiary (Art. 1(d)).

Art. 1(c) indeed requires the Member State of the permanent establishment – re-   **457** ceiving the distribution of profits – to treat it like a parent company, thus either exempting or granting a tax credit according to Art. 4 of the Directive.[61] As argued by tax scholars, such a rule is a clarification of the principles deriving from the *Saint-Gobain* decision.[62] In particular, Art. 1(c) deals with a **triangular situation**, i.e. a situation involving three Member States, namely the Member State of the parent company, the Member State of the subsidiary and the Member State of the permanent establishment. In this case, (i) the Member State of the subsidiary is obliged to eliminate juridical double taxation by exempting from withholding tax the profits distributed by a company resident therein under Art. 1(b) and Art. 5 of the Directive; (ii) the Member State of the parent company is obliged to eliminate economic double taxation under Art. 1(a) and Art. 5 of the Directive and, finally, (iii) the Member State of the permanent establishment is also obliged to eliminate economic double taxation according to the applicable method whenever the profits are received by resident parent companies. Such a result stems from the combined reading of Art. 1(a) and Art. 4 of the Directive.

Art. 1(d) deals with a bilateral situation, in which the parent and the subsidiary are   **458** resident in the same Member State whereas the permanent establishment is resident in another Member State.[63] It was uncertain whether, prior to the 2003 amending Directive, this situation was covered by the Directive.[64] The main argument against the application of the Directive was the absence of a cross-border distribution of profits, as the parent company resides in the same State as the subsidiary.[65] How-

---

61 Should the permanent establishment belong to a non-EU parent, the Directive would no longer apply.
62 For some Member States, which had meanwhile aligned their domestic law with the *Saint-Gobain* decision, the addition of this paragraph did not require any further amendment to domestic law. See Maisto, The 2003 amendments to the EC Parent-Subsidiary Directive: What's next?, *EC Tax Review* 2004, p. 166; Zanotti, Taxation of Inter-Company Dividends in the Presence of a PE: The impact of EC Fundamental Freedoms (Part One), *ET* 2004, p. 504; Thömmes, in: Thömmes/Fuks (eds.), *EC Corporate Tax* Law (loose leaf) p. 32.
63 Should the permanent establishment be located in a non-EU Member State, the Directive would no longer apply.
64 Maisto, The 2003 amendments to the EC Parent-Subsidiary Directive: What's next?, *EC Tax Review* 2004, p. 167; Zanotti, Taxation of Inter-Company Dividends in the Presence of a PE: The impact of EC Fundamental Freedoms (Part One), *ET* 2004, p. 505; Hausner, in: Aigner/Loukota (eds.), *Source Versus Residence in International Tax Law* (2005) p. 496.
65 Also in this case it could be argued that the denial of the application of the Directive in the source State would hinder the freedom of establishment of the parent, which would be obliged to exercise

ever, one should take into account that the profits are also taxed in the permanent establishment State, as they are attributed to a permanent establishment therein. The application of the Directive in such a situation is therefore in line with its general aim, i.e. the elimination of economic double taxation. In particular, the permanent establishment State would be required to eliminate economic double taxation, as a result of Art. 1(d) and Art. 4, whereas the State of the subsidiary will be required to exempt the distribution, according to Art. 1(d) and Art. 5 of the Directive.

459 Two more **cases not covered by the 2003 amending Directive**, although still involving the presence of a permanent establishment, need to be analysed. First, one could wonder whether the Directive applies where the **permanent establishment is located in the same Member State as the subsidiary** in circumstances in which the parent company is resident in another Member State. In such a scenario, the distribution of profits would still be taxable in both the Member State of the subsidiary – which is also the State where the permanent establishment is located – and the Member State of the parent company.[66] As for the application of the Directive, different positions have been argued in the tax literature. According to the view of some scholars, which is also shared by the author, this scenario would fall outside the scope of the Directive, i.e. the State of the subsidiary would not be obliged to exempt the profits and the State of the parent company would not be required to eliminate economic double taxation.[67] According to others, the Directive would only bind the State of the parent company to eliminate economic double taxation according to Art. 4.[68] Some others argue that the Directive would bind the State of the parent company and would prevent the State of the subsidiary from levying a withholding tax on the dividends. However, the latter State would not be prevented from taxing the dividends when received by the permanent establishment, according to domestic and tax treaty rules. Finally, others argue that such a scenario should be dealt with under domestic law as suggested in Recital no. 8 of the 2013 amending Directive.[69]

460 Second, one could wonder whether the presence of a **permanent establishment in a non-EU Member State** is covered by the application of the Directive. Certainly, the definition of permanent establishment contained in Art. 2 makes reference exclusively to permanent establishments "situated in a Member State". Even though there are no specific provisions in this respect, the Directive should apply since the profits are still being distributed by a subsidiary resident in a Member State (Art. 4(1)(b)) and are still received by a company of a parent company resident in another Member

such freedom by setting up a company instead of a permanent establishment. As for the State of the permanent establishment, once again the *Saint Gobain* decision would require such a State to treat it like a parent resident therein.

66   According to the tax treaty between such two states, if any and if similar to the OECD MC, the dividends will be taxed in the subsidiary State (or the permanent establishment State) according to Art. 7(1). The State of the parent will have to grant double taxation relief according to Art. 23 OECD MC.

67   Maisto, The 2003 amendments to the EC Parent-Subsidiary Directive: What's next?, *EC Tax Review* 2004, p. 167.

68   Garcia Prats, Application of the Parent-Subsidiary to Permanent Establishment, *ET* 1995, p. 181.

69   Thömmes/Nakhai, in: Thömmes/Fuks (eds.), *EC Corporate Tax Law* (loose leaf) p. 34.

State (Art. 4(1)(a)). The fact that the profits are attributable to a permanent establishment located in a non-EU Member State should therefore be immaterial.[70]

E. Overview of the Scope of the Directive (Art. 1)

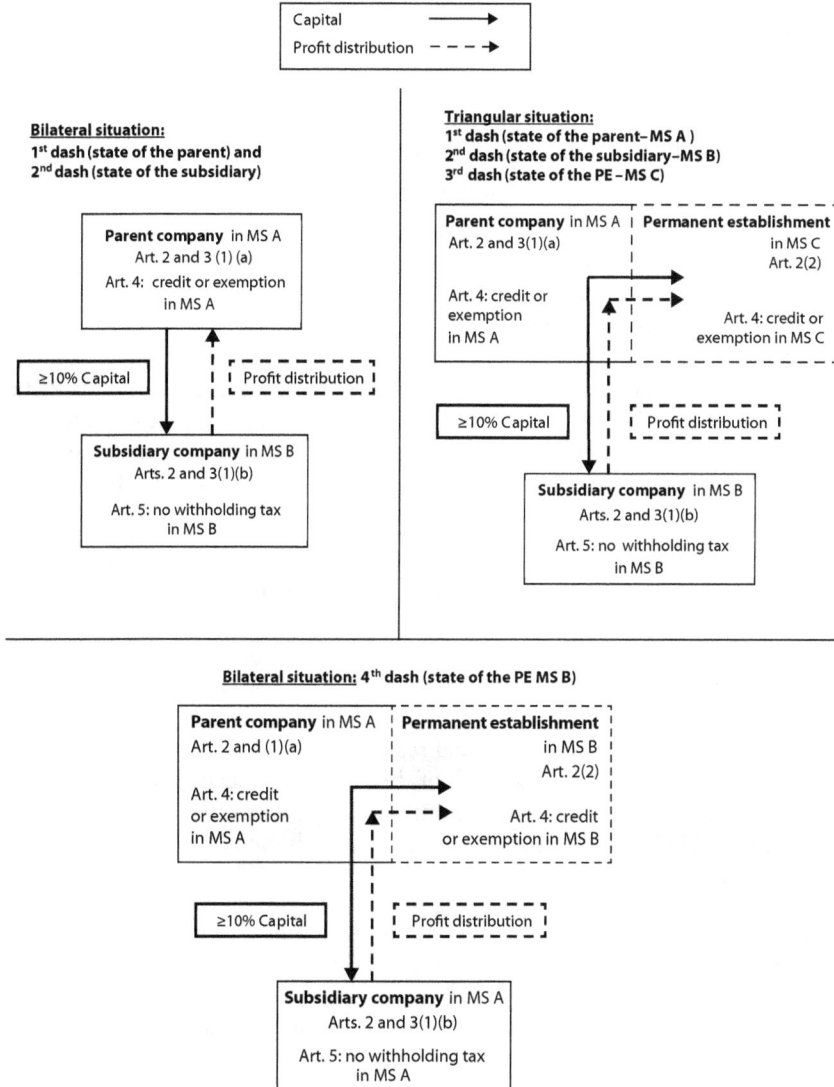

461

Capital	⟶
Profit distribution	– – – ➔

Bilateral situation:
1st dash (state of the parent) and
2nd dash (state of the subsidiary)

Triangular situation:
1st dash (state of the parent– MS A)
2nd dash (state of the subsidiary–MS B)
3rd dash (state of the PE – MS C)

Parent company in MS A
Art. 2 and 3 (1) (a)
Art. 4: credit or exemption
in MS A

≥10% Capital   Profit distribution

Subsidiary company in MS B
Arts. 2 and 3(1)(b)
Art. 5: no withholding tax
in MS B

Parent company in MS A | **Permanent establishment**
Art. 2 and 3(1)(a) | in MS C
Art. 2(2)
Art. 4: credit or exemption in MS A | Art. 4: credit or exemption in MS C

≥10% Capital   Profit distribution

Subsidiary company in MS B
Arts. 2 and 3(1)(b)
Art. 5: no withholding tax
in MS B

Bilateral situation: 4th dash (state of the PE MS B)

Parent company in MS A | **Permanent establishment**
Art. 2 and (1)(a) | in MS B
Art. 2(2)
Art. 4: credit or exemption in MS A | Art. 4: credit or exemption in MS B

≥10% Capital   Profit distribution

Subsidiary company in MS A
Arts. 2 and 3(1)(b)
Art. 5: no withholding tax
in MS A

---

70   In such a case Council Directive 2003/49/EC of 3 June 2003 on a Common System of Taxation Applicable to Interest and Royalty Payments Made Between Companies of Different Member States, OJ L157, 26 June 2003, would not be applicable.

IV. Abuse

462 In the 'Danish cases',[71] the CJEU clarified that Member States are obliged to deny the benefits of the Directive if these benefits have been claimed abusively in accordance with the general principle prohibiting abusive practices.[72] It also clarified that the benefits of the Directives should be denied if the tax advantage is the essential aim (and not necessarily the sole aim) of the transactions carried out by the taxpayer.[73] The CJEU pointed out that the previously mentioned conclusion applies regardless of the existence of domestic or agreement based anti-abuse provisions.[74] As a consequence of the CJEU's judgment in the 'Danish cases', the relevance of the anti-abuse provision – introduced in 2015 by the amending Directive – ends up being very limited.

463 In particular, Art. 1(2) and (3) of the Directive contains a general anti-abuse clause ("**GAAR**") that will prevent Member States from granting the benefits of the Directive to arrangements that are not "genuine", i.e. that have been put into place to obtain a tax advantage without reflecting any economic reality. The GAAR sets the minimum standards for countering such practices, while allowing the Member States to apply stricter national or treaty rules. Therefore, all Member States now have an obligation to counter abusive practices, which did not exist before.[75] The GAAR broadly coincides with that of Art. 6 of the Directive (EU) 2016/1164 laying down rules against tax avoidance practices that directly affect the functioning of the internal market.

464 The GAAR contained in the Directive is based on **four conditions** which must be cumulatively met,[76] namely (1) there must be an arrangement or a series of arrangements, (2) these arrangements must have been put into place for the main purpose or one of the main purposes of obtaining a tax advantage (known as the "*subjective test*"),[77] (3) the tax advantage defeats the object and purpose of the Directive ("*objective test*")[78] and (4) the arrangement(s) is (are) not genuine, i.e. not put into place for valid commercial reasons that reflect economic reality. The consequences, effectiveness and reach of the GAAR application are not clear and (although not explicitly mentioned in either of the aforementioned provisions) the GAAR should have effects on both the State of the subsidiary and on the State of the parent company.[79]

---

71 CJEU, 26 February 2019, Case C-116/16 to C-117/16, *Skatteministeriet v. T Danmark and Y Denmark Aps*, EU:C:2019:135.
72 Para. 72.
73 Para. 79.
74 As a consequence of the implementation of the ATAD, all Member States should have a GAAR in their respective tax systems.
75 Tavares/Bogenschneider, *Intertax* 2015, p. 486.
76 See Debelva/Luts, The General Anti-Abuse Rule of the Parent-Subsidiary Directive, *ET* 2015, p. 224.
77 *Ibid.*
78 *Ibid.*
79 *Ibid.*, p. 228, "… *Member States will thus be obliged to deny the benefits of the PSD once the conditions of the GAAR are fulfilled; they have no discretion in this regard. The benefits of the PSD in respect of*

The GAAR has a different function vìs-à-vìs the provision contained in Art. 4(1)(a) **465** with a view countering double non-taxation (see m.no 441 above). The GAAR is aimed at preventing abusive practices, which may not always be identified in the aggressive tax planning schemes caught by Art. 4(1)(a) of the Directive (whereby the taxpayer seeks to obtain the deduction in one country and the non-inclusion of the income in the other country). The scope of the GAAR is therefore much broader than the latter provision, which applies to "hybrid-entity mismatches" only.[80] The GAAR targets "directive shopping", which takes place through the channelling of investment by non-EU taxpayers though the use of intermediary EU sub-holding companies.[81] It has been argued that when such companies are "minimally functional" they should be "entitled to a right of establishment" with the consequence that the GAAR should be interpreted in line with the general concept of abuse developed in the direct tax case law of the CJEU.[82] The CJEU pointed out that where the non-resident parent company manages its subsidiaries' assets, this does not per se indicate the existence of a wholly artificial arrangement that does not reflect economic reality. The fact that the management of assets is not considered to constitute an economic activity for the purposes of value-added tax is irrelevant, since the tax at issue in the main proceedings and value-added tax are governed by distinct legal regimes, each pursuing difference objectives.[83]

In the context, *inter alia*, of the Directive, in the so called 'Danish cases', the Court established a set of *indicia*[84] that the national court must take into account for the purpose of assessing the existence of an abusive transaction,[85] in particular:

---

profit distributions falling within its scope are twofold, i.e. (1) an exemption from withholding taxes in the Member State of the subsidiary company (article 5 of the PSD) and (2) elimination of double taxation (by way of exemption or credit) in the Member State of the parent company (article 4 of the PSD). A literal reading of the new anti-abuse provision implies that both of these benefits are to be denied if an arrangement (or series thereof) falls within the scope of the new anti-abuse provision of the PSD. This may have far-reaching consequences and, in fact, creates international (juridical and economic) multiple taxation in the hands of a shareholder/company that is involved in an alleged abusive arrangement. One could validly question the proportionality thereof."

80 For a comparison between the GAAR and Art. 4(1)(a) of the Directive, see Tavares/Bogenschneider, The New *De Minimis* Anti-abuse Rule in the Parent Subsidiary Directive: Validating EU Tax Competition and Corporate Tax Avoidance?, *Intertax* 2015, pp. 489-490.

81 Tavares/Bogenschneider, The New *De Minimis* Anti-abuse Rule in the Parent Subsidiary Directive: Validating EU Tax Competition and Corporate Tax Avoidance?, *Intertax* 2015, p. 486, *citing* Pistone, *Tax L. Rev.* 2008, p. 75.

82 *Ibid*, p. 492.

83 A similar conclusion was reached by the Austrian VwGH (27 March 2019, Ro 2018/13/0004) in respect of a company engaged in a financial activity. According to the Court, a company is considered to have its own economic activity if three employees are involved in strategic business development, exploitation of investment opportunities, financial administration and reporting, compliance, office administration and the management of financial accounts.

84 Bærentzen/van 't Riet, Limitation of Holding Structures for Intra-EU Dividends: An End to Tax Avoidance?, *WTJ* 2020,

85 CJEU, 26 February 2019, Joined Cases C-116/16 to C-117/16, *Skatteministeriet v. T Danmark and Y Denmark Aps*, EU:C:2019:135, para. 104 et seq.

- the role of a conduit of the immediate recipient that is obliged to pass on the income (in a short timeframe) to entities that, being established in third countries, would have been subject to withholding tax in the State of source had they received the payments directly. Such an obligation can be grounded in a formal contractual or legal obligation but may also be a *de facto* obligation that results from the analysis of various factual circumstances (such as whether the conduit entities actually have the right to use and enjoy the income received);
- the lack of economic substance at the level of the immediate recipient and the carrying out by the latter of very limited activities (including the receipt of the income and its transfer to the beneficial owner or to other conduit companies). Such a circumstance must be inferred from an analysis of all the relevant facts, including the management of the company, the cost structure, and the presence of staff, premises and equipment; and
- whether the group structure was put in place at the same time as or shortly after the introduction of changes in the law that would otherwise have created additional tax burdens had the group not changed its structure.

466 In addition to the GAAR, Art. 1(4) of the Directive[86] retains the right of Member States to apply their domestic and agreement-based provisions aimed at preventing "**fraud or abuse**". By reference to the old Art. 1(2) of Directive 90/435/EU (now Art. 1(4) of the Directive) the CJEU confirmed that such a provision reflects the general principle of EU law according to which any abuse of right is prohibited.[87] The Court reiterated its case law that Member States are allowed to deny the benefits of the Directive by applying domestic rules (if any) that counter wholly artificial arrangements not reflecting economic reality and that are aimed at achieving undue tax advantages. In contrast, Member States are not allowed to apply provisions establishing a general presumption of fraud and abuse that are not proportionate and conflict therefore with the Directive.[88]

---

86 If read in the light of the position held by the Court in CJEU, 5 July 2007, Case C-321/05, *Kofoed*, EU:C:2007:408, this provision lacks direct effect and corresponds to that contained in the old Art. 1(2) of the Directive (i.e. prior to the 2015 amending Directive).

87 CJEU, 7 September 2017, Case C-6/16, *Eqiom*, EU:C:2017:641, p. 36; CJEU, 20 December 2017, Joined Cases C-504/16 and C-613/16), *Deister Holding and Juhler Holding*, paras. 60-62 and 74.

88 CJEU, 20 December 2017, Joined Cases C-504/16 and C-613/16), *Deister Holding and Juhler Holding*, paras. 61 and 69-70.

V. Overview of the Functioning of the Directive

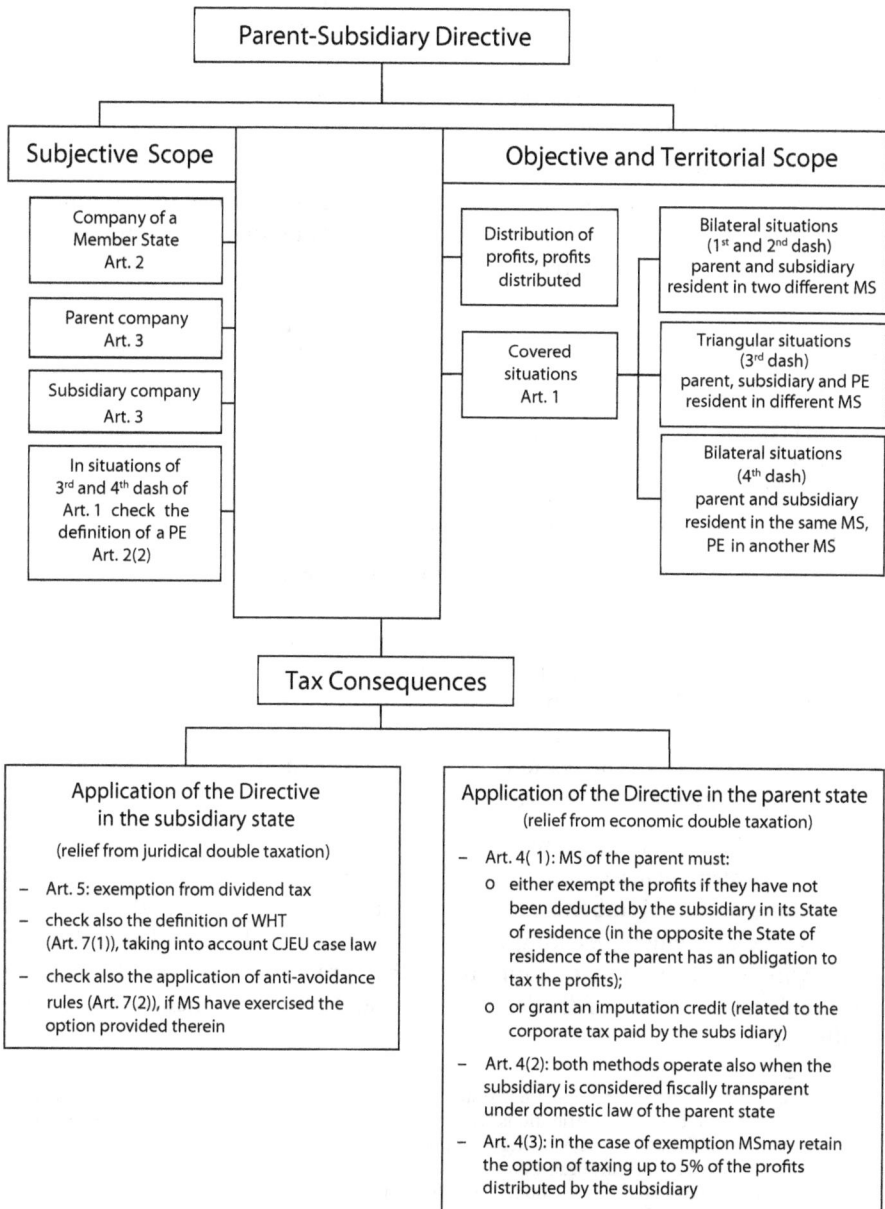

467

```
                    ┌─────────────────────────────┐
                    │ Parent-Subsidiary Directive │
                    └─────────────────────────────┘
```

Subjective Scope		Objective and Territorial Scope
Company of a Member State Art. 2	Distribution of profits, profits distributed	Bilateral situations (1st and 2nd dash) parent and subsidiary resident in two different MS
Parent company Art. 3	Covered situations Art. 1	Triangular situations (3rd dash) parent, subsidiary and PE resident in different MS
Subsidiary company Art. 3		Bilateral situations (4th dash) parent and subsidiary resident in the same MS, PE in another MS
In situations of 3rd and 4th dash of Art. 1 check the definition of a PE Art. 2(2)		

```
                    ┌──────────────────┐
                    │ Tax Consequences │
                    └──────────────────┘
```

Application of the Directive in the subsidiary state

(relief from juridical double taxation)

– Art. 5: exemption from dividend tax
– check also the definition of WHT (Art. 7(1)), taking into account CJEU case law
– check also the application of anti-avoidance rules (Art. 7(2)), if MS have exercised the option provided therein

Application of the Directive in the parent state

(relief from economic double taxation)

– Art. 4(1): MS of the parent must:
  o either exempt the profits if they have not been deducted by the subsidiary in its State of residence (in the opposite the State of residence of the parent has an obligation to tax the profits);
  o or grant an imputation credit (related to the corporate tax paid by the subs idiary)
– Art. 4(2): both methods operate also when the subsidiary is considered fiscally transparent under domestic law of the parent state
– Art. 4(3): in the case of exemption MSmay retain the option of taxing up to 5% of the profits distributed by the subsidiary

VI. The Relationship with Double Taxation Conventions

468   The application of the Directive prevails over domestic and tax treaty law. Art. 7(2), however, contains a derogation to this principle, wherein it is provided that the Directive may not affect the application of domestic or agreement-based **provisions aimed at eliminating or lessening economic double** taxation, such as the repayment of an indirect tax credit to foreign shareholders.[89]

469   Should the tax treatment of the distributed profits be **more favourable** under the regime provided for in a DTC, or ultimately under that provided under domestic law, then parent companies may opt for the application of either regime instead of that provided for in the Directive.

VII. Extension of the EU Parent-Subsidiary Directive to Switzerland

470   Art. 15(1) of the **EU-Swiss Savings Tax Agreement**[90] extends the application of the Directive as adopted in 1990 (i.e. before amendments effective as from 1 January 2005) in relations with Switzerland. The application of the aforementioned regime is subject to the following cumulative conditions:

- the parent company has a direct shareholding of at least 25 % in the capital of the subsidiary for at least two years;
- one company is resident for tax purposes in a Member State and the other company is resident for tax purposes in Switzerland;
- under any DTC with any third states neither company is resident for tax purposes in that third state; and
- both companies are subject to corporation tax without being exempted[91] and both companies adopt the form of a limited company.[92]

471   The aforementioned regime applies without prejudice to the application of domestic or agreement-based provisions for the prevention of **fraud or abuse in Switzerland and in Member States.** Moreover, under Art. 15(3) of the EU-Swiss Savings Tax Agreement, existing DTCs between Switzerland and the Member States which – at the time of adoption of the agreement – provide for a more favourable tax treatment of dividends, interest and royalty payments shall remain unaffected.

---

89   Usually, States adopting an imputation system only provide for an indirect tax credit in respect of purely domestic dividend distributions. However, such States may exceptionally extend such tax credits to foreign shareholders, whether or not reciprocally, through a double tax convention.

90   Agreement between the European Community and the Swiss Confederation providing for measures equivalent to those laid down in Council Directive 2003/48/EC of 3 June 2003 on taxation of savings income in the form of interest payments.

91   Thus, companies with federal tax holidays do not qualify.

92   The term "limited company" covers for Switzerland the share corporation ("AG"), the corporation with unlimited partners ("KommanditAG"), as well as the limited liability company ("GmbH").

The scope of application of Art. 15(3) is more restrictive than the scope of application of the Directive. For example, it does not cover certain legal forms that were not included in the old 1990 Directive and distributed profits accruing to a permanent establishment; in addition, Art. 15(1) of the EU-Swiss Savings Tax Agreement requires a higher holding requirement (25 % instead of 10 %). **472**

Since the Directive has been amended a number of times over the years, its current wording contains several differences compared to Art. 15(1) and Art. 15(3) of the EU-Swiss Savings Tax Agreement, which replicates the text of the original Directive, dating from 1990. As rightly pointed out by some authors, later versions of the Parent-Subsidiary Directive are not relevant for the purpose of the EU-Swiss Savings Tax Agreement unless and until legislative action is taken to amend the text of the latter agreement.[93] Accordingly, amendments that have been made to the Directive over the years, such as the lowering of the holding thresholds (which has been brought down to 10 %) are not relevant to the EU-Swiss Savings Tax Agreement. **473**

Literature

Arginelli, The Subject-to-Tax Requirement in the EU Parent-Subsidiary Directive (2011/96), *ET* 2017; Bærentzen, Lejour & M. van 't Riet, Limitation of Holding Structures for Intra-EU Dividends: An End to Tax Avoidance?, WTJ (2020); Brokelind, The Proposed Amendments to the Parent-Subsidiary Directive: Some progress, *ET* 2003, p. 451; Brokelind, *Une interprétation de la directive sociétés mères et filiales du 23 juillet 1990* (2000); Da Camara, Parent-Subsidiary Directive: The Epson case, *ET* 2001, p. 307; Debelva/Luts, The General Anti-Abuse Rule of the Parent-Subsidiary Directive, *ET* 2015, p. 223; European Team of the IBFD, The *Océ Van Der Grinten* Case: Implications for other EU Member States, A critical assessment, *ET* 2003, p. 394; Garcia Prats, Application of the Parent-Subsidiary to Permanent Establishment, *ET* 1995, p. 181; H.T.P.M. van den Hurk, Proposed Amended Parent-Subsidiary Directive Reveals the European Commission's Lack of Vision, *BIT* 2014; Hausner, Source and Residence aspects in the amended parent subsidiary directive, in: Aigner/Loukota (eds.), *Source Versus Residence in International Tax Law* (2005); Helminen, *The Dividend Concept in International Tax Law* (1999); Maisto, Current Issues on the Interpretation of the Parent-Subsidiary Directive, in: Maisto/Weber (eds.), *EU Income Tax Law: Issues for the Years Ahead* (2013) p. 1; Maisto, The 2003 amendments to the EC Parent-Subsidiary Directive: What's next?, *EC Tax Review* 2004, p. 164; Schonewille, Some questions on the Parent-Subsidiary Directive and the Merger Directive, *Intertax* 1992, p. 14; Stavropoulos, ECJ: Greek Income Tax Provision is a Withholding Tax within the Meaning

---

93 H.T.P.M. van den Hurk, Proposed Amended Parent-Subsidiary Directive Reveals the European Commission's Lack of Vision, *BIT* 2014.

of the Parent-Subsidiary Directive, *ET* 2002, p. 94; Tavares/Bogenschneider, The New *De Minimis* Anti-abuse Rule in the Parent Subsidiary Directive: Validating EU Tax Competition and Corporate Tax Avoidance?, *Intertax* 2015, p. 484; Tenore, Taxation of dividends: a comparison of selected issues under Article 10 OECD MC and the Parent-Subsidiary Directive, *Intertax* 2010, p. 222; Terra/Wattel, *European Tax Law* (2019); Thömmes/Nakhai, Commentary on the Parent-Subsidiary Directive, in: Thömmes/Fuks (eds.) *EC Corporate Tax Law* (loose leaf); Zanotti, Taxation of Inter-Company Dividends in the Presence of a PE: The impact of EC Fundamental Freedoms (Part One), *ET* 2004, p. 493.

Legal Basis: Council Directive 2011/96/EU of 30 November 2011 on common system of taxation applicable in the case of parent companies and subsidiaries of Member States, OJ L 225 of 20 August 1990, pp. 6-9; Council Directive (EU) 2015/121 of 27 January 2015 amending Directive 2011/96/EU on the common system of taxation applicable in the case of parent companies and subsidiaries of different Member States, OJ L 21 of 28 January 2015, pp. 1-3; Council Directive 2014/86/EU of 8 July 2014 amending Directive 2011/96/EU on the common system of taxation applicable in the case of parent companies and subsidiaries of different Member States, OJ L 219 of 25 July 2014, pp. 40-41.

Chapter 6 – The Merger Directive

Matthias Hofstätter/Daniela Hohenwarter-Mayr

I. The Necessity of Tax-Neutral Reorganizations in the European Union

474 **Reorganizations** – in absence of any specific tax provisions – will generally **trigger taxation of capital gains as barter-like transactions.** For **domestic reorganizations,** Member States typically provide for tax deferral of the capital gains tax levied on the hidden reserves of the transferred assets under their domestic tax law. Often, losses not yet utilized by the transferring company may also be carried over to the acquiring company. Therefore, domestic reorganizations are tax neutral, i.e. they do not trigger immediate taxation at the time of reorganization since taxation of the capital gain is deferred until a later disposal of those assets.

475 Similar tax provisions for **reorganizations of companies of different Member States** are necessary for the completion of an internal market within the European Union. Thus, cross-border reorganizations ought not to be hampered by restrictions, disadvantages or distortions arising from the tax provisions of the Member States. It is therefore necessary to have tax provisions that are neutral from the point of view of competition, in order to allow enterprises to adapt to the requirements of the common market, increase their productivity and improve their competitive strength at the international level. Consequently, tax provisions that put cross-border reorganizations at a disadvantage in comparison with reorganizations involving companies established in the same Member State have to be abolished.

476 However, it was considered that simply extending the rules for domestic reorganizations to cross-border reorganizations was not feasible because of the differences between the regimes in force in the Member States. (New) Distortions were expected. Only a **common tax system for cross-border reorganizations** was thought to provide a satisfactory solution. Therefore, the Council adopted Council Directive 90/434/EEC of 23 July 1990 on the common system of taxation applicable to mergers, divisions, transfers of assets and exchanges of shares concerning companies of different Member States (hereinafter the Merger Directive or Directive).[1]

477 The **aim** of the common tax system for cross-border reorganizations is to **avoid the imposition of an income or capital gains tax** in connection with mergers, divisions, partial divisions, transfers of assets, exchanges of shares and transfers of the registered office of an SE or SCE between Member States. At the same time, the **financial interests of the Member State** of the transferring or acquired company should be safeguarded. Thus, the taxing rights of the Member States should be protected.

---

1   Now Council Directive 2009/133/EC of 19 October 2009 on the common system of taxation applicable to mergers, divisions, partial divisions, transfers of assets and exchanges of shares concerning companies of different Member States and to the transfer of the registered office of an SE or SCE between Member States (codified version), OJ L 310 of 25 November 2009, pp. 34-46.

Initial proposals for a Merger Directive date back to 1969. However, it took more **478** than 20 years before the final text was **adopted by the Council in 1990**. The Merger Directive adopted in 1990 covered mergers, divisions, transfers of assets and exchanges of shares concerning companies of different Member States and had to be **implemented by 1 January 1992**. In 2003, the Commission issued a proposal to substantially amend the Directive,[2] a modified version of which was finally adopted by the Council in 2005.[3] The **changes in 2005** included a **broadening of the personal and the objective scope** of the Directive. The personal scope was enlarged to include the SE, the SCE and several entities previously not covered, as well as hybrid entities.[4] With respect to the objective scope, partial divisions and the transfer of the registered office of an SE or SCE from one Member State to another were included. The 2005 amendments had to be **implemented in part by 1 January 2006 and in part by 1 January 2007**. Because of the numerous amendments,[5] the Merger Directive was codified in 2009 to enhance clarity and rationality. However, the codification did not lead to changes in terms of content.

II. Scope

A. Personal Scope

The Merger Directive requires the companies involved in the operations covered[6] **479** to qualify as a "company from a Member State". To be characterized as a "company from a Member State", the respective company has to meet **three requirements**: Firstly, the company has to take one of the legal forms listed in the annex to the Merger Directive. Secondly, the company has to be resident, for tax purposes, within the European Union. Thirdly, the company has to be subject to one of the taxes listed in the annex to the Merger Directive.

With respect to the first requirement (Art. 3(a)), the company has to take **one** **480** **of the legal forms listed in the annex** to the Merger Directive. Under the 2005 amendment, the list of eligible legal forms was enlarged considerably to broaden the Directive's personal scope. Nevertheless, not all companies qualifying as companies for domestic corporate income tax purposes qualify as companies under the Merger Directive.

2　COM(2003) 613.
3　Council Directive 2005/19/EC of 17 February 2005 amending Directive 90/434/EEC 1990 on the common system of taxation applicable to mergers, divisions, transfers of assets and exchanges of shares concerning companies of different Member States, OJ L 58 of 4 March 2005, pp. 19-26.
4　For the tax treatment of hybrid entities in the context of operations covered by the Merger Directive see Fibbe/Stevens, *Hybrid Entities and the EU Tax Directives* (2015), p. 18 et seq., as their treatment will not be further elaborated on in this chapter.
5　E.g. Council Directive 2006/98/EC of 20 November 2006 adapting certain Directives in the field of taxation, by reason of the accession of Bulgaria and Romania, OJ L 363 of 20 December 2006, pp. 129-136; Council Directive 2013/13/EU of 13 May 2013 adapting certain directives in the field of taxation, by reason of the accession of the Republic of Croatia, OJ L 141 of 28 May 2013, pp. 30-31.
6　See m.no. 484 et seq.

481   The second requirement is that the company be **resident for tax purposes in one Member State** on the basis of the **domestic tax law** of that State. Additionally, the company must not, according to a **double taxation convention (DTC) concluded with a third State** (non-Member State) be resident for tax purposes outside the EU (Art. 3(b)). This is especially relevant for dual resident companies that are also resident under the domestic tax law of a third State. If there is a DTC similar to the OECD Model 2014 (and the previous Models) with the tie-breaker rule being the place of effective management, this company would not have access to the benefits of the Merger Directive if the place of effective management was in that third State. If, however, the DTC with the third State contains the MAP (mutual agreement procedure) as a coporate residence tie-breaker, as the OECD Model 2017 does, the treatment of the dual-resident company for the period of time before the contracting states mutually agree on its tax residence would be unclear.[7] Notwithstanding the above, dual-resident companies having both tax residences within the EU (but in two different Member States) are generelly not excluded from the Directive's personal scope according to Art. 3(b), and neither are dual-resident companies having one residence within and one residence outside the EU in circumstances in which no DTC is available between the respective states.

482   According to Art. 3(c), the third requirement for being covered is that the company be **subject to a tax listed in the annex to the Merger Directive,** i.e. corporate income tax in the respective Member States without being exempt and without the possibility of an option.

483   All three conditions must be cumulatively met to qualify as a company within the meaning of the Merger Directive. However, it is **not required that all three conditions be met within one Member State.** This being said, it is evident that companies, within the meaning of the Merger Directive, may also qualify as taxpayers under Art. 1 of Council Directive 2016/1164 of 12 July 2016 laying down rules against tax avoidance practices that directly affect the functioning of the internal market (herinafter ATAD 1),[8] which could cause an overlap.[9]

B. Objective Scope

1. Operations Covered in General

484   Under Art. 1 of the Merger Directive, it is required that a "company from a Member State" is involved in operations covered and specified by Art. 2. This **list of operations** is **exhaustive.** Since the 2005 amendment, the Merger Directive applies

---

7   Either the company is provisionally regarded as tax resident within the EU for the purposes of the Merger Directive until it is decided otherwise (i.e. the outcome of the MAP is that the company has its tax residence for treaty purposes in the third country) or the company is considered to meet the "tax residence test" only after the mutual agreement procedure has been closed and the states have come to that result. In the latter case, this decision should, however, have retroactive effect.

8   See Chapter 8 m.no. 587 et seq.

9   See m.no. 505.

to mergers, divisions, partial divisions, transfers of assets, exchanges of shares and a transfer of the registered office of an SE or SCE from one Member State to another. Other types of reorganizations are not covered.

2. Mergers

For the purposes of the Merger Directive, Art. 2(a) defines a merger as an operation whereby one or more companies **transfer all of their assets and liabilities to another company**. The transferring companies are dissolved without going into liquidation. Therefore, the transferring companies cease to exist. **485**

The **receiving company** is the legal successor of the assets and liabilities. In return for the assets and liabilities received, it **issues shares** to the shareholders of the transferring company or companies. An additional cash payment not exceeding 10 % of the nominal value, or in absence of a nominal value, of the accounting par value of those securities (i.e. the shares in the receiving company issued to the shareholders of the transferring company in exchange) to match the values of the shares in the transferring and in the receiving company is allowed. Thus, remaining differences in value can be compensated for in cash. **486**

Under Art. 2(a), three different subtypes of mergers are defined. Firstly (i), one or more existing companies may **merge into another existing company**. Secondly (ii), two or more existing companies may **merge into a newly formed company**. Thirdly (iii), a wholly owned subsidiary may be **merged with its parent company (up-stream merger)**. Notwithstanding the lack of a special provision, the merger of the parent company with its subsidiary (down-stream merger) should also be covered by the Merger Directive, as it fulfils the criteria of Art. 2(a)(i). **487**

3. Divisions and Partial Divisions

Divisions and partial divisions are covered under Art. 2(b) and (c). A division is an operation whereby **one company transfers all of its assets and liabilities to two or more new or existing companies in exchange for shares** representing the capital of the companies receiving the assets and liabilities. The transferring company ceases to exist but is dissolved without liquidation. As is the case with mergers, cash payments up to 10 % are eligible. **488**

Although Art. 2(b) requires an "issue" of shares by the receiving company, thus implying that **new shares** are required, a division should also be protected if the receiving company transfers **existing shares** to the shareholders of the transferring company.[10] This also holds true for mergers covered by Art. 2(a). **489**

Since the 2005 amendment, partial divisions are also covered by the Merger Directive. A partial division as defined under Art. 2(c) is an operation whereby a **490**

---

10   Wattel/Marres/Vermeulen (eds.), *European Tax Law*, Volume I (2019) p. 285.

company **transfers, without being dissolved, one or more branches of activity to one or more existing or new companies,** leaving at least one branch of activity in the transferring company. Unlike a division, the transferring company does not cease to exist but is left with at least one branch of activity. The operation covered by Art. 2(c) is therefore also referred to as a split-off.

491   The term "**branch of activity**" is defined by Art. 2(j) as all the assets and liabilities of a division of a company that, from an organizational point of view, constitute an independent business, i.e. an entity capable of functioning by its own means. Based on this definition, the transfer of a single asset is not covered by a partial division under Art. 2(c).

4. Transfer of Assets

492   Art. 2(d) adds the transfer of assets to the objective scope of the Merger Directive. The transfer of assets is an operation whereby a **company transfers without being dissolved**[11] **all or one or more branches of its activity to another existing or newly established company** in exchange for securities representing the capital of the company receiving the transfer. The transferring company has to transfer at least one **branch of activity** defined under Art. 2(j). Here too a transfer of unrelated assets does not result in access to the benefits of the Merger Directive. Contrary to the other reorganization types covered by the Directive, cash payments are not provided for in the context of Art. 2(d).

493   In return for the transfer of activities, the transferring company receives shares in the capital of the receiving company. Unlike a merger, a division or a partial division it is the **transferring company itself that receives the shares as consideration** and not the shareholders of the transferring company.

5. Exchange of Shares

494   Art. 2(e) defines an exchange of shares. An exchange of shares is an operation whereby the **acquiring company pays for the shares in the acquired company by issuing shares of its own capital** to the former shareholders of the acquired company. Thereby, the acquired company becomes a subsidiary of the acquiring company and the former shareholders of the acquired company become shareholders of the acquiring company.

495   The application of the "exchange of shares" provision is made conditional upon the fact that the acquiring company obtains the **majority of the voting rights** in the acquired company, or, when already holding such a majority, acquires a further holding. Similar to mergers, divisions and partial divisions, cash payments not exceeding 10 % of the nominal or accounting par value of the securities issued in exchange, do not exclude the application of the "exchange of shares" provision.

---

11   The transferring company, thus, continues to exist.

6. Transfer of the Registered Office of an SE and SCE

With the 2005 amendment to the Merger Directive, a transfer of the registered office **496** of an SE or SCE from one Member State to another became possible. Although Art. 1(b) includes such transfers in the objective scope of the Merger Directive, a transfer of a registered office has **nothing to do with merging or demerging**. Art. 1(b) deals with the emigration of an SE or SCE, which is not a transaction but a movement of the management from one Member State to another. Under the other operations covered by the Merger Directive, only ownership is transferred. As such, there is usually no (physical) movement of assets and liabilities.

In respect of the transfer of the registered office of an SE or SCE, the objective scope **497** of the Merger Directive partially addresses circumstances that are also covered by ATAD 1, i.e. Art. 5(1)(c) dealing with a "transfer of tax residence to another Member State or to a third country". Nevertheless, there is no conflict of laws, as the directives complement one another in terms of their legal consequences.[12]

III. Tax Consequences

A. Rationale of the Merger Directive

The essence of the Merger Directive is the **deferral of capital gains tax** on the **498** occasion of an operation covered by the Directive. This is basically achieved **by a roll-over of basis**, i.e. by carrying over the value for tax purposes of the assets, liabilities and shares involved. In other words, the Directive requires the Member States to refrain from taxing any capital gains triggered by the qualifying reorganization. However, the benefit of the Directive is not a tax exemption but a tax deferral. Thus, in a merger, (partial) division or transfer of assets, the potential tax due on the hidden reserves accruing prior to the transaction (= latent tax claim) is shifted to the receiving company, which must enter the transferred assets and liabilities in its accounts at the same tax value as that assigned to them in the transferring company's accounts prior to the transfer. When the receiving company later on disposes of the assets transferred, tax may be due on the difference between the disposal value and the original value for tax purposes. In fact, this difference also encompasses those hidden reserves that arose prior to the reorganization, the tax on which was deferred by means of the Merger Directive. Similarly, shareholders who – in the course of a merger, (partial) division or exchange of shares – exchange shares they own in one company for shares in another company, will not be taxed at the time of the swap, provided the same value for tax purposes of the substituted shares is attributed to the shares being substituted. In this case as well, taxes only become due when the shares received are sold by the shareholder and thereby the hidden reserves are finally realized. Corresponding

---

12   See m.no. 507.

deferral rules also apply when an SE or SCE transfers its registered office from one Member State to another.

499 From the above, it becomes clear that with respect to the tax consequences, the Merger Directive distinguishes between **taxation at the level of the companies** involved and **taxation at the level of the shareholders** affected. This pattern will also be followed in the following discussion.

B. Taxation of the Companies Involved

1. Deferral of Capital Gains Tax and Carry-Over of Tax Values

500 Art. 4(1) provides the basic rule for taxation at the level of the transferring company in the Member State of the transferring company.[13] Accordingly, a **merger, division or partial division may not give rise to any taxation of capital gains** calculated as the difference between the real value of the assets and liabilities transferred and their value for tax purposes. This "value for tax purposes" is defined in Art. 4(2)(a) as the value on the basis of which any gain or loss would have been computed by the transferring company if the assets or liabilities had been sold at the time of the reorganization but independently of it.

501 However, Art. 4(4) makes the **tax deferral conditional upon** the receiving company computing any new depreciation and any gains or losses in respect of the assets and liabilities transferred according to the same rules that would have applied to the transferring company (or companies) had the reorganization not taken place. This mechanism is therefore also known as **roll-over of basis**, since the tax values of the assets and liabilities of the transferring company have to be taken over by the receiving company in the Member State of the transferring company. Thereby the tax basis in the form of the hidden reserves that accrued at the level of the transferring company until the merger or (partial) division is shifted to the receiving company.

502 Deviations in the value for tax purposes of the assets and liabilities transferred, such as a step-up in basis, partially frustrate the relief provided by the Directive. Consequently, as clarified by Art. 4(5), **where** – under the laws of the Member State of the transferring company – the **receiving company is entitled to have such a step-up in the tax value of the transferred assets**, the **tax neutrality** at the level of the transferring company as set out in Art. 4(1) **does not apply** to the assets and liabilities in respect of which the option was exercised.[14]

---

13 Although Art. 4 does not explicitly state which Member State must apply the rules contained therein, from the scope, system and history of the Directive it is evident, however, that Art. 4 addresses only the State of the transferring company. See also Van den Broek, *Cross-Border Mergers within the EU* (2012) p. 203.

14 Since Arts. 4(4) and 4(5) do not address the Member State of the receiving company, the valuation of the transferred assets and liabilities in that State is irrelevant to their valuation in the Member State of the transferring company.

Another important feature of Art. 4 is the **"remaining PE requirement"** as provided **503** for by Art. 4(2)(b). Prima facie, it makes the tax deferral and the carry-over of values conditional upon the **transferred assets and liabilities remaining effectively connected with a PE** of the receiving company in the Member State of the transferring company. Furthermore, it is required that these assets and liabilities play a part in generating the profits and losses taken into account for tax purposes. The rationale of this remaining PE requirement is obviously the safeguarding of taxing rights and thereby the financial interests of the Member State of the transferring company, since under current international tax (treaty) law, a State may only tax profits derived by non-residents if that profit is sourced within its territory. In respect of profits stemming from a business operation, this requirement is, as a rule, fulfilled if the business is carried on through a PE in that State. If the assets and liabilities transferred in a cross-border reorganization do not form part of a PE in the State of the transferring company, then that State, as a rule, loses its tax claim on the capital gains and fiscal reserves represented by those assets because at a later stage they belong to a non-resident taxpayer and their disposal cannot be taxed in the original source State. Art. 4(2)(b) is therefore regarded as a **"claim saver"**, ensuring that the future realization of the deferred capital gains will be part of the tax base allocated to the State of the transferring company;[15] thus, to the State under whose tax jurisdiction they were generated. However, in order to achieve this goal, it is not always necessary that the transferred assets remain effectively connected with a PE, such as in respect of immovable property. In this context, the PE requirement is excessive. The **PE concept also fails when the State in which the PE is situated does not have the right to tax the PE** because of specific provisions in a DTC similar to the provision of Art. 8 of the OECD Model. To overcome this problem, the Commission and the Council agreed in the Council minutes that Art. 4 of the Directive should not prevent the Member State of a transferring company from taxing, at the time of the reorganization, gains that would otherwise, by virtue of DTC provisions, escape tax in that State altogether.[16]

The crucial question in this respect is, however, whether an immediate taxation of **504** hidden reserves (unrealized capital gains) that would otherwise escape taxation in the State of the transferring company is in line with the requirements of the fundamental freedoms of primary EU law. Even though the Merger Directive seems to tolerate this, it has to be noted that the Merger Directive, as a part of secondary EU law, still has to comply with the higher-ranking fundamental freedoms.[17] As the cases on exit taxation of individuals[18] and legal entities[19] reveal, the compulsory

---

15 See Wattel/Marres/Vermeulen (eds.), *European Tax Law*, Volume I (2019) p. 303 et seq.

16 Thömmes, in: Thömmes/Fuks (eds.), *EC Corporate Tax Law* (December 2004) Merger Directive para. 163.

17 See e.g. CJEU, 23 February 2006, Case C-471/04, *Keller Holding*, EU:C:2006:143, para. 45.

18 Such as CJEU, 11 March 2004, Case C-9/02, *Lasteyrie du Saillant*, EU:C:2004, para. 138; CJEU, 7 September 2006, Case C-470/04, *N.*, EU:C:2006:525; CJEU, 12 July 2012, Case C-269/09, *Commission v Spain*, EU:C:2012:439.

19 Such as CJEU, 29 November 2011, Case C-371/10, *National Grid Indus*, EU:C:2011:785; CJEU, 6 September 2012, Case C-38/10, *Commission v Portugal*, EU:C:2012:521; corporate exit taxation was also

immediate taxation of unrealized capital gains upon emigration to another Member State, whereas no such taxation is provided for in purely domestic situations, runs the risk of infringing the fundamental freedoms, primarily the freedom of establishment according to Art. 49 TFEU. If we transpose the arguments used by the Court to situations in which companies "emigrate" by means of a cross-border reorganization,[20] the remaining PE requirement of Art. 4(2)(b) and Art. 10(1), if interpreted in such a way that it tolerates compulsory immediate tax collection, would contravene the obligations imposed by the fundamental freedoms of primary EU law.[21] The underlying object and purpose of such taxation – namely the safeguarding of tax claims – may be achieved by less restrictive measures than immediate tax collection. These concerns, therefore, suggest an interpretation of Art. 4(2)(b) and Art. 10 (1) that is in conformity with primary EU law.

505 In the meantime, the CJEU has already elaborated on the substantive elements of a system that safeguards the taxing rights of the Member State of origin (i.e. the Member State in which the hidden reserves accrued) in "exit scenarios" of corporate entities or business undertakings in a manner that meets the requirements of primary EU law.[22] As result of a coherent understanding of the principle of fiscal territoriality linked to a temporal component, the CJEU leaves no doubt that Member States are entitled to tax increases in value that were generated while the respective taxpayer or taxable object had a sufficient nexus to the taxing State.[23] However, taxation is only justifiable to the extent that the taxing Member State is

---

the subject matter in CJEU, 25 April 2013, Case C-64/11, *Commission v Spain*, EU:C:2013:264 and CJEU, 31 January 2013, Case C-301/11, *Commission v* Netherlands, EU:C:2013: 47. On the issue of capital taxes in the context of a transfer of seat, see CJEU, 6 September 2012, Case C-380/11, *DI. VI. Finanziaria di Diego della Valle & C.*, EU:C:2012:552.

20 Due to the structural relationship between exit taxation in situations of corporate emigration and the taxation of cross-border reorganizations, the findings of the Court in its case law on exit taxation can be applied *mutatis mutandis* to reorganizations. This can also be inferred from the Court's case law. In the *DMC* judgment the CJEU transposed its case law on exit taxes in the strict sense to a cross-border transfer of an interest in a partnership to a limited liability company in exchange for shares not covered by the Merger Directive (CJEU, 23 January 2014, *DMC*, Case C-164/12, EU:C:2014:20). Similarly, in the *A Oy* case, the CJEU used its "exit tax reasoning" to decide on the disproportionality of an immediate collection of taxes levied in the context of a transfer of assets pursuant to Art. 10(2) of the Merger Directive (CJEU, 23 November 2017, Case C-292/16, *A Oy*, EU:C:2017:888, para. 20 in conjunction with para. 34 et seq.). Also in *Verder LabTec* the CJEU applied the arguments used in the context of companies transferring their tax residence to the situation in which only assets are transferred and thereby lose their qualifying tax nexus for later taxation in the State of origin (CJEU, 21 May 2015, Case C-657/13, *Verder LabTec*, EU:C:2015:331, in particular para. 42 et seq.). The immediate taxation resulting from the interplay between reorganizations and exit scenarios was also at stake in the *Commission v. Portugal* case (CJEU, 21 December 2016, Case C-503/14, *Commission v Portugal*, EU:C:2016:979), which the CJEU, in the end, did not treat differently from straight exit scenarios. The *Jacob* and *Lassus* decision of the CJEU (CJEU, 22 March 2018, Joined Cases C-327/16 and C-421/16, *Jacob and Lassus*, EU:C:210) has not changed that reasoning, as it concerned the tax consequences of an exchange of shares within the meaning of Art. 8 of the Merger Directive at the shareholder level. See m.no. 525.

21 See Schön, Tax Issues and Constraints on Reorganizations and Reincorporations in the European Union, *TNI* 2004, p. 202 et seq.

22 See also Chapter 3, m.no. 293.

23 CJEU, 29 November 2011, Case C-371/10, *National Grid Indus*, EU:C:2011:785, para. 46 et seq.

actually prevented from exercising its power of taxation in respect of such income at a later point in time.[24] Against the background of the principle of proportionality, the Court, furthermore, rejects a mandatory immediate payment of the taxes due on the hidden reserves disclosed at the time of exit. At this point, the CJEU distinguishes between the establishment of the amount of tax due and its recovery. Whereas an immediate tax assessment is allowed, immediate recovery is not.[25] The recovery of the tax debt has to be postponed until the time of actual realization of the capital gain or an equivalent chargeable event in the host Member State, instead. To counterbalance the resultant administrative burden, the CJEU suggested an optional system, offering taxpayers the choice between immediate payment of the tax or deferred payment, possibly together with interest in accordance with the applicable national legislation.[26] Beyond that, the Court also accepted the ability to spread the payment of the tax due on the disclosed hidden reserves over a fixed period of time as a satisfactory and proportionate alternative to postponement until actual realization.[27] Furthermore, the Member States may also take into account the risk of non-recovery of the tax in the event of deferral by measures such as the provision of a bank guarantee, provided that the requirement to supply collateral is imposed on

---

24 CJEU, 23 January 2014, Case C-164/12, *DMC*, EU:C:2014:20, para. 56; also CJEU, 23 November 2017, Case C-292/16, *A Oy*, EU:C:2017:888, para. 30 et seq. In this context it should be noted, however, that the CJEU in the *A Oy* case obviously did not regard the tax jurisdiction in relation to the shares received in consideration for the transferred assets as sufficient compensation for the loss of tax jurisdiction over the transferred assets. As put by Advocate General Kokott in her opinion on the case, the jurisdiction to tax shares in a foreign company situated abroad is a different matter as compared with the power to tax the assets of a foreign permanent establishment. The shares received are not the same as the assets of the PE. See Opinion of Advocate General Kokott, 13 July 2017, Case C-292/16, *A Oy*, EU:C:2017: 555, para. 36.

25 Thus, the amount of tax due may be fixed definitively at the time the Member State of origin loses its tax jurisdiction over the transferred assets. As a consequence, decreases in value that occur subsequent to the transfer need not be taken into account. CJEU, 29 November 2011, Case C-371/10, *National Grid Indus*, EU:C:2011:785, para. 52 et seq.; CJEU, 16 April 2015, Case C-591/13, *Commission v Germany*, EU:C:2015:230, para. 66. The *Jacob* and *Lassus* decision of the CJEU does not question this result, as the case did not concern the definite determination of the tax due at the time the taxpayer ceases to be subject to tax in the Member State of origin and that state thereby loses its fiscal competence, but a deferral of taxation. Accordingly, at the time of the reorganization in question (i.e. exchange of shares according Art. 2(e)) only the amount of the capital gain (i.e. the hidden reserves that accrued up to this point in time) is established; taxation, as such, takes place at a later stage, i.e. when the securities received in exchange are alienated or otherwise transferred. This implies, however, that the Member State applying such a system of deferral exercises its fiscal competence in respect of that capital gain at the time when the deferral ends and taxation takes place. In doing so, the Member State is also, other than in the classical exit tax scenarios, obliged to take into account capital losses that arise at that time. CJEU, 22 March 2018, Joined Cases C-327/16 and C-421/16, *Jacob and Lassus*, EU:C:210, in particular para. 82 et seq.

26 CJEU, 29 November 2011, Case C-371/10, *National Grid Indus*, EU:C:2011:785, para. 73; CJEU, 16 April 2015, Case C-591/13, *Commission v Germany*, EU:C:2015:230, para. 67.

27 CJEU, 23 January 2014, Case C-164/12, *DMC*, EU:C:2014:20, para. 64; CJEU, 21 May 2015, Case C-657/13, *Verder LabTec*, EU:C:2015:331, para. 53. Thereby, the Court seems to take into account the fact that the assets and liabilities structure of a business undertaking can be complex and, consequently, deferring the recovery of the tax debt until the time of actual realization or a comparable point in time is not only difficult but the collection of the tax may even be undermined if the assets are not destined for alienation but for use in the ordinary course of the business.

the basis of the actual risk of non-recovery of the tax.[28] This reasoning has recently also been "codified" in Art 5(2) and (3) of ATAD 1, according to which taxpayers in intra-EU/EEA cases[29] shall be given the right to defer the payment of the taxes triggered by measures within the meaning of Art 5(1) by paying the tax in instalments over five years.[30] Since the implementation of the ATAD 1 measures in exit scenarios is mandatory, it is expected that there will be some sort of tacit harmonization also in other instances where taxes are levied to counter a loss of taxing rights.

506   Since Art. 9 explicitly refers to Art. 4, the **tax deferral rules of Art. 4 also apply to transfers of assets.** Consequently, also in a qualifying transfer of assets, the transferring company must not tax any hidden reserves built into the assets and liabilities attributable to the branch of its activity that is transferred, provided the receiving company takes over the tax values attached to them prior to the transfer.

507   In respect of a **transfer of the registered office of an SE or an SCE or the cessation of residence** of such a corporation, Art. 12(1) likewise provides that the emigration of the corporation may not give rise to any taxation on capital gains within the meaning of Art. 4(1). Analogous to the remaining PE requirement of Art. 4(2)(b), Art. 12(1)(b) also requires the assets and liabilities of the emigrating SE or SCE to remain effectively connected with a PE of that company in the Member State of departure for the tax deferral to apply. In fact, the same concerns as outlined in m.no. 504 et seq. arise also with respect to Art. 12(1)(b). The second precondition for the tax neutrality of the transfer is – along the lines of Art. 4(4) – that the SE or SCE compute any new depreciation and any gains or losses in respect of the assets and liabilities that remain effectively connected with the PE in the Member State of departure as if the "corporate emigration" has not taken place. In this respect, the Merger Directive has been complemented by ATAD 1. Under Art. 12(1)(b) of the Merger Directive, the exit tax triggered by the transfer of residence under Art. 5(1)(c) of the ATAD only applies to assets that do not remain effectively connected with a permament establishment in the Member State of departure. Thus, for assets that do not remain effectively connected with a PE in the Member State of departure of an SE or SCE and that therefore fall outside the scope of Art. 12(1) of the Merger Directive, ATAD 1 requires that any taxes levied on the difference between the market value and book value of the transferred assets be eligible for tax deferral under Art. 5(2)(c) of ATAD 1. Inversely, the Member State of destination henceforth has to accept the value established by the Member State of departure as the starting value of the assets for tax purposes.

---

28   CJEU, 23 January 2014, Case C-164/12, *DMC*, EU:C:2014:20, para. 65 et seq.

29   The legal requirement for the tax deferral is – in line with the case law of the CJEU – that the transfer takes place within the EU or the EEA subject to the condition that the respective EEA country has concluded an agreement with the Member State of the taxpayer or with the Union on mutual assistance for the recovery of tax claims equivalent to the mutual assistance provided for in Council Directive 2010/24/EU of 16 March 2010 concerning mutual assistance for the recovery of claims relating to taxes, duties and other measures.

30   See Chapter 8 m.no. 610.

In this regard, it has to be noted that the Merger Directive only covers the legal **508** transfer of assets as a result of a reorganization and therefore does not address any physical transfer of assets carried out collaterally. Such an additional physical transfer of assets in connection with a transaction covered by the Merger Directive may, however, fall under Art 5(1) of ATAD 1.[31]

2. Carry-Over of Tax-Free Provisions and Reserves

According to Art. 5 of the Directive, the **Member State of the transferring company** **509** in a merger or (partial) division **must refrain from recapturing any tax-deductible provisions or tax-free reserves** formed by the transferring company in respect of assets and liabilities transferred to the receiving company. Such provisions and reserves must be carried over with the same tax exemption to the remaining PEs of the receiving company that are situated in the Member State of the transferring company. Thereby, the receiving company assumes the rights and obligations attached to the provisions and reserves and may continue to use them in the same way as the transferring company.

An **exception** is made **for provisions or reserves** that were set up in connection **510** with assets and liabilities **of foreign PEs** of the transferring company. As a result of the transfer, such PEs become PEs of the receiving company, which, however, is not a resident of the Member State of the transferring company. Consequently, the assets and liabilities concerned are, as a rule, not subject to tax in that State if they are disposed of or realized in the future. For this reason, the Merger Directive allows the Member State of the transferring company to recapture and tax such provisions and reserves at the moment of the reorganization, i.e. when the Member State of the transferring company loses its taxing power over the foreign PEs concerned. This, again, raises the question of whether such immediate taxation is in line with the fundamental freedoms of EU law provided that a comparable domestic reorganization would not cause an immediate recapture.[32]

According to Art. 9, **Art. 5 also applies to a transfer of assets.** Rules similar to those **511** as contained in Art. 5 are also enshrined in Art. 13(1) concerning the **transfer of the registered office** of an SE or an SCE.

3. Takeover of Losses

The treatment of losses is, in many instances, decisive in restructuring a business. **512** This is also true for cross-border reorganizations. **Art. 6 of the Merger Directive addresses the issue of losses,** but inadequately. If, for purely domestic mergers, (partial) divisions and asset transfers,[33] the respective national laws allow losses

---

31 In particular Art. 5(1)(d) ATAD 1.
32 See m.no. 504 et seq.
33 This is the result of the references contained in Art. 9 on the transfer of assets to applying Art. 6 *mutatis mutandis.*

connected with the transferred assets and not yet exhausted to be taken over by the receiving company to be set off there, such a takeover must also be available for the equivalent cross-border operation covered by the Merger Directive. Only then does the Merger Directive require the Member State of the transferring company to allow the takeover of such losses by the receiving company's PEs situated within its territory. Thus, the Directive **only contains a non-discrimination rule** that, in the light of the case law of the CJEU on the fundamental freedoms, has become obsolete.

513 Like Art. 6 of the Merger Directive, Art. 13(2) requires the "State of departure" of an SE or SCE that transfers its registered office to another Member State to allow the remaining PE in its jurisdiction to set off the losses of the SE or SCE not yet utilized if it would allow such compensation in a comparable domestic situation in which the corporation continued to have its registered office or continued to be tax resident in that Member State.

514 From the above, it is evident that Arts. 6 and 13(2) of the Merger Directive only address the treatment of losses in the Member State in which the PEs of the receiving company or emigrating SE/SCE are located but not the treatment by the State of residence of the receiving or emigrating company. Discriminatory treatment resulting from cross-border reorganizations in these circumstances has to be resolved by primary EU law.[34]

4. Cancellation of Shares

515 The objective of Art. 7 is a relief of the tax burden of the receiving company in situations in which it has a holding in the capital of the transferring company (**upstream merger**). Upon merging, the **participation the receiving company holds in the transferring company is cancelled**, since the transferring company ceases to exist. However, this cancellation of shares may trigger a taxable profit if the holding was assessed at a lower value than the value of the assets and liabilities that take the place of that holding in the balance sheet of the receiving company. **Art. 7(1)** of the Merger Directive now **prohibits any taxation of gains** that accrue **in connec-**

---

34   The key issue is whether losses that, as a result of the reorganization or emigration, can no longer be used in the Member State of origin have to be regarded as "final losses" under the *Marks & Spencer* doctrine (CJEU, 13 December 2005, Case C-446/03, *Marks & Spencer*, EU:C:2005:763) and therefore have to be compensated for in the Member State of the receiving company or in the new Member State of residence of the emigrating company. The CJEU ruled that losses may be "final" under the *Marks & Spencer* doctrine in respect of cross-border mergers even if the domestic tax law of the state of the transferring company generally does not provide for a transfer of losses to another company and therefore losses become automatically legally exhausted in the event of a merger or similar transaction (see CJEU, 19 June 2019, Case C-607/17, *Memira Holding*, EU:C:2019:510; similarly CJEU, 19 June 2019, Case C-608/17, *Holmen*, EU:C:2019:511). As a result, the tax burden that is caused by the deliberate choice of an EU Member State to preclude a transfer of losses as part of mergers in general is economically passed on to other Member States, leading to an export of losses by means of a (voluntary) cross-border merger under the doctrine of "final losses". This result is not convincing (see also Van den Broek, Final Losses in Respect of Cross-Border Mergers: *Memira* (Case C-607/17) and *Holmen* (Case C-608/17), *ET* 2020, pp. 54 and 57 et seq.).

tion with such a **cancellation of shares**.[35] Furthermore, the Directive only covers the cancellation of shares in respect of up-stream mergers. The reverse situation, where the transferring company holds a participation in the capital of the receiving company, as is the case in a **down-stream merger**, is **not covered** by the Directive, even though (book) gains may also arise in these circumstances.

Moreover, **Art. 7(2)** grants the Member States the **right to derogate from the tax exemption in Art. 7(1)** provided the amount of the shares held by the receiving company in the transferring company is below a certain threshold. This threshold corresponds to the **minimum shareholding** of Art. 3(1)(a) of Council Directive 2011/96/EU of 30 November 2011 on the Common System of Taxation Applicable in the Case of Parent Companies and Subsidiaries of Different Member States (hereinafter Parent-Subsidiary Directive).[36] Consequently, this minimum amount was reduced from the original 25 % to 10 % as of 1 January 2009.

5. Valuation of Shares Received in a Transfer of Assets

The Directive contains **no rules on how the transferring company** in a transfer of assets according to Art. 2(d) in conjunction with Art. 9 **should assess the value of the shares issued to it by the receiving company**. If, therefore, the transferring company has to enter those shares in its tax accounts at the book value of the transferred assets and liabilities, the **hidden reserves** contained in the transferred assets and liabilities **are doubled**. This means that both the receiving company (because of the roll-over of basis according to Art. 4) and the transferring company may later be taxed on the same capital gain; the receiving company, when disposing of the assets and liabilities received, and the transferring company, when selling the shares in the receiving company that it obtained in exchange for the assets transferred.[37]

6. Valuation of Shares by the Acquiring Company in an Exchange of Shares

Similarly, the **Directive does not include rules on the valuation of the shares acquired by the acquiring company in an exchange of shares** according to Art. 2(e). Art. 8(3) only provides for a roll-over of tax values at the shareholder level. Again,

516

517

518

---

35 From the fact that the wording of the provision is restricted to "gains" it is inferred that Art. 7(1) does not apply to losses in connection with the cancellation of shares. See e.g. BFH, 30 July 2014, I R 58/12.

36 See Chapter 5, m.no. 418 et seq.

37 This consequence was confirmed by the CJEU in the *3D I Srl* case (CJEU, 19 December 2012, Case C-207/11, *3D I Srl*, EU:C:2012:818, para. 29 et seq.; Rossi-Maccanico, The *3D I* Case: Useful Clarification from the Court on the Boundaries of the EU Merger Directive, *EC Tax Review* 2013, p. 197 et seq. In order to avoid the doubling of hidden reserves and the economic double taxation that is thereby triggered, the proposal for the 2005 amendment to the Merger Directive added to Art. 9 a paragraph 2. These new rules should have provided that the transferring company had to attribute to the shares received in exchange the real value of the assets and liabilities transferred. However, no political agreement could be reached on this part of the proposal. Consequently, the proposed paragraph 2 was not included in Directive 2005/19/EC.

if the acquiring company is obliged to value the shares obtained from the former shareholders of the acquired company at their book value, economic double taxation due to a doubling of hidden reserves is the result.[38] In the *A.T.* case,[39] the CJEU only held that Art. 8(1) and (2) of the Merger Directive preclude domestic tax rules according to which, as a consequence of an exchange of shares, the shareholders of the acquired company are taxed on the capital gains arising from the transfer,[40] unless the acquiring company carries over the historical book value of the shares transferred in its own tax balance sheet.[41] A "double book value carry-over" was, thus, not regarded as being in conformity with the Merger Directive. Apart from that, the issue of valuation at the level of the acquiring company has, however, not yet been conclusively dealt with by the CJEU.

7. Transfer of a Foreign Permanent Establishment

519   **Art. 10(1)** sentence 1 in conjunction with sentence 3 of the Merger Directive addresses the **transfer of a PE in a triangular situation,** in other words the transfer of a branch of activity in the form of a PE situated in one Member State by a company resident in another Member State to a company resident in a third Member State.

520   **Tax neutrality in the Member State that hosts the PE** is achieved by Art. 10(1) sentence 3, which requires that the State of the PE and the Member State of the receiving company apply the provisions of the Merger Directive as if the transferring company was situated in the State of the PE. Consequently, the State of the PE may not tax any capital gains on the assets and liabilities of the PE and must allow a carry-over of tax-free provisions and reserves, provided that, within the PE, the original book values and depreciation methods are retained.

521   Art. 10(1) sentence 4 clarifies that the rules of Art. 10(1) providing for tax neutrality also apply to a transaction commonly known as an **incorporation of a branch into a subsidiary**, i.e. where the PE that is to be transferred is situated in the same Member State as that in which the receiving company is resident (**transfer of a PE in a bilateral situation**).

522   Even though the Member State of the transferring company may not tax any unrealized capital gains upon the transfer of the foreign PE, Art. 10(1) sentence 2 entitles that Member State to **recapture** any **loss deductions** granted in the past to the transferring company in respect of losses incurred by its foreign PE, provided these losses had not been recovered by the time of the transfer. Since, after

---

38   In this scenario the proposal for the 2005 amendment of the Directive included its own valuation rule, according to which the acquiring company would be able to enter the shares acquired in its tax account at their real (market) value. Since no political agreement could be reached, this part of the amendment was dropped altogether.

39   CJEU, 11 December 2008, Case C-285/07, *A.T.*, EU:C:2008:705.

40   With these gains being deemed to correspond to the difference between the initial cost of acquiring the shares transferred and their market value.

41   CJEU, 11 December 2008, Case C-285/07, *A.T.*, EU:C:2008:705, para. 39.

the transfer, the PE no longer belongs to the transferring company but is part of the receiving company's enterprise that is resident in another Member State, this recapture rule is regarded as necessary to safeguard the financial interests of the Member State of the transferring company. The question in this respect is, however, whether an immediate claw-back of the losses concerned is also proportionate within the meaning of primary EU law.

Art. 10(2) particularly addresses those Member States that apply the credit method **523** for the avoidance of double taxation. By way of **derogation from paragraph 1, the Member State of the transferring company is allowed to include the capital gains** of the foreign PE's assets and liabilities **in the taxable income of the transferring company.** However, it is then **obliged to credit a notional amount of tax,** i.e. the amount of tax that the Member State in which the PE is situated would have levied on those gains, had it not been required to grant tax neutrality on the transaction under the rules of the Merger Directive. In this way, double taxation should be avoided. Since neither Art. 10(2) nor any other article of the Merger Directive contains provisions on how the collection of the tax due has to take place, the respective national provisions also have to be in line with the fundamental freedoms. Accordingly, Member States applying such a notional tax credit system must also offer taxpayers a choice between immediate payment of the tax so calculated or deferred payment in instalments. Compulsory immediate collection of the tax established at the time of the reorganziation (despite the notional tax credit) is disproportionate.[42]

C. Taxation of the Shareholders Involved

Art. 8(1) of the Merger Directive **defers taxation** with respect to capital gains in **524** an exchange of shares **at the shareholder level resulting from a merger, division or an exchange of shares** within the meaning of Art. 2(e) of the Directive. With regard to a merger or division, the exchange of shares concerns the shareholders of the (dissolved) transferring companies, who, in exchange for their shares, get shares in the receiving companies, whereas in an exchange of shares transaction according to Art. 2(e), Art. 8(1) covers the shares in the acquired company that are transferred to the acquiring company in return for (new) shares that are issued to the former shareholders of the acquired company. Similarly, **Art. 8(2) defers taxation of the allotment of shares issued in the course of a partial division,** where the receiving companies issue shares to the shareholders of the transferring company.

Consequently, no tax will be levied on the capital gain realized on the shares that **525** were substituted or on the allotment of shares. This **deferral** is, however, **conditional upon the shareholders' carry-over of tax values.** According to Art. 8(4)

---

42   CJEU, 23 November 2017, Case C-292/16, *A Oy*, EU:C:2017:888, para. 36 et seq.

and (5), the shareholders therefore have to attribute to the shares received in exchange the same value for tax purposes as that attached to the "old" shares. In most instances, this mechanism ensures that the Member State in whose tax jurisdiction the hidden reserves in the exchanged shares accumulated is still able to tax them when the shareholder sells the shares in the acquiring or receiving company. Taxation at the time of subsequent disposal is also confirmed by **Art. 8(6)**, which **permits the Member States to tax the gain arising out of a subsequent transfer of the securities** received in exchange in the same way as gains arising out of a transfer of securities that existed before the acquisition. Nevertheless, there may be situations in which the Member State of the acquired company loses its taxing power over the hidden reserves that accumulated in the acquired shares upon the exchange without being compensated by a corresponding possibility to tax the shares received in exchange. Nevertheless, the Member States are not forced to accept a complete erosion of their taxing rights. As the CJEU decided in the joined *Jacob* and *Lassus* cases, Art. 8(1), in conjunction with Art. 8(6), in principle permits a mechanism to defer taxation of a capital gain calculated at the time of the exchange until the shares received in exchange are actually realized, provided that capital losses arising after the exchange are also taken into account if such an advantage would have been granted in a purely domestic situation.[43] Not covered by the tax deferral is any additional cash payment within the 10 % limitation as provided for by Art. 2(a) to (c), as well as Art. 2(e).[44]

526   If, however, the respective **national laws in the State in which the shareholders are resident allow them to opt for a step-up in tax basis** and the shareholders, by exercising this option, voluntarily choose to be taxed on the capital gain arising from the exchange of shares, then the **tax deferral rules**, of course, **do not apply**. This is provided for by Art. 8(8) of the Merger Directive.

527   The **Directive lacks a comprehensive definition of the term "shareholder".** From this lack of any further requirement as to the shareholder, it has been deduced that the benefits of the Merger Directive must also apply to shareholders resident in a third (non-EU) country. Under the 2005 amendments, these issues should have been addressed by the insertion of a new Art. 8(12), which was supposed to extend tax neutrality to shareholders resident in third countries. In the final version of the amending Directive, this provision was, however, dropped, obviously because of the fear of negative revenue repercussions.[45] Consequently, it is still not entirely clear whether the benefits of the Merger Directive have to be granted

---

43   CJEU, 22 March 2018, Joined Cases C-327/16 and C-421/16, *Jacob and Lassus*, EU:C:210.
44   Art. 8(9) of the Merger Directive; for the 10 % limitation, see also m.no. 486, 488 and 495.
45   In its legislative resolution on the proposal of the amending Directive, it was proposed that the tax relief provided for by Art. 8 only be granted if the taxing rights of the Member States with regard to third countries' shareholders were not significantly infringed. European Parliament of 10 March 2004, P5_TA(2004)0159, Amendment 4.

to shareholders resident in non-EU countries in the same way as EU-resident shareholders.[46]

Although a **transfer of the registered office of an SE or SCE** does not trigger an exchange of shares at the shareholder level, **Art. 14 also stipulates corresponding deferral rules** upon the emigration of SEs or SCEs. The reason behind this is the danger that the Member States could otherwise regard the act of emigration of an SE or SCE as a taxable event for the shareholders. Consequently, Art. 14(1) provides that the transfer of the registered office in itself may not give rise to any taxation of the shareholders of the emigrating company. Again, the Directive does not preclude the Member States from taxing gains arising out of a subsequent alienation of the shares in the SE or the SCE that transferred its registered office previously (Art. 14(2)).   **528**

IV. Transactions Not Covered

The common tax system for cross-border reorganizations under the Merger Directive was introduced to create, within the European Union, conditions analogous to those of an internal market. The scope of the Merger Directive is, however, **limited in several respects**. The **personal scope** of the Merger Directive is restricted to companies specified under Art. 3. The Directive is also limited with respect to the **objective** and **territorial scope**. Only the specified reorganizations and operations under Art. 2,[47] involving companies of two or more Member States, are covered by the Merger Directive. Therefore, in particular, reorganizations involving third State companies or purely domestic situations are not covered.   **529**

Furthermore, a merger, division, partial division or exchange of shares falls outside the Merger Directive's scope if the consideration for the reorganization includes cash payments, if any, **exceeding 10 % of the nominal value** or, in absence of a nominal value, of the accounting par value of the securities issued to the (former) shareholders of the transferring or acquired company by the receiving or acquiring company in exchange for the transfer.   **530**

---

46   When adopting the final version of the amending Directive, the Council and the European Commission agreed that Art. 8 of the Directive does not deprive shareholders resident in Member States of the benefits of the Directive in a situation in which the majority holding is acquired from Community residents and from residents of third countries (Council of the European Union of 8 March 2005, 6504/05 ADD 1, Item 1). For a discussion of the issue see also Gordillo Fernández de Villavicencio, Applying the Merger Directive beyond Its Scope in Third-Country Scenarios: An Alternative Approach to *A Oy* (Case C-48/11) – Part 2, *ET* 2013, p. 65 et seq. (in particular footnote 82).

47   Based on the *Cartesio* case (CJEU, 16 December 2008, Case C-210/06, *Cartesio*, EU:C:2008: 327) and the *Vale* case (CJEU, 12 July 2012, Case C-378/10, *Vale*, EU:C:2012:440) the limitation of tax-neutral transfers of registered offices to an SE and an SCE seems to be too narrow. Subject to the condition that the fundamental freedoms of the TFEU are applicable, other legal forms should also have the possibility of benefitting from a tax-neutral corporate emigration (compare also CJEU, 6 September 2012, Case C-38/10, *Commission v Portugal*, EU:C:2012; CJEU, 25 October 2017, Case C-106/16, *Polbud*, EU:C:804). To this end see also Wattel/Marres/Vermeulen (eds.), *European Tax Law*, Volume I (2019) pp. 280 et seq.

531 In the *Kofoed* case, the CJEU held that dividend distributions immediately after an exchange of shares under Art. 2(e) of the Merger Directive do not necessarily have to be considered in determining the 10 % threshold for eligible cash payments. As there was no agreement between the parties participating in the exchange of shares that would characterize the dividend distribution as binding consideration for shares exchanged, the dividend distribution was not regarded as an excessive "cash payment" according to Art. 2(e) of the Merger Directive.[48] Consequently, the Merger Directive remained applicable.

532 Since the scope of the Merger Directive is limited in several respects, for cross-border reorganizations the **fundamental freedoms may also offer a "safety net"**. As most Member States have provisions for domestic reorganizations not triggering immediate taxation at the time of the reorganization, under non-discrimination principles, the Member States may in general not discriminate against comparable cross-border situations. Differences in treatment would only be permissible if they can be justified under the rule of reason doctrine. Furthermore, the measures taken have to be proportionate. A consistent application of the non-discrimination principles enshrined in the fundamental freedoms of the TFEU or the EEA Treaty may, therefore, under certain circumstances, lead to an extension of the benefits of the Merger Directive to cases not covered.

V. Withdrawal of the Benefits of the Directive due to Tax Evasion and Tax Avoidance[49]

533 The Merger Directive includes in Art. 15(1)(a) a clause providing that a Member State **may refuse** to apply or withdraw the benefit of all or any part of the Directive where it appears that the reorganization has as its principal or as one of its principal objectives tax evasion or tax avoidance without providing a definition of tax evasion or tax avoidance.[50] However, as the Member States are, in addition, bound by the mandatory GAAR in Art. 6 of ATAD 1, reorganizations are also covered there.[51]

---

48 CJEU, 5 July 2007, Case C-321/05, *Kofoed*, EU:C:2007:408, para. 33.

49 Art. 15 not only contains a tax specific anti-abuse provision but also includes a rather peculiar rule on the representation of employees on the companies' board of directors. According to Art. 15(1)(b), Member States may withdraw the benefit of all or any part of the Directive if the transaction generally covered by the Merger Directive results in a reduction or cancellation of employee representation on the companies' board of directors. However, this is a provision that applies to the extent that no EU law provisions containing equivalent rules on representation of employees on company organs are applicable to companies covered by the Merger Directive (Art. 15(2)). This is rarely the case, as multiple secondary law acts contain such provisions; see e.g. with respect to limited liability companies, Art. 133 of Directive (EU) 2017/1132 relating to certain aspects of company law (OJ L 169 of 30 June 2017, pp. 45-12).

50 The CJEU has already decided upon Art. 15(1)(a) in some cases: CJEU, 17 July 1997, Case C-28/95, *Leur-Bloem*, EU:C:1997:369; CJEU, 5 July 2007, Case C-321/05, *Kofoed*, EU:C:2007:408; CJEU, 20 May 2010, Case C-352/08, *Zwijnenburg*, EU:C:2011:282.

51 Art. 6 ATAD 1 refers to "arrangements" or "series of arrangements", which may also include reorganizations.

First of all, the implementation of the anti-abuse clause of the Merger Directive in **534** domestic tax law does **not necessarily lead to legislative action**. The transposition of a directive may also be achieved through the general legal context so that a formal and express transposition of the provisions of the directive in the form of specific national provisions is not necessary. If a Member State does not implement a specific anti-abuse provision based on Art. 15(1)(a) and also does not have a domestic anti-abuse clause that may be applicable to cross-border reorganizations covered by the Merger Directive, they may nevertheless reject the application by arguing abuse based on general principles of EU law as discussed in the recent *Danish cases*.[52] Under the "older"case law of the CJEU the anti-abuse clause under the Merger Directive itself was regarded as not having direct effect, as directives themselves cannot impose obligations on an individual.[53] The *Danish* cases have, however, further shifted the weight in the area of abuse. Even though they were not addressing the Merger Directive, but dealt with the Interest and Royalties Directive and the Parent-Subsidiary Directive, general conclusions concerning the Member States' right not to formulate their own anti-abuse clauses can be drawn. As a result of the *Danish* cases, the question whether there is still a need for the anti-abuse clause in the Merger Directive is even more pressing. Beyond that, the question arises whether the general anti-abuse principles of EU law can even replace codified anti-abuse rules.

Art. 15(1)(a) provides that if a reorganization generally covered by the Merger **535** Directive is not undertaken for valid commercial reasons, it may be **presumed that the whole reorganization has tax evasion or avoidance** as its principal objective or as one of its principal objectives. Tax evasion or avoidance need not necessarily be the only goal behind the reorganization, as long as it is one of the main objectives. And even if there are some **commercial reasons**, the attainment of a pure **tax advantage** (like the utilization of losses) was and still is not accepted as a valid commercial reason by the CJEU.[54]

Against this background, it was for example decided in the *Foggia* case on a merger **536** between two companies of the same group, that such an operation is not carried out for valid commercial reasons if the acquired company does not carry out any activity, does not have any financial holdings and transfers to the acquiring company only substantial tax losses of undetermined origin, even though that operation has a positive effect in terms of cost structure.[55] Since the *Zwijnenburg* judgment, it is also clear that Art. 15(1)(a) only addresses the evasion or avoidance of income

---

52 CJEU, 26 February 2019, Joined Cases C-116/16 and C-117/16, *T Danmark / Y Denmark Aps*, EU:C:135; CJEU, 26 February 2019, Joined Cases C-115/16, C-118/16, C-119/16 and C-299/16, *N Luxembourg 1, X Denmark A/S, C Danmark I* and *Z Denmark ApS*, EU:C:134.
53 See chapter 3, m.no. 269.
54 CJEU, 17 July 1997, Case C-28/95, *Leur-Bloem*, EU:C:1997:369, para. 50 et seq.; CJEU, 10 November 2011, Case C-126/10, *Foggia*, EU:C:2011:718, para. 34 et seq.
55 CJEU, 10 November 2011, Case C-126/10, *Foggia*, EU:C:2011:718, para. 52.

(capital gains) taxes, thus taxes to which the Merger Directive relates.[56] Consequently, the avoidance of other taxes (e.g. transaction taxes on immovable property) does not justify precluding the Directive's benefits. In the *Danish* cases, it was decided that abusive practices require, first, a combination of objective circumstances under which, despite formal observance of the conditions laid down by the EU rules, the purpose of those rules has not been achieved and, second, a subjective element consisting in an intention to obtain an advantage from the EU rules by artificially creating the conditions laid down for obtaining it.[57]

537 In order to determine whether a planned or realized operation runs counter to the purposes of the Merger Directive and has the objective of tax avoidance or tax evasion, the **application of general, predetermined criteria is not permissible.**[58] In fact, an examination on a case-by-case basis has to take place, which must be open to judicial review.[59] Thus, the laying down of a rule automatically excluding certain operations from the benefits of the Merger Directive would go further than is necessary in preventing tax evasion or tax avoidance and **would** therefore **infringe the principle of proportionality.**[60] Such an impermissible general presumption of tax evasion or tax avoidance may, as the *Euro Park Services* decision reveals, also exist if a provision of national law systematically and generally requires the taxpayer to show that the operation intended does not have as its principal objective, or as one of its principal objectives, tax evasion or tax avoidance, without the tax authorities being required to provide even prima facie evidence that there are no valid commercial reasons or evidence of tax evasion or tax avoidance.[61] Furthermore, a process of prior approval may only be allowed if the procedural rules laid down for the preliminary produre are not less favourable than those governing similar domestic situations (principle of equivalence) and provided that they do not make it impossible, in practice, or excessively difficult to exercise the rights conferred by the Merger Directive (principle of effectiveness).[62] National legislation that does not specify detailed rules for the application of such a preliminary procedure is not in line with the requirements of Art. 15 of the Merger Directive. Moreover, negative decisions must always be reasoned so that the taxpayer may ascertain whether the reasons that led the authority not to grant him the advantage were well founded and, where appropoiate, seek judicial review.[63]

---

56   CJEU, 20 May 2010, Case C-352/08, *Zwijnenburg*, EU:C:2011:282, para. 47 et seq.
57   CJEU, 26 February 2019, Joined Cases C-116/16 and C-117/16, *T Danmark and Y Denmark Aps*, EU:C:135; CJEU, 26 February 2019, Joined Cases C-115/16, C-118/16, C-119/16 and C-299/16, *N Luxembourg 1, X Denmark A/S, C Danmark I and Z Denmark ApS*, EU:C:134.
58   CJEU, 8 March 2017, Case C-14/16, *Euro Park Services*, EU:C:2017:177, para. 54 et seq.
59   CJEU, 10 November 2011, Case C-126/10, *Foggia*, EU:C:2011:718, para. 37.
60   CJEU, 17 July 1997, Case C-28/95, *Leur-Bloem*, EU:C:1997:369, para. 52 et seq.
61   CJEU, 8 March 2017, Case C-14/16, *Euro Park Services*, EU:C:2017:177, para. 56.
62   For the interaction of the principle of effectiveness with the principle of legal certainty in respect of procedural rules see also CJEU, 18 October 2012, Case C-603/10, *Pelati*, EU:C:2012:639, para. 32 et seq.
63   CJEU, 8 March 2017, Case C-14/16, *Euro Park Services*, EU:C:2017:177, para. 43 et seq.

VI. Overview of the Functioning of the Directive

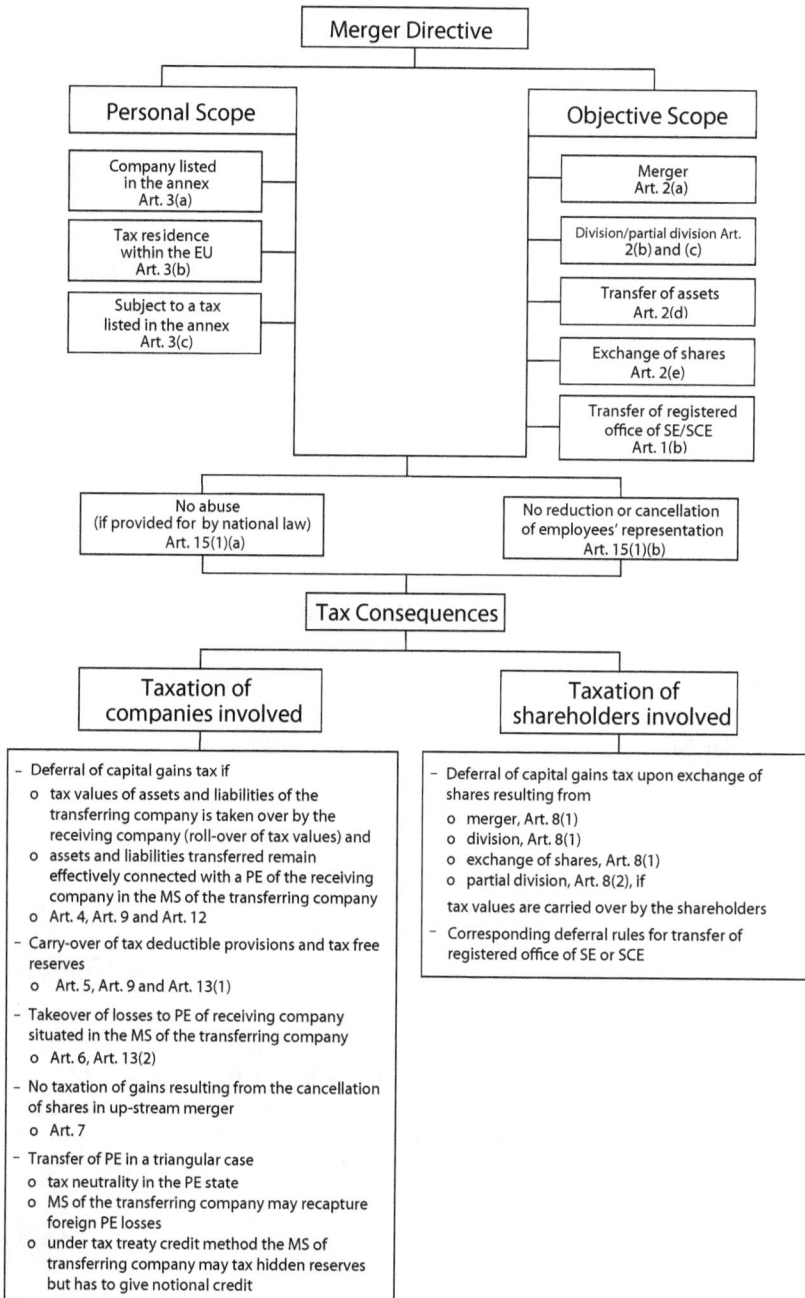

538

```
                           ┌──────────────────┐
                           │ Merger Directive │
                           └──────────────────┘
```

Personal Scope

- Company listed in the annex Art. 3(a)
- Tax residence within the EU Art. 3(b)
- Subject to a tax listed in the annex Art. 3(c)

Objective Scope

- Merger Art. 2(a)
- Division/partial division Art. 2(b) and (c)
- Transfer of assets Art. 2(d)
- Exchange of shares Art. 2(e)
- Transfer of registered office of SE/SCE Art. 1(b)

No abuse (if provided for by national law) Art. 15(1)(a)

No reduction or cancellation of employees' representation Art. 15(1)(b)

Tax Consequences

Taxation of companies involved

- Deferral of capital gains tax if
  - tax values of assets and liabilities of the transferring company is taken over by the receiving company (roll-over of tax values) and
  - assets and liabilities transferred remain effectively connected with a PE of the receiving company in the MS of the transferring company
  - Art. 4, Art. 9 and Art. 12
- Carry-over of tax deductible provisions and tax free reserves
  - Art. 5, Art. 9 and Art. 13(1)
- Takeover of losses to PE of receiving company situated in the MS of the transferring company
  - Art. 6, Art. 13(2)
- No taxation of gains resulting from the cancellation of shares in up-stream merger
  - Art. 7
- Transfer of PE in a triangular case
  - tax neutrality in the PE state
  - MS of the transferring company may recapture foreign PE losses
  - under tax treaty credit method the MS of transferring company may tax hidden reserves but has to give notional credit

Taxation of shareholders involved

- Deferral of capital gains tax upon exchange of shares resulting from
  - merger, Art. 8(1)
  - division, Art. 8(1)
  - exchange of shares, Art. 8(1)
  - partial division, Art. 8(2), if
  tax values are carried over by the shareholders
- Corresponding deferral rules for transfer of registered office of SE or SCE

Literature

Bezzina, The Treatment of Losses under the EC Merger Directive 1990, ET 2002, p. 57; Boulogne, A Proposal to Expand and Improve Article 6 of the EU Merger Directive, Intertax 2014, p. 70; Boulogne, Shortcomings in the European Unions Merger Directive: Lessons for Future Harmonization, intertax 2016, p. 810; Boulogne/Gooijer, Merger Directive: Conceptual Clarity of the Term "Branch of Activity" Needed, ET 2013, p. 243; De Broe/Beckers, The General Anti-Abuse Rule of the Anti-Tax Avoidance Directive: An Analysis Against the Wider Perspective of the European Court of Justice's Case Law on Abuse of EU Law, EC Tax Review 2017, p. 133; Fibbe/Stevens, Hybrid Entities and the EU Tax Directives (2015); Gordillo Fernández de Villavicencio, Applying the Merger Directive beyond Its Scope in Third-Country Scenarios: An Alternative Approach to A Oy (Case C-48/11) – Part 2, ET 2013, p. 62; Helminen, EU Tax Law Direct Taxation (2019); Helminen, Must EU Merger Directive Benefits Be Made Available where EEA States are involved?, ET 2011, p. 179; Helminen, Must the Losses of a Merging Company be Deductible in the State of Residence of the Receiving Company in EU?; EC Tax Review 2011, p. 172; Hohenwarter, Verlustverwertung im Konzern (2010); O'Shea, CJEU finds French Merger Rules in Breach of EU Law, TNI 2017, p. 691; Pinetz/Schaffer, Exit Taxation in Third Country Situations, ET 2014, p. 432; Rossi-Maccanico, The 3D I Case: Useful Clarification from the Court on the Boundaries of the EU Merger Directive, EC Tax Review 2013, p. 197; Schön, Tax Issues and Constraints on Reorganizations and Reincorporations in the European Union, TNI 2004, p. 197; Thömmes, Commentary on the Merger Directive, in: Thömmes/Fuks (eds.), EC Corporate Tax Law, 28th suppl. (December 2004); Van den Broek, Cross-Border Mergers within the EU – Proposals to Remove the Remaining Tax Obstacles (2012); Van den Broek, Final Losses in Respect of Cross-Border Mergers: Memira (Case C-607/17) and Holmen (Case C-608/17), ET 2020, p. 53; Vande Velde, How Does the CJEU's Case Law on Cross-Border Loss Relief Apply to Cross-Border Mergers and Divisions?, EC Tax Review 2016, p. 132; Wattel/Marres/Vermeulen (eds.), European Tax Law, Volume I, 7th edition (2019); Zalasinski, The ECJ's Decisions in the Danish "Beneficial Ownership" Cases: Impact on the Reaction to Tax Avoidance in the European Union, International Tax Studies 4/2019, p. 1.

Legal Basis: Council Directive 2009/133/EC of 19 October 2009 on the common system of taxation applicable to mergers, divisions, partial divisions, transfers of assets and exchanges of shares concerning companies of different Member States and to the transfer of the registered office of an SE or SCE between Member States (codified version), OJ L 310 of 25 November 2009.

Chapter 7 – The Interest and Royalties Directive

Dimitar Hristov

I. Principles

539 On 1 January 2004, Council Directive 2003/49/EC of 3 June 2003 on a Common System of Taxation Applicable to Interest and Royalty Payments Made Between Companies of Different Member States (the Interest and Royalties Directive)[1] entered into force after many years of preparatory work and dispute. The Interest and Royalties Directive is based on the notion that, in the Single Market, interest and royalty payments between associated companies of different Member States should not be subject to less favourable tax conditions than those applicable to the same payments made between associated companies of the same Member State. Less favourable tax conditions could entail double taxation of such EU cross-border payments since bilateral and multilateral tax treaties do not always ensure the elimination of double taxation. For example, not all double taxation conventions (DTCs) provide for a reduction at source in the source state and a credit in the residence state of the recipient; furthermore, DTCs, in particular, do not contain solutions to triangular situations[2] and have not been concluded between all EU Member States. Although, in many instances, double taxation is avoided through the application of DTCs, the application of the specific DTC and, in particular, source taxation often causes additional administrative burdens, cash-flow problems, interest and other opportunity costs.[3] Thus, according to Recital (1) of the Interest and Royalties Directive, **equal treatment** of EU cross-border and domestic interest and royalty payments is to be achieved by the Directive. Additionally, less favourable tax conditions, as well as double taxation and double non-taxation, should also be avoided. However, from a practical point of view, it should be mentioned that, due to the burdensome application requirements of the Interest and Royalties Directive, companies often prefer to rely on a "zero" source tax rate (e.g. as provided for in Art. 12 OECD Model) if applicable under the respective DTC. In relation to Switzerland, Art. 9 para. 2 of the Swiss-EU Agreement (among other instruments) on interest and royalty payments contains provisions similar to the Interest and Royalties Directive.[4]

540 The main principle of the Interest and Royalties Directive is found in Art. 1(1), which provides for an **exemption from source state tax** (in most cases this is a domestic withholding tax) for interest and royalty payments made by

(a) a **company** of a Member State
or by
(b) a **permanent establishment** situated in another Member State of a company of a Member State,

---

1   Council Directive 2003/49/EC of June 2003 on a common system of taxation applicable to interest and royalty payments, OJ L 157 of 26 June 2003.

2   See, on the issue of triangular cases, Gusmeroli, Triangular cases and the Interest and Royalties Directive: Untying the Gordian knot? – Parts 1, 2 and 3, *ET* 2005, p. 2 et seq., p. 39 et seq. and p. 86 et seq.

3   See e.g. Eicker/Aramini, Overview on the recent developments of the EC Directive on withholding taxes on royalty and interest payments, *EC Tax Review* 2004, p. 134 et seq.

4   Agreement as of 26 October 2004 between Switzerland and the EU, amended by the Amendment Protocol as of 27 May 2017.

provided that the **beneficial owner** of the interest or royalty payments is

(i) an **associated company** of another Member State or
(ii) a **permanent establishment** situated in another Member State of an associated company of a Member State.

In applying the benefits of the Interest and Royalties Directive, it is generally irrelevant whether source tax was levied by way of a deduction at "source" or an "assessment"; source tax is generally abolished according to Art. 1(1) if the application requirements of the Interest and Royalties Directive are met (see m.no. 547 et seq.). In this context, it has to be pointed out that, according to the *Scheuten Solar Technology GmbH* case,[5] Art. 1(1) does not preclude a provision of the national (German in this case) tax law according to which loan interest paid by a (German) company to another associated (Netherlands) company is included in the assessment/tax base of the trade tax payable by the German company. In this context, it should be noted that Council Directive 2016/1164 of 12 July 2016 laying down rules against tax avoidance practices that directly affect the functioning of the internal market (Anti-Tax Avoidance Directive; ATAD)[6] contains, in Art. 4, an interest deduction limitation, which in fact could lead to a hidden source tax, as interest will not be recognized as a tax deductible expense in the state of the payer. This provision in the ATAD should be in line with the Interest and Royalties Directive in the context of the ECJ decision in the *Scheuten Solar Technology GmbH* case. Further, it is important to note that, according to Art. 1(7), the company that is the **payer**, or the company whose permanent establishment is treated as the payer of the interest or royalty payment, has to be an **associated company** of the company that is the **beneficial owner**, or whose permanent establishment is treated as the beneficial owner, of that interest or royalty payment.

Art. 9 furthermore contains a **delimitation clause** whereby the applicability of **541** more favourable national or DTC provisions may not be excluded by application of the Directive. This is also a tax harmonization clause,[7] as a result of which the harmonization obligations of the Member States are kept to a minimum. Moreover, when implementing the Interest and Royalties Directive into national law, the Member States have to keep in mind the decision of the CJEU in the *Bosal Holding* case, in which it ruled that Member States must take into consideration the non-discrimination principle and the fundamental freedoms of the EU in implementing directives.[8] As regards the fundamental freedoms of the EU, it should be pointed out that the compatibility with the fundamental freedoms must be assessed only when the (Interest and Royalties) Directive provides Member States

---

5   CJEU, 21 July 2011, Case C-397/09, *Scheuten Solar Technology GmbH*, EU:C:2011:499.
6   Council Directive 2016/1164/EC of 12 July 2016 laying down rules against tax avoidance practices that directly affect the functioning of the internal market, OJ L 193 of 12 July 2016, p. 1.
7   Rodriguez, in: Thömmes/Fuks (eds.), *EC Corporate Tax Law* (October 2004) para. 291.
8   CJEU, 18 September 2003, Case C-168/01, *Bosal Holding*, EU:C:2003:479, para. 26 et seq.; Rodriguez, in: Thömmes/Fuks (eds.), *EC Corporate Tax Law* (October 2004) para. 292.

with discretion.[9] If the (Interest and Royalties) Directive fully harmonizes a certain aspect, then domestic legislation can be tested only vis-à-vis the Directive but not the fundamental freedoms.

542 Further, it has to be mentioned that the legal terms used by the Interest and Royalties Directive are obviously similar to some definitions of the **OECD Model**, the **Parent-Subsidiary Directive** and the **Merger Directive**. The relationship between the Interest and Royalties Directive and the OECD Model and the above-mentioned directives will be discussed in more detail where the similarities have relevance to the interpretation and application of the Interest and Royalties Directive. However, in any event, it should be noted that the terms used by the Interest and Royalties Directive have a meaning that is **autonomous** from the terms of the OECD Model,[10] unless it transpires from the preparatory work that the OECD Model was relied on by the Union legislator.[11]

II. Historical Development

543 In 1990/91, the Commission prepared the **first proposal** on a common tax treatment of EU cross-border interest and royalty payments between parent companies and subsidiaries in different Member States.[12] Due to the fact that the Council was unable to agree on certain specific issues, the first proposal was withdrawn by the Commission in 1994.[13]

544 In 1997, the Commission was asked to submit a new proposal. Hence, in 1998, the Commission released a **second proposal** on a common tax treatment of interest and royalty payments made between associated companies.

545 The final **adoption** of the Interest and Royalties Directive by the Council took place on 3 June 2003. Ultimately, the Directive was restricted to direct holdings, whereas the second proposal from 1998 also covered indirect holdings. The justification for this restriction was probably the apprehension of some Member States that the Directive, as amended in the second proposal, could have a major financial impact on the tax revenue of the Member States.[14] According to Art. 7(1), the final date for implementation was 1 January 2004. However, Art. 6 provides for transitional rules for some countries.

---

9   CJEU, 18 September 2003, Case C-168/01, *Bosal Holding*, EU:C:2003:479, para. 26.
10   Van Dongen, Thin capitalization legislation and the EU Corporate Tax Directives, *ET* 2012, p. 22.
11   CJEU, 16 May 2017, Case C-682/15, *Berlioz Investment Fund SA v Directeur de l'administration des contributions directes*, para. 67; CJEU, 26 February 2019, Joined Cases C-115/16, *N Luxembourg 1 v Skatteministeriet*, and C-118/16, *X Denmark A/S v Skatteministeriet*, and C-119/16, *C Danmark I v Skatteministeriet*, and C-299/16, *Z Denmark ApS v Skatteministeriet*, para. 91.
12   See Proposal for a Council Directive on a common system of taxation applicable to interest and royalty payments made between parent companies and subsidiaries in different Member States, COM(1990) 571 final of 6 December 1990, OJ C 53 of 28 February 1991, p. 26 et seq.
13   Commission Press Release IP/94/1023 of 8 November 1994.
14   Distaso/Russo, The EC Interest and Royalties Directive – A comment, *ET* 2004, p. 144; Rodriguez, in Thömmes/Fuks (eds.) *EC Corporate Tax Law* (October 2004) para. 23.

In **2011,** the Commission adopted a **proposal containing amendments** to the **546** Interest and Royalties Directive.[15] The proposal is rooted in the 2009 Report from the Commission to the Council (which has its origins in Art. 8) on the functioning of the Interest and Royalties Directive.[16] Under the proposal, the Commission intended, on the one hand, to extend the list of companies (legal forms) covered by the Directive. On the other hand, the Commission wanted to reduce the shareholding (threshold) requirements for associated companies from a 25 % minimum direct holding to a 10 % direct or indirect holding. Further, the Commission wanted to make it clear that Member States would have to grant the benefits only to companies that are not exempt from corporate taxation; this addresses, in particular, companies that, while subject to corporate tax, also benefit from a special national tax (incentive) scheme explicitly exempting foreign interest or royalty payments received or income covering – among other items – interest and royalties (e.g. "tax holidays" for a specific period of time, or "IP-box regimes", etc., see m.no. 550). The fact that interest and royalties are not taxed due to special circumstances at the level of the receiving company, such as existing loss carry-forwards or group taxation regimes, does not, however, give the Member States the right to deny the applicability of the Interest and Royalties Directive.

III. Application Requirements

A. Personal Scope

1. Company of a Member State

As mentioned in m.no. 540, the exemption from source state tax is applicable **547** only if the payer of the interest or royalty is a company of a Member State or a permanent establishment of a company of a Member State and if the beneficial owner of the interest or royalty payment is an associated company of a Member State or a permanent establishment of an associated company of a Member State. Thus, in either case, a **company of a Member State** is required in order for the Directive to be applicable. Art. 3(a) contains the definition of the term "company of a Member State" and makes the definition dependent on the fulfilment of three cumulative requirements.[17]

As a first requirement, according to Art. 3(a)(i), the company has to take one of **548** the legal forms listed in the annex to the Interest and Royalties Directive. The

---

15 See the Proposal for a Council Directive on a common system of taxation applicable to interest and royalty payments made between associated companies of different Member States of 11 November 2011, COM (2011), 714.

16 Report from the Commission to the Council in accordance with Article 8 of Council Directive 2003/49/EC on a common system of taxation applicable to interest and royalty payments made between associated companies of different Member States, COM (2009) 179.

17 Distaso/Russo, The EC Interest and Royalties Directive – A comment, *ET* 2004, p. 143.

annex provides an **exhaustive list of companies**[18] – similar to the (broader) list of the Parent-Subsidiary Directive – to which the Interest and Royalties Directive applies so that a legal entity not expressly mentioned may not benefit from the Directive, either as payer or as payee. As regards the SE and the SCE, the Commission proposed to broaden the scope of the Interest and Royalties Directive to these two legal forms,[19] which are not yet expressly contained in the Annex to the Directive.[20] Nevertheless, e.g. *Herzig/Griemla*[21] support the notion that the Interest and Royalties Directive is already applicable to the SE. Another important issue in the tax literature is the question of whether unincorporated **tax-transparent companies** (e.g. partnerships) may benefit from and fall within the scope of the Interest and Royalties Directive in particular on the basis of Art. 54 TFEU (ex Art. 48 EC).[22] This question and the related problems do not seem to have been resolved. In this context it further has to be mentioned that the Directive covers, in any event, some legal forms of partnership from the Eastern-European countries that, as limited partnerships or open partnerships/companies, are treated (wholly or partly) for tax purposes as non-transparent entities in their residence state but are characterized for tax purposes as transparent entities in another Member State.

549   According to Art. 3(a)(ii), the second requirement is the necessity for the company – mentioned in the Annex to the Interest and Royalties Directive – to be **resident for tax purposes in a Member State** and not to be – within the meaning of a DTC – a resident for tax purposes in a third state. This provision is especially of importance for dual-resident companies.[23] To solve the problem of dual residence the Interest and Royalties Directive refers to the relevant DTC concluded with a third state. Normally DTCs contain a tie-breaker-provision and provide – as Art. 4(3) of the OECD Model does – that with respect to dual resident companies the place of effective management is the preferred criterion. If, according to the DTC, the company is resident in a Member State, the Interest and Royalties Directive is applicable; otherwise, the benefits of the Directive are denied. As regards (especially Eastern-European) partnerships mentioned in the Annex to the Directive, the problem could arise that e.g. an interest-receiving partnership is characterized as tax resident by one Member State (e.g. where the interest or royalty payment is

---

18   The list was amended by Council Directive 2006/98/EC of 20 November 2006 adapting certain Directives in the field of taxation, by reason of the accession of Bulgaria and Romania, OJ L 363 of 20 December 2006, p. 129 et seq.

19   See Proposal for a Council Directive on a common system of taxation applicable to interest and royalty payments made between associated companies of different Member States of 11 November 2011, COM(2011) 714, p. 7 et seq.

20   Van Dongen, Thin capitalization legislation and the EU Corporate Tax Directives, *ET* 2012, p. 22.

21   Eicker/Aramini, Overview on the recent developments of the EC Directive on withholding taxes on royalty and interest payments, *EC Tax Review* 2004, p. 144, at footnote 53.

22   Russo, Partnerships and Other Hybrid Entities and the EC Corporate Direct Tax Directives, *ET* 2006, p. 478; Weber, The proposed EC Interest and Royalty Directive, *EC Tax Review* 2000, p. 17 et seq.; see Pt. 3.3.5.2. COM (2009) 179.

23   See Pt. 3.3.5.3. COM (2009) 179.

received) but not by the other Member State (where e.g. the interest or royalty payment arose) as e.g. the other Member State does not recognize foreign partnerships as taxable entities (and therefore denies residence status altogether) or e.g. the interest is received via a foreign permanent establishment of the partnership and the permanent establishment is situated in a Member State that does not recognize foreign partnerships as taxable entities either (and therefore denies their residence status altogether). Nevertheless, in the author's opinion, the Directive will apply in all such situations, as the respective partnership (mentioned in the Annex to the Directive) is, in any event, resident for tax purposes in one Member State. Otherwise the aim of Art. 3(a)(i) to cover specific legal forms of companies may simply be circumvented by a Member State under its own national tax law by denying the residence status of a partnership mentioned in the Annex to the Directive.

The **subject-to-tax condition** of Art. 3(a)(iii) is the third and final requirement **550** that has to be met in order for the Interest and Royalties Directive to be applicable. In this context, the company has to be – as the Parent-Subsidiary Directive and the Merger Directive similarly provide – subject to one of the taxes listed in Art. 3(a)(iii) without being exempt, or to a tax that is identical or substantially similar and that is imposed after the date of entry into force of the Interest and Royalties Directive in addition to, or in place of, the taxes listed in Art. 3(a)(iii). As regards the interpretation of the subject-to-tax requirement it has been disputed in the tax literature whether the company itself may not be personally exempt from tax (subjective requirement)[24] or whether the income of the company may not be exempt from tax (objective requirement).[25] In *X Denmark A/S and C Danmark I and Z Denmark ApS v the Danish Ministry of Finance* (the "interest cases") the CJEU explicitly follows the approach that the subject-to-tax condition is to be interpreted as an objective requirement.[26]

2. Permanent Establishments

Permanent Establishments: According to Art. 1(1), the payer (see m.no. 565 et seq.) **551** or the beneficial owner (see m.no. 567 et seq.) of interest and royalty payments may also be a **permanent establishment** belonging to a company of a Member State that is situated in a different Member State. Thus, it is important to point out that, according to Art. 1(8), the exemption from source state tax in Art. 1(1) is not applicable if the payer or payee is a permanent establishment situated in a third state of a company of a Member State and the business of that company is wholly or partly carried on through that permanent establishment. Correspond-

---

24   Distaso/Russo, The EC Interest and Royalties Directive – A comment, *ET* 2004, p. 143; Rodriguez, in: Thömmes/Fuks (eds.), *EC Corporate Tax Law* (October 2004) para. 36.
25   Weber, The proposed EC Interest and Royalty Directive, *EC Tax Review* 2000, p. 20 et seq.
26   CJEU, 26 February 2019, Joined Cases C-115/16, N Luxembourg 1 v Skatteministeriet, and C-118/16, X Denmark A/S v Skatteministeriet, and C-119/16, C Danmark I v Skatteministeriet, and C-299/16, Z Denmark ApS v Skatteministeriet, para. 153.

ingly, Art. 3(c) defines a "permanent establishment" as a fixed place of business situated in a Member State through which the business of a company of another Member State is wholly or partly carried on. The similarity of this definition to Art. 5(1) of the OECD Model and Art. 2(2) of the Parent-Subsidiary Directive is obvious and the interpretation problems arising as a result of this definition (e.g. concerning building sites or construction or installation projects) have been discussed frequently in the tax literature.[27] Ultimately, the CJEU will have to find an autonomous interpretation of the term "permanent establishment".

552 By extending the personal scope, the Interest and Royalties Directive seems to resolve, within the EU, dual source problems in connection with **triangular and quadrangular cases** involving permanent establishments.[28] In such cases, a separate DTC generally does not contain real solutions due to its bilateral character. Nevertheless, it should be mentioned that the Interest and Royalties Directive resolves triangular and quadrangular situations only if the companies to which the payer or the payee-permanent establishment belongs are associated companies according to Art. 3(b) (see m.no. 553 et seq.). Outside the scope of association, reference has to be made to the particular DTC concluded between the various Member States. Furthermore, in the tax literature, it has been also noted that even within the scope of the Interest and Royalties Directive not all problems connected with triangular and quadrangular situations seem to be resolved.[29]

3. Associated Companies

553 The source tax exemption applies only if the company that is the payer or the company whose permanent establishment is treated as the payer of interest or royalty payments is an **associated company** of the company that is the beneficial owner or whose permanent establishment is treated as the beneficial owner of that interest or royalty payment. This requirement is laid down in Art. 1(7) and made concrete in Art. 3(b). As mentioned in m.no. 547 et seq., the association may only exist between companies of EU Member States within the meaning of Art. 3(a). To benefit from the Interest and Royalties Directive, companies of third states are excluded from the personal scope of the Directive.

554 For purposes of the Interest and Royalties Directive, Art. 3(b) provides for **two different forms of association**. The first form is a direct vertical association (Art. 3(b)(i) and (ii)), which requires that the company that is the payer or whose permanent establishment is treated as the payer of the interest or royalty payments have a

---

27 Distaso/Russo, The EC Interest and Royalties Directive – A comment, *ET* 2004, p. 146 et seq.; Rodriguez, in: Thömmes/Fuks (eds.), *EC Corporate Tax Law* (October 2004) para. 82 et seq.; Weber, The proposed EC Interest and Royalty Directive, *EC Tax Review* 2000, p. 23 et seq.

28 Eicker/Aramini, Overview on the recent developments of the EC Directive on withholding taxes on royalty and interest payments, *EC Tax Review* 2004, p. 141.

29 Gusmeroli, Triangular cases and the Interest and Royalties Directive: Untying the Gordian knot? – Parts 1, 2 and 3, *ET* 2005, p. 2 et seq., p. 39 et seq. and p. 86 et seq.

direct minimum holding of 25 % in the capital of the company that is the benefi-cial owner or whose permanent establishment is treated as the beneficial owner of that interest or royalty payment (**downstream payments**). The vertical association covers the reverse situation, which requires that the company that is the beneficial owner or whose permanent establishment is treated as the beneficial owner of the interest or royalty payments have a direct minimum holding of 25 % in the capital of the company that is the payer or whose permanent establishment is treated as the payer of that interest or royalty payment (**upstream payments**). The second form of association is a direct horizontal association (Art. 3(b)(iii)), which requires that a parent company, which is neither the payer nor the beneficial owner of interest or royalty payments, have a direct minimum holding of 25 % both in the capital of the subsidiary company that is the payer or whose permanent establish-ment is treated as the payer of the interest or royalty payments and in the capital of the other subsidiary company that is the beneficial owner or whose permanent establishment is treated as the beneficial owner of that interest or royalty payment (**sidestream payments**). For potential developments regarding the forms of asso-ciation covered see m.no. 546.

As regards the required **quality of the association**, attention should be paid to the **555** following three issues. First of all, the Interest and Royalties Directive requires a direct holding, in other words an indirect holding[30] is insufficient and the applica-bility of the Directive could be denied if the participation is not a direct one (see also m.no. 547).[31] Second, Art. 3(b) allows the Member States to replace the require-ment of a minimum holding in the capital with that of a minimum holding of voting rights. Third, Art. 1(10) provides that a Member State has the option of not apply-ing the Interest and Royalties Directive to a company in circumstances where the required forms of association "have not been maintained" for an uninterrupted period of at least two years (temporal criterion). In the tax literature, the applica-bility of the CJEU's decision in the *Denkavit-VITIC-Voormeer* case[32] has been dis-cussed due to the similarity of Art. 1(10) to the provision of Art. 3(2) of the Parent-Subsidiary Directive and due to the fact that the Interest and Royalties Directive uses the past tense and the Parent-Subsidiary Directive uses the present tense. One of the opinions in the literature – and from the author's point of view the correct one – is that the *Denkavit-VITIC-Voormeer* decision is fully applicable to Art. 1(10), with the consequence that it is, in principle, not necessary for the required two-year holding period to have ended at the time the interest or royalty payment is made, provided the companies complete the required period of two years after the

---

30   E.g. if a parent company is holding a participation in a subsidiary company through an intermediary (non-transparent) partnership or if a grandparent company is holding a participation in a sub-subsidiary through an intermediary company.
31   See on this issue Distaso/Russo, The EC Interest and Royalties Directive – A comment, *ET* 2004, p. 145 et seq.; Rodriguez, in: Thömmes/Fuks (eds.), *EC Corporate Tax Law* (October 2004) para. 67 et seq.
32   CJEU, 17 October 1996, Joined Cases C-283/94, C-291/94 and C-292/94, *Denkavit, VITIC and Voormeer*, EU:C:1996:387.

payment.[33] A question connected with the minimum holding period is also whether a period started in relation to or by one company may be continued by another company due to a transfer of the shares (e.g. sale/acquisition, exchange of shares, spin-off) or a change of the corporate statute of a company (e.g. merger, split-up or liquidation). In the author's opinion, a holding period already started by one company with regard to an existing qualifying participation (association, i.e. at least 25 %) could be continued by the successor, depending on whether the legal successor of the qualifying participation has acquired from the applicable civil law perspective the qualifying shareholding by way of a **singular succession** (e.g. acquisition of shares by the purchaser by sale-and-purchase-agreement, by a contribution in kind or after liquidation of a subsidiary in combination with an in-kind distribution of the subsidiary's assets, i.e. the qualifying shareholding; spin-off of shares, if singular succession is provided for by civil law) or **universal succession** (merger or split-up of companies without liquidation). If the qualifying shareholding (i.e. the association) was acquired by singular succession, in the author's opinion the minimum period cannot assumed by the successor; if, however, the qualifying shareholding was acquired by way of universal succession, the universal successor continues the holding period. The differentiation depends on the different nature of both succession forms, as the singular succession ends legal ties between the transferring and the receiving company and creates a new legal position for the receiving company, whereas the concept of universal succession implies that the receiving company is the successor as regards all assets and liabilities of the transferring company.

B. Substantive Scope

1. Cross-Border Interest or Royalty Payments

556 On the one hand, the source tax exemption of the Interest and Royalties Directive applies to **interest** payments. According to the definition in Art. 2(a), interest payments mean "income from debt-claims of every kind, whether or not secured by mortgage and whether or not carrying a right to participate in the debtor's profits, and in particular, income from securities and income from bonds or debentures, including premiums and prizes attaching to such securities, bonds or debentures; penalty charges for late payment shall not be regarded as interest." The definition of "interest" in the Interest and Royalties Directive mirrors Art. 11(3) of the OECD Model and obviously refers to the definition in the OECD Model except for the exclusion of government securities.[34] Unlike the OECD Model, the Interest and Royalties Directive contains in Art. 4(1) an explicit catalogue of specific payments that are excluded from the definition of "interest" (see m.no. 558 et seq.). Despite

---

33 Distaso/Russo, The EC Interest and Royalties Directive – A comment, *ET* 2004, p. 151; Rodriguez, in: Thömmes/Fuks (eds.), *EC Corporate Tax Law* (October 2004) para. 74 et seq.

34 See e.g. Distaso/Russo, The EC Interest and Royalties Directive – A comment, *ET* 2004, p. 149 et seq.; Van Dongen, Thin capitalization legislation and the EU Corporate Tax Directives, *ET* 2012, p. 23.

the similar definitions of Art. 2(a) of the Interest and Royalties Directive and Art. 11(3) of the OECD Model, EU law should be interpreted autonomously[35] although a reference of the CJEU to the interpretation concepts concerning Art. 11(3) of the OECD Model seems to be useful.[36]

On the other hand, the source tax exemption of the Interest and Royalties Directive **557** also applies to **royalty** payments. According to the definition in Art. 2(b), royalty payments mean "payments of any kind received as a consideration for the use of, or the right to use, any copyright of literary, artistic or scientific work, including cinematograph films and software, any patent, trade mark, design or model, plan, secret formula or process, or for information concerning industrial, commercial or scientific experience; payments for the use of, or the right to use, industrial, commercial or scientific equipment shall be regarded as royalties." Although the definition of royalty payments also seems to mirror the definition of Art. 12(2) of the OECD Model, the definition in the OECD Model is narrower since it does not mention software royalty payments and includes only payments for information concerning industrial, commercial or scientific knowledge, but not for the use of, or the right to use, industrial, commercial or scientific equipment. In contrast, the Interest and Royalties Directive covers royalty payments for the use of, or the right to use, software[37] and also royalty payments for the use of, or the right to use industrial, commercial or scientific equipment (i.e. mobile leasing and also franchise contracts).[38]

2. Exclusion of Specific Payments

Art. 4(1) allows the source Member State to exclude specific – in the majority of **558** cases, interest – payments from the benefits of the Interest and Royalty Directive. The **exclusion catalogue**[39] contains, in principle, hybrid financial instruments that fall between equity and debt.[40] In this context, attention should be paid to the fact that if income received from these hybrid instruments does not fall under the Interest and Royalties Directive it could fall under the Parent-Subsidiary Directive.[41] In this case, the requirements for application of the Parent-Subsidiary Directive should be scrutinized.[42] One of the aims of the exclusion catalogue could

---

35 Van Dongen, Thin capitalization legislation and the EU Corporate Tax Directives, *ET* 2012, p. 22.
36 See e.g. Rodriguez, in: Thömmes/Fuks (eds.), *EC Corporate Tax Law* (October 2004) para. 105 et seq.
37 See e.g. Rodriguez, in: Thömmes/Fuks (eds.), *EC Corporate Tax Law* (October 2004) para. 125 et seq.
38 See e.g. Brokelind, Royalty Payments: Unresolved issues in the Interest and Royalties Directive, *ET* 2004, p. 252 et seq.; Rodriguez, in: Thömmes/Fuks (eds.), *EC Corporate Tax Law* (October 2004) para. 136 et seq.
39 See Distaso/Russo, The EC Interest and Royalties Directive – A comment, *ET* 2004, p. 149 et seq.; Rodriguez, in: Thömmes/Fuks (eds.), *EC Corporate Tax Law* (October 2004) para. 140 et seq.
40 See for details Bundgaard, Classification and treatment of hybrid financial instruments and income derived therefrom under EU Corporate Tax Directives – Parts 1 and 2, *ET* 2010, p. 442 et seq.
41 Rodriguez, in: Thömmes/Fuks (eds.), *EC Corporate Tax Law* (October 2004) para. 170 et seq.; see also Van Dongen, Thin capitalization legislation and the EU Corporate Tax Directives, *ET* 2012, p. 20.
42 Bundgaard, Classification and treatment of hybrid financial instruments and income derived therefrom under EU Corporate Tax Directives – Parts 1 and 2, *ET* 2010, p. 445.

be the avoidance of "double-dip situations" (i.e. a situation in which interest is paid without withholding tax and remains a tax-deductible expense in the payer's state; however, the interest is treated in the payee's state as a tax-exempt dividend). However, in any event, the exceptions mentioned in the list in Art. 4(1) have to be **interpreted restrictively,** as they are meant as exceptions to the general rule of application of the Directive stipulated in Art. 1(1) and 2.[43] It should further be mentioned that there could also be cases where hybrid financial instruments fall neither under the Parent-Subsidiary Directive nor under the Interest and Royalties Directive.

559 Art. 4(1)(a) refers to payments that are treated as a **distribution of profits or as a repayment of capital** under the domestic[44] law of the source Member State. This exclusion has a wide scope, including several forms of hybrid financial instruments and especially **interest subject to thin capitalization rules** in the source state if the source state reclassifies the interest as dividends.[45] As regards the relationship between the Interest and Royalties Directive and domestic thin capitalization rules, according to *Van Dongen*, the Interest and Royalties Directive is not applicable with respect to interest payments on which the respective domestic thin capitalization rule is applicable.[46] Art. 4(1)(a) mentions further the "repayment of capital". Despite the fact that in most Member States the repayment of capital should not be a taxable event (and should not be a tax-deductible expense either) subject to withholding tax, the Directive would, nevertheless, allow a withholding tax.[47]

560 Art. 4(1)(b) mentions payments from debt-claims that carry a right to participate in the profits of the debtor (i.e. **profit-sharing loans**).[48] This provision would potentially exclude some profit-participating loans, participating bonds, jouissance rights and silent partnerships from the scope of the Directive.[49] According to *Eberhartinger/Six*, this provision, in combination with the Parent-Subsidiary Directive, provides a Member State with the possibility of totally excluding jouissance rights and silent partnerships from the directives by treating them as debt under domestic law.[50]

---

43   Ibid.

44   Explicitly, Distaso/Russo, The EC Interest and Royalties Directive – A comment, *ET* 2004, p. 150.

45   Bundgaard, Classification and treatment of hybrid financial instruments and income derived therefrom under EU Corporate Tax Directives – Parts 1 and 2, *ET* 2010, p. 444; see for details van Dongen, Thin capitalization legislation and the EU Corporate Tax Directives, *ET* 2012, p. 20 et seq.

46   See for details Van Dongen, Thin capitalization legislation and the EU Corporate Tax Directives, *ET* 2012, p. 22 et seq.

47   Bundgaard, Classification and treatment of hybrid financial instruments and income derived therefrom under EU Corporate Tax Directives – Parts 1 and 2, *ET* 2010, pp. 445 and 446 for other questions with respect to the Directive.

48   Rodriguez, in: Thömmes/Fuks (eds.), *EC Corporate Tax Law* (October 2004) para. 156 et seq.

49   Bundgaard, Classification and treatment of hybrid financial instruments and income derived therefrom under EU Corporate Tax Directives – Parts 1 and 2, *ET* 2010, p. 445.

50   Eberhartinger/Six, in: Andersson et al. (eds.), *National Tax Policy in Europe* (2007) p. 225 et seq.; see further Bundgaard, Classification and treatment of hybrid financial instruments and income derived therefrom under EU Corporate Tax Directives – Parts 1 and 2, *ET* 2010, p. 445.

Furthermore, Art. 4(1)(c) contains the possibility for the source Member State to **561** exclude payments from debt-claims that entitle the creditor to exchange his right to interest for a right to participate in the profits of the debtor (i.e. **convertible debt instruments**).[51] A literal interpretation of this provision would exclude convertible bonds/loans and warrant bonds/loans from the Directive.[52]

Finally, Art. 4(1)(d) enables the source Member State to exclude payments from debt- **562** claims that contain no provision for repayment of the principal amount or where the repayment is due more than 50 years after the date of issue (i.e. **quasi-equity**).[53] Super-maturity debt and perpetual debt fall under the scope of this provision.[54]

Attention should also be paid to the provision of Art. 4(2), which follows the **arm's** **563** **length** approach of Art. 11(6) of the OECD Model and Art. 12(4) of the OECD Model and is very similar to these provisions. Thus, Art. 4(2) precludes the application of the Interest and Royalties Directive to payments that are not at arm's length. The Interest and Royalties Directive assumes payments to not be at arm's length whereby "reason of a special relationship between the payer and the beneficial owner of interest or royalties, or between one of them and some other person, the amount of the interest or royalties exceeds the amount which would have been agreed by the payer and the beneficial owner in the absence of such a relationship." In this case, the Interest and Royalties Directive applies only to the amount that would have been agreed by the payer and the beneficial owner in the absence of such a relationship.

3. Sourcing Rules

The sourcing rules are connected with the question of where interest or royalty **564** payments arise. If the interest or royalty payment has been made by a **company** of a Member State (see Art. 3(b) and m.no. 547 et seq.), Art. 1(2) provides that this payment is deemed to arise in that Member State. That Member State is also treated as the source Member State for purposes of the Interest and Royalties Directive. This sourcing rule seems to be self-evident.

As regards interest or royalty payments made by a **permanent establishment** be- **565** longing to a company of a Member State that is situated in a different Member State, Art. 1(2) provides for the same sourcing rule as for companies of a Member State.[55] Thus, payments made by a permanent establishment belonging to a company

---

51   Rodriguez, in: Thömmes/Fuks (eds.), *EC Corporate Tax Law* (October 2004) para. 159 et seq.
52   Distaso/Russo, The EC Interest and Royalties Directive – A comment, *ET* 2004, footnote 16, p. 150; Eberhartinger/Six, in Andersson et al. (eds.), *National Tax Policy in Europe* (2007) footnote 25, p. 228; see further Bundgaard, Classification and treatment of hybrid financial instruments and income derived therefrom under EU Corporate Tax Directives – Parts 1 and 2, *ET* 2010, p. 445.
53   Rodriguez, in: Thömmes/Fuks (eds.), *EC Corporate Tax Law* (October 2004) para. 162 et seq.
54   Bundgaard, Classification and treatment of hybrid financial instruments and income derived therefrom under EU Corporate Tax Directives – Parts 1 and 2, *ET* 2010, p. 445.
55   For details see Kofler/Rodriguez, in: Lang/Pistone/Schuch/Staringer/Storck (eds.), *Beneficial Ownership: Recent Trends* (2013) p. 215 et seq.

of a Member State that is situated in a different Member State are deemed to arise in the first-mentioned (other) Member State where the permanent establishment is situated. That Member State is also treated as the source Member State for purposes of the Directive. The Interest and Royalties Directive reiterates this aim in Art. 1(6) when pointing out that if a permanent establishment is treated as the payer of interest or royalty payments then obviously no other part of the company to which the permanent establishment, in principle, belongs may be treated as the payer of that interest or royalty payment. However, in Art. 1(3), the Interest and Royalties Directive contains another more problematic requirement for permanent establishments. This provision provides that a permanent establishment is considered to be the payer of an interest or royalty payment only if that payment is a tax-deductible expense for the permanent establishment in the Member State where the permanent establishment is situated.[56] Otherwise, the source Member State may exclude the permanent establishment from the benefits of the Interest and Royalties Directive.[57] *Distaso/Russo* suggest that this rule could infringe EU primary law due to the different treatment of permanent establishments and companies resulting from this provision.[58]

4. Beneficial Ownership

566 The beneficial ownership provisions in the Interest and Royalties Directive are related to the concept of "beneficial ownership" in international tax law (see Arts. 11(1) and 12(2) of the OECD Model)[59] and concern the question as to which company or which permanent establishment should be treated as the effective payee of the interest or royalty payments and also (Art. 1(9)) which Member State has the right to ultimately tax the interest or royalty payments. For companies, Art. 1(4) provides that a company of a Member State is treated as the beneficial owner of these payments if the payments are received for the company's own benefit and not as an intermediary for another person (e.g. agent, trustee, authorized signatory). The aim of the provision is to prevent a circumvention of the goal of the Interest and Royalties Directive to not grant indirectly the benefits of the Directive to companies from third states.

---

56 As regards the relationship of this provision to the *Scheuten Solar Technology GmbH* case and thin capitalization rules see Van Dongen, Thin capitalization legislation and the EU Corporate Tax Directives, *ET* 2012, p. 23.

57 The provision could have relevance especially where the tax base of the permanent establishment is a notional one or where it is based on the cost-plus method; furthermore, if the payments were made from a branch to the foreign head office or if the source Member State applies thin capitalization legislation. See, on this issue, e.g. Rodriguez, in: Thömmes/Fuks (eds.), *EC Corporate Tax Law* (October 2004) para. 187 et seq.

58 Distaso/Russo, The EC Interest and Royalties Directive – A comment, *ET* 2004, p. 151; Van Dongen, Thin capitalization legislation and the EU Corporate Tax Directives, *ET* 2012, p. 23.

59 Distaso/Russo, The EC Interest and Royalties Directive – A comment, *ET* 2004, p. 148 et seq.; Eicker/Aramini, Overview on the recent developments of the EC Directive on withholding taxes on royalty and interest payments, *EC Tax Review* 2004, p. 142 et seq.; Rodriguez, in: Thömmes/Fuks (eds.), *EC Corporate Tax Law* (October 2004) para. 191 et seq.

The determination of the beneficial ownership of permanent establishments is **567** important due to Art. 1(6), which provides that if a permanent establishment of a Member State is treated as the beneficial owner of interest or royalty payments, no other part of the company, to which the permanent establishment in principle belongs, may be treated as the beneficial owner of that interest or royalty payment. Concerning permanent establishments, the provisions on the determination of beneficial ownership differ from the above-mentioned provisions for companies. In this context, Art. 1(5) lays down **two exhaustive requirements** the fulfilment of which is necessary for the characterization of a permanent establishment as beneficial owner of interest or royalty payments.

The first requirement is the **effective connection** of the permanent establishment **568** with the debt-claim or the right to use information (or equipment)[60] in respect of which the interest or royalty payments have been made (Art. 1(5)(a)). The tax literature interprets the term "effective connection" as a necessary genuine economic link[61] between the debt-claim or the right to use from which the interest or royalty payment arises and the permanent establishment. In other words, it is important e.g. whether the payments have been received for the benefit of the permanent establishment, whether the interest or royalty income is attributable to the permanent establishment[62] or whether the debt-claim or the right to use is part of the business assets of the permanent establishment.

Furthermore, Art. 1(5)(b) lays down a **subject-to-tax condition** pursuant to which **569** the interest or royalty payment has to represent income in respect of which the recipient permanent establishment is subject, in the Member State in which it is situated, to one of the taxes mentioned in Art. 3(a)(iii)[63] or to a tax that is identical or substantially similar and that is imposed after the date of the entry into force of the Interest and Royalties Directive in addition to or instead of the taxes in Art. 3(a)(iii).

The requirement of **beneficial ownership** is the subject of the decisions of the ECJ **570** in *T Denmark and Y Denmark v the Danish Ministry of Taxation* and *N Luxembourg 1* [64] and, in particular, in *X Denmark A/S and C Danmark I and Z Denmark ApS v the Danish Ministry of Finance.*[65] The underlying question in the cases (especially the interest cases) was whether dividend and interest payments were to be exempt

---

60 Art. 1(5)(a) of the Interest and Royalties Directive does not explicitly mention the right to use equipment. However, Art. 2(b) of the Interest and Royalties Directive covers payments for the right to use specific equipment. Thus, a systematic view results in the interpretation that Art. 1(5)(a) of the Directive also covers the right to use equipment.

61 See e.g. Distaso/Russo, The EC Interest and Royalties Directive – A comment, *ET* 2004, p. 149.

62 Rodriguez, in: Thömmes/Fuks (eds.), *EC Corporate Tax Law* (October 2004) para. 196.

63 In the case of Belgium and Spain permanent establishments are subject to a non-resident income tax to which Art. 1(5)(a) of the Interest and Royalties Directive refers.

64 CJEU, 26 February 2019, Joined Cases C-116/16, *T Denmark Aps v Skatteministeriet*, and C-117/16, *Y Denmark Aps v Skatteministeriet*.

65 CJEU, 26 February 2019, Joined Cases C-115/16, *N Luxembourg 1 v Skatteministeriet*, and C-118/16, *X Denmark A/S v Skatteministeriet*, and C-119/16, *C Danmark I v Skatteministeriet*, and C-299/16, *Z Denmark ApS v Skatteministeriet*.

from withholding tax when the payments were made by a Danish company to a company resident in the EU and subsequently were forwarded to a company resident in a third state. The CJEU stated in this respect that the term "beneficial owner" concerns not a formally identified recipient but rather the entity that benefits economically from the (interest) payments, whereby the term "beneficial owner" has to be interpreted in line with the OECD Model Commentary, i.e. the entity needs, in particular, to have the power to freely determine the use of the interest payment to which it is put. It also has to be analysed in connection with the fraud and abuse provisions in Art. 5 (as regards the conclusions in these cases see m.no. 571 et seq.).[66]

IV. Fraud and Abuse

571 The Interest and Royalties Directive contains numerous specific anti-avoidance provisions (e.g. Arts. 1(4), 1(5)(b), 1(8), 1(10), 3(a)(iii) and 4). Art. 5 contains two **general anti-avoidance provisions** whereas, according to Art. 5(1), the application of the Interest and Royalties Directive does not preclude the application of domestic or agreement-based provisions for the prevention of fraud and abuse. According to Art. 5(2), the Member States have the option to withdraw the benefits of the Interest and Royalties Directive or to refuse to apply the Interest and Royalties Directive if the principal motive or one of the principal motives for the transaction is tax evasion, tax avoidance or abuse. The obvious similarity of Art. 5(1) to the former version of Art. 1(2) of the Parent-Subsidiary Directive (Art. 1(4) in the amended version as of 27 January 2015)[67] and of Art. 5(2) to Art. 11(1)(a) of the Merger Directive[68] has often been discussed in the tax literature.[69] Thus, the decisions of the CJEU in the *Leur-Bloem* and *Kofoed* decisions[70] and, in particular, the proportionality principle[71] should be relevant to an interpretation of Art. 5 of the Interest and Royalties Directive.[72] As regards these decisions, reference can be made to Chapter 6, m.no. 533 et seq.

572 Furthermore, in *T Denmark and Y Denmark v the Danish Ministry of Taxation and N Luxembourg 1* (in relation to the Parent-Subsidiary Directive)[73] and in *X Denmark*

---

66 CJEU, 26 February 2019, Joined Cases C-115/16, *N Luxembourg 1 v Skatteministeriet*, and C-118/16, *X Denmark A/S v Skatteministeriet*, and C-119/16, *C Danmark I v Skatteministeriet, and* C-299/16, *Z Denmark ApS v Skatteministeriet*, para. 89 et seq.

67 See Chapter 5, m.no. 462 et seq.

68 See Chapter 6, m.no. 533 et seq.

69 See e.g. Rodriguez, in: Thömmes/Fuks (eds.), *EC Corporate Tax Law* (October 2004) para. 225 et seq.

70 CJEU, 17 July 1997, Case C-28/95, *Leur-Bloem*, EU:C:1997:369; CJEU, 5 July 2007, Case C-321/05, *Kofoed*, EU:C:2007:408.

71 See Chapter 3, m.nos. 289 et seq.

72 See Distaso/Russo, The EC Interest and Royalties Directive – A comment, *ET* 2004, p. 152; Eicker/Aramini, Overview on the recent developments of the EC Directive on withholding taxes on royalty and interest payments, *EC Tax Review* 2004, p. 144, at footnote 56; Rodriguez, in: Thömmes/Fuks (eds.), *EC Corporate Tax Law* (October 2004) para. 241 et seq.; Weber, The proposed EC Interest and Royalty Directive, *EC Tax Review* 2000, p. 28 et seq.

73 CJEU, 26 February 2019, Joined Cases C-116/16, *T Denmark Aps v Skatteministeriet*, and C-117/16, *Y Denmark Aps v Skatteministeriet*.

A/S and C Danmark I and Z Denmark ApS v the Danish Ministry of Finance (in relation to the Interest and Royalties Directive)[74] the CJEU provided an interpretation of the beneficial ownership requirement from the perspective of EU law. This has a direct impact on Art. 5 of the Interest and Royalties Directive. According to the CJEU, there is a general principle that EU law cannot be relied on for abusive ends and hence the benefits of the Interest and Royalties Directive must be refused in instances of abusive behaviour, even in the absence of domestic anti-abuse provisions. The finding of abuse will require establishing both objective and subjective elements,[75] assessed in conjunction with various indicators. Such indicators include, for example, the existence of conduit companies without economic justification and the purely formal nature of the arrangement.[76] Moreover, in reaching a conclusion regarding abuse, the national authority is not required to identify the entity that it regards as being the beneficial owner of that interest.

Distinctions between the interpretation of fraud and abuse in the Interest and Royalty Directive and in the Parent Subsidiary Directive could arise due to the different wording of the anti-avoidance provisions in the Interest and Royalties Directive. This could become especially relevant for future interpretation, as Art. 1(2) of the Parent-Subsidiary Directive has been amended (see Chapter 5, m.no. 462 et seq.) and allows (Art. 1(2) and (3)) the Member States to not grant the benefits of the Parent-Subsidiary Directive to an arrangement or a series of arrangements that, having been put into place for the main purpose or one of the main purposes of obtaining a tax advantage that defeats the object or purpose of the Parent-Subsidiary Directive, are not genuine, having regard to all relevant facts and circumstances. An arrangement may comprise more than one step or part and must be regarded as not genuine to the extent that such steps are not put into place for valid commercial reasons that reflect economic reality. So far, the Interest and Royalties Directive does not contain such a clause, i.e. the Interest and Royalties Directive has not been amended. In the author's opinion, however, irrespective of this fact, due to the very general wording of fraud and abuse clauses and also the common and very similar interpretation of "fraud and abuse" clauses by the CJEU (under secondary and primary law) and, in particular, based on the background of the case law as described in m.no. 572, the wording of new Art. 1(2) and (3) of the Parent-Subsidiary Directive could be used in interpreting Art. 5(2) of the Interest and Royalties Directive. Further, as the Interest and Royalties Directive itself will be amended at some point (see m.no. 546), this could be used to reduce the number of attestation requirements.

573

---

74   CJEU, 26 February 2019, Joined Cases C-115/16, *N Luxembourg 1 v Skatteministeriet*, and C-118/16, *X Denmark A/S v Skatteministeriet*, and C-119/16, *C Danmark I v Skatteministeriet*, and C-299/16, *Z Denmark ApS v Skatteministeriet*.
75   As to the elements of abuse, see Chapter 3, m.nos. 268-273.
76   For a more comprehensive overview of the indications see Chapter 5, m.no. 465.

V. Procedural Provisions

A. Attestation of Fulfilment of Application Requirements

574 Art. 1(11) to (16) contains procedural provisions for the functioning of the Interest and Royalties Directive whereas Art. 1(11) to (14) regulates the **attestation procedure**.[77] Under the attestation procedure, the Interest and Royalties Directive differentiates between a simplified attestation procedure and an attestation procedure based on a decision. According to Art. 1(11), the simplified attestation procedure entails that the source Member State may require an attestation by which the fulfilment of the requirements laid down in Arts. 1 and 3 is established. The attestation must include the information listed in Art. 1(13) (proof of residence for tax purposes, proof of beneficial ownership of the receiving company, fulfilment of subject-to-tax requirement according to Art. 3(a)(iii), proof of minimum holding, proof of holding period).[78] In the attestation procedure, the source Member State has the right to make it a condition for the granting of the benefits of the Interest and Royalties Directive that its tax authority has issued a decision on source tax exemption based on the above-mentioned attestation. Thus, such a decision on source tax exemption is an optional additional requirement for the Member States when granting an attestation. It also should be mentioned that, according to Art. 1(14), if the requirements for exemption cease to be fulfilled, the receiving company or permanent establishment has an obligation to immediately inform the paying company or permanent establishment and, if the source Member State so requires, the competent authority of that source Member State. It has to be asked in this respect whether all the attestation requirements are still proportionate at a time in which the (European and worldwide) automatic exchange of information is making fast progress (see on that issue in detail Chapter 8). Probably, as the Interest and Royalties Directive itself will be amended sooner or later (see m.no. 546), it is likely that, in addition to the amendments discussed, Art. 5 of the Interest and Royalties Directive may also be changed.

B. Repayment of Tax Withheld at Source

575 If the source tax exemption requirements have not been attested to at the time of the interest or royalty payment, the source Member State may oblige the payer of the interest or royalty to withhold the tax at the time of the payment. As a consequence of a later attestation, the source Member State has to provide for a **reimbursement procedure**, the principles of which are laid down in Art. 1(15) and (16).[79]

---

77   Distaso/Russo, The EC Interest and Royalties Directive – A comment, *ET* 2004, p. 152 et seq.; Rodriguez, in: Thömmes/Fuks (eds.), *EC Corporate Tax Law* (October 2004) para. 252 et seq.
78   In the tax literature it is not exactly clear who should make the attestation; see on this issue Rodriguez, in: Thömmes/Fuks (eds.), *EC Corporate Tax Law* (October 2004) para. 263 et seq.
79   Distaso/Russo, The EC Interest and Royalties Directive – A comment, *ET* 2004, p. 153; Rodriguez, in: Thömmes/Fuks (eds.), *EC Corporate Tax Law* (October 2004) para. 265 et seq.

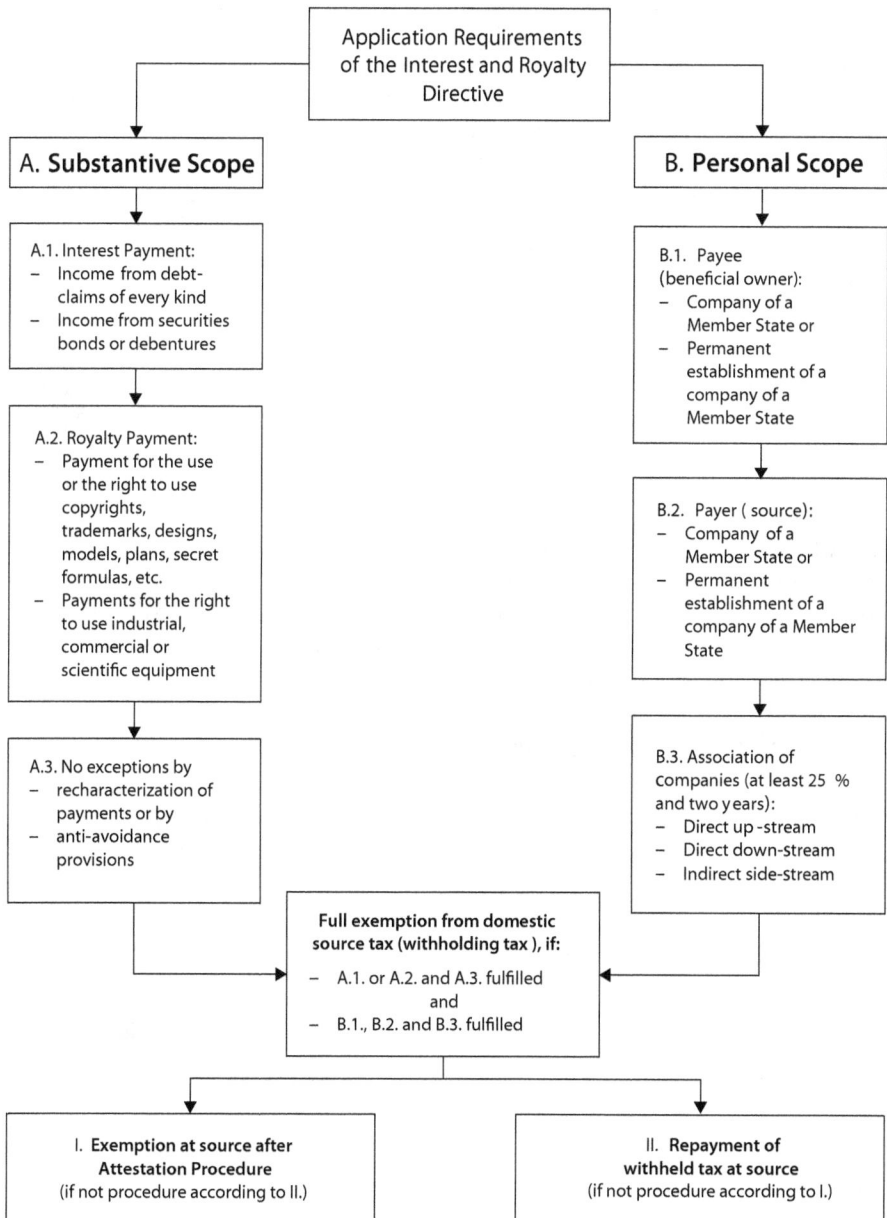

VI. Overview of the Functioning of the Directive

576

```
                    ┌─────────────────────────┐
                    │ Application Requirements │
                    │ of the Interest and Royalty │
                    │        Directive         │
                    └─────────────────────────┘
```

A. Substantive Scope

B. Personal Scope

A.1. Interest Payment:
- Income from debt-claims of every kind
- Income from securities bonds or debentures

A.2. Royalty Payment:
- Payment for the use or the right to use copyrights, trademarks, designs, models, plans, secret formulas, etc.
- Payments for the right to use industrial, commercial or scientific equipment

A.3. No exceptions by
- recharacterization of payments or by
- anti-avoidance provisions

B.1. Payee (beneficial owner):
- Company of a Member State or
- Permanent establishment of a company of a Member State

B.2. Payer (source):
- Company of a Member State or
- Permanent establishment of a company of a Member State

B.3. Association of companies (at least 25 % and two years):
- Direct up-stream
- Direct down-stream
- Indirect side-stream

Full exemption from domestic source tax (withholding tax), if:
- A.1. or A.2. and A.3. fulfilled and
- B.1., B.2. and B.3. fulfilled

I. Exemption at source after Attestation Procedure
(if not procedure according to II.)

II. Repayment of withheld tax at source
(if not procedure according to I.)

Literature

Weber, The proposed EC Interest and Royalty Directive, *EC Tax Review* 2000, p. 15; Brokelind, Royalty Payments: Unresolved issues in the Interest and Royalties Directive, *ET* 2004, p. 252; Distaso/Russo, The EC Interest and Royalties Directive – A comment, *ET* 2004, p. 143; Eicker/Aramini, Overview on the recent developments of the EC Directive on withholding taxes on royalty and interest payments, *EC Tax Review* 2004, p. 134; Rodriguez, Commentary on the EC Interest and Royalties Directive, in: Thömmes/Fuks (eds.), *EC Corporate Tax Law* (2004); Gusmeroli, Triangular cases and the Interest and Royalties Directive: Untying the Gordian knot? – Parts 1, 2 and 3, *ET* 2005, pp. 2, 39 and 86; Russo, Partnerships and Other Hybrid Entities and the EC Corporate Direct Tax Directives, *ET* 2006, p. 478; Eberhartinger/Six, National Tax Policy, the Directives and Hybrid Finance, in: K. Andersson et al. (eds.), *National Tax Policy in Europe* (2007) p. 225; Report from the Commission to the Council in accordance with Article 8 of Council Directive 2003/49/EC on a common system of taxation applicable to interest and royalty payments made between associated companies of different Member States, COM (2009) 179; Bundgaard, Classification and treatment of hybrid financial instruments and income derived therefrom under EU Corporate Tax Directives – Parts 1 and 2, *ET* 2010, pp. 442 and 490; Proposal for a Council Directive on a common system of taxation applicable to interest and royalty payments made between associated companies of different Member States of 11 November 2011, COM (2011), 714; van Dongen, Thin capitalization legislation and the EU Corporate Tax Directives, *ET* 2012, p. 20; and Kofler/Rodriguez, Beneficial Ownership and EU Law, in: Lang/Pistone/Schuch/Staringer/Storck (eds.), *Beneficial Ownership: Recent Trends* (2013).

Legal Basis: Council Directive 2003/49/EC of 3 June 2003 on a common system of taxation applicable to interest and royalty payments made between associated companies of different Member States, OJ L 157 of 26 June 2003, pp. 49-54.

Chapter 8 – The Anti-Tax Avoidance Directive

Sriram Govind/Stephanie Zolles[1]

---

[1]   The opinions expressed in this chapter are personal opinions of the authors and do not reflect the position of any organization to which the authors are affiliated.

I.   Introduction

A. Background and Origins

577 The fight against tax evasion and tax avoidance has attracted significant media attention over the past few years. This is mostly due to instances of tax avoidance by multinational enterprises revealed through various media reports, the Luxemburg-Leaks (2014), the Swiss-Leaks (2015) and the Panama-Leaks (2016). In an attempt to multilaterally tackle this issue, at the behest of the G-20, the OECD released reports on 15 actions dealing with the fight against base erosion and profit shifting (BEPS) in 2013, which were 'finalized' in 2015.[2] As countries work towards implementing the BEPS actions, the efforts of the EU toward coordinated action in this regard has assumed great significance.[3]

578 The implementation of measures against tax avoidance and aggressive tax planning becomes even more challenging in the context of a common internal market guaranteeing free movement and free establishment among strongly diverging direct tax legislations.[4] The danger of aggressive tax planning and tax avoidance has been recognized politically at the EU level.[5] Even prior to the BEPS reports, the European Commission (Commission) issued several resolutions,[6] communications (containing action plans)[7] and recommendations[8] in this regard. Tax avoidance was also addressed by means of rules on automatic exchange of information[9] and on advance tax rulings.[10] Furthermore, double non-taxation was addressed, in particular, through the inclusion of rules dealing with mismatches[11] and a common general anti-abuse rule[12] in the Parent-Subsidiary Directive.

---

2   OECD, Addressing Base Erosion and Profit Shifting (2013) and OECD, Action Plan on Base Erosion and Profit Shifting (2013), leading to the final reports on the action plans, which were released in October 2015.

3   *See* Chapter 2 for a general discussion of this issue.

4   The internal market allows for free movement, which generally restricts discriminatory national measures. See in that regard CJEU, 5 February 1963, Case C-26/62, *van Gend en Loos*, EU:C:1963:1.

5   See 14 February 1975, AB. EG 1975 Nr. C 35/1; see the preamble to Council Directive 77/799/EEC of 19 December 1977 concerning mutual assistance by the competent authorities of the Member States in the field of direct taxation, OJ L 336 of 27 December 1977.

6   Initiated by the Council Resolution of 10 February 1975 on the measures to be taken by the Community in order to combat international tax evasion and avoidance.

7   COM(2012)722 (6 December 2012); COM(2015)136final (18 March 2015); COM (2015)302final (17 June 2015).

8   COM(2012)8806 (6 December 2012); SWD(2012)403 final (6 December 2012).

9   Council Directive 2014/107/EU of 9 December 2014 amending Directive 2011/16/EU as regards mandatory automatic exchange of information in the field of taxation, OJ L 359/1 of 16 December 2014.

10   Council Directive (EU) 2015/2376 of 8 December 2015 amending Directive 2011/16/EU as regards mandatory automatic exchange of information in the field of taxation, OJ L 332/1 of 18 December 2015.

11   Council Directive 2014/86/EU of 8 July 2014 amending Directive 2011/96/ EU on the common system of taxation applicable in the case of parent companies and subsidiaries of different Member States, OJ L 219 of 25 July 2014, pp. 40-41.

12   Council Directive (EU) 2015/121 of 27 January 2015 amending Directive 2011/96/EU on the common system of taxation applicable in the case of parent companies and subsidiaries of different Member States, OJ L 21 of 28 January 2015, pp. 1-3.

In January 2016, the Commission released a proposal[13] for a directive to tackle tax   **579**
avoidance practices, as a part of its **Anti-Tax Avoidance Package**.[14] The proposal
was largely **based on the BEPS reports** and seeks to implement these recommendations in the EU context.[15] The Council adopted the Anti-Tax Avoidance Directive (ATAD)[16] on 12 July 2016. This rapidly obtained and unanimous political
consensus may be owing to the general mood among governments, which favours
combating BEPS, as well as the political pressure stemming from the public opinion on 'fair taxation'. The idea of introducing a directive to combat aggressive tax
planning and tax avoidance was also attractive from a governmental perspective
since the ATAD promises increased revenue collection.[17]

On 17 July 2016, the ECOFIN requested further rules on hybrid mismatches.[18] The   **580**
Commission immediately responded to the need for an amendment through a further proposal (ATAD 2),[19] which was once again adopted swiftly.[20] With the ATAD
a new EU instrument was introduced to the area of abuse in direct taxation.
The proposed measures are highly complex and their effects in relation to EU primary and secondary law are yet unclear.

B. Aims and Measures

Unlike other directives in the area of direct taxation, such as the Parent-Subsid-   **581**
iary Directive or the Merger Directive, the ATAD does not specifically aim to
ease cross-border operations or to confer rights on taxpayers.[21] The Commission
mentions in its working paper that the ATAD proposal was aimed at **effectively
countering tax avoidance** and ensuring that "*income cannot go untaxed*".[22] Never-

---

13 Proposal for a Council Directive Laying Down the Rules against Tax Avoidance Practices that Directly
    Affect the Functioning of the Internal Market, COM (2016) 26 final of 28 Jan. 2016.
14 Communication from the Commission to the European Parliament and the Council Anti-Tax Avoid-
    ance Package: Next steps towards delivering effective taxation and greater tax transparency in the EU,
    COM(2016) 23 final.
15 Commission Staff Working Document, Accompanying the document Communication from the
    Commission to the European Parliament and the Council Anti- Tax Avoidance Package: Next Steps
    towards delivering effective taxation and greater tax transparency in the EU, SWD (2016) 6 final 9.
16 Council Directive 2016/1164 of 12 July 2016 laying down rules against tax avoidance practices that
    directly affect the functioning of the internal market, OJ L 193/1 of 19 July 2016.
17 Politically, it may also be that some of the larger Member States have already implemented measures
    contained in the ATAD. For example, Germany provided for an interest limitation rule even before
    the ATAD. See Blum, Controlled Foreign Companies: Selected Policy Issues – or the Missing Elements
    of BEPS Action 3 and the Anti Tax Avoidance Directive, *Intertax* 2018, p. 298.
18 ECOFIN meeting of 17 July 2016, FISC 104, p. 33 available at http://data.consilium.europa.eu/doc/
    document/ST-10426-2016-INIT/en/pdf.
19 Proposal for Council Directive Amending Directive (EU) 2016/1164 as Regards Hybrid Mismatches
    with Third Countries, COM (2016) 687 final of 25 October 2016.
20 See Council Directive (EU) 2017/952 of 29 May 2017 amending Directive (EU) 2016/1164 as regards
    hybrid mismatches with third countries, OJ L 144 of 7 June 2017.
21 See also Smit, The Anti-Tax-Avoidance Directive (ATAD) in: Terra/Wattel (eds.), *European Tax Law*
    (2019), p. 490.
22 Commission Staff Working Document, Accompanying the document Communication from the
    Commission to the European Parliament and the Council Anti-Tax Avoidance Package: Next Steps
    towards delivering effective taxation and greater tax transparency in the EU, SWD (2016) 6 final 26.

theless, the ATAD neither provides for an obligation to introduce a corporate tax, nor for a single tax rate since direct taxation generally falls within the sovereignty of the Member States.

582   According to Recitals 1, 2 and 3 of the preamble, the ATAD aims towards:

- restoring trust in the fairness of tax systems;
- ensuring the good functioning of the internal market and prevent fragmentation of the internal market by implementing BEPS in a coordinated manner and
- ensuring a minimum level of protection against aggressive tax planning in the internal market.

583   In order to attain the above-mentioned aims, the ATAD prescribes five measures:

- An Interest Limitation Rule (Art. 4)
- An Exit Tax Rule (Art. 5)
- A General Anti-abuse Rule (GAAR) (Art. 6)
- A Controlled Foreign Company (CFC) Rule (Arts. 7 and 8)
- A Hybrid Mismatch Rule (Art. 9)

584   The ATAD, hence, contains four rules that counter very specific instances of tax avoidance and one general rule. The GAAR may be applied to instances where the specific rules leave loopholes (Recital 11).

585   The proposed measures on interest limitation, CFCs and hybrid mismatches were strongly influenced by the BEPS action plans. In contrast, exit taxation and a GAAR are hardly addressed in the BEPS reports. Rather, the rules on exit taxation and the GAAR in the ATAD codify principles laid down in the case law of the CJEU, although in the context of the fundamental freedoms (see m.nos. 610 and 614).

586   In addition to these rules, the directive provides for a **minimum standard** (Art. 3), allowing States to introduce stricter rules to provide "*a higher level of protection for domestic corporate tax bases*" per their discretion.

II. Scope of the Directive

A. Scope (Art. 1)

587   The Directive applies to **all taxpayers** that are **subject to corporate tax** in one or more Member States. In addition to taxpayers residing in the EU, **permanent establishments (PEs) of third-country resident entities** located in at least one Member State are also covered by the ATAD. The personal scope of the ATAD is clearly restricted to entities subject to corporate tax; **individuals are thus, excluded** from the scope.

Although third-country PEs are explicitly included in the scope, **a PE definition** **588** **is lacking**. Member States may use different standards arising from tax treaties or from domestic law.[23] Similar problems arise with regard to the **concept of 'residence'**: Although Art. 1 ATAD does not refer to residence, some measures, such as the CFC and in some cases, even the exit tax rules and the hybrid mismatch rules, provide for obligations particularly for the residence State or the PE State. The ATAD does not define residence and **does not include a tie-breaker rule**[24]. With regard to the CFC rules in particular, this might raise concerns: The CFC rules in the ATAD capture certain income of the controlled company and add it to the tax base of the parent company. If an entity is considered a resident in more than one State at the same time the taxpayer might, in the absence of a tie breaker rule, be treated as a resident by several States and, thus, be subject to CFC measures in all those States. This may lead to double taxation, as the foreign income will be added to the tax base of the controlled company in all those States.

Some ATAD measures apply regardless of requirements such as residence or the existence of a PE, such as the interest limitation rules. Where a taxpayer is subject to worldwide taxation in several Member States, it will have to face national interest limitation rules in each country with respect to its taxable income in each State. Such situations may be problematic especially considering that these rules may be heterogeneously implemented by States following the 'minimum standard' provision.

Third country entities have not been excluded from the scope of the ATAD, while **589** benefits arising from other directives in the area of direct taxation often do not apply to residents of a third country, regardless of the transactions they carry out in a Member State.[25] This may lead to a situation where companies that are third-country residents may not enjoy the benefits under the other direct taxation directives but are still subject to the rigours of the ATAD.

The wording of Art. 1 ATAD, which refers to entities subject to corporate tax "*in* **590** *one or more Member States*" also provides room for interpretation. Based on a strict reading, a Member State may even have to apply the ATAD measures to an entity that is **not** subject to corporate tax under its domestic law as long as the entity is subject to corporate tax in another Member State. For example, the exit tax may be applied to a transfer of assets by an entity not subject to corporate tax in the State of origin.

---

23 Smit, The Anti-Tax-Avoidance Directive (ATAD) in: Terra/Wattel (eds.), *European Tax Law* (2019), p. 493.

24 As regards tax residency mismatches between Member States Art. 9b ATAD makes reference to residence as assigned under the DTC between these Member States.

25 E.g. under Art. 2 of the Parent-Subsidiary Directive, a company is not considered 'a company of a Member State' where its residence, under a DTC, is in a third State outside the EU. *See* Chapter 5 m.no. 417; Smit, The Anti-Tax-Avoidance Directive (ATAD) in: Terra/Wattel (eds.), *European Tax Law* (2019), p. 492.

591   Moreover, **the expression 'subject to corporate tax' is not defined.**[26] Therefore, it is important to consider whether the ATAD would apply even where a taxpayer generally falls within the scope of the corporate tax system, but is exempted or subject to a zero tax rate. In the context of the Parent-Subsidiary Directive, the CJEU found, in its decision in *Wereldhave*, that a zero rate is 'tantamount' to not subjecting such entities to tax.[27] However, the relevant provision in the Parent-Subsidiary Directive substantially differs in its wording, aim and context from Art. 1 ATAD.[28] Furthermore, Art. 7 ATAD, in the context of CFC rules, uses the phrasing 'not subject to tax or exempt from tax'. It may be inferred from this that (per the drafters of the ATADq not being subject to tax is different from being exempted from tax. Accordingly, exempted taxpayers – being different from taxpayers 'not subject to tax' – may fall within the scope of the ATAD.

B.   Minimum Standard (Art. 3)

592   Art. 3 ATAD clarifies that the ATAD only provides a **minimum level of protection** and thus shall not preclude the application of domestic or agreement based provisions that provide **higher levels of protection to domestic corporate tax bases.** Member States are free to implement the provisions of the ATAD with more rigour per their discretion. This provision ensures that a national measure that is stricter than the corresponding ATAD measure would not be contrary to the ATAD and thus, inapplicable. This does not, however, mean that the Member States have unlimited discretion. National measures going beyond the minimum standard, as well as the minimum standard itself, are restricted by EU primary law and, in particular, by the fundamental freedoms.[29] National measures going beyond the minimum standard may hence be in line with the ATAD but nevertheless be illegitimate if they violate EU primary law. Where primary law does not allow for stricter measures than those provided in the ATAD, the ATAD provisions do not, in fact, function as a 'minimum standard'.[30]

593   Besides allowing for greater protection against tax avoidance, the introduction of a minimum standard in the ATAD could lead to **heterogeneous implementation.**[31] However, while directives may require the Member States to achieve a certain result, the means to achieve that result is generally left to them.[32] Given that the

---

26   It is questionable whether the distinction between 'liable to tax' and 'subject to tax' as made in the tax treaty literature may be extended here and whether, owing to such a distinction, this expression would imply actually being subject to tax and not legal liability.

27   CJEU, 8 March 2017, Case C-448/15, *Wereldhave Belgium*, EU:C:2017:180, para. 34.

28   *See* also Smit, The Anti-Tax-Avoidance Directive (ATAD) in: Terra/Wattel (eds.), *European Tax Law* (2019), p. 492.

29   *See* Section V.B of this chapter for a discussion of such situations.

30   Docclo, The European Union's Ambition to Harmonize Rules to Counter the Abuse of Member States' Disparate Tax Legislations, *BIT* 2017, p. 368. On the relevance of the fundamental freedoms for direct taxation see also Chapter 3.

31   The importance of 'coordinated' action is highlighted in Recital 2 ATAD.

32   Terra/Wattel, *European Tax Law* (2019) p. 23; Eisenberg/Ramello, *Comparative Law and Economics* (2016) p. 464.

goal of the ATAD is to combat tax avoidance and aggressive tax planning in a harmonized manner, the introduction of a minimum standard may be considered legitimate.

Another issue that may be pointed out is that Member States may now assume the **594** freedom to remove the safeguards provided in the ATAD (and recommended in the BEPS reports) under the pretext of providing a 'higher' level of protection to their tax bases, subject to the limits created by primary law.

III. Substantive Provisions of the Directive

A. Interest Limitation Rules (Art. 4)

Multinational enterprises may engage in aggressive tax planning by accumulating **595** **excessive interest deductions** through loan agreements. Typically, such agreements involve the borrowing of money by an entity in a high-tax jurisdiction from another entity in a low or no tax jurisdiction, leading to interest payments. While the company paying the interest will be entitled to fully deduct the interest payments from its taxable profits in the high-tax jurisdiction as expenses, the corresponding income from interest will be subject to low or no taxation at the level of the entity receiving the interest. This leads to an erosion of the tax base in the high tax jurisdiction. In response, States have sought to counter such planning by **limiting the deductibility of interest payments.**[33]

Prior to the BEPS Project, there was **no coordinated action** on the limitation of **596** interest deduction within the EU and Member States followed different practices. The most common approach was the classic debt-equity ratio based **thin capitalization rule** that disallows an interest deduction where the maximum amount of debt on which interest may be deducted is fixed by a ratio as against equity. However, since such rules mostly cover cross-border debt and not domestic debt, the CJEU has, on several occasions, discussed the compatibility of such rules with the fundamental freedoms.[34] Further, many authors have pointed out that the differences in the various interest limitation rules within the EU have led to several practical problems, including (economic) double taxation, calling for harmonization of such rules.[35]

---

33   Commission Staff Working Document accompanying the document Communication from the Commission to the European Parliament and the Council Anti-Tax Avoidance Package: Next steps towards delivering effective taxation and greater tax transparency in the EU, COM(2016) 23 final.

34   See e.g. CJEU, 12 December 2002, Case C-324/00, *Lankhorst-Hohorst*, EU:C:2002:749; 13 March 2007, Case C-524/04, *Test Claimants in the Thin Cap Group Litigation*, EU:C:2007:161; 3 October 2013, Case C-282/12, *Itelcar*, EU:C:2013:629, etc. In response to this concern, many States have moved to an 'interest barrier' or 'earnings stripping' rule to limit interest deductions so that the rules would not be discriminatory (at least overtly).

35   Dourado/de la Feria, Thin Capitalization and Outbound Investment, in Thin Capitalization Rules in the Context of the CCCTB, in: Lang et al. (eds.), *Common Consolidation Corporate Tax Base* (2008) pp. 381–382.

597 Rules limiting the deductibility of interest were covered in the form of **'interest barrier' rules** in Action 4 of the BEPS Project. The final report on Action 4 recommended, as a best practice, that States introduce domestic legislation **limiting an entity's net interest deductions to a fixed percentage of its profits**. Art. 4 ATAD broadly aims to implement these proposals at the EU level by introducing an interest barrier rule, termed **'earning's stripping rule'**.[36]

598 Art. 4(1) ATAD codifies the **'fixed ratio rule'** under which deductible interest of an entity is limited to a certain percentage of earnings. 'Exceeding borrowing costs'[37] shall generally be deductible in the tax period in which they are incurred only up to 30 % of the taxpayer's 'earnings'. The 'earnings' used in calculating the deductible amount is meant to be **earnings before interest, taxes, depreciation and amortization (EBITDA)**.[38] Recital 6 to the ATAD allows Member States to use alternatives to the EBITDA in determining earnings, such as earnings before interest and taxes (EBIT).[39] In principle, the interest limitation rule in the ATAD presumes that non-deductible borrowing costs cannot be deducted in **previous or future tax periods**. However, Member States are given certain options to provide for a carry forward or a carry back of non-deductible borrowing costs (Art. 4(6) ATAD).

599 The interest limitation rule in the ATAD also provides for a **group ratio rule** as suggested in BEPS Action 4. It allows Member States to treat entities that are part of 'groups' per national tax law as **one taxpayer** for the purpose of this rule. While Art. 4 ATAD does not provide for any restrictions in terms of which entities can be considered part of a group, Recital 7 seems to support a restriction to *"entities in the same State"*. Where Member States opt for the group ratio rule, 'exceeding borrowing costs' and EBITDA may be calculated at the level of the group, comprising the results of all the member entities.

600 If the taxpayer is a member of a consolidated financial group for financial accounting purposes, the Member State may allow either of two options under Art. 4(5) ATAD:

---

36 The wording of this provision was inspired by Art. 14a of the CCCTB Compromise Proposal added in 2012 and discussed until 2014 with added input from the Action Plan 4 suggestions. *See* Proposal for a Council Directive on a Common Consolidated Corporate Tax Base (CCCTB)- Compromise Proposal, 9180/13, 2 May 2012 and 10177/14, 26 May 2014. It may be noted that Art. 14 of the 2016 CCCTB directive proposal closely mirrors Art. 4 ATAD, without, however, allowing States a choice in terms of how to implement the provision according to their needs.

37 The term 'Borrowing costs' is defined in Art. 2(1) ATAD exhaustively to include not just interest expenses from all forms of debt, but also all other economic equivalents incurred in connection with the raising of finance per national law. 'Exceeding borrowing costs' means the amount by which deductible borrowing costs of a taxpayer exceed taxable interest revenues (or equivalent taxable revenues) that the taxpayer receives per national law.

38 Art. 4(2) ATAD clarifies that the EBITDA shall be calculated by adding back to the income subject to corporate tax, the tax adjusted amounts for exceeding borrowing costs, depreciation and amortization, excluding tax exempt income of the taxpayer.

39 Note that in BEPS Action 4, EBITDA and EBIT were considered equally legitimate approaches: OECD, Final Report on Action Plan 4 (2015), pp. 23 and 48. Furthermore, Art. 3 ATAD, on the minimum standard, may serve as a legal basis for different definitions of earnings.

- an equity escape rule, allowing the taxpayer the right to fully deduct excess borrowing costs if the ratio of its equity to its total assets is equal to or higher than the equivalent ratio of the group
- deduction of exceeding borrowing costs up to the limit calculated as provided below:

$$\frac{\text{Exceeding borrowing costs of the group vis-à-vis third parties}}{\text{Group EBITDA}} \times \text{Taxpayer EBITDA}$$

Member States may introduce a *de minimis* **threshold** allowing deductions for **601** exceeding borrowing costs up to EUR 3 000 000 for each entity or for a group as a whole. The threshold is aimed at reducing the administrative and compliance burden associated with the interest limitation rule for taxpayers with low borrowing costs (Recital 8). However, the threshold has been criticised for neither fully combatting tax avoidance nor mitigating the bias against equity for taxpayers that fall below the threshold.[40]

Further exemptions from the interest limitation rule are provided for in Art. 4(3), **602** (4) and (7) ATAD: A Member State may allow a deduction of excess borrowing costs if the taxpayer qualifies as a **'standalone entity'**. A 'standalone entity' is a taxpayer who is not part of a consolidated group for financial accounting purposes and has no associated enterprise or PE. Member States may exclude loans concluded before 17 June 2016 unless modified afterwards and loans used to fund a **'long-term public infrastructure project'**[41] where the project operator, the borrowing costs, the assets and the income are all in the EU. Finally, Member States may also exclude **financial undertakings** from the scope of the interest limitation rule. The European Commission has recently taken the view that limiting such exclusions to those contained in the ATAD is an obligation and has commenced infringement proceedings against Belgium for not doing so.[42]

While Recital 6 ATAD provides that Art. 4 ATAD is intended to counter BEPS **603** resulting from excessive interest deductions, the scope of the provision has been criticized for not fully being in line with this aim: It has been contended that the rule is too strict, as it also applies to cases involving no profit shifting, i.e. *inter alia* to domestic situations where the interest would be taxable in the same State where the deduction is available.[43] Further, it has been pointed out that a taxpayer's

---

40 For a critique on this point, *see* Van Os, Interest Limitation under the Adopted Anti-Tax Avoidance Directive and Proportionality, *EC Tax Rev.* 2016, p. 191.

41 Defined in Art. 4(4) as *"a project to provide, upgrade, operate and/or maintain a large-scale asset that is considered in the general public interest by a Member State."*

42 Commission, July Infringement package: key decisions, 2 July 2020, available at: https://ec.europa.eu/commission/presscorner/detail/en/INF_20_1212 (accessed on 28 July 2020).

43 *See* Van Os, Interest Limitation under the Adopted Anti-Tax Avoidance Directive and Proportionality, *EC Tax Rev.* 2016, p. 193.

earnings tend to change with time and linking interest deductions to earnings may be commercially damaging for companies facing a temporary downturn in business.[44] The interest limitation rule has also been criticised for not covering all cases of profit shifting, such as where the minimum threshold is not exceeded.[45] Finally, it has also been observed that, while the deduction of interest is restricted, the corresponding income may be taxed at the level of the creditor and a withholding obligation may be imposed on the borrower outside the scope of the Interest and Royalty Directive, creating the possibility of double taxation.[46]

B. Exit Tax Rules (Art. 5)

604 **Exit taxation** denotes the taxation of unrealized capital gains at the moment a taxpayer moves either (i) its residence, (ii) a business or (iii) certain assets from one State to another. Since the State of departure may lose its power to tax the unrealized gains (either due to domestic rules or pursuant to a DTC), rules on exit taxation ensure taxation of the capital gains in the State of departure, although the gain has not yet been realized.[47]

605 Rules on exit taxation were not included in the BEPS Action Plans. BEPS Action 6 merely mentioned that such rules are in line with DTCs insofar as income accruing after the exit is not taxed.[48] Similar to the OECD's BEPS Project, the legal framework of the EU before the ATAD did not provide for explicit rules on exit taxation. Rather, exit taxation provisions were an aspect of the sovereignty of the Member States in matters of direct taxation. However, there is a large number of **CJEU cases on exit taxation rules** and their compliance with the fundamental freedoms. In *National Grid Indus,* the CJEU concluded that Member States are principally allowed to apply exit taxes on unrealized capital gains at the time of the relocation, but must not collect such taxes immediately at the time of the transfer.[49] In *DMC*, the CJEU was satisfied with a rule that granted the possibility for the taxpayer to decide whether he would pay such tax immediately or would spread the payment over a period of five years.[50] Prescribing security[51] or interest

---

44 Smit, The Anti-Tax-Avoidance Directive (ATAD) in: Terra/Wattel (eds.), *European Tax Law* (2019), p. 499.

45 *See* van Os, Interest Limitation under the Adopted Anti-Tax Avoidance Directive and Proportionality, *EC Tax Rev.* 2016, p. 193 referring to Opinion of Advocate General Geelhoed, 29 June 20016, Case C-524/04, *Test Claimants in the Thin Cap Group Litigation*, EU:C:2007:161, para. 68.

46 Soom, Double Taxation Resulting from the ATAD: Is there Relief?, *Intertax* 2020, p. 274 et seq.

47 Recital 10 ATAD; Commission Staff Working Document of 28 February 2016 accompanying the Communication from the Commission, SWD(2016) 6 final 27.

48 OECD/G20 BEPS Project Action 6, Preventing the Granting of Treaty Benefits in Inappropriate Circumstances, Final Report, paras. 65-67 (2015).

49 CJEU, 29 November 2011, Case C-371/10, *National Grid Indus*, EU:C:2011:785, paras. 42-48.

50 CJEU, 23 January 2014, Case C-164/12, *DMC*, EU:C:2014:20, paras. 62-64; 21 May 2015, Case C-657/13, *Verder Lab Tec*, EU:C:2015:331, para. 52.

51 CJEU, 29 November 2011, Case C-371/10, *National Grid Indus*, EU:C:2011:785, para. 74; 23 January 2014, Case C-164/12, *DMC*, EU:C:2014:20, paras. 65-68.

payments[52] in the event of a deferral of payments is also in line with the freedom of establishment.

The ATAD introduces a harmonized legal framework for exit taxation of corpora- **606**
tions in the EU. Though the provision is formally a minimum standard owing to Art. 3 ATAD, in light of the CJEU's case law, it seems difficult to find an exit tax scheme in line with the fundamental freedoms that provides for a higher protection of the domestic corporate tax base. Rather, the ATAD seems to be a **codification** of the case law decided on this subject. However, while the CJEU has never pre-scribed the application of an exit tax in its case law, the ATAD (at least formally) **obliges** the Member States to introduce exit taxation rules for entities subject to corporate tax. While the amount subject to exit tax is addressed in the ATAD, it does not provide for any rules on how the amount should be taxed, nor does it provide for any minimum level of taxation.[53]

The ATAD mentions three instances of **transference** that are subject to exit tax if **607**
the state of departure loses its taxing rights: (i) a transfer of assets from a Member State to another State,[54] (ii) a transfer of residence,[55] (iii) a transfer of a business carried on by a PE.[56] However, as discussed in chapter II.A., the ATAD does not define 'residence' or 'PE'. The terms may arguably have autonomous meanings and therefore, may be interpreted the same way in all Member States. On the other hand, it may also be that the intention was to use the meanings as derived from the national law of the Member State applying the rule. Consequently, the terms would have a different meaning in each Member State, with the result that they may apply the exit tax rules differently.

The exit tax is to be applied '*at the time of exit of the assets*'. The amount of un- **608**
realized capital gains subject to the exit tax is equal to the difference between the '*market value*' of the transferred assets at the time of exit and the 'value' of the transferred assets 'for tax purposes'. The **market value** is "*the amount for which an asset can be exchanged or mutual obligations can be settled between willing un-related buyers and sellers in a direct transaction*" (Art. 5 para. 6 ATAD) and is cal-culated based on an **arm's length approach** (Recital 10, ATAD). The ATAD is, however, silent on the meaning of 'arm's length', which may lead to the result that the Member States may use substantially different tests to establish 'arm's length'.

---

52 CJEU, 29 November 2011, Case C-371/10, *National Grid Indus*, EU:C:2011:785, para. 73; 23 January 2014, Case C-164/12, *DMC*, EU:C:2014:20, para. 61; 6 September 2012, Case C-38/10; *Commission/Portugal*, EU:C:2012:521, para. 32.

53 Peeters, Exit Taxation: From an Internal Market Barrier to a Tax Avoidance Prevention Tool, *EC Tax Rev.* 2017, p. 122 at 130, 131; Docclo, The European Union's Ambition to Harmonize Rules to Coun-ter the Abuse of Member States' Disparate Tax Legislations, *BIT* 2017, p. 368.

54 Exit tax must be applied if a Member State loses its taxing right on assets due to a transfer of the assets (a) from the taxpayer's head office to a PE in another State or (b) *vice versa* from a domestic PE to its head office (or a PE) situated in another State.

55 A carve out is provided for assets that remain "*effectively connected with a permanent establishment*" in the Member State of departure.

56 Exit tax must be applied in so far as the State of departure no longer has (as a consequence of the departure) a taxing right over the transferred assets.

609 Under Art. 5 para. 5 ATAD, i.e. the '**step up**' provision, the State of destination must accept the value established by the State of departure as the starting value for tax purposes, unless this value does not reflect the market value. The step up has an impact on the calculation of future depreciation and amortization, as well as on the determination of the gain or loss from a future disposal of the asset.[57]

610 Art. 5 paras. 2 and 3 ATAD are evidently strongly inspired by the CJEU's decisions in *National Grid Indus*[58] and *DMC*.[59] They provide an option for taxpayers to pay in instalments over five years and a possibility for the Member States to require the payment of interest. A Member State may, in principle, require the taxpayer to provide for a bank guarantee as a condition for the granting a deferral if there is a demonstrable and actual risk of non-recovery. The deferral must be discontinued immediately in certain circumstances, such as where the taxpayer disposes of the transferred assets or transfers them to a third country (Art. 5 para. 4 ATAD).

611 The exit tax rules do not apply to certain **temporary transfers** (Art. 5 para. 7 ATAD), where the assets revert back to the departure State in less than 12 months: the transfer is related to the financing of securities, the asset is posted as collateral, the transfer is required to meet prudential capital requirements or the transfer serves the purpose of liquidity management. As Member States are allowed to apply measures that provide for a 'higher' level of protection to their tax bases, applying exit tax rules also to temporary transfers serving the above-mentioned purposes may be legitimate. However, this may be considered contrary to the wording of the provision ('shall not apply') and might be inconsistent with the EU legislator's approach of explicitly providing for options for Member States throughout the ATAD (e.g. Art. 7(3) ATAD) and the aim of preventing the fragmentation of the internal market.

C. General Anti-Avoidance Rule (Art. 6)

612 Prior to the adoption of the ATAD, general rules tackling abusive practices have already been introduced to the Parent Subsidiary Directive,[60] Merger Directive[61] and the Interest and Royalties Directive.[62] In addition to these various GAARs

---

57 Peeters, Exit Taxation: From an Internal Market Barrier to a Tax Avoidance Prevention Tool, *EC Tax Rev.* 2017, p. 131.

58 CJEU, 29 November 2011, Case C-371/10, *National Grid Indus*, EU:C:2011:785.

59 CJEU, 23 January 2014, Case C-164/12, *DMC*, EU:C:2014:20.

60 See Art. 1(4) Council Directive (EU) 2015/121 of 27 January 2015 amending Directive 2011/96/EU on the common system of taxation applicable in the case of parent companies and subsidiaries of different Member States, OJ L 21 of 28 January 2015, pp. 1-3.

61 Art. 15 Council Directive 2009/133/EC of 19 October 2009 on the Common System of Taxation Applicable to Mergers, Divisions, Partial Divisions, Transfers of Assets and Exchanges of Shares Concerning Companies of Different Member States and to the Transfer of the Registered Office of an SE or SCE between Member States (Codified Version), OJ L 310 of 25 November 2009, pp. 34-46.

62 Art. 5 Council Directive 2003/49/EC of June 2003 on a common system of taxation applicable to interest and royalty payments, OJ L 157 of 26 June 2003, pp. 49-54.

in Directives other than the ATAD, Art. 6 ATAD introduced, for the first time, a GAAR to cover corporate taxation as a whole.

Art. 6 ATAD requires Member States to ignore certain arrangements, the main **613** purpose or one of the main purposes of which, is to **obtain a tax advantage**, thereby defeating the purpose of the applicable tax law. The arrangement should then be ignored and taxed according to national law. The rule applies to arrangements that are – considering all relevant facts and circumstances – **not 'genuine'**. An arrangement is to be considered genuine to the extent it is put into place for valid commercial reasons reflecting economic reality.

While employing a number of unclear and subjective criteria, the Explanatory **614** Memorandum of the initial ATAD proposal states that the GAAR in the ATAD is designed to reflect the CJEU's case law on abusive practices.[63] In fact, a huge number of CJEU cases in the area of direct taxation deal with combatting abuse: Besides cases concerning GAAR provisions explicitly included in a directive,[64] in settled case law the CJEU also accepts the prohibition of abuse as a justifying objective when testing the compatibility of national measures with the fundamental freedoms.[65] In the decision of the Grand Chamber in *N Luxembourg 1*, the CJEU affirmed the existence of **a general principle of prohibiting abusive practices** even in the area of direct taxation.[66] Although direct taxation is not fully harmonized in the EU, the principle is inter alia applicable where harmonizing measures exist. Since the ATAD is a further step towards harmonizing corporate tax law, the scope of the principles of EU law has been extended to the areas governed by the ATAD. It also remains to be seen whether a general principle prohibiting abusive practices would affect how the GAAR in the ATAD is interpreted and *vice versa*. From hitherto case law, it appears likely that the CJEU would use a similar concept of prohibiting abuse under primary and secondary law measures.[67]

When qualifying an arrangement as abusive, the CJEU applies a two-step test:[68] **615** (i) the objective test, which requires that the purpose and object of an EU rule, such as the freedom of establishment, have not been achieved in light of objective circumstances and (ii) a subjective test, focusing on whether a taxpayer has the intention to create wholly artificial conditions to obtain an advantage.

---

63   Proposal for a Council Directive Laying Down the Rules against Tax Avoidance Practices that Directly Affect the Functioning of the Internal Market, COM (2016) 26 final of 28 Jan. 2016.
64   See e.g. CJEU, 5 July 2007, Case C-321/05, *Kofoed*, EU:C:2007:408; 8 March 2017, Case C-14/16, *Euro Park Service*, EU:C:2017:177; 7 September 2017, *Eqiom*, Case C-6/16, EU:C:2017:641.
65   E.g. CJEU, 12 September 2006, Case C-196/04, *Cadbury Schweppes and Cadbury Schweppes Overseas*, EU:C:2006:544.
66   CJEU, 26 February 2019, Case C-115/16, *N Luxembourg 1*, EU:C:2019:134, para. 101 et seq.
67   See CJEU, 8 March 2017, Case C-14/16, *Euro Park Service*, EU:C:2017:177, para. 87; 7 September 2017, *Eqiom*, Case C-6/16, EU:C:2017:641, para. 64. See also Cordewener, Anti-Abuse Measures in the Area of Direct Taxation: Towards Converging Standards under Treaty Freedoms and EU Directives?, *EC Tax Rev.* 2017, p. 60 at 63.
68   CJEU, 14 December 2000, Case C-110/99, *Emsland-Stärke GmbH*, EU:C:2000:695, para. 52 et seq.; 12 September 2006, Case C-196/04, *Cadbury Schweppes and Cadbury Schweppes Overseas*, EU:C:2006:544, para. 64.

616 In principle, the CJEU considers a measure restricting the fundamental freedoms justified by the prohibition of tax avoidance only if the objective of the measure is *"to prevent conduct involving the creation of **wholly artificial arrangements** which **do not reflect economic reality**, with a view to escaping **the tax normally due** on the profits generated by activities carried out on national territory [emphasis added]"*.[69] In *Cadbury Schweppes*, the CJEU held that an arrangement reflects 'economic reality' if it is aimed at carrying out a 'genuine' economic activity.[70] It appears that Art. 6 ATAD is strongly inspired by this case law. Despite the lack of reference to 'wholly artificial arrangements', it generally corresponds to the principles laid down, i.e. focusing on whether economic reality is reflected, referring to 'non-genuine' activities and requiring that an arrangement defeat the object and purpose of national law.[71]

617 Throughout its case law, the CJEU refers to the **purpose** of an arrangement to determine whether it is abusive. However, the Court seems to be inconsistent, sometimes deeming an operation abusive where its 'sole' purpose is to obtain a tax advantage,[72] sometimes when the 'essential' purpose is to obtain a tax advantage[73] and sometimes where its 'principal' purpose is to obtain such an advantage.[74] By contrast, the ATAD's concept of abuse requires only that obtaining a tax advantage be 'one of the main purposes'.[75]

618 Significantly, the GAAR in the ATAD is not limited to cross-border transactions but applies also to **purely internal tax matters.** Due to the similarities between the wording of the ATAD and the formulation used by the CJEU to describe abusive practices, it seems that the CJEU's observations on fundamental freedoms will play a growing role also in purely national situations.[76] Apart from its relevance for

---

69   CJEU, 7 January 2008, Case C-105/07, *NV Lammers & Van Cleeff*, EU:C:2008:24, para. 28; 13 March 2007, Case C-524/04, *Test Claimants in the Thin Cap Group Litigation*, EU:C:2007:161, para. 74; 12 September 2006, Case C-196/04, *Cadbury Schweppes and Cadbury Schweppes Overseas*, EU:C:2006:544, para. 55; see also 7 November 2013, Case C-322/11, *K*, EU:C:2013:716, para. 61; 17 December 2015, Case C-388/14, *Timac Agro*, EU:C:2015:829, para. 42; 7 September 2017, Case C-6/16, *Eqiom*, EU:C:2017:641, para. 30; 20 December 2017, Joined Cases C-504/16 and C-613/16, *Deister Holding and Juhler Holding*, EU:C:2017:1009, para. 60.

70   CJEU, 12 September 2006, Case C-196/04, *Cadbury Schweppes and Cadbury Schweppes Overseas*, EU:C:2006:544, para. 66.

71   For a critique on this point, *see* de Broe/Beckers, The General Anti-Abuse Rule of the Anti-Tax Avoidance Directive: An Analysis Against the Wider Perspective of the European Court of Justice's Case Law on Abuse of EU Law, *EC Tax Rev.* 2017, p. 113 at 143.

72   CJEU, 8 March 2017, Case C-14/16, *Euro Park Service*, EU:C:2017:177, para. 53.

73   CJEU, 21 February 2006, Case C-255/02, *Halifax*, EU:C:2006:121, para. 75.

74   CJEU, 21 February 2008, Case C-425/06, *Part Service*, EU:C:2008:108, para. 45; 7 September 2017, Case C-6/16, *Eqiom*, EU:C:2017:641, para. 36.

75   The *Multilateral Convention to Implement Tax Treaty Related Measures to Prevent Base Erosion and Profit Shifting* (24 Nov. 2016), as well as BEPS Action Plan 6 use similar language and it will be interesting to see whether the interpretation of this provision will influence the GAAR in the ATAD and vice versa. *See also* Chapter 3 m.no. 268 et seqq.

76   *See* de Broe/Beckers, The General Anti-Abuse Rule of the Anti-Tax Avoidance Directive: An Analysis Against the Wider Perspective of the European Court of Justice's Case Law on Abuse of EU Law, *EC Tax Rev.* 2017, p. 140.

the future interpretation of Art. 6 ATAD, the CJEU's case law will also be pivotal where Member States make use of the minimum standard provision. Arguably, Art. 3 ATAD may allow the Member States to introduce a broader GAAR into their national laws.[77] The scope of any national law must, however, be compliant with the CJEU's case law.

D. CFC Rules (Arts. 7 and 8)

CFC structures involve the shielding of income from taxation in a State by creating   **619** a subsidiary (a CFC) in a low-tax jurisdiction whereto profits are shifted. Since the parent company will not be taxable on the income attributed to the subsidiary, a tax deferral is created by delaying repatriation. Such a structure may also allow for the sheltering of income from taxation due to a different characterization by the Member States or due to participation exemptions.[78] CFC rules tackle such arrangements by including the non-distributed income of the controlled subsidiary in the tax base of the parent company in its State of residence.

CFC rules were ubiquitous in the domestic law of Member States for several years   **620** before the ATAD. Although there was no harmonization of such rules prior to the ATAD, the CJEU has, on several occasions, and most significantly in the *Cadbury Schweppes* case, held that CFC rules restrict the freedom of establishment. However, the CJEU accepts that CFC rules could, in principle, be justified on the ground of prevention of abusive practices if they target wholly artificial arrangements that do not reflect economic reality.

In *Cadbury Schweppes*, the CJEU held that the existence of substantial economic   **621** activity through the presence of staff, equipment, assets and premises means that an arrangement is not 'wholly artificial'. Consequent to the *Cadbury Schweppes* decision, the Commission released a recommendation laying down 'best practices' as regards CFC rules in 2007.[79] Furthermore, there was political agreement on CFC rules at the Code of Conduct Group among Member States as early as in 2010.[80] Best practices with regard to CFC rules were also laid down as part of the BEPS Project in Action 3. Action 3 also clarifies that EU Member States should implement CFC rules giving due importance to the *Cadbury Schweppes* doctrine.

Arts. 7 and 8 ATAD build on the BEPS proposals and provide for the 'minimum   **622** standard' for CFC rules. Per these rules, a Member State is obliged to treat an entity

---

77 Docclo, The European Union's Ambition to Harmonize Rules to Counter the Abuse of Member States' Disparate Tax Legislations, *BIT* 2017, p. 368. *See* also m.no. 592 et seqq.

78 de Broe, *International Tax Planning and Prevention of Abuse* (2008) p. 41.

79 Communication from the Commission to the Council, the European Parliament and the European Economic and Social Committee, 10 December 2007, The application of anti-abuse measures in the area of direct taxation — within the EU and in relation to third countries [COM(2007) 785 final, p. 5 et seq.

80 Code of conduct group (business taxation), report to the Council of 22 November 2010, 16766/10 LIMITE, FISC 139, para. 16.

or a PE that is not subject to tax in that State as a CFC under certain circumstances. The income of a low-taxed entity or PE then has to be **included in the tax base of the controlling company**.

623 With regard to an entity, the ATAD lays down two cumulative conditions for the application of the CFC rules: (i) the taxpayer by itself or along with its associated enterprises[81] must hold or own 50% or more of the voting rights or capital directly or indirectly or be entitled to receive more than 50% of the profits of that entity and (ii) the actual corporate tax paid by the entity must be lower than 50% of the corporate tax that would have been charged to the entity, as computed under the laws of the Member State of the taxpayer.

624 With regard to a PE, only condition (ii) must be met. While DTCs usually allocate the primary taxing right for income attributable to a PE to the State where the PE is situated, under the ATAD CFC rule, the residence State would tax the income of the PE at the level of the domestic company. However, a PE of a CFC shall not be taken into account for the calculation provided in (ii) if the PE is not taxable in the jurisdiction of the CFC. Since income of a CFC's PE that is exempted in the CFC State is not included, tax planning opportunities by way of shifting income from the CFC State to an even lower taxed State arise.[82] Moreover, though transparent entities are not specifically included, a transparent entity may be treated as a PE and may be covered by the CFC rule, where condition (ii) is met.

625 The CFC income is generally aittributed to the controlling taxpayer in proportion to the holding/participation in profits as mentiond in m.no. 623 (Art. 8(3) ATAD). Where an entity or PE is deemed a CFC, either of the following rules may be implemented:

a) The Member State of the taxpayer may choose to include certain non-distributed income of the entity or the PE in the tax base of the taxpayer.[83] However, to keep in line with the *Cadbury Schweppes* doctrine, it should be emphasized that this inclusion shall not apply where the CFC carries on a '**substantive economic activity**' supported by staff, equipment, assets and premises per the relevant facts and circumstances. States may choose to not apply this exception where the CFC is situated in a third country outside the European Economic Area (Art. 7(2)(a) ATAD); or

b) The Member State of the taxpayer may choose to include only non-distributed income of the entity or PE arising from **non-genuine arrangements** that have been put in place for the essential purpose of obtaining a tax advantage. An

---

81 For a definition of associated enterprise see Art. 2(4) ATAD.

82 Moser/Hentschel, The Provisions of the EU Anti-Tax Avoidance Directive Regarding Controlled Foreign Company Rules: A Critical Review Based on the Experience with the German CFC Legislation, *Intertax* 2017, pp. 612-613.

83 This list includes interest, royalties, dividends, capital gains, financial income or service income involving associated enterprise transactions without adding much economic value.

arrangement would be considered non-genuine where the CFC would not have owned the assets or undertaken the risks required in generating all or part of its income, were it not controlled by the parent company where significant people functions relating to the assets, risks and generation of income are carried out (Art. 7(2) (b) ATAD).

Depending on which of the above mentioned options is applicable, different computation rules as regards the attributable income (see Art. 8(1) and Art. 8(2) ATAD) and exceptions (Art. 7 (3) and (4) ATAD) apply. In general, Art. 8(1) refers to the domestic corporate tax rules and Art. 8(2) ATAD follows the arm's length principle for such computation.

Where the controlled entity distributes profits or where the taxpayer disposes of a **626** participation in the controlled entity, the tax due on such action shall be calculated by deducting from the tax base the amount that was previously included for the purpose of taxation pursuant to the CFC rules (Art. 8(5) and (6) ATAD). This rule is aimed at **preventing double taxation.**[84] Further, a deduction from tax liability or a credit shall be allowed for the tax paid by the entity or the PE in its State of residence or location, calculated per national law (Art. 8(7) ATAD). In spite of the minimum standard provision (Art. 3 ATAD), the European Commission has taken the view that implementing Art. 8(7) ATAD is an obligation and has commenced infringement proceedings against Belgium for not implementing the measure.[85]

Since the ATAD CFC rule does not provide for specific rules covering multi-tier **627** structures, a CFC may be created even though the income is cumulatively not low-taxed. Finally, it has been pointed out that since CFC rules are broad in nature, leaving room for heterogeneous implementation, numerous possibilities of double taxation may arise.[86]

E. Hybrid Mismatch Rules (Arts. 9, 9a and 9b ATAD)

Hybrid mismatches are situations arising from the **differences in the legal char-** **628** **acterization** of the same instruments, payments or entities per domestic laws of different States. For example: An instrument may be considered as equity in State A and debt in State B. State B treats payments arising out of such instrument to be deductible interest, whereas State A considers such payments to be dividends and allows a participation exemption. The taxpayers enjoy tax favourable treatment in both jurisdictions owing to the difference in qualification of the instrument. Similar mismatches could be created using transparent entities, PEs, dual-resident entities, etc.

---

84   It may, however, be that the amount included in the tax base as CFC income exceeds the actual amount attributable to such actions – thus, not preventing double taxation all together.

85   Commission, July Infringement package: key decisions, 2 July 2020, available at: https://ec.europa.eu/commission/presscorner/detail/en/INF_20_1212 (accessed on 28 July 2020).

86   Soom, Double Taxation Resulting from the ATAD: Is there Relief?, *Intertax* 2020, pp. 276-278.

629 Hybrid mismatch arrangements were dealt with in BEPS Action 2, where best practice proposals were made to tackle such mismatches. Action 2 focused on hybrid mismatches where a deduction is granted in one State, without a corresponding inclusion as taxable income in the other State (hereinafter referred to as 'deduction/non-inclusion'). It also dealt with double deduction situations caused by the use of hybrid or dual-resident entities and imported mismatches. The ATAD provisions on hybrid mismatch arrangements were initially much more limited in scope than the proposals contained in BEPS Action 2. The Commission released a proposal to revise the ATAD on 25 October 2016. Thereby, the Commission aimed to bring the rule in line with the BEPS Action 2 proposals and to extend the scope to mismatches involving third countries. Following discussions and revisions, ATAD 2 was finally enacted on 29 May 2017. In essence, the hybrid mismatch measures can be divided into three groups: a) **deduction/non-inclusion outcomes**, b) **double deduction outcomes** and c) **imported mismatches**.

630 a) Deduction/non-inclusion outcomes

Per Art. 2(9) ATAD, a 'hybrid mismatch' includes outcomes resulting in a deduction in one State without a corresponding inclusion as taxable income in the other. A deduction/non-inclusion may result from hybrid instrument mismatches, hybrid transfers, hybrid entity mismatches, PE mismatches or reverse hybrid mismatches.

631 *Hybrid instrument mismatches*

Hybrid instrument mismatches result from differences in the characterization of a financial instrument or a payment made thereunder where the payment is not included within a reasonable period of time.

Example: A, resident in State A, grants a convertible loan to B, resident in State B. B pays a fixed 'coupon' to A. In State B, the coupon is characterized as interest and deductible, while in State A, the coupon is characterized as an exempted 'dividend' and not included in A's tax base.

Such situations are countered primarily by denying a deduction in the payer jurisdiction. Where such a primary rule is not applied, a defensive rule, which entails inclusion as taxable income in the payee jurisdiction, shall be applied (Art. 9(2) ATAD).

632 *Hybrid transfers*

A hybrid transfer is a transfer of a financial instrument treated differently by two States, following which the States disagree as to whether the transferor or the transferee has ownership of the asset. Deduction/non-inclusion outcomes resulting from a hybrid transfer are neutralized in the same way as hybrid instrument mismatches (Recital 23 ATAD 2).

A hybrid transfer could also be designed to provide for relief from withholding tax on the return from the transferred asset at the level of more than one taxpayer involved. In such a situation, the Member State of the taxpayer shall limit such relief in proportion to the net taxable income regarding such payment (Art. 9(6) ATAD).

Hybrid entity mismatches 633

The ATAD also covers differences in the allocation of payments made to a **hybrid entity** between the jurisdiction where the entity is established and the jurisdiction of any person having a participation in that entity. A '**hybrid entity**' is defined as any entity or arrangement that is regarded as a taxable entity under the laws of one jurisdiction, while treated as transparent under the laws of another jurisdiction.

Example: A partnership established in Member State A makes a payment to its partner residing in State B. State A considers the partnership a taxable entity, whereas Member State B treats the partnership as transparent. Accordingly, State A would deduct the payments from the tax base of the partnership, whereas State B would not tax the payment at the level of the partner since it does not recognize the transaction between the partnership and the partner.

In the above example, the mismatch would be countered primarily by denying the deduction at the level of the partnership in State A (Art. 9(2), ATAD). Where State A does not have such a primary rule, State B may include the payment as taxable income at the level of the partners.

PE mismatches 634

PE mismatches are caused by differences in the allocation of payments between a head office and a PE or between two or more PEs of the same entity per the laws of the jurisdictions where the entity operates. Such mismatches are also resolved by denying the deduction in the payer jurisdiction or, where there is no such rule, including the income in the payee jurisdiction.

Mismatches may also be caused by payments made to a **disregarded PE**. A disregarded PE is defined as an arrangement that is treated as a PE under the laws of the head office jurisdiction but not under the laws of the other jurisdiction.

Example: A company has its head office in State A and establishes a PE in State B. State A attributes income received by the PE to the PE, while State B – disregarding the PE – attributes the receipts to the head office and thus, does not tax them at all. Given that State A and State B have concluded a tax treaty under which the residence State has to exempt foreign PE income, State A will also not tax the receipts.

To the extent that a hybrid mismatch involves disregarded PE income that is not subject to tax in the Member State in which the taxpayer resides, that Member

State shall require the taxpayer to include the income, except where the State is required to exempt the income under a DTC (Art. 9(5) ATAD).

635 *Reverse hybrid mismatches*

In a **reverse hybrid situation,** an entity is transparent in its State of formation and treated as opaque in the State of its shareholder.

Example: Company A in State A has 90% of the voting rights in a subsidiary B in State B. State B treats the subsidiary as transparent, but State A treats it as opaque. Profits may be received by B in State B without tax consequences in either State A or State B.

Subject to the conditions in Art. 9a, the hybrid entity shall be regarded as a resident of the Member State of its shareholder and taxed on its income to the extent it is not otherwise taxed in any other jurisdiction on that income.

636 b) Double deduction outcomes

The ATAD also provides rules on hybrid mismatches resulting from double deductions, e.g. at the level of a head office and a PE.

Example: If company A in State A has a PE in State B that is not recognized in State A, interest payments made by the PE may be deductible in both State B and in State A.

Per Art. 9 ATAD, double deduction outcomes would be countered primarily by a denial of deduction in the investor jurisdiction. Where a deduction in the investor jurisdiction takes place, a defensive rule that entails a denial of a deduction in the payer jurisdiction shall be applied (Art. 9(1) ATAD). The rules only apply to the extent that the payer jurisdiction allows the deduction to be set off against an amount that is not income that is included in both jurisdictions.

637 Double deductions resulting from dual-residence of the taxpayer are dealt with in Art. 9b ATAD: If payments, expenses or losses of a dual-resident taxpayer are deductible in both jurisdictions, the Member State of the taxpayer shall deny the deduction to the extent the other jurisdiction allows the (duplicate) deduction to be set off against income that is not dual-inclusion income. If both jurisdictions are Member States, the taxpayer is deemed to be a resident in the State per the DTC between the two States.

638 c) Imported mismatches

Imported mismatch situations involve importing benefits from a hybrid mismatch arrangement through another related transaction.

Example: A deductible payment under a non-hybrid instrument is used to fund an expenditure in a hybrid mismatch arrangement.

To counter such imported mismatches, a Member State has the right to deny deductions in respect of any payment that directly or indirectly funds deductible expenditure giving rise to a hybrid mismatch through a transaction or series of transactions between associated enterprises or through a structured arrangement. It may not do so where one of the other jurisdictions involved has made an equivalent adjustment to remedy such mismatch (Art. 9(3) ATAD).

IV. Implementation and Application of the ATAD

The ATAD generally had to be transposed into domestic law by the Member **639** States by 31 December 2018. However, longer **transposition periods** applied or may apply as regards certain measures: Member States were given the option to transpose the rules on exit taxation by 31 December 2019. With the ATAD 2, the implementation period for the rules on hybrid mismatches had also been extended to 31 December 2019, while the implementation period for the rules on reverse hybrid mismatches (Art. 9a ATAD) was extended to 31 December 2021. In addition, Member States may apply national interest limitation rules until 1 January 2024, if they are 'equally effective' to those of the ATAD.[87]

The CJEU requires national courts to **interpret national law** as far as possible in **640** conformity with a directive.[88] This obligation becomes particularly relevant where Member States fail to transpose the ATAD into their national laws. However, the CJEU emphasizes in its settled case law that an interpretation of domestic law by referring to a directive must not lead to an interpretation *contra legem*.[89]

A future concern may be whether ATAD measures that are not implemented by **641** Member States within the required period may be given **direct effect**. In this regard, the CJEU repeatedly emphasizes that a directive "*may not of itself impose obligations on a private individual and may not therefore be relied on as such against such a person*".[90] Thus, a directive does not take direct effect to the detriment of the taxpayer. Where the ATAD or parts of it are not transposed into national law, tax authorities may not be able to rely on the provisions in the directive to the disadvantage of the taxpayer. The taxpayer, on the other hand, may rely on the

---

87 In November 2019, the European Commission took the view that Austria and Ireland did not have 'equally effective' interest limitation rules and did not allow such deferral. *See* Commission, November infringements package: key decisions, 27 November 2019, available at: https://ec.europa.eu/commission/presscorner/detail/en/inf_19_6304 (accessed on 28 July 2020).

88 CJEU, 13 November 1990, Case C-106/89, *Marleasing SA v La Comercial Internacional de Alimentacion SA*, EU:C:1990:395, para. 8. *See* also Chapter 1, m no. 16.

89 CJEU, 15 April 2008, Case C-268/06, *Impact*, EU:C:2008:223, para. 100; 21 September 2016, Case C-605/15, *Aviva*, EU:C:2017:718, para. 37; 21 September 2017, Case C-326/15, *DNB Banka*, EU:C: 2017:719, para. 42.

90 CJEU, 22 February 1990, Case C-221/88, *Busseni*, EU:C:1990:84, para. 23; 14 September 2000, Case C-343/98, *Collino*, EU:C:2000:441, para. 20; 21 September 2016, Case C-605/15, *Aviva*, EU:C:2017:718, para. 36. *See also* Chapter 1, m no. 12 et seq.

ATAD provision if advantageous. This is particularly important in the context of the ATAD, as the measures provided therein are predominantly detrimental to the taxpayer and will often lead to a higher tax burden than under national law. Thus, in light of hitherto case law, it might be that the ATAD will have direct effect only in very rare instances since, in respect of a non- or incorrect implementation, the tax authorities are not allowed to rely on the direct effect of the ATAD to the disadvantage of the taxpayer. However, the ATAD also provides for a few rules under which the taxpayer may, in concrete cases, receive advantageous treatment, such as the 'step up' rule used in the exit tax provision (see m.no. 609). The taxpayer may thus, rely on the direct effect of these provisions in case of non- or incorrect implementation.

642 The direct effect of the ATAD is further restricted by the CJEU's case law under which the taxpayer is not allowed to take advantage of EU provisions 'improperly or fraudulently.[91] Since the ATAD aims at countering such actions, it may – depending on the circumstances involved – neither be relied on by the tax authorities, nor by the taxpayer.

643 For interpretation purposes, as well as for purposes of the direct effect, the 'minimum standard' provision may be relied on by States to claim that existing or newly introduced domestic law is merely an over-implementation of the ATAD as allowed by Art. 3.

V. Interaction with EU Primary law

A. Enacting a Directive Dealing with Abuse in Direct Taxation

644 The EU has no exclusive competence in the area of direct taxation. Consequently, harmonization in direct taxation has, apart from a few exceptions,[92] not taken place as yet. The ATAD takes the EU one step forward in achieving harmonization in the area of corporate taxation.

645 The legal basis for the **legislative competence** of the EU to enact the ATAD is Art. 115 TFEU. This provision allows for secondary measures in direct taxation if – in addition to certain procedural conditions – the measure contributes to the **functioning of the internal market**.[93] The relevance of the ATAD to the functioning

---

91 CJEU, 12 September 2006, Case C-196/04, *Cadbury Schweppes and Cadbury Schweppes Overseas*, EU:C:2006:544, para. 35. See also the decision of the CJEU in *Cussens* concerning VAT wherein the CJEU refers to a *"principle that abusive practices are prohibited"* (CJEU, 22 November 2017, Case C-251/16, *Cussens*, EU:C:2017:881, para. 30).

92 The CCCTB Directive proposal is the most significant attempt to change this situation (European Commission, Proposal for a Council Directive on a Common Consolidated Corporate Tax Base (CCCTB), COM(2011) 121 final of 16 March 2011). *See* Chapter 2 m no. 132 et seqq.

93 *See* Chapter 1 m no. 32.

of the internal market has been called into question in literature:[94] In contrast to former directives in the field of direct taxation, the ATAD does not aim to reduce barriers within the internal market, but rather allows Member States to exercise their tax sovereignty in the area of abuse. The preamble to the ATAD explicitly claims that the ATAD contributes to the functioning of the internal market and emphasizes that the ATAD aims to prevent fragmentation of the market by coordinating efforts to counteract tax avoidance and ensures **fair taxation** and **taxation where value is created**. Since a heterogeneous implementation of BEPS measures amongst the Member States may arguably have led to further fragmentation and thus to increasing compliance costs for taxpayers, the ATAD may complement the functioning of the internal market.

B. Interaction with the Fundamental Freedoms

In principle, the provisions of ATAD aim to prevent or mitigate tax avoidance **646** and aggressive tax planning within the EU. The ATAD measures must, however, be in line with the fundamental freedoms and thus, must not discriminate against cross-border situations. Compared to violations of primary law by national measures, CJEU case law, to date, points towards a rather reluctant approach when examining the compatibility of secondary law with primary law.[95] Hitherto case law may nevertheless be applied in the context of ATAD measures or vice versa be reconsidered in light of the measures adopted implemeting the ATAD.

In principle, a proceeding before the CJEU may concern the provisions of the ATAD **647** itself or the national law implementing the measure, depending on whether the particular provision in the ATAD provides for **exhaustive harmonization**. As regards the review of national measures in light of EU law, the CJEU has clarified that national measures in an area that is exhaustively harmonized must be assessed in light of the harmonizing measure, and not in light of the provisions of primary law.[96] Hence, where a directive provides for exhaustive harmonization, national measures may be reviewed only in light of the directive and violations of primary law may be ascribed to the corresponding provision in the directive. Where secondary law does not lead to exhaustive harmonization, the national measure may not only be assessed with respect to its compatibility with the directive, but also with primary law. This was, for example, the case in the decision in *Euro Park Service*,[97]

---

94 *See* De Graaf/Visser, ATA Directive: Some Observations Regarding Formal Aspects, *EC Tax Rev.* 2016, p. 203; Govind/Lazarov, Carpet-Bombing Tax Avoidance in Europe: Examining the Validity of the ATAD Under EU Law, *Intertax*, 2019, p. 852.
95 See in this regard CJEU, 15 June 1994, Case C-137/92 P, *Commission v BASF and Others*, EU:C:1994: 247; para. 48; 5 October 2004, Case C-245/92 P *Chemie Linz v Commission*, para. 93; 5 October 2004, Case C-475/01, *Commission v the Hellenic Republic*, EU:C:2004:585, para. 18, wherein the CJEU states that measures of the EU are *"presumed to be lawful."*
96 CJEU, 8 September 2017, Case C-14/16, *Euro Park Service*, EU:C:2017:177, para. 19; 7 September 2017, Case C-6/16, *Eqiom*, EU:C:2017:641, para. 15; 20 December 2017, Joined Cases C-504/16 and C-613/16, *Deister Holding and Juhler Holding*, EU:C:2017:1009, para. 45.
97 CJEU, 8 March 2017, Case C-14/16, *Euro Park Service*, EU:C:2017:177, paras. 22 and 24.

wherein the CJEU considered the anti-abuse provision in the Merger Directive as non-exhaustive, emphasizing that the provision does not provide for more details, thus leaving the adoption of modalities up to the Member States. In the end, the CJEU concluded that the national measure was neither compatible with the directive, nor with primary law. Following this reasoning, national measures implementing the ATAD may – depending on the degree of harmonization – be assessed not only in light of the ATAD but also in light of primary law. The minimum standard provision may play a major role in this respect: Where national measures go beyond the minimum standard set up in the ATAD, a Member State exercises its discretion provided for in the ATAD, rather than transposing exhaustive harmonized secondary law measures. Such national provisions that are within the discretion of the Member States can thus be (directly) assessed in light of primary law.

648　Especially where measures apply only to cross-border situations, such as the exit tax rules or the CFC rules, a restriction of the fundamental freedoms seems to be important to consider. Restrictions may nevertheless be compatible with the fundamental freedoms if they can be justified on the grounds of a **legitimate objective**. Prominent examples of justifying objectives in the area of direct taxation are the **safeguarding of a balanced allocation of taxing rights** and the **coherence** of the national legal system. In the case of ATAD measures, the most obvious legitimate objective is most likely the **prevention of abusive practices**.[98] In its settled case law on the freedom of establishment, the CJEU considers measures justified by the prevention of tax avoidance only if they specifically target 'wholly artificial arrangements'.[99] As regards the process of qualifying an arrangement as abusive, the CJEU rejects predetermined general criteria and requires that an individual examination of the whole arrangement take place.[100] Further, the CJEU does not allow for rules that do not even require the tax authorities to provide for prima facie evidence.[101]

Interest limitation Rules

649　The interest limitation rules and, in particular, a possible implementation of the group ratio rule applying only to entities within one State, as proposed in Recital 7, may be assessed in light of the fundamental freedoms:[102] Domestic members of a group would then be treated as one taxpayer for the purposes of the interest limi-

---

98　See Section III. C of this Chapter.

99　See CJEU, 7 November 2013, Case C-322/11, *K*, EU:C:2013:716, para. 62, wherein the Court ignored the objective of tax avoidance since the legislation was not "*specifically intended to prevent wholly artificial arrangements*" (emphasis added) but was directed at a very general situation. Similar in CJEU, 7 September 2017, Case C-6/16, *Eqiom*, EU:C:2017:641, para. 30; 20 December 2017, Joined Cases C-504/16 and C-613/16, *Deister Holding and Juhler Holding*, EU:C:2017:1009, para. 60.

100　CJEU, 7 September 2017, Case C-6/16, *Eqiom*, EU:C:2017:641, para. 32; 20 December 2017, Joined Cases C-504/16 and C-613/16, *Deister Holding and Juhler Holding*, EU:C:2017:1009, para. 62.

101　CJEU, 7 September 2017, Case C-6/16, *Eqiom*, EU:C:2017:641, para. 36; 20 December 2017, Joined Cases C-504/16 and C-613/16, *Deister Holding and Juhler Holding*, EU:C:2017:1009, para. 62.

102　See e.g. Douma, EU report: BEPS and European Union Law Vol 1, *IFA Cahiers* 2017, pp. 77-78. The OECD acknowledged this as a concern in the public discussion draft on BEPS Action 4.

tation rule. As a result, the interest limitation rule could not apply to interest payments between the domestic group members. The rule may be considered to favour domestic situations as opposed to identical cross-border situations. Similar concerns become especially evident from the CJEU's decision of 22 February 2018 on the joint cases *X BV* and *X NV*. [103] The Netherlands' legislation prohibited an interest deduction in respect of a loan taken out in order to finance a capital contribution to a subsidiary. However, the rule did not apply where two companies 'form a single entity', an option available only to domestic companies. The CJEU found that this different treatment of domestic and cross-border companies violated the freedom of establishment and could not be justified.

In light of this decision, there may be concerns as regards possible implementation of the option in Art. 4(1) (a) ATAD allowing Member States to treat a group as **one** entity per national law if they do not allow the inclusion of foreign companies in a group. In such a situation, the interest limitation rule will factually not apply to transactions within the group, while a company with a foreign subsidiary is fully subjected to the limitation rule. A justification of the interest limitation rule on the basis of the need to prevent tax avoidance seems difficult in light of the parallels to the *X BV* case (see m.no. 649) and the fact that the interest limitation applies in a general manner, i.e. regardless of whether a taxpayer acts abusively.[104] **650**

Exit Taxes

It has been pointed out that the exit tax rules seem to be questionable where realized gains on certain assets are not subject to taxation in the Member State of departure at all.[105] In such cases, the Member State of departure faces an obligation imposed by the ATAD to apply an exit tax notwithstanding the national legal treatment of similar realized assets. It is thus possible that a gain arising from the sale of an asset might not be subjected to tax by national law, while at the same time the ATAD provides for an obligation to tax such an asset if the requirements of Art. 5 of the ATAD are met. Imposing an exit tax on certain assets while not taxing similar realized gains in a purely domestic context may constitute a disproportionate restriction of the freedom of establishment.[106] A possible solution for a Member State to avoid potential discrimination issues could be the applcation of a zero-exit tax rate to such situations. **651**

Art. 5 ATAD does not take into account decreases in value arising after the transfer. Similar concerns have already been discussed in previous CJEU proceedings: In *N*,[107] on exit tax imposed on natural persons, the CJEU considered such exit tax **652**

---

103 See CJEU, 22 February 2018, Joined Cases C-398/16 and C-399/16, *X BV and X NV*, EU:C:2018:110.
104 Smit, The Anti-Tax-Avoidance Directive (ATAD) in: Terra/Wattel (eds.), *European Tax Law* (2019), p. 504.
105 Peeters, Exit Taxation: From an Internal Market Barrier to a Tax Avoidance Prevention Tool, *EC Tax Rev.* 2017, p. 122 at 130.
106 Ibid.
107 CJEU, 7. September 2006, Case C-470/04, *N*, EU:C:2006:525, para. 54 et seq.

rules to be a violation of the freedom of establishment. Despite the fact that, unlike Art. 5 ATAD, the *N* case concerned a natural person, the decision in *N* conflicts with the CJEU's position in subsequent decisions such as *National Grid Indus*[108] and *Kommission/Portugal*,[109] wherein the CJEU took the position that national exit tax rules that do not take decreases in value occurring after the transfer of a company's place of effective management into account can be justified. Thus, in light of this case law, the primary law requirements on exit tax rules arising from *N* seem to have been lowered.

GAAR

653 The CJEU has elaborated on the concept of tax avoidance in a large number of cases concerning violations of the fundamental freedoms (see m.no. 614 et seqq.). Therein, preventing tax evasion and tax avoidance is mentioned as a justifying objective. Since the GAAR in the ATAD is meant to be a codification of the CJEU's case law,[110] the CJEU's case law on the fundamental freedoms may nevertheless play a pivotal role in the interpretation of the ATAD.

654 Generally, the GAAR applies equally to purely internal situations and cross-border situations. However, the GAAR may in specific cases be applied in such a way that it targets cross-border arrangements more than domestic arrangements. This may give rise to concerns as to whether it constitutes a restriction on the fundamental freedoms.[111] In such cases, it may be important to analyse whether the GAAR, as implemented by Member States and applied by courts and the tax authorities, indeed fulfils the requirements set out in the settled case law of the CJEU.

CFC Rules

655 The CJEU has discussed the compliance of CFC rules with the fundamental freedoms in several cases, the most prominent example being the decision in *Cadbury Schweppes*. Therein, the CJEU took the position that CFC rules involve a difference in the treatment of resident companies based on the level of taxation imposed on the company in which they have a controlling holding. Such a disadvantageous treatment cannot be justified by the objective of preventing abusive practices, unless it relates only to *"wholly artificial arrangements which do not*

---

108   CJEU, 29 November 2011, Case C-371/10, *National Grid Indus*, EU:C:2011:785, para. 56.
109   CJEU, 21 December 2016, Case C-503/14, *European Commission v Portuguese Republic*, EU:C:2016: 979.
110   See Commission Staff Working Document, Accompanying the document Communication from the Commission to the European Parliament and the Council Anti-Tax Avoidance Package: Next Steps towards delivering effective taxation and greater tax transparency in the EU, SWD (2016) 6 final 28: "*The proposed GAAR provides for the artificiality tests present in the case law*".
111   For instance, *see* Decision No. 8165/16.06.2014, Case No. 11534/2013 of the Supreme Administrative Court of Bulgaria wherein the application of the GAAR to a cross-border structure, in circumstances in which it would not have applied in respect of an identical domestic structure, was found to be restrictive of the fundamental freedoms.

reflect economic reality, with a view to escaping the tax normally due on the profits generated by activities carried out on national territory."[112] The CJEU also emphasized that the controlled company should carry out a *"genuine economic activity"* for an arrangement to not be classified as 'wholly artificial' and that such a finding should be supported by objective, determinable factors such as physical existence in terms of premises, staff and equipment.[113]

Art. 7(2) and Recital 12 seem to replicate the *Cadbury Schweppes* criteria: Under **656** the option included in Art. 7(2)(a), the application of the CFC rule is denied where the controlled company carries on a '**substantive economic activity' supported by premises, staff and equipment.** The wording does not correspond to the wording used by the CJEU in *Cadbury Schweppes,* i.e. 'genuine economic activity'. However, the provision refers to 'premises, staff and equipment' as required by the CJEU and the term 'substantive' should be broad enough to allow for an interpretation in line with the CJEU case law. The second option provided in Art. 7(2)(b) adopts an **'essential purpose' test** in respect of **non-genuine arrangements**. Under this provision, an arrangement is non-genuine if two conditions are met. First, the entity or PE involved should not own the assets or should not have undertaken the risks that generate all, or part of, its income if it were not controlled by another company. Second, the significant people functions, which are relevant to those assets and risks and instrumental in generating the income of the entity or the PE must be carried out by the controlling company. This differs from the CJEU's approach of determining genuineness based on the mere existence of objective factors such as premises, staff and equipment in the CFC State. Furthermore, when testing whether an arrangement is wholly artificial, the requirements set out in the decision in *Eqiom* and *Deister* [114] need to be fulfilled as discussed above.

As regards **third-country situations**, it is questionable whether companies can **657** rely on the free movement of capital rule. This is because rules applying **only** to shareholdings *"which enable the holder to exert a definite influence on a company's decisions and to determine its activities"* generally fall within the scope of the freedom of establishment as opposed to the free movement of capital, thereby protecting only EU nationals.[115] However, where the freedom of establishment does not apply, which may be the case specifically where a Member State uses Art. 3 to allow smaller shareholdings to apply the CFC rules (as is allowed under CFC rules

---

112 CJEU, 12 September 2006, Case C-196/04, *Cadbury Schweppes and Cadbury Schweppes Overseas,* EU:C:2006:544, para. 55.
113 CJEU, 12 September 2006, Case C-196/04, *Cadbury Schweppes and Cadbury Schweppes Overseas,* EU:C:2006:544, paras. 54 and 67.
114 CJEU, 20 December 2017, Joined Cases C-504/16 and C-613/16, *Deister Holding and Juhler Holding,* EU:C:2017:1009.
115 CJEU, 13 November 2912, C-35/11, *Test Claimants in the FII Group Litigation,* EU:C:2012:707, para. 91. *See also* Chapter 3, m no. 213 et seq.

in several Member States at present) or where the CFC rules apply owing to the profit share and not based on the holding, the free movement of capital may be called into question.[116]

Hybrid Mismatch

658   The hybrid mismatch provisions raise interesting questions as regards compatibility with the fundamental freedoms since they apply **only** in cross-border situations and can result in denial of deductions or compensatory inclusion of income only in such situations. In contrast, identical domestic arrangements would not be subject to such actions. Since hybrid mismatches arise owing to **different characterizations in different Member States,** the circumstances cannot arise in a purely domestic situation and it may be argued that the purely domestic situation and the cross-border situation are not comparable,[117] for example, due to differences in the legal circumstances or in light of the aim of the hybrid mismatch rules.

C. Interaction with the Charter of Fundamental Rights of the European Union

659   The Charter of Fundamental Rights of the European Union is another instrument of **primary law** that imposes limits on measures of secondary law and national law. The Charter came into force with effect from 1 December 2009. However, as the Charter only applies where EU law is implemented (Art. 51 of the Charter), it has so far played only a minor role in the area of direct taxation. With the ATAD, the Charter is gaining increasing relevance in the area of direct taxation, leading to additional requirements as regards corporate income tax provisions reflecting ATAD measures.

660   The most significant freedom to mention in relation to the ATAD may be the **equality principle** in Art. 20 of the Charter. This provision is a codification of the unwritten principle of equality established in the CJEU's case law. In contrast to the fundamental freedoms, Art. 20 of the Charter tackles not only discrimination against taxpayers with cross-border activities but also discrimination against domestic taxpayers provided that the national measure falls within the implementation of EU law. Hence, the equality principle can – unlike the fundamental freedoms – also be invoked where ATAD measures create inequalities between purely domestic situations. The ATAD, in fact, creates the risk of unequal treatment as it only applies to entities subject to corporate tax but not to natural persons,

---

116   See CJEU, 10 February 2012, Joined Cases C-436/08 and C-437/08, *Haribo*, ECLI:EU:C:2011:61, 34 et seq. *See* also the EFTA Court decision in *Fred Olsen* wherein such CFC rules in Norway were found to be in conflict with the free movement of capital provision in the EEA agreement (EFTA Court, 9 July 2014, Joined Cases E-3/13 and E-20/13, *Fred Olsen and ors*).

117   Fibbe, *EC Aspects of Hybrid Entities* (2009).

thus providing for disadvantageous treatment of corporations solely owed to the legal form. Arguably, however, natural persons and corporations may not be in comparable situations as regards the need to combat aggressive tax planning or tax avoidance.

In addition to the substantive provisions, the Charter has also an effect on **procedural law** applied in connection with the ATAD or applied in proceedings concerning such measures. E.g. Art. 47 of the Charter on the right to an effective remedy and to a fair trial may play a major role in the future application of procedural law provisions or such proceedings. **661**

Yet, the CJEU has applied the Charter in very rare cases concerning taxation. Although some of the fundamental rights included in the Charter already existed in EU law as unwritten general principles prior to the Charter, the codification of these rights in the form of the Charter may give them more visibility. While various Member States have (constitutional) national laws that provide for similar rights as the Charter, the Charter offers additional protection. For example, a taxpayer may rely on both protection under Art. 20 of the Charter and on protection by a national constitutional right to equality, given that the scope of each is fulfilled. Where national courts interpret the constitutional right to equality restrictively, the taxpayer may be successful in a proceeding before the CJEU by invoking Art. 20 of the Charter. **662**

D. Interaction with State Aid Rules

In addition to the fundamental freedoms and the Charter, Art. 107 TFEU on **State aid** rules also provides for restrictions on state measures. The limitations of the State aid rules apply – unlike the fundamental freedoms and the Charter – not to secondary law measures, but solely to aid granted by the Member States. Unlike the fundamental freedoms and the Charter, provisions of the ATAD should be implemented in such a way that they do not constitute unlawful State aid.[118] Generally, an advantage, including an exemption from taxation that is not imputable to a State but stems from an act of the EU does not qualify as aid.[119] Member States acting per the dictate of secondary law, such as the ATAD, may hence generally not be considered to provide State aid. Recital 8 seems to refer to this effect, stating that the ATAD not only foresees the implementation of interest limitation rules but also allows the Member States to introduce exceptions, such as for loans used to fund long-term public infrastructure projects, without prejudice to State aid rules.[120] **663**

---

118 *See* Chapter 4, m.no. 325 et seqq. on the conditions for State aid.
119 CJEU, 5 April 2006, Case T-351/02, *Deutsche Bahn AG*, EU:T:2006:104, para. 101 et seq and the case law cited therein.
120 In the context of the ATAD, it may however also be argued that the States are exercising their choice in applying certain exemptions that may create State aid in the context of their tax system.

664   State aid concerns may nevertheless arise where Member States make use of the possibility to go beyond the minimum standard or where a Member State fails to implement or apply an ATAD provision correctly. For example, investigations by the Commission on tax rulings elucidated that even the failure to apply the GAAR in specific situations may lead to State aid concerns.[121]

VI. Interaction with Secondary Law

665   Alongside the ATAD, there are several other directives regulating matters of direct taxation.[122] The ATAD may, in certain situations, lead to a denial of benefits arising from these directives, e.g. when applying the GAAR. Notably, there is **no general hierarchy** between secondary law measures.

666   Art. 1(4) of the Parent-Subsidiary Directive explicitly states that it does not preclude other instruments required for the prevention of fraud, evasion or abuse. A similar provision is contained in Art. 5 of the Interest and Royalties Directive. In light thereof, it appears that in relation to these two directives, the measures provided for in the ATAD may prevail, depending on whether they are 'required' for the prevention of abuse. However, Recital 30 of ATAD 2 specifically provides that where the Parent-Subsidiary Directive applies, there is no room for applying the hybrid mismatch rules in the ATAD.[123]

667   The Merger Directive does not contain a provision similar to those mentioned in m.no. 666, which is why the relationship to the ATAD requires discussion: The Merger Directive only concerns **legal transfers** of assets as a result of a reorganization, while the exit tax rules of the ATAD generally apply to **physical transfers** of assets.[124] The GAAR in Art. 15 of the Merger Directive is optional, while the one in the ATAD is obligatory for Member States. Despite the option in the Merger Directive, Member States are thus obliged to introduce the GAAR in the ATAD.

The Mutual Assistance Directive may also have an interesting interaction with the ATAD since States may use information gathered under this Directive to enforce action under the measures implemented pursuant to the ATAD.

668   Where the directives do not contain specific rules that determine their relationships, potential conflicts may generally be avoided by means of interpretation. Remaining conflicts between the ATAD and other directives may be solved with

---

121   *See* Chapter 4, m.no. 310 et seq.
122   *See* Chapters 5, 6 and 7.
123   *See* Chapter 5, m.no. 466. However, if the anti-hybrid rule in the Paret-Subsidiary Directive and the anti-hybrid rules in the ATAD are read harmoniously, there should be no conflict. This is because the former rule only allows for inclusion where a deduction is allowed, similar to the latter rule, under which denial of a deduction is the primary rule and allowing for inclusion is the defensive rule where a deduction is allowed.
124   See Chapter 6, m.nos. 508.

different instruments, such as the *lex posterior* rule, under which the later law takes precedence over the earlier law, or the *lex specialis* rule, under which a more specific law takes precedence over a general law rule. These are rules of national and international law for solving norm conflicts. While the *"lex posterior"* rule has not played a substantial role in hitherto case law, the CJEU referred to *lex specialis* in several decisions.[125] Another means of solving conflicts of law may be an analysis of the proportionality of the conflicting norms.

VII. Concluding Remarks

In general, the ATAD aims to pursue coordinated action against aggressive tax **669** planning and tax avoidance in the EU, in both domestic and cross-border situations, including cases involving third countries. While some of the rules are **inspired by the BEPS Project**, others, such as the GAAR and the exit tax rules were created rather independently from BEPS, **reflecting the CJEU's case law.**

The ATAD has a great impact on the current landscape of EU law on direct taxa- **670** tion. Despite its harmonizing objective, the ATAD does not lead to full harmonization in the area of combating aggressive tax planning and abusive practices in corporate taxation. This becomes particularly evident from the 'minimum standard' provision and the various options provided for the Member States, which may also result in **heterogeneous implementation** of the ATAD, going against the base motive of coordinated action in this area. This is, for example, evident in the differences in implementation of CFC rules by the Member States.[126] The ATAD also contains several terms that are not defined (yet) and may also lead to heterogeneous application of some measures.[127]

In light thereof, concerns as regards the competence of the EU to enact the ATAD, **671** as well as the compatibility of the ATAD with primary law, were raised in literature. As time passes, the CJEU may be called into action to clarify these issues. Moreover, the scope of the ATAD, the impact of its measures on the taxpayer and the obligations imposed on the Member States will need to be defined by the CJEU in the future. As evident from *N Luxembourg 1*, this may also mean that the position of the CJEU as regards anti-abuse in direct taxation may be affected by the enactment of the ATAD.

---

125 CJEU, 3 July 2012, Case C-128/11, *UsedSoft*, EU:C:2012:407, para. 56; 23 November 2014, Case C-355/12, *Nintendo*, EU:C:2014:25; 30 April 2014, Case C-280/13, *Barclays Bank SA*, EU:C:2014:279, para. 44.
126 *See* in general, Lang et al. (eds.), *Implementing Key BEPS Actions: Where Do We Stand?* (2018).
127 For example, 'participation' in Art. 7, which may lead to double CFC attribution if two different tests are fulfilled by two different 'controlling entities'. However, per Moser/Hentschel, The Provisions of the EU Anti-Tax Avoidance Directive Regarding Controlled Foreign Company Rules: A Critical Review Based on the Experience with the German CFC Legislation, *Intertax* 2017, p. 611, a harmonious interpretation of this provision should lead to attributable income being linked to profit participation irrespective of which test triggers the creation of the CFC.

672 Although the ATAD represents a clear step forward in the fight against aggressive tax planning and tax avoidance in the EU, it may still not lead to an end to such practices. Eventually, the ATAD may even give rise to different tax avoidance practices. This becomes evident from the scope of the ATAD, which is restricted to persons subject to corporate tax. Changing the nature of the controlling entity or setting up controlling companies in low-tax countries may, for instance, help to avoid CFC rules.[128] It remains to be seen whether Member States will use the GAAR to also attack situations of tax planning, which are not covered by the ATAD, or only take advantage of it by filling loopholes left from the specific rules in the ATAD.

673 Therefore, the ATAD deserves a close and intricate study to ensure that the different layers of complexity and uncertainty are unravelled as we progress.

Literature

Balco, ATAD 2: Anti-Tax Avoidance Directive, *ET* 2017, p. 127; Blum, Controlled Foreign Companies: Selected Policy Issues – or the Missing Elements of BEPS Action 3 and the Anti-Tax Avoidance Directive, *Intertax* 2018, p. 298; Cordewener, Anti-Abuse Measures in the Area of Direct Taxation: Towards Converging Standards Under Treaty Freedoms and EU Directives?, *EC Tax Rev.* 2017, p. 60 et seq.; de Broe, *International Tax Planning and Prevention of Abuse* (2008); de Broe/Beckers, The General Anti-Abuse Rule of the Anti-Tax Avoidance Directive: An Analysis Against the Wider Perspective of the European Court of Justice's Case Law on Abuse of EU Law, *EC Tax Rev.* 2017, p. 113, at 143; De Graaf/Visser, ATA Directive: Some Observations Regarding Formal Aspects, *EC Tax Rev.* 2016, p. 203; Docclo, The European Union's Ambition to Harmonize Rules to Counter the Abuse of Member States' Disparate Tax Legislations, *BIT* 2017, p. 368; Douma, EU report: BEPS and European Union Law Vol 1, *IFA Cahiers* 2017, pp. 77-78; Dourado/de la Feria, Thin Capitalization and Outbound Investment, in Thin Capitalization Rules in the Context of the CCCTB, in: Lang et al. (eds.), *Common Consolidation Corporate Tax Base* (2008) pp. 381–382; Eisenberg/Ramello, Comparative Law and Economics (2016) p. 464; Fibbe, *EC Aspects of Hybrid Entities* (2009); Govind/Lazarov, Carpet-Bombing Tax Avoidance in Europe: Examining the Validity of the ATAD Under EU Law, *Intertax*, 2019, p. 852; Moser/Hentschel, The Provisions of the EU Anti-Tax Avoidance Directive Regarding Controlled Foreign Company Rules: A Critical Review Based on the Experience with the German CFC Legislation, *Intertax* 2017, p. 612; Peeters, Exit Taxation: From an Internal Market Barrier to a Tax Avoidance Prevention Tool, *EC Tax Rev.* 2017, p. 122; Smit, The Anti-Tax-Avoidance Directive (ATAD) in: Terra/Wattel (eds.), *European Tax Law* (2019); Soom, Double Taxation Resulting from the ATAD: Is

---

128 Smit, The Anti-Tax-Avoidance Directive (ATAD) in: Terra/Wattel (eds.), *European Tax Law* (2019).

there Relief?, *Intertax* 2020, p. 273; Terra/Wattel, *European Tax Law* (2019) p. 23; Van Os, Interest Limitation under the Adopted Anti-Tax Avoidance Directive and Proportionality, *EC Tax Rev.* 2016/4, p. 191.

Legal Basis: Council Directive 2016/1164 of 12 July 2016 laying down rules against tax avoidance practices that directly affect the functioning of the internal market, OJ L 193/1 of 19 July 2016; Council Directive (EU) 2017/952 of 29 May 2017 amending Directive (EU) 2016/1164 as regards hybrid mismatches with third countries, OJ L 144 of 7 June 2017.

Chapter 9 – Mutual Assistance in Direct Tax Matters

Michael Schilcher/Karoline Spies/Sabine Zirngast

I. The Directive on Administrative Cooperation in the Field of Direct Taxation

A. Background and History

The first Directive on mutual assistance in the assessment of taxes in the field of **674** direct taxation entered into force in December 1977.[1] The Directive was drafted with a view to providing for an efficient exchange of information between the Member States in order to counter new forms of tax evasion and avoidance, which are increasingly assuming a multinational character.[2] This first Directive provided a framework for exchange of information **on request only** and was **revised several times.**

In 2003, the Council adopted Directive 2003/48/EC (hereinafter: the **Savings** **675** **Directive**),[3] which was aimed at effective taxation of cross-border interest payments in the State of residence of individuals. This ultimate aim was achieved by introducing obligatory and **automatic exchange of information** at regular intervals for the first time. The focus on more pro-active automatic exchange of information, instead of request-based exchange, started in 2009 and got a strong boost in 2014, driven by international developments.

In 2011, provoked by successive financial crises, the Council adopted a **completely** **676** **new Directive on Administrative Cooperation** in the field of taxation (hereinafter: "**DAC**").[4] The DAC improved effectiveness in many areas: in particular, mandatory automatic exchange was introduced in areas other than interest payments (see m.no. 707 et seq.) and bank secrecy could no longer justify refusing information requests (see m.no. 748). Since then, the DAC has been amended several times to address specific challenges Member States' tax administrations were facing. The amending Directives are known as DAC 2 to DAC 6.

In 2014, the Council agreed on **DAC 2,** which introduced **automatic exchange of** **677** **financial account information** (see m.no. 707 et seq.).[5] The driving force behind these developments was international pressure by the OECD, as well as the US, for more efficient exchange of information in order to tackle tax avoidance and evasion. Under the Foreign Account Tax Compliance Act (**FATCA**), published in 2010, the US is requiring foreign financial institutions around the world to

---

1   Council Directive 77/799/EEC of 19 December 1977 concerning mutual assistance by the competent authorities of the Member States in the field of direct taxation and taxation of insurance premiums, OJ L 336 of 27 December 1977.

2   Preamble to Council Directive 77/799/EEC of 19 December 1977.

3   Council Directive 2003/48/EC of 3 June 2003 on taxation of savings income in the form of interest payments, OJ L 157/38 of 26 June 2003. The legal basis for this Directive was Art. 94 EC (now Art. 115 TFEU).

4   Council Directive 2011/16/EU of 15 February 2011 on administrative cooperation in the field of taxation and repealing Directive 77/799/EEC, OJ L 64/1 of 11 March 2011.

5   Council Directive 2014/107/EU of 9 December 2014 amending Directive 2011/16/EU as regards mandatory automatic exchange of information in the field of taxation, OJ L 359/1 of 16 December 2014.

provide the US tax authorities with information regarding US clients. Inspired by the US approach, the OECD developed a Standard for Automatic Exchange of Financial Account Information (hereinafter: "**Common Reporting Standard**", CRS) in 2014. Finally, in 2014 and 2015, 61 jurisdictions (including 24 EU Member States) signed a multilateral competent authority agreement on exchange of financial account information, committing themselves to the automatic exchange of financial account information as from 2017/2018.[6] In order to avoid parallel and uncoordinated agreements between the Member States, a Union-wide harmonization of automatic exchange of financial data resting with banks was seen as indispensable. The provisions of DAC 2 were implemented by the Member States **by 1 January 2016** (see m.nos. 690 and 710). To avoid duplication and overlapping EU legislation in the area of financial account information, the Savings Directive was repealed (see m.no. 814).

678 In 2015, the Council adopted **DAC 3**, which introduced **automatic exchange of tax rulings** (see m.no. 714 et seq.).[7] This Directive was part of the **Tax Transparency Package**,[8] which represented the Commission's reaction to the "**Luxembourg leaks**" case (public exposure of preferential rulings granted to multinationals by Luxembourg tax authorities; on the State aid issue in this regard see Chapter 4, m.no. 311 et seq.). Only a few days prior to the adoption of DAC 3, the OECD/G20 had also reached political agreement that automatic exchange of rulings on a global basis is needed to fight harmful tax practices (OECD BEPS Action 5).[9]

679 In 2016, the Council agreed on **DAC 4,** introducing **automatic exchange of Country-by-Country reports** ("**CbC reports**"; see m.no. 722 et seq.).[10] The aim of this amending directive is to oblige **multinational enterprise groups (MNE groups)** to report annually important key figures for each tax jurisdiction in which they do business. This reform also has its roots in global developments. Automatic exchange of CbC reports is part of the minimum standard of OECD BEPS Action 13.[11] As of December 2019, 84 States have signed the Multilateral Competent Authority Agreement on the Exchange of CbC reports (**CbC MCAA**) to implement automatic exchange of CbC reporting on a global basis.[12]

---

6   See in detail http://www.oecd.org/tax/exchange-of-tax-information/multilateral-competent-authority-agreement.htm (accessed on 6 March 2020).

7   Council Directive (EU) 2015/2376 of 8 December 2015 amending Directive 2011/16/EU as regards mandatory automatic exchange of information in the field of taxation, OJ L 332/1 of 18 December 2015.

8   Communication of 18 March 2015 from the Commission to the European Parliament and the Council on tax transparency to fight tax evasion and avoidance, COM(2015) 136 final.

9   OECD/G20, BEPS Action Plan, Final Report on Action 5: Countering Harmful Tax Practices More Effectively (2015) p. 45 et seq.

10   Council Directive (EU) 2016/881 of 25 May 2016 amending Directive 2011/16/EU as regards mandatory automatic exchange of information in the field of taxation, OJ L 146/8 of 3 June 2016.

11   OECD/G20, BEPS Action Plan, Final Report on Action 13: Guidance on Transfer Pricing Documentation and Country-by-Country Reporting (2015) p. 29 et seq.

12   See www.oecd.org/tax/beps/country-by-country-reporting.htm (accessed on 10 February 2020).

The Council, also in 2016, agreed on **DAC 5,** which, in contrast to previous amend- **680**
ing directives, does not broaden the scope of automatic exchange of information but rather ensures that tax authorities have access to beneficial ownership
information collected pursuant to the **anti-money laundering** legislation (see also
m.no. 708).[13]

In 2018, the Council adopted **DAC 6,** which implements a **mandatory disclosure** **681**
regime (MDR) for potentially aggressive tax planning schemes, combined with
automatic exchange of the disclosed arrangements between Member States (see in
more detail m.no. 729 et seq.).[14] Again, this amending directive is linked to international developments, namely OECD BEPS Action 12, which aims to enable tax
authorities and legislatures to quickly respond to tax revenue risks by providing
early access to relevant information.[15]

Moreover, in 2016, the Commission also proposed to make CbC reports of MNE **682**
groups publicly available (**public CbC reporting**).[16] According to this proposal,
MNEs would need to publish key information on where they make their profits
and where they pay their tax on a country-by-country basis, which should give
the public society the possibility to scrutinize the tax behaviour of multinationals.
It has been proposed to include these provisions in the Accounting Directive[17]
(not the DAC). The proposed change to the Accounting Directive is based on
Art. 50(1) TFEU (rather than Art. 115 TFEU). Thus, the proposed directive needs
to be adopted by the **European Parliament and the Council by qualified majority**
voting (rather than unanimity!). Due to the close connection of the public CbC
proposal to the area of tax law, it is disputed whether Art. 50 TFEU requiring
majority voting only is the suitable legal basis.[18] After three years of discussions in
the Council and the Parliament, no political agreement could be reached. Some
Member States fear that public CbC reporting could conflict with fundamental
rights and put EU businesses at a disadvantage in the global market, since the
OECD/G20 BEPS Action Plan does not promote public CbC. Note, that public CbC
reporting is, however, already known and has applied in the extractive industry
and the banking sector in the European Union for many years.

---

13   Council Directive (EU) 2016/2258 of 6 December 2016 amending Directive 2011/16/EU as regards
      access to anti-money-laundering information by tax authorities, OJ L 342/1 of 16 December 2016.
14   Council Directive (EU) 2018/822 of 25 May 2018 amending Directive 2011/16/EU as regards manda-
      tory automatic exchange of information in the field of taxation in relation to reportable cross-border
      arrangements, OJ L 139/1 of 5 June 2018.
15   OECD/G20, BEPS Action Plan, Final Report on Action 12: Mandatory Disclosure Rules (2015).
16   Proposal for a Directive of the European Parliament and of the Council amending Directive 2013/34/EU
      as regards disclosure of income tax information by certain undertakings and branches, COM(2016)
      198 final.
17   Directive 2013/34/EU of the European Parliament and of the Council of 26 June 2013 on the annual
      financial statements, consolidated financial statements and related reports of certain types of under-
      takings, OJ L 182/19 of 29 June 2013.
18   See Joint statement by Cyprus, the Czech Republic, Estonia, Hungary, Ireland, Latvia, Luxembourg,
      Malta, Slovenia and Sweden, 28 November 2019, Interinstitutional File 2016/0107(COD).

683 In February 2020, the Commission anounced that it will start working on a **proposal for a DAC 7**, which should implement **mandatory reporting for online market places** on sales conducted via their platform combined with automatic exchange of information.[19]

684 Member States are obliged to submit a **yearly assessment on the application of the DAC** including statistical data to the Commission (Art. 23). In a report from 2017,[20] the Commission assumed that the Directive has had a "**significant deterrent effect**", which is a key tool in the fight against tax evasion. A 2019 evaluation report, however, admits that the available evidence is in fact insufficient to allow for overall conclusions on whether the intervention has had a deterrent effect and contributed to the perceived fairness of the tax system.[21]

B. Scope of the Directive

1. Objective Scope

685 The DAC has a **wide scope**: According to Art. 1(1), as a matter of principle, any **information** that is "**foreseeably relevant**" to the **administration and enforcement** of the domestic laws of the Member States concerning taxes is covered by the Directive and must be exchanged. The cooperation is not limited to information relevant to the determination of tax liability, but also includes e.g. information relevant to recovery, the service of documents and penalties with respect to the taxes covered. However, the wording is also intended to clarify that Member States are not at liberty to engage in "fishing expeditions" or to request information that is unlikely to be relevant to the tax affairs of a given taxpayer.[22] The wording "foreseeably relevant" has been copied from Art. 26 OECD MC. In *Berlioz*, the CJEU confirmed that the Commentary on Art. 26 OECD MC, hence, plays a vital role in interpreting these provisions.[23]

686 Note that this definition is, in particular, relevant to exchange on request (Art. 5), spontaneous exchange (Art. 9) and participation in administrative enquiries abroad (Art. 11(1)). Automatic exchange of information (Arts. 8 and 8a) does not require that the information be "foreseeably relevant".

2. Substantive Scope

687 According to Art. 2(1), the DAC applies to **all taxes of any kind** levied by, or on behalf of, a Member State or its territorial or administrative subdivisions and local

---

19 Commission, Inception Impact Assessment, Ref. Ares(2020)795980 – 07/02/2020. As of the date this book went to print, no proposal had been published.

20 Report from the Commission to the European Parliament and the Council, on the application of Council Directive (EU) 2011/16/EU on administrative cooperation in the field of direct taxation, COM(2017) 781 final.

21 Commission Staff Working Document, Evaluation of the Council Directive 2011/16/EU, SWD(2019) 328 final.

22 See Recital 9 of the preamble to Directive 2011/16/EU.

23 CJEU, 16 May 2017, C-682/15, *Berlioz*, EU:C:2017:373, para. 63.

authorities. Art. 2(2) and (3), however, enumerate taxes that may not be covered by the Directive in an exhaustive list. According to these provisions, the Directive explicitly does not apply to value added tax, customs and excise duties covered by other Union legislation,[24] compulsory social security contributions (Art. 2(2)), fees for certificates and other public documents and dues of a contractual nature (Art. 2(3)). All taxes not listed in Art. 2(2) and (3) are covered by the Directive. This negative list approach adds to legal clarity. The Directive, thus, covers, in particular, taxes on income and capital, including inheritance and wealth taxes, real estate transfer taxes, car taxes, environmental taxes, wage taxes, taxes on insurance premiums, and taxes on capital appreciation.[25]

3. Personal and Territorial Scope

In general, the nationality or residence of the taxpayers involved is not relevant. **688** Therefore, even an exchange of information involving persons who are **neither nationals nor residents of any of the Member States** is possible.[26] Only the automatic exchange of information listed in Art. 8(1) and of financial account information is limited to information concerning residents of a Member State (see Art. 8(1), Art. 3(9)(b), and Annex I, Section VIII.D.2).[27] Moreover, the legal status of the persons affected – individuals, corporations or hybrid entities – is also not relevant. This may be derived from Art. 3(11), which defines the term "person" in a **very wide sense,** including associations of persons (e.g. partnerships) and any other legal arrangements owning or managing assets (e.g. trusts) that are subject to the taxes covered.

As regards the territorial scope, the Directive applies in **all EU Member States**. **689** The EEA Member States Iceland, Liechtenstein and Norway are not covered (see m.no. 781).

4. Temporal Scope

The Directive only regulates the temporal scope of the application of the auto- **690** matic exchange of information and the admissibility of bank secrecy as a ground for refusing assistance. Art. 8(1) provides that mandatory automatic exchange of information on specific categories of income listed therein may include information regarding taxable periods as from 1 January 2014 only. Mandatory automatic

---

24 Council Regulation (EU) No 904/2010 of 7 October 2010 on administrative cooperation and combating fraud in the field of value added tax, OJ L 268/1 of 12 October 2010; Council Regulation (EU) No 389/2012 of 2 May 2012 on administrative cooperation in the field of excise duties and repealing Regulation (EC) No 2073/2004, OJ L 121/1 of 8 May 2012.
25 Terra/Wattel, *European Tax Law* (2018) p. 553.
26 See Terra/Wattel, *European Tax Law* (2018) p. 553.
27 The Directive is silent on how to determine the State of residence. This term will require an unlimited tax liability based on residence or a comparable territorial link (Helminen, *EU Tax Law* (2017) section 6.1.3.1).

exchange of financial account information takes place for information regarding taxable periods as from 1 January 2016 only (Art. 8(3a)).[28] With regard to tax rulings, all rulings issued, amended or renewed after 31 December 2016 are covered (see in more detail m.no. 714 et seq.). Mandatory automatic exchange of CbC reports covers any fiscal year of an MNE group commencing on or after 1 January 2016 (Art. 8aa(4)). Potentially aggressive cross-border arrangements are to be reported if the first step of the arrangement was implemented after 25 June 2018 (Art. 8ab(12)).

691 With regard to **bank secrecy**, Art. 18(3) permits Member States to refuse the transmission of requested information held by a bank or financial institution where such information concerns taxable periods prior to 1 January 2011 and where the transmission of such information could have been refused on the basis of the old Directive. This means that for requests received after 1 January 2013, Member States applying domestic banking secrecy provisions (Austria, Belgium and Luxembourg) are, as a rule, forced to provide information residing with banks relating to taxable periods after 1 January 2011.

692 Besides these provisions, no general rules on the taxable periods to which the requested information has to relate are included in the Directive. Thus, in all cases not regulated it seems to be **immaterial which taxable period** a request relates to, even if that tax year predates the entry into force of the Directive.[29] This conclusion can also be drawn from the *Tsalapos and Diamantakis* case, in which the CJEU held that the old Tax Collection Directive[30] is to be interpreted as applying to customs claims that arose in one Member State before the Directive entered into force in the other Member State.[31]

C. Organization (Art. 4)

693 Art. 4 distinguishes between **four types** of entities engaged in the cooperation proceeding: the **competent authority, the single central liaison office ('CLO'), liaison departments and competent officials.** Each Member State has to designate a single competent authority for the purposes of the Directive, which will be made public by the Commission.[32] The Member State's competent authority must then designate a single central liaison office, which has the principal responsibility for contact with other Member States. In addition, the competent authority is permitted,

---

28   Austria is obliged to apply these provisions on automatic exchange to financial information relating to taxable periods as from 1 January 2017 only (Art. 2(2) amending Directive 2014/107/EU).

29   See Terra/Wattel, *European Tax Law* (2018) p. 556.

30   Council Directive 2008/55/EC of 26 May 2008, OJ L 150/28 of 26 May 2008.

31   CJEU, 1 July 2004, Joined Cases C-361/02 and C-362/02, *Tsapalos and Diamantakis*, EU:C:2004:401, para. 23.

32   See List of competent authorities referred to in Art. 4(1) of Council Directive 2011/16/EU, OJ C 191, 2 July 2013.

but not obliged, to set up liaison departments and appoint any number of competent officials.

The DAC, thus, provides, as opposed to the old Directive,[33] a legal basis for **direct** **694** **communication between two internal revenue services** of different Member States, on the basis that these authorities are appointed as liaison departments or competent officials by the Member States' competent authorities.[34] Moreover, based on the recitals to the Directive, it seems that direct communication between the national delegated departments and officials should be the rule.[35]

As regards **automatic exchange of information,** according to Arts. 8(3a), 8a, 8aa **695** and 8ab, specific detailed rules on the organization are set out in the Annex to the DAC and the Council Implementing Regulation (EU) 2015/2378.[36] Note, in particular, that Art. 8(3a) on financial account information requires the Member States to shift certain responsibilities to financial institutions (see m.no. 707 et seq.) Art. 8aa on CbC reporting requires Member States to subject MNE groups to reporting obligations (see m.no. 722) and Art. 8ab on cross-border arrangements requires Member States to involve intermediaries in the reporting (see m.no. 729). Member States are obliged to impose **penalties** if those private entities do not meet their reporting obligations. The DAC does not specify the criteria and severity of such penalties, but merely states that they shall be "effective, proportionate and dissuasive" (Art. 25a).

D. Exchange of Information

1. Overview

The Directive distinguishes between **three types** of exchange of information: ex- **696** change on request (Art. 5 et seq.), mandatory automatic exchange (Arts. 8, 8a, 8aa and 8ab), and spontaneous exchange (Art. 9). One can distinguish the three types of exchange by their passive and active character: Exchange on request depends on the initiative of another Member State. With regard to spontaneous exchange, a State has to decide on its own account whether information obtained may be relevant to another Member State. Finally, automatic exchange is carried out at pre-defined regular intervals without the need for investigations as to whether the information may be useful to the receiving State at all. Due to its automatic character, **automatic exchange** is seen as the **most effective type**.[37] However, it might also lead to **big data**, which has to be analysed, and to problems in terms of taxpayer rights and confidentiality of the information.

---

33   See Terra/Wattel, *European Tax Law* (2008) p. 667.
34   See Gabert, Council Directive 2011/16/EU on Administrative Cooperation in the Field of Taxation, *ET* 2011, p. 343.
35   See Recital 8 of the preamble to Directive 2011/16/EU.
36   Commission Implementing Regulation (EU) 2015/2378; amended by Commission Implementing Regulation (EU) 2016/1963 and Commission Implementing Regulation (EU) 2018/99.
37   Recital 10 of the preamble to Directive 2011/16/EU.

2. Exchange on Request (Art. 5 et seq.)

697 Any designated authority of a Member State laid down in Art. 4 **may** request from a designated authority of another Member State **any information** according to Art. 1(1) (see m.no. 685). Although the opportunities for making a request are very extensive, it is necessary for a request to relate to a **specific case** (Art. 3(8)).[38] "Fishing expeditions" should, thus, not be permitted under the Directive.[39] In order to demonstrate the foreseeable relevance of the information requested, the request has to include at least the **identity of the person** under investigation and the **tax purpose** for which the information is sought (Art. 20(2)).[40] Additional information, such as the name and address of persons that might be in possession of the requested information and other helpful elements, must be provided by the requesting authority only *"to the extent known and in line with international developments."*[41] If these conditions are met, the requested State is, in principle, **obliged** to answer such a request, unless it can rely on a ground for refusal provided for in the Directive (discussed in m.no. 748 et seq.). Based on these requirements for a valid request, "group requests", i.e. asking for information on a group of taxpayers characterized by specific criteria without naming them individually (permitted based on the Commentary on Art. 26 OECD MC since the 2012 update) are not, in principle, possible under the DAC.

698 In *Berlioz*, the CJEU ruled that the requesting authority enjoys rather broad discretion in deciding whether information is "foreseeably relevant"; however, it has to provide the requested authority with an adequate statement of reasons explaining the purpose of the information sought. The requested authority can only challenge the validity of the request if the information sought appears to be manifestly devoid of any foreseeable relevance.[42]

699 Art. 6 obliges the requested State to carry on **any administrative enquiries** necessary to obtain such information and the same procedures as it would when acting for its own purposes ('national treatment'), which also includes audits.[43] It is

---

38   See also, on the old Directive 77/799/EEC, CJEU, 11 June 2009, Joined Cases C-155/08 and C-157/08, *X and Passenheim*, EU:C:2008:308, para. 64.

39   See Recital 9 of the Preamble to Directive 2011/16/EU.

40   As of the date this book went to print, two referrals by Luxembourg courts on the condition of "foreseeable relevance" were pending before the CJEU (Pending Cases C-245/19 and C-437/19, *État du Grand-duché de Luxembourg*). The Court is being asked to decide, amongst others, whether a request can also be admissible if a person is only identified by his status as shareholder and beneficial owner of a company (but not individually by name) and how detailed the description of the tax purpose must be.

41   One has to wonder, however, how the wording, in particular "in line with international developments", should be interpreted and what the meaning and consequences of this provision should be. The developments on the OECD level, in particular with regard to Art. 26 OECD MC, the TIEA Model and the corresponding Commentaries could be of relevance here. This approach, however, would lead to a dynamic interpretation depending on the future decisions in a non-EU body and this could be criticized from a democratic and policy point of view.

42   CJEU, 16 May 2017, Case C-682/15, *Berlioz*, EU:C:2017:373, paras. 70-71 and 80-82.

43   See Terra/Wattel, *European Tax Law* (2018) p. 557-558.

immaterial to this obligation that the requested information is irrelevant to the requested State's own tax purposes (Art. 18(1)). The requesting authority is also permitted to ask the requested authority to carry out a specific administrative enquiry upon a reasoned request (Art. 6(2)). Based on Art. 11, officers of the requesting State may also take part in the investigations conducted by the requested State (see m.no. 744 et seq.).

The requested authority has to provide the information as quickly as possible, **700** **at the very latest within six months** from the date of receipt of the request. If the requested authority is already in possession of the relevant information, the information has to be transmitted within two months (Art. 7(1)). In addition, the requested authority is obliged to confirm receipt of the request (within seven working days at the latest, Art. 7(3)), to inform the requesting authority about any deficiencies or the need for additional information (within one month at the latest, Art. 7(4)), to provide information about the inability to respond on time (within three months at the latest, Art. 7(5)) or about the refusal of assistance and the reason thereof (within one month at the latest, Art. 7(6)).

According to the CJEU, the Directive itself does not lay down any obligation for the **701** competent authorities of the Member States to consult and involve the taxpayer during the exchange proceedings.[44] Taxpayer rights may, however, be inferred from domestic law and the fundamental rights laid down in the ECHR and CFR (see m.no. 763 et seq.).

Moreover, according to established CJEU case law, Member States are **not obliged** **702** **to make use of the Directive** and request information from another Member State if the taxpayer has not provided or is not even in a position to provide the necessary evidence for applying a certain tax benefit.[45] The burden of proof for relying on a tax benefit, as a rule, is on the taxpayer.

3. Mandatory Automatic Exchange of Information (Art. 8 et seq.)

a) Overview

Mandatory automatic exchange of information without preconditions is consid- **703** ered the **most effective means** of enhancing the correct assessment of taxes in cross-border situations and of fighting tax fraud. As opposed to the old Directive from 1977, which only permitted the Member States to introduce a system of automatic exchange of information for certain categories of cases,[46] under the scope of the DAC, automatic exchange of information is mandatory for specific categories

---

44 CJEU, 22 October 2013, Case C-276/12, *Sabou*, EU:C:2013:678.
45 CJEU, 27 September 2007, Case C-184/05, *Twoh International*, EU:C:2007:550, para. 32; CJEU, 10 February 2011, Joined Cases C-436/08 and C-437/08, *Haribo and Österreichische Salinen*, EU:C:2009:17, para. 102; contrary on the VAT Regulation 904/2010/EU CJEU, 17 December 2015, Case C-419/14, *WebMindLicenses Kft*, EU:C:2015:832, paras. 55-59.
46 Art. 3 Directive 77/799/EEC.

of income and capital (see m.no. 704 et seq.), for financial account information (DAC 2, see m.no. 707 et seq.), in respect of advance cross-border tax rulings (DAC 3, see m.no. 714 et seq.), CbC reports (DAC 4, see m.no. 722 et seq.) and cross-border arrangements (DAC 6, see m.no. 729 et seq.). For the automatic exchange of information pursuant to Arts. 8, 8a, 8aa and 8ab, **standard computerized formats** are to be used (see m.no. 755).

b) Specific Categories of Income and Capital (Art. 8(1))

704   In Art. 8(1), the DAC introduces a means of **systematic communication** of predefined information to another Member State, without prior request, **at pre-established regular intervals** for specific categories of income. The competent authority of each Member State must communicate to the competent authority of another Member State information that is "available" concerning residents in that other Member State on the following **five specific categories of income and capital:** income from employment, director's fees, life insurance products not covered by other Union legislation, pensions, and the ownership of and income from immovable property.[47]

705   Only information that is "**available**", which means retrievable in the tax files in accordance with national procedures for gathering and processing information in the Member State communicating the information (Art. 3(9)(a)), needs to be exchanged under Art. 8(1). This precondition may lead to significant imbalances of exchange content among the Member States.[48] Member States may also indicate that they do not wish to receive information on certain of the categories of income and capital listed.[49] In this event, other Member States are not under any obligation to provide this information automatically to this specific Member State. In addition, if a Member State has no information on any single category of income or capital listed available in its tax files, this Member State will automatically be considered to not wish to receive any information. This rule serves as an "**anti-free-riding**" provision motivating the Member States to make at least one category available.

706   The information must be communicated **at least once a year, within six months** following the end of the tax year of the Member State during which the information became available (Art. 8(6)(a)). Only information regarding taxable periods as from **1 January 2014** is covered (Art. 8(1)). The first exchange, therefore, already took place before 1 July 2015, covering information relating to 2014.

---

47   For the specific definitions of the categories listed, the understandings under the national legislation of the Member State that communicates the information may be relied on.

48   Terra/Wattel, *European Tax Law* (2018) p. 559 et seq.

49   Initially, Art. 8(3) also permitted the Member States to indicate that they do not wish to receive information on income or capital not exceeding a certain threshold amount. This threshold limitation was deleted in the amending Directive 2014/107/EU, since it was considered not to be manageable in practice (Recital 15 of the preamble to the amending Directive 2014/107/EU).

c) Financial Account Information (Art. 8(3a)) – DAC 2

In December 2014, the Council adopted a directive (DAC 2)[50] amending Directive **707**
2011/16/EU, which brings **interest, dividends, gross proceeds from the sale of
financial assets** and other income, as well as **account balances,** within the scope
of the automatic exchange of information (newly inserted paragraph 3a of Art. 8).
The scope of the DAC hence now also covers provisions of substance and procedure previously contained in the EU Savings Directive[51] (also refer to m.no. 814).
As the provisions of Art. 8(3a) and Annexes I and II are largely inspired by the
Common Reporting Standard (CRS) developed by the OECD, the OECD materials
may serve as a source of interpretation.[52]

In Art. 8(3a), in conjunction with Art. 3(9)(b), the DAC obliges the **competent** **708**
authority of each Member State to systematically communicate to the competent
authority of any other Member State, **without prior request, at pre-established
intervals,** predefined information concerning "**reportable accounts**". A "reportable account" is essentially defined as a financial account (of a depositary, custodial or similar character)[53] that is maintained by a Member State "reporting financial institution" and is held by one or more "reportable persons".[54] "**Reporting
financial institutions**" are, in particular, custodial institutions, depository institutions, investment entities or specified insurance companies, unless they fall
within one of the following categories that transform them into non-reporting
financial institutions: governmental entities, international organizations, central
banks, particular retirement funds, qualified credit card issuers and similar.[55]
"**Reportable persons**", in turn, are individuals and entities that are **resident in
another Member State**, other than corporations the stock of which is regularly
traded on one or more established securities markets, governmental entities,
international organizations, central banks and financial institutions.[56] Accounts
held by a (resident) passive entity[57] are also subject to the exchange procedure if
its controlling natural persons[58] are resident in another Member State. In order
to enable tax authorities to identify the controlling persons of such intermediary

---

50   Council Directive 2014/107/EU of 9 December 2014 amending Directive 2011/16/EU as regards man-
      datory automatic exchange of information in the field of taxation, OJ L 359/1 of 16 December 2014.
51   Council Directive 2003/48/EC of 3 June 2003 on taxation of savings income in the form of interest
      payments, OJ L 157/38 of 26 June 2003; repealed on 10 November 2015.
52   See Recital 13 of the preamble to the amending Directive 2014/107/EU.
53   See the definition of "financial account" in Annex I, Section VIII C of the Directive.
54   See the definition of "reportable account" in Annex I, Section VIII D of the Directive.
55   See the definitions of "reporting financial institution" and "non-reporting financial institution" in
      Annex I, Section VIII A and B, respectively, of the Directive.
56   See the definition of "reportable person" in Annex I, Section VIII D 2 (in conjunction with 3) of the
      Directive.
57   Entities qualify as passive if e.g. more than 50 % of their income is related to passive activities or if
      more than 50 % of their assets may generate passive income (see the definition in Annex I, Section
      VIII D 6-8 of the Directive).
58   See the definition of "controlling persons" in Annex I, Section VIII D 5 of the Directive. The "con-
      trolling persons" are to be treated as "reportable persons".

structures, Art. 22(1a) (introduced by DAC 5) ensures that the tax authorities have access to beneficial ownership information collected pursuant to the **anti-money laundering** (AML) legislation.[59]

709 The **information** to be exchanged under this title covers the following:

- the name, address, tax identification number(s) and date and place of birth (in the case of an individual) of each reportable person that is an account holder of the account;
- the account number;
- the name and identifying number (if any) of the reporting financial institution;
- the **account balance** or value as of the end of the relevant reporting period or, if the account was closed during the relevant period, the closure of the account;
- for custodial accounts: the total gross amount of **interest** and **dividends**; the total gross amount of **other income** generated with respect to assets held in the account; and the total gross proceeds from the sale or redemption of financial assets paid or credited to the account during the reporting period with respect to which the reporting financial institution acted as an agent for the account holder; and
- for depository accounts: the total gross amount of **interest** paid or credited to the account during the reporting period.

710 The communication of the information must take place **annually, within nine months** following the end of the reporting period (calendar year or other appropriate reporting period) to which the information relates (Art. 8(6)(b)). Only information regarding taxable periods as from **1 January 2016** is covered (Art. 8(3a)). It follows that the information was first exchanged by **30 September 2017**.[60] Practical evidence shows that the network of bilateral exchanges is centered around Luxembourg and, to a much smaller extent, Ireland.[61]

---

59 Council Directive (EU) 2016/2258 of 6 December 2016 amending Directive 2011/16/EU as regards access to anti-money-laundering information by tax authorities, OJ L 342/1 of 16 December 2016.

60 Austria was obliged to apply these provisions on automatic exchange to financial account information as from 1 January 2017 and with respect to taxable periods as from that date only (Art. 2(2) amending Directive 2014/107/EU; unused one-year extension). An overview of the Member States' state of transposition and implementation is provided in chapter 3.3 of the Commission's 2019 Evaluation Report: European Commission, Evaluation of Administrative Cooperation in Direct Taxation, Final Report, 24 April 2019; https://ec.europa.eu/taxation_customs/sites/taxation/files/2019_evaluation_study_on_dac_kp0219284enn.pdf (accessed on 9 January 2020).

61 Report from the Commission to the European Parliament and the Council on overview and assessment of the statistics and information on the automatic exchanges in the field of direct taxation, COM(2018) 844 final, 17 December 2018, 9; and chapter 4.2.2 of the Commission's 2019 Evaluation Report (fn. 75). A detailed evaluation of the DAC, as amended by, inter alia, DAC 2, covering the issues of effectiveness, efficiency, relevance, coherence, and EU added value, is provided by the recent Commission Staff Working Document, Evaluation of the Council Directive 2011/16/EU on administrative cooperation in the field of taxation and repealing Directive 77/799/EEC, SWD(2019) 327 final of 12 September 2019.

In order to be able to comply with the reporting requirement set out above, each **711** Member State is obliged to require its **reporting financial institutions** to follow specific **reporting and due diligence rules,** which are further detailed in Annexes I and II of the Directive. The information eventually to be communicated by the competent authority of each Member State to the competent authority of any other Member State is to be provided by each reporting financial institution to the competent authority of its (own) Member State under the "**General Reporting Requirement**".[62] The reporting obligations are consistent with those set out in the Common Reporting Standard (CRS) developed by the OECD in order to allow for one single set of rules within the EU and in relation to third countries.[63]

Specific **due diligence requirements** with the **aim of identifying reportable** **712** **accounts** depend on the nature of the account at stake. The Directive distinguishes between pre-existing and new accounts (depending on whether the account was maintained by a reporting financial institution as of 31 December 2015[64] or not) and between individual and entity accounts (depending on whether the account is held by one or more individuals or entities, respectively):[65]

- *Pre-existing individual accounts* (Section III of Annex I): The due diligence procedure to be pursued depends on whether the account qualifies as a "lower value account" or as a "high value account", with enhanced review procedures applying to the latter. The review of pre-existing lower and higher value accounts must be completed by 31 December 2017 and 2016,[66] respectively.
- *New individual accounts* (Section IV of Annex I): Upon an account being opened, the reporting financial institution must obtain a self-certification,[67] which may be part of the account opening documentation, that allows the reporting financial institution to determine the account holder's residence(s) for tax purposes and confirm the reasonableness of such self-certification based on the information obtained by the reporting financial institution in connection with the opening of the account, including any documentation collected pursuant to AML/KYC procedures.
- *Pre-existing entity accounts* (Section V of Annex I): Only pre-existing entity accounts held by reportable persons that have (i) an aggregate account balance or value that exceeds, as of 31 December 2015,[68] an amount that corresponds

---

62 See Section I of Annex I of the Directive.

63 See Recital 9 of the preamble to amending Directive 2014/107/EU.

64 In the case of pre-existing accounts held by reporting financial institutions located in Austria: 31 December 2016; see Annex I, Section X of the Directive.

65 See the relevant definitions in Annex I, Section VIII C 9 to 16 of the Directive.

66 In the case of reporting financial institutions located in Austria: 31 December 2018 and 2017; see Annex I, Section X of the Directive.

67 A reporting financial institution may not rely on a self-certification or documentary evidence if the reporting financial institution knows or has reason to know that the self-certification or documentary evidence is incorrect or unreliable; see Section VII A of Annex I.

68 In the case of pre-existing accounts held by reporting financial institutions located in Austria: 31 December 2016; see Annex I, Section X of the Directive.

to USD 250 000, and (ii) with regard to lower pre-existing entity accounts an aggregate account balance or value that exceeds such amount as of the last day of any subsequent calendar year must be reviewed. The review of pre-existing entity accounts must be completed by 31 December 2017[69] with regard to (i) and within the calendar year following the year in which the aggregate account balance or value exceeds such amount with regard to (ii).

- *New entity accounts* (Section VI of Annex I): The reporting financial institution must obtain a self-certification, which may be part of the account opening documentation, that allows it to determine the account holder's residence(s) for tax purposes, whether an entity qualifies as passive, and the residency of controlling persons of such passive entities. Moreover, the financial institution must confirm the reasonableness of such self-certification based on the information obtained by the reporting financial institution in connection with the opening of the account, including any documentation collected pursuant to AML/KYC procedures.

713 Each Member State may allow reporting financial institutions to apply the due diligence procedures for new accounts to pre-existing accounts, and the due diligence procedures for high value accounts to lower value accounts.[70]

d) Tax Rulings (Art. 8a) – DAC 3

714 The mandatory automatic exchange of **tax rulings** became part of the DAC due to the amendment in December 2015 (**DAC 3**; on the background to DAC 3 see m.no. 678).[71] Although Art. 9(1)(a) already obliged Member States to spontaneously exchange information in cases where there may be a loss of tax in another Member State, exchange of rulings under this provision did not work in practice.

715 According to Art. 8a(1), the competent authority of a Member State issuing a ruling is obliged to communicate information on "**advance cross-border rulings**" and "**advance pricing arrangements**" by automatic exchange to all other Member States. Both terms are defined in the **broadest possible sense** and cover **any agreement**, communication, or any other instrument or action with similar effects, including one issued in the context of a tax audit, which is issued, amended or renewed by, or on behalf of, the government or the tax authority of a Member State, or any territorial or administrative subdivisions thereof, **to a particular person or a group of persons** (Art. 3(14) and (15)). Art. 8a(3) and (4) only explicitly exclude two forms of rulings: (i) bi- or multilateral advance pricing agreements with third countries, where the international tax agreement with the third country does not permit such a disclosure; and (ii) rulings that exclusively concern natural persons.

---

69 In the case of reporting financial institutions located in Austria: 31 December 2018; see Annex I, Section X of the Directive.

70 See Section II E of Annex I of the Directive.

71 Council Directive, (EU) 2015/2376 of 8 December 2015 amending Directive 2011/16/EU as regards mandatory automatic exchange of information in the field of taxation, OJ L 332/1 of 18 December 2015.

Moreover, the Directive sets up three other general criteria in Art. 3(14) and (15), **716** which apply to both definitions: First, both terms require that the person(s) be entitled to rely on the ruling, meaning the ruling must be **legally binding**. Second, the ruling must be made **in advance**, meaning before the transactions to which the ruling relates are carried out. Third, the two terms require that the ruling relate to a **cross-border transaction**.[72]

In addition to these general criteria, the two terms "advance cross-border ruling" **717** and "advance pricing arrangement" ask that specific criteria be met regarding their content: In order to qualify as an "**advance cross-border ruling**" the ruling has to concern the **interpretation or application** of a legal or administrative provision concerning the administration or enforcement of national laws relating to taxes of the Member State, or its territorial or administrative subdivisions (Art. 3(14)(c)). In order to qualify as an "**advance pricing arrangement**" the action needs to relate to transactions between **associated enterprises**[73] and either set up an appropriate set of criteria for the determination of the **transfer pricing** or determine the **attribution of profits** to a permanent establishment (Art. 3(15)(c)).

With regard to temporal scope, all tax rulings **issued, amended or renewed after** **718** **31 December 2016** are covered. Moreover, according to Art. 8a(2), the Member States are also obliged to communicate information on certain "**old" rulings** issued, amended or renewed **after 31 December 2011**.[74]

Automatic exchange does not cover the original full text of the rulings, but rather **719** the following information (Art. 8a(6)):

- the **identification** of the person and, where appropriate, the group of companies to which it belongs;
- a **summary of the content** of the ruling, including an abstract description of relevant business activities or transactions;
- the **scope and nature of the ruling** (type of ruling, date of issue, start and end of the period of validity (if specified));
- the **amount** of the transaction;
- the identification of the **other Member States** likely to be directly or indirectly concerned by the advance cross-border ruling or advance pricing arrangement;
- the identification of any **person**, other than a natural person, in the other Member States **likely to be directly or indirectly affected** by the ruling;

---

72 According to Art. 3(16) a cross-border transactions exists if not all parties to the transaction are resident in the Member State giving the ruling, if one of the parties to the transaction is dual resident, if one of the parties to the transaction carries on business in another State through a permanent establishment or if the transactions "have a cross-border impact".

73 According to Art. 3(15), enterprises are associated enterprises where one enterprise participates directly or indirectly in the management, control or capital of another enterprise or the same persons participate directly or indirectly in the management, control or capital of the enterprises.

74 However, ruling issued in 2012 and 2013 only had to be exchanged if still valid on 1 January 2014. Moreover, Member States had the option to exclude rulings issued before 1 April 2016 to small groups of companies (annual group turnover of less than EUR 40 million) from the scope of application if these companies did not conduct mainly financial or investment activities.

- in the case of **advance pricing arrangements**: the description of the set of criteria used and the identification of the method used for the determination of the **transfer pricing** or transfer price itself.

720 The European Commission developed a **secure central directory** where the information on the rulings is recorded and to which competent authorities of all Member States have access (Art. 21(5)). The Commission only has limited access to the information and, in particular, cannot read the abstract content of the ruling and the persons affected (Art. 8a(8)).

721 The exchange of the rulings by the competent authorities takes place **within three months following the half of the calendar year during which the ruling has been issued** (meaning a maximum of twice per year: by the end of March and September). In respect of "old" rulings, the exchange had to take place before 1 January 2018 (Art. 8a(5)).

e) Country-by-Country Reports (Art. 8aa) – DAC 4

722 **Country-by-Country (CbC) reports** became part of the categories of information **subject to mandatory automatic exchange of information** due to the DAC amendment in **May 2016** (DAC 4; on the background to DAC 4 see m.no. 679).[75] The information included in the CbC reports should enable the Member States´ tax authorities to react to harmful tax practices by making changes in legislation or by undertaking adequate risk assessments and tax audits, and to identify whether companies have engaged in practices that have the effect of artificially shifting substantial amounts of income into tax-advantaged environments.[76]

723 The **reporting obligation** only applies to MNE groups with annual consolidated group revenue of at least **EUR 750 million**. An "MNE group" is defined as a collection of enterprises related through **ownership or control** such that it is required to prepare consolidated financial statements under applicable accounting principles and which has enterprises resident in two or more different jurisdictions or a permanent establishment in a jurisdiction other than the State of residence. Both **Union MNE groups and non-Union MNE groups,** in respect of which one or several of their entities are located in the Union, **are subject to the reporting obligation.**

724 If the **ultimate parent company** of an MNE group is resident in the EU, that parent company has to submit the CbC report (Art. 8aa(1)). If the ultimate parent company of the MNE group is, however, resident outside the EU, the reporting obligation is shifted to another constituent entity tax resident within the EU if the Member States do not receive the CbC report from the third State where the ultimate parent is resident. Member States shall provide for **penalties** if these filing obligations are not fulfilled (Art. 25a).

---

75   Council Directive (EU) 2016/881 of 25 May 2016 amending Directive 2011/16/EU as regards mandatory automatic exchange of information in the field of taxation, OJ L 146/8 of 3 June 2016.
76   See Recital 4 of the preamble to amending Directive (EU) 2016/881.

In the CbC report, MNE groups have to provide **annually** and **for each tax juris-** 725
diction in which they do business, the following information (Art. 8aa(3)):

- **tax-related information**: the amount of revenue, profit/loss before income tax and income tax paid and accrued.
- **other information related to their business activities**: number of their employees, stated capital, accumulated earnings and tangible assets in each tax jurisdiction.

Finally, MNE groups should also identify each entity within the group doing 726
business in a particular tax jurisdiction and provide an indication of the **business**
activities in which each entity engages. The same holds true for permanent establishments with separate financial statements ("constituent entity"). **Three standard**
forms shall be used for reporting an MNE group's allocation of income, taxes and
business activities on a tax jurisdiction-by-tax jurisdiction basis.[77]

The "**reporting entity**" has to file a CbC report with respect to a fiscal year of the 727
MNE group **within 12 months** of the last day of the reporting fiscal year of the
MNE group ((Art. 8aa(1)). The first CbC report had to be filed for any fiscal year
of the MNE group **commencing on or after 1 January 2016** ((Art. 8aa(4)). The
competent authority of a Member State that receives the CbC report shall **auto-**
matically communicate the CbC report to **any other Member State** in which one
or more constituent entities of the MNE group are either resident for tax purposes
or subject to tax with respect to the business carried out through a permanent establishment ((Art. 8aa(2)). The CbC report shall be **automatically exchanged** among
Member States **within 15 months from the end of that fiscal year**, except for the
first communication for which 18 months is allowed ((Art. 8aa(4)). A proposal to
make CbC reports also publicly available was still under discussion when this book
went to print (see m.no. 682).

DAC 4 includes a special safeguard clause as regards the use of CbC reports: 728
transfer pricing (TP) **adjustments** by the receiving Member State **shall not be**
based on the information exchanged **on CbC reporting** (Art. 16(6), see m.no. 759).

f) Reportable Cross-Border Arrangements (Art. 8ab) – DAC 6

An initiative in 2018 – linked to BEPS Action 12 (see m.no. 681) –, led to a fifth 729
amendment of the DAC (DAC 6),[78] aiming to capture, via disclosure by intermediaries, **potentially aggressive tax planning arrangements** and subject them
to **mandatory automatic exchange of information**. Under the new regime, each
Member State shall take the necessary measures to require so-called "intermediaries"

---

77 Table 1: Overview of allocation of income, taxes and business activities by tax jurisdiction; Table 2: List of all the constituent entities of the MNE group included in each aggregation per tax jurisdiction; Table 3: Additional information.

78 Council Directive (EU) 2018/822 of 25 May 2018 amending Directive 2011/16/EU as regards manda-tory automatic exchange of information in the field of taxation in relation to reportable cross-border arrangements, OJ L 139/1 of 5 June 2018.

to **file information** that is within their knowledge, possession or control on a "reportable cross-border arrangement" with the competent tax authorities. These reporting obligations are being critizised as being in conflict with EU primary law by some scholars (see m.nos 737, 767, 770).

730 The **intermediaries** referred to by this provision are, inter alia, all persons that design, market, organise or make available for implementation, or manage the implementation of a reportable cross-border arrangement (Art. 3(21)). Examples for intermediaries covered include: lawyers, tax consultants and financial institutions. Member States have the option to grant intermediaries a waiver from filing information on a reportable cross-border arrangement where the reporting obligation would breach **legal professional privilege** under the national law of that Member State. If a Member States uses this option and the cross-border arrangement is covered by the domestic legal professional privilege, the obligation to file information shall be the responsibility of any other intermediary involved or, if there is no such intermediary, the taxpayer (both to be notified by the intermediary applying the waiver). If there is no intermediary (e.g. in-house design), the obligation to report also lies with the taxpayer (Art. 8ab(5) and (6)). Member States shall provide for **penalties** if these filing obligations are not fulfilled (Art. 25a). Note, that the freedom from self-incrimination deriving from Art. 48(2) CFR may set limits on the reporting obligations (see m.nos 770).

731 DAC 6 also includes rules for **multiple reporting** situations: If an intermediary or taxpayer is subject to reporting obligations for the same arrangement in more than one Member State, Art. 8ab(3) and (7) provide a ranking order to ensure that he only reports to one Member State. By contrast, if more than one intermediary or more than one taxpayer is subject to reporting obligations for the same arrangement in the same Member State, as a general rule, all of them have to file the information with the competent authority, unless the intermediary or taxpayer has proof that the arrangement has already been reported (Art. 8ab(9) and (10)).

732 Each **cross-border arrangement**, i.e. an arrangement in either more than one Member State or a Member State and a third country, that meets at least one of the conditions set out in Art. 3(18),[79] has to be examined in terms of whether or not it is reportable. The hallmarks of **reportable cross-border arrangements** are set out in a new Annex IV (introduced to the DAC by DAC 6) and cover a "main benefit test", as well as a number of generic and specific hallmarks. The "**main benefit test**" will be satisfied where (one of) the main benefit(s) that a person may reasonably expect to derive from an arrangement is the obtaining of a tax advantage. **Generic hallmarks** (category A) cover three exhaustively listed situations: among others, arrangements where the intermediary is entitled to receive a fee that is

---

79 E.g., not all of the participants in the arrangement are resident for tax purposes in the same jurisdiction; or one or more of the participants in the arrangement carries on a business in another jurisdiction through a permanent establishment situated in that jurisdiction and the arrangement forms part or the whole of the business of that permanent establishment.

fixed by reference to the amount of the tax advantage derived from the arrangement, and arrangements where the taxpayer undertakes to comply with a condition of confidentiality as regards the tax planning scheme. **Specific hallmarks** occur in four further detailed categories, namely:

- Category B: hallmarks linked to the "main benefit test" (inter alia: circular transactions);
- Category C: hallmarks related to cross-border transactions (inter alia: deductible payments to low-tax jurisdictions, situations of double deduction or double relief);
- Category D: hallmarks concerning automatic exchange of information and beneficial ownership (inter alia: avoiding the reporting of financial income); and
- Category E: hallmarks concerning transfer pricing (inter alia: use of unilateral safe harbour rules).

An arrangement should be subject to the reporting obligation if it cumulatively **733** fulfils the main benefit test and one (or more) general hallmark(s) or one (or more) of the specific hallmark(s) in category B or one (or more) specifically mentioned hallmark(s) in category C. Furthermore, an arrangement would also be subject to reporting if it, on a standalone basis, meets one (or more) of the residual specific hallmark(s) listed in category C or one (or more) of the specific hallmark(s) listed in categories D or E, irrespective of whether or not the main benefit test is satisfied.

The competent authority of a Member State where the information, on a reportable **734** cross-border arrangement, was filed is obliged to **automatically communicate** the information specified in Art. 8ab(14) to the competent authorities of all other Member States (Art. 8ab(13)) via a secure central directory to be developed by the European Commission (Art. 21(5)). The **information** to be exchanged includes:

- the identification of intermediaries and taxpayers, including their name, residence for tax purposes, and taxpayer identification number (TIN);
- details of the hallmarks set out in Annex IV that make the cross-border arrangement reportable, including an abstract description of the relevant business activities;
- a summary of the content of the reportable cross-border arrangement;
- the date on which the first step in implementing the arrangement has been made or will be made;
- details of the national tax provisions that form the basis of the reportable cross-border arrangement;
- the **value** of the reportable cross-border arrangement;
- identification of the Member States that are likely to be concerned by the reportable cross-border arrangement; and
- identification of any person in the other Member States, if any, likely to be affected by the reportable cross-border arrangement indicating to which Member States such person is linked.

735 The intermediary (or the taxpayer if professional legal privilege applies or no intermediary is present) has to file the necessary information with the authorities **within 30 days** from the day after the reportable cross-border arrangement is made available for implementation by the intermediary, after it is ready for implementation, or when the first step in its implementation has been taken, whichever occurs first (Art. 8ab(1) and (7)). In addition, with regard to marketable arrangements (i.e. those that do not need to be substantially customized),[80] periodic reports are to be made by the intermediary every three months (Art. 8ab(2)).

736 The new provisions have to be applied by Member States **from 1 July 2020**. Because of the COVID-19 pandemic, Member States may however defer time limits for filing information on reportable cross-border arrangements (Art. 27a).[81] Thus, they may allow the period of 30 days for filing information on **"new" reportable cross-border arrangements** referred to in Article 8ab(1) and (7) to begin by 1 January 2021 where the reporting requirement is triggered between 1 July 2020 and 31 December 2020 (Art. 27a(2)b)). Not all Member States have used this optional deferral.

737 Additionally, reporting obligations already apply for arrangements implemented prior to 1 July 2020, more specifically for all arrangements the first step of which was implemented between the date of entry into force of DAC 6, i.e. **25 June 2018**, and 1 July 2020. This "**retroactivity**" of DAC 6 has been critizised as being in conflict with the principle of legal certainty and legitimate expectations.[82] These **"old" arrangements** need to be reported by 31 August 2020 at the latest, unless Member States defer this time limit because of the COVID-19 pandemic to 28 February 2021 (Art. 27a(1)). Not all Member States have used this optional deferral.

738 Member States have to exchange the information **within one month of the end of the quarter** in which the information was filed. The first exchange in general takes place by 31 October 2020 (Art. 8ab(18)), but because of the COVID-19 pandemic Member States may allow the first information to be communicated by 30 April 2021(Art. 27a(2)a)). Similar to tax rulings (m.no. 720), the Commission has no full access to the information exchanged (Art. 8ab(17)).

4. Spontaneous Exchange of Information (Art. 9 et seq.)

739 Besides exchange on request and automatic exchange, the Directive establishes rules for spontaneous exchange, meaning a non-systematic communication between

---

80   See Art. 3(24) of the DAC.

81   Council Directive (EU) 2020/876 of 24 June 2020 amending Directive 2011/16/EU to address the urgent need to defer certain time limits for the filing and exchange of information in the field of taxation because of the COVID-19 pandemic, OJ L 204/46 of 26 June 2020. Additionally, the Council, acting unanimously on a proposal from the Commission, may take an implementing decision to extend the period of deferral of the time limits set out in Article 27a by three months, provided that severe risks to public health, hindrances and economic disturbance caused by the COVID-19 pandemic continue to exist and Member States apply lockdown measures (Art. 27b).

82   See Čičin-Šain, New Mandatory Disclosure Rules for Tax Intermediaries and Taxpayers in the European Union, WTJ 2019, pp. 79-90.

authorities at any time without prior request (Art. 10(3)). Spontaneous exchange is partly mandatory (Art. 9(1)) and partly voluntary (Art. 9(2)).

In Art. 9(1), the Directive mentions cases in which a Member State **"shall"** inform **740** the other State without prior request. These provisions largely correspond to the provisions on spontaneous exchange in the first Directive, in respect of which the CJEU has already clarified that this amounts to an **obligation** for the Member States.[83] A Member State **must** therefore, of its own motion, forward information in the five cases listed below:[84]

- Where there is a possible loss of tax (**unjustified saving of tax**) in another Member State;[85]
- Where a taxpayer obtains a tax reduction or exemption that should be followed by a corresponding tax liability or increase in another Member State (e.g. as the amount of the tax credit would be reduced);[86]
- Where there are business dealings between taxpayers in two different Member States that are liable to reduce tax (tax planning, not necessarily "tax avoidance");
- Where there is a possible loss of tax as a result of artificial transfers of profits within groups of enterprises (transfer pricing not in line with the arm's length principle); and
- *do ut des*: when information obtained from Member State B enabled Member State A to obtain new, interesting information, which is also relevant to Member State B, Member State A has to forward that new information to State B.

Information on foreign residents **unlawfully obtained**, e.g. data stolen by a bank **741** employee and subsequently sold to the local tax administration, should be covered by the obligation on spontaneous exchange under Art. 9(1)(a), as the DAC does not set limits in this respect. Using this information in a tax, civil or criminal procedure in the receiving State may, however, be subject to limitations based on the CFR (see also m.no. 760 et seq.).

If one of the circumstances requiring mandatory spontaneous exchange under **742** Art. 9(1) is at hand, the competent authority must forward the information to the competent authority of the other Member State concerned as quickly as possible, and **no later than one month** after the information has become available (Art. 10(1)).

Moreover, Art. 9(2) **allows** a Member State, in all other cases, to forward any **743** information of which it is aware to another Member State by way of spontaneous exchange if this information "may be useful" to the other Member State. Finally, it has to be kept in mind that the Tax Collection Directive also permits the Member States to spontaneously exchange information in specific situations (see m.no. 792).

---

83 CJEU, 13 April 2000, Case C-420/98, *W.N.*, EU:C:2000:209, para. 13.
84 See Terra/Wattel, *European Tax Law* (2018) p. 576 et seq.
85 CJEU, 13 April 2000, Case C-420/98, *W.N.*, EU:C:2000:209, paras. 22–24.
86 Concerning this obligation, there is an overlap with the spontaneous exchange of information under the Tax Collection Directive (see m.no. 792).

E. Other Forms of Cooperation

1. Collaboration among Officials in the State Concerned (Art. 11)

744   Under international public law, tax officials of one Member State may not conduct investigations in another Member State on their own. The DAC does not revoke that principle. However, Art. 11 offers the opportunity to **authorize the presence of tax officials of the requesting State** in the offices of administrative authorities or during administrative enquiries carried out in the territory of the requested Member State.

745   Note, that the opportunity conceded in Art. 11 is **subject to prior bilateral agreement** by the Member States concerned. Moreover, Art. 11 is limited to the presence of foreign officials (Art. 11(1)) and the possibility to interview individuals and examine records (Art. 11(2)); officers of the requesting State are still not allowed to enact audit activities of the requesting authority.[87] In addition, the officials involved need to be authorized by the requesting Member State and be able to produce written confirmation of their identity and authorization at any time (Art. 11(1) and (3)).

2. Simultaneous Controls (Art. 12)

746   Art. 12 provides for procedures and rules for simultaneous controls (joint audits) of one or more persons of interest in different Member States. Simultaneous controls are tax audits where the audited persons, the audited cases and the time schedules are coordinated between two or more States. However, the Member States still remain sovereign, as they still conduct these coordinated audits **only in their own territory**. Only the information thus obtained will be exchanged between the Member States involved. Simultaneous audits can be more effective than controls conducted by a single Member State in particular with regard to multinational enterprises (e.g. transfer pricing issues between a German parent company and its Belgian subsidiary). The Commission announced that it will consider proposing more comprehensive rules for joint audits in the field of direct taxation.[88]

3. Request for Notification (Art. 13)

747   In addition to presence in the territory of another Member State and simultaneous controls, Member States may also ask for assistance in notifying addressees. The object of notification may be **any instrument and decision** that emanates

---

87   See Seer, Recent Development in Exchange of Information within the EU for Tax Matters, *EC Tax Review* 2013, p. 72.

88   Report from the Commission to the European Parliament and the Council, on the application of Council Directive (EU) 2011/16/EU on administrative cooperation in the field of direct taxation, COM(2017) 781 final, p. 6.

from the administrative authorities of the requesting Member State. The requested Member State has to carry out the notification as if it were its own similar decision or instrument. An authority may only make a request for notification when it is unable to notify in accordance with the national rules governing the notification, or where such notification would lead to **disproportional difficulties** (Art. 13(4)).

F. Grounds for Refusal of Assistance

1. Invalid and Valid Grounds

The Directive leads to a far-reaching obligation of Member States to exchange **748** information between one another. Such an obligation to cooperate is not only derived from the Directive itself, but also from EU law, namely the principle **of Union loyalty** (Art. 4(3) TEU). The Directive explicitly refers to two important invalid grounds for refusal of assistance: Art. 18(1) provides that Member States cannot refuse to cooperate on the ground that they have **no domestic interest** in the information asked for. In addition, according to Art. 18(2), **national bank secrecy** is no longer recognized as a valid ground for refusal.[89]

However, the Directive itself also lists **five specific grounds** that give the Member **749** States the right to refuse cooperation (Art. 17). These limits on the obligations under the Directive are mainly relevant to exchange on request and mandatory spontaneous exchange of information. With regard to automatic exchange for specific categories of income and capital, financial account information, tax rulings, CbC reports and cross-border arrangements, Art. 17(1), (2) and (3) do not seem to be applicable. Only commercial secrets under Art. 17(4) might arguably be a valid ground for refusal in respect of automatic exchange (see also m.no. 753).

2. Subsidiarity Principle (Art. 17(1))

Art. 17(1) allows the requested State to refuse its co-operation if it appears as if **750** the requesting State has not exhausted its own "usual sources" of obtaining the information sought prior to the request, in so far as these means could be utilized without jeopardizing the result desired. This provision leads to a number of **uncertainties**: It seems unclear how the requested State can verify whether this requirement has been met. Furthermore, there are doubts whether "usual sources" also cover more burdensome increased procedural obligations for taxpayers in cross-border situations than in purely domestic situations.[90]

---

89 This had been a valid ground for refusal under the old Directive 77/799/EEC. See Schilcher in Lang et al., *Introduction to European Tax Law on Direct Taxation* (2010) m.no. 617.

90 E.g. Art. 90(2) German Tax Code. From a fundamental freedoms perspective, increased procedural obligations for cross-border situations seem to be acceptable (CJEU, 10 February 2011, Joined Cases C-436/08 and C-437/08, *Haribo and Österreichische Salinen*, EU:C:2009:17, para. 95 et seq.).

3. National Treatment (Art. 17(2))

751 The Directive does not oblige the requested State to carry out enquiries or to provide information if this would be **contrary to its domestic law** (except for domestic bank secrecy provisions, see m.no. 748). However, if information is already readily available in the requested State and there is consequently no need to conduct enquiries to collect it, the wording of Art. 17(2) does not seem to provide grounds for refusal to forward that specific information, even where collection would be contrary to the national law of the requested State.[91]

4. Reciprocity (Art. 17(3))

752 The principle of reciprocity allows a Member State to refuse to provide information when the requesting State itself is **legally unable** to provide similar information on request. This provision only covers reasons of law and not reasons of fact. This means that if a competent authority does not have the necessary administrative possibilities to collect the information requested, this is not a valid excuse.[92] In fact, this provision permits Member States, in particular, to decline the forwarding of banking information to Austria and Luxembourg related to tax years prior to 2011.

5. Commercial Secrets (Art. 17(4))

753 Member States may refuse to provide information if this would lead to the disclosure of a commercial, industrial or professional secret or a commercial process. The aim of this provision is to protect the legitimate competitive edge of the undertakings concerned.[93] Economic and industrial espionage should be hindered.[94] Art. 18(2) clarifies that banking secrets and ownership secrets are not covered by this exception. This ground for refusal is emphasized in particular with respect to **tax rulings and cross-border arrangements**: According to Art. 8a(6)(b) and Art. 8ab(14)(c), Member States shall communicate to other States an abstract description of the underlying facts only in order to avoid the disclosure of a commercial, industrial or professional secret.

6. Ordre Public (Art. 17(4))

754 Member States may refuse to exchange information the disclosure of which would be contrary to **public policy**. The public policy reservation allows a Member State to refuse an exchange of information if one of its fundamental interests would be affected. According to some scholars, a Member State may also refuse to supply

---

91 See Terra/Wattel, *European Tax Law* (2018) p. 583-584.
92 Under the old Directive, declining for reasons of law and for reasons of fact was possible. See Terra/Wattel, *European Tax Law* (2012) p. 839.
93 See Terra/Wattel, *European Tax Law* (2018) p. 585.
94 See Seer, Recent Development in Exchange of Information within the EU for Tax Matters, *EC Tax Review* 2013, p. 73.

information based on public policy grounds where the request originates from the acquisition of illegally obtained information by the requesting State.[95]

G. Standard Forms and Language (Arts. 20 and 21)

To guarantee efficient information exchange, Art. 20 sets up **standard forms and computerized formats,** which must be used for all types of exchange. The use of these standard forms is accompanied by provisions concerning the use of the Common Communication Network (**CCN**), an electronic data exchange system.[96] Information communicated must "as far as possible" be provided by electronic means using this network. Detailed rules including forms and templates are laid down in the Commission Implementing Regulation (EU) 2015/2378 and its Annex I-XIII.[97]

755

Requests for information may be made in **any language** agreed between the co-operating authorities. Asking for translations into the official language of the requested State is only permitted in "special cases" (Art. 21(4)). As regards the automatic exchange of tax rulings, CbC reports and cross-border arrangements, Member States are also permitted to make use of any of the official languages of the Union (Art. 20(5) and (6)). **Key elements,** however, have to also be provided in **English.**

756

H. Use of Information Received

As regards the use of the information received, Art. 16 follows the **"national treatment"** principle. Art. 16(1) provides that all information made known to a Member State under this Directive must be kept secret in that State in the same manner as information received under its domestic legislation. Moreover, according to Art. 16(5), information received may be invoked as evidence by the requesting State on the same basis as similar information provided by an authority of the requesting State.

757

More specifically, information received from another State may be used for the **administration and enforcement** concerning taxes covered by the Directive and compulsory social security contributions. In addition, the receiving State may also use the information received in the assessment and enforcement of taxes covered by the Tax Collection Directive, which extends the use notably to value added tax, excise duties and customs; and for judicial and administrative proceedings involving penalties, meaning criminal proceedings against tax offenders, provided their defence rights are respected (Art. 16(1)). Any other use legally permitted in the requesting State is only allowed upon the consent of the requested State. Permission, however, has to be granted if the envisaged use is legal in the requested State as well (Art. 16(2)).

758

---

95   See Baker/Pistone, General Report on Subject 2, IFA Cahiers (2015), p. 63.
96   This system is already in use for value added tax and excise purposes.
97   Commission Implementing Regulation (EU) 2015/2378 amended by: Commission Implementing Regulation (EU) 2016/1963, Commission Implementing Regulation (EU) 2018/99, and Commission Implementing Regulation (EU) 2019/532.

759   The Directive includes more specific rules only as regards **CbC reports**: Art. 16(6) stipulates that CbC reports shall be used for the purposes of assessing high-level transfer-pricing risks and other risks related to base erosion and profit shifting and for statistical purposes. As a safeguard in favour of the taxpayer, the Directive explicitly provides that **transfer-pricing adjustments shall not be based directly on the data included in CbC reports**. However, the CbC report may still serve as a basis for making further enquiries (e.g. tax audits) that, in the end, lead to appropriate adjustments.

760   It is disputed whether the receiving State may also use **unlawfully obtained information** in its national tax or criminal proceedings. Examples might include: stolen data by a bank employee subsequently sold to the tax authorities (as was the case in Germany and France) or information obtained by illegal interception of telecommunications and seizure of emails.[98] Limits to the use of information that was initially obtained unlawfully in another State may be found in domestic law and fundamental rights laid down in the **ECHR or the CFR**.[99] As regards the implications of the CFR, the CJEU held, in the *WebMindLicences* case in 2015, that Art. 47 CFR prohibits domestic tax authorities from using evidence in a VAT proceeding that has been obtained by domestic authorities in breach of the rights guaranteed by the Charter.[100] Hence, it seems advisable that the evidence provided by the requested State should be accompanied by details about how the evidence was collected.

761   **Forwarding information to other Member States** is, as a rule, permissible if the information "is likely to be useful" to the administration and enforcement of taxes in this third Member State. The Member State of origin must be informed beforehand about the intention to forward the information, in order to be in a position to oppose such a sharing of information (within ten working days of receipt at the latest, Art. 16(3)). **With regard to the forwarding of information to third States** see m.no. 771.

I.   Taxpayer Rights

1.   Legal framework

762   Besides references to rights under the Data Protection Directive in Art. 25 (see m.no. 765 et seq), the DAC does not contain any provision on protection for taxpayers. This was explicitly confirmed by the CJEU in the *Sabou* case in 2013, wherein the Court clarified that the Directive *"does not [...] confer specific rights*

---

98   See e.g. CJEU, 17 December 2015, Case C-419/14, *WebMindLicenses Kft*, EU:C:2015:832.

99   See on the diverging opinions Calderón Carrero/Quintas Seara, The Taxpayer's Right of Defence in Cross-Border Exchange-of-Information Procedures, *BIT* 2014, p. 502; Parada, Intergovernmental Agreements and the Implementation of FATCA in Europe, *WTJ* 2015, p. 212 et seq.

100   CJEU, 17 December 2015, Case C-419/14, *WebMindLicenses Kft*, EU:C:2015:832, paras. 87-91.

on the taxpayer," but coordinates the transfer of information between competent authorities of the Member States only.[101] Member States are, however, at liberty to grant taxpayer rights with regard to exchange proceedings under **domestic law**.[102] Persons potentially affected by an exchange of tax information can thus rely on domestic legislation, e.g. for an injunction or claim for damages in the case of unlawful exchange.[103] The possibility to implement domestic safeguards is limited by the soft law obligations set by the **OECD Global Forum** and its peer review process, according to which procedural protection should not unduly prevent or delay the **effective exchange** of information.[104]

In addition to domestic law, taxpayer rights can also be inferred from the ECHR **763** and EU primary law, in particular the **fundamental right to the protection of personal data in Art. 8 CFR, the freedom to conduct a business in Art. 16 CFR, the fundamental right to good administration, including the right to be heard and the right to have access to own files in Art. 41 CFR, the right to an effective remedy and to a fair trial in Art. 47 CFR and the right of defence including the freedom from self-incrimination in Art. 48 CFR** (see Chapter 1, m.no. 36 et seq.). Domestic provisions implementing the DAC, including legislation on penalties, fall within the scope of the CFR.[105] The effects of the fundamental rights stipulated in the CFR on exchange of information proceedings have not been fully clarified by the Court to date. When this book went to print, two referals from Luxembourgh courts on the scope of data protection rights and defensive rights of the taxpayer and third-party information holders deriving from Arts. 8 and 47 CFR were pending before the CJEU.[106] Besides the fundamental rights of the CFR, **general legal principles** that are recognized under EU primary law (e.g. the principle of legal certainty and legitimate expectations) and the **fundamental freedoms** may also set limits on reporting obligations and information exchange proceedings.

2. Right to data protection

Whether the DAC and its extensive reporting obligations, in particular as regards **764** financial account information, CbC reports, tax rulings and cross-border arrangements, may lead to a violation of the **fundamental right to data protection** is debated by scholars.[107] According to the prevailing opinion, the scope of the fun-

---

101 CJEU, 22 October 2013, Case C-276/12, *Sabou*, EU:C:2013:678, para. 36 et seq.; confirmed in CJEU, 16 May 2017, Case C-682/15, *Berlioz*, EU:C:2017:373, para. 46.
102 CJEU, 22 October 2013, Case C-276/12, *Sabou*, EU:C:2013:678, paras. 45 and 49.
103 Terra/Wattel, *European Tax Law* (2018) p. 586.
104 OECD Global Forum on Transparency and Exchange of Information for Tax Purposes, 2016 terms of reference to monitor and review progress transparency and exchange of information on request for tax purposes (2016) Section B.2.1, p. 6.
105 CJEU, 16 May 2017, Case C-682/15, *Berlioz*, EU:C:2017:373, paras. 32-42.
106 Pending Cases C-245/19 and C-437/19, *État du Grand-duché de Luxembourg*.
107 In detail, Wöhrer, *Data Protection and Taxpayers' Rights: Challenges created by Automatic Exchange of Information* (2018).

damental right to data protection is limited to natural persons. Similar effects for legal entities may, however, derive from the freedom to conduct a business in Art. 16 CFR[108] (see m.nos 767). The CJEU seems to apply a rather lenient standard in favour of tax legislatures: In the *Commission v. Germany* case in 2018, the Court ruled that the obligation for travel agents, under the VAT Directive, to disclose the profit margin on the invoice does not infringe these fundamental rights, since the measure is justified by the aim of simplifying tax rules and of allocating VAT revenues between Member States.[109] Similarly, in the *Puškár* case in 2017, the CJEU ruled that the publication of a list of straw men, including personal data, without their consent, can be justified by the aim of ensuring tax collection and combating tax fraud.[110] As the DAC, however, leads to massive reporting obligations for scenarios that are neither fraudulent nor abusive and the reported information is automatically exchanged with Member States to which this information may not be at all useful, it is nevertheless questionable whether the DAC measures are indeed proportionate in the light of the objective they pursue.[111]

765 Art. 25(1) clarifies that all exchange of information pursuant to the Directive (on request, spontaneously and automatically) is, in principle, subject to the provisions of the **Data Protection Directive 95/46/EC**,[112] which enshrines the **fundamental right to the protection of personal data guaranteed by Art. 8 CFR**. As the Data Protection Directive has been replaced by the **General Data Protection Regulation** (EU) 2016/679 of 25 May 2018,[113] the references in the DAC still need to be updated. However, within the same paragraph, it is specified that the Member States **are obliged** to restrict some of these rights for the purposes of the correct application of the DAC to the extent required in order to safeguard important economic or financial interests, including taxation matters.[114] As a result, Member States are, in principle, based on the Directive, **not obliged to inform the taxpayer** about the processing of data and the exchange of information (except for financial account information, see m.no. 766). Moreover, according to Art. 25(4), any information processed is to be retained for no longer than necessary to achieve the purpose of

---

108   See Blum/Langer, At a Crossroads: Mandatory Disclosure under DAC 6 and EU Primary Law – Part 2, *ET* 2019, p. 314.

109   CJEU, 8 February 2018, Case C-380/16, *Commission v Germany*, EU:C:2018:76, paras. 62-73.

110   CJEU, 27 September 2017, Case C-73/16, *Puškár*, EU:C:2017:725, paras. 108-117.

111   With respect to DAC 6, Blum/Langer, At a Crossroads: Mandatory Disclosure under DAC 6 and EU Primary Law – Part 2, *ET* 2019, pp. 315-317.

112   Directive 95/46/EC of the European Parliament and of the Council of 24 October 1995 on the protection of individuals with regard to the processing of personal data and on the free movement of such data, OJ L 281/31 of 23 November 1995.

113   Regulation (EU) 2016/679 of the European Parliament and of the Council of 27 April 2016 on the protection of natural persons with regard to the processing of personal data and on the free movement of such data, and repealing Directive 95/46/EC (General Data Protection Regulation), OJ L 119/1 of 4 April 2016.

114   Information on taxable income will meet the requirement of "important economic or financial interest" (see Opinion of Advocate General Cruz Villalón, 9 July 2015, Case C-201/14, *Bara*, EU:C:2015:461, point 82).

the Directive, and, in any case, in accordance with each data controller's domestic rules on the statute of limitations.

A different data protection standard only applies with respect to **financial account information**: Art. 25(2) clarifies that reporting financial institutions and the competent authorities of each Member State are considered to be data controllers for the purpose of the Data Protection Directive 95/46/EC, resulting in data quality obligations and information duties.[115] According to Art. 25(3), Member States have to ensure that the reporting financial institution **informs each person concerned** about the exchange of the financial account information in sufficient time to exercise his data protection rights[116] and, in any case, before the financial institution reports the information to the competent authority.

766

3. Freedom to conduct a business

767

The reporting obligations and information exchange proceedings deriving from the DAC might raise conflicts with the right to conduct a business of several stakeholders. In particular, DAC 2 and DAC 6 put compliance burdens on private entities (financial institutions and intermediaries) and oblige them to report certain customer data to the authorities. This risk of reporting could prevent potential clients from engaging with them. Moreover, as the reporting obligations are limited to cross-border situations, conflicts with the fundamental freedoms could arise.[117] It is questionable whether this interference with EU primary law is proportionate in light of the objective of safeguarding tax revenues and fighting tax abuse and evasion.

4. Right of defence and right to fair trial

768

According to the 2013 *Sabou* decision, the requesting State is, based on the fundamental right of defence, not obliged to inform the taxpayer of the request and to allow his participation in the exchange proceedings. Defensive rights for the taxpayer might potentially only be available in the contentious stage of the proceedings (tax assessment) rather than in the investigation stage (collection of information).[118]

In the 2017 *Berlioz* case,[119] the CJEU confirmed that procedural rights may also exist in the investigation stage, namely at the level of a **third-party information holder**. A Luxembourg investment fund was subject to a penalty because it refused

769

---

115 See Arts. 6, 10 and 11 Data Protection Directive 95/46/EC.
116 This seems, in particular, to refer to Art. 14 Data Protection Directive, which lays down the right for the data subject to object to the processing of data if there are compelling legitimate grounds in his particular situation. Moreover, the Data Protection Directive guarantees the following rights: the right to obtain from the controller confirmation whether data is being processed, information on the purpose of the processing, information on the categories of data concerned and information on the recipients to whom the data is disclosed (Art. 12).
117 See Blum/Langer, At a Crossroads: Mandatory Disclosure under DAC 6 and EU Primary Law – Parts 1 and 2, *ET* 2019, pp. 288 and 314.
118 CJEU, 22 October 2013, Case C-276/12, *Sabou*, EU:C:2013:678.
119 CJEU, 16 May 2017, C-682/15, *Berlioz*, EU:C:2017:373; in more detail on this case Pantazatou, in: Lang et al (eds.) *CJEU – Recent Developments in Direct Taxation 2017* (2018) p. 127 et seq.

to provide specific information to the Luxembourg authorities that they ought to have in answering an information request by the French authorities. The Court held that, based on Art. 47 CFR, the investment fund must be entitled to **challenge the legality of the decision** to provide information and the "foreseeable relevance" of the information before an independent and impartial tribunal (see also m.no. 698). The whole of the request of information, however, may not need to be provided to the third-party information holder, as this could impair the effectiveness of the underlying investigation. When reconciling the *Sabou* and *Berlioz* cases, this right to a judicial review seems to be limited to third parties that have no possibility of challenging the request and use of information in a contentious stage in the requesting State.[120] More case law on defensive rights is to be expected in the upcoming years.

5. Freedom from self-incrimination (nemo tenetur)

770 The reporting obligations deriving from the DAC, in particular the mandatory disclosure rules for cross-border arrangements introduced by DAC 6, could also lead to a conflict with the freedom from self-incrimination deriving from Art. 48(2) CFR.[121] As the hallmarks in the Annex to DAC 6 are of a rather general nature, not every arrangement that meets one of the hallmarks (e.g. transfer of hard-to-value intangibles abroad) will qualify as tax evasion or tax fraud. However, in those limited scenarios where it is clear that the information that should be reported is likely to be used to initiate a criminal proceeding, the intermediary and the relevant taxpayer should be able to refuse to disclose the arrangement by relying on Art. 48(2) CFR and should not be penalized for this non-disclosure.

J. Exchange of Information and Third Countries

771 The Directive also gives guidance on the exchange of information with regard to third countries. According to Art. 24(1), Member States may also **forward information received from a third country to other Member States,** upon request or spontaneously, if this information is "foreseeably relevant" to the administration or enforcement of the other Member State and in so far as the agreement with that third country so permits. The scope of this provision seems rather narrow, since, under the current OECD standard, a contracting State to a DTC or TIEA is only permitted to request information that is needed for **its own tax purposes** (not for the purposes of another State). In addition, under the prevailing opinion, the current OECD standard also does not permit the spontaneous passing on of information received from a contracting State to another State not party to the treaty, unless explicitly stipulated otherwise.

---

120   Opinion of Advocate General Wathelet, 10 January 2017, Case C-682/15, *Berlioz*, EU:C: 2017:2, paras. 115-117.

121   Čičin-Šain, New Mandatory Disclosure Rules for Tax Intermediaries and Taxpayers in the European Union, *WTJ* 2019, pp. 90-107; Blum/Langer, At a Crossroads: Mandatory Disclosure under DAC 6 and EU Primary Law – Part 2, *ET* 2019, p. 317.

Vice versa, Art. 24(2) regulates the **forwarding of information received from a** 772
Member State to third countries. Information received from another Member
State can be provided to a third country, provided that the Member State of origin
agrees, and the third country is prepared to reciprocate by exchanging information
for the purposes of tax avoidance.

Moreover, with respect to agreements on mutual assistance of Member States with 773
third countries, Art. 19 sets up a **most-favoured-nation clause.** If a Member State
agrees on wider cooperation with a third country than that provided for under
the DAC, this Member State is obliged to extend this cooperation to any other
Member State asking for it. The most-favoured-nation clause does not apply within
the European Union (i.e. for treaties signed between Member States).

Member States mainly enter into bilateral agreements on exchange of information 774
with third countries. Only in the special field of **automatic exchange of financial
account information** is the European Commission, since 2014, concluding **agreements in the name of the European Union** effective for all Member States with
those third countries where important financial centres are located (see m.no. 814).

K. Comparison and Relationship to Bi- and Multilateral Provisions on the Exchange of Information

Alongside the national provisions based on the DAC, bilateral provisions based on 775
Art. 26 OECD MC, as well as on the Model on Tax Information Exchange Agreements (**TIEA Model**) and the Convention on Mutual Administrative Assistance
in Tax Matters (**MAATM Convention**), also allow for exchange of information.
With respect to automatic exchange of financial account information, on a global
level, the intergovernmental agreements with the US based on the FATCA obligations and the multilateral competent authority agreements based on the **OECD
CRS** are counterparts. As regards CbC reports, a multilateral competent authority
agreement was signed in 2017 (**CbC MCAA**) in order to implement **BEPS Action 13**.
With respect to tax rulings, the political commitment on automatic exchange laid
down by the OECD/G20 in the final report to **BEPS Action 5** is of relevance.
Finally, the counterpart to DAC 6 on reportable cross-border arrangements is
BEPS Action 12.

Art. 26 OECD MC, the TIEA Model, the MAATM Convention and the various 776
international agreements on exchange of specific categories of information are, **to
a large extent, comparable** to the DAC.[122] However, there are also a number of
differences:

---

122   For example, comparable to the Directive, the OECD MC, the TIEA Model and the MAATM Con-
      vention also provide for exchange of information upon request, automatically or spontaneously (the
      TIEA Model itself does not provide for automatic exchange; however, the Model Protocol to the
      TIEA Model does). Moreover, they all contain secrecy provisions (Art. 26(2) OECD MC, Art. 8 TIEA
      Model, Art. 22 MAATM), which are, to a large extent, similar to Art. 16 of the Directive.

- *Scope*: In practice, bilateral provisions based on Art. 26 OECD MC may either provide for a restricted "**narrow**" exchange of information (only information that is relevant to the proper application of the respective convention may be exchanged) or an unrestricted "**broad**" exchange of information (information that is only relevant to the correct application of domestic law may be exchanged as well). Only a "broad" information clause equals the standard laid down in Art. 5 of the DAC.

- *Exchange on Request*: The OECD MC, the TIEA Model, the MAATM Convention and the Directive permit a request only if the requested information is "foreseeably relevant" to the assessment or enforcement of taxes in the requesting State. However, the details in order to fulfil this requirement differ: Based on the Commentary to Art. 26 OECD MC (after the 2012 update) "**group requests**" (asking for information on a group of taxpayers characterized by specific criteria without naming them individually) are permitted under the OECD MC.[123] In contrast, based on the requirements for a valid request in Art. 5, in conjunction with Art. 20(2) of the DAC (identity of the person is a must), "group requests" are not possible under the DAC.

- *Grounds for Refusal*: The OECD MC allows the requested State to refuse its cooperation (Art. 26(3) OECD MC) in situations that are equivalent to Art. 17 of the DAC. The TIEA Model and the MAATM Convention, however, include more grounds for refusal of cooperation than the Directive.[124]

- *Automatic Exchange:* The Directive obliges the Member States to automatically exchange data on certain categories of income and capital (e.g. financial income, employment income, etc., see m.no. 704 et seq.), tax relevant documents (tax rulings, CbC reports) and reportable cross-border arrangements. The OECD MC, the MAATM Convention and the protocol to the TIEA Model merely permit an automatic exchange. Comparable mandatory rules, however, derive from a number of specific international agreements at the OECD level. These international counterparts are to a large extent comparable to the obligations set by the DAC. In some areas, the **EU even goes beyond the international agreements.** For example, BEPS Action 12 only recommends implementing mandatory disclosure rules for potentially aggressive tax planning schemes, but does not require the automatic exchange of this data. Moreover, whereas the OECD is critical of making CbC reports publicly available within the EU, public CbC is under discussion (see m.no. 682).

- *Time Limits and Organization:* Art. 26 OECD MC, the TIEA Model and the MAATM Convention do not contain any time limits for responding to a request and are less specific when it comes to organizational and procedural

---

123   See Commentary to Art. 26 OECD MC, para 5.
124   E.g. declining a request is also permitted in the case of discrimination against a national of the requested State as compared with a national of the applicant State in the same circumstances.

aspects. However, the OECD MC (since the 2012 update) at least provides for a proposal for time limits to answer a request to be included in a bilateral agreement.[125]

As a rule, the **most effective rule applies** between EU Member States, since the EU rules are the **minimum level** of cooperation to be extended. Art. 1(3) clarifies that **provisions with a broader scope** than the DAC are not in any way affected by the provisions of the Directive.[126] Hence, e.g., if a DTC between Member States only provides for a "narrow" information clause, the possibilities for exchanging information are broadened by the DAC. In contrast, a group request might be based on a DTC in line with the latest OECD MC between two Member States, as the EU Directive does not allow for group requests. **777**

If the DAC and the bi- or multilateral agreement have a comparable scope, the Member States can, in principle, **freely decide** whether to base a request for information to another Member State on the DAC or the bi- or multilateral agreement. However, a decision to base a request on the DTC rather than the DAC should not exclude the jurisdiction of the CJEU and the applicability of general EU principles, including the fundamental rights laid down in the CFR, since any domestic legislation on exchange of information, enacted prior to or subsequent to the entry into force of the DAC, can be considered as **implementation of EU law**.[127] **778**

With respect to agreements with third countries refer to m.no. 774. **779**

L. Relevance of the Directive in the CJEU's Case Law on the Fundamental Freedoms

The DAC has also influenced the CJEU's jurisprudence concerning the relationship between Member States' direct tax systems and the **fundamental freedoms**. Repeatedly, the CJEU has referred to the Directive and held that a Member State may rely on it in order to obtain from another Member State all information enabling it to ascertain the correct amount of income or all information it considers necessary to ascertain the correct amount of income tax payable by a taxpayer.[128] Thus, Member States cannot justify discriminatory tax measures applicable to cross-border situations within the EU by the need to ensure the **effectiveness of fiscal supervision** (see also Chapter 3, m.no. 274 et seq.). The Member States are not, however, obliged to make use of the Directive, but may ask the taxpayer for **780**

---

125 Commentary to Art. 26 OECD MC, para 10.4.
126 See, on the old Directive, CJEU, 11 October 2007, Case C-451/05, *Elisa*, EU:C:2007:594, paras. 42–48.
127 Cf Opinion of Advocate General Wathelet, 10 January 2017, Case C-682/15, *Berlioz*, EU:C:2017:2, point 47.
128 CJEU, 28 January 1992, Case C-204/90, *Bachmann*, EU:C:1992:35; CJEU, 29 March 2007, Case C-347/04, *Rewe Zentralfinanz*, EU:C:2007:194; CJEU, 11 October 2007, Case C-451/05, *Elisa*, EU:C:2007:594.

evidence on conditions for a tax benefit beforehand.[129] Thereby, the CJEU seems to accept increased procedural obligations for taxpayers in cross-border situations to be in line with the fundamental freedoms.

781 By contrast, the CJEU generally accepts the justification of the effectiveness of fiscal supervision for discriminatory tax measures in **third-country situations within the scope of the free movement of capital under Art. 63 TFEU,** as the DAC is not applicable vis-à-vis third countries, including EEA Member States.[130] Third countries may, thus, only escape discriminatory treatment of capital movements in the tax law systems of the Member States if they agree on an exchange of information system "equivalent" to the Directive with the respective Member State (see also Chapter 3, m.no. 276). Bi- or multilateral agreements (e.g. DTCs and the MAATM Convention) may qualify as equivalent, although they lack comparable enforcement possibilities (no jurisdiction by the CJEU).[131] Asking for an agreement on mutual assistance with a third country as a prerequisite for a tax benefit may be disproportionate only if the necessary information does not require a complex assessment and may thus be effectively verified without relying on a mutual assistance mechanism.[132]

---

129 CJEU, 10 February 2011, Joined Cases C-436/08 and C-437/08, *Haribo and Österreichische Salinen*, EU:C:2009:17, para. 102.

130 CJEU, 18 December 2007, Case C-101/05, *A*, EU:C:2007:804; CJEU, 19 November 2009, Case C-540/07, *Commission v Italy*, EU:C:2009:717; concerning EEA States see CJEU, 28 October 2010, Case C-72/09, *Etablissements Rimbaud*, EU:C:2010:645.

131 CJEU, 10 April 2014, Case C-190/12, *Emerging Markets*, EU:C:2014:249, para. 85 et seq.; see also Binder/Pinetz, Ensuring the Effectiveness of Fiscal Supervision in Third Country Situations, *EC Tax Review* 2014, p. 328 et seq.

132 CJEU, 17 October 2013, Case C-181/12, *Welte*, EU:C:2013:662, para. 64 et seq.

M. Overview of the Directive on Administrative Cooperation

782

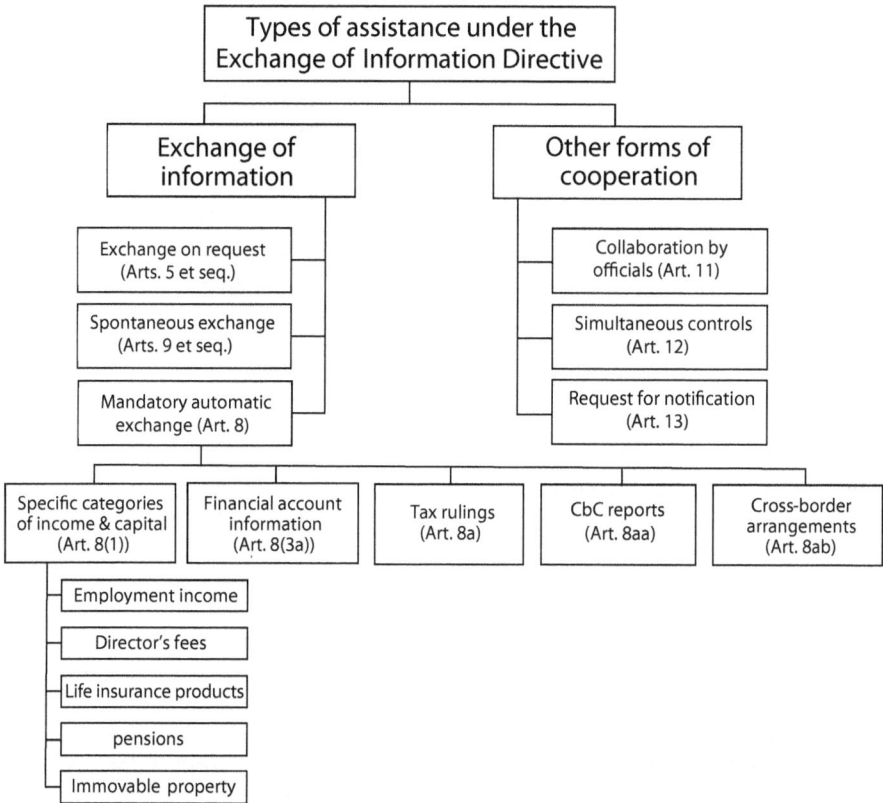

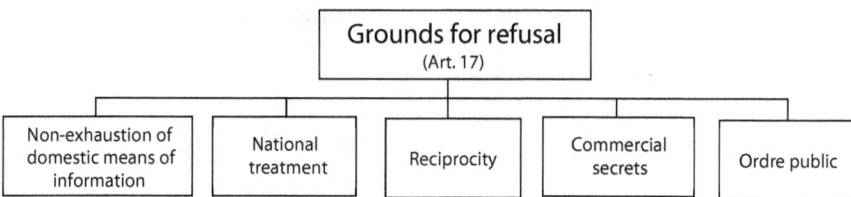

II. The Directive on Mutual Assistance in the Recovery of Tax Claims

A. Background and History

783 In 2010, the Council adopted Directive 2010/24/EU on Mutual Assistance in the Recovery of Tax Claims (hereinafter the "**Tax Collection Directive**"), which entered into force 1 January 2012.[133] National provisions relating to recovery are applicable only within national territories, which could, in itself, be an obstacle to the establishment and functioning of the common market.[134] Thus, the Tax Collection Directive provides for common rules on mutual assistance for the cross-border recovery of tax claims. Similar rules on assistance in the recovery of tax claims can also be found in Art. 27 OECD MC and in the MAATM Convention.

B. Scope of the Directive

1. Objective Scope

784 The Tax Collection Directive has a **wide scope**, since it covers assistance between the Member States for the recovery of any claims covered by the Directive (Art. 1).

2. Substantive Scope

785 The Tax Collection Directive covers **all taxes and duties of any kind** levied by or on behalf of a Member State or its territorial or administrative subdivisions, or on behalf of the Union (Art. 2(1)(a)). It also applies to refunds, interventions and other measures forming part of the system of total or partial financing of the European Agricultural Guarantee Fund (EAGF) and the European Agricultural Fund for Rural Development (EAFRD), including sums to be collected in connection with these actions (Art. 2(1)(b)) and to levies and other duties provided for under the common organization of the market for the sugar sector (Art. 2(1)(c)). Moreover, the Tax Collection Directive also covers fees and surcharges relating to these claims, fees for certificates and similar documents issued in connection with administrative procedures related to taxes and duties, as well as interest and costs relating to these claims (Art. 2(2)). The Tax Collection Directive does not apply to

---

133 The Tax Collection Directive 2010/24/EU replaced the Council Directive 2008/55/EC of 26 May 2008, OJ L 150/28 of 26 May 2008 on mutual assistance for the recovery of claims relating to certain levies, duties, taxes and other measures, which codified Council Directive 76/308/EEC of 15 March 1976 on mutual assistance for the recovery of claims resulting from operations forming part of the system of financing the European Agricultural Guidance and Guarantee Fund, and of agricultural levies and customs duties, and in respect of value-added tax, OJ L 73/18 of 19 March 1976, and the acts amending it (Council Directive 79/1071/EEC of 7 December 1979, OJ L 331 of 27 December 1979, and Council Directive 2001/44/EC of 15 July 2001, OJ L 175 of 28 June 2001). For a comparison between the new and the old Directive see Schilcher/Spies/Zirngast in: Lang et al. (eds.), *Introduction to European Tax Law on Direct Taxation* (2016) m.no. 707 et seq.

134 Preamble to Council Directive 76/308/EEC.

compulsory social security contributions, dues of a contractual nature and criminal penalties (Art. 2(3)).

3. Personal and Territorial Scope

The **definition** of *"person"* in the Directive (Art. 3(c)) is aligned with the DAC   **786** (Art. 3(11), see m.no. 688). This wide definition should allow Member States to carry out cross-border assistance for all possible debtors. Only the spontaneous exchange of information laid down in Art. 6 between Member States is limited to information concerning residents of a Member State. The Directive only applies to EU Member States; EEA States are not under an obligation to implement the rules.

4. Temporal Scope

Any request for recovery assistance by a Member State as from 1 January 2012 is   **787** based on the provisions of the Tax Collection Directive. As there are no general rules in the Directive on the taxable periods to which requested recovery assistance has to relate, it is **immaterial to which tax year** a request relates, even if that tax year predates the entry into force of the Directive provision on which the requesting State is relying.[135]

C. Organization (Art. 4)

Art. 4 provides for detailed rules on the designation of the competent authorities   **788** for applying the Tax Collection Directive that are similar to the rules on organization included in the DAC. The key aspect of Art. 4 is the designation of a **single central liaison office ("CLO")** in each Member State, which is to have principal responsibility for any administrative cooperation with other Member States covered by the Tax Collection Directive (Art. 4(2)).

D. Types of Assistance

The Tax Collection Directive provides for **four main types of assistance** in the   **789** recovery of tax claims, which include exchange of the relevant information in relation to a tax claim (Arts. 5-7), notification to the addressee of a tax claim (Art. 8), recovery of a tax claim upon request (Arts. 10-15), as well as the enforcement of precautionary measures (Arts. 16-17).

1. Exchange of Information (Art. 5 et seq.)

The Directive distinguishes between three types of exchange of information: exchange on request (Art. 5), spontaneous exchange (Art. 6) and the presence of   **790** officials of the requesting Member State in the requested Member State (Art. 7).

---

135   CJEU, 1 July 2004, Joined Cases C-361/02 and C-362/02, *Tsapalos and Diamantakis*, EU:C:2004:401, para. 23. See m.no. 692.

a) On Request (Art. 5)

791 At the **request** of the requesting authority, the requested authority **must** provide **any information** that is "**foreseeably relevant**" to the requesting authority in the recovery of its tax claims (see on this term m.no. 685 et seq.). For the purpose of providing that information, the requested authority must arrange for the carrying out of any administrative enquiries necessary to obtain it.

b) Spontaneous exchange of information (Art. 6)

792 Art. 6 of the Directive allows for a spontaneous exchange of information in respect of refunds of tax other than VAT relating to a resident of another Member State, which is similar to the spontaneous exchange under the DAC. It is worth noting that the spontaneous exchange of information on refunds of taxes covered by the DAC is mandatory under Art. 9(1) DAC. In the authors' view, the wider obligation to exchange information under the DAC in such cases takes precedence over the permission under Art. 6 Tax Collection Directive according to Art. 24(1) Tax Collection Directive.

c) Collaboration by Officials in the State Concerned (Art. 7)

793 In order to promote the exchange of information under this Directive, Art. 7 offers the opportunity to authorize the presence of tax officials of the requesting Member State in the offices of administrative authorities or during administrative enquiries carried out in the territory of the requested Member State, as well as the assistance of the competent officials during court proceedings in the requested Member State.[136]

2. Notification to Addressee (Art. 8)

794 At the request of the requesting Member State, the requested Member State must notify to the addressee all documents issued by the requesting Member State that relate to a tax claim or its recovery. The request for notification must be accompanied by a standard form (Art. 8(1)). Similar to the DAC, a Member State may notify documents under the Tax Collection Directive directly to addressees in another Member State by registered mail or electronically (Art. 9(2)) and, therefore, may only request notification assistance when it is unable to notify in accordance with its domestic notification rules (Art. 8(2), see m.no. 747).

3. Recovery upon Request (Arts. 10-15)

795 Arts. 10-15 lay down rules for the collection and cross-border enforcement of a tax claim. Art. 10 provides that, at the request of the requesting authority, the requested authority must recover claims that are the subject of an instrument

---

136   Apart from the assistance of the competent officials during court proceedings in the requested Member State, the provision is aligned with Art. 11 DAC. For more details see m.no. 744.

permitting their enforcement. Moreover, the tax claim must be treated by the requested State **as if it were a domestic claim** (Art. 13(1)). Any request for recovery assistance must be accompanied by the **EU uniform instrument** permitting enforcement in the requested State (Art. 12(1), see in detail m.no. 798).

According to Art. 11(2), the requesting State **must**, as a rule, first use its domestic **796** recovery remedies before requesting recovery assistance. However, there are two cases listed where a Member State is permitted to ask for assistance under the Directive without actually **using domestic remedies beforehand**: first, when it is obvious that there are no recoverable assets in the requesting State and the requesting authority has specific information indicating recoverable assets in the requested State; second, when using its own remedies would be disproportionately difficult. A request may not be made if the tax claim and/or the instrument permitting enforcement is legally challenged by the taxpayer in the requesting State (Art. 11(1)). However, despite such a challenge, the requesting State may insist that the requested State proceeds anyway if the laws of both States nevertheless allow for enforcement (Art. 14(4) 3rd subpara.).

4. Precautionary Measures with respect to a Reasoned Request (Arts. 16 and 17)

At the request of the requesting authority, the requested State must take **precau-** **797** **tionary measures** to ensure recovery where a claim is contested in the requesting State if the laws of both States allow for such measures (Art. 16(1)). The Directive also allows for **early action** to guarantee recovery of a future claim when an instrument permitting enforcement has not yet been issued (Art. 16(1) 1st subpara.).[137] The EU uniform instrument forms the sole basis for the precautionary measures taken in the requested State (see m.no. 798).

E. Uniform Instrument Permitting Enforcement (Art. 12)

The Tax Collection Directive provides for a **uniform instrument permitting** **798** **enforcement** in the requested State.[138] Any request for recovery assistance must be accompanied by the EU uniform instrument permitting enforcement in the requested State (Art. 12(1)). The uniform instrument must reflect the content of the original domestic enforcement instrument (e.g. warrant, writ or judgment) and constitutes the **sole basis for recovery and precautionary measures** in the requested State. Thus, its validity may not be dependent on any act of recognition, supplement or replacement by judicial or other authorities of the requested State. Moreover, the bodies of the requested State have no power to review the acts of

---

137 See Vascega/Van Thiel, Council Adopts New Directive on Mutual Assistance in Recovery of Tax and Similar Claims, *ET* 2010, p. 236.
138 See also Baker et al., International Assistance in the Collection of Taxes, *BIT* 2011, p. 285.

the requesting State (Art. 14(1)), since the Tax Collection Directive is based on the **principle of mutual trust.**[139]

F. Standard Forms and Language (Arts. 21 and 22)

799 Like the DAC, the Tax Collection Directive sets up **standard forms** and **computerized formats** that must be used for all types of assistance. These documents are to be sent by electronic means as far as possible. Notification requests are based on the **uniform notification form,** which is transmitted to the addressee of the notification. Recovery requests are based on the **uniform instrument permitting enforcement** in the requested State. Both documents are available in all official languages.[140]

800 According to the *Kyrian* case, the notification of the enforcement instrument to the taxpayer can be made in an official language of the requested Member State and does not need to include a translation in the language of the requesting Member State, subject to the condition that this ensures the full effectiveness of Union law.[141]

G. Grounds for Refusal of Assistance

801 The Tax Collection Directive provides for a far-reaching obligation on Member States to provide the four main forms of assistance covered by the Directive. Similar to the DAC, national bank secrecy is not recognized as a valid ground for refusal (Art. 5(3), see m.no. 748 et seq). Art. 5(2) of the Directive lists **three grounds** that give the Member States the right to refuse cooperation that are also aligned with the DAC, i.e. national treatment, commercial secrets and ordre public (see m.no. 749 et seq.).

802 Moreover, the Tax Collection Directive includes **three additional valid grounds for refusal:** The requested State is not obliged to grant recovery assistance or to take precautionary measures if the recovery of the claim, because of the situation of the debtor, creates **serious economic or social difficulties** in the requested State, provided national law also allows for such exceptions for national claims (Art. 18(1)). The requested State is not obliged to grant any assistance under the Directive if the **claim is more than five years old** (Art. 18(2)). Finally, there is also no obligation for the requested State to grant any assistance under the Directive if the total amount of the **claim is less than EUR 1 500** (Art. 18(3)).

---

139 See CJEU, 26 April 2018, Case C-34/17, *Donnellan*, EU:C:2018:282, paras. 42-46; similar to the old Tax Collection Directive 76/308/EEC CJEU, 14 January 2010, C-233/08, *Kyrian*, EU:C:2010:11, paras. 41-44.

140 They are annexed to Commission Implementing Regulation (EU) No 1189/2011 of 18 November 2011, OJ L 302/16 of 19 November 2011; amended by Commission Implementing Regulation (EU) 2017/1966.

141 See on the old Tax Collection Directive 76/308/EEC CJEU, 14 January 2010, Case C-233/08, *Kyrian*, EU:C:2010:11, paras. 51-63.

According to the **Donnellan** case from 2018, the requested Member States can 803 also refuse enforcement assistance if the taxpayer did not receive the original decision raising the respective claim and the reasoning for that decision and, thus, was never in a position to effectively assert his defensive rights in the requesting Member State. The Court did not make it fully clear whether this situation falls within the category "ordre public" or is an additional ground for refusal deriving from Art. 47 CFR.[142]

H. Statute of Limitation (Art. 19)

The limitation periods for a claim are solely governed by the **law of the requesting** 804 **State** (Art. 19(1)). However, suspension, interruption or prolongation of that period is, in principle, determined by the law of the requested State, unless that law does not provide for suspension, interruption or prolongation, in which case the steps taken in the requested State are deemed to have been taken in the requesting State in so far as they would produce suspension, interruption or prolongation under the law of the requesting State (Art. 19(2)).

I. Costs (Art. 20)

The requested State must seek to **recover from the debtor** and retain for itself 805 the costs linked to the recovery incurred according to its national rules applicable to similar domestic claims (Art. 20(1)). No reimbursement of costs from the requesting State arising from any assistance is allowed under the Directive except in exceptional cases involving a specific problem, concerning a very large amount of costs or relating to organized crime, in which case the Member States involved may agree to reimbursement on a case-by-case basis (Art. 20(2)). However, the requesting State remains liable for costs and losses resulting from actions held to be unfounded if the tax claim or the enforcement proves to be legally invalid (Art. 20(3)).

J. Use of Information Received and Secrecy Provisions (Art. 23)

Art. 23 of the Tax Collection Directive provides for rules on the allowable use 806 of information received under the Directive and secrecy standards (i.e. **"national treatment"** of the information) in a similar way to Art. 16 DAC (see m.no. 757 et seq).

---

142   CJEU, 26 April 2018, Case C-34/17, *Donnellan*, EU:C:2018:282, paras. 47-62.

K. Taxpayer Rights

807 The Tax Collection Directive deals with the issue of **disputes** in Art. 14. According to these rules, disputes concerning the claim and the initial instrument permitting enforcement fall within the competence of the requesting Member State only, whereas disputes concerning the enforcement measures taken in the requested Member State or concerning the validity of a notification made by the requested Member State shall be brought before the competent body of the requested Member State in accordance with its laws and regulations.[143] Besides these **competence rules**, the Directive does not deal with taxpayer rights.

808 In the 2018 *Donnellan* case,[144] the CJEU confirmed that domestic rules implementing the Tax Collection Directive are within the scope of the CFR and that, thus, fundamental rights have to be considered when interpreting and applying these rules.[145] The Member States therefore, in particular, need to ensure that the taxpayer can effectively make use of his **defensive rights** deriving from Arts. 47 and 48 CFR regarding the validity of the tax claim in the requesting Member State and regarding the validity of the enforcement measures in the requested Member State.

L. Comparison and Relation to Bi- and Multilateral Provisions on the Recovery of Tax Claims

809 In addition to national provisions based on the Tax Collection Directive, bi- and multilateral provisions based on **Art. 27 OECD MC, as well as the MAATM Convention** allow for assistance in the recovery of tax claims. Art. 27 OECD MC and the provisions on recovery assistance in the MAATM Convention are, to a large extent, comparable to the Tax Collection Directive.

810 Art. 27 OECD MC and the MAATM Convention mainly differ from the Directive in respect of the **grounds for refusal of assistance, as they permit restricting assistance in additional cases** that are not listed in the Directive:

- Art. 27(8)(c) OECD MC allows assistance to be refused if the requesting State has not pursued all reasonable measures of collection or conservancy.
- Art. 27(2) OECD MC and Art. 21(2)(e) MAATM[146] permit restricting assistance in cases where the underlying taxation is contrary to the DTC between the requesting and requested State.

---

143 See also CJEU, 26 April 2018, Case C-34/17, *Donnellan*, EU:C:2018:282, paras. 43-44; CJEU, 14 March 2019, Case C-695/17, *Metirato*, EU:C:2019:209, paras. 33-34.

144 CJEU, 26 April 2018, Case C-34/17, *Donnellan*, EU:C:2018:282, paras. 45-62.

145 See also recital 21 of the preamble to the Tax Collection Directive.

146 The MAATM Convention also permits restricting assistance if taxation would be contrary to generally accepted taxation principles or against any other convention that the requested State has concluded with the requesting State.

- Art. 27(8)(d) OECD MC allows assistance to be refused in those cases where the administrative burden on that State is clearly disproportionate to the benefit to be derived by the other contracting State.[147]

Bi- or multilateral provisions on the recovery of tax claims and national provisions based on the Tax Collection Directive can be applied **in parallel** by Member States. Like the DAC, the Tax Collection Directive does not limit in any way wider bi- or multilateral forms of cooperation (Art. 24(1)).   **811**

M. Relevance of the Directive in the CJEU's Case Law on the Fundamental Freedoms

According to the CJEU's case law, the need to ensure the effective collection of   **812** taxes constitutes a justification for restrictions on the fundamental freedoms (see Chapter 3, m.no. 278 et seq.). Still, Member States cannot simply justify discriminatory tax rules in cross-border situations within the EU based on the **need to ensure the recovery of tax claims** if the Tax Collection Directive is applicable, as, according to the CJEU, the Directive – in a less restrictive way for the taxpayer – enables them to obtain assistance in the cross-border recovery of tax claims. The Court, in particular, has emphasized this in its exit tax jurisprudence.[148] However, the approach of the Court is not totally consistent. For example, the CJEU has ruled that an obligation to withhold tax at source and the liability risk connected to it, applicable to cross-border situations only, is justified by the need to ensure the effective collection of tax. According to the Court, this measure does not go beyond what is necessary, even though Member States can rely on the mechanisms of the Tax Collection Directive, since the aim of the Directive *"was not to replace the taxation at source as a method of collecting tax"* (see also m.no. 278).[149]

---

147   However, the de minimis threshold of EUR 1,500 in the Tax Collection Directive seems to serve a similar goal.
148   CJEU, 6 October 2011, Case C-493/09, *Commission v Portugal*, EU:C:2011:635, para. 49; CJEU, 29 November 2011, Case C-371/10, *National Grid Indus BV*, EU:C:2011:785, para. 78.
149   CJEU, 18 October 2012, Case C-498/10, *X NV*, EU:C:2012:635, para. 47. Critical Kemmeren, Recovery of Income Taxes: ECJ Tends to Allow Member States more Leeway, *EC Tax Review* 2013, p. 4 et seq.

N. Overview of the Tax Collection Directive

813

```
                    ┌────────────────────────────┐
                    │   Types of assistance under │
                    │     the Tax Collection      │
                    └────────────────────────────┘
```

Exchange of information (Arts. 5 to 7)	Notification to addressee (Art. 8)	Recovery on request (Arts. 10 to 15)	Precautionary measures (Arts. 16 to 17)

```
                    ┌────────────────────────────┐
                    │      Grounds fo refusal      │
                    │         (Arts 5(2)           │
                    └────────────────────────────┘
```

No obligation to exchange information	No obligation to grant recovery assistance or to take precautionar

- National treatment
- Commercial secrets
- Ordre public
- Claims older than five years
- Claims less than EUR 1,500
- Serious economic or social

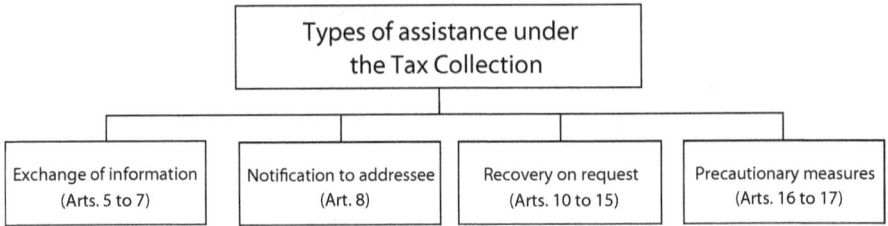

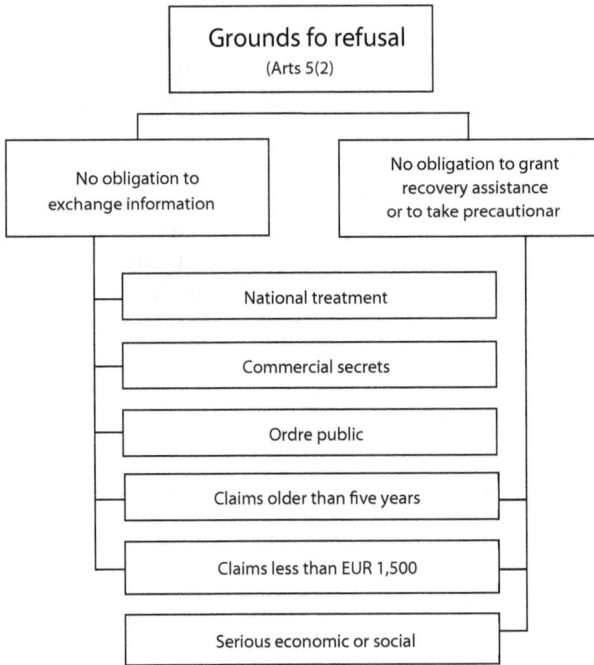

III. Savings Agreements

814 In 2003, as part of the larger tax package to tackle harmful tax competition, the Council adopted the **Savings Directive**[150] aimed at effective taxation of cross-border interest payments in the State of residence of the beneficial owner. The Savings Directive's ultimate aim was to be achieved through obligatory and automatic exchange of information between the competent authorities of the Member States

---

150   Council Directive 2003/48/EC of 3 June 2003 on taxation of savings income in the form of interest payments, OJ L 157/38 of 26 June 2003.

involved. The adoption of the DAC 2[151] in December 2014 (for details refer to m.no. 707 et seq.) led to a repeal of the Savings Directive on 10 November 2015.[152] Under transitional arrangements, the Savings Directive continued to be operational until the end of 2015.[153] In an attempt to thwart the threat of capital flight to a number of particular third country financial markets, the Commission, in 2015 and 2016, signed protocols of amendment to replace the rules of the third-country **Savings Agreements** concluded with Andorra, Liechtenstein, Monaco, San Marino and Switzerland that originally flanked the Savings Directive with a (reciprocal) system of **automatic exchange of financial account information** based on the global standard. These revised agreements entered into force in 2016 and 2017. Over the years, all dependent or associated territories of the Member States that had not done so from the start of the application of the respective Savings Agreements also moved to automatic exchange of information.[154]

Literature

Baker/Czakert/van Eijseden/Grau Ruiz/Kana, International Assistance in the Collection of Taxes, *BIT* 2011, p. 281; Bal, Extraterritorial Enforcement of Tax Claims, *BIT* 2011, p. 598; Baker/Pistone, General Report on Subject 2: The practical protection of taxpayers' fundamental rights, *IFA Cahiers de Droit Fiscal International* 2015, p. 61; Binder/Pinetz, Ensuring the Effectiveness of Fiscal Supervision in Third Country Situations, *EC Tax Review* 2014, p. 324; Blum/Langer, At a Crossroads: Mandatory Disclosure under DAC 6 and EU Primary Law – Parts 1 and 2, *ET* 2019, pp. 282 and 313; Calderón Carrero/Quintas Seara, The Taxpayer's Right of Defence in Cross-Border Exchange-of-Information Procedures, *BIT* 2014, p. 498; Čičin-Šain, New Mandatory Disclosure Rules for Tax Intermediaries and Taxpayers in the European Union, *WTJ* 2019, p 77; De Troyer, Tax Recovery Assistance in the EU: Analysis of Directive 2010/24/EU, *EC Tax Review* 2014, p. 135; Furuseth, Can Procedural Rules Create Obstacles to Fundamental Freedoms in European Law, *Intertax* 2007, p. 256; Gabert, Council Directive 2011/16/EU on Administrative Cooperation in the Field of Taxation, *ET* 2011, p. 342; Grau Ruiz, *Mutual Assistance for the Recovery of Tax Claims* (2003); Helminen, *EU Tax Law – Direct Taxation* (2017) Chapter 6; Hemels, References to the Mutual Assistance Directive in the Case Law of the ECJ: A Systematic Approach, *ET* 2009, p. 583;

---

151 Council Directive 2014/107/EU of 9 December 2014 amending Directive 2011/16/EU as regards mandatory automatic exchange of information in the field of taxation, OJ L 359/1 of 16 December 2014.

152 Council Directive (EU) 2015/2060 of 10 November 2015 repealing Directive 2003/48/EC on taxation of savings income in the form of interest payments, OJ L 301 of 18 November 2015, p. 1.

153 For a full overview, including the history of the Directive, details on essential concepts of the exchange of information mechanism and the withholding tax regime (transitionally) in force for a number of Member States, refer to Chapter 7 of the third edition of this book.

154 For an overview also refer to https://ec.europa.eu/taxation_customs/individuals/personal-taxation/taxation-savings-income/international-developments_en (accessed 10 January 2020).

Kemmeren, Recovery of Income Taxes: ECJ Tends to Allow Member States more Leeway, *EC Tax Review* 2013, p. 2; Krähenbühl, Personal Data Protection Rights with the Framework of International Automatic Exchange of Financial Account Information, *ET* 2018, p. 354; Michel, Exchange of Information on Request: Whenever, Wherever? Shakira's (and Berlioz's) Right to Judicial Review of the Foreseeable Relevance Standard, *BIT* 2019, p. 90; Nijkeuter, Exchange of Information and the Free Movement of Capital between Member States and Third Countries, *EC Tax Review* 2011, p. 232; Pantazatou, Luxembourg: Fundamental rights in the era of information exchange – The Berlioz case (C-682/15), in: Lang et al (eds.) *CJEU – Recent Developments in Direct Taxation 2017* (2018) p. 127; Parada, Intergovernmental Agreements and the Implementation of FATCA in Europe, *WTJ* 2015, p. 201; Rust/Fort (eds.), *Exchange of Information and Bank Secrecy* (2012); Seer, Recent Development in Exchange of Information within the EU for Tax Matters, *EC Tax Review* 2013, p. 66; Seer/Gabert, European and International Tax Cooperation: Legal Basis, Practice, Burden of Proof, Legal Protection and Requirements, *BIT* 2011, p. 88; Terra/Wattel, *European Tax Law* (2018); Vanistendael, Automatic Exchange of Tax Rulings in the EU, *TNI* 2015, p. 261; Wöhrer, *Data Protection and Taxpayers' Rights: Challenges created by Automatic Exchange of Information* (2018).

Legal Basis: Council Directive 77/799/EEC of 19 December 1977 concerning mutual assistance by the competent authorities of the Member States in the field of direct taxation and taxation of insurance premiums, OJ L 336/15 of 27 December 1977; Council Directive 76/308/EEC of 15 March 1976 on mutual assistance for the recovery of claims resulting from operations forming part of the system of financing the European Agricultural Guidance and Guarantee Fund, and of agricultural levies and customs duties, and in respect of value-added tax, OJ L 73/18 of 19 March 1976; Council Directive 2003/48/EC of 3 June 2003 on taxation of savings income in the form of interest payments, OJ L 157/38 of 26 June 2003; Council Directive 2008/55/EC of 26 May 2008 on mutual assistance for the recovery of claims relating to certain levies, duties, taxes and other measures, OJ L 150/28 of 26 May 2008; Council Directive 2010/24/EU of 16 March 2010 concerning mutual assistance for the recovery of claims relating to taxes, duties and other measures, OJ L 84/1 of 31 March 2010; Council Directive 2011/16/EU of 15 February 2011 on administrative cooperation in the field of taxation and repealing Directive 77/799/EEC, OJ L 64/1 of 11 March 2011; Commission Implementing Regulation (EU) No 1189/2011 of 18 November 2011 laying down detailed rules in relation to certain provisions of Council Directive 2010/24/EU concerning mutual assistance for the recovery of claims relating to taxes, duties and other measures, -/16 of 19 November 2011; Council Directive 2014/107/EU of 9 December 2014 amending Directive 2011/16/EU as regards mandatory automatic exchange of information in the field of taxation, OJ L 359/1 of 16 December 2014; Council Directive (EU) 2015/2376 of 8 December 2015 amending Directive 2011/16/EU as regards mandatory automatic exchange of information in the field of taxation, OJ L 332/1 of 18 December 2015; Commission Implementing Regulation (EU) 2015/2378 of 15 December 2015 laying down detailed rules for implementing certain provisions of Council Directive 2011/16/EU on administrative cooperation in the field of taxation and repealing Implementing Regulation (EU) No 1156/2012, OJ L 332/19 of 18 December 2015; Council Directive (EU) 2016/881 of 25 May 2016 amending Directive 2011/16/EU as regards mandatory automatic exchange of information in the field of taxation, OJ L 146/8 of 3 June 2016; Commission Implementing Regulation (EU) 2016/1963 of 9 November 2016 amending Implementing Regulation (EU) 2015/2378 as regards standard forms and linguistic arrangements to be used in relation to Council Directives (EU) 2015/2376 and (EU) 2016/881, OJ L 303/4 of 10 November 2016; Council Directive (EU) 2016/2258 of 6 December 2016 amending Directive 2011/16/EU as regards access to anti-money-laundering information by tax authorities, OJ L 342/1 of 16 December 2016; Commission Implementing Regulation (EU) 2017/1966 of 27 October 2017 amending Implementing Regulation (EU) No 1189/2011 as regards the communication of assistance requests and the follow-up to those requests, OJ L 279/38 of 28 October 2017; Commission Implementing Regulation (EU) 2018/99 of 22 January 2018 amending Implementing Regulation (EU) 2015/2378 as regards the form and conditions of communication for the yearly assessment of the effectiveness of the automatic exchange of information and the list of statistical data to be provided by Member States for the purposes of evaluating of Council Directive 2011/16/EU, OJ L 17/29 of 23 January 2018; Proposal for a Council Directive amending Directive 2011/16/EU as regards mandatory automatic exchange of information in the field of taxation in relation to reportable cross-border arrangements, COM(2017) 335 final; Council Directive (EU) 2018/822 of 25 May 2018 amending Directive 2011/16/EU as regards mandatory automatic exchange of information in the field of taxation in relation to reportable cross-border arrangements, OJ L 139/1 of 5 June 2018; Commission Implementing Regulation (EU) 2019/532 of 28 March 2019 amending Implementing Regulation (EU) 2015/2378 as regards the standard forms, including linguistic arrangements, for the mandatory automatic exchange of information on reportable cross-border arrangements, OJ L 88/25 of 29 March 2019; Council Directive (EU) 2020/876 of 24 June 2020 amending Directive 2011/16/EU to address the urgent need to defer certain time limits for the filing and exchange of information in the field of taxation because of the COVID-19 pandemic, OJ L 204/46 of 26 June 2020.

Chapter 10 – The EU Arbitration Convention and Dispute Resolution Directive

Jean-Philippe Van West/Christiane Zöhrer[1]

---

[1]   The 4th edition of this chapter, authored by Patrick Plansky, was substantially reworked by Jean-Philippe Van West and Christiane Zöhrer for the 5th edition. Van West updated the chapter for this version of the book.

I.   Aim and History

815   Convention 90/436/EEC on the elimination of double taxation in connection with the adjustment of profits of associated enterprises (hereinafter: Arbitration Convention) and Council Directive (EU) on tax dispute resolution mechanisms in the European Union (2017/1852) (hereinafter: Dispute Resolution Directive) are both instruments that can be used to resolve double taxation disputes within the European Union. The introduction of these two legal instruments was the result of a long process.[2] In 1976, the Commission proposed a directive for the elimination of double taxation as regards profit adjustments in transfer pricing scenarios.[3] This directive was never implemented but, in 1990, the **Arbitration Convention**[4] was concluded. The aim of the Arbitration Convention is to establish a procedure to **eliminate double taxation** resulting from a profit adjustment by the competent authorities in one contracting state without a corresponding adjustment in the other contracting state. It is not an EU law instrument, but a multilateral international law convention; however, it is part of the *acquis communautaire*.[5] The validity of the Arbitration Convention was initially limited to five years from the date of ratification of the last EU Member State, but has, in the meantime, been made subject to an implicit periodical renewal. Its scope has been extended three times and it now **applies in all EU Member States**.

816   The Commission has identified difficulties in the practical implementation of the Arbitration Convention and therefore established the **EU Joint Transfer Pricing Forum** (JTPF) in 2001 to examine possibilities to enhance, *inter alia,* its implementation. The JTPF prepared a **Code of Conduct** for the effective implementation of the Convention on the elimination of double taxation in connection with the adjustment of profits of associated enterprises, which was adopted by the Council in 2006.[6] The Code of Conduct is a mere **political commitment** and does not affect the rights and obligations of the contracting states. Although the Code of Conduct is a **soft law tool**, it can be a useful instrument for the interpretation of the Arbitration Convention. In 2009, a **Revised Code of Conduct,** which aims to resolve more cases within a three-year time frame, was adopted by the Council.[7] In 2015, as a last step in the evolution of the Code of Conduct, and as a consequence of

---

2   For a detailed overview see Pit, *Dispute Resolution in the EU; The EU Arbitration Convention and the Dispute Resolution Directive* (2018) Part I, Chapter 1; History and Recent Developments.

3   Proposal for a Council directive on the elimination of double taxation in connection with the adjustment of transfers of profits between associated enterprise (Arbitration Procedure), COM(1976) 611 final.

4   Convention on the elimination of double taxation in connection with the adjustment of profits of associated enterprises (90/436/EEC), OJ T 225 of 20 August 1990, pp. 10-25.

5   See Hinnekens, The Uneasy Case and Fate of Article 293 Second Indent EC, Intertax 2009, p. 604.

6   Code of conduct for the effective implementation of the Convention on the elimination of double taxation in connection with the adjustment of profits of associated enterprises (2006/C 176/02), OJ C 176 of 28 July 2006, p. 8.

7   Revised Code of Conduct for the effective implementation of the Convention on the elimination of double taxation in connection with the adjustment of profits of associated enterprises (2009/C 322/01), OJ C 322 of 30 December 2009.

a comprehensive exercise to monitor the proper functioning of the Arbitration Convention and the Revised Code of Conduct, the Commission (JTPF) issued its **Final Report** on Improving the Functioning of the Arbitration Convention.[8] It proposed changes to the Revised Code of Conduct. To complement the EU strategy to resolve transfer pricing disputes, in addition to the *ex post* resolution of transfer pricing disputes by way of the Arbitration Convention, the Commission (JTPF) issued **Guidelines for Advance Pricing Agreements** (APA), thereby also promoting the *ex ante* possibility of preventing transfer pricing disputes.

Despite constituting a huge step forward in achieving an effective resolution of **817** transfer pricing disputes within the EU, the **Arbitration Convention** also has significant **drawbacks,** as well as **structural flaws.** The main issue is the Arbitration Convention's narrow scope, which is limited to transfer pricing disputes. Others include the lack of effective remedy against the rejection of complaints as unfounded, extensive delays and the lack of flexibility.[9]

In October 2016, the European Commission, attempting to improve the current **818** mechanisms to resolve double taxation disputes in the European Union and to address the aforementioned drawbacks of the Arbitration Convention, proposed a draft of a new **Dispute Resolution Directive.**[10] A revised version of the draft proposal of the European Commission was adopted by the Council of the European Union on 10 October 2017.[11] The aim of the Directive is to create an effective and efficient framework for the resolution of cross-border tax disputes that ensures legal certainty and a business friendly environment.[12] The Dispute Resolution Directive represents an important step forward in creating an effective mechanism to solve cross-border tax disputes within the European Union. The main achievements of the Directive are that it (i) has a broad scope, (ii) provides for enforceable time restrictions and therefore guarantees that the dispute is resolved in a timely manner and (iii) improves the rights of the taxpayer.

The Directive had to be implemented by the Member States by 30 June 2019. **819** Although most Member States now have legislation in force implementing the Directive, many have failed to transpose the Directive into domestic law in a timely manner.[13] A few EU Member States have still not transposed the Directive into

---

8   EU Joint Transfer Pricing Forum: Final Report on Improving the Functioning of the Arbitration Convention (Meeting of 12 March 2015); JTPF/002/2015/EN.

9   Govind/Turcan, Cross-Border Dispute Resolution in the 21st century, A Comparative Study of Existing Bilateral and Multilateral Remedies, *Derivs. & Fin. Instrums* 2017

10   Proposal for a Council Directive on Double Taxation Dispute Resolution Mechanisms in the European Union, COM (2016) 686 final of 2016.

11   Council Directive (EU) 2017/1852 of 10 October 2017 on tax dispute resolution mechanisms in the European Union, OJ L 265/1 of 14 October 2017.

12   5th recital Dispute Resolution Directive.

13   For example, in the following Member States the bill on implementation of the Dispute Resolution Directive was gazetted after 30 June 2019: Austria, Bulgaria, Croatia, Estonia, Germany, Hungary, Ireland, Latvia, Luxembourg, Malta, the Netherlands, Poland, Portugal, Romania and Spain. For an overview of implementation of the Dispute Resolution Directive see IBFD Tax Dossier – Tax Dispute Resolution.

national law.[14] The Directive acts as an **alternative to the other mechanisms** for dispute resolution that are available, namely the Arbitration Convention and the procedures that are included in both the OECD Model and the MLI,[15] which was signed by almost 70 states on 7 June 2017 and entered into force on 1 July 2018.[16] Part V of the MLI includes two clauses on improving dispute resolution and part VI contains several provisions that enhance the functioning of arbitration in double taxation conventions (DTCs) as a tool for settling cross-border tax disputes. The adoption of Part VI is optional and only 26 states have, to date, opted for its implementation.

820 While taxpayers, in the 20th century, had to employ domestic legal remedies to minimize the impact of cross-border tax disputes, much has changed in the 21st century. Nowadays, affected taxpayers have up to three options for requesting the settlement of such disputes within the European Union.

821 The introduction of mutual agreement procedures in Art. 25 of the 1963 OECD Model marks the starting point of the evolution process for settling cross-border tax disputes. However, for various reasons, these mechanisms do not lead to satisfactory results in all cases.[17] This is mostly due to the fact that the authorities of the contracting states are not obliged to actually come to a solution that eliminates double taxation under Art. 25 of the OECD Model.[18] Furthermore, there are no time limits on dispute settlement. Although some tax treaties contain a provision on arbitration procedures, they do not necessarily solve the problem of eliminating double taxation. While the OECD Commentary states that it is a duty of the authorities to initiate the mutual agreement procedure,[19] some authors are of the opposite opinion.[20] Moreover, DTCs do not exist with regard to all possible constellations within the European Union. Additionally, not all DTCs between Member States contain the corresponding adjustment requirement of Art. 9(2) of the OECD Model. But even if there is a provision equivalent to Art. 9(2) of the OECD Model in the respective DTC, double taxation may arise due to different views on the correct interpretation of the arm's length principle.

---

14   For example, Cyprus, Czech Republic, Italy and Greece have not yet transposed the Directive into national law.

15   *Multilateral Convention to Implement Tax Treaty Related Measures to Prevent Base Erosion and Profit Shifting* (24 Nov. 2016).

16   As of 28 February 2020, 94 jurisdictions had signed the MLI.

17   See Thömes/Hagenbucher/Hasenoehrl, in: Thömmes/Fuks (eds.), EC Corporate Tax Law (October 1992) para. 34 et seq.; Ribes Ribes, Compulsory Arbitration as a Last Resort in Resolving Tax Treaty Interpretation Problems, ET 2002, p. 400 with further references.

18   See Terra/Wattel, European Tax Law (2008) p. 564 et seq.: Under Art. 25(3) of the OECD Model, the authorities of the contracting states must only "endeavour" to resolve by mutual agreement any difficulties or doubts arising as to the interpretation or application of the convention. For a detailed comparison between the EU Arbitration Convention and the Mutual Agreement Procedure under Art. 25 of the OECD Model, see Thömmes/Hagenbucher/Hasenoehrl, in: Thömmes/Fuks (eds.), EC Corporate Tax Law (October 1992) Law.

19   See OECD Commentary 2010, Art. 25 para. 33.

20   Thömmes/Hagenbucher/Hasenoehrl, in: Thömmes/Fuks (eds.), EC Corporate Tax Law (October 1992) para. 58.

In 2007, the OECD issued a report[21] proposing a new provision (Art. 25(5)) on an **822** arbitration process for the OECD Model. For new DTCs modelled along the lines of this new paragraph 5 of Art. 25 of the OECD Model, although the level of tax-payer protection has increased, as the **arbitration process under Art. 25(5) of the OECD Model** covers all disputes arising from "taxation not in accordance with the Convention", several issues remain problematic.

II.   The EU Arbitration Convention[22]

A. Scope and Principles

The scope of the EU Arbitration Convention is limited to transfer pricing disputes. **823** The **substantive scope** covers taxes on income, in particular income tax and corporate tax.[23] The **personal scope** applies to any situation in which the profits of an enterprise of one contracting state are also included in the profits of an enterprise in another contracting state. The term "enterprise" is not defined in the Convention but the concept is broad, covering permanent establishments of an enterprise of another contracting state.[24] Two constellations are covered by the Convention: (i) violations of the arm's length principle between **associated enterprises** (Art. 4(1) of the Arbitration Convention)[25] and (ii) violations of the arm's length principle between **independent parts of an enterprise,** i.e. head office and permanent establishment or between permanent establishments (Art. 4(2) of the Arbitration Convention).[26] The Arbitration Convention only allows for an **adjustment of profits** that are not determined in accordance with the arm's length principle.[27]

---

21 OECD, Improving the Resolution of Tax Treaty Disputes (Report adopted by the Committee on Fiscal Affairs on 30 January 2007), February 2007.

22 This chapter is largely based on Plansky, in: Lang/Pistone/Schuch/Staringer (eds), *Introduction to European Tax Law on Direct Taxation*, 4th Edition, Chapter 9 – The EU Arbitration Convention (2016).

23 Art. 2 Arbitration Convention.

24 Art. 1(2) Arbitration Convention; see also joint declaration on Art. 4(1) in the Annex to the Convention, which states that Art. 4(1) of the Arbitration Convention also applies to permanent establishments of the other enterprise situated in a third country.

25 Art. 4(1) of the Arbitration Convention is an (almost) literal rendition of Art. 9(1) of the OECD Model. These arm's length profit adjustments for associated enterprises are applicable in two constellations: first, where an enterprise of a contracting state participates directly or indirectly in the management, control or capital of an enterprise of another contracting state (horizontal affiliation) and, second, where the same persons participate directly or indirectly in the management, control or capital of an enterprise of one contracting state and an enterprise of another contracting state (vertical affiliation).

26 As regards independent parts of an enterprise, Art. 4(2) of the Arbitration Convention, which is an (almost) literal rendition of Art. 7(2) of the OECD Model (up to and including the OECD Model 2008), provides that those profits must be attributed to the permanent establishment that it might be expected to form if it were a distinct and separate enterprise, engaged in the same or similar activities under the same or similar conditions and dealing wholly independently from the enterprise of which it is a permanent establishment. Violations of these principles may lead to profit adjustments and to the procedures described herein.

27 Adjustments other than arm's length profit adjustments are not covered by the Convention. Therefore, if one contracting state adjusts the profits of an enterprise as a result of the recharacterization of income or costs, this adjustment may lead to double taxation, as the other contracting state possibly will not follow this recharacterization by that state.

B. Procedure

1. Complaint Stage

824   The tax authority of a contracting state that intends to adjust the profits of an enterprise in accordance with the arm's length principle is **obliged to inform** the respective enterprise of the intended step and give the enterprise the possibility to inform the other enterprise in the other contracting state of the intended step. This enterprise must, in turn, be able to inform its contracting state of the intended step of the other contracting state. The contracting state wishing to adjust the profits does not need to wait for the other contracting state's reaction to adjust the profits; nevertheless, the Revised Code of Conduct, which is just a soft law tool, proposes to suspend the collection of taxes derived from a profit adjustment.[28] If both states agree to the adjustment, there is no need for a further mutual agreement or arbitration procedure. Instead, the second contracting state would have to adjust the profits correspondingly.

825   If, however, no agreement can be reached and the enterprise is of the opinion that the arm's length principle has not been observed, it may present its case (a **complaint**) to the competent authority of the contracting state in which the enterprise is situated. This complaint must be made within three years of initial notification. In this context, the Revised Code of Conduct refers to the "date of the first tax assessment notice or equivalent" that results or may result in double taxation as the starting point for the calculation of the three-year period.[29] At the same time, the enterprise must notify the competent authorities of any other relevant contracting states.

2. MAP Stage

826   It is possible that the competent authority will not be willing or able to provide a unilateral solution.[30] In this instance, Art. 6(2) of the Arbitration Convention obliges the contracting state to open a **mutual agreement procedure**. While the notification phase happens at the domestic level, the opening of the mutual agreement procedure occurs at the cross-border level. If the competent authorities fail to reach a solution that eliminates double taxation within two years of submitting the case to the competent authority,[31] the **arbitration procedure** must be initiated.

---

28   See Point 8 of the Revised Code of Conduct for the effective implementation of the Convention on the elimination of double taxation in connection with the adjustment of profits of associated enterprises (2009/C 322/01), OJ C 322 of 30 December 2009, p. 10.

29   See Point 4 of the Revised Code of Conduct for the effective implementation of the Convention on the elimination of double taxation in connection with the adjustment of profits of associated enterprises (2009/C 322/01), OJ C 322 of 30 December 2009, p. 3.

30   Art. 6(2) of the Arbitration Convention uses the wording "if the complaint appears to be well-founded", which seems to confer the competent authorities with a discretionary power, nevertheless this phrase has to be interpreted as simply enabling the competent authorities to "dismiss manifestly ill-founded applications"; see Terra/Wattel, *European Tax Law* (2012) p. 375.

31   Point 5 of the Revised Code of Conduct contains more details on the starting point of this two-year-period; see Revised Code of Conduct for the effective implementation of the Convention on the elimination of double taxation in connection with the adjustment of profits of associated enterprises (2009/C 322/01), OJ C 322 of 30 December 2009, p. 3 et seq.

The Aritration Convention is silent on taxpayer rights and involvement during the MAP stage.

3. The Arbitration Stage

If no satisfactory result regarding the elimination of double taxation under the mutual agreement procedure is achieved, the first step in the arbitration procedure is to set up an **advisory commission, which** is required to deliver an opinion on the dispute submitted for arbitration.[32] According to the Revised Code of Conduct, the contracting state that issued the first tax assessment on the additional income takes the initiative to establish the advisory commission and arranges for its meetings.[33] Additionally, the enterprises involved may simultaneously appeal before national courts. In this instance, the two-year period for achieving a solution starts only after the judgment of the final court of appeal. **827**

The **composition** of the advisory commission is laid down in Art. 9(1) of the Arbitration Convention. The advisory commission consists of (i) a chairman, (ii) one[34] or two representatives of each competent authority and (iii) an even number of independent persons. Independent persons, within the meaning of Art. 9 of the Arbitration Convention, are appointed by mutual agreement or by the drawing of lots. In respect of the drawing of lots, each competent authority may, under certain circumstances, object to the appointment of any independent person.[35] For each independent person, one alternate has to be appointed. These independent persons must be nationals of a contracting state and resident in one of the signatory countries to the Arbitration Convention. Moreover, they must be competent and independent.[36] The chairman is then elected by the representatives and independent persons. The chairman of the advisory commission must have the highest qualifications, i.e. possess the qualifications for the highest judicial office or be a jurisconsult of recognized competence.[37] There is always an uneven number of members. Usually the advisory commission consists of five persons (one chairman, one representative of each competent authority and two independent persons). As a consequence of this composition, the votes of the independent persons will normally be decisive.[38] **828**

Art. 10 of the Arbitration Convention lays down the **procedure before the advisory commission**. All members of the advisory commission have to keep the proceedings confidential. On the one hand, the enterprises concerned may provide **829**

---

32 Art. 7(1) Arbitration Convention.
33 See Point 7.2. of the Revised Code of Conduct for the effective implementation of the Convention on the elimination of double taxation in connection with the adjustment of profits of associated enterprises (2009/C 322/01), OJ C 322 of 30 December 2009, p. 8.
34 Art. 9(1) of the Arbitration Convention proposes two representatives of each competent authority but also allows this number to be reduced to one representative per competent authority by agreement.
35 Art. 9(3) Arbitration Convention.
36 Art. 9(4) Arbitration Convention.
37 Art. 9(5) second sentence Arbitration Convention.
38 See Terra/Wattel, *European Tax Law* (2012) p. 377.

the advisory commission with any information, evidence or documents that seem to be of use to the advisory commission in forming its opinion. On the other hand, the enterprises are obliged to present all the information, evidence or documents requested by the advisory commission. Oral hearings may also be held and taxpayers may submit any evidence they consider relevant and may request an appearance or to be represented before the commission. Indeed, in contrast to the MAP stage, the Arbitration Convention provides for limited participation of the taxpayer during the arbitration stage. It is limited because, for example, the Arbitration Convention does not provide the taxpayer with a right to be informed about the progress of the advisory commission, or a right to rebut the arguments made by the competent authoritires or the evidence put forward by them.

830   After the investigation, the advisory commission is obliged to **deliver an opinion** within a period of six months from the date on which the case was referred to it. The term "referred to it" is not defined in the Convention. Under the Revised Code of Conduct, the matter "is referred to" the advisory commission as soon as the chairman confirms that its members have received all relevant documentation and information.[39] The opinion must be adopted by a simple majority of its members. The enterprises bear their own costs. The costs of the procedure are shared equally by the competent authorities.

831   The advisory commission must base its opinion on Art. 4 of the Arbitration Convention, which lays down the arm's length principle based on the wording of Art. 9(1) of the OECD Model. Although the Arbitration Convention does not provide special rules for the modality, procedures and criteria, other than those laid down in Art. 4 of the Arbitration Convention, the **OECD Transfer Pricing Guidelines** must be taken into consideration.[40]

832   As a last step in the arbitration procedure, the competent authorities have to make a **decision** within six months of having received the opinion of the advisory commission. The competent authorities may reach an agreement that deviates from the opinion of the advisory commission. If they cannot reach an agreement, they are bound by the opinion of the advisory commission.[41] The decision may be published if the competent authorities, as well as the enterprises involved, agree.

833   While the Arbitration Convention provides for a rather tight schedule, experience shows that the actual time required to complete the procedure may, in fact, be much longer. There are various reasons for this time lag including problems concerning the appointment of arbitrators and other related situations in which the states involved present different views.

---

39   See Point 7.3.(b) of the Revised Code of Conduct for the effective implementation of the Convention on the elimination of double taxation in connection with the adjustment of profits of associated enterprises (2009/C 322/01), OJ C 322 of 30 December 2009, p. 8.
40   Andonnino, Some Thoughts on the EC Arbitration Convention, *ET* 2003, p. 403.
41   Art. 12 Arbitration Convention.

4. Chart Illustrating the Procedure

834

```
                                                      ┌──────────────┐
                    ┌────────────────────┐            │  To submit   │
                    │     Complaint      │────────────│  within 3    │
                    └────────────────────┘            │  years from  │
                              │                       │ notification │
                              ▼                       └──────────────┘
                    ┌────────────────────┐
                    │ Competent authority│
                    │     concerned      │
                    └────────────────────┘
                     │                  │
          ┌──────────┘                  └──────────┐
          ▼                                        ▼
┌────────────────────┐              ┌────────────────────┐
│ Competent authority│              │ Competent Authority│          ┌──────────┐
│ decides the        │              │ decides the        │          │ Agreement│
│ complaint is       │              │ complaint is       │          │ should be│
│ not well founded   │              │ well founded       │          │ reached  │
└────────────────────┘              └────────────────────┘          │ within   │
          │                                   │                      │ 2 years  │
          ▼                                   ▼                      └──────────┘
┌────────────────────┐              ┌────────────────────┐
│  End of procedure  │              │        MAP         │──────────
└────────────────────┘              └────────────────────┘
                                     │                  │
                          ┌──────────┘                  └──────────┐
                          ▼                                        ▼
                ┌────────────────────┐              ┌────────────────────┐
                │ Agreement –        │              │ No agreement –     │
                │ Elimination        │              │ Matter referred to │
                │ of double taxation │              │ an Advisory        │
                └────────────────────┘              │ Commission         │
                                                    └────────────────────┘
          ┌──────────┐                                       │
          │ Must take│                              ┌────────────────────┐
          │ a decision│─────────────────────────────│ The Advisory       │
          │ within   │                              │ Commission delivers│
          │ 6 months │                              │ its opinion        │
          └──────────┘                              └────────────────────┘
                                                             │
                                                    ┌────────────────────┐
                                                    │ Competent          │
                                                    │ authorities        │
                                                    │ concerned take a   │
                                                    │ decision           │
                                                    │ eliminating double │
                                                    │ taxation within 6  │
                                                    │ months or the      │
                                                    │ opinion becomes    │
                                                    │ binding            │
                                                    └────────────────────┘
```

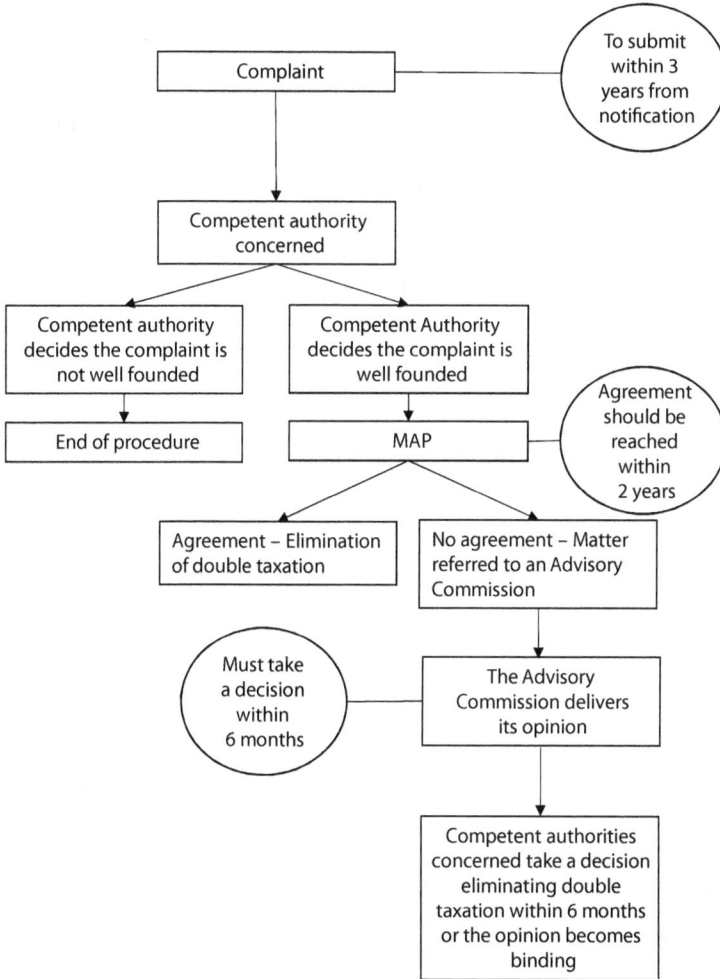

III. The EU Dispute Resolution Directive

A. Scope and Principles

Art. 1 determines the personal, substantive and territorial scope of the Dispute **835** Resolution Directive.

Any **affected person** falls under the **personal scope** of the Dispute Resolution **836** Directive. An affected person means "any person, including an individual, that is a resident of a Member State for tax purposes, and whose taxation is directly affected by a question in dispute."[42] Compared to the Arbitration Convention, the Dispute Resolution Directive has a wider personal scope and is not limited to enterprises of a contracting state.

837 The Dispute Resolution Directive has a wide **substantive scope** covering disputes arising from "the interpretation and application of agreements and conventions that provide for the elimination of double taxation of income and, where applicable, capital." This includes **disputes arising from the interpretation and application of bilateral tax treaties and of the Arbitration Convention.**[43] The scope is not limited to disputes regarding the interpretation and application of DTCs or the Arbitration Convention leading to double taxation but includes other disputes regarding the interpretation and application of tax treaties. However, Art. 16(7) of the Dispute Resolution Directive allows Member States to deny access to the dispute resolution procedure when the dispute does not involve double taxation.

838 The territorial scope of the Dispute Resolution Directive is limited to disputes between Member States. This implies that not all DTCs concluded by the Member States fall under the territorial scope of the Dispute Resolution Directive. DTCs concluded by Member States with third countries fall outside the territorial scope of the Dispute Resolution Directive. If we read the territorial scope together with the substantive scope, the Dispute Resolution Directive does not apply when a tax dispute arises between two Member States insofar as these two Member States have not concluded a DTC. In this regard, the Arbitration Convention can offer a solution for taxpayers in relation to transfer pricing disputes.[44]

839 The Dispute Resolution Directive applies to complaints submitted as from 1 July 2019 concerning disputes relating to a tax year starting on or after 1 January 2018. The competent authorities of the Member States concerned may, however, agree to apply the Directive with regard to any complaint that was submitted prior to that day or to earlier tax years.[45]

B. Procedure

1. Complaint

840 The procedure starts with the **submission of a complaint** by an affected person.[46] In principle, the affected person has to submit the complaint to **the competent authorities** of each Member State concerned. However, the Directive provides for

---

42   Art. 2(1)(d) Dispute Resolution Directive.
43   First and sixth recital.
44   Note that almost all EU Member States have concluded a DTC with one another. A few exceptions exist, however. For example, currently no DTC is in force between Denmark and France, Denmark and Spain, and Finland and Portugal.
45   Art. 23 Dispute Resolution Directive.
46   Art. 3 Dispute Resolution Directive.

an **exception for individuals, and undertakings that are not large and that do not form part of a large group**, which only have to submit the complaint to the competent authority of the Member State in which they are resident.[47] The affected person has to submit the complaint within a period of three years following initial notification of the action resulting in the dispute.[48] The complaint must be submitted in **one of the official languages** of each Member State concerned or any other language that such Member State accepts for this purpose. The affected person can submit the complaint regardless of the availability of other remedies under the domestic law of any of the Member States concerned. The complaint must contain the information requested in Art. 3(3) of the Dispute Resolution Directive, such as information about the taxpayer and the case under dispute.

The competent authority of each Member State concerned has the **obligation to** **841** **acknowledge receipt** of the complaint within two months from the receipt of the complaint.[49] The authorities may **request specific additional information** within three months of receipt of the complaint and the affected person must reply within three months of receiving the request for further information.[50] The competent authority of each of the Member States concerned must make a **decision on the acceptance or rejection of the complaint** within six months of receipt of the complaint, or, in the event a competent authority has requested further information, within six months of receipt of such further information.[51] If a competent authority fails to make a decision within six months, the complaint is **deemed to be accepted** by that competent authority.[52] This measure guarantees that the taxpayer will receive a timely decision on acceptance or rejection of the complaint.

The Dispute Resolution Directive provides for the possibility to resolve the ques- **842** tion in dispute on a **unilateral basis**.[53] A competent authority of a Member State concerned may decide, within six months of receipt of the complaint or receipt of the additional information requested, to resolve the dispute on a unilateral basis, without the involvement of the competent authorities of the other Member States concerned. In such a scenario, the competent authority concerned has to notify the affected person and the competent authorities of the other Member States concerned. When a Member State concerned decides to do so, the proceedings under the Dispute Resolution Directive will end. If no competent authority of a Member State concerned decides to resolve the dispute on a unilateral basis,

---

47 Art. 17 Dispute Resolution Directive. The Dispute Resolution Directive refers to Directive 2013/34/EU of the European Parliament and of the Council of 26 June 2013 on the annual financial statements, consolidated financial statements and related reports of certain types of undertakings for the definition of the terms 'large undertaking' and 'large group', OJ L 182 of 29 June 2013.
48 Art. 3(1) Dispute Resolution Directive.
49 Art. 3(2) Dispute Resolution Directive.
50 Art. 3(4) Dispute Resolution Directive.
51 Art. 3(5) Dispute Resolution Directive
52 Art. 5(2) Dispute Resolution Directive.
53 Art. 3(5) Dispute Resolution Directive.

the continuation of the procedure depends on the decision of the competent authority of each of the Member States concerned. **Three different situations** are possible.

843 First, if **all competent authorities accept the complaint,** the mutual agreement procedure will be initiated.[54] Second, if **at least one, but not all competent authorities, accepts the complaint,** the affected person may request that the competent authorities concerned set up an **advisory commission** within 50 days of receipt of the decision.[55] The advisory commission must be set up within 120 days of receipt of the request. Once set up, the advisory commission shall decide on acceptance of the complaint within six months. Although not explicitly stated in the Dispute Resolution Directive itself, it seems that the proceedings under the Dispute Resolution Directive will end if the advisory commission rejects the complaint.[56] If the advisory commission accepts the complaint, there are two possibilities.[57] Upon the request of one of the competent authorities, the mutual agreement procedure will be initiated. If none of the competent authorities request that mutual agreement procedure be initiated within 60 days from the decision of the advisory commission, the arbitration stage shall be initiated.

844 Third, it is also possible that **all competent authorities of the Member States concerned could reject the complaint.** A competent authority may reject a complaint (i) if the complaint does not contain the information required under Art. 3(3) or if the affected persons fail to deliver the requested additional information, (ii) if it considers there is no question in dispute, or (iii) if the complaint is not submitted within three years of initial notification of the action resulting in the dispute.[58] The competent authority of the Member State concerned must provide the affected person with general reasons for the rejection. If all competent authorities of the Member States concerned reject the complaint, the **affected person is entitled to appeal** the decision before the competent national court. Although the Dispute Resolution Directive does not state this explicitly, it seems that if all of the competent courts reject the appeal, the proceedings under the Dispute Resolution Directive will end.[59] If at least one national court accepts the appeal, the affected person may request that the competent authorities concerned set up an advisory commission under the procedure described above. The request must be made within 50 days of the date of the decision of the competent national court.

---

54   Art. 4(1) Dispute Resolution Directive.
55   Art. 6(1) Dispute Resolution Directive.
56   See also Debelva/Luts, Directive on Tax Dispute Resolution Mechanisms in the EU, *Tax Notes International* 2018, p. 76
57   Art. 6(2) Dispute Resolution Directive.
58   Art. 5(3) Dispute Resolution Directive.
59   See also Debelva/Luts, Directive on Tax Dispute Resolution Mechanisms in the EU, *Tax Notes International* 2018, p. 76

It is important to note that all proceedings under the Dispute Resolution Direc- **845** tive will end at the complaint stage if an affected person withdraws its complaint or if the question in dispute ceases to exist.[60]

2. MAP Stage

The mutual agreement procedure will be initiated if (i) all competent authorities **846** concerned accept the complaint[61] or (ii) if the advisory commission accepts the complaint and one of the competent authorities of the Member States concerned initiates the mutual agreement procedure.[62] Once the mutual agreement procedure is initiated, **the competent authorities concerned must endeavour to resolve the question in dispute within two years** starting from (i) the last notification of acceptance of the complaint or (ii) the date of notification by the advisory commission of acceptance of the complaint.[63] The period of two years **may be extended by up to one year** upon the request of one of the competent authorities if the requesting competent authority provides a written justification. The Dispute Resolution Directive is silent on judicial control of the validity of a request to extend the period.

If the **competent authorities of the Member States concerned do not reach an** **847** **agreement** on how to resolve the question in dispute within the aforementioned time period, they will notify the affected person and the **arbitration stage** will be initiated.[64] The competent authorities of the Member States concerned must inform the affected person of the general reasons for the failure to reach an agreement. When the **competent authorities of the Member States concerned have agreed on how to resolve the question in dispute**, they will notify the affected person of such agreement. If the affected person accepts the agreement, **the agreement is binding upon the competent authorities** of the Member States concerned, provided that the affected person renounces the right to any other remedy.[65] Where the affected person has already initiated a proceeding to pursue another remedy, for example a procedure under domestic law, the said person has to provide evidence, within 60 days of the date the agreement was notified to the affected person, that action has been taken to terminate any such proceeding.

The Dispute Resolution Directive does not confer the right **to be heard or to inter-** **848** **vene during the MAP stage**. The Dispute Resolution Directive only provides that the affected person deliver any specific additional information that the competent authorities of the Member States concerned consider to be necessary.[66]

---

60   Art. 3(6) Dispute Resolution Directive.
61   Art. 4(1) Dispute Resolution Directive.
62   Art. 6(2) Dispute Resolution Directive.
63   Arts. 4(1) and 6(2) Dispute Resolution Directive.
64   Arts. 4(3) and 6 (1)(b) Dispute Resolution Directive.
65   Art. 4(2) Dispute Resolution Directive.
66   Art. 3(4) Dispute Resolution Directive.

3. Arbitration Stage

849 The arbitration stage will be initiated (i) if, after a positive decision of the advisory commission, no competent authority concerned has requested that a mutual agreement procedure be initiated within 60 days of notification of a positive decision of the advisory commission,[67] or (ii) if the competent authorities concerned have not reached an agreement under the mutual agreement procedure.[68] However, a Member State may **deny access to the arbitration procedure (i) where penalties were imposed** in that Member State in relation to the adjusted income or capital for tax fraud, wilful default and gross negligence or **(ii) where the question in dispute does not involve double taxation.**[69]

850 The arbitration stage can take place before either of two bodies, i.e. an **advisory commission**[70] or an **alternative dispute resolution commission.**[71] The **advisory commission** shall be **composed** of one chair, one representative of each of the Member States concerned, and one independent person of standing who shall be appointed by each of the Member States.[72] If the Member States agree, the number of representatives and the number of independent persons may be increased to two. The Directive provides for specific provisions that are intended to guarantee the independence of the members of the advisory commission.[73] The advisory commission must deliver an **opinion** on how to resolve the question in dispute within six months of being set up.[74] This period may be extended by three months if the advisory commission or the alternative dispute resolution commission considers that this is necessary to resolve the question in dispute. The advisory commission must inform the competent authorities of the Member States concerned and the affected persons of any such extension.

851 Instead of an advisory commission, an **alternative dispute resolution commission** may be established if the competent authorities of the Member States concerned agree to do so. The **composition and form of the alternative dispute resolution commission may differ from the advisory commission**, but the same rules regarding the independence of the members apply.[75] The alternative dispute resolution commission may apply any **alternative dispute resolution process or technique** to resolve the question in dispute if the competent authorities of the Member States involved agree on this.[76] Consequently, Member States could, for example, use the "last best offer" or "final offer" arbitration process.[77] The last best offer or final offer arbitration process entails that each of the competent authorities of the Member States concerned

---

67 Art. 6(2) Dispute Resolution Directive.
68 Art. 6(1)(b) Dispute Resolution Directive.
69 Art. 16(6) and 16(7) Dispute Resolution Directive.
70 Art. 6 Dispute Resolution Directive.
71 Art. 10 Dispute Resolution Directive.
72 Art. 8(1) Dispute Resolution Directive.
73 Art. 8(4) and 8(5) Dispute Resolution Directive.
74 Art. 14 Dispute Resolution Directive.
75 Art. 10(2) Dispute Resolution Directive.
76 Art. 10(2) Dispute Resolution Directive.
77 Art. 10(2) Dispute Resolution Directive.

submit a proposal on how to resolve the issue in dispute to an arbitration panel. The arbitration panel then has to choose one of the proposals submitted.[78] Like the advisory commission, the alternative dispute resolution commission delivers an opinion on how to resolve the question in dispute.[79] The same time restrictions apply.

The competent authorities of the Member States concerned must agree within six **852** months of notification of the opinion of the advisory commission or the alternative dispute resolution commission on how to resolve the question in dispute.[80] They do not have to follow the opinion of the advisory commission or the alternative dispute resolution commission; however, if they fail to agree on how to resolve the disputed question they will be bound by the opinion of the advisory commission or the alternative dispute resolution commission.[81] The final decision of the competent authorities concerned shall be **binding on the Member States concerned** and shall be implemented provided that (i) the affected person accepts the decision and renounces the right to any domestic remedy and (ii) the relevant national court does not decide that there was a lack of independence.[82]

The possibility for the affected person to be involved in the procedure during the **853** arbitration stage depends on the **consent of the competent authorities of the Member States concerned**. Only when the competent authorities of the Member States agree may the affected person submit any information, evidence or documents that may be relevant to the advisory commission or the alternative dispute resolution commission.[83] The affected person and the competent authorities of the Member States concerned must, however, provide such information upon the request of the advisory commission or the alternative dispute resolution commission. The competent authorities of the Member States concerned can refuse to provide such information under the circumstances determined in Art. 13(1) of the Dispute Resolution Directive. Furthermore, the affected person may only appear or be represented before an advisory committee or an alternative dispute resolution commission with the consent of the competent authorities of the Member States concerned. The affected person, however, has to appear or be represented before the advisory committee or the alternative dispute resolution commission upon request.[84]

Subject to the consent of the persons concerned, the competent authorities can **854** decide to **publish the final decision.**[85] If the competent authorities or the affected persons do not consent to publication of the final decision, an abstract of the decision shall be published, which shall at least contain a description of the issue and the subject matter, the legal basis, a short description of the outcome and a description of the method of arbitration used.

---

78   OECD, *Model Tax Convention on Income and on Capital: Condensed Version* (2017) Art. 25, p. 474.
79   Art. 14(1) Dispute Resolution Directive.
80   Art. 15(1) Dispute Resolution Directive.
81   Art. 15(2) Dispute Resolution Directive.
82   Art. 15(4) Dispute Resolution Directive.
83   Art. 13(1) Dispute Resolution Directive.
84   Art. 13(2) Dispute Resolution Directive.
85   Art. 18 Dispute Resolution Directive.

4. Chart Illustrating the Procedure

855

```
                              ┌──────────────────┐          ╭──────────────╮
                              │    Complaint     │──────────│  To submit   │
                              └──────────────────┘          │   within 3   │
                                       │                    │  years from  │
                                       │                    │ notification │
                                       ▼                    ╰──────────────╯
                              ┌──────────────────┐          ╭──────────────╮
                              │    Competent     │          │  Must take   │
                              │ authorities of   │──────────│  a decision  │
                              │    each MS       │          │   within 6   │
                              │   concerned      │          │    months    │
                              └──────────────────┘          ╰──────────────╯
```

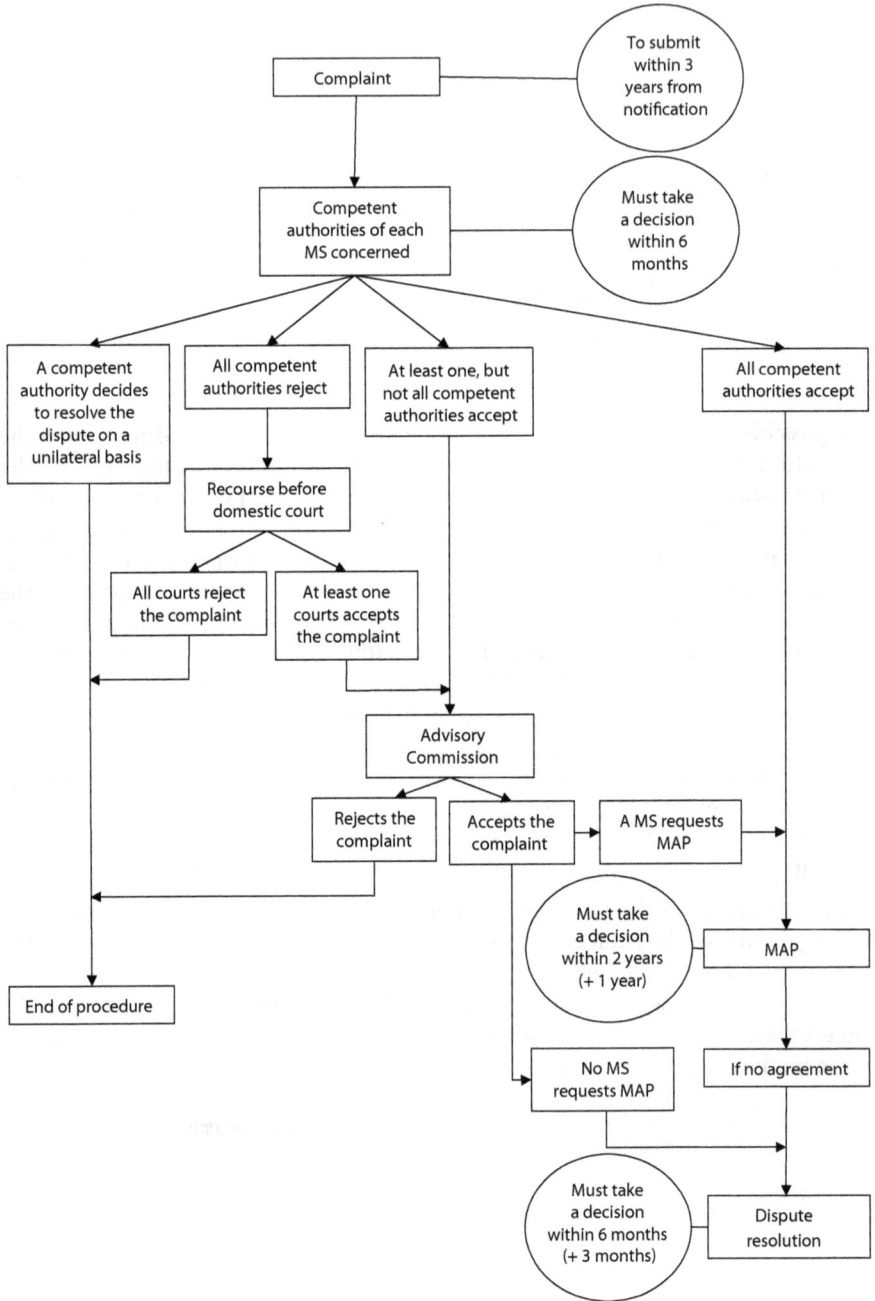

IV. Relationship between the Directive and Other Procedures

A. Interaction with Domestic Procedures

The Dispute Resolution Directive does not prevent a taxpayer from bringing a **856** dispute that falls within the scope of the Dispute Resolution Directive before a **domestic court or judicial body**. The taxpayer decides which procedure to initiate. However, recourse to a domestic court or judicial body in order to resolve cross-border tax disputes might not always lead to a desirable outcome. Although the Dispute Resolution Directive does not exclude the possibility of a dispute being brought simultaneously before a domestic court or judicial body and under the Dispute Resolution Directive, a taxpayer should carefully analyse its actions. Under certain circumstances, a Member State is allowed to terminate the proceeding under the Dispute Resolution Directive if a domestic court gives a decision on a question in dispute, from which national law does not allow it to derogate. This will be the case if (i) such a decision of the domestic court is given before the competent authorities of the Member States concerned come to an agreement under the MAP procedure, or (ii) if such a decision of the domestic court is given before the advisory commission or alternative dispute resolution commission has delivered its opinion.[86]

B. Interaction with the MLI

Part V of the **MLI** aims to improve **dispute resolution**. Art. 16 of the MLI, which **857** constitutes part of the minimum standard, encompasses the changes to be made to the mutual agreement procedure, including allowing access to either competent authority under a mutual agreement procedure. This change is a welcome improvement, as access to the opinion of the other competent authority ensures that a taxpayer will not be prevented from making use of a mutual agreement procedure for purely domestic policy reasons. However, the provision does not fully address the primary concerns regarding mutual agreement procedures, such as the fact that there is no obligation to arrive at an agreement, as well as the lack of time limits, taxpayer participation and suspension of domestic recovery procedures until the mutual agreement is settled.[87]

Also, a detailed chapter on **mandatory binding arbitration** was included **in part VI** **858** of the **MLI**. This part provides for greater procedural clarity than the current Models.[88] The arbitration process under the MLI may either be "independent opinion" arbitration or "baseball" arbitration, which serves as the default option. As part VI is not

---

86 Art. 16(4) Dispute Resolution Directive.
87 Govind/Turcan, The Changing Contours of Dispute Resolution in the International Tax World: Comparing the OECD Multilateral Instrument and the Proposed EU Arbitration Directive, *BIT* 2017.
88 For further information on the MLI's provisions on arbitration see Govind/Turcan, Cross-Border Tax Dispute Resolution in the 21st century: A Comparative Study of Existing Bilateral and Multilateral Remedies, *Derivs. & Fin. Instrums.* 2017.

part of the minimum standard, states are not required to apply it. To date, about 30 states have opted to commit to implementing the arbitration provision set forth in the MLI. Due to certain reservations, part VI may even become inapplicable if both treaty partners choose to apply part VI. While the MLI provides for significantly more procedural clarity than the Models, the procedures are not yet complete, as they require an additional competent authority agreement. Furthermore, under the provisions of the MLI, the commencement of the arbitration process may be extended without time limit, the appointment and transparency rules that lead to the OECD appointing an arbitrator in the event of default may be perceived as not guaranteeing even-handedness in the appointment of arbitrators by developing countries and unpublished opinions may raise concerns of arbitrariness. Also, the legal standing of the taxpayer is not clarified either at the MAP or arbitration stage.[89]

859 Thus, while it is effectively **up to taxpayers to decide which procedure** they wish to initiate, the procedure provided for by the **Dispute Resolution Directive** seems to be **more favourable**, as this instrument contains more details in many areas. For example, while the Dispute Resolution Directive provides for strict time limits that cannot be extended indefinitely, the MLI contains no such limits. Furthermore, the detailed procedural rules in the Directive provide for much greater legal certainty than the MLI. The Dispute Resolution Directive is also more favourable than the MLI with regard to the rights of the taxpayer, as it gives the taxpayer the option to participate in the proceedings, to access courts in order to challenge inaction or unfavourable decisions and also requires the publication of decisions.[90] Furthermore, the EU Charter on Fundamental Rights applies to the Dispute Resolution Directive and Member States must respect the rights provided therein in respect of cases covered by the Directive. In this regard, it is stated explicitly in the preamble that the Dispute Resolution Directive seeks to respect the principles recognized by the Charter of Fundamental Rights of the European Union.[91] Amongst others, the right to property (Art. 17 of the Charter), the right of access to documents (Art. 42 of the Charter)[92]

---

89 For a detailed discussion of taxpayer rights under a MAP and arbitration see Baker/Pistone, BEPS Action 16: The Taxpayers´ Right to an Effective Legal Remedy Under European Law in Cross-Border Situations, *EC Tax Review* 2016, p. 341.

90 If there is no consent to publish the decision, abstracts summarizing the key aspects will at least be made publicly available for transparency purposes.

91 9th recital Dispute Resolution Directive.

92 Although Art. 42 of the Charter refers to European Parliament, Council and Commission documents, Kokott argues that the right of access to documents could also be of relevance for disputes falling under the scope of the Dispute Resolution Directive. She finds arguments for this position in the case law of the CJEU in the area of VAT, in which the CJEU has decided that a taxpayer should have, at his request, access to the documents on which the tax authorities base their assessment, unless public interest objectives warrant restricting access to that information and those documents. Consequently, the right of access to documents is not only relevant for European Parliament, Council and Commission documents, but can apply in respect of documents of Member State institutions. Kokott, Taxpayer's Rights, *ET* 2020, pp. 5-6 with reference to CJEU, 9 Nov. 2017, Case C-298/16, *Teodor Ispas, Anduţa Ispas v Direcţia Generală a Finanţelor Publice Cluj*. Note that no reference is made in Case C-298/16 to Art. 42 of the Charter, at least not directly. The Court had to decide on the scope of the general principle of EU law of respect for the rights of the defence. Consequently, the potential relevance of Art. 42 of the Charter is disputable.

and the right to an effective remedy and to a fair trial (Art. 47 of the Charter) have been identified in the literature as being potentially of significant relevance.[93]

It should be noted that the procedure under the MLI shall come to an end when a complaint is submitted under the Directive effective the date that the complaint was first received by any of the competent authorities in the Member States concerned. This is also true for any other ongoing international procedure based on DTCs (MAP or arbitration) or the EU arbitration convention.[94]

C. Chart Illustrating the Main Differences between the Arbitration Procedure under the Directive, the Convention, the MLI and Art. 25(5) OECD Model

860

	Art. 25(5) OECD Model Convention	Arbitration Convention	Dispute Resolution Directive	MLI
Dispute subjects	Competent authority disputes	Only transfer pricing disputes	Disputes arising from the interpretation and application of agreements and conventions that provide for the elimination of double taxation of income and, where applicable, capital	Taxation not in accordance with the provisions of the Covered Tax Agreement
Threshold period of MAP before arbitration is triggered	Disputes that remain unsolved after two years (may be replaced by a three-year period, or may be extended indefinitely in specific cases)	Disputes that remain unsolved after two years (time limit may be waived if competent authorities mutually agree and with consent of the taxpayers concerned)	Disputes that remain unsolved after two years (period may be extended by up to one year)	Disputes that remain unsolved after two years (period may be replaced by a three-year period, or may be extended indefinitely in specific cases)

---

93   See, for example, Kokott, Taxpayer's Rights, *ET* 2020, p. 3 et seq.
94   Art. 16(5) Dispute Resolution Directive; For further information see Debelva/Luts, Directive on Tax Dispute Resolution Mechanisms in the EU, *Tax Notes International* 2018, p. 81 et seq.

	Art. 25(5) OECD Model Convention	Arbitration Convention	Dispute Resolution Directive	MLI
Persons involved in the procedure	The two competent authorities	The two competent authorities. Under certain conditions limited involvement of taxpayer	The two competent authorities. Under certain conditions limited involvement affected person(s)	The two competent authorities
Composition of the decision making body	Each competent authority appoints an arbitrator; the two arbitrators appoint a third arbitrator who chairs the panel	Advisory commission composed of independent president, two authority representatives (this number may be reduced to one by agreement between the competent authorities) and two independent members	Advisory commission composed of one chair, one representative of each competent authority and one independent person of standing.[95] If an alternative dispute resolution committee (ADRC) is set up, such ADRC might have a different composition.	Each competent authority appoints an arbitrator; the two arbitrators appoint a third arbitrator who chairs the panel
Result	Panel may issue its own opinion or chose between the two settlements proposed by the competent authorities (dependent on respective DTC)	Advisory commission delivers opinion	Advisory commission or ADRC delivers opinion. If ADRC is set up possibility to opt for any alternative dispute resolution processes (e.g. last best offer arbitration process)	Panel may issue its own opinion or chose between the two settlements proposed by the competent authorities (dependent on the type of arbitration process)
Binding decision	Decision binding on the competent authorities (not binding if the competent authorities agree on a different resolution of all unresolved issues within six months)	Competent authorities may find alternative solution within six months; if ,they fail, they are bound by the opinion	Competent authorities may find alternative solution within six months of notification of the opinion of the advisory commission or ADRC; if they fail, they are bound by the opinion	Decision binding on the competent authorities (not binding if the competent authorities agree on a different resolution of all unresolved issues within three months)

---

95   If the competent authorities agree, the number of representatives of each country and/or independent persons of standing may be increased to two for each competent authority.

Literature

Baker/Pistone, BEPS Action 16: The Taxpayers´ Right to an Effective Legal Remedy Under European Law in Cross-Border Situations, *EC Tax Review* 2016, p. 341; Debelva/Luts, Directive on Tax Dispute Resolution Mechanisms in the EU, *Tax Notes International* 2018, p. 71; Govind/Turcan, Cross-Border Dispute Resolution in the 21st century, A Comparative Study of Existing Bilateral and Multilateral Remedies, *Derivs. & Fin. Instrums.* 2017; Govind/Turcan, The Changing Contours of Dispute Resolution in the International Tax World: Comparing the OECD Multilateral Instrument and the Proposed EU Arbitration Directive, *BIT* 2017; Hinnekens, European Arbitration Convention: Thoughts on Its Principles, Procedures and First Experience, *EC Tax Review* 2010, p. 109; Pit, *Dispute Resolution in the EU; The EU Arbitration Convention and the Dispute Resolution Directive* (2018); Kokott, Taxpayer's Rights, *ET* 2020, p. 3 et seq.

Legal basis: Convention on the elimination of double taxation in connection with the adjustment of profits of associated enterprises (90/436/EEC), OJ L 225 of 20 August 1990, pp. 10-25; Council Directive (EU) on tax dispute resolution mechanisms in the European Union (2017/1852), OJ L 265 of 10 October 2017, pp. 1-14.

Table of CJEU Case Law

This table contains all CJEU judgments mentioned in the book, listed alphabetically in the first column, with relevant information on the marginal number of the book and the chapter in which they are quoted.

CJEU cases listed alphabetic	Date	Case	Sources of EU Law — Chapter 1	Coordination of Tax Policies — Chapter 2	Fundamental Freedoms — Chapter 3	State Aid — Chapter 4	Parent-Subsidiary Directive — Chapter 5	Merger Directive — Chapter 6	Interest and Royalty Directive — Chapter 7	ATAD — Chapter 8	Mutual Assistance Directives — Chapter 9	Arbitration Convention & Directive — Chapter 10
3D I Srl	19 December 2012	C-207/11						517				
A	18 December 2007	C-101/05			210, 249, 280, 284						781	
A Oy	23 November 2017	C-292/16						504, 505, 523				
A.T.	11 December 2008	C-285/07						518				
Aberdeen Property	18 June 2009	C-303/07			232		450					
AceaElectrabel Produzione SpA v Commission	16 December 2010	C-480/09				326						
Adria-Wien Pipeline	8 November 2001	C-143/99				346						
A-Fonds	2 May 2019	C-598/17				321						
Air Liquide Industrie Belgium	15 June 2006	C-393/04 C-41/05				390						
Åkerberg Fransson	26 February 2013	C-617/10	44, 52									
Alzetta Mauro	15 June 2000	Joined Cases T-298/97, T-312/97				358						
Argenta Spaarbank	17 October 2019	C-459/18			225							
Argenta Spaarbank NV	4 July 2013	C-350/11			261							

CJEU cases listed alphabetic	Date	Case	Sources of EU Law Chapter 1	Coordination of Tax Policies Chapter 2	Fundamental Freedoms Chapter 3	State Aid Chapter 4	Parent-Subsidiary Directive Chapter 5	Merger Directive Chapter 6	Interest and Royalty Directive Chapter 7	ATAD Chapter 8	Mutual Assistance Directives Chapter 9	Arbitration Convention & Directive Chapter 10
Argenta Spaarbank NV	26 October 2017	C-39/16					448					
Asscher v Staatssecretaris van Financien	27 June 1996	C-107/94			200							
Asteris	27 September 1988	Joined Cases C-106/87-C-120/87				335						
Athinaiki Zithopiia	4 October 2001	C-294/99					453					
Atzeni and others	23 February 2006	C-346/03 C-529/03				371						
AURES Holding	27 February 2020	C-405/18			200, 229, 231, 232, 264, 266							
Austria v Germany	12 September 2017	C-648/15	24		252							
Aviva	21 September 2016	C-605/15								640, 641		
Bachmann	28 January 1992	C-204/90			261							
Banco Exterior de España	15 March 1994	C-387/92				332, 384						
Barclays Bank SA	30 April 2014	C-280/13								668		
Baumbast	17 September 2002	C-413/99			203							
Bautiaa and Société française maritime	13 February 1996	C-197/94 and C-252/94					455					
Bechtel	22 June 2017	C-20/16			243, 263							
Becker	19 January 1982	8/81	14									
Beker	28 February 2013	C-168/11			213, 244							

CJEU cases listed alphabetic	Date	Case	Sources of EU Law	Coordination of Tax Policies	Fundamental Freedoms	State Aid	Parent-Subsidiary Directive	Merger Directive	Interest and Royalty Directive	ATAD	Mutual Assistance Directives	Arbitration Convention & Directive
			Chapter 1	Chapter 2	Chapter 3	Chapter 4	Chapter 5	Chapter 6	Chapter 7	Chapter 8	Chapter 9	Chapter 10
Belgische Staat v Wereldhave Belgium Comm. VA and others	8 March 2017	C-448/15					416					
Belgium and Forum 187 v Commission	22 June 2006	Joined Cases C-182/03 and C-217/03				406						
Belgium v Commission (Magnetrol)	14 February 2019	Joined Cases T-131/16 and T-263/16				310						
Belvedere Costruzioni	29 March 2012	C-500/10	51									
Berlioz Investment Fund	16 May 2017	C-682/15	54								685, 698, 762, 763, 769, 778	
Bevola	12 June 2018	C-650/16			231, 232, 263, 294							
Blanco and Fabretti	22 October 2014	C-344/13			224, 259, 290							
Block	12 February 2009	C-67/08		113	252, 294							
Bosal Holding	18 September 2003	C-168/01					448		541			
Bouanich	19 January 2006	C-265/04			253							
Bouanich	13 March 2014	C-375/12			213, 256, 261							
Brisal and KBC Finance Ireland	13 July 2016	C-18/15			207, 220, 233, 278, 283							
British Aggregates Association v Commission	7 March 2012	T-210/02				346						

CJEU cases listed alphabetic	Date	Case	Sources of EU Law (Chapter 1)	Coordination of Tax Policies (Chapter 2)	Fundamental Freedoms (Chapter 3)	State Aid (Chapter 4)	Parent-Subsidiary Directive (Chapter 5)	Merger Directive (Chapter 6)	Interest and Royalty Directive (Chapter 7)	ATAD (Chapter 8)	Mutual Assistance Directives (Chapter 9)	Arbitration Convention & Directive (Chapter 10)
British Aggregates v Commission	22 December 2012	C-487/06				346						
Burda	26 June 2008	C-284/06					454					
Busseni	22 February 1990	C-221/88								641		
Cadbury Schweppes	12 September 2006	C-196/04			220, 222, 232, 247, 268, 271					614, 615, 616		
Cartesio	16 December 2008	C-210/06						529				
Case Opinion	18 December 2014	2/13	18, 40									
Cassa di Risparmio di Firenze SpA	10 January 2006	C-222/04				326, 327, 328, 359, 361						
Caster and Caster	9 October 2014	C-326/12		192	226, 283, 285, 292							
CELF	12 February 2008	C-199/06				401, 402						
CETA	30 April 2019	1/17	74									
Chakroun	4 March 2010	C-578/08	39									
Chartry	1 March 2011	C-467/09	50									
CILFIT	6 October 1982	283/81	88									
Ciola	29 April 1999	C-224/97	6									
Cobelfret	12 February 2009	C-138/07					440					
Cofaz	28 January 1986	C-169/84				395						
College Pension Plan of British Columbia	13 November 2019	C-641/17			281							

CJEU cases listed alphabetic	Date	Case	Sources of EU Law Chapter 1	Coordination of Tax Policies Chapter 2	Fundamental Freedoms Chapter 3	State Aid Chapter 4	Parent-Subsidiary Directive Chapter 5	Merger Directive Chapter 6	Interest and Royalty Directive Chapter 7	ATAD Chapter 8	Mutual Assistance Directives Chapter 9	Arbitration Convention & Directive Chapter 10
Collino	14 September 2000	C-343/98								641		
Columbus Container	6 December 2007	C-298/05			252							
Comité d'entreprise de la Société française de production and others	23 May 2000	C-106/98				395						
Commission v Philip Morris	17 September 1980	730/79				360, 371						
Commission v Austria	27 November 2001	C-424/99	37									
Commission v Austria	29 September 2011	C-387/10			292							
Commission v Belgium	6 June 2013	C-383/10			217							
Commission v Belgium ("flat-rate transference duty")	5 May 1970	Case 77/69	103									
Commission v Belgium ("deductibility of insurance contributions")	28 January 1992	C-300/90			261							
Commission v France	7 May 1985	Case 18/84			192							
Commission v France	26 September 1996	C-241/94				343						
Commission v France ("Avoir Fiscal")	28 January 1986	270/83			191, 237, 287							
Commission v France ("Boussac")	14 February 1990	C-301/87				397, 399						
Commission v France ("vineyards in Charentes")	12 December 2002	C-456/00				371						
Commission v Germany	15 July 2010	C-271/08	39									
Commission v Germany	20 October 2011	C-284/09			267							

CJEU cases listed alphabetic	Date	Case	Sources of EU Law — Chapter 1	Coordination of Tax Policies — Chapter 2	Fundamental Freedoms — Chapter 3	State Aid — Chapter 4	Parent-Subsidiary Directive — Chapter 5	Merger Directive — Chapter 6	Interest and Royalty Directive — Chapter 7	ATAD — Chapter 8	Mutual Assistance Directives — Chapter 9	Arbitration Convention & Directive — Chapter 10
Commission v Germany	16 April 2015	C-591/13			261, 288			505				
Commission v Germany	8 February 2018	C-380/16									767	
Commission v Germany ("The New German Länder")	19 September 2000	C-156/98				321						
Commission v Gibraltar	15 November 2011	C-106/09 C-107/09				332, 336, 342, 345, 346, 347, 352, 354, 355, 356						
Commission v Greece	20 January 2011	C-155/09			217							
Commission v Greece	26 May 2016	C-244/15			233							
Commission v Italy ("Alfa Romeo II")	4 April 1995	C-348/93				405						
Commission v Italy ("conditions of recovery")	9 December 2003	C-129/00	103									
Commission v Italy ("Italgrani")	30 June 1992	C-47/91				397						
Commission v Italy ("outbound dividends")	19 November 2009	C-540/07									781	
Commission v Italy ("EFIM group")	23 February 1995	C-349/93				405						
Commission v MOL	4 June 2015	C-15/14				352						
Commission v Netherlands	8 September 2011	C-279/08				333						
Commission v Netherlands	31 January 2013	C-301/11						504				

CJEU cases listed alphabetic	Date	Case	Sources of EU Law	Coordination of Tax Policies	Fundamental Freedoms	State Aid	Parent-Subsidiary Directive	Merger Directive	Interest and Royalty Directive	ATAD	Mutual Assistance Directives	Arbitration Convention & Directive
			Chapter 1	Chapter 2	Chapter 3	Chapter 4	Chapter 5	Chapter 6	Chapter 7	Chapter 8	Chapter 9	Chapter 10
Commission v Netherlands ("outbound dividends to EEA")	11 June 2009	C-521/07			217, 247, 277							
Commission v Netherlands ("The MINAS System")	29 April 2004	C-159/01				352						
Commission v Parliament/Council	21 January 2003	C-378/00				394						
Commission v Portugal	6 October 2011	C-493/09		192	274, 292						781, 812	
Commission v Portugal	6 September 2012	C-38/10						504, 529		605		
Commission v Portugal	21 December 2016	C-503/14			202, 263, 267, 293			504		652		
Commission v Portugal	5 May 2011	C-267/09			217							
Commission v Portugal ("Azores and Madeira")	6 September 2006	C-88/03				340, 341, 346, 349, 350						
Commission v Spain	6 October 2009	C-153/08			224							
Commission v Spain	3 June 2010	C-487/08			225							
Commission v Spain	12 July 2012	C-269/09						504				
Commission v Spain	25 April 2013	C-64/11						504				
Commission v Spain	11 December 2014	C-678/11		192	283							
Commission v Spain ("Cook II")	14 January 1997	C-169/95				371						
Commission v Spain ("VAT – services by a settlement office of a mortgage district")	12 November 2009	C-154/08	103									

CJEU cases listed alphabetic	Date	Case	Sources of EU Law — Chapter 1	Coordination of Tax Policies — Chapter 2	Fundamental Freedoms — Chapter 3	State Aid — Chapter 4	Parent-Subsidiary Directive — Chapter 5	Merger Directive — Chapter 6	Interest and Royalty Directive — Chapter 7	ATAD — Chapter 8	Mutual Assistance Directives — Chapter 9	Arbitration Convention & Directive — Chapter 10
Commission v The Hellenic Republic	5 October 2004	C-475/01								646		
Commission v. France	8 October 2018	C-416/17	87									
Congregación de Escuelas	27 June 2017	C-74/16				328, 342, 378						
Conijn	6 July 2006	C-346/04			244							
Costa v. E.N.E.L.	15 July 1964	6/64	6			390						
Cussens, Jennings, Kingston v. T.G. Brosnan	22 November 2017	C-251/16	13		272					642		
D.	5 July 2005	C-376/03			244, 247							
Damseaux	16 July 2009	C-128/08		113	253							
Dansk Rørindustri and Others	28 June 2005	Joined Cases C-189/02 P, C-202/02 P, C-205/02 P to C-208/02 P and C-213/02 P		153								
De Groot	12 December 2002	C-385/00			244							
Deister Holding and Juhler Holding	20 December 2017	Joined Cases C-504/16 and C-613/16			201, 214, 270, 271, 273, 288, 295		465			616, 647, 648, 656		
Deka	30 January 2020	C-156/17			210, 222							
Demesa and Territorio Historico de Alava	11 November 2004	C-183/02 C-187/02				406						
Denkavit International & Denkavit France	14 December 2006	C-170/05			224							

CJEU cases listed alphabetic	Date	Case	Sources of EU Law Chapter 1	Coordination of Tax Policies Chapter 2	Fundamental Freedoms Chapter 3	State Aid Chapter 4	Parent-Subsidiary Directive Chapter 5	Merger Directive Chapter 6	Interest and Royalty Directive Chapter 7	ATAD Chapter 8	Mutual Assistance Directives Chapter 9	Arbitration Convention & Directive Chapter 10
Denkavit, VITIC and Voormer	17 October 1996	C-283/94 C-291/94 C-292/94	14				424		555			
Deutsche Bahn AG v Commission	5 April 2006	T-351/02				320				663		
DI. VI. Finanziaria di Diego della Valle & C	6 September 2012	C-380/11						504				
Dijkman	1 July 2010	C-233/09			285							
Dilly's Wellnesshotel	21 July 2016	C-493/14				381						
Dirk Andres	28 June 2018	C-203/16				347, 395						
DMC Beteiligungs-gesellschaft	23 January 2014	C-164/12			214, 220			504, 505		605		
DNB Banka	21 September 2017	C-326/15								640		
Donnellan	26 April 2018	C-34/17									798, 803, 807, 808	
Edis	15 September 1998	C-231/96	92									
Elisa	11 October 2007	C-451/05			292						777, 780	
Emerging Markets Series of DFA	10 April 2014	C-190/12	104		280, 282, 285, 292						781	
Emmott	25 July 1991	C-208/90	92									
Emsland-Stärke	14 December 2000	C-110/99		174								
Epson	8 June 2000	C-375/98					453			615		
Eqiom and Enka	7 September 2017	C-6/16			270		465			614, 616, 617, 647, 648		

CJEU cases listed alphabetic	Date	Case	Sources of EU Law Chapter 1	Coordination of Tax Policies Chapter 2	Fundamental Freedoms Chapter 3	State Aid Chapter 4	Parent-Subsidiary Directive Chapter 5	Merger Directive Chapter 6	Interest and Royalty Directive Chapter 7	ATAD Chapter 8	Mutual Assistance Directives Chapter 9	Arbitration Convention & Directive Chapter 10
Eribrand	19 June 2003	C-467/01	37									
Établissements Rimbaud	28 October 2010	C-72/09									781	
État belge	24 October 2019	C-35/19			199, 258							
Ettwein	28 February 2013	C-425/11			244							
Euro Park Services	8 March 2017	C-14/16						537		614, 617, 647		
EV	20 September 2018	C-685/16			280, 281							
Exécutif régional wallon and SA Glaverbel v Commission	8 March 1988	Joined Cases 62 and 72/87				371						
Fallimento Olimpiclub	3 September 2009	C-2/08	98									
Farrugia v Commission	21 March 1996	Case T-230/94				394						
Fédéreation nationale du Commerce Extérieur des Produits Alimentaires (FNCE) and others	21 November 1991	C-354/90				390						
Ferrero e C. SpA v Agenzia delle Entrate – Ufficio di Alba	24 June 2010	C-338/08 C-339/08					454					
Fiat Chrysler Finance Europe	24 September 2019	Joined Cases T-755/15 and T-759/15				310, 336						
Fidium Finanz	3 October 2006	C-452/04			215							
Fisher	12 October 2017	C-192/16			194							
Foggia	10 November 2011	C-126/10						535, 536, 537				

CJEU cases listed alphabetic	Date	Case	Sources of EU Law — Chapter 1	Coordination of Tax Policies — Chapter 2	Fundamental Freedoms — Chapter 3	State Aid — Chapter 4	Parent-Subsidiary Directive — Chapter 5	Merger Directive — Chapter 6	Interest and Royalty Directive — Chapter 7	ATAD — Chapter 8	Mutual Assistance Directives — Chapter 9	Arbitration Convention & Directive — Chapter 10
France Télécom SA	8 December 2011	C-81/10				339, 356, 400, 405, 406						
Francovich	19 November 1991	C-6/90 C-9/90	91, 101									
Free Trade Agreement Between the European Union and the Republic of Singapore	16 May 2017	2/15	74									
Frucona Kosice	24 January 2013	C-73/11				333						
Futura Participations	15 May 1997	C-250/95			241, 275						780	
Gaz de France	1 October 2009	C-247/08					415					
Gebhard	30 November 1995	C-55/94			221							
Germany v Commission	30 September 2003	C-301/96				365						
Gerritse	12 June 2003	C-234/01			244							
Gilly	12 May 1998	C-336/96	34		252							
Google Ireland	3 March 2020	C-482/18			223							
Greece vs Commission	29 April 2004	C-278/00				365, 368						
Groupe Steria	2 September 2015	C-386/14			234, 263							
Grundig Italiana	24 September 2002	C-255/00	91									
Gschwind	14 September 1999	C-391/97			244							
GVC Services (Bulgaria)	2 April 2020	C-458/18			209, 248, 259							
Halifax	21 February 2006	C-255/02			272					617		

CJEU cases listed alphabetic	Date	Case	Sources of EU Law Chapter 1	Coordination of Tax Policies Chapter 2	Fundamental Freedoms Chapter 3	State Aid Chapter 4	Parent-Subsidiary Directive Chapter 5	Merger Directive Chapter 6	Interest and Royalty Directive Chapter 7	ATAD Chapter 8	Mutual Assistance Directives Chapter 9	Arbitration Convention & Directive Chapter 10
Haribo Lakritzen and Österreichische Salinen	10 February 2011	C-436/08 C-437/08			216, 247, 256, 257, 277, 292						702, 750	
Hein	13 December 2018	C-385/17	44									
Heinrich Heine	15 April 2010	C-511/08				390						
Heylens and others	15 October 1987	222/86	37					514				
Hirvonen	19 November 2015	C-632/13			204, 245							
Holböck	24 May 2007	C-157/05			201, 281							
Holmen AB	19 June 2019	C-608/17			294							
Hornbach Baumarkt	31 May 2018	C-382/16			264, 271, 295							
Huijbrechts	22 November 2018	C-679/17			290							
Ianelli & Volpi	22 March 1977	Case 74/76				322, 323						
Imfeld and Garcet	12 December 2013	C-303/12			244, 252							
Impact	15 April 2008	C-268/06								640		
IN & JM	24 October 2019	Joined Cases C-469/18 and C-470/18	52									
Ingeborg Wagner-Raith	21 May 2015	C-560/13			213, 280, 281							
Intermills	14 November 1984	Case 323/82				395						
Internationale Handelsgesellschaft	17 December 1970	Case 11/70	6, 38									
Italy v Commission	15 December 2005	C-66/02				330, 338, 342						

CJEU cases listed alphabetic	Date	Case	Sources of EU Law Chapter 1	Coordination of Tax Policies Chapter 2	Fundamental Freedoms Chapter 3	State Aid Chapter 4	Parent-Subsidiary Directive Chapter 5	Merger Directive Chapter 6	Interest and Royalty Directive Chapter 7	ATAD Chapter 8	Mutual Assistance Directives Chapter 9	Arbitration Convention & Directive Chapter 10
Itelcar	3 October 2013	C-282/12			201, 295					596		
Jacob and Lassus	22 March 2018	Joined Cases C-327/16 and C-421/16			231, 232, 267, 293			504, 505, 525				
Johnston	15 May 1986	222/84	37									
Jundt	18 December 2007	C-281/06			204							
K	7 November 2013	C-322/11			262					616, 648		
Kadi II	18 July 2013	C-584/10 P, C-593/10 P and C-595/10 P	20									
Kapferer	16 March 2006	C-234/04	96									
KBC Bank NV	4 June 2009	C-439/07 C-499/07					440					
Keller Holding	23 February 2006	C-471/04	78		200			504				
Kerckhaert-Morres	14 November 2006	C-513/04		113	223							
Köbler	30 September 2003	C-224/01	103									
Kofoed	5 July 2007	C-321/05					465	531, 533	571			
Kohll and Kohll-Schlesser	26 May 2016	C-300/15			263							
Kolpinghuis Nijmegen	8 October 1987	80/86	16									
Konstantinos Adeneler	4 July 2006	C-212/04	16									
Krankenheim Ruhesitz am Wannsee-Senioren-heimstatt	23 October 2008	C-157/07			262							
Kronos International	11 September 2014	C-47/12			214, 216, 235, 253		438					

CJEU cases listed alphabetic	Date	Case	Sources of EU Law — Chapter 1	Coordination of Tax Policies — Chapter 2	Fundamental Freedoms — Chapter 3	State Aid — Chapter 4	Parent-Subsidiary Directive — Chapter 5	Merger Directive — Chapter 6	Interest and Royalty Directive — Chapter 7	ATAD — Chapter 8	Mutual Assistance Directives — Chapter 9	Arbitration Convention & Directive — Chapter 10
Kühne & Heitz	13 January 2004	C-453/00	94									
Kyrian	14 January 2010	C-233/08									798, 800	
Ladbroke v Commission	27 January 1998	Case T-67/94				338						
Lakebrink	18 July 2007	C-182/06			244							
Lankhorst-Hohorst	12 December 2002	C-324/00					431					
Lasteyrie du Saillant	11 March 2004	C-9/02						504				
Lawrie-Blum	3 July 1986	66/85			216							
Les Vergers du Vieux Tauves SA	22 December 2008	C-48/07					419					
Leur-Bloem	17 July 1997	C-28/95						533, 535, 537	571			
Libert	8 May 2013	C-197/11				375						
Littlewoods Retail	19 July 2012	C-591/10	100									
Lorenz	11 December 1973	120/73				390, 393, 404						
Lucchini	18 July 2007	C-119/05	97			322						
Manninen	7 September 2004	C-319/02			222, 254, 283							
Marks & Spencer	13 December 2005	C-446/03			220, 234, 264, 290, 294			514				
Marleasing SA v La Comercial Internacional de Alimentacion SA	13 November 1990	C-106/89	16							640		

CJEU cases listed alphabetic	Date	Case	Sources of EU Law — Chapter 1	Coordination of Tax Policies — Chapter 2	Fundamental Freedoms — Chapter 3	State Aid — Chapter 4	Parent-Subsidiary Directive — Chapter 5	Merger Directive — Chapter 6	Interest and Royalty Directive — Chapter 7	ATAD — Chapter 8	Mutual Assistance Directives — Chapter 9	Arbitration Convention & Directive — Chapter 10
Max-Planck-Gesellschaft zur Förderung	6 November 2018	C-684/16	44									
Memira Holding	19 June 2019	C-607/17			294			514				
Metirato	14 March 2019	C-695/17									807	
Montag	6 December 2018	C-480/17			243							
MOTOE	1 July 2008	C-49/07				326						
N Luxembourg 1	26 February 2019	Joined Cases C-115/16, C-118/16, C-119/16 and C-299/16		187	268, 269, 273			534, 536	542, 550, 570, 572	614		
N.	7 September 2006	C-470/04			211, 220, 293			504				
National Grid Indus	29 November 2011	C-371/10			202, 220, 222, 291, 293			504, 505		605, 610, 652	812	
Niki Luftfahrt GmbH	13 May 2015	Case T-511/09				324						
Nintendo	23 November 2014	C-355/12								768		
Nordea Bank Danmark	17 July 2014	C-48/13			228, 229, 230, 240, 263							
NV Lammers & Van Cleeff	7 January 2008	C-105/07								617		
Nygard	23 April 2002	C-234/99				324						
Océ van der Grinten	25 September 2003	C-58/01					453					
Ospelt	23 September 2003	C-452/01	78									

CJEU cases listed alphabetic	Date	Case	Sources of EU Law Chapter 1	Coordination of Tax Policies Chapter 2	Fundamental Freedoms Chapter 3	State Aid Chapter 4	Parent-Subsidiary Directive Chapter 5	Merger Directive Chapter 6	Interest and Royalty Directive Chapter 7	ATAD Chapter 8	Mutual Assistance Directives Chapter 9	Arbitration Convention & Directive Chapter 10
Oy AA	18 July 2007	C-231/05			264, 287							
P Chemie Linz v Commission	5 October 2004	C-245/92								646		
P Commission v BASF and others	15 June 1994	C-137/92								646		
P Oy	18 July 2013	C-6/12				343, 350, 351, 353, 355						
P Unión de Pequeños Agricultores v Council	25 July 2002	C-50/00	37									
Paint Graphos	8 September 2011	C-78/08, C-80/08				332, 333, 341, 346, 352, 361						
Paola Faccini Dori v Recreb Srl.	14 July 1994	C-91/92	15									
Papillon	27 November 2008	C-418/07			262, 292							
Part Service	21 February 2008	C-425/06								618		
Pavlov and others	12 September 2000	Joined Cases C-180/98 to C-184/98				326						
Pelati	18 October 2012	C-603/10						537				
Pensioenfonds Metaal en Techniek	2 June 2016	C-252/14			278							
Persche	27 January 2009	C-318/07			274						702, 750, 780	
Petersen	28 February 2013	C-544/11			277							

Lang et al (Eds), Introduction to European Tax Law on Direct Taxation[6], Linde

CJEU cases listed alphabetic	Date	Case	Sources of EU Law	Coordination of Tax Policies	Fundamental Freedoms	State Aid	Parent-Subsidiary Directive	Merger Directive	Interest and Royalty Directive	ATAD	Mutual Assistance Directives	Arbitration Convention & Directive
			Chapter 1	Chapter 2	Chapter 3	Chapter 4	Chapter 5	Chapter 6	Chapter 7	Chapter 8	Chapter 9	Chapter 10
Pfeiffer a. o.	5 October 2004	Joined cases C-397/01 to C-403/01	16									
Philip Morris	4 May 2016	C-547/14	87									
Polbud	25 October 2017	C-106/16						529				
Polydor and others	9 February 1982	Case 270/80	17									
PPU, J. McB v L.E. Case	5 October 2010	C-400/10	42									
Preussen Elektra	13 March 2001	C-379/98				337						
Prunus	5 May 2011	C-384/09			208							
Puffer v Unabhängiger Finanzsenat Außenstelle Linz	23 April 2009	C-460/07				318						
Punch Graphix	18 October 2012	C-371/11					439					
Puškár	27 September 2017	C-73/16									764	
Q	18 December 2014	C-133/13			210							
Ratti	5 April 1979	Case 148/78	12									
Regione Sardegna	17 November 2009	C-169/08				322, 336						
Renneberg	16 October 2008	C-527/06			244							
Rewe	16 December 1976	Case 33/76	90									
Rewe Zentralfinanz	29 March 2007	C-347/04			315						780	
Rewe-Zentral "Cassis de Dijon"	20 February 1979	Case 120/78			221, 260							
Rijn-Schelde-Verolme v Commission	24 November 1987	Case 223/85				406						

CJEU cases listed alphabetic	Date	Case	Sources of EU Law Chapter 1	Coordination of Tax Policies Chapter 2	Fundamental Freedoms Chapter 3	State Aid Chapter 4	Parent-Subsidiary Directive Chapter 5	Merger Directive Chapter 6	Interest and Royalty Directive Chapter 7	ATAD Chapter 8	Mutual Assistance Directives Chapter 9	Arbitration Convention & Directive Chapter 10
Riskin and Timmermans	30 June 2016	C-176/15			248, 252							
RPO	7 March 2017	C-390/15		193						640		
Rüffler	23 April 2009	C-544/07			203							
Sabou	22 October 2013	C-276/12									701, 762, 763	
Saint-Gobain	21 September 1999	C-307/97			238, 252, 253							
San Giorgio	9 November 1983	Case 199/82	99									
Santander Asset Management SGIIC and Others	10 May 2012	Joined Cases C-338/11 to C-347/11	104									
Savaş	11 May 2000	C-37/98	17									
SCA Group Holding	12 June 2014	Cases C-39/13, C-40/13 and C-41/13			220							
Schempp	12 July 2005	C-403/03		114	204							
Scheuten Solar Technology	21 July 2011	C-397/09							540			
Schröder	31 March 2011	C-450/09			244							
Schumacker	14 February 1995	C-279/93			231, 242, 243							
Scorpio	3 October 2006	C-290/04			220, 278							
SECIL	24 November 2016	C-464/14			213, 214, 250, 254							
SFEI and others	11 July 1996	C-39/94				390						
SIAT	5 July 2012	C-318/10			272							

CJEU cases listed alphabetic	Date	Case	Sources of EU Law	Coordination of Tax Policies	Fundamental Freedoms	State Aid	Parent-Subsidiary Directive	Merger Directive	Interest and Royalty Directive	ATAD	Mutual Assistance Directives	Arbitration Convention & Directive
			Chapter 1	Chapter 2	Chapter 3	Chapter 4	Chapter 5	Chapter 6	Chapter 7	Chapter 8	Chapter 9	Chapter 10
Simmenthal	9 March 1978	106/77	6									
Slovak Republic v Achmea BV	6 March 2018	C-284/16	74									
Société de Gestion Industrielle	21 January 2010	C-311/08			216, 232, 271, 273, 291							
Sopora	24 February 2015	C-512/13			248							
Sparkasse Allgäu	14 April 2016	C-522/14			275							
Staatssecretaris van Financien v Schoenimport Italmoda Mariano Previti vof a. o.	18 December 2014	Joined Cases C-131/13, C-163/13 and C-164/13	13									
Starbucks Manufacturing Emea BV	24 September 2019	Joined Cases T-760/15 and T-636/16				310						
Stauder v City of Ulm	12 November 1969	Case 29/69	37									
STEKO Industriemontage	22 January 2009	C-377/07			231							
Strojírny Prostějov	19 June 2014	C-53/13 and C-80/13			278, 294							
Surgicare – Unidades de Saúde SA v Fazenda Pública	12 February 2015	C-662/13	55									
T Danmark	26 February 2019	Joined Cases C-116/16 and C-117/16			269, 270		414, 462, 465	534, 536	570, 572			
Taricco and others	8 September 2015	C-105/14	55									

CJEU cases listed alphabetic	Date	Case	Sources of EU Law Chapter 1	Coordination of Tax Policies Chapter 2	Fundamental Freedoms Chapter 3	State Aid Chapter 4	Parent-Subsidiary Directive Chapter 5	Merger Directive Chapter 6	Interest and Royalty Directive Chapter 7	ATAD Chapter 8	Mutual Assistance Directives Chapter 9	Arbitration Convention & Directive Chapter 10
Teodor Ispas	9 November 2017	C-298/16										859
Tesco-Global Áruházak	3 March 2020	C-323/18			224							
Test Claimants in the FII Group Litigation	12 December 2006	C-446/04	90		250, 254, 280		438					
Test Claimants in the FII Group Litigation	13 November 2012	C-35/11	90		213, 214, 256, 262		438			657		
Test Claimants in the FII Group Litigation	12 December 2013	C-362/12	90									
Test Claimants in the Thin Cap Group Litigation	13 March 2007	C-524/04	99		271					596, 603, 617		
Test Claimants in Class IV of the ACT Group Litigation	12 December 2006	C-374/04			210, 232							
The Gilbraltar Betting and Gaming Association Limited and The Queen	13 June 2017	C-591/15			192							
The Queen on the application of Delena Wells v Secretary of State for Transport Local Government and the Regions	7 January 2004	C-201/02	15									
The Trustees of the BT Pension Scheme	14 September 2017	C-628/15			210							
Timac Agro	17 December 2015	C-388/14			231, 240, 263					617		
Traghetti del Mediterraneo	13 June 2006	C-173/03	102									

CJEU cases listed alphabetic	Date	Case	Sources of EU Law (Chapter 1)	Coordination of Tax Policies (Chapter 2)	Fundamental Freedoms (Chapter 3)	State Aid (Chapter 4)	Parent-Subsidiary Directive (Chapter 5)	Merger Directive (Chapter 6)	Interest and Royalty Directive (Chapter 7)	ATAD (Chapter 8)	Mutual Assistance Directives (Chapter 9)	Arbitration Convention & Directive (Chapter 10)
Tsapalos and Diamantakis	1 July 2004	C-361/02 C-362/02									692, 787	
Turpeinen	9 November 2006	C-520/04			204, 245							
Twoh International	27 September 2007	C-184/05									702, 762, 780	
Unibet	22 June 2017	C-49/16	37									
Unicredito Italiano	15 December 2005	C-148/04				342						
Unión General de Trabajadore de La Rioja (UGT-Rioja) v Juntas Generales del Territorio Histórico de Vizcaya	11 September 2008	C-428/06 C-434/06				349						
UsedSoft	3 July 2012	C-128/11								668		
Vale	12 July 2012	C-378/10						529				
Van der Weegen and others	8 June 2017	C-580/15			212, 222							
Van Duyn	4 December 1974	Case 41/74	12									
Van Gend & Loos	5 February 1963	Case 26/62	9							578		
Varec	14 February 2008	C-450/06	42									
Vatsouras	4 June 2009	Joined Cases C-22/08 and C-23/08			198							
Verder LabTec	21 May 2015	C-657/13			220, 234, 291			504, 505		606		
Verest and Gerards	11 September 2014	C-489/13			252, 253							
Verkooijen	6 June 2000	C-35/98			210							

CJEU cases listed alphabetic	Date	Case	Sources of EU Law Chapter 1	Coordination of Tax Policies Chapter 2	Fundamental Freedoms Chapter 3	State Aid Chapter 4	Parent-Subsidiary Directive Chapter 5	Merger Directive Chapter 6	Interest and Royalty Directive Chapter 7	ATAD Chapter 8	Mutual Assistance Directives Chapter 9	Arbitration Convention & Directive Chapter 10
Vestergaard	28 October 1999	C-55/98			207							
Vodafone Magyarország	3 March 2020	C-75/18			224							
von Colson	10 April 1984	14/83	16									
Vorarlberger Landes- und Hypothekenbank AG	22 November 2018	C-625/17			212							
W.N.	13 April 2000	C-420/98									740	
Wächtler	26 February 2019	C-581/17			293							
Wallentin	1 July 2004	C-169/03			244							
Weber's Wine World	2 October 2003	C-147/01	93									
WebMindLicences Kft.	17 December 2015	C-419/14	56								702, 760	
Welte	17 October 2013	C-181/12									781	
Westzucker	14 March 1973	Case 57/72				371						
Weyl Beef Products	31 January 2001	Case T-197/97				324						
World Duty Free Group SA	21 December 2016	C-20/15				342, 347, 357						
X	9 February 2017	C-283/15			199, 244							
X	15 February 2017	C-317/15			280, 281							
X	17 May 2017	C-68/15			202, 220, 239		453					
X AB and Y AB	18 November 1999	C-200/98			203, 244							
X BV and TBG Limited	5 June 2014	C-24/12 and C-27/12			209							

CJEU cases listed alphabetic	Date	Case	Sources of EU Law Chapter 1	Coordination of Tax Policies Chapter 2	Fundamental Freedoms Chapter 3	State Aid Chapter 4	Parent-Subsidiary Directive Chapter 5	Merger Directive Chapter 6	Interest and Royalty Directive Chapter 7	ATAD Chapter 8	Mutual Assistance Directives Chapter 9	Arbitration Convention & Directive Chapter 10
X BV and X NV	22 February 2018	Joined Cases C-398/16 and C-399/16			220, 235, 263					649		
X GmbH	26 February 2019	C-135/17			236, 249, 269, 270, 280							
X Holding	25 February 2010	C-337/08			228, 244, 282							
X NV	18 October 2012	C-498/10			278						812	
Yoshikazu Lida v Stadt Ulm	8 November 2012	C-40/11	49									
Zanotti	20 May 2010	C-56/09			205, 207							
Zurstrassen	16 May 2000	C-87/99			244							
Zweckverband Tierkörperbeseitigung v Commission	16 July 2014	Case T-309/12				396						
Zwijnenburg	20 May 2010	C-352/08						533, 536				
Zyla	23 January 2019	C-272/17			244							

Index

www.ingramcontent.com/pod-product-compliance
Lightning Source LLC
Chambersburg PA
CBHW060759220326
41598CB00022B/2489